HARCOURT

Math

VIRGINIA EDITION

Orlando   Austin   New York   San Diego   Toronto   London

Visit *The Learning Site!*
www.harcourtschool.com

ISBN 0-15-340408-6

3 4 5 6 7 8 9 10 048 10 09 08 07 06 05

Senior Author

Evan M. Maletsky
Professor of Mathematics
Montclair State University
Upper Montclair, New Jersey

Mathematics Advisor

Richard Askey
Professor of Mathematics
University of Wisconsin
Madison, Wisconsin

Authors

Angela Giglio Andrews
Math Teacher, Scott School
Naperville District #203
Naperville, Illinois

Jennie M. Bennett
Houston Independent School District
Houston, Texas

Grace M. Burton
Professor, Watson School of Education
University of North Carolina
 at Wilmington
Wilmington, North Carolina

Lynda A. Luckie
K–12 Mathematics Coordinator
Gwinnett County Public Schools
Lawrenceville, Georgia

Joyce C. McLeod
Visiting Professor
Rollins College
Winter Park, Florida

Vicki Newman
Classroom Teacher
McGaugh Elementary School
Los Alamitos Unified School District
Seal Beach, California

Tom Roby
Associate Professor of Mathematics
California State University
Hayward, California

Janet K. Scheer
Executive Director
Create A Vision
Foster City, California

Program Consultants and Specialists

Janet S. Abbott
Mathematics Consultant
California

Elsie Babcock
Director, Mathematics and
 Science Center
Mathematics Consultant
Wayne Regional
 Educational Service
 Agency
Wayne, Michigan

William J. Driscoll
Professor of Mathematics
Department of
 Mathematical Sciences
Central Connecticut State
 University
New Britain, Connecticut

Lois Harrison-Jones
Education and
 Management Consultant
Dallas, Texas

Rebecca Valbuena
Language Development
 Specialist
Stanton Elementary School
Glendora, California

iii

UNIT 1
CHAPTERS 1-4

Use Whole Numbers and Decimals

1 PLACE VALUE OF WHOLE NUMBERS

2 PLACE VALUE OF DECIMALS 20

Technology Link

Harcourt Mega Math: *Chapter 1, p. 2;
Chapter 2, p. 26; Chapter 3, pp. 46, 48;
Chapter 4, pp. 67, 72*

The Harcourt Learning Site:
www.harcourtschool.com

Multimedia Math Glossary:
www.harcourtschool.com/mathglossary

UNIT 2
CHAPTERS 5-6
Data and Graphing

Technology Link

Harcourt Mega Math:
Chapter 5, p. 102
Chapter 6, p. 120

The Harcourt Learning Site:
www.harcourtschool.com

Multimedia Math Glossary:
www.harcourtschool.com/mathglossary

UNIT 3
CHAPTERS 7-8

Multiply Whole Numbers and Decimals

 Technology Link

Harcourt Mega Math:
Chapter 7, p. 153
Chapter 8, p. 171

The Harcourt Learning Site:
www.harcourtschool.com

Multimedia Math Glossary:
www.harcourtschool.com/mathglossary

UNIT 4
CHAPTERS 9-12

Divide Whole Numbers and Decimals

Technology Link

Harcourt Mega Math:
Chapter 9, p. 199
Chapter 10, p. 213
Chapter 11, p. 231
Chapter 12, pp. 248, 251, 255

The Harcourt Learning Site:
www.harcourtschool.com

Multimedia Math Glossary:
www.harcourtschool.com/mathglossary

UNIT 5
CHAPTERS 13-15

Number Theory and Fractions

Technology Link

Harcourt Mega Math:
Chapter 13, p. 277; Chapter 14, p. 303;
Chapter 15, p. 321

The Harcourt Learning Site:
www.harcourtschool.com

Multimedia Math Glossary:
www.harcourtschool.com/mathglossary

Operations with Fractions

Technology Link

Harcourt Mega Math:
Chapter 16, p. 346; Chapter 17, p. 373;
Chapter 18, p. 388; Chapter 19, p. 403

The Harcourt Learning Site:
www.harcourtschool.com

Multimedia Math Glossary:
www.harcourtschool.com/mathglossary

UNIT 7
CHAPTERS 20-23

Geometry and Algebra

Technology Link

Harcourt Mega Math:
*Chapter 20, pp. 443, 447; Chapter 21, pp. 457, 462, 471;
Chapter 22, pp. 481, 484; Chapter 23, pp. 503, 506*

The Harcourt Learning Site: www.harcourtschool.com

Multimedia Math Glossary:
www.harcourtschool.com/mathglossary

UNIT 8 Measurement
CHAPTERS 24-27

Technology Link

Harcourt Mega Math:
Chapter 24, pp. 533, 535
Chapter 26, p. 564
Chapter 27, p. 593

The Harcourt Learning Site:
www.harcourtschool.com

Multimedia Math Glossary:
www.harcourtschool.com/mathglossary

UNIT 9
CHAPTERS 28-30

Ratio, Percent, and Probability

Technology Link

Harcourt Mega Math:
Chapter 29, p. 642
Chapter 30, pp. 655, 658

The Harcourt Learning Site:
www.harcourtschool.com

Multimedia Math Glossary:
www.harcourtschool.com/mathglossary

Why Learn Math?

◀ You use addition and multiplication to keep score when you play games.

You use computation skills when you earn, save, and spend money. ▼

▲ You use mean, median, mode, and range when you track individual and team sports data.

You will use the mathematics that you learn in **Harcourt Math** every day. The skills you learn will help you **build success** both now and in the future.

▶ Building Success for the Future

◀ If you become a computer animator, algebra and geometry skills will help you create complex images for animated films.

If you become a building contractor, you will use measurement skills to construct a house. ▼

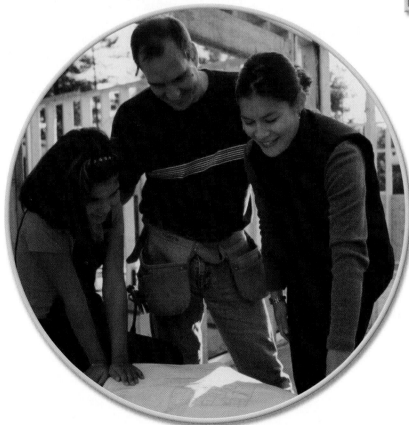

▲ If you become a scientist, you might use measurement and geometry to conduct experiments in space.

Have a great year and enjoy learning Math!

PRACTICE WHAT YOU LEARN

It's in the Bag

PROJECT In each unit of this book, you'll do a project that will help you practice the math skills you've learned. Make the Math Pockets Plus below to hold some of these projects.

Materials

- 9 paper lunch bags (size 12)
- Clear, wide packaging tape
- Scissors
- Markers, crayons, and color pencils

Directions

1. Cut off the bottom of each bag. (*Picture A*) Then open each bag by unfolding the pleats, and lay the bag flat. Tape the bottom of each bag closed to make a pocket.

2. Turn down the top of each bag. Cut along each end of the turned-down part, and cut off the bottom flap. (*Picture B*) Cut off the corners of the top flap, making an envelope-like closing.

3. Lay the bags next to each other, and tape them together at the edges. (*Picture C*) Then fold them accordion-style to make an organizer.

4. Decorate and label each bag with the unit number on the flap and the unit title on the pocket. Apply a hook-and-loop fastener to the opening of each bag, if desired.

A

B

C

SHOW WHAT YOU LEARN

Taking a test is one way to show what you've learned. Being a good test taker is like being a good problem solver. When you answer test questions, you are solving problems.

Each time you take a test, remember to:

- Listen carefully to your teacher's instructions.
- Read all the directions.
- Pay attention to where and how to mark the test.
- Read the problems carefully.
- If you don't understand a problem, read it again.
- Mark or write your answers clearly.
- Answer questions you are sure about first.
- Work quickly but carefully.
- If you finish early, go back and check your work.
- Relax and do the best that you can.

GETTING READY!

Practice Addition and Subtraction

You can use mental math strategies and regrouping to find sums and differences.

BREAK APART STRATEGY

Find the sum.   Think: $79 = 70 + 9$
$79 + 37$ $37 = 30 + 7$

$70 + 30 = 100$ Add the tens.
$9 + 7 = 16$ Add the ones.
$100 + 16 = 116$ Add the sums.

So, $79 + 37 = 116$.

MAKE A TEN STRATEGY

Find the difference.   Think: Add 2 to 38 to
$285 - 38$ get 40.

$38 + 2 = 40$ Add 2 to 285 to
$285 + 2 = 287$ adjust the difference.
$287 - 40 = 247$ Subtract $287 - 40$.

So, $285 - 38 = 247$.

REGROUPING IN ADDITION

$$\begin{array}{r} 1 \\ 643 \\ +\ 95 \\ \hline 738 \end{array}$$

Think: Regroup 13 tens as 1 hundred 3 tens.

REGROUPING IN SUBTRACTION

$$\begin{array}{r} 9 \\ 3\ 10\ 10 \\ \cancel{400} \\ -\ 176 \\ \hline 224 \end{array}$$

Think:
Regroup 4 hundreds as 3 hundreds 9 tens 10 ones.

▶ ## Practice

Find the sum or difference.

1. $\begin{array}{r} 62 \\ +\ 18 \\ \hline \end{array}$ **2.** $\begin{array}{r} 75 \\ -\ 49 \\ \hline \end{array}$ **3.** $\begin{array}{r} 80 \\ -\ 36 \\ \hline \end{array}$ **4.** $\begin{array}{r} 93 \\ +\ 25 \\ \hline \end{array}$

5. $\begin{array}{r} 73 \\ -\ 24 \\ \hline \end{array}$ **6.** $\begin{array}{r} 138 \\ +\ 57 \\ \hline \end{array}$ **7.** $\begin{array}{r} 300 \\ -\ 124 \\ \hline \end{array}$ **8.** $\begin{array}{r} 419 \\ +\ 68 \\ \hline \end{array}$

9. $\begin{array}{r} 503 \\ -\ 146 \\ \hline \end{array}$ **10.** $\begin{array}{r} 783 \\ +\ 544 \\ \hline \end{array}$ **11.** $\begin{array}{r} 250 \\ -\ 193 \\ \hline \end{array}$ **12.** $\begin{array}{r} 639 \\ +\ 754 \\ \hline \end{array}$

13. $\begin{array}{r} 32 \\ 57 \\ +\ 28 \\ \hline \end{array}$ **14.** $\begin{array}{r} 42 \\ 68 \\ +\ 59 \\ \hline \end{array}$

Practice Multiplication and Division

You can use multiplication fact families, place value, and regrouping to review multiplication and division.

EXAMPLES

Use place value and regrouping to find products.

$$
\begin{array}{r}
1 \\
62 \\
\times\ 47 \\
\hline
434 \\
+\ 2480 \\
\hline
2{,}914
\end{array}
$$

Think: Multiply by 7 ones, then by 4 tens, or 40.

7×62

40×62

Use place value to place the first digit in the quotient.
Then, use the order of division.

$$
\begin{array}{r}
56\ \text{r}3 \\
7\overline{)395} \\
-\ 35 \\
\hline
45 \\
-\ 42 \\
\hline
3
\end{array}
$$

$3 < 7$, so look at the tens.
$39 > 7$, so use 39 tens.
Place the first digit in the tens place.

Divide.
Multiply.
Subtract.
Compare.

▶ Practice

Multiply or divide.

1. 17
    × 49

2. 67
    × 15

3. 40
    × 38

4. 66
    × 24

5. 307
    × 65

6. 514
    × 87

7. 148
    × 52

8. 760
    × 19

9. 114
    × 23

10. 5)79

11. 4)83

12. 6)78

13. 7)294

14. 9)470

15. 8)809

Place Value of Whole Numbers

Satellite image of North America at night

≡FAST FACT • SOCIAL STUDIES
One person is added to the United States population every 17 seconds. Much of the population lives in just a few areas.

PROBLEM SOLVING   Look at the graph. Which two states have about the same populations? List the states in order from the greatest population to the least population.

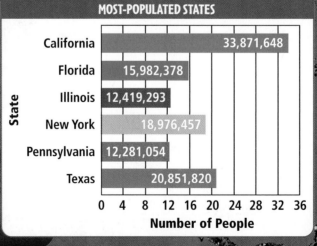

MOST-POPULATED STATES

State	Number of People
California	33,871,648
Florida	15,982,378
Illinois	12,419,293
New York	18,976,457
Pennsylvania	12,281,054
Texas	20,851,820

0 4 8 12 16 20 24 28 32 36
Number of People

CHECK WHAT YOU KNOW

Use this page to help you review and remember
important skills needed for Chapter 1.

PLACE VALUE

Write the value of the digit 6 in each number.

1. 62,980 **2.** 368 **3.** 56,709 **4.** 906

Write the value of the blue digit.

5. 560 **6.** 3,072 **7.** 47,092 **8.** 30,561

9. 6,257 **10.** 13,348 **11.** 97,812 **12.** 20,465

READ AND WRITE WHOLE NUMBERS

Write each number in two other forms.

13. sixteen thousand, forty **14.** 50,000 + 4,000 + 200 + 4

15. eighty-seven thousand, forty-two **16.** 20,000 + 3,000 + 50 + 6

Write the number in expanded form.

17. 387 **18.** 2,412 **19.** 43,671 **20.** 35,902

21. 60,234 **22.** 12,084 **23.** 13,087 **24.** 92,530

Write the number in word form.

25. 409 **26.** 2,010 **27.** 5,102 **28.** 73,249

29. 14,013 **30.** 89,738 **31.** 30,952 **32.** 16,870

VOCABULARY POWER

REVIEW

digit [di′jit] *noun*

Digit is one of the oldest mathematical
words. In addition to meaning "a numeral,"
digit can also mean "a finger or a toe."
Name two ways the word *digital* is used
today.

PREVIEW

billion

benchmark

www.harcourtschool.com/mathglossary

Understand Place Value

▶ **Learn**

BUSY BEES Mr. Howard is a beekeeper. He raises bees for the honey they produce. His two colonies have about 128,000 bees. To understand how many bees this is, you need to understand the place value of each digit in 128,000.

MATH IDEA Each digit in a number has a place value. The value of a digit depends on its place, or position, in the number.

The place value of the digit 8 in 128,000 is thousands. The value of 8 in 128,000 is $8 \times 1,000 = 8,000$.

Remember

Starting from the right, each group of three digits forms a period. Commas separate the periods.

--- PERIOD ---

THOUSANDS			ONES		
Hundreds	Tens	Ones	Hundreds	Tens	Ones
1	2	8,	0	0	0
$1 \times 100,000$	$2 \times 10,000$	$8 \times 1,000$	0×100	0×10	0×1
100,000	20,000	8,000	0	0	0

Technology Link

More Practice: Harcourt Mega Math The Number Games, *Tiny's Think Tank,* Level A

Standard Form: 128,000

Expanded Form: $100,000 + 20,000 + 8,000$

Word Form: one hundred twenty-eight thousand

Examples

A

    Standard Form: 2,641

    Expanded Form: $2,000 + 600 + 40 + 1$

    Word Form: two thousand, six hundred forty-one

B

    Standard Form: 97,508

    Expanded Form: $90,000 + 7,000 + 500 + 8$

    Word Form: ninety-seven thousand, five hundred eight

1. **Explain** how to find the value of the digit 4 in the number 2,467.

Write the value of the blue digit.

2. 567   **3.** 38   **4.** 6,459   **5.** 45,088   **6.** 123,047

Write each number in expanded form and in word form.

7. 430   **8.** 36,025   **9.** 8,922   **10.** 12,608   **11.** 690,000

▶ **Practice and Problem Solving**   Extra Practice, page 16, Set A

Write the value of the blue digit.

12. 979   **13.** 345,671   **14.** 23,874   **15.** 861,113   **16.** 909,904

Write each number in expanded form and in word form.

17. 653   **18.** 44,703   **19.** 1,922   **20.** 723,651   **21.** 400,230

Write each number in standard form.

22. 70,000 + 6,000 + 400 + 10 + 8   **23.** 600,000 + 20,000 + 1,000 + 70 + 3

24. twenty-five thousand, seventy-five   **25.** four hundred sixteen thousand, three hundred twelve

26. A truck driver delivers 20,000 honey jars to 3 grocery stores. If 10,200 jars are delivered to the first grocery store, 1,600 to the second, and the remaining jars to the third store, how many jars are delivered to the third store?

27. A butterfly migrated four thousand, eight hundred twenty-eight kilometers! Write this number in standard form.

28. Vocabulary Power In some sports, *periods* are the equal portions of time into which a game is divided. How does this relate to the *periods* of a number?

Mixed Review and Test Prep

USE DATA For 29–30, use the graph.

29. Which school has the most students? the fewest?

30. Which school has the most male students?

31. 9 × 8   **32.** 30 ÷ 6

33. Which is the sum 80,444 + 812,045?

     A 792,489   **C** 892,589
     B 892,489   **D** 902,489

SCHOOL POPULATION

■ males
■ females

Number of Students: 0, 100, 200, 300, 400, 500, 600

Parker   Delaney   Polytech
School

Millions and Billions

▶ **Learn**

MOONWALK   An estimated 1 million people crowded Florida roads and beaches to see the launch of *Apollo 11*. You can use a grid to understand the size of 1 million.

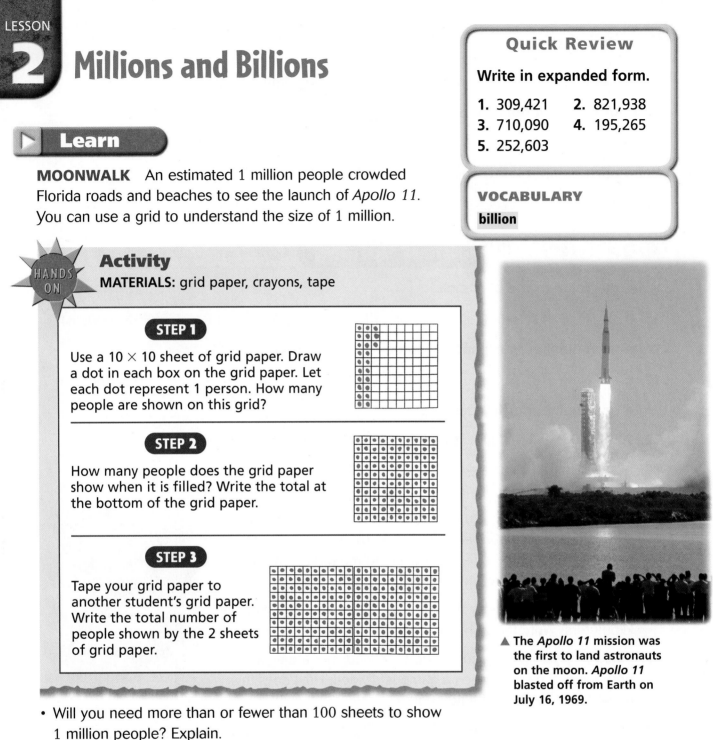

Activity

MATERIALS: grid paper, crayons, tape

STEP 1

Use a 10 × 10 sheet of grid paper. Draw a dot in each box on the grid paper. Let each dot represent 1 person. How many people are shown on this grid?

STEP 2

How many people does the grid paper show when it is filled? Write the total at the bottom of the grid paper.

STEP 3

Tape your grid paper to another student's grid paper. Write the total number of people shown by the 2 sheets of grid paper.

▲ The *Apollo 11* mission was the first to land astronauts on the moon. *Apollo 11* blasted off from Earth on July 16, 1969.

• Will you need more than or fewer than 100 sheets to show 1 million people? Explain.

An estimated 726,300,000 people watched Neil Armstrong take the first step on the moon. You can show this number on a place-value chart.

MILLIONS			THOUSANDS			ONES		
Hundreds	Tens	Ones	Hundreds	Tens	Ones	Hundreds	Tens	Ones
7	2	6,	3	0	0,	0	0	0

Standard Form: 726,300,000

Expanded Form: 700,000,000 + 20,000,000 + 6,000,000 + 300,000

Word Form: seven hundred twenty-six million, three hundred thousand

Billions

The National Aeronautics and Space Administration (NASA) funding for Project Apollo's human spaceflights was $19,407,134,000.

A billion has one more period than a million. One **billion** is 1,000 million.

BILLIONS			MILLIONS			THOUSANDS			ONES		
Hundreds	Tens	Ones	Hundreds	Tens	Ones	Hundreds	Tens	Ones	Hundreds	Tens	Ones
	1	9,	4	0	7,	1	3	4,	0	0	0

Standard Form: 19,407,134,000

Expanded Form: 10,000,000,000 + 9,000,000,000 + 400,000,000 + 7,000,000 + 100,000 + 30,000 + 4,000

Word Form: nineteen billion, four hundred seven million, one hundred thirty-four thousand

• How do periods help you read a number?

REASONING   There are 1,000 millions in 1 billion. How many 10 millions are in 10 billion?

MATH IDEA   Place value and periods help you read and write greater numbers.

Check

1. Explain how the word form and the expanded form for 3,450,632 are alike. How are they different?

▲ Neil Armstrong snapped this picture of Buzz Aldrin as Aldrin stepped onto the moon.

Write each number in standard form.

2. five million, three hundred fourteen

3. two billion, six hundred eleven thousand, one hundred seven

4. thirty-three million, two hundred seven thousand, twelve

5. eighty million, three hundred eight thousand, four

Use the number 4,302,698,051.

6. Write the name of the period that has the digits 698.

7. Write the name of the period that has the digits 302.

8. Write the digit in the ten-millions place.

9. Write the place value of the digit 4.

LESSON CONTINUES

Write each number in standard form.

10. twenty-one million, eleven thousand, two hundred twelve

11. fifty-three billion, two million, one hundred sixteen thousand, seven

Write the value of the blue digit.

12. 35,427,231 **13.** 780,904,652 **14.** 413,916,102 **15.** 19,413,572

16. 8,102,673,124 **17.** 14,956,630,210 **18.** 9,124,432,212 **19.** 424,984,127

In which number does the digit 7 have the greater value? Explain.

20. a. 17,854
　　b. 105,079

21. a. 7,089,000,000
　　b. 7,089,000

22. a. 760
　　b. 750,000

For 23–24, copy and complete.

23. The number 2,984,052,681 represents two billion, __?__ hundred eighty-four million, fifty-two thousand, __?__ hundred eighty-one.

24. ✦ALGEBRA
$5{,}000{,}000 + \blacksquare + 10{,}000 + 6{,}000 + \blacksquare + 50 + 1 = 5{,}716{,}651$

Write each number in two other forms.

25. two million, three hundred six thousand, fifteen

26. $1{,}000{,}000{,}000 + 10{,}000{,}000 + 10{,}000 + 100 + 1$

27. 65,200,108 **28.** 207,111,006 **29.** 1,480,200,965

USE DATA For 30–31, use the table.

30. Which planet is about ninety-two million, nine hundred thousand miles from the sun?

31. About how many billion miles is Neptune from the sun?

32. ❓ **What's the Error?** Mary wrote the number 5,67,890. Explain her error. Write the number correctly in standard form.

33. **REASONING** If your printer could print a number every second, about how many hours would it take for it to print all the numbers from 1 to 1,000,000?

DISTANCE FROM THE SUN	
Planet in the Solar System	**Approximate Average Distance From the Sun (in Miles)**
Mercury	35,960,000
Earth	92,900,000
Neptune	2,793,000,000
Pluto	3,664,000,000

The sun ▶

34. **≡FAST FACT** • SCIENCE The distance between Earth and the moon is about 240,250 miles. Write this number in expanded form.

35. **REASONING** Write the least 9-digit number possible without repeating a digit. What is the value of the digit 2?

Mixed Review and Test Prep

Write the value of the blue digit. (p. 2)

36. 73,215   **37.** 678,621

There are 100 dimes in a roll.

38. How much money is each roll worth?

39. How many rolls of dimes do you need for $1,000,000?

Copy and complete.

40. $6 \times 2 = 4 \times \blacksquare$ **41.** $50 - 34 = 4 \times \blacksquare$

42. Write the factors of 24.

Choose the letter of the next three numbers in the pattern.

43. **TEST PREP**   9, 12, 15, 18
    A 19, 20, 21   **C** 21, 23, 26
    B 21, 24, 27   **D** 23, 25, 27

44. **TEST PREP**   1, 2, 4, 7, 11
    F 16, 22, 29   **H** 16, 24, 31
    G 14, 18, 23   **J** 13, 15, 17

Problem Solving Thinker's Corner

WHAT'S THE NUMBER'S SIZE? The students at Forest Lake Elementary School collected pennies for one year to pay for new band uniforms. At the end of the year, they had collected one million pennies.

Is the value of one million pennies greater than or less than $1,000,000?

Since it takes 100 pennies to make one dollar, then 1,000,000 pennies has to be less than $1,000,000.

Use these questions to help you see how 1,000,000 relates to other numbers.

1. Is 1,000,000 greater than or less than 100,000?

2. Does your school library have more than or fewer than 1,000,000 books?

3. Is 1,000,000 books more than or fewer than 850,000 books?

4. Is 1,000,000 closer to 900,000 or closer to 1,500,000?

For 5–7, use the numbers 680,000; 850,000; and 2,450,000.

5. Which two numbers are closest to each other?

6. Name a number that is less than all 3 numbers.

7. Name a number between 680,000 and 850,000.

3 Benchmark Numbers

Quick Review

Write the value of the digit 8.

1. 108   **2.** 4,801
3. 38,234   **4.** 56,980
5. 89,095

VOCABULARY

benchmark

▶ **Learn**

TO COUNT OR NOT TO COUNT! A **benchmark** is a familiar number used as a point of reference. You can use a benchmark to determine a reasonable estimate.

Notre Dame Stadium is in South Bend, Indiana. In the top photo each outlined section seats about 1,000 people. About how many people can sit in the 3 outlined sections?

The benchmark is 1,000 people. The larger section is about 3 times as great.

So, about 3,000 people can sit in the 3 outlined sections.

Examples

A Which estimate of the number of trading cards is more reasonable, 500 or 1,500?

Benchmark: 100 cards

The taller stack of cards is about 5 times the benchmark amount.
5 × 100 = 500

So, the more reasonable estimate of the number of trading cards in the taller stack is 500.

B What is a reasonable estimate of the number of pieces of macaroni in the full jar?

Benchmark: 500 pieces

The full jar of macaroni holds about 4 times the benchmark amount.
4 × 500 = 2,000

So, a reasonable estimate of the number of pieces of macaroni in the full jar is 2,000.

• In Example A, why is 1,500 not a reasonable estimate?

▲ Notre Dame Stadium

▶ **Check**

1. Explain how a benchmark of 20 people in one row could help you estimate the number of people in a movie theater.

Use the benchmark to find a reasonable estimate.

2. dog food in a full jar

100 pieces   _?_

3. baseballs in a full carton

30 baseballs   _?_

▶ Practice and Problem Solving   Extra Practice, page 16, Set C

Use the benchmark to find a reasonable estimate.

4. bricks in a wall

100 bricks   _?_

5. CDs in a stack

50 CDs   _?_

6. ESTIMATION In every major league baseball game, about 6 dozen baseballs are used. If 5 games are played in a week, how many baseballs will be used?

7. 📖 **Write About It** Explain how you can use a benchmark of 50 bike riders per grade to estimate the number of bicycles at your school.

Mixed Review and Test Prep

8. Write thirty-eight million, six thousand, nine hundred forty-five in standard form.
(p. 4)

9. Write $1,000,000 + 500,000 + 7,000 + 400 + 90 + 8$ in standard form. (p. 4)

10. The number 528,390,467 represents _?_ twenty-eight million, three hundred _?_ thousand, _?_ hundred sixty-seven. (p. 4)

11. $4 \times 5 = \blacksquare + 8$

12. ⭐ **TEST PREP** Which is the value of the digit 7 in 176,495,283? (p. 4)

  A 7,000
  B 700,000
  C 7,000,000
  D 70,000,000

LESSON

4

Compare and Order

Quick Review

Write the value of the blue digit.

1. 60   **2.** 4,260

3. 5,209   **4.** 2,854

5. 11,463

▷ **Learn**

POPULAR POOCHES The dachshund and the beagle are two popular dog breeds in the United States. In a recent year, there were 50,478 dachshunds and 50,419 beagles registered with the American Kennel Club. Which breed had more dogs registered?

One Way Use a number line to compare 50,478 and 50,419.

50,478   **Think:** 50,478 is to the right
50,419   of 50,419, so 50,478 > 50,419.

50,000 50,100 50,200 50,300 50,400 50,500 50,600 50,700 50,800 50,900 51,000

Another Way Use place value. Start at the left. Compare the digits in each place-value position until the digits are different.

STEP 1	STEP 2	STEP 3	STEP 4
Compare the ten thousands.	Compare the thousands.	Compare the hundreds.	Compare the tens.
50,478	50,478	50,478	50,478
↓ same	↓ same	↓ same	↓ 7 > 1
50,419	50,419	50,419	50,419
			So, 50,478 > 50,419.

Since 50,478 > 50,419, there were more dachshunds registered than beagles.

• How does aligning the digits by place value help you compare numbers?

Examples   Compare.

Ⓐ 84,200,000
       ↓   2 < 9
   84,900,000

So, 84,200,000 < 84,900,000.

Ⓑ 1,024,850
       ↓   1 > 0
     643,850

There are no millions in 643,850.

So, 1,024,850 > 643,850.

10

Order Whole Numbers

In that same year, there were 40,005 poodles, 42,025 Yorkshire terriers, and 37,035 boxers registered. Order these breeds from the least number of dogs registered to the greatest.

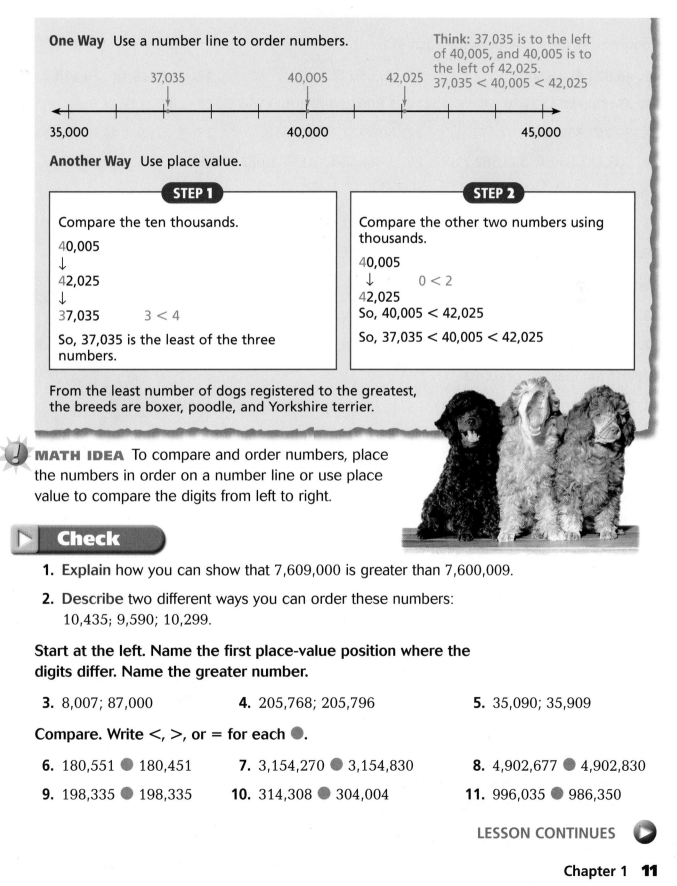

One Way Use a number line to order numbers.

Think: 37,035 is to the left of 40,005, and 40,005 is to the left of 42,025.
37,035 < 40,005 < 42,025

Another Way Use place value.

STEP 1

Compare the ten thousands.

40,005
↓
42,025
↓
37,035   3 < 4

So, 37,035 is the least of the three numbers.

STEP 2

Compare the other two numbers using thousands.

40,005
↓   0 < 2
42,025
So, 40,005 < 42,025

So, 37,035 < 40,005 < 42,025

From the least number of dogs registered to the greatest, the breeds are boxer, poodle, and Yorkshire terrier.

MATH IDEA To compare and order numbers, place the numbers in order on a number line or use place value to compare the digits from left to right.

▷ Check

1. **Explain** how you can show that 7,609,000 is greater than 7,600,009.

2. **Describe** two different ways you can order these numbers: 10,435; 9,590; 10,299.

Start at the left. Name the first place-value position where the digits differ. Name the greater number.

3. 8,007; 87,000
4. 205,768; 205,796
5. 35,090; 35,909

Compare. Write <, >, or = for each ●.

6. 180,551 ● 180,451
7. 3,154,270 ● 3,154,830
8. 4,902,677 ● 4,902,830
9. 198,335 ● 198,335
10. 314,308 ● 304,004
11. 996,035 ● 986,350

LESSON CONTINUES ▷

Start at the left. Name the first place-value position where the digits differ. Name the greater number.

12. 6,712; 61,365   **13.** 680,742; 680,789   **14.** 351,604; 351,408

Compare. Write <, >, or = for each ●.

15. 48,922 ● 49,800   **16.** 15,650 ● 5,650   **17.** 187,418 ● 178,418

18. 451,300 ● 452,030   **19.** 1,800,250 ● 1,800,250   **20.** 28,792 ● 28,790

21. 20,767,300 ● 2,767,071   **22.** 602,717 ● 602,718   **23.** 7,451,950 ● 7,045,950

24. 509,782,650 ● 509,562,710   **25.** 1,098,254,701 ● 1,082,276,535

Find the missing digit.

26. 1,988,678 < 1,98■,678   **27.** 192,717,568 > 19■,717,568

28. 5,323,134 > 5,323,■34   **29.** 537,691,432 > 537,69■,432

Order from greatest to least.

30. 26,295; 216,925; 219,625   **31.** 235,289; 236,287; 236,178

32. 78,935; 77,590; 178,286   **33.** 234,650,200; 234,850,100; 38,950,500

Order from least to greatest.

34. 895,000; 8,595,000; 859,000   **35.** 4,210,632; 2,410,781; 4,120,681

36. 49,086; 49,680; 48,690   **37.** 335,219; 336,007; 336,278

USE DATA For 38–40, use the graph.

38. Order from greatest to least the number of terriers registered.

39. How much greater is the number of Yorkshire terriers than the total number of silky, Boston, Scottish, cairn, and Airedale terriers?

40. When comparing the number of Scottish terriers to Airedale terriers, in which place value do the digits first differ?

41. ✒ Write About It Explain how to compare 1,879,987 and 1,979,987.

42. ✨❓ What's the Question? There are 3 numbers: 345,789; 355,984; and 355,798. The answer is 355,984.

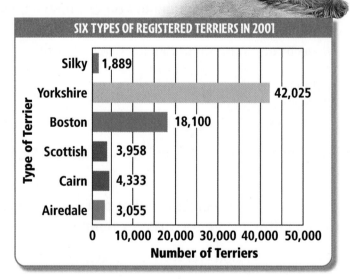

SIX TYPES OF REGISTERED TERRIERS IN 2001

Silky: 1,889
Yorkshire: 42,025
Boston: 18,100
Scottish: 3,958
Cairn: 4,333
Airedale: 3,055

Type of Terrier

Number of Terriers: 0 10,000 20,000 30,000 40,000 50,000

REASONING Kim, Juan, and Karen went to the annual dog show. Kim drove 455 miles to get there. Juan drove 110 miles farther than Kim. Karen drove 150 miles less than Juan. Use this information for 43–44.

43. How far did each person drive to the dog show?

44. Who drove the least distance? Who drove the greatest distance?

Mixed Review and Test Prep

45. $36 \div 3$

46. 9×6

47. Write $3,000,000,000 + 60,000,000 + 8,000,000 + 20,000 + 6,000 + 9$ in standard form. (p. 5)

48. $9,011 - 1,235$

49. TEST PREP How many dimes are in $55?

   A 55   **C** 550

   B 500   **D** 5,050

50. 9×3

51. 8×4

Write the number that is 1,000 more.

52. 4,099

53. 56,230

54. TEST PREP Which number is one million, seventeen thousand, four hundred sixty-five written in standard form? (p. 4)

   F 1,170,465   **H** 1,017,465

   G 1,017,645   **J** 1,017,346

Problem Solving Thinker's Corner

VISUAL THINKING Rachel is using base-ten blocks to help her compare 1,380 and 1,365. She uses cubes to represent thousands, flats to represent hundreds, rods to represent tens, and units to represent ones.

1. Look at the photo. Which number is represented by the base-ten blocks, 1,380 or 1,365?

2. Use base-ten blocks to show 1,380 and 1,365.

3. Draw your models.

4. Explain how you can use the blocks or drawings to help you decide which number is greater.

Use base-ten blocks to model. Draw your models. Write <, >, or = for each ●.

5. 432 ● 408

6. 1,521 ● 1,512

7. 1,055 ● 1,505

8. 290 ● 209

Problem Solving Skill
Use a Table

UNDERSTAND ▷ PLAN ▷ SOLVE ▷ CHECK

SIZE IT UP Rhode Island is the smallest state in the United States. Delaware is the second smallest state. What is the difference between the areas of Delaware and Rhode Island?

AREA AND POPULATION OF STATES

Name	Area (sq mi)	Population
Delaware	2,396	783,600
Florida	65,755	15,982,378
Indiana	36,418	6,080,485
Michigan	58,527	9,938,444
New Jersey	8,215	8,414,350
Rhode Island	1,231	1,048,319

Find the areas of Delaware and Rhode Island. Then subtract to find the difference.

Area of Delaware   2,396 square miles
Area of Rhode Island −1,231 square miles
                              1,165 square miles

So, the difference in areas is 1,165 square miles.

Talk About It

• How are the states ordered in the table? How would you change the table to show the state populations in order from greatest to least?

• Explain how reading the data from a table helps you solve problems.

Problem Solving Practice

USE DATA   For 1–4, use the table.

CAPITAL CITIES	
City and State	**Population**
Baton Rouge, LA	227,818
Indianapolis, IN	791,926
Nashville, TN	569,891
Oklahoma City, OK	506,132
Richmond, VA	197,790

1. Which city has the greatest population? the least?

3. **ALGEBRA**   Which equation shows the combined populations of Nashville and Richmond if *n* represents the total population?

  A $569,891 + 197,790 = n$
  B $n + 197,790 = 569,891$
  C $n = 197,790 - 569,891$
  D $569,891 + n = 197,790$

2. How much greater is the population of Nashville than the population of Oklahoma City?

4. Which states' capital cities have populations of 1 million when rounded to the nearest million?

  F VA, IN, OK   **H** IN, TN, OK
  G IN, TN, VA   **J** LA, TN, OK

Mixed Applications

5. The clock shows the time Mike's 1-hour flight landed in Richmond. It took him 30 minutes to drive to the airport, and he was 45 minutes early for his flight. At what time did he leave his house?

6. Sasha's family is planning a trip. They can go to either Orlando or New York. They can drive, fly, or take the train to their destination. Make a list of their choices.

7. Bill said, "The greater the state's area, the greater the population." How can you use the table on page 14 to decide whether Bill's statement is correct?

8. **ALGEBRA**   The Smiths drove a total of 540 miles in 2 days. They drove twice as far on Tuesday as they did on Monday. How many miles did they drive on Monday? on Tuesday?

9. Write a problem using the "Capital Cities" table above. Then solve the problem.

Extra Practice

Set A (pp. 2–3)

Write the value of the blue digit.

1. 14,350   **2.** 54,079   **3.** 635,017   **4.** 3,980

Write each number in expanded form and in word form.

5. 34   **6.** 6,080   **7.** 123,689   **8.** 991

Write each number in word form.

9. 642,007   **10.** 2,311   **11.** 1,078   **12.** 601

Set B (pp. 4–7)

Write each number in standard form.

1. 3,000,000 + 40,000 + 9,000 + 200 + 7

2. 50,000,000 + 1,000,000 + 400,000 + 10,000 + 300 + 20 + 5

3. forty-three million, three hundred ten thousand, five hundred seven

4. six billion, five hundred six million, thirteen thousand, four hundred twenty

Write the value of the blue digit.

5. 9,450,180   **6.** 47,329,052   **7.** 8,506,332,189

Set C (pp. 8–9)

Use the benchmark to find a reasonable estimate.

1. nails in a bucket

50 nails   ?

2. buttons in a box

200 buttons   ?

Set D (pp. 10–13)

Compare. Write <, >, or = for each ●.

1. 18,276 ● 18,287   **2.** 845,418 ● 845,418   **3.** 50,967,300 ● 5,967,021

Order from greatest to least.

4. 12,945; 12,693; 12,990

5. 10,235,561; 1,235,561; 10,253,561

Order from least to greatest.

6. 436,042,303; 463,054,119; 64,332,989

7. 1,525,202; 1,252,202; 1,522,202

Review/Test

✔ CHECK VOCABULARY AND CONCEPTS

Choose the best term from the box.

million
billion
benchmark
period

1. A thousand thousands is equal to one ___?___ . (p. 4)

2. A familiar number used as a point of reference is called a ___?___ . (p. 8)

✔ CHECK SKILLS

Write the value of the blue digit. (pp. 2–7)

3. 162,408

4. 27,140,652

Write each number in two other forms. (pp. 4–7)

5. 2,030,909

6. three billion, two hundred three million, forty-two thousand, five

Use the benchmark to find a reasonable estimate. (pp. 8–9)

7. peanuts in a jar

100 peanuts   ___?___

Compare. Write < , > , or = for each ●. (pp. 10–13)

8. 104,690 ● 140,690

9. 3,250 ● 13,250

10. 9,782,650 ● 9,782,650

Order from least to greatest. (pp. 10–13)

11. 9,519; 10,003; 9,195

12. 1,502,369; 1,501,369; 1,507,369

✔ CHECK PROBLEM SOLVING

USE DATA   For 13–14, use the table. (pp. 14–15)

13. Order the lakes from the least area to the greatest area.

14. List the lakes in order from the greatest maximum depth to the least maximum depth.

15. In the future, a spaceship might be built that could travel 100,000 miles a second. How long would it take to travel 1 million miles? 10 million miles? (pp. 4–7)

AREAS OF THE GREAT LAKES		
Lake	Area (sq mi)	Maximum Depth (ft)
Michigan	22,300	923
Erie	9,910	210
Ontario	7,550	802
Superior	31,700	1,330
Huron	23,000	750

Standardized Test Prep

NUMBER SENSE, CONCEPTS, AND OPERATIONS

1. This table shows languages other than English that are spoken in the United States. Which language is spoken by the **greatest** number of these people?

SOME LANGUAGES IN THE U.S.	
Language	**Number of Speakers**
French	1,702,000
Greek	388,000
Chinese	1,249,000
Spanish	17,339,000

A French

B Greek

C Chinese

D Spanish

2. Randi read about the heights of mountains in the United States. Mt. Bear is 14,831 feet tall; Mt. Elbert is 14,433 feet; Mt. Rainier is 14,410 feet, and Mt. Whitney is 14,494 feet. Which shows the heights in order from **greatest** to **least**?

F 14,831; 14,494; 14,433; 14,410

G 14,494; 14,433; 14,831; 14,410

H 14,410; 14,433; 14,494; 14,831

J 14,831; 14,410; 14,433; 14,494

3. Explain It A bookstore sold 249 books on Friday and 475 books on Saturday. ESTIMATE the number of books sold during the two days. Explain your estimate.

MEASUREMENT

4. Which weighs about 3 kilograms?

A a balloon

B a watermelon

C a pencil

D a refrigerator

TIP **Decide on a plan.** See item 5. Using the strategy *draw a diagram* may help you find the perimeter of the park. Draw a square and label the sides 115 m.

5. Timothy jogs around the park every morning. The park is a square with sides 115 meters long. What is the perimeter of the park?

F 460 meters

G 450 meters

H 345 meters

J 330 meters

6. Which of these units is the most reasonable unit to use when measuring the distance between Atlanta and Miami?

A inch

B foot

C yard

D mile

7. Explain It A juice bottle holds 4 pints. Is this enough to serve one cup each to 4 people? Explain how you know.

⭐ DATA ANALYSIS AND PROBABILITY

8. Lara tossed a coin and drew this bar graph of the results. How many times did the coin land on tails?

F 5 **H** 15

G 10 **J** 25

9. Suppose you have the following cards in a bag.

Which statement below is true?

A The probability of drawing a red card is less than the probability of drawing a yellow card.

B The probability of drawing a red card or a yellow card is the same.

C The probability of drawing a red card is greater than the probability of drawing a yellow card.

D The probability of drawing a red card or a yellow card is 0.

10. Explain It Carlos can choose from these pizza crusts and toppings.

Crusts: thin, thick
Toppings: pepperoni, sausage, ham, mushroom, peppers, onion

How many different choices of crust and one topping does he have? Explain how you found your answer.

⭐ GEOMETRY AND SPATIAL SENSE

11. Which of the following is an obtuse angle?

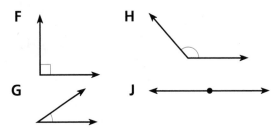

12. Which **best** describes the lines in the figure?

A intersecting and parallel

B parallel and perpendicular

C intersecting and perpendicular

D intersecting and NOT perpendicular

13. Which word **best** describes how the figure was moved?

F translation **H** reflection

G rotation **J** tessellation

14. Explain It Name the ordered pair that shows the location of the pool. Explain how you know.

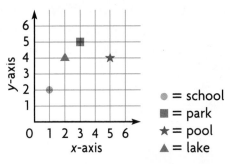

Place Value of Decimals

≡FAST FACT • SCIENCE

Pollen grains produced by plants are microscopic. Wind, water, and animals can carry pollen grains to new locations. Pollen can drift in from 400 miles out at sea and 2 miles high in the air.

PROBLEM SOLVING The main features that make one type of pollen different from another are size, shape, and the surface of the grain. Look at the graph. Order the sizes of the pollen grains from greatest to least.

POLLEN GRAINS

Type	Grain Size (in millimeters)
Giant water lily	0.2
Forget-me-not	0.006
Daisy	0.025
Snapdragon	0.015

0   0.05   0.1   0.15   0.2   0.25

Grain Size (in millimeters)

Pollen of giant water lilies

Forget-me-not and pollen

Daisies and pollen

Snapdragon and pollen

CHECK WHAT YOU KNOW

Use this page to help you review and remember
important skills needed for Chapter 2.

ORDER WHOLE NUMBERS

Write the numbers in order from least to greatest.

1. 8,945; 8,962; 8,974

2. 890,104; 809,192; 899,110

3. 45,325; 44,254; 42,124

4. 3,004; 3,040; 3,404

Write the numbers in order from greatest to least.

5. 3,257; 3,268; 3,284

6. 743,125; 734,216; 763,326

7. 23,322; 23,321; 23,335

8. 302,233; 326,799; 328,232

READ AND WRITE DECIMALS

Write as a decimal.

9.

10.

11.

Write the number in two other forms.

12. fourteen and three tenths

13. 7,000 + 4 + 0.1

14. 3,000 + 20 + 7 + 0.2

15. 16.4

VOCABULARY POWER

REVIEW

equivalent [i•kwiv′ə•lənt] *adjective*

Equivalent is the combination of two Latin
roots, *aequus* and *valere*. The word *aequus*
means "equal" and *valere* means "value."
Explain how this information helps you find
the number that is equivalent to 72 ÷ 9.

PREVIEW

decimal
tenth
hundredth
thousandth
ten-thousandth
equivalent decimals

GO ON-LINE

www.harcourtschool.com/mathglossary

LESSON 1

Decimal Place Value

▷ Learn

TINY GRAINS! **Decimals** name wholes and parts of a whole. Scientists use decimals to measure pollen.

One whole is shaded.	One tenth is shaded.	One hundredth is shaded.
1	$\frac{1}{10}$	$\frac{1}{100}$
1.0	0.1	0.01
one	one tenth	one hundredth

Example 1 Use a place-value chart to find the value of each digit in the number 1.75. Then write the decimal in standard form, in expanded form, and in word form.

Ones	Tenths	Hundredths
1	7	5
$1 \times 1 = 1.0$	$7 \times 0.1 = 0.7$	$5 \times 0.01 = 0.05$

Standard Form: 1.75   **Expanded Form:** $1 + 0.7 + 0.05$

Word Form: one and seventy-five hundredths

▲ The marrow pollen grain is one of the largest pollen grains. Its size is 0.2 mm.

- How are $1\frac{75}{100}$ and 1.75 related?

MATH IDEA As you move from left to right on the place-value chart, the value of each place is one-tenth of the value of the place to its left.

You can locate decimals on a number line.

Remember

A *mixed number* is made up of a whole number and a fraction.

$1\frac{75}{100}$ is a mixed number.

Example 2

Locate 1.75, 0.35, and 0.8 on a number line.

- What if you were to locate 1.23 on the number line above? Would it be closer to 1.2 or closer to 1.3?

22

Thousandths and Ten-Thousandths

If you divide one whole by 1,000, you get one **thousandth**. If one square of a hundredth decimal model were magnified and one column of it were shaded, you could see one thousandth.

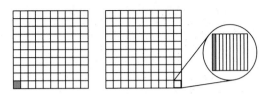

one hundredth   one thousandth

If you divide one whole by 10,000, you get one **ten-thousandth**.

$$1 \div 10,000 = \frac{1}{10,000} = 0.0001 = \text{one ten-thousandth}$$

You can also use a place-value chart to find the value of each digit in decimals to ten-thousandths. The chart below shows 2.7835.

▲ The forget-me-not pollen grain is the smallest pollen grain. Its size is 0.006 mm.

Ones	Tenths	Hundredths	Thousandths	Ten-thousandths
2	7	8	3	5
2 × 1	7 × 0.1	8 × 0.01	3 × 0.001	5 × 0.0001
2.0	0.7	0.08	0.003	0.0005

Standard Form: 2.7835
Expanded Form: 2 + 0.7 + 0.08 + 0.003 + 0.0005
Word Form: two and seven thousand, eight hundred thirty-five ten-thousandths

- How many thousandths are in one hundredth? in one tenth? in one?

Check

1. Explain a rule for the pattern: 10, 1, $\frac{1}{10}$, $\frac{1}{100}$. Write the next number.

Write as a decimal and as a fraction or mixed number.

2.

3.

4.

5. 3 + 0.57   6. eight and two tenths   7. thirty-two thousandths

LESSON CONTINUES

Write as a decimal and as a fraction or mixed number.

8. **9.** **10.**

11. 4 + 0.7

12. 10 + 7 + 0.7 + 0.01

13. 0.3 + 0.04

14. nine and six tenths

15. eighteen hundredths

16. one and six hundredths

Write each decimal in expanded form and in word form.

17. 1.067   **18.** 11.03   **19.** 1.045   **20.** 0.1234   **21.** 2.9

Write in standard form.

22. eight thousandths

23. fifty-four ten-thousandths

24. five hundredths

25. one and sixty-two thousandths

For 26–29, copy the number line below. Then locate each decimal.

```
 <——+++++++|+++++++|+++++++|+++++++|+++—>
    0      0.5     1.0      1.5     2.0
```

26. 0.45   **27.** 1.8   **28.** 0.07   **29.** 1.65

USE DATA For 30–33, use the circle graph.

30. How many people voted?

31. Mary says more than half of the voters chose daisies or sunflowers. Is Mary correct? Explain.

32. What fraction of the people voted for daisies?

33. 📓 Write a problem that can be solved by using the circle graph.

VOTES FOR FAVORITE FLOWERS

Key:
- carnations
- daisies
- roses
- sunflowers

40 25 15 20

REASONING In 34–37, the decimal point in some of the numbers has been placed incorrectly. Write the correct decimal number for each.

34. A car usually travels on the highway at 5.05 miles per hour.

35. When Wanda was sick, her temperature was 10.15 degrees.

36. In the fishing tournament, only fish 9 inches or longer can be kept. Joe threw back his fish because it measured 85 inches.

37. The long jump was won by Jake, whose jump measured 0.99 feet.

38. ≡**FAST FACT** • **SCIENCE** One of the greatest producers of pollen is the ragweed. A plant can release 8,000,000 pollen grains in just 5 hours. How many grains can one plant release in 10 hours?

39. Vocabulary Power When you write a number in *expanded form,* you actually "unfold" the place values and show the number in more detail. Write the expanded form of 0.327.

Mixed Review and Test Prep

40. Order 3,019,531; 3,019,643; and 3,019,639 from greatest to least. (p. 10)

41. The time is 5:25. What time will it be in 1 hour 35 minutes?

42. 700 + 850 **43.** 1,031 − 103

44. **TEST PREP** How many hours are in one week?
   A 168   **C** 60
   B 148   **D** 24

45. Write the factors of 42.

46. How is 9,000 + 20 + 2 written in standard form? (p. 2)

47. 3 × 40   **48.** 10 × 20

49. **TEST PREP** Which describes the number of sides of a hexagon?
   F 3 sides   **H** 6 sides
   G 4 sides   **J** 8 sides

Problem Solving LiNKÜP...to Science

BOTANIST Botanists are scientists who study plants and trees. Sequoias are the tallest trees in the world. The tallest sequoias are as tall as 26-story buildings. The heaviest sequoias can be 10 times the weight of the world's largest animal, the blue whale.

Giant sequoias begin life as tiny seeds. When botanists measure the very small parts of sequoias, they use decimals.

Use the Sequoia Fact Box to solve.

1. Use expanded form to write the width of a sequoia cone.

2. Write the length of a sequoia cone in word form.

3. Write the length of a sequoia seed as a fraction.

4. Use standard form to write the weight of a sequoia seed.

SEQUOIA FACT BOX	
Average length of cone	2.75 in.
Average width of cone	1.875 in.
Average weight of seed	three ten-thousandths oz
Average length of seed	0.1875 in.

Equivalent Decimals

Quick Review

Write in expanded form.

1. 3.7   **2.** 0.72

3. 4.908   **4.** 8.365

5. 13.004

VOCABULARY

equivalent decimals

▶ Learn

SAME BUT DIFFERENT Newborn red kangaroos, called joeys, are just 2.5 cm long. Adult red kangaroos can grow to a height of 1.6 m. Write an equivalent decimal for 1.6.

Equivalent decimals are different names for the same number or amount. These are some different ways to express the decimal 1.6 or its equivalent.

one and six tenths   1 + 0.6   1.60   1.600

To determine if two decimals are equivalent, draw models or line up the decimal points and compare the digits in the same place-value positions.

Examples

A Equivalent

0.4   0.40
0.4
0.40

B Not Equivalent

0.8   0.08
0.8
0.08

▲ The red kangaroo is Australia's largest kangaroo.

MATH IDEA Placing a zero to the right of the decimal point, after the last digit in a decimal, does not change its value.

▶ Check

Technology Link

More Practice: Harcourt Mega Math Fraction Action, *Number Line Mine,* Level M

1. Explain how to determine if 0.046 is equivalent to 0.0406.

Write *equivalent* or *not equivalent* to describe each pair of decimals.

2. 0.09 and 0.009   **3.** 3.8 and 3.80   **4.** 4 and 4.0   **5.** 7.2 and 7.02

Write an equivalent decimal for each number.

6. 5.3   **7.** 0.034   **8.** 0.1230   **9.** 9.030

26

Write *equivalent* or *not equivalent* to describe each pair of decimals.

10. 1.02 and 1.20   **11.** 6 and 6.0   **12.** 3.007 and 3.07

13. 7.02 and 7.020   **14.** 4.09 and 4.099   **15.** 4.008 and 4.08

Write an equivalent decimal for each number.

16. 0.03   **17.** 4.630   **18.** 0.2   **19.** 5.600   **20.** 0.83

21. 5.550   **22.** 7.10   **23.** 0.900   **24.** 0.103   **25.** 2.4

Write the two decimals that are equivalent.

26. 0.0502   **27.** 0.017   **28.** 1.00050   **29.** 8.01
0.00502   0.01700   1.0050   8.0010
0.05020   0.00170   1.005   8.01000

USE DATA For 30–31, use the table.

30. Which two animals have tails which are equivalent in length?

31. Write an equivalent decimal for the length of a leopard's tail.

32. A 0.5-pound block of cheddar cheese costs $1.89. The Swiss cheese costs $2.98 per pound. Which cheese is less expensive per pound? Explain.

33. The cash register showed change of $2.50. Miko said this is two and one half dollars. Is Miko correct? Explain.

34. ? **What's the Error?** Jeb's batting average is .309, and Tom's is .390. Tom says they have the same average. Describe Tom's error.

| MAMMALS WITH THE LONGEST TAILS ||
Mammal	Tail Length (in meters)
African buffalo	1.1
African elephant	1.3
Asian elephant	1.5
Giraffe	1.1
Leopard	1.4

35. **REASONING** Explain how to use a number line to show that 0.4 is not equivalent to 0.04.

Mixed Review and Test Prep

36. 70 + 80 + 90

37. 320 + 110 + 440

38. Order from greatest to least. 60,692; 605,962; 60,962 (p. 10)

39. Is 909,909 > 909,099? Write *yes* or *no*. (p. 10)

40. **TEST PREP** Which shows three million, four hundred fifty-six thousand, four hundred thirty-two in standard form? (p. 4)
   A 3,456,423
   B 3,456,432
   C 3,000,000 + 400,000 + 50,000 + 6,000 + 400 + 30 + 2
   D 3,465,432

Compare and Order Decimals

Quick Review
Compare.
1. 34 ● 43
2. 250 ● 205
3. 600 ● 600
4. 450 ● 4,500
5. 26,983 ● 29,683

▶ **Learn**

FIRST PLACE! The cardinal is the most popular state bird. The seven states which have adopted the cardinal are Indiana, North Carolina, Virginia, West Virginia, Illinois, Kentucky, and Ohio. Suppose two cardinal eggs weigh 0.28 oz and 0.32 oz. Which egg is heavier?

You can use decimal models or a number line to compare decimals.

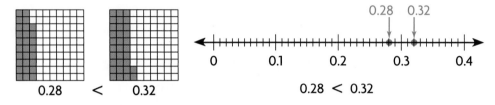

0.28 < 0.32   0.28 < 0.32

So, the egg weighing 0.32 oz is heavier.

You can also use place value to compare decimals.

Example 1 Compare 1.42 and 1.46. First, line up the decimal points. Then, compare the digits from left to right until they are different.

STEP 1
Begin at the left. Compare the ones.
1.42
↓   same
1.46

STEP 2
Compare the tenths.
1.42
↓   same
1.46

STEP 3
Compare the hundredths.
1.42
↓   6 > 2, or 2 < 6
1.46

So, 1.46 > 1.42, or 1.42 < 1.46.

• Show how you could use decimal models or a number line to compare 1.42 and 1.46.

Example 2 Order 2.853, 2.844, and 2.862 from least to greatest.

STEP 1
Begin at the left.
Compare the ones and tenths.
2.853
↓↓
2.844   same
↓↓
2.862

STEP 2
Compare the hundredths.

2.853
↓   different
2.844   4 < 5 < 6
↓
2.862

STEP 3
Order the numbers.

2.844 < 2.853 < 2.862

So, 2.844 < 2.853 < 2.862.

1. **Explain** how you can use a number line to order 1.468, 1.452, and 1.469 from least to greatest.

Write <, >, or = for each ●. Use the number line.

← + + + + + + + + + + + →
6.10   6.11   6.12   6.13   6.14   6.15   6.16   6.17   6.18   6.19   6.20

2. 6.152 ● 6.125   **3.** 6.14 ● 6.140   **4.** 6.114 ● 6.118

5. 6.19 ● 6.198   **6.** 6.170 ● 6.175   **7.** 6.176 ● 6.167

▶ **Practice and Problem Solving**   Extra Practice, page 32, Set C

Write < , > , or = for each ●. You may wish to use a number line.

8. 0.65 ● 0.63   **9.** 0.307 ● 0.037   **10.** 0.759 ● 0.769

11. 132.94 ● 132.48   **12.** 156.93 ● 156.98   **13.** 99.989 ● 99.998

14. 0.905 ● 0.905   **15.** 63.938 ● 63.939   **16.** 476.069 ● 476.096

Order from least to greatest.

17. 6.58, 6.38, 6.29, 7.08   **18.** 13.393, 13.309, 13.339, 13.039

19. 4.102, 4.105, 4.118, 4.110   **20.** 15.259, 15.389, 15.291, 15.301

USE DATA   For 21–23, use the menu.

21. Write the salads in order from the least expensive to the most expensive.

22. Name two items that cost more than yogurt but less than onion soup.

23. **NUMBER SENSE** Lisa has $5 in her wallet. Which two soups can she buy?

24. ✎ Write About It Explain how to compare 1.23 and 1.27.

Power Lunch Menu
Bean Soup $2.25
Onion Soup $2.95
Tomato Soup $2.75
Taco Salad $1.89
Garden Salad $1.80
Fruit Salad $1.85
Yogurt $1.95

Mixed Review and Test Prep

25. Is 2.05 equal to 2.50? Write *yes* or *no*.
(p. 26)

26. Write 3.025 in word form. (p. 22)

27. 1,401 − 989   **28.** 260 × 10

29. **TEST PREP**   Which decimal is NOT equivalent to five hundred ten thousandths? (p. 26)

A 0.501   **C** 0.510
B 0.5100   **D** 0.51

Problem Solving Skill
Draw Conclusions

UNDERSTAND ⟩ PLAN ⟩ SOLVE ⟩ CHECK ⟩

THINK FOR YOURSELF   Sometimes you will need to analyze data to draw conclusions.

The table and the bar graph below display data about an experiment involving five plants all of the same type. You can use the data to draw conclusions.

PLANT FOOD DROPS USED

Plant	Number of Plant Food Drops
A	1
B	5
C	9
D	13
E	17

PLANT GROWTH

▲ This Pacific giant kelp can grow 18 inches in one day.

ANALYZE	CONCLUSION
• Look at the graph. Which plant grew the tallest?	Plant C grew the tallest.
• Look at the table. How many drops of plant food did the tallest plant receive?	Plant C received 9 drops.
• What relationship do you notice between the number of drops of plant food and the plant's growth?	Up to 9 drops, more plant food helped the plants grow taller. With 13 and 17 drops, growth decreased.

• What conclusion can you draw about Plants A, B, and C?
  about Plants D and E?

• **What if** the total growth for Plant D had been 35.89 cm and for
  Plant E, 38 cm? What conclusion could you draw about all five plants?

▶ Problem Solving Practice

For 1–4, can the conclusion be drawn from the information given?
Write *yes* or *no*. Explain your choice.

Mrs. Carson measured the heights of her fifth graders. The
shortest student is 50 inches tall, and the tallest student is
64 inches tall. There are 25 students in Mrs. Carson's class.

1. All of the students are taller
than 5 feet.

2. The tallest student in the class
is taller than 5 feet.

3. All of the students are shorter
than Mrs. Carson.

4. The difference between the tallest
student and the shortest student
in the class is 14 inches.

Lena thinks that the smaller box of cereal is a better buy than the
larger box. The larger box has 10 servings, and the smaller box has
8 servings. The smaller box costs $3.20, and the larger box costs $3.90.

5. Which expression describes
the price per serving for the
smaller box?
  A $3.20 × 8
  B $3.20 ÷ 20
  C $3.20 ÷ 8
  D $3.20 × 20

6. What conclusion can you draw
from the data?
  F The smaller box costs less per serving.
  G The larger box costs less per serving.
  H Both boxes cost the same per serving.
  J The smaller box costs twice as much
per serving.

⌐Mixed Applications ━━━━━━━━━━

USE DATA For 7–11, use the table.

7. Does the weight of the animal determine its
speed? Explain.

8. ⚡❓ **What's the Error?** Don says that the
more an animal eats, the more it sleeps.
Explain the error in Don's conclusion.

9. Which animal eats the greatest amount
of fruits and vegetables?

10. How many more hours does the bear
sleep than the elephant? than the giraffe?

11. ⚡❓ **What's the Question?** Use the data
from the table. The answer is 2 times as
many kilograms.

ANIMALS			
	Elephant	**Bear**	**Giraffe**
Weight	5,450 kg	725 kg	1,180 kg
Speed	51 kph	48 kph	51 kph
Sleep per day	180 min	8 hours	240 min
Fruits and vegetables eaten per day	1.8 kg	0.9 kg	0.1 kg

1 hour = 60 minutes (min)
kph = kilometers per hour

Extra Practice

Set A (pp. 22–25)

Write in expanded form and in standard form.

1. two hundred sixteen ten-thousandths

2. five and five hundredths

3. two and seven hundred two thousandths

Write in word form.

4. 44.009   **5.** 2.0189   **6.** 0.8   **7.** 0.505

Write as a decimal and as a fraction or mixed number.

8. 4 + 0.07   **9.** 10 + 0.3 + 0.09   **10.** 8 + 0.8 + 0.01

11. thirteen and four hundredths   **12.** fifty-seven hundredths

13. Mike rode his bike three and four hundredths of a mile. Write this number in standard form.

Set B (pp. 26–27)

Write *equivalent* or *not equivalent* to describe each pair of decimals.

1. 3.45 and 3.450   **2.** 0.097 and 0.970   **3.** 23.504 and 23.50

Write an equivalent decimal for each number.

4. 5.2   **5.** 9.320   **6.** 87.0800   **7.** 2.02

Set C (pp. 28–29)

Order from greatest to least.

1. 54.453, 54.59, 54.811   **2.** 7.564, 17.4, 11.94

Order from least to greatest.

3. 31.104, 31.05, 31.94   **4.** 6.309, 6.42, 6.341

5. Leslie has $4.68 in her pocket. Which of the following items can she buy?

Notebook $2.30   Box of Pencils $4.67
Binder $8.53   Markers $4.69

Review/Test

✓ CHECK VOCABULARY AND CONCEPTS

Choose the best term from the box.

tenth
hundredth
decimal
thousandth
ten-thousandths

1. A decimal or fraction that names one part of ten equal parts is one __?__. (p. 22)

2. If you divide one whole by 1,000, you get one __?__. (p. 22)

3. A decimal or fraction that names one part of 100 equal parts is one __?__. (p. 22)

4. The decimal 0.0016 is sixteen __?__. (p. 22)

✓ CHECK SKILLS

Write as a decimal and as a fraction or mixed number. (pp. 22–25)

5. twenty-one and one hundredth

6. seven and six tenths

7. three hundred forty-nine thousandths

Write each decimal in expanded form and in word form. (pp. 22–25)

8. 17.0002

9. 1.002

10. 13.201

11. 4.076

Write *equivalent* or *not equivalent* to describe each pair of decimals. (pp. 26–27)

12. 0.650 and 0.65

13. 9.502 and 9.52

14. 3.0040 and 3.040

15. 10.01 and 10.010

Order from least to greatest. (pp. 28–29)

16. 0.057; 0.56; 0.05

17. 5.98; 5.908; 5.809

18. 6.969; 9.696; 6.696

✓ CHECK PROBLEM SOLVING

Solve. (pp. 30–31)

19. Jim worked 5 hours last week and earned $31.25. Sara earned $43.75 and worked 7 hours. Latasha earned $56.25 and worked 9 hours. Draw a conclusion about this information.

20. Kerry, Stu, Beth, and Julio are in line. Kerry is first in line. Julio is between Kerry and Stu. Beth is after Stu. Beth is last in line. Draw a conclusion about where Julio stands in line.

Standardized Test Prep

NUMBER SENSE, CONCEPTS, AND OPERATIONS

1. Use the table to order the meats from **greatest** number of calories to **least**.

CALORIES IN MEATS	
Type (3 oz)	**Calories**
Ham	205
Liver	185
Ground Beef	245
Steak	240

A liver, ham, steak, ground beef

B ham, steak, ground beef, liver

C steak, ham, liver, ground beef

D ground beef, steak, ham, liver

2. The average annual precipitation in Miami is fifty-five and ninety-one hundredths inches. How is this number written in standard form?

F 5.91

G 50.91

H 55.90

J 55.91

> **TIP** **Look for important words.** See item 3. *Estimate* is an important word. It tells you to round the addends to estimate rather than find the exact answer.

3. Explain It The table shows the results of a survey. ESTIMATE to find the total number of people who have pets. Explain your estimate.

SURVEY RESULTS	
Pet	**Number of People**
Cat	30,482
Dog	27,407

DATA ANALYSIS AND PROBABILITY

4. The bar graph shows the average airport departure delays. Which airport had the shortest average departure delays in 2000?

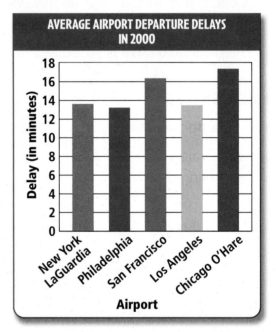

A New York LaGuardia

B Philadelphia

C Los Angeles

D Chicago O'Hare

5. Jodi has 3 dimes, 1 quarter, and 2 pennies in her wallet. She takes one coin out. What is the probability that it is a quarter?

F one out of six   **H** three out of five

G two out of six   **J** three out of three

6. Explain It A spinner has 6 equal sections, 2 red, 2 blue, and 2 yellow. Explain how you can determine the probability of spinning red, blue, or yellow.

⭐ ALGEBRAIC THINKING

7. Rafael drew this geometric pattern.

Which figure did he draw next in the pattern?

A □

B □

C ▽

D ▭

8. Which is the missing number in the pattern below?

3, 7, 11, 15, ■, 23, 27

F 15

G 17

H 19

J 21

9. Explain It Describe the relationship between *x* and *y* in this table.

INPUT	OUTPUT
x	*y*
1	4
2	5
3	6
4	7
5	8

⭐ GEOMETRY AND SPATIAL SENSE

10. Suppose four bright stars are located at *A*, *B*, *C*, and *D*. Which is the correct location of star *C*?

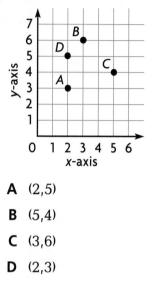

A (2,5)

B (5,4)

C (3,6)

D (2,3)

11. Which two lines are perpendicular?

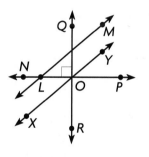

F $\overleftrightarrow{NP}$ and $\overleftrightarrow{QR}$

G $\overleftrightarrow{LM}$ and $\overleftrightarrow{NP}$

H $\overleftrightarrow{QR}$ and $\overleftrightarrow{XY}$

J $\overleftrightarrow{QR}$ and $\overleftrightarrow{LM}$

12. Explain It A polygon has sides of 4 feet, 5 feet, 4 feet, 5 feet, and 6 feet. Draw and name the polygon.

Add and Subtract Whole Numbers and Decimals

▤ *FAST FACT* • SCIENCE

The rarest of all sea turtles is the Kemp's ridley turtle. It weighs between 80 and 100 pounds.

PROBLEM SOLVING The heaviest sea turtle is the leatherback turtle. It can weigh 1,000 pounds more than the heaviest turtle shown in the graph. What is the maximum weight of a leatherback?

MAXIMUM WEIGHTS OF SEA TURTLES

The hawksbill turtle was so named because it has a beaklike mouth.

CHECK WHAT YOU KNOW

Use this page to help you review and remember
important skills needed for Chapter 3.

✔ ROUND WHOLE NUMBERS AND DECIMALS

Round each number to the nearest thousand.

1. 17,922 **2.** 308,389 **3.** 3,278,623 **4.** 45,325

5. 82,390 **6.** 3,569,203 **7.** 20,344 **8.** 23,056

9. 12,005 **10.** 4,035,654 **11.** 28,138 **12.** 456,979

Round each number to the nearest hundredth.

13. 4.108 **14.** 0.598 **15.** 12.835 **16.** 3.652

17. 9.305 **18.** 0.133 **19.** 2.846 **20.** 9.673

✔ ADD AND SUBTRACT MONEY

Find the sum or difference. Estimate to check.

21. $5,789
+$4,569

22. $9,468
−$4,263

23. $2,635
+$3,508

24. $7,545
−$5,023

25. $6,390
+$4,743

26. $8,092
−$1,953

27. $7,597
+$8,146

28. $6,204
−$2,132

29. $6.87 + $3.87 **30.** $8.75 − $6.43 **31.** $4.99 + $12.64 **32.** $2.03 + $27.89

33. $56.78 − $6.89 **34.** $76.02 + $34.85 **35.** $25.83 + $20.40 **36.** $65.47 − $31.23

VOCABULARY POWER

REVIEW

sum [sum] *noun*

Sum is originally from the Latin root word *summus,* which means "highest." The Greeks and Romans added numbers from the bottom and wrote the answer or sum at the top. What word for the top of a mountain comes from *summus*?

PREVIEW

estimate

front-end estimation

www.harcourtschool.com/mathglossary

Round Whole Numbers

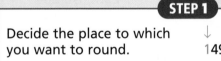

Quick Review

What is the value of each 5?

1. 582,017
2. 3,456
3. 5,034,768
4. 57,316
5. 17,063,521

CROWD PLEASERS The programs for this year's women's college basketball championships need to be ordered. The programs come in boxes of 10,000 each. Last year, 29,619 people attended the championships. How many boxes of programs should be ordered?

To be sure enough programs are ordered, round 29,619 up to the next ten thousand. You can use a number line to round.

29,619

```
20,000        25,000        30,000
```

29,619 rounded to the next ten thousand is 30,000.

So, 3 boxes of 10,000 programs should be ordered.

Another way to round is to use the rounding rules.

▲ 1982 was the first year the NCAA held championships for women's basketball. About 10,000 people attended.

Example

Round 149,987 to the nearest hundred thousand.

STEP 1

Decide the place to which you want to round.
149,987

STEP 2

If the digit to the right is less than 5, round down.
If the digit to the right is 5 or greater, round up.
149,987
100,000   4 < 5   Round down.

More Examples

Round 1,265,483 to the place of the blue digit.

A

1,265,483
1,000,000   2 < 5   Round down.

1,265,483 rounded to the nearest million is 1,000,000.

B

1,265,483
1,300,000   6 > 5   Round up.

1,265,483 rounded to the nearest hundred thousand is 1,300,000.

C

1,265,483
1,270,000   5 = 5   Round up.

1,265,483 rounded to the nearest ten thousand is 1,270,000.

1. **Explain** why 735,489 rounded to the nearest ten thousand is 740,000.

Round each number to the place of the blue digit.

2. 2,681 **3.** 178,365 **4.** 1,532,300 **5.** 33,689 **6.** 6,023,490

Round 1,654,508 to the place named.

7. thousands **8.** ten thousands **9.** hundred thousands

10. hundreds **11.** tens **12.** millions

▷ **Practice and Problem Solving** (Extra Practice, page 58, Set A)

Round each number to the place of the blue digit.

13. 78,210 **14.** 350,962 **15.** 5,811,326 **16.** 606,310 **17.** 890,352

Round 2,908,365 to the place named.

18. thousands **19.** ten thousands **20.** hundred thousands

21. hundreds **22.** tens **23.** millions

Name the place to which each number was rounded.

24. 191,562 to 190,000 **25.** 4,236,810 to 4,000,000 **26.** 80,154 to 80,200

USE DATA For 27–29, use the table.

27. Which 2 years had the same attendance, rounded to the nearest thousand?

28. How many people in all attended the NCAA Women's Championships in 1999, 2000, and 2001?

29. **? What's the Error?** Sean says that, rounded to the nearest thousand, the attendance in 1997 was the same as in 1998. Describe Sean's error.

NCAA Women's Basketball Championship Game Attendance

Year	Attendance
1996	23,291
1997	16,714
1998	17,976
1999	17,733
2000	20,060
2001	20,551

⌐Mixed Review and Test Prep

30. $68 + 25 = $ ■ **31.** $71 - 29 = $ ■

32. Use mental math to find the sum $15 + 8 + 2 + 5$.

33. How many sides does a quadrilateral have?

34. **TEST PREP** The orchestra has 18 violins and violas. There are 8 more violins than violas. How many violins are in the orchestra?

A 13 **B** 10 **C** 8 **D** 5

LESSON 2 Round Decimals

Learn

WINGING IT The Pygmy Blue is the smallest butterfly in the United States. Its average width is 0.563 inch. What is the width rounded to the nearest hundredth of an inch?

You can use a number line to round 0.563 to the nearest hundredth.

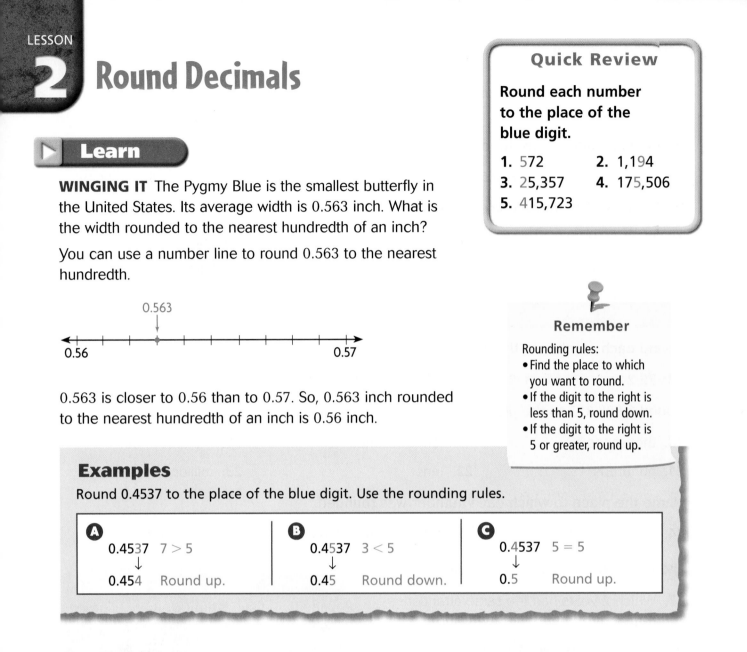

0.563 is closer to 0.56 than to 0.57. So, 0.563 inch rounded to the nearest hundredth of an inch is 0.56 inch.

Quick Review

Round each number to the place of the blue digit.

1. 572   2. 1,194
3. 25,357   4. 175,506
5. 415,723

Remember

Rounding rules:
- Find the place to which you want to round.
- If the digit to the right is less than 5, round down.
- If the digit to the right is 5 or greater, round up.

Examples

Round 0.4537 to the place of the blue digit. Use the rounding rules.

A
0.4537 $7 > 5$
↓
0.454   Round up.

B
0.4537 $3 < 5$
↓
0.45   Round down.

C
0.4537 $5 = 5$
↓
0.5   Round up.

Check

1. **Explain** how you can use the rounding rules to round $8.49 to the nearest dollar and to the nearest tenth of a dollar.

Round each number to the place of the blue digit.

2. 0.783   3. 0.256   4. 0.1732

5. 0.685   6. 0.66

Round 0.6285 to the place named.

7. tenths   8. hundredths

9. thousandths   10. ones

Round each number to the place of the blue digit.

11. 3.193 **12.** 29.423 **13.** 2.0475 **14.** 0.86 **15.** 1.234

Round 2.5438 to the place named.

16. tenths **17.** hundredths **18.** thousandths **19.** ones

Name the place to which each number was rounded.

20. 0.562 to 0.56 **21.** 6.8354 to 6.835 **22.** 80.154 to 80.2

23. 1.7592 to 1.759 **24.** 5.9273 to 6 **25.** 2.3625 to 2.36

Round to the nearest tenth of a dollar and to the nearest dollar.

26. $10.56 **27.** $0.42 **28.** $0.98 **29.** $5.45

30. $4.02 **31.** $32.36 **32.** $9.49 **33.** $10.91

Round each number to the nearest hundredth.

34. nine hundred thirty-four thousandths **35.** $10 + 5 + 0.2 + 0.06 + 0.002$

36. seven and eighty-three thousandths

37. $2 + 0.8 + 0.09 + 0.005 + 0.0003$

USE DATA For 38–40, use the graph.

38. Round the width of the Dwarf Blue to the nearest tenth of an inch.

39. Which two butterflies are the same width when each width is rounded to the nearest hundredth of an inch?

40. Which butterfly is 0.88 inch wide when its width is rounded to the nearest hundredth of an inch?

41. Vocabulary Power *Round* means "to increase or decrease to the nearest unit." What is another math definition for *round*?

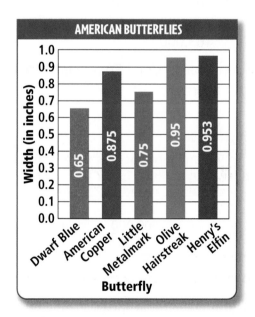

AMERICAN BUTTERFLIES

Width (in inches)

Dwarf Blue 0.65
American Copper 0.875
Little Metalmark 0.75
Olive Hairstreak 0.95
Henry's Elfin 0.953

Butterfly

Mixed Review and Test Prep

42. Write nine thousandths in standard form. (p. 22)

43. Round 4,807 to the nearest ten. (p. 38)

44. Order 1.65, 1.56, and 1.6 from greatest to least. (p. 28)

45. Write 3.024 in word form. (p. 22)

46. TEST PREP Tim ran the first half of a race 1.9 seconds faster than the second half. He ran the second half in 20.6 seconds. What was Tim's total time?

A 18.7 sec **C** 39.3 sec

B 22.5 sec **D** 43.1 sec

Estimate Sums and Differences

Quick Review

Round to the nearest thousand.

1. 457,986   2. 2,057,516
3. 2,954   4. 9,051,687
5. 326,198

VOCABULARY

estimate
front-end estimation

UNDERWATER FLORIDA John Pennekamp Coral Reef State Park, located on Key Largo, off the coast of southern Florida, was the first undersea park in the United States. The park consists of 60,124 underwater acres and includes the famous coral reef. It also has 2,960 acres of coastal land. About how many total acres does the park have?

You can round to estimate sums and differences of whole numbers. When you **estimate**, you find a number that is close to an exact amount.

$$\begin{array}{r} 60,124 \rightarrow 60,000 \\ + \ 2,960 \rightarrow + \ 3,000 \\ \hline 63,000 \end{array}$$ Round to the nearest thousand. Then add.

So, John Pennekamp Coral Reef State Park has about 63,000 acres.

Example 1

About how many more people visited the park in 2000–2001 than in 1991–1992? Use the table.

$$\begin{array}{r} 1,050,749 \rightarrow 1,100,000 \\ - \ \ 782,421 \rightarrow - \ \ 800,000 \\ \hline 300,000 \end{array}$$ Round to the nearest hundred thousand. Then subtract.

| JOHN PENNEKAMP STATE PARK ATTENDANCE ||
Year	Number of Visitors
1991–1992	782,421
2000–2001	1,050,749

So, about 300,000 more people visited the park in 2000–2001.

You can also round to estimate sums and differences of decimals.

More Examples

A Round to the nearest whole number. Then subtract.

$$\begin{array}{r} 89.5 \rightarrow 90 \\ - \ 1.83 \rightarrow - \ 2 \\ \hline 88 \end{array}$$

B Round to the nearest tenth. Then add.

$$\begin{array}{r} 3.675 \rightarrow 3.7 \\ 2.502 \rightarrow 2.5 \\ +0.32 \rightarrow +0.3 \\ \hline 6.5 \end{array}$$

C Round to the nearest dollar. Then add.

$$\begin{array}{r} \$10.00 \rightarrow \$10 \\ +\$ \ 8.19 \rightarrow +\$ \ 8 \\ \hline \$18 \end{array}$$

Front-End Estimation

Another way to estimate a sum or difference is to use **front-end estimation**. When you use front-end estimation, you add or subtract the values of the front digits of each number.

Jacksonville

FLORIDA

Orlando

420.9 miles

289.5 miles

John Pennekamp State Park

Example 2

About how much farther is the park from Jacksonville than from Orlando?

$420.9 \rightarrow$	400	Subtract the values of the
$-289.5 \rightarrow$	-200	front digits of each number.
	200	

So, the park is about 200 miles farther from Jacksonville than from Orlando.

More Examples

A 3,287 + 4,501

$3,287 \rightarrow$	$3,000$
$+4,501 \rightarrow$	$+4,000$
	$7,000$

B 587 − 435

$587 \rightarrow$	500
$-435 \rightarrow$	-400
	100

C 13.6 + 22.9

$13.6 \rightarrow$	10
$+22.9 \rightarrow$	$+20$
	30

- In Example A, how would a rounded estimate differ from the front-end estimate?

- When you use front-end estimation to estimate a sum, is your estimate greater than or less than the actual sum? Explain.

Check

1. **Explain** how you use front-end estimation to estimate the sum $73.25 + 91.02$.

2. How is estimating sums and differences of decimals like estimating sums and differences of whole numbers?

Estimate by rounding.

3.	85,476	4.	845,008	5.	1.22	6.	$1.78	7.	4.87
	−41,131		+124,895		+3.51		−$1.04		+2.94

LESSON CONTINUES

Estimate by using front-end estimation.

8.	9.	10.	11.	12.
752,401	21,421	$52.89	5.681	4.35
−491,922	+32,970	−$18.78	+3.025	−0.78

Practice and Problem Solving   Extra Practice, page 58, Set B

Estimate by rounding.

13.	14.	15.	16.	17.
93,582	82,631	$7.92	30.23	$7.36
+82,785	−22,965	+$5.39	+13.65	−$6.41

18. 397,352 + 187,590   **19.** 512,824 − 495,008   **20.** 1,289,405 + 3,321,945

21. 2.39 + 8.06   **22.** 0.702 − 0.397   **23.** 14.782 + 8.110

Estimate by using front-end estimation.

24.	25.	26.	27.	28.
502,963	42,110	2.704	$500.00	7.153
−132,631	+16,850	+1.818	−$279.65	+4.099

29. 5,278 + 3,621   **30.** 13,500 − 11,693   **31.** 6,345,672 − 1,254,789

32. 24.89 − 17.34   **33.** 33.872 + 12.946   **34.** 37.054 + 27.922

Estimate to compare. Write < or > for each ⬤.

35. 69,210 + 24,391 ⬤ 68,258 + 45,924   **36.** 74,361 + 24,391 ⬤ 91,308 − 25,924

37. 82,356 − 14,638 ⬤ 86,551 − 13,725   **38.** 8.14 − 4.89 ⬤ 7.45 − 2.37

39. 2.8 + 9.1 ⬤ 11 + 5   **40.** 7.925 + 5.392 ⬤ 15.431 − 4.974

USE DATA For 41–42, use the table.

41. About how much farther is it to John Pennekamp State Park from Chattanooga, TN, than from Montgomery, AL?

42. Josh drove from his home in Greensboro, NC, to John Pennekamp State Park, and then he drove to visit his cousin in Tallahassee, FL. About how many miles did he drive?

DISTANCE TO JOHN PENNEKAMP STATE PARK (in miles)	
Chattanooga, TN	836.22
Greensboro, NC	850.34
Montgomery, AL	746.49
Tallahassee, FL	539.02

43. 📓 Write a problem in which front-end estimation gives an estimate closer to the exact answer than rounding.

44. Three duffel bags weigh 49.49 pounds, 53.73 pounds, and 77.89 pounds. Estimate the total weight to the nearest pound.

45. **? What's the Question?** Ally and three friends are in line to buy tickets for a snorkeling trip. Ally is right behind Eric and in front of Lynn. Lee is last. Eric is the answer.

46. **REASONING** There are 1.609344 kilometers in 1 mile. Estimate to the nearest tenth the number of kilometers in 3 miles.

Mixed Review and Test Prep

47. $4{,}954 + 2{,}608 = \blacksquare$

48. True or false: $505{,}736 > 505{,}746$ (p. 10)

49. Compare 7.064 and 7.644 using $<$, $>$, or $=$. (p. 28)

50. Round 1,435,987 to the nearest hundred thousand. (p. 38)

51. **TEST PREP** Which is 5,567,398 rounded to the nearest million? (p. 38)

    A 5,000,000   **C** 6,000,000

    B 5,600,000   **D** 6,500,000

52. What is $7 + 0.03 + 0.009$ written in standard form? (p. 22)

Write an equivalent decimal for each. (p. 26)

53. 0.105   **54.** 2.720

55. **TEST PREP** In which number does the digit 8 have the greatest value? (p. 2)

    F 91,358   **H** 38,195

    G 53,891   **J** 19,583

Problem Solving Thinker's Corner

Another way to estimate is called clustering. **Clustering** is a method used when all addends are close to, or clustered around, a number.

Estimate: $24.8 + 26.82 + 24.3 + 25.7$

Look at the number line. These four numbers all cluster around 25.

24.3 24.8 25.7 26.82   Each addend is close to 25.

20   25   30

Use $25 + 25 + 25 + 25$ or $4 \times 25 = 100$.

So, the estimated sum is 100.

Use clustering to estimate each sum.

1. $445 + 463 + 455$

2. $891 + 904 + 912 + 885$

3. $10.51 + 11.2 + 9.9 + 9.65$

4. $1{,}891 + 1{,}975 + 2{,}004$

4

Add and Subtract Whole Numbers

Quick Review

1.   450
    +550

2.   5,700
    −2,200

3.   4,200
    − 600

4.   24,000
     48,000
    +86,000

5. 73 + 27 + 42 + 58

MAKE A DIFFERENCE!   At the Wildlife Center, volunteers are helping scientists place black-footed ferrets back into their natural habitats. This year's volunteers have logged 12,385 hours of service. Last year they logged 10,098 hours. How many hours did they log for both years?

Example 1

Add. 12,385 + 10,098

Estimate. 12,000 + 10,000 = 22,000

1 1	
12,385	Start with the ones.
+10,098	Regroup as needed.
22,483	

So, the volunteers logged 22,483 hours for both years. This is close to the estimate, so the answer is reasonable.

Example 2

How many more hours were logged this year than last year?

Subtract. 12,385 − 10,098

Estimate. 12,000 − 10,000 = 2,000

17 2 7 15	
12,385	Start with the ones.
−10,098	Regroup as needed.
2,287	

So, the volunteers logged 2,287 more hours this year than last year. This is close to the estimate, so the answer is reasonable.

• How do you use place value when you add and subtract?

▲ **A black-footed ferret**

Technology Link

More Practice: Harcourt Mega Math The Number Games, *Tiny's Think Tank*, Levels B, C

1. Explain how you know which place values to regroup when adding.

Find the sum or difference. Estimate to check.

2. 6,317 +8,903	**3.** 12,911 −10,260	**4.** 11,004 + 8,986	**5.** 607,411 −249,897	**6.** 998,623 −771,128

Practice and Problem Solving

Extra Practice, page 58, Set C

Find the sum or difference. Estimate to check.

7. 5,752 −1,842	**8.** 8,875 +4,908	**9.** 327,032 −109,986	**10.** 17,620 − 9,003	**11.** 675,531 +318,746

12. 234 + 125 + 681   **13.** 6,010 − 498   **14.** 2,943 + 7,894

15. 1,298 + 786 + 412   **16.** 511,832 + 238,778   **17.** 61,933 − 12,040

18. 208 + 816 + 7,049   **19.** 17,001 − 8,542   **20.** 209,123 − 146,897

USE DATA For 21–23, use the circle graphs.

21. How many species of birds are *not* threatened and *not* extinct? How many species of reptiles? How many species of mammals?

22. How many threatened and extinct species are there in all three classes of animals?

23. ✎ **Write About It** How many more bird species are threatened than reptile species? Explain.

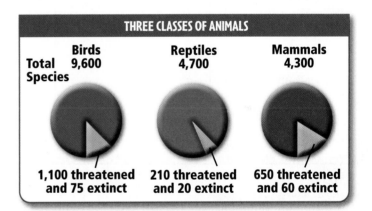

THREE CLASSES OF ANIMALS

Total Species

Birds 9,600 — 1,100 threatened and 75 extinct

Reptiles 4,700 — 210 threatened and 20 extinct

Mammals 4,300 — 650 threatened and 60 extinct

24. During track practice, four runners ran the $\frac{1}{4}$-mile run. Greg finished after Sean. Alex finished before Sean but after Louis. Who finished first?

Mixed Review and Test Prep

25. Round 5,567,398 to the nearest million. (p. 38)

For **26–27**, write each number in word form. (p. 22)

26. 0.98   **27.** 0.675

28. Order 2,430,717; 2,340,717; and 2,470,717 from least to greatest. (p. 10)

29. **TEST PREP** Which is two and one hundred ninety-three ten-thousandths? (p. 22)

A 2.93   **C** 2.0193
B 2.193   **D** 2.0093

Add and Subtract Decimals

Quick Review

1. 321 + 40
2. 64 − 17
3. 1,643 + 2,309
4. 969 − 333
5. 1,075 + 762 + 956

▶ **Learn**

SPLISH SPLASH Tyler's science class recorded the weather for the first week in March. Tyler's job was to measure the rainfall. It rained 2 days during that week. On Tuesday, Tyler recorded 1.95 inches of rain, and on Friday another 0.85 inch fell. How much rain did Tyler record during the first week in March?

Technology Link

More Practice: Harcourt Mega Math The Number Games, *Tiny's Think Tank,* Level L *Buggy Bargains,* Level I

Example 1 Add. 1.95 + 0.85

Estimate. 2 + 1 = 3

STEP 1	**STEP 2**	**STEP 3**
Line up the decimal points to align place-value positions. Add the hundredths.	Add the tenths.	Add the ones. Place the decimal point in the sum.
$\begin{array}{r} 1 \\ 1.95 \\ +0.85 \\ \hline 0 \end{array}$	$\begin{array}{r} 1\ 1 \\ 1.95 \\ +0.85 \\ \hline 80 \end{array}$	$\begin{array}{r} 1\ 1 \\ 1.95 \\ +0.85 \\ \hline 2.80 \end{array}$

So, Tyler recorded 2.80 inches of rain during the first week of March. This is close to the estimate, so the answer is reasonable.

More Examples

A 2.69 + 3.83

Line up the decimal points.

$\begin{array}{r} 1\ 1 \\ 2.69 \\ +3.83 \\ \hline 6.52 \end{array}$

Place the decimal point in the sum.

B 13.76 + 8.5

$\begin{array}{r} 1\ 1 \\ 13.76 \\ +\ 8.50 \\ \hline 22.26 \end{array}$ ← Place a zero for an equivalent decimal.

• When is it helpful to show an equivalent decimal in addition?

Subtract Decimals

Tyler recorded 2.75 inches of rain during the first week in April, and then he measured 4.92 inches of rain for the entire month of April. How much rain fell in April after the first week?

Example 2 Subtract. 4.92 − 2.75

Estimate. 5 − 3 = 2

STEP 1

Line up the decimal points to align place-value positions. Subtract the hundredths. Regroup if needed.

$$\begin{array}{r} \overset{8\,12}{4.9\cancel{2}} \\ -\ 2.75 \\ \hline 7 \end{array}$$

STEP 2

Subtract the tenths. Regroup if needed.

$$\begin{array}{r} \overset{8\,12}{4.\cancel{9}\cancel{2}} \\ -\ 2.75 \\ \hline 17 \end{array}$$

STEP 3

Subtract the ones.

$$\begin{array}{r} \overset{8\,12}{4.\cancel{9}\cancel{2}} \\ -\ 2.75 \\ \hline 2.17 \end{array}$$ Place the decimal point.

So, 2.17 inches of rain fell in April after the first week.
This is close to the estimate, so the answer is reasonable.

More Examples

A 5.12 − 1.08

$$\begin{array}{r} \overset{0\,12}{5.\cancel{1}\cancel{2}} \\ -\ 1.08 \\ \hline 4.04 \end{array}$$

B 24.23 − 11.6

$$\begin{array}{r} \overset{3\,12}{24.\cancel{2}\cancel{3}} \\ -\ 11.60 \\ \hline 12.63 \end{array}$$ Place a zero to show an equivalent decimal.

C 1.6 − 0.342

$$\begin{array}{r} \overset{9}{\underset{5\ 10\ 10}{1.6\cancel{0}\cancel{0}}} \\ -\ 0.342 \\ \hline 1.258 \end{array}$$ Place zeros to show an equivalent decimal.

• Where do you place the decimal point in the answer?

MATH IDEA You can add and subtract decimals the same way you add and subtract whole numbers if you line up the decimal points first.

▷ Check

1. **Explain** why placing zeros to the right of the decimal point, after the last digit in a decimal, does not change its value.

Find the sum. Estimate to check.

2. 0.3
    +0.9

3. 2.7
    1.15
    +0.62

4. 11.74
    5.12
    6.3
    + 1.54

5. 5.08
    +4.18

6. 12.1
    + 9.01

LESSON CONTINUES ▶

Find the difference. Estimate to check.

7.   0.8
       −0.3

8.   1.23
       −0.47

9.   4.06
       −2.85

10.   10.2
        − 8.67

11.   23.05
        −12.8

12. 4.3 − 3.6

13. 1.6 − 0.8

14. 7.2 − 5.69

15. 17.13 − 10.9

▶ **Practice and Problem Solving** ⟩ Extra Practice, page 58, Set C

Find the sum or difference. Estimate to check.

16.   5.6
        7.8
      +1.7

17.   40.8
        25.17
      +16.3

18.   6.008
      +1.883

19.   45.903
        9.374
      +51.28

20.   13.046
      + 0.298

21.   1.5
       −0.7

22.   4.12
       −1.852

23.   7.095
       −5.64

24.   16.1
       − 7.34

25.   43.18
       −29.9

26.   20.1
       − 8.652

27.   3.15
       − 1.99

28.   5.07
       −0.68

29.   22.6
       − 9.45

30.   21.064
       − 9.33

31. 1.84 + 1.92

32. 1.34 + 4.61

33. 2.05 + 0.97

34. 3.1 + 0.42 + 8.3

ALGEBRA **Find a pattern. Write a rule. Use your rule to find the missing numbers in the pattern.**

35. 2.3, 2.5, 2.4, 2.6, 2.5, ■, 2.6, 2.8, ■

36. 0.45, 0.55, 0.65, ■, ■, 0.95, 1.05, 1.15

37. 3.96, 3.98, ■, 4.02, 4.04, ■, 4.08, 4.10

38. 1.25, 1.50, 1.75, 2.00, 2.25, 2.50, ■, ■

USE DATA For 39–40, use the graph.

39. Between which two months does the average monthly precipitation have the greatest increase? How many inches?

40. The record in Indianapolis for the most precipitation in one month occurred in July 1875, when 13.12 inches of rain fell. How much greater was this than the average precipitation for July?

41. **GEOMETRY** Bob is enclosing a rectangular field with fencing. The field is 120 feet long and 50 feet wide. How much fencing does he need?

42. **REASONING** Without adding, how do you know that the sum of 36.179 and 8.63 will have a 9 in the thousandths place?

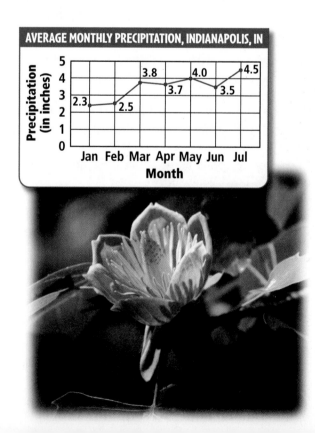

AVERAGE MONTHLY PRECIPITATION, INDIANAPOLIS, IN

Precipitation (in inches) — vertical axis: 0, 1, 2, 3, 4, 5

Data points: 2.3, 2.5, 3.8, 3.7, 4.0, 3.5, 4.5

Month (horizontal axis): Jan Feb Mar Apr May Jun Jul

43. ≣**FAST FACT** • SCIENCE In August 1992, during Hurricane Andrew, 57.68 inches of rain fell in Florida. The average amount of rainfall for an entire year in Florida is 53.52 inches. How much greater was the hurricane's rainfall than Florida's annual rainfall?

44. Steve spent $9.45 on a ticket to the game and $3.75 for snacks. He had $7.35 left at the end of the day. How much did he have at the beginning of the day?

Mixed Review and Test Prep

45. What is 0.017 rounded to the nearest hundredth? (p. 40)

Write the value of the blue digit.

46. 34,097,829 (p. 4)   **47.** 561.087 (p. 22)

Complete.

48. $3 \times 6 = 4 +$ ■

49. $63 - 43 = 2 \times$ ■

50. List the factors of 25.

51. $847 + 916$ (p. 46)

52. $1,240 - 623$ (p. 46)

Choose the letter of the next three numbers in the pattern.

53. ⭐ **TEST PREP**   15, 17, 16, 18, 17

A 18, 20, 22   **C** 19, 18, 20
B 18, 17, 19   **D** 19, 21, 20

Problem Solving LiNKUP... to Science

Scientists use weather instruments to collect data about rainfall. The graph below shows the average annual precipitation for five cities in the United States.

USE DATA For 1–3, use the graph.

1. How much less was the precipitation in Roanoke, VA, than in Memphis, TN?

2. How much greater was the precipitation in Miami, FL, than in Asheville, NC?

3. How much greater was the precipitation in the city with the greatest precipitation than in the city with the least precipitation?

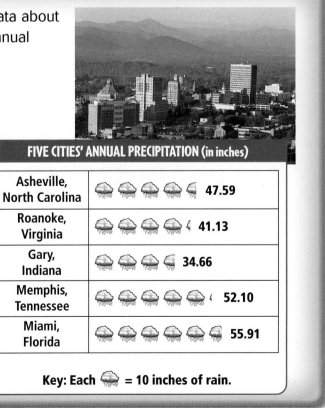

FIVE CITIES' ANNUAL PRECIPITATION (in inches)

Asheville, North Carolina	🌧️🌧️🌧️🌧️🌢 47.59
Roanoke, Virginia	🌧️🌧️🌧️🌧️🌢 41.13
Gary, Indiana	🌧️🌧️🌧️🌢 34.66
Memphis, Tennessee	🌧️🌧️🌧️🌧️🌧️🌢 52.10
Miami, Florida	🌧️🌧️🌧️🌧️🌧️🌢 55.91

Key: Each 🌧️ = 10 inches of rain.

Choose a Method

Quick Review

1.   1,000
      800
  +16,000

2.   800
  −500

3.   11,900
  − 9,300

4.   151,000
   27,000
 +419,000

5.   220,000
  110,000
 +440,000

▶ **Learn**

AD TIME ADDS UP! During Super Bowl XXXVI, the average cost for a 30-second commercial was $1,900,000. A 1-minute commercial cost $3,800,000. If a company bought a 1-minute commercial and a 30-second commercial, how much was the combined cost?

Example 1

Use Mental Math Find the combined cost of a 30-second and a 1-minute commercial.

1,900,000 + 3,800,000 = 5,700,000

So, the combined cost was $5,700,000.

Example 2 A survey showed that 42,663,850 households watched Super Bowl XXXVI. Of those, 3,041,660 said they watched just to see the commercials. How many households tuned in to see the game?

Use a Calculator To find the exact answer, subtract using a calculator. Calculators are especially useful when computing with greater numbers.

Subtract. 42,663,850 − 3,041,660

Estimate. 43,000,000 − 3,000,000 = 40,000,000

$$4\;2\;6\;6\;3\;8\;5\;0$$
$$-\;3\;0\;4\;1\;6\;6\;0\;=\;\boxed{=39\,'622'190}$$

Use Paper and Pencil The answer can also be computed using paper and pencil.

```
   3 12    7 15
  42,663,850   Start with the ones.
 − 3,041,660   Regroup as needed.
  39,622,190
```

So, 39,622,190 households tuned in to see the game. This is close to the estimate, so the answer is reasonable.

Decimals

At the Super Bowl, Kasey had $40.00 to spend. She bought a sandwich for $8.25 and a soda for $2.75. How much money did Kasey have left?

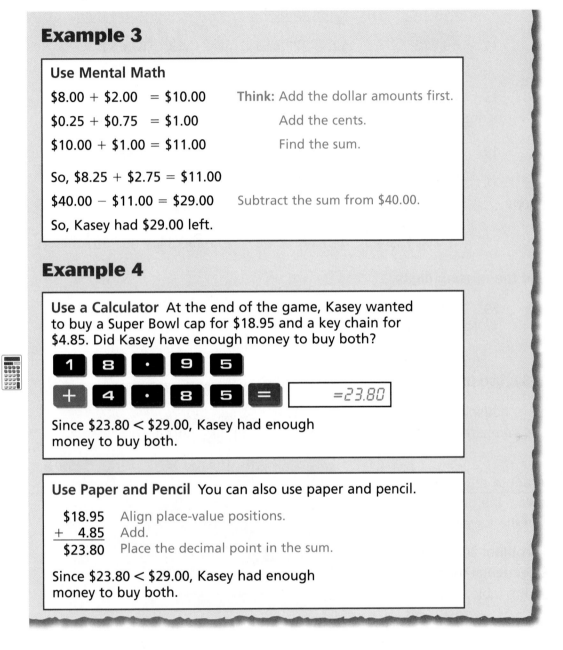

Example 3

Use Mental Math

$8.00 + $2.00 = $10.00   **Think:** Add the dollar amounts first.

$0.25 + $0.75 = $1.00   Add the cents.

$10.00 + $1.00 = $11.00   Find the sum.

So, $8.25 + $2.75 = $11.00

$40.00 − $11.00 = $29.00   Subtract the sum from $40.00.

So, Kasey had $29.00 left.

Example 4

Use a Calculator At the end of the game, Kasey wanted to buy a Super Bowl cap for $18.95 and a key chain for $4.85. Did Kasey have enough money to buy both?

$$\boxed{1}\ \boxed{8}\ \boxed{\cdot}\ \boxed{9}\ \boxed{5}$$
$$\boxed{+}\ \boxed{4}\ \boxed{\cdot}\ \boxed{8}\ \boxed{5}\ \boxed{=}\quad \boxed{=23.80}$$

Since $23.80 < $29.00, Kasey had enough money to buy both.

Use Paper and Pencil You can also use paper and pencil.

$18.95   Align place-value positions.
+ 4.85   Add.
$23.80   Place the decimal point in the sum.

Since $23.80 < $29.00, Kasey had enough money to buy both.

Check

1. Explain which method you could choose to find $7.08 + $73.92.

Choose a method. Find the sum or difference.

2.	3.	4.	5.
56,219	5,462,000	4,234.85	$40.50
+62,793	−3,450,000	+2,567.76	− $20.75

LESSON CONTINUES ▶

Choose a method. Find the sum or difference.

6. 3,432,213
   +3,513,568

7. 743,041
   −244,130

8. 45,000
   +35,000

9. 2,001,005
   +7,011,300

10. 990,000
    −840,000

11. 49,672
    −18,770

12. 873,450
    +234,684

13. 87,654
    +12,345

14. $9.15
    − $8.85

15. 145.000
    −125.000

16. $87.96
    + $13.13

17. 143.097
    − 29.798

18. 10.357
    + 4.321

19. 4.000
    −0.832

20. $87.00
    + $23.00

21. 2,480.50
    −1,240.25

22. 47,205 − 32,000

23. 3,556,014 + 879,843

24. 7,800,000 − 4,200,000

25. 38.00 + 21.5

26. 1,234.5 − 927.68

27. 450.34 + 387.56

★ᵃ⁺ᵇ**ALGEBRA** **Find the missing digits.**

28. 7,2■5
    +6,■72
    1■,357

29. 8,47■
    −4,3■8
    ■,145

30. 1,369,36■
    − 526,■23
    84■,239

31. 4,382,1■7
    + 4■8,287
    4,■20,404

USE DATA **For 32–34, use the table.**

32. How many more households watched Super Bowl XX compared to Super Bowl XVI?

33. What is the order of the Super Bowls from the one with the highest ratings to the one with the lowest ratings?

34. 🖊 **Write a problem** that can be solved by using mental math. Use the information in the table.

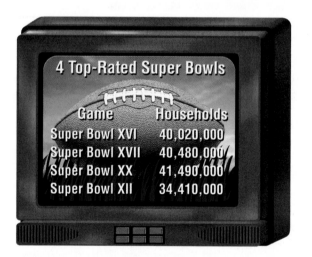

4 Top-Rated Super Bowls

Game	Households
Super Bowl XVI	40,020,000
Super Bowl XVII	40,480,000
Super Bowl XX	41,490,000
Super Bowl XII	34,410,000

35. **ESTIMATION** Angie estimates that 234,678 + 785,000 is about 100,000. Is she correct? Explain.

36. **NUMBER SENSE** Write a decimal that is less than 10.55 + 12.45 but greater than 31.75 − 19.25.

37. The computer club has raised $119.25 for new software. The club wants to buy 3 programs that cost $34.95, $24.99, and $69.99. About how much more money does the club need to raise to buy the 3 programs?

38. India, Ukraine, and the United States combined have more than 40,000 movie theaters. India has 8,975 theaters. Ukraine has 8,702 fewer than the U.S. and 5,985 more than India. How many theaters are in the U.S.?

39. The cost of a 30-second commercial in the 1967 Super Bowl was $42,500. In 2001, the cost of a 30-second commercial was $2,157,500 more than in 1967. What was the cost of a 30-second commercial in 2001?

40. After the game, Colleen spent $3.50 for a snack, $2.25 for a drink, and $10.95 for a shirt. She then had $8.30 left in her wallet. How much money did she have in her wallet before she went shopping?

Mixed Review and Test Prep

For 41–42, round each to the nearest hundred thousand. (p. 38)

41. 685,321

42. 1,095,302

43. $28 - \blacksquare = 17$

44. Round 1.3609 to the nearest thousandth. (p. 40)

45. TEST PREP In which does the digit 3 have the least value? (p. 22)

A 3.158   **B** 5.139   **C** 5.319   **D** 9.153

46. $69,201 - 23,641$ (p. 52)

47. $7.865 + 0.603$ (p. 48)

48. Write 0.107 in word form. (p. 22)

49. TEST PREP Emily bought a pack of paper for $1.50, a pencil for $0.45, and 2 pens. She spent $3.75. How much did Emily pay for both pens? (p. 48)

F $2.80   **G** $1.80   **H** $0.90   **J** $0.25

Problem Solving Thinker's Corner

MENTAL MATH Compatible numbers are numbers that are easy to compute mentally. Two decimals which have a whole-number sum are compatible numbers.

$3.2 + 4.8 = 8$ 3.2 and 4.8 are compatible numbers.

3.9 and 2.1 are compatible numbers

Using the Commutative and Associative Properties, along with mental math strategies, can help you solve problems.

2.5 and 7.5 are compatible numbers

Find the sum. $3.9 + 2.5 + 2.1 + 7.5$

$3.9 + 2.5 + 2.1 + 7.5 = 3.9 + 2.1 + 2.5 + 7.5$ Commutative Property
$= (3.9 + 2.1) + (2.5 + 7.5)$ Associative Property
$= 6 + 10$
$= 16$

So, the sum is 16.

Use compatible numbers and the Commutative and Associative Properties to find each sum.

1. $2.6 + 3.0 + 1.4 + 4.0$

2. $0.25 + 3.7 + 2.3 + 0.75$

3. $2.3 + 8.2 + 3.8 + 5.7$

4. $1.5 + 2.5 + 8.5 + 2.5$

Problem Solving Strategy
Use Logical Reasoning

Quick Review

1. $\begin{array}{r} 12,000 \\ +\ 8,000 \\ \hline \end{array}$ 2. $\begin{array}{r} 30,000 \\ -\ 4,000 \\ \hline \end{array}$

3. $\begin{array}{r} 420,000 \\ -230,000 \\ \hline \end{array}$ 4. $\begin{array}{r} 156,000 \\ +\ 8,000 \\ \hline \end{array}$

5. $1,500,000 + 3,500,000$

PROBLEM   Paco, Rob, Shawna, and Milly each won an award at Field Day. Rob's total score was less than 5,000 points. Shawna scored the fewest points. Paco scored 355 more points than Shawna. How many points did they each score?

UNDERSTAND

- What do you need to find out?

- What information will you use?

FIELD DAY
Points Scored
1ST Award 6,050 pts.
2ND Award 4,230 pts.
3RD Award 1,820 pts.
4TH Award 1,465 pts.

PLAN

- What strategy can you use?

  You can *use logical reasoning* to organize the information in a table.

SOLVE

- How can you solve the problem?

  Make a table to show the information you know. Since each person won an award, there can be only one *yes* in each row of the table.

  Shawna scored the fewest points. Put *yes* in the 1,465 column for Shawna and *no* in the remaining columns.

  Paco scored 355 + 1,465 points. Put *yes* in the 1,820 column for Paco.

  Rob must have scored 4,230 points, since his total score was less than 5,000 points.

  So, *Milly* won the remaining award, with 6,050 points.

FIELD DAY SCORES				
	6,050	**4,230**	**1,820**	**1,465**
Paco	No	No	Yes	No
Rob	No	Yes	No	No
Shawna	No	No	No	Yes
Milly	Yes	No	No	No

CHECK

- Look back at the problem. Does the answer make sense for the problem? Explain.

Problem Solving Practice

Strategies

Draw a Diagram or Picture
Make a Model or Act It Out
Make an Organized List
Find a Pattern
Make a Table or Graph
Predict and Test
Work Backward
Solve a Simpler Problem
Write an Equation
▶ **Use Logical Reasoning**

Use logical reasoning to solve.

1. **What if** the problem did not say that Shawna scored the fewest points? Could you still solve the problem? Explain.

2. Tom, Andy, and Neil mixed up their clothes at the beach. Each one had someone else's hat and sandals. Andy had Tom's hat and Neil's sandals. Whose hat and sandals did each person have?

Ari, Sue, and Jack are hauling truckloads of fruit. The loads weigh 87,500; 76,750; and 91,250 pounds. Ari's load weighs more than Sue's, but their loads weigh the same when rounded to the nearest ten thousand. Jack's load is lighter than Ari's.

3. If you listed the weights of Ari's, Sue's, and Jack's truckloads in order from greatest to least, which list is correct?

    A Ari, Jack, Sue
    B Ari, Sue, Jack
    C Sue, Jack, Ari
    D Jack, Ari, Sue

4. Which information is *not* necessary to solve problem 3?

    F Ari's load weighs more than Sue's.
    G Ari's and Sue's weights rounded to the nearest ten thousand are equal.
    H Jack's load is lighter than Ari's.
    J Weights: 87,500; 76,750; 91,250

Mixed Strategy Practice

5. Decimals A, B, C, D, and E are shown at the right. C is the least of the decimals. D is greater than A. C and E have the same thousandths digit. D is less than B. Which decimal goes with which letter?

6. **REASONING** You have two sand-filled egg timers, one for 9 minutes and one for 2 minutes. How can you use them to time a 5-minute egg?

7. Lightning can be as hot as 50,000°F. The surface of the sun is about 11,000°F. How much hotter can lightning be than the surface of the sun?

8. Last year, the West Plant of the Citrus Company processed 809,309 lemons. The East Plant processed 978,503 grapefruits. If the Citrus Company processed 689,444 more oranges than grapefruits and lemons, how many oranges were processed?

CHAPTER 3

Extra Practice

Set A (pp. 38–39, 40–41)

Round each number to the place of the blue digit.

1. 2,517
2. 450,339
3. 724,950
4. 3,620,740
5. 7,852,060
6. 2.0647
7. 1.3686
8. 34.0685
9. 7.3168
10. 79.5063

Set B (pp. 42–45)

Estimate by rounding.

1. 48,502
   +37,154
2. 518,273
   −284,043
3. 3.85
   +7.07
4. 7.948
   −2.034

Estimate by using front-end estimation.

5. 35,704
   +40,355
6. 547,041
   −231,454
7. 32.75
   +50.15
8. 9.68
   −3.50

Set C (pp. 46–47, 48–51)

Find the sum or difference. Estimate to check.

1. 9,002
   −7,784
2. 16,456
   + 9,023
3. 31,216
   −18,927
4. 48,898
   +61,124

5. $5.83
   +$3.74
6. 6.57
   −3.45
7. 15.04
   − 4.835
8. $367.09
   +$ 14.52

9. 80.54 + 29.06
10. 482.37 − 129.693
11. 83.6 + 154.73

12. There were 11,561 fans at Game 1 and 15,907 fans at Game 2. How many more fans attended Game 2?

Set D (pp. 52–55)

Choose a method. Find the sum or difference.

1. 78,000
   +23,000
2. 89,504
   −43,750
3. 8,400,000
   − 600,000
4. 2,600,898
   + 452,917

5. $6.18
   −$4.79
6. $89.36
   +$14.89
7. 132.65
   + 58.936
8. 5,104.8
   −1,987.36

9. 403,687 + 280,321
10. 8,311,298 − 6,901,283
11. 6,352.839 + 4,972.42

Review/Test

✓ CHECK VOCABULARY AND CONCEPTS

Choose the best term from the box.

┌─────────────────────────┐
│ front-end estimation   │
│ round   │
│ estimate   │
└─────────────────────────┘

1. To find an answer that is close to an exact amount, you can __?__ a sum or difference first. (p. 43)

2. When you estimate by using the values of the front digits of numbers, it is called __?__. (p. 42)

✓ CHECK SKILLS

Round 4,508,684 to the place named. (pp. 38–39)

3. ten thousands   4. hundred thousands   5. millions

Name the place to which each number was rounded. (pp. 40–41)

6. 0.784 to 0.78   7. 0.11 to 0.1   8. 7.5748 to 7.575

Estimate by rounding. (pp. 42–45)

9.	507,294	10.	0.404	11.	129,054	12.	4.807
	+ 45,602		−0.231		+562,081		−3.746

Estimate by using front-end estimation. (pp. 42–45)

13.	604,485	14.	32,153	15.	$55.84	16.	6.954
	+735,327		−15,407		+$34.06		−4.013

Choose a method. Find the sum or difference. (pp. 46–47, 48–51, 52–55)

17.	5,000	18.	950,729	19.	6,074,851	20.	8,382,900
	+2,000		−563,072		+5,733,509		−3,985,631

21. 6.062 + 17.581   22. 23.009 − 5.3   23. 840,000 + 670,000

✓ CHECK PROBLEM SOLVING

Solve. (pp. 56–57)

24. José, Mary, and Rick played cards. The scores were 725, 510, and 225 points. Rick was *not* third. Mary scored about 300 points more than José. Who earned which score?

25. Ann, Linda, and Hugh have pets. One of them has a turtle, one has a cat, and the other has a goldfish. Ann's pet has 4 feet, but it cannot climb trees. Hugh is allergic to fur. Who has which pet?

Standardized Test Prep

⭐ NUMBER SENSE, CONCEPTS, AND OPERATIONS

1. What is the difference between the longest jump and the shortest jump listed in the table below?

LONGEST LONG JUMPS		
Year	Distance (in meters)	Athlete
1991	8.87	Lewis
1991	8.95	Powell
1987	8.86	Emmiyan
1968	8.90	Beamon

A 0.03 meter   **C** 0.30 meter

B 0.09 meter   **D** 0.90 meter

2. Carl Lewis won the gold medal for the long jump in four of the Olympic Games.

CARL LEWIS'S LONG JUMPS	
Year	Distance (in meters)
1984	8.54
1988	8.72
1992	8.67
1996	8.50

Which shows Carl Lewis's jumps listed from shortest to longest?

F 8.72, 8.54, 8.50, 8.67

G 8.54, 8.50, 8.67, 8.72

H 8.50, 8.54, 8.67, 8.72

J 8.54, 8.67, 8.72, 8.50

3. Explain It Darla bought a 395-page book. If she reads 15 pages each evening, will she finish the book in one month? Explain how you know by using an estimation strategy.

⭐ DATA ANALYSIS AND PROBABILITY

4. At the school carnival's Win-a-Stamp booth, students spin a wheel to win animal stamps. What is the probability of winning a shark stamp if you spin the wheel once?

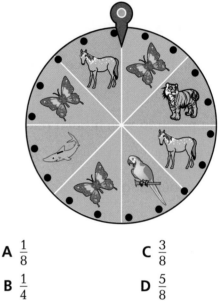

A $\frac{1}{8}$ **C** $\frac{3}{8}$

B $\frac{1}{4}$ **D** $\frac{5}{8}$

5. April recorded her math quiz scores on a stem-and-leaf plot.

Stem	Leaves
7	6 9 9 9
8	3 5 8
9	0 0 1 3

What is the mode of her scores?

F 17   **H** 85

G 79   **J** 90

6. Explain It Serena is designing a board game that will have 16 squares all the same size. She wants the probability of landing on a green square to be $\frac{1}{2}$. How many squares should she color green? Explain your answer.

⭐ **GEOMETRY AND SPATIAL SENSE**

7. Beth is sewing a patchwork quilt that will be 10 feet wide and 8 feet long. The quilt will be made from squares that are 1 foot on each side. How many squares does Beth need for the quilt?

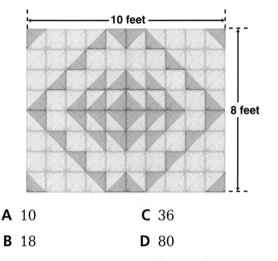

10 feet

8 feet

A 10   C 36

B 18   D 80

8. Brad covered his math book with a paper book cover. He drew a plane figure on the cover. The figure had 3 angles and 3 sides. No two sides were congruent. Which term **best** describes the figure Brad drew?

F equilateral triangle

G isosceles triangle

H scalene triangle

J trapezoid

9. Explain It How many lines of symmetry does a square have? Draw a square and show all the lines of symmetry. Explain how you know that the lines you drew are lines of symmetry.

⭐ **MEASUREMENT**

TIP **Decide on a plan.** See item 10. Find the elapsed time for each movie.

10. Katie wants to see the longest movie. Which movie should she choose?

GRAND

MOVIE	TIMES
SPACE EXPLORATION	3:35 to 5:15
HAPPY-GO-LUCKY	2:55 to 4:45
THE WORLD AROUND US	3:05 to 4:40
CLOWNING AROUND	2:40 to 4:05

A *Space Exploration*

B *Happy-Go-Lucky*

C *The World Around Us*

D *Clowning Around*

11. A large egg weighs about 2.5 ounces. About how much will a dozen large eggs weigh?

1 Dozen Large Eggs

F about 1 pound

G about 2 pounds

H about 2.5 pounds

J about 12 pounds

12. Explain It Daniel's goal is to jog 6 kilometers each week. He jogged 2,350 meters on Monday and 1,900 meters on Tuesday. If he jogs 2,000 meters on Wednesday, will he meet his goal? Explain how you know.

CHAPTER 4

Algebra: Use Addition and Subtraction

FAST FACT • SCIENCE During the Great Backyard Bird Count, bird enthusiasts across North America count birds for four days. In 2002, a total of 4,727,536 individual birds were counted.

PROBLEM SOLVING During the count, a total of 201 belted kingfishers were sighted across Florida. The greatest count in one location was 29 kingfishers in Merritt Island, Florida. Write an equation to find how many were counted in the rest of Florida.

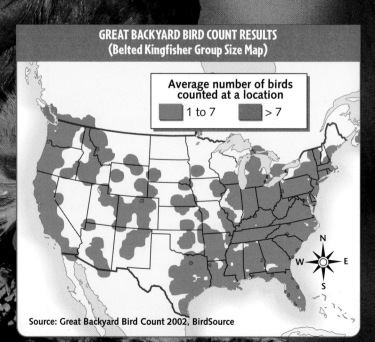

GREAT BACKYARD BIRD COUNT RESULTS
(Belted Kingfisher Group Size Map)

Average number of birds counted at a location

■ 1 to 7   ■ > 7

Source: Great Backyard Bird Count 2002, BirdSource

CHECK WHAT YOU KNOW

Use this page to help you review and remember
important skills needed for Chapter 4.

MISSING ADDENDS

Find the missing addend.

1. $9 + \blacksquare = 15$

2. $13 + \blacksquare = 17$

3. $8 + \blacksquare = 14$

4. $\blacksquare + 6 = 20$

5. $\blacksquare + 3 = 15$

6. $9 + \blacksquare = 18$

7. $\blacksquare + 7 = 15$

8. $\blacksquare + 6 = 13$

9. $\blacksquare + 8 = 21$

ADDITION PROPERTIES

Write the letter of the addition property used in
each equation.

A. Order Property

B. Grouping Property

C. Identity Property

10. $9 + 8 = 8 + 9$

11. $24 + 0 = 24$

12. $(5 + 6) + 3 = 5 + (6 + 3)$

13. $0 + 12 = 12$

14. $23 + 9 = 9 + 23$

15. $7 + (1 + 4) = (7 + 1) + 4$

EXPRESSIONS

Find the value.

16. $(8 + 12) - 6$

17. $8 + (15 - 5)$

18. $17 + (21 - 5)$

19. $(21 + 60) - 30$

20. $(12 + 9) - 11$

21. $50 - (14 + 6)$

VOCABULARY POWER

REVIEW

Order Property [ôr´dər prä´ pər•te] *noun*

The word *order* can be used to mean an
arrangement such as alphabetical or
numerical order. Explain what the word
order means in this example of the
Order Property.

$6 + 10 + 5 = 10 + 5 + 6$

PREVIEW

expression   inequality

variable   Commutative Property

equation   Associative Property

solution   compensation

 www.harcourtschool.com/mathglossary

Expressions and Variables

Quick Review

Write the words for each.

1. $3 + 5$
2. $6 - 2$
3. $10 + 2 + 8$
4. $(2 + 7) - 4$
5. $9 - (5 + 1)$

VOCABULARY

expression
variable

Learn

GO FISH An **expression** is a mathematical phrase that combines numbers, operation signs, and sometimes variables. It does *not* have an equal sign. These are some expressions:

$$15 + 4 \qquad 9 - 7 \qquad (4 + 6) - 11 \qquad 3 \times 2$$

You can write an expression and find its value.

Example 1

Matt had 12 fish in his tank. Then he added 3 more fish. How many fish are in his tank now?

12 fish in tank	plus	3 more fish
↓	↓	↓
12	+	3

15

So, Matt has 15 fish in the tank now.

An expression *may* have a variable. A **variable** is a letter or symbol that stands for one or more numbers. These are some expressions with a variable:

$$4 + n \qquad f - 5 \qquad 6 \times a \qquad 3 + x - 2$$

You can use a variable in an expression to model a situation.

Example 2

Julie had 16 fish in her tank. She gave some fish to her sister. Write an expression to show this.

16 fish in tank	minus	some fish
↓	↓	↓
16	−	f

• What can you use to represent a number that you do not know in an expression?

Find the Value

MATH IDEA You can find a value of an expression by replacing the variable with a number and using that number to compute the result.

More Examples

A Sara had 15 apples in a basket. Some were eaten.

Let a = the number of apples eaten.

apples in a basket		apples eaten
↓		↓
15	−	a

Expression: $15 - a$

If 10 apples were eaten, how many were left?

Let $a = 10$.

$15 - a$
↓   ↓
$15 - 10 = 5$

So, 5 apples were left.

B There are 11 people joining the swim team.

Let p = people already on the swim team.

on swim team		joining swim team
↓		↓
p	+	11

Expression: $p + 11$

If 23 people were already on the team, how many people are on the swim team now?

Let $p = 23$.

$p + 11$
↓   ↓
$23 + 11 = 34$

So, there are 34 people on the swim team now.

C Tom had 18 baseball cards. He traded some of his cards for 3 of Tammy's cards.

Let c = number of cards Tom traded.

cards Tom had		cards Tom traded		cards Tom received
↓		↓		↓
(18	−	c)	+	3

Expression: $(18 - c) + 3$

If Tom traded 6 cards, how many cards does Tom have now?

Let $c = 6$.

$(18 - c) + 3$
   ↓   ↓
$(18 - 6) + 3$
   ↓
$12 + 3 = 15$

So, Tom has 15 baseball cards.

▷ Check

1. **Explain** why 6 is an unreasonable value for n in this expression: Lyle has some fish. He buys 3 more fish and then sells 10 fish. Expression: $(n + 3) - 10$.

Write an expression. Find the value.

2. Sam had 10 dimes. He gave Gary 4.

3. eleven added to five

4. Kim had 24 cookies, ate 6, and then baked 12 more.

Write an expression with a variable. Explain what the variable represents.

5. Rona had 96 pencils and then sold some.

6. Tim had 17 cards. Joe gave him more.

7. Lee gave me 12 cookies. I ate 6 and then baked more.

LESSON CONTINUES

PROBLEM SOLVING ON LOCATION in *Virginia*

THE ASSATEAGUE LIGHTHOUSE

The Assateague Lighthouse was built about 170 years ago. It is located on Assateague Island near Chincoteague, Virginia. This area has had the opposite problem of beach erosion. Sand bars have filled in the area which used to be water along the coast. Now, the lighthouse is actually one mile inland from the coast.

THE ASSATEAGUE LIGHTHOUSE	
1833	First lighthouse built
1867	Current lighthouse built
1910	Current keeper's quarters built
1933	Lighthouse electrified
1965	Lighthouse automated
1972	Lighthouse added to National Registry of Historic Places

The Assateague Lighthouse, painted with distinctive red and white stripes, can be seen for miles. ▼

USE DATA For 1–3, use the table.

1. How many years after the current lighthouse was built did it get electric lights?

2. How many years after the first lighthouse was built did the lighthouse join the National Registry of Historic Places?

3. The lighthouse is narrower at the top than it is at the base. Near the top of the lighthouse, the diameter of the tower is 13 feet 7 inches. Near the base, the diameter is 14 feet greater. What is the diameter of the lighthouse near its base?

4. In 1832, the government spent $333.33 to buy the land on which the lighthouse would be built. In 1833, it cost $55,000 to build the first tower. How much more did it cost to build the tower than to buy the land?

THE PONIES OF CHINCOTEAGUE

Before the Assateague Lighthouse was built, many ships sank off the shore of nearby Chincoteague Island. According to legend, 17 horses survived such a shipwreck over 500 years ago. Their descendants are known as the wild ponies of Chincoteague. Each year, some of their foals are sold at auction.

USE DATA For 1–5, use the table.

AUCTION PRICES FOR PONIES OF CHINCOTEAGUE				
Year	Highest Price	Average Price	Lowest Price	Ponies Sold
2002	$7,800	$1,818	$950	89
2001	$10,500	$1,961	$1,000	85
2000	$7,500	$2,060	$1,300	84
1999	$4,200	$1,620	$800	86

▲ Each year thousands of people gather to watch the wild ponies swim from Assateague Island to Chincoteague Island.

1. In which year was the highest price paid for a pony? How much greater was the highest price than the lowest price in that same year?

2. Order the average prices for ponies from least to greatest.

3. Which year had the greatest difference between the average price and the lowest price? How much was the difference?

4. What was the average price paid for ponies in 2000? Round this number to the nearest hundred.

5. In 2003 a number of ponies were sold. Suppose there were 5 more ponies sold in 2003 than in 2002. Write an equation to find the number of ponies sold in 2003.

Analyze Data and Graphs

⌷FAST FACT • SPORTS

Dr. James Naismith invented basketball in 1891. The first official college basketball game took place in 1897, when Yale University defeated the University of Pennsylvania, 32–10. The graph shows the average points per game scored by college basketball's top scorers for 1997 through 2001.

PROBLEM SOLVING

How much greater was Ronnie McCollum's average than Courtney Alexander's? Can you tell from the graph how many total points Charles Jones scored during the 1997 season? Explain.

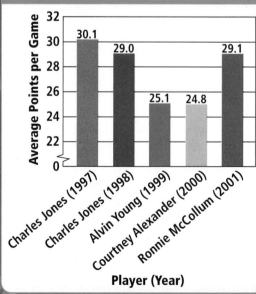

NCAA MEN'S BASKETBALL LEADING SCORERS

CHECK WHAT YOU KNOW

Use this page to help you review and remember
important skills needed for Chapter 5.

FREQUENCY TABLES

For 1–4, use the frequency table.

1. How many students scored 90 on the test?

2. How many students scored either 90 or 100?

3. How many students took the test?

4. How many students scored less than 90?

TEST SCORES	
Score	Frequency
70	12
80	15
90	17
100	12

READ GRAPHS

For 5–8, use the line graph.

5. Which two months had equal amounts of snowfall?

6. Which month had the greatest amount of snow?

7. Which month had the least amount of snow?

8. What was the total snowfall for November and December?

MONTHLY SNOWFALL

For 9–11, use the circle graph.

9. What flavor received the most votes?

10. How many people chose vanilla?

11. How many people voted?

FAVORITE ICE CREAM FLAVORS

Strawberry 3 · Mint Chip 6 · Vanilla 9 · Chocolate 12

VOCABULARY POWER

REVIEW

data [dā′tə] *noun*

Data are information collected about
people or things. Data can be numbers,
words, pictures, photos, or videos. List
three ways to collect data.

PREVIEW

survey   outlier

sample   mean

population   median

random sample   mode

GO ON-LINE

www.harcourtschool.com/mathglossary

Collect and Organize Data

Quick Review

1. $9 + 14$ **2.** $13 + 24$
3. $40 + 18$ **4.** $15 + 220$
5. $240 + 160$

VOCABULARY

survey
sample
population
random sample
cumulative frequency
outlier

▶ **Learn**

WHAT'S THE QUESTION? A survey can be used to gather information about a group. Often, a part of the group, called a sample, is chosen to represent the whole group, or population.

A sample must represent the population fairly. In a random sample each person in the population has an equal chance of being chosen.

Example

Suppose a television network wants to find the time of day that most children ages 9–12 watch TV. Which sample represents the population?

a. a random sample of 100 girls, ages 9–12

b. a random sample of 100 children, ages 9–12

c. a random sample of 100 children

d. a random sample of 100 adults

Choice **a** leaves out boys. Choice **c** could include children who are younger than 9 or older than 12, and choice **d** does not include children. Only choice **b** represents the population.

HANDS ON

Activity

Design your own survey and collect data.

• Select one of the topics listed below.
   a. Hours spent studying each week
   b. Favorite type of movie
   c. Favorite breakfast food

• Decide what population you want to survey. Do you want to include all students at your school, or just fifth graders?

• Write a question for your survey.

   The question should be clear and simple, use words that have the same meaning to everyone, and have only one response, or answer, per person.

• Survey a random sample of at least 30 students.

• Make a recording sheet for your data.

Frequency Tables and Line Plots

A frequency table shows the total for each category or group. The **cumulative frequency** column is a running total of the frequencies.

Remember

The range is the difference between the greatest and least numbers in a set of data.

Examples

May Elementary had a pet fair. The student council surveyed students by asking, "How many pets do you have at home?"

A Read from the frequency column to find how many students have just 3 pets at home.

Five students have 3 pets at home.

B Read from the cumulative frequency column to find how many students have 3 or fewer pets at home.

Twenty-seven students have 3 or fewer pets at home.

C Read the last entry in the cumulative frequency column to find how many students were surveyed.

Thirty students were surveyed.

Pet Survey

Pets	Tally
0	ЖЖ II
1	ЖЖ I
2	ЖЖ IIII
3	ЖЖ
4	II
7	I

PET SURVEY

Number of Pets	Frequency	Cumulative Frequency	
0	7	7	
1	6	13	← 7 + 6 = 13
2	9	22	← 13 + 9 = 22
3	5	27	← 22 + 5 = 27
4	2	29	← 27 + 2 = 29
5	0	29	← 29 + 0 = 29
6	0	29	← 29 + 0 = 29
7	1	30	← 29 + 1 = 30

You can graph these data by using a line plot.

The line plot gives a visual picture of the data. You can quickly see that the most common number of pets is 2.

Some students have no pets, and one student has 7 pets. So, the range for these data is 7 − 0, or 7.

- Organize your data from the Activity on page 96 in a frequency table. Draw a line plot or other graph to display the data.

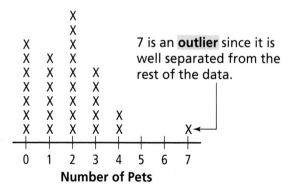

7 is an **outlier** since it is well separated from the rest of the data.

LESSON CONTINUES

1. **Explain** one way to select a random sample of the fifth-grade students at your school.

A toy company surveyed children ages 8–12. Tell whether the sample represents the population. If it does not, explain.

2. a random sample of 250 boys, ages 8–12

3. a random sample of 250 children, ages 8–12

▷ **Practice and Problem Solving** (Extra Practice, page 110, Set A)

Nelton Elementary wants to name the new school mascot. Tell whether the sample represents the population. If it does not, explain.

4. a random sample of 100 students from a list of all students in school

5. a random sample of 100 fifth-grade students

Write *yes* or *no* to tell whether the question would be a good survey question. If it would not, explain.

6. Is your favorite sport soccer or tennis?

7. Which state would you most like to visit?

For 8–10, use the tally table.

8. Make a cumulative frequency table for the data.

9. Which time was selected by the greatest number of students?

10. If each student took part in only one event, how many students participated in Field Day?

SIGN-UP FOR FIELD EVENT TIMES	
Event Times	Number of Students
9:30 A.M.	ЖЖ ЖЖ ЖЖ I
10:30 A.M.	ЖЖ ЖЖ III
1:30 P.M.	ЖЖ ЖЖ ЖЖ II
2:30 P.M.	ЖЖ ЖЖ ЖЖ III

11. **Vocabulary Power** In physics, the word *frequency* means "rate of repetition," as in a vibration. Explain what *frequency* means in a frequency table.

12. **Write About It** Explain why a sample is often used rather than a population when conducting a survey.

Find the range for each set of data.

13. 8, 12, 17, 15, 20, 9

14. 34, 26, 37, 31, 37, 22

15. 100, 110, 105, 103

16. 96, 74, 83, 81, 64

17. 156, 147, 145, 168, 155

18. 38, 45, 59, 32, 47, 51

19. Survey 20 people to find the number of servings of fruit they eat each week. Make a frequency table and a line plot. Find the range, and describe the results.

20. Find survey results from a newspaper or magazine. Identify the sample size and the question. Describe the results of the survey.

21. Write an expression for this situation. Lisa read 4 fewer pages than Karen. Karen read n pages. (p. 64)

22. Solve. $n - 9 = 21$ (p. 70)

23.   4.32 (p. 48)   **24.**   10.5   (p. 48)
      $+3.57$ $- 1.46$

25. Round 2,497,629 to the nearest million. (p. 38)

26. Round 6.058 to the nearest tenth. (p. 40)

27. $4.2 - 0.3$ (p. 48) **28.** $1.02 - 0.9$ (p. 48)

For 29–30, choose the letter of the number written in standard form. (p. 22)

29. TEST PREP   five and nine tenths

   A 5.09   **C** 9.5
   B 5.9   **D** 509

30. TEST PREP   twenty-six hundredths

   F 0.026   **H** 1.26
   G 0.26   **J** 2.6

Problem Solving   LiNKÜP... to Reading

STRATEGY • USE GRAPHIC AIDS   Examining each part of a table can help you understand the data presented. The title tells you what data are represented. The labels on the columns and rows give you more details about the data. As you read a problem about data in a table, match what you read with what you see.

For 1–6, use the frequency table.

1. What does the title tell you?

2. What does the frequency column tell you?

3. Where would you look in the table to find the total number of students represented by the data?

4. How many students read for 60 minutes during the week?

5. How many more students read for 40 minutes or more than read for less than 40 minutes?

6. Explain how using a graphic aid, such as a table or graph, can help you analyze data.

MINUTES STUDENTS SPENT READING MAGAZINES (1 WEEK)		
Minutes	**Frequency**	**Cumulative Frequency**
20	5	5
30	9	14
40	10	24
50	14	38
60	11	49

Find the Mean

Learn

"WHEN IN THE COURSE . . ."
The table shows the ages of some of the youngest signers of the Declaration of Independence. What is the mean age of these signers?

The **mean**, or average, is one number that is representative of the data. You can find the mean by dividing the sum of a set of numbers by the number of addends.

SIGNERS OF DECLARATION OF INDEPENDENCE	
Signer	**Age**
Edward Rutledge	26
Benjamin Rush	30
Elbridge Gerry	31
Thomas Jefferson	33

VOCABULARY

mean

▲ Starting on August 2, 1776, 56 members of Congress signed the Declaration of Independence.

Example

STEP 1

Add all the data.

$$\begin{array}{r} 26 \\ 30 \\ 31 \\ +33 \\ \hline 120 \end{array}$$

STEP 2

Divide the sum by the number of addends.

$$\begin{array}{r} 30 \\ 4\overline{)120} \end{array}$$

So, the mean age is 30.

▲ Edward Rutledge

• What if the table included the oldest signer, Benjamin Franklin, who was 70 years old? How would that affect the mean?

More Examples Find the mean for each set of data.

Ⓐ 74, 91, 63, 92, 85

$$\begin{array}{r} 74 \\ 91 \\ 63 \\ 92 \\ +\ 85 \\ \hline 405 \end{array}$$

number of → addends

$$\begin{array}{r} 81 \\ 5\overline{)405} \\ \underline{40} \\ 05 \\ \underline{5} \\ 0 \end{array}$$

Ⓑ 357, 562, 411, 584, 294, 372

$$\begin{array}{r} 357 \\ 562 \\ 411 \\ 584 \\ 294 \\ +\ 372 \\ \hline 2,580 \end{array}$$

number of → addends

$$\begin{array}{r} 430 \\ 6\overline{)2580} \\ \underline{24} \\ 18 \\ \underline{18} \\ 00 \\ \underline{0} \\ 0 \end{array}$$

▲ Benjamin Franklin

You can also use a calculator to find the mean.

(357 + 562 + 411 + 584 + 294 + 372) ÷ 6 =   = 430

▷ Check

1. **Look** at this set of data: 5, 16, 17, 17, 17, 18. Do you think the mean will be closer to 5 or to 16? Explain.

Find the mean for each set of data.

2. 18, 22, 14

3. 58, 105, 172, 45

4. 33, 36, 35, 37, 39

▷ Practice and Problem Solving   Extra Practice, page 110, Set B

Find the mean for each set of data.

5. 9, 6, 5, 9, 11

6. $6, $7, $9, $10

7. 19, 25, 28, 32

8. 1,250; 980; 350

9. 110, 75, 135, 160

10. 147, 116, 148, 128, 116

11. 95, 84, 72, 73, 76

12. 124, 130, 100, 122, 124

13. 202, 213, 315, 285, 285

14. 100, 150, 200, 170, 250, 300

15. 1,200; 2,400; 1,320; 2,560

ALGEBRA **Use the given mean to find the missing number in each data set.**

16. $1, $3, $5, ▨; mean: $4

17. 5, 7, 10, 13, ▨; mean: 10

18. 12, 15, 18, 10, ▨; mean: 13

19. 20, 25, 30, ▨, 32, 18; mean: 25

For 20–24, use the table.

20. What is the average of Andrew's test scores?

21. How can you tell what Lin's test average is without calculating it?

22. Who had the highest test mean, or average, Ally, Andrew, or Lin?

23. **REASONING** What score does Karen need to get on Test 4 to raise her average to 85?

24. ✎ Write a problem using the information in the table. Then solve the problem.

HISTORY TEST SCORES				
Name	Test 1	Test 2	Test 3	Test 4
Ally	87	93	100	80
Andrew	95	92	89	76
Karen	81	86	82	absent
Lin	85	85	85	85

25. Ally, Andrew, Karen, and Lin sit in the same row. Ally sits in front of Karen and behind Lin. Andrew sits in the front seat. Who sits right behind Andrew?

Mixed Review and Test Prep

26. Find the range for the scores 88, 79, 84, and 88. (p. 96)

27. 85,941 (p. 46)
   + 5,357

28. 3,105,568 (p. 52)
   −1,387,555

29. Round 32.5876 to the nearest thousandth. (p. 40)

30. **TEST PREP** Which is the solution of the equation $13 + n = 29$? (p. 70)

  A $n = 13$ **C** $n = 29$
  B $n = 16$ **D** $n = 42$

Chapter 5 **101**

Find the Median and Mode

Quick Review

Give the number halfway between the numbers in each pair.

1. 6 and 8
2. 12 and 14
3. 14 and 18
4. 32 and 36
5. 68 and 72

VOCABULARY

median   mode

▶ **Learn**

WHAT'S THE SCORE?   The Eagles basketball team has played 9 games so far this season. The coach recorded their scores.

To analyze the data, the coach can find the median and mode of the scores.

The **median** is the middle number when the data are arranged in order.

The **mode** is the number or item that occurs most often in a set of data. There may be one mode, more than one mode, or no mode.

HANDS ON   **Activity**

STEP 1

Put the basketball points in order from least to greatest. Find the median.

STEP 2

Make a line plot of the points.

- Draw a horizontal line.
- Label vertical tick marks in units of 1 from 40–50.
- Plot the data. Then title the graph.

STEP 3

Use the line plot to find the mode.

- Where are the data clustered on the line plot?
- What if the Eagles score 45 points in their tenth game? Will that change the mode? Explain.

EAGLES

GAME	POINTS	GAME	POINTS
1	42	6	43
2	50	7	40
3	45	8	42
4	42	9	45
5	44	10	

- What fraction of the basketball points are greater than the median? What fraction are less than the median?

When there are two middle numbers, the median is the mean of the two numbers.

The median for 3, 5, 7, 9 is between 5 and 7.

$$(5 + 7) \div 2 = 12 \div 2 = 6$$ The median is 6.

Technology Link

More Practice:
Harcourt Mega Math
The Number Games,
ArachnaGraph, Level F

▷ Check

1. Explain how the median and the mode differ from the mean of a set of data.

Find the median and the mode.

2. 12, 14, 11, 11, 9, 16, 17, 19

3. 24, 32, 28, 45, 19, 24, 50, 32

▷ Practice and Problem Solving   (Extra Practice, page 110, Set C)

Find the median and the mode.

4.

KATIE'S TEST SCORES							
Test	1	2	3	4	5	6	7
Score	94	93	95	87	94	78	85

5.

CARD COLLECTIONS					
Name	Tony	Kara	Ray	Sue	Jay
Number	240	200	200	265	285

Find the mean, median, mode, and range.

6. 9, 6, 5, 9, 11

7. $4, $1, $8, $6, $3, $8

8. 124, 130, 100, 122, 124

9. 95, 84, 72, 73, 76

10. 202, 213, 315, 285, 285

11. 749, 751, 1,298, 202

For 12–15, use the line plot.

12. How many players were measured, and what is the range of their heights?

13. What is the most common height?

14. What is the median height for the basketball team?

Heights of Fifth-Grade Basketball Players (in.)

15. Two players with heights of 56 in. and 63 in. join the team. How does this affect the median and the mode of the heights?

16. ❓ **What's the Error?**   Julio said the median of the scores 90, 80, 82, 95, 78, 84, and 86 is 95. Explain Julio's error. What is the correct median of the scores?

Mixed Review and Test Prep

17. 345,000 + 9,004,356 (p. 52)

18. Round 34,576 to the nearest thousand. (p. 38)

19. Find the values of $15 + b$ if $b = 12$ and if $b = 20$. (p. 64)

20. Solve: $120 + t = 200$. (p. 70)

21. **TEST PREP**   Which is closest to 5.247? (p. 48)

A 4.247   **C** 5.499

B 5.098   **D** 5.647

Problem Solving Strategy
Make a Graph

PROBLEM   A store recorded the ages of all the people who bought a pair of in-line skates last month. Which age group bought the most skates: people 10–19, people in their 20's, in their 30's, in their 40's, or in their 50's?

VOCABULARY
stem-and-leaf plot

UNDERSTAND

- What are you asked to find?

- What information will you use?

PLAN

- What strategy can you use to solve the problem?

  You can *make a graph* to organize the data.

SOLVE

- How can you use the strategy to solve the problem?

  You can make a **stem-and-leaf plot** to help you see how data are clustered, or grouped.

  List the tens digits of the data in order from least to greatest. These are the stems.

  Beside each tens digit, record the ones digits of the data, in order from least to greatest. These are the leaves.

  So, the most skate buyers were in the 10–19 age group.

Ages of People Who Bought In-Line Skates

26	18	41	51
12	34	23	19
31	44	45	14
34	16	37	23
13	27	12	22

The tens digit of each number is its stem.

The ones digit of each number is its leaf.

Stem	Leaves
1	2 2 3 4 6 8 9
2	2 3 3 6 7
3	1 4 4 7
4	1 4 5
5	1

4 | 5   represents 45.

Ages of In-Line Skate Buyers

CHECK

- Look back. Does the answer make sense? Explain.

Problem Solving Practice

Strategies

Draw a Diagram or Picture
Make a Model or Act It Out
Make an Organized List
Find a Pattern
▶ **Make a Table or Graph**
Predict and Test
Work Backward
Solve a Simpler Problem
Write an Equation
Use Logical Reasoning

Make a graph to solve.

1. **What if** three more people, ages 25, 28, and 32, bought skates? Which age group would have bought the most skates then?

2. Angela's bowling scores are 71, 87, 96, 73, 76, 95, 84, 95, and 97. Does she bowl more often in the 70's, 80's, or 90's?

Mr. Brown recorded the class test scores. Make a stem-and-leaf plot, using the table below.

TEST SCORES										
84	81	85	75	81	87	70	90	82	92	86

3. Jim and Tamara got the same score on the test. What was their score?

   A 90   **C** 81
   B 85   **D** 75

4. Which is true about the test scores?

   F The mode for the test scores is 87.
   G The mean test score is 85.
   H The range for the test scores is 12.
   J The median test score is 84.

Mixed Strategy Practice

For 5–6, use the table.

5. Make a stem-and-leaf plot of the number of home runs. Which stem has the most leaves?

6. What are the range, median, and mode for the data set?

NATIONAL LEAGUE HOME-RUN RECORDS 1992–2001			
Year	Home Runs	Year	Home Runs
1992	35	1997	49
1993	46	1998	70
1994	43	1999	65
1995	40	2000	50
1996	47	2001	73

7. **FAST FACT** • SPORTS The New York Yankees won their first World Series championship in 1923. They won their twenty-sixth championship 77 years later. What year was that?

8. Brenda is older than June. Alice is younger than June. Cindy's age is between Alice's and June's. Write the names in order from oldest to youngest.

9. The Ricardos family paid $14.00 for parking. Parking cost $5.00 for the first hour and $1.50 for each additional hour. How many hours were they parked?

10. Antonio has 6 coins that are dimes and quarters. He has a total of $1.05. What combination of coins does he have?

Analyze Graphs

Quick Review

Give the next number in the pattern.

1. 16, 17, 18, ■
2. 0, 2, 4, 6, ■
3. 7, 10, 13, ■
4. 4, 10, 16, 22, ■
5. 80, 84, 88, ■

▶ **Learn**

GRAPHS GALORE! A **pictograph** displays countable data with symbols or pictures. Pictographs have a *key* to show how many each picture represents.

Look at the Aerobics Class Size pictograph. How many people are in the 3:00 and 4:00 aerobics classes altogether?

AEROBICS CLASS SIZE

3:00	🙌🙌🙌
4:00	🙌🙌🙌🙌🙌
5:00	🙌🙌🙌🙌🙌
6:00	🙌🙌🙌

Key: 🙌 = 2 people

VOCABULARY

pictograph   bar graph
line graph   circle graph
trend

There are 8 whole symbols and 1 half symbol in the 3:00 and 4:00 classes combined.

$$(8 \times 2) + 1 = 17$$

So, there are 17 people altogether.

A **bar graph** uses horizontal or vertical bars to display countable data. Bar graphs allow you to compare facts about groups of data.

Look at the exercise bar graph. Which type of exercise is more popular, jogging or weights?

The jogging bar is taller, so that exercise is more popular.

How many more students chose jogging over weights?

There were 14 students who chose jogging and 10 who chose weights.

$$14 - 10 = 4$$

So, 4 more students chose jogging.

FAVORITE TYPES OF EXERCISE

Number of Students / Type of Exercise (Aerobics, Treadmill, Jogging, Weights)

More Graphs

A **line graph** shows how data change over time. All or part of the graph may show a **trend**, or a pattern over time, such as increasing, decreasing, or staying the same.

Look at the line graph. The distance increases by 6 miles each hour. Predict how long it will take to travel 30 miles by bike if the trend continues.

You can extend the line to see that it will probably take 5 hours to travel 30 miles if the trend continues.

BIKING AT 6 MILES PER HOUR

Total Distance (in mi) — 30, 24, 18, 12, 6, 0

Time (in hr) — 1, 2, 3, 4

KAREN'S 60-MINUTE WORKOUT

10 min Warm-up
10 min Stretch
30 min Jog
10 min Cool-Down

A **circle graph** shows how parts of the data are related to the whole and to each other.

Look at the circle graph of Karen's workout. On which activity does Karen spend the most time? How long does she spend on this activity?

Jogging fills half of the circle. So, Karen spends the most time jogging. Half of 60 minutes is 30 minutes. So, Karen jogs for 30 minutes.

MATH IDEA When you know how to analyze graphs, you can draw conclusions, answer questions, and make predictions about the data.

Check

1. **Explain** which type of graph would be the most appropriate to compare the high temperatures for a week.

For 2–5, use the graphs above.

2. How long does it take to travel 12 miles?

3. Estimate the distance that can be traveled in $1\frac{1}{2}$ hours.

4. How does the amount of time Karen jogs compare to the amount of time she stretches?

5. What fraction of her workout does Karen spend warming up?

LESSON CONTINUES

For 6–10, use the pictograph.

6. Which profession has the most walking?

7. Which two professions have about the same amount?

8. What does each footprint symbol represent?

9. About how far do doctors walk in a year?

10. Real estate agents walk about 600 miles in a year. How would this amount be displayed on the pictograph?

PROFESSIONS WITH MUCH WALKING

Police Officer	👣👣👣👣👣👣👣👣👣
Mail Carrier	👣👣👣👣👣👣
TV Reporter	👣👣👣👣👣
Doctor	👣👣👣👣

Key: 👣 = 200 mi/yr

For 11–13, use the line graph.

11. Between which ages did Sam's dog gain the most weight? About how much did the dog gain?

12. Estimate the dog's weight at 5 months and at 11 months.

13. **What if** Sam's dog stays at 105 pounds for the next 3 months? How would this trend be displayed on the line graph?

WEIGHT OF SAM'S DOG

14. Sam spent $30 on dog food, $20 on a collar, $15 on toys, and $35 for a dog bed. What type of graph would best display how Sam spent $100?

For 15–16, use the circle graph.

15. About what part of all the pets in the United States are either cats, birds, or fish?

16. Do dogs or fish account for about one quarter of all the pets in the United States?

PETS IN THE U.S.

17. Rosa works at a dog kennel. She feeds each dog 0.2 pound of dry food each day. How much dry food does she use for 5 dogs in 2 weeks?

18. Of the 25 students in Mr. Reeve's class, 7 ride a bus to school, 8 ride in a carpool, and the rest walk to school. How many students walk to school?

Mixed Review and Test Prep

19. 1,369,501
+3,695,224
(p. 52)

20. 82,954
−60,387
(p. 46)

21. $11 + n = 57$ (p. 70)   **22.** $n − 16 = 38$ (p. 70)

23. TEST PREP   Find the mean for 26, 35, 87, 13, 4, 25, 20. (p. 100)

A 83
B 38
C 30
D 25

24. $12.7945 − 1.68$ (p. 48)

25. $0.69 + 1.577$ (p. 48)

26. $42 − n = 28$ (p. 10)   **27.** $n + 8 = 25$ (p. 70)

28. TEST PREP   Round 36,582,367 to the nearest hundred thousand. (p. 38)

F 36,500,000
G 36,580,000
H 36,600,000
J 37,000,000

Problem Solving   LiNKUP...to Science

The cheetah is the fastest land animal, reaching speeds of 70 miles per hour. The slowest land animal is the snail, moving at top speeds of 0.03 miles per hour, or about 3 feet per minute.

For 1–6, use the bar graph.

1. Which animal runs faster, a rabbit or a zebra?

2. About how fast can an elephant run?

3. A slow-moving truck is traveling at 37 miles per hour. Which animals can run faster than the truck is moving?

4. A greyhound runs faster than a rabbit but slower than a zebra. How fast can a greyhound run?

5. ⭐ **What's the Error?**   Lisa read the graph and said that a pig can run about 20 miles per hour. How fast can a pig run? Explain Lisa's error.

6. ⭐ **What's the Question?**   The answer is 40 miles per hour.

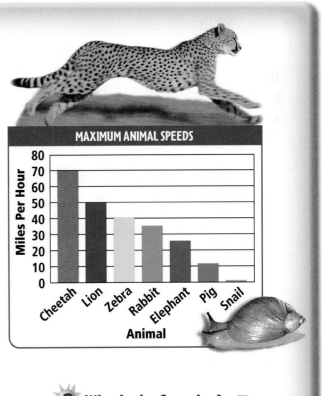

MAXIMUM ANIMAL SPEEDS

Miles Per Hour — Animal: Cheetah, Lion, Zebra, Rabbit, Elephant, Pig, Snail

Extra Practice

Set A (pp. 96–99)

For 1–4, use the frequency table.

SCHOOL FRUIT SURVEY		
Fruits Eaten Each Day	Frequency	Cumulative Frequency
1	6	6
2	3	9
3	4	13
4	2	15
5	5	20

1. How many students eat 2 fruits each day? 5 fruits each day?

2. How many students eat fewer than 4 fruits each day?

3. What is the range of the fruits eaten each day?

4. How many students were surveyed?

Set B (pp. 96–99, 100–101)

Find the mean for each set of data.

1. 8, 21, 18, 17

2. 45, 31, 20, 27, 52

3. 15, 64, 33, 18, 22, 40

For 4–5, use the line plot.

4. What is the mean of the students' ages?

5. What is the range of the students' ages?

```
                    X    X
     X              X    X
     X    X    X    X         X
     +----+----+----+----+
     8    9    10   11   12
```
Ages of Students

Set C (pp. 102–103)

Find the median and the mode.

1.

SAVINGS									
Weeks	1	2	3	4	5	6	7	8	9
Amount	$10	$14	$8	$7	$10	$12	$10	$12	$12

2.

POINTS SCORED							
Game	1	2	3	4	5	6	7
Points	23	17	28	20	24	30	20

3. 16, 24, 11, 29, 20

4. 25, 50, 75, 25, 80

5. 26, 28, 28, 36, 40, 28

Set D (pp. 106–109)

For 1–3, use the bar graph.

1. How many students voted for cake? ice cream?

2. Which two foods got the same number of total votes?

3. How many more students voted for cake than for popcorn?

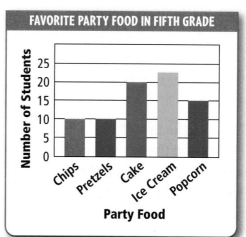

FAVORITE PARTY FOOD IN FIFTH GRADE

Review/Test

✔ CHECK VOCABULARY AND CONCEPTS

Choose the best term from the box.

1. When you add all of the data and divide by the number of addends, you find the __?__ of the data. (p. 100)

2. To find the __?__ for a data set, subtract the least value from the greatest value. (p. 97)

3. In a survey, the whole group is known as the __?__. (p. 96)

mean
mode
range
population
sample

✔ CHECK SKILLS

For 4–6, use the tally table. (pp. 96–99)

4. Make a cumulative frequency table for the data.

5. During which hour were the most salads sold? the fewest?

6. How many more salads were sold during the first two hours than in the last two hours?

SALADS SOLD	
Hour	**Salads**
1	卌 l
2	卌 卌 ll
3	卌 llll
4	卌

Find the range, mean, median, and mode for each. (pp. 96–103)

7. $8, $9, $11, $5, $8, $7

8. 15, 11, 20, 12, 12

9. 635, 499, 717, 601

For 10–12, use the circle graph. (pp. 106–109)

10. In which activity does Austin spend the most time?

11. Which two activities take up about the same part of Austin's day?

12. Does Austin spend more than or less than half the day sleeping?

HOW AUSTIN SPENDS A TYPICAL DAY

School / Sleep / Eat / TV / Football / Homework

✔ CHECK PROBLEM SOLVING

Solve. Use the test score data. (pp. 104–105)

13. Make a stem-and-leaf plot for the data.

14. What are the range, median, mean, and mode for the test scores?

15. Two more students score 79 and 97 on the test. How does this affect the range, median, mean, and mode of the scores? Explain.

5th Grade Test Scores			
76	92	82	88
89	68	72	
70	94	89	

Standardized Test Prep

DATA ANALYSIS AND PROBABILITY

1. Jan's table shows the high and low temperatures for the past five days. What was the median low temperature?

DAILY TEMPERATURES (in °F)

Day	High	Low
Monday	76°	60°
Tuesday	84°	64°
Wednesday	75°	57°
Thursday	77°	60°
Friday	83°	64°

A 60°F   **C** 62°F

B 61°F   **D** 64°F

2. Look at the table above. What was the mean high temperature?

F 77°F

G 78°F

H 79°F

J 84°F

3. **Explain It** Thomas is playing a game with these spinners. He spins both pointers.

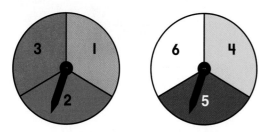

If his total is greater than 7, he wins a prize. List all the possible outcomes of the two spins. Explain the ways that Thomas can win.

MEASUREMENT

TIP   **Look for important words.** See item 4. *About* is an important word. You do not need to find the exact length in yards of the average blue whale. You can estimate the number of yards in 110 feet.

4. The table shows facts about blue whales. About how many yards long is the average blue whale?

BLUE WHALE	
Average length	110 feet
Average weight	209 tons

A 10   **C** 300

B 40   **D** 1,320

5. Look at the table above. How many pounds does an average blue whale weigh?

F 418,000 pounds

G 209,000 pounds

H 41,800 pounds

J 2,090 pounds

6. **Explain It** Heather went to the store to buy a gallon of milk.

$2.89

She gave the clerk $10 to pay for the milk and received $5.11 in change. ESTIMATE to explain how much change Heather should have received.

⭐ NUMBER SENSE, CONCEPTS, AND OPERATIONS

7. The table shows the prices of four electronic items. Which costs less than $18.90?

ELECTRONICS STORE PRICE LIST	
Item	**Price**
Headphones	$18.89
Portable radio	$18.99
Clock radio	$19.98
CD player	$19.95

A headphones

B portable radio

C clock radio

D CD player

8. Look at the table above. Jared bought a CD player and a set of headphones. He gave the clerk two $20 bills. How much change did he get?

F $0.16

G $1.06

H $1.16

J $2.16

9. What is the **greatest** 4-digit number that can be made from the digits 7, 0, 1, and 6?

A 6,017   **C** 7,061

B 6,701   **D** 7,610

10. Explain It Marilee went on a 5-hour beach walk to collect shells. Her goal was to collect 500 shells to make a wreath. She collected 108 shells the first hour, 83 the second hour, 78 the third hour, 84 the fourth hour, and 103 the fifth hour. ESTIMATE to decide whether she reached her goal. Explain your solution.

⭐ ALGEBRAIC THINKING

11. Cleo gained 3 pounds and then lost 7 pounds. If p represents Cleo's beginning weight, which expression represents Cleo's weight now?

F $(p + 3) + 7$

G $(p + 3) - 7$

H $(p - 3) + 7$

J $(p - 3) - 7$

12. Shania spent $45 for a pair of new shoes. She had $13 left. Let m represent the amount of money Shania started with. Which equation could be used to find the amount of money she started with?

A $45 - m = 13$

B $m + 13 = 45$

C $13 - m = 45$

D $m - 45 = 13$

13. Which is a rule for this pattern?

54, 62, 70, 78, 86

F Add 18.

G Add 16.

H Add 8.

J Subtract 8.

14. Explain It Look at the equations in the chart.

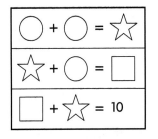

Find the number represented by each symbol. Explain your reasoning.

Make Graphs

Polar bear at the North Carolina Zoological Park in Asheboro, North Carolina

≡FAST FACT • SCIENCE The world population of polar bears is estimated to be between 22,000 and 27,000. Polar bears spend much of their lives on the arctic ice.

PROBLEM SOLVING The graph shows how the amount of arctic ice in the Nordic Sea area of the Arctic Ocean has changed. Approximately how many fewer square kilometers of ice were in the Nordic Sea area in 2000 than in 1900?

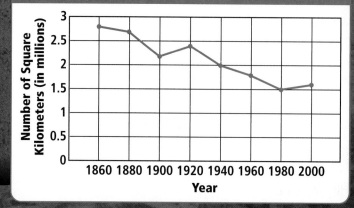

NORDIC SEA AREA ICE

Use this page to help you review and remember
important skills needed for Chapter 6.

✔ NUMBER PATTERNS

Write a rule for each pattern. Then find the missing numbers.

1. 0, 6, 12, 18, ■, ■, ■

2. 0, 10, 20, 30, ■, ■, ■

3. 0, 3, 6, 9, ■, ■, ■

4. 0, 4, 8, 12, ■, ■, ■

5. 0, 50, 100, 150, ■, ■, ■

6. 0, 25, 50, 75, ■, ■, ■

7. 0, 12, 24, 36, ■, ■, ■

8. 0, 100, 200, 300, ■, ■, ■

9. 0, 15, 30, 45, ■, ■, ■

10. 0, 500, 1,000, 1,500, ■, ■, ■

11. 0, 200, 400, 600, ■, ■, ■

12. 0, 150, 300, 450, ■, ■, ■

✔ IDENTIFY POINTS ON A GRID

For 13–22, use the ordered pair to name
the point on the grid.

13. (1,3)   **14.** (2,6)

15. (5,4)   **16.** (4,1)

17. (6,8)   **18.** (0,5)

19. (7,5)   **20.** (2,9)

21. (9,10)   **22.** (8,0)

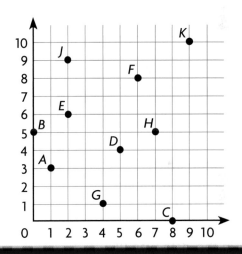

REVIEW

mean [mēn] *noun*
median [mē′•dē•ən] *noun*

In math, the mean is sometimes confused
with the median. This is not surprising
because both words come from the same
root word, *medhyo*, and both words
originally meant the same thing, "middle."
Explain the difference between the mean
and the median.

PREVIEW

scale
interval
ordered pair
histogram

www.harcourtschool.com/mathglossary

CHAPTER 7 Multiply Whole Numbers

The twin Keck Telescopes stand eight stories tall on the 13,800-foot Mauna Kea summit.

≡FAST FACT • SCIENCE The largest reflecting telescopes are the twin Keck Telescopes, weighing 300 tons each. Reflecting telescopes use mirrors to help us see distant objects in our solar system and beyond. Each telescope has an opening that allows light to be gathered by a mirror. The larger the opening, the more powerful the telescope and the farther you can see.

PROBLEM SOLVING The mirror diameter of the twin Keck telescopes is about two times the Hale Telescope's mirror diameter, which is shown in the graph. How big are the mirrors of the Keck I and Keck II?

FOUR OF THE WORLD'S LARGEST REFLECTING TELESCOPES

Telescopes:
- **Bol'shoi Teleskop Azimutal'ny** Nizhny Arkhyz, Russia
- **Hale** Palomar Mountain, California
- **4-Meter** Cerro Tololo, Chile
- **Canada-France-Hawaii** Mauna Kea, Hawaii

Mirror Diameter (in inches): 0 50 100 150 200

Use this page to help you review and remember
important skills needed for Chapter 7.

✔ MULTIPLY BY TENS AND HUNDREDS

Find the product.

1. 1×100	**2.** 2×10	**3.** 5×40	**4.** 7×60
5. 8×90	**6.** 9×600	**7.** 3×700	**8.** 6×300
9. 2×600	**10.** 5×300	**11.** 4×800	**12.** 7×900

✔ MULTIPLY 2-DIGIT NUMBERS

Find the product.

13. $\begin{array}{r} 12 \\ \times\ 6 \\ \hline \end{array}$	**14.** $\begin{array}{r} 19 \\ \times\ 9 \\ \hline \end{array}$	**15.** $\begin{array}{r} 14 \\ \times 12 \\ \hline \end{array}$	**16.** $\begin{array}{r} 17 \\ \times\ 4 \\ \hline \end{array}$
17. $\begin{array}{r} 50 \\ \times\ 9 \\ \hline \end{array}$	**18.** $\begin{array}{r} 24 \\ \times 15 \\ \hline \end{array}$	**19.** $\begin{array}{r} 28 \\ \times\ 3 \\ \hline \end{array}$	**20.** $\begin{array}{r} 20 \\ \times\ 6 \\ \hline \end{array}$
21. $\begin{array}{r} 32 \\ \times\ 7 \\ \hline \end{array}$	**22.** $\begin{array}{r} 64 \\ \times\ 2 \\ \hline \end{array}$	**23.** $\begin{array}{r} 54 \\ \times 23 \\ \hline \end{array}$	**24.** $\begin{array}{r} 94 \\ \times\ 7 \\ \hline \end{array}$
25. $\begin{array}{r} 29 \\ \times 24 \\ \hline \end{array}$	**26.** $\begin{array}{r} 34 \\ \times 27 \\ \hline \end{array}$	**27.** $\begin{array}{r} 72 \\ \times 31 \\ \hline \end{array}$	**28.** $\begin{array}{r} 93 \\ \times 45 \\ \hline \end{array}$

VOCABULARY POWER

REVIEW

factor [fak´•tər] *noun*

The Latin root of *factor* means "to do."
Factories are used to put goods together
to make something. How are factors used
in multiplication?

PREVIEW

multiples

GO ON-LINE www.harcourtschool.com/mathglossary

Estimation: Patterns in Multiples

Quick Review

Round to the nearest 10.

1. 93   2. 16

3. 139   4. 147

5. 998

VOCABULARY

multiples

▶ **Learn**

ORBITING NUMBERS The **multiples** of a whole number are all of the whole numbers that are products of the given number and another whole number. For example, multiples of 10 include 10, 20, 30, and 40 since $1 \times 10 = 10$, $2 \times 10 = 20$, $3 \times 10 = 30$, and $4 \times 10 = 40$.

Use multiples of 10 to help you estimate mentally.

Each hour, the Hubble Space Telescope transmits enough data to fill about 83 computer floppy disks. About how many computer floppy disks are filled with data in a day?

Estimate. 24×83
                 ↓   ↓
                 20×80 Round each factor.

$2 \times 8 = 16$ **Think:** Use the basic fact 2×8.
$2 \times 80 = 160$ Look for patterns in multiples of 10.
$20 \times 80 = 1,600$

So, about 1,600 computer floppy disks are filled.

▲ **Each day, the Hubble Space Telescope collects enough data to fill an encyclopedia. Since 1990, over 2.5 terabytes of data (1 terabyte = 1 million megabytes) have been collected.**

- Look for a pattern in the factors and products. What do you notice?

Examples

A Estimate. 8×522

8×500 Think: $8 \times 5 = 40$
$8 \times 500 = 4,000$
     ↑   ↑
2 zeros   2 zeros
So, 8×522 is about 4,000.

B Estimate. 73×862

70×900 Think: $7 \times 9 = 63$
$70 \times 900 = 63,000$
     ↑   ↑   ↑
1 zero + 2 zeros   3 zeros
So, 73×862 is about 63,000.

MATH IDEA You can use multiples of 10 to estimate products mentally. Count the number of zeros in the rounded factors. Place that number of zeros at the end of the product of the basic fact.

1. **Explain** why 400 × 5 has more zeros in the product than 300 × 5.

Estimate each product.

2. 4 × 1,453

3. 67 × 824

4. 32 × 1,839

5. 8 × 2,347

6. 6 × 3,609

7. 42 × 690

8. 99 × 2,092

9. 23 × 3,041

▶ **Practice and Problem Solving** (Extra Practice, page 158, Set A)

Estimate each product.

10. 34 × 123

11. 5 × 960

12. 82 × 53

13. 69 × 681

14. 58 × 2,234

15. 2 × 490

16. 7 × 2,589

17. 42 × 524

18. 301
   × 12

19. 291
   × 8

20. 341
   × 86

21. 915
   × 52

22. 5,451
   × 83

23. 290
   × 82

24. 723
   × 3

25. 963
   × 42

26. 389
   × 49

27. 6,715
   × 39

28. The product 20 × 600 has 3 zeros. How many zeros does the product 20 × 600,000 have?

29. How can you tell without multiplying that 3,000,000 × 6,000 = 30,000 × 600,000?

30. **? What's the Question?** Juan bought 52 bicycles for his store. Each bicycle cost $117. The estimate is $5,000.

31. The product of two 2-digit numbers is 2,000. Their sum is 90. What are the numbers?

32. Gail received $10 as a gift. She bought a magazine that cost $2 and a marker set. She has $3.45 left. How much did she spend on the marker set?

33. ✏ **Write About It** Explain how you can tell if the estimated products in the Examples on page 148 are greater than or less than the actual product.

Mixed Review and Test Prep

Find the value of each expression.

34. 18 + n if n = 3
   (p. 64)

35. (6 − 4) + n if n = 9
   (p. 64)

36. Identify the addition property you use to solve 20 + (3 + 2) = (20 + n) + 2. (p. 76)

37. Write four and six hundred fifty-nine ten-thousandths in standard form. (p. 22)

38. **TEST PREP** Which number is between 10 million and 100 million? (p. 4)
   A 999,999
   B 9,999,999
   C 99,999,999
   D 999,999,999

Multiply by 1-Digit Numbers

Quick Review
1. 29×3 2. 39×3
3. 41×5 4. 49×5
5. 92×6

▶ **Learn**

HEAVYWEIGHTS An African elephant, the heaviest land mammal, weighs 14,632 pounds. A humpback whale weighs as much as 4 African elephants. How much might a humpback whale weigh?

Example 1

Find $4 \times 14,632$.

$4 \times 15,000 = 60,000$ Estimate. Round 14,632 to the nearest thousand.

STEP 1

Multiply the ones and tens.
$4 \times 2 = 8$ ones
$4 \times 3 = 12$ tens
Regroup.

$$\begin{array}{r} 1 \\ 14{,}632 \\ \times \quad 4 \\ \hline 28 \end{array}$$

STEP 2

Multiply the hundreds.
$4 \times 6 = 24$ hundreds
Add the 1 regrouped hundred. Regroup.

$$\begin{array}{r} 2\ 1 \\ 14{,}632 \\ \times \quad 4 \\ \hline 528 \end{array}$$

STEP 3

Multiply the thousands.
$4 \times 4 = 16$ thousands
Add the 2 regrouped thousands. Regroup.

$$\begin{array}{r} 1\ 2\ 1 \\ 14{,}632 \\ \times \quad 4 \\ \hline 8{,}528 \end{array}$$

STEP 4

Multiply the ten thousands.
$4 \times 1 = 4$ ten thousands
Add the 1 regrouped ten thousand.

$$\begin{array}{r} 1\ 2\ 1 \\ 14{,}632 \\ \times \quad 4 \\ \hline 58{,}528 \end{array}$$

So, a humpback whale might weigh about 58,528 pounds. This is close to the estimate of 60,000, so the answer is reasonable.

MATH IDEA To multiply a greater number by a 1-digit number, use the same method you use for 2-digit numbers. Just repeat the same steps for all the digits.

▼ The heaviest known 90-foot female blue whale weighed 418,000 pounds. That's about the weight of 29 African elephants!

Example 2

Use place value and expanded form.

$5 \times 3,014 = n$ Think: $3,014 = 3,000 + 10 + 4$

$(5 \times 3,000) + (5 \times 10) + (5 \times 4) = n$

$15,000 \quad + \quad 50 \quad + \quad 20 \quad = n$

$15,070 = n$

So, $n = 15,070$.

1. Explain how you know that 115,275 is a reasonable product for 38,425 × 3.

Find the product. Estimate to check.

2. 2,231	**3.** 348	**4.** 52,113	**5.** 608,123	**6.** 391,224
× 3	× 5	× 2	× 7	× 4

7. 36,825 × 9   **8.** 5 × 309,224   **9.** 649,321 × 4

▶ **Practice and Problem Solving**   (Extra Practice, page 158, Set B)

Find the product. Estimate to check.

10. 4,567	**11.** 8,112	**12.** 24,531	**13.** 417,263	**14.** 882,917
× 8	× 7	× 9	× 4	× 6

15. 8 × 52,379   **16.** 826,243 × 3   **17.** 7,952,344 × 5

ALGEBRA   Solve for *n*.

18. 20,450 × 6 = *n*   **19.** 292,453 × 9 = *n*

USE DATA   For 20–21, use the table.

20. To ship animals to new locations, a zoo needs to estimate how much the animals weigh. About how much would 8 hippopotamuses weigh?

21. MENTAL MATH   Suppose the shipping weight limit is 50,000 pounds. Can a zoo ship 6 white rhinoceroses together? Explain.

22. ✎ **Write About It**   Explain the steps you follow to multiply by a 1-digit number.

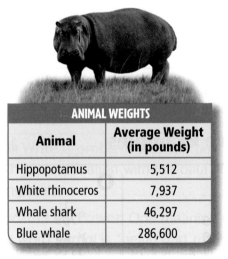

ANIMAL WEIGHTS	
Animal	**Average Weight (in pounds)**
Hippopotamus	5,512
White rhinoceros	7,937
Whale shark	46,297
Blue whale	286,600

Mixed Review and Test Prep

23. 52,954	**24.** 62,752
−48,393	+ 3,694
(p. 52)	(p. 52)

25. Write 2.057 in word form. (p. 22)

26. Order 9.004, 9.400, 9.040, and 9.404 from greatest to least. (p. 28)

27. TEST PREP   Rosa and Kate went to the mall. Kate bought a scarf for $9 and a blouse. Rosa paid $14 for a belt and $22 for a purse. They both spent the same amount. How much did Kate spend on the blouse? (p. 80)

A $20   **B** $27   **C** $36   **D** $37

Standardized Test Prep

⭐ NUMBER SENSE, CONCEPTS, AND OPERATIONS

1. The table shows the mean distance in miles of some planets from the sun.

MEAN DISTANCE FROM THE SUN	
Planet	**Mean Distance**
Mercury	36 million miles
Mars	141 million miles
Jupiter	480 million miles
Saturn	900 million miles

How many miles **farther** from the sun is Jupiter than Mercury?

A 454,000,000 miles

B 444,000,000 miles

C 344,000,000 miles

D 44,400,000 miles

2. Which of the following is **greater than** 948,026 and has a 5 in the ten thousands place?

F 965,160

G 958,347

H 947,051

J 943,529

3. Explain It There are 12 inches in 1 foot and 5,280 feet in 1 mile. Explain how you would ESTIMATE the number of inches in 1 mile. Then find the exact answer.

⭐ ALGEBRAIC THINKING

4. Jacob bought 12 doughnuts. He ate 1 and gave some to his brother. Let d represent the number of doughnuts Jacob gave to his brother. Which expression shows how many doughnuts Jacob has left?

A $(d - 12) - 1$ **C** $(12 - 1) + d$

B $(d - 12) + 1$ **D** $(12 - 1) - d$

5. The pictures on the wall of an art classroom are arranged in rows, with one picture in the first row, two in the second row, three in the third row, and so on. If there are 7 rows of pictures, how many pictures are on the wall?

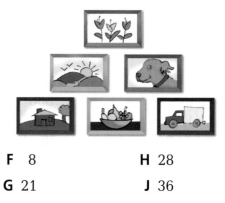

F 8   **H** 28

G 21   **J** 36

6. Explain It Carly is saving money to buy a new bike. In January she saved $3, in February she saved $9, in March she saved $27. This pattern continued for the next two months.

CARLY'S SAVINGS					
Month	**Jan**	**Feb**	**Mar**	**Apr**	**May**
Amount Saved	$3	$9	$27	■	■

How much money did Carly save in May? Explain how you solved the problem.

⭐ DATA ANALYSIS AND PROBABILITY

7. The graph shows the number of sneakers sold by Joe during 5 months. During which month were sales the **greatest**?

A January   **C** March

B February   **D** May

8. Mrs. Green bought sneakers for each of her children. The table shows the price she paid for each child's sneakers.

Child	Price Paid
Matthew	$45
Lisa	$56
Daniel	$38
Julie	$29

What was the average price Mrs. Green paid for a pair of sneakers?

F $27   **H** $42

G $41.50   **J** $56

9. Explain It Marliss is going on vacation. She can travel by bus, train, or car. She can leave on Monday, Tuesday, Wednesday, or Thursday. How many possible choices for type of transportation and day does she have? Explain your answer.

⭐ GEOMETRY AND SPATIAL SENSE

10. Which of the following describes how the figure was moved?

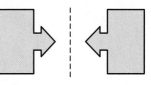

A translation   **C** rotation

B reflection   **D** tessellation

> **TIP** **Decide on a plan.** See item 11. Use the strategy *draw a diagram* to help you find the dimensions of the picture frame.

11. Kira's dad is making a picture frame. The length is 8 inches. The width is 2 inches greater than the length. Which of the following shows the perimeter of the picture frame?

F 80 inches   **H** 28 inches

G 36 inches   **J** 18 inches

12. Explain It Josh has plotted two of three points that form a right triangle when connected.

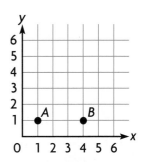

Name an ordered pair for a third point that can be used to form a right triangle. Then, name the ordered pairs for *A* and *B*. Explain what you notice about the *x*- and *y*-coordinates of the ordered pairs.

Multiply Decimals

≡FAST FACT • SCIENCE

There are about 10 million different kinds of animals in the world. Some are very light. A bee hummingbird and a golf ball are about the same size, but the weight of a golf ball is about 28 times as great as that of a bee hummingbird.

PROBLEM SOLVING
The table lists some of the lightest and heaviest animals. About how much does a golf ball weigh?

The bee hummingbird measures 60 millimeters long.

ANIMAL WEIGHTS		
Record	**Animal**	**Weight (kilograms)**
Lightest bird	Bee hummingbird	0.0016
Lightest land mammal	Bumblebee bat	0.002
Heaviest insect	Goliath beetle	0.099
Heaviest bird	Ostrich	148.5
Heaviest bony fish	Ocean sunfish	1,980
Heaviest land mammal	African elephant	7,000

Use this page to help you review and remember important skills needed for Chapter 8.

MULTIPLY 2-DIGIT NUMBERS

Find the product.

1.	13 × 8	2.	24 × 5	3.	52 × 7	4.	76 ×49
5.	39 × 3	6.	67 × 4	7.	53 ×83	8.	84 × 8
9.	48 ×27	10.	17 ×26	11.	92 ×56	12.	63 ×15

MULTIPLY MONEY

Multiply.

13. $0.10 × 2   **14.** $0.05 × 20   **15.** $0.25 × 4

16. $0.25 × 3   **17.** $0.10 × 10   **18.** $0.50 × 5

19.	$0.01 × 9	20.	$0.05 × 5	21.	$0.25 × 8
22.	$0.25 × 2	23.	$0.10 × 8	24.	$0.05 × 9
25.	$0.01 × 12	26.	$0.25 × 6	27.	$0.50 × 6

VOCABULARY POWER

REVIEW

decimal [de′sə•məl] *noun*

Decimal is derived from the Latin *decimus*, meaning "tenth." Explain why this meaning helps you understand decimals.

 www.harcourtschool.com/mathglossary

Multiply Decimals and Whole Numbers

HANDS ON

▶ **Explore**

The red kangaroo, the world's largest marsupial, uses its tail for balance when jumping. Its tail is about 0.53 times as long as its body. Its body is about 2 meters long. How long is its tail to the nearest meter?

Activity 1

Make a model to show how to multiply 2 by 0.53.

What is 2 × 0.53?

STEP 1

Use hundredths models. Shade 0.53, or 53 hundredths, two times. Use a different color each time.

STEP 2

Count the number of shaded hundredths. There are 106 shaded hundredths. This is 1 whole and 6 hundredths.

So, 2 × 0.53 = 1.06.

So, the red kangaroo's tail is about 1 meter long.

- How is multiplying 2 × 0.53 similar to multiplying 2 × 53?

- Is the product of 3 and 0.53 greater than or less than 3? Why?

Try It

Make a model to find the product.

a. 4 × 0.12
b. 3 × 0.03
c. 5 × 0.5
d. 3 × 0.3

The orange squares show 1 × 0.12. How do you show 4 × 0.12?

You can write a multiplication sentence for your model.

Activity 2
What is 3×0.6?

Model

Use tenths models. Shade 0.6, or 6 tenths, three times. Use a different color each time. Count the number of shaded tenths. There are 18 shaded tenths, or 1 whole and 8 tenths.

Record

Record.

$$\begin{array}{r} 0.6 \\ \times\ \ 3 \\ \hline 1.8 \end{array}$$

Use the model to place the decimal point. 3×0.6 is 3×6 tenths, or 18 tenths, which is 1.8. So, $3 \times 0.6 = 1.8$.

▶ Practice and Problem Solving

Make a model to find each product.

1. 3×0.8 **2.** 6×0.4 **3.** 5×0.6 **4.** 2×0.82

5. 7×0.03 **6.** 2×0.12 **7.** 4×0.19 **8.** 9×0.18

Joy is shopping at the pet store. For 9–12, use the table to find the total cost.

9. 3 neon tetras, 2 zebra danios

10. 2 albino danios, 3 leopard danios

11. 4 neon tetras, 2 zebra danios, 1 leopard danio

12. 5 albino danios, 3 zebra danios

13. ✎ **Write about it** Explain how to draw a picture to find 3×0.9.

TROPICAL FISH	
Item	**Price**
Neon tetra	$0.74
Zebra danio	$0.89
Albino danio	$0.99
Leopard danio	$0.95

Mixed Review and Test Prep

14. Aponi recorded temperatures of 78°, 82°, 65°, 66°, and 83°. What is the range of the data? (p. 96)

15. What is the value of the expression $\$10 + (\$4 - n)$ if n is $2? (p. 64)

16. Round 82,394,021 to the nearest million. (p. 38)

17. Write an equivalent decimal for 8.02. (p. 26)

18. **TEST PREP** Which number is 900 less than the product of 217 and 508? (p. 154)

A 101,236   **C** 110,146

B 109,336   **D** 111,136

Algebra: Patterns in Decimal Factors and Products

Quick Review

1. 10×12
2. 100×12
3. $1,000 \times 12$
4. $10,000 \times 12$
5. $100,000 \times 12$

▶ **Learn**

MEASURE UP The smallest frog in the Northern Hemisphere is found in Cuba and grows to about 0.98 centimeters in body length. The photos show the frog at its actual size and enlarged 5 times. What would be the length of the frog in a photo enlarged 1,000 times?

▲ Frog enlarged 5 times

Example

What is $0.98 \times 1,000$?

Look for a pattern.

$0.98 \times 1 = 0.98$

$0.98 \times 10 = 9.8$ ← The decimal point moves 1 place to the right.

$0.98 \times 100 = 98.$ ← The decimal point moves 2 places to the right.

$0.98 \times 1,000 = 980.$ ← The decimal point moves 3 places to the right.

▲ Actual size of frog

So, in the photo enlarged 1,000 times, the frog would be 980 centimeters long.

- **What if** you enlarge the frog photo 100 times? What will be the length of the frog in the photo?

⚠ **MATH IDEA** The decimal point moves one place to the right when you multiply by 10, two places to the right when you multiply by 100, and three places to the right when you multiply by 1,000.

More Examples

Ⓐ	Ⓑ	Ⓒ
$\$3.25 \times 1 = \$3.25$	$0.478 \times 1 = 0.478$	$0.0009 \times 1 = 0.0009$
$\$3.25 \times 10 = \$32.50$	$0.478 \times 10 = 4.78$	$0.0009 \times 10 = 0.009$
$\$3.25 \times 100 = \$325.00$	$0.478 \times 100 = 47.8$	$0.0009 \times 100 = 0.09$
$\$3.25 \times 1,000 = \$3,250.00$	$0.478 \times 1,000 = 478$	$0.0009 \times 1,000 = 0.9$

- **REASONING** How can you use the pattern to place the decimal point in $\$32.50 \times 100$?

1. **Explain** why the product 4.56×100 is the same as the product $4.56 \times 10 \times 10$? What is 4.56×100?

Use mental math to complete.

2. $1 \times 0.3 = 0.3$
   $10 \times 0.3 = 3$
   $100 \times 0.3 = \blacksquare$
   $1,000 \times 0.3 = \blacksquare$

3. $1 \times 2.845 = 2.845$
   $10 \times 2.845 = 28.45$
   $100 \times 2.845 = \blacksquare$
   $1,000 \times 2.845 = 2,845$

4. $1 \times 0.3459 = 0.3459$
   $10 \times 0.3459 = \blacksquare$
   $100 \times 0.3459 = 34.59$
   $1,000 \times 0.3459 = 345.9$

Practice and Problem Solving   Extra Practice, page 178, Set A

Use mental math to complete.

5. $1 \times 0.005 = 0.005$
   $10 \times 0.005 = \blacksquare$
   $100 \times 0.005 = 0.5$
   $1,000 \times 0.005 = 5$

6. $1 \times 4.761 = 4.761$
   $10 \times 4.761 = 47.61$
   $100 \times 4.761 = \blacksquare$
   $1,000 \times 4.761 = \blacksquare$

7. $1 \times 0.45 = 0.45$
   $10 \times 0.45 = \blacksquare$
   $100 \times 0.45 = \blacksquare$
   $1,000 \times 0.45 = \blacksquare$

Multiply each number by 10, by 100, and by 1,000.

8. 0.9

9. 0.51

10. 0.007

11. 0.015

12. 0.2178

13. $0.25

14. 45.69

15. 1.0608

ALGEBRA   Find the value of n.

16. $10 \times 0.009 = n$

17. $n \times 0.08 = 0.8$

18. $100 \times n = 4.5$

19. $1.5 \times n = 15$

20. $n \times 100 = 1.9$

21. $n \times 1,000 = 3.1$

22. A half dollar is 0.50 of a dollar. What is the value of 100 half dollars? of 1,000 half dollars?

23. If a snail moves 8 inches a minute, how many minutes would it take it to move 12 feet?

24. **Write About It** Explain why multiplying a decimal by 10, by 100, and by 1,000 is easy to compute mentally.

25. **REASONING**   How does the position of the decimal point change when you multiply 6.7 by 10,000?

Mixed Review and Test Prep

26. $1,456 \times 8$ (p. 150)

27. 345×23 (p. 152)

Write <, >, or = for each ●. (p. 28)

28. 0.89 ● 0.98

29. 3.9 ● 3.09

30. **TEST PREP**   Find the value of n.
   $90 = n + 32 + 28$ (p. 70)

   A $n = 20$ **C** $n = 30$

   B $n = 28$ **D** $n = 32$

Model Decimal Multiplication

▷ Learn

FAST FOOD The bee hummingbird weighs about 0.2 dekagram. It needs to eat half its body weight in food every day to stay alive. About how much food does a bee hummingbird need to eat every day?

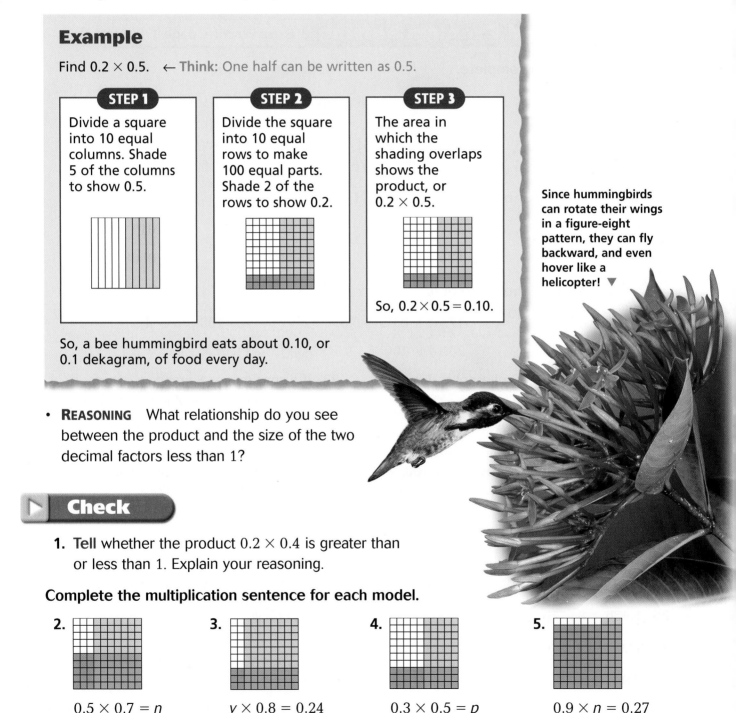

Example

Find 0.2 × 0.5. ← **Think:** One half can be written as 0.5.

STEP 1

Divide a square into 10 equal columns. Shade 5 of the columns to show 0.5.

STEP 2

Divide the square into 10 equal rows to make 100 equal parts. Shade 2 of the rows to show 0.2.

STEP 3

The area in which the shading overlaps shows the product, or 0.2 × 0.5.

So, 0.2 × 0.5 = 0.10.

Since hummingbirds can rotate their wings in a figure-eight pattern, they can fly backward, and even hover like a helicopter! ▼

So, a bee hummingbird eats about 0.10, or 0.1 dekagram, of food every day.

- **REASONING** What relationship do you see between the product and the size of the two decimal factors less than 1?

▷ Check

1. **Tell** whether the product 0.2 × 0.4 is greater than or less than 1. Explain your reasoning.

Complete the multiplication sentence for each model.

2.
0.5 × 0.7 = n

3.
y × 0.8 = 0.24

4.
0.3 × 0.5 = p

5.
0.9 × n = 0.27

Make a model to find the product.

6. 0.1×0.5 **7.** 0.4×0.7 **8.** 0.3×0.3 **9.** 0.8×0.4

Practice and Problem Solving   Extra Practice, page 178, Set B

Complete the multiplication sentence for each model.

10.

11.

12.

13.

$0.4 \times 0.6 = n$ $0.5 \times y = 0.25$ $p \times 0.9 = 0.18$ $0.1 \times 0.4 = n$

Make a model to find the product.

14. 0.8×0.8 **15.** 0.1×0.9 **16.** 0.6×0.2 **17.** 0.8×0.3

Find the product.

18. 0.7×0.8 **19.** 0.2×0.8 **20.** 0.9×0.6 **21.** 0.6×0.7

22. 0.5×0.6 **23.** 0.8×0.9 **24.** 0.5×0.4 **25.** 0.3×0.6

ALGEBRA   **For 26–29, find the value of n.**

26. $n \times 0.2 = 0.14$ **27.** $0.6 \times n = 0.48$ **28.** $0.9 \times n = 0.63$ **29.** $n \times 0.7 = 0.35$

30. Vocabulary Power *Deca-* and *deka-* are variations of the same prefix. A *decagon* is a polygon with 10 sides. Use the meaning of *decagon* to explain the meaning of *dekagram*.

31. At the pet store, Jason bought 2 birdcages at $12.98 each and 5 boxes of birdseed at $3.49 each. If he gave the clerk five $10-bills, what would be his change?

32. **? What's the Error?** Marco said $0.1 \times 0.6 = 0.6$. Describe his error. Draw a model.

33. **FAST FACT • SCIENCE** A grasshopper can leap about 0.7 meter. A flea can jump 0.5 times as far. About how far can a flea jump?

Mixed Review and Test Prep

Round to the nearest million. (p. 38)

34. 4,099,999   **35.** 16,399,999

Order from least to greatest. (p. 10)

36. 87,314; 87,413; 81,341

37. 109,721; 190,271; 109,271

38. TEST PREP Which shows three and two tenths written as a decimal and a fraction? (p. 22)

A $3.2; 3\frac{2}{10}$ **C** $3.12; 3\frac{12}{100}$

B $2.3; 2\frac{3}{10}$ **D** $3.02; 3\frac{2}{100}$

4 Place the Decimal Point

Quick Review

Round to the nearest whole number.

1. 3.4   **2.** 99.2   **3.** 0.38
4. 0.68   **5.** 5.3

▶ **Learn**

TIP TO TIP   From the tip of its nose to the end of its tail, a pygmy shrew measures 6.1 centimeters long. A house mouse is 2.7 times as long. How long is the house mouse?

You can use estimation to help you place the decimal point in a decimal product and to determine if your answer is reasonable.

Example 1   Find 2.7 × 6.1.

STEP 1
Estimate the product. Round each factor.

2.7 × 6.1
↓   ↓
3 × 6 = 18

STEP 2
Multiply as with whole numbers.

$$\begin{array}{r} 6.1 \\ \times 2.7 \\ \hline 427 \\ +1220 \\ \hline 1647 \end{array}$$

STEP 3
Use the estimate to place the decimal point in the product.

$$\begin{array}{r} 6.1 \\ \times 2.7 \\ \hline 427 \\ +1220 \\ \hline 16.47 \end{array}$$

Since the estimate is 18, place the decimal point so there is a two-digit whole number in the product.

So, the house mouse is 16.47 centimeters long.

The pygmy shrew, one of the world's smallest mammals, could sleep in a spoon! And it weighs about as much as a table-tennis ball! ▼

More Examples

Ⓐ Find 12 × 0.48.

10 × 0.5 = 5 ← Estimate.

$$\begin{array}{r} 0.48 \\ \times \quad 12 \\ \hline 96 \\ +480 \\ \hline 5.76 \end{array}$$

Since the estimate is 5, place the decimal point so there is a one-digit whole number in the product.

Ⓑ Find 0.75 × $1.25.

0.8 × $1 = $0.8, or $0.80 ← Estimate.

$$\begin{array}{r} \$1.25 \\ \times \ 0.75 \\ \hline 625 \\ +8750 \\ \hline \$0.9375 \end{array}$$

Since the estimate is $0.80, place the decimal point so there is less than 1 dollar in the product.

Count Decimal Places

You can also place the decimal point by finding the total number of decimal places in the factors. Then count that many places from the right in the product.

Technology Link

More Practice: Harcourt Mega Math The Number Games, *Buggy Bargains*, Levels K, L

Example 2 Find 0.7 × 0.2.

STEP 1

Multiply as with whole numbers.

```
   0.7
 ×0.2
   14
```

STEP 2

Find the total number of decimal places in the factors. Place the decimal point that number of places from the right in the product.

```
   0.7  ← 1 decimal place in the factor
 ×0.2  ← 1 decimal place in the factor
 0.14  ← 1 + 1, or 2 decimal places in the product
```

So, 0.7 × 0.2 is 0.14.

More Examples

C
```
     23  ← 0 decimal places in the factor
 ×0.04  ← 2 decimal places in the factor
   0.92  ← 0 + 2, or 2 decimal places in
            the product
```

D
```
     7.52  ← 2 decimal places in the factor
   ×0.23  ← 2 decimal places in the factor
     2256
  +15040
   1.7296  ← 2 + 2, or 4 decimal places in
              the product
```

MATH IDEA You can use estimation or the total number of decimal places in the factors to determine where to place the decimal point in the product.

▼ House mouse

▶ Check

1. **Explain** how you can check that the answer to Example D is reasonable.

Choose the better estimate. Write *a* or *b*.

2. 34 × 0.8   **a.** 24   **b.** 2.4   **3.** 4.2 × 3.9   **a.** 16   **b.** 1.6

Copy each exercise. Place the decimal point in the product.

4.
```
    29
 ×0.7
   203
```

5.
```
   2.98
 ×  0.7
   2086
```

6.
```
    1.8
 ×0.2
    36
```

7.
```
   0.37
 ×0.64
   2368
```

Find the product. Estimate to check.

8. 9 × 1.7   **9.** 0.2 × 12   **10.** 95 × 0.64   **11.** 1.25 × 0.5

12. 0.9 × 0.4   **13.** 0.37 × 0.6   **14.** 0.211 × 18

LESSON CONTINUES ▶

Choose the better estimate. Write *a* or *b*.

15. 22 × 0.6   **a.** 12   **b.** 1.2   **16.** 2.3 × 4.8   **a.** 10 **b.** 1.0

17. 0.82 × 6   **a.** 0.48 **b.** 4.8   **18.** 42 × 0.5   **a.** 20 **b.** 2.0

Copy each exercise. Place the decimal point in the product.

19.	**20.**	**21.**	**22.**
3.4	0.58	5.48	2.32
× 5	× 2	×0.726	×4.68
170	116	397848	108576

Find the product. Estimate to check.

23. 0.3 × 14   **24.** 0.5 × 1,206   **25.** 6.8 × 4.5   **26.** 7.25 × 3.8

27. 5.1 × 2.7   **28.** 12.92 × 7.2   **29.** 19 × 0.21   **30.** 38.8 × 4.62

31. 0.7 × 0.8   **32.** 6.9 × 3.1   **33.** 0.12 × 0.9   **34.** 0.325 × 82

35. 0.68 × 0.4   **36.** 2.36 × 0.9   **37.** 0.3 × 0.918   **38.** 9.2 × 0.07

39. 0.25 × 0.75   **40.** 0.8 × 0.201   **41.** 2.7 × 5.6   **42.** 43.3 × 6.2

43. 24.37 × 0.8   **44.** 0.848 × 3.2   **45.** 9.748 × 0.42   **46.** 436.3 × 0.181

47. Which product will have 6 decimal places?

  a. 0.12 × 0.0456   **b.** 1.2 × 0.0456   **c.** 12 × 0.0456

48. Which product will have 5 decimal places?

  a. 0.283 × 1.078   **b.** 2.83 × 1.078   **c.** 28.3 × 1.078

49. ✎ **Write About It** How can you use an estimate to help you place the decimal point? Give an example.

USE DATA For 50–52, use the graph.

50. Which aquarium has a capacity that is 0.20 times as great as that of the shark aquarium?

51. Is the total capacity of the five aquariums greater than or less than 500,000 gallons? Explain.

52. Which aquariums have capacities that are greater than twice that of the river otter aquarium?

53. The largest male killer whale weighed 55 times the weight of a dolphin. If an average dolphin weighs 400 lb, how much did the largest killer whale weigh?

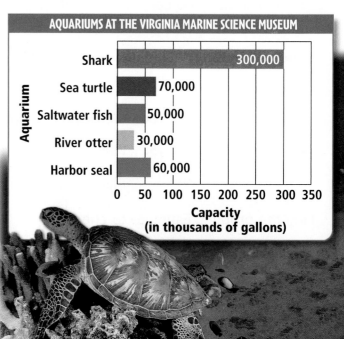

AQUARIUMS AT THE VIRGINIA MARINE SCIENCE MUSEUM

Aquarium

Shark — 300,000
Sea turtle — 70,000
Saltwater fish — 50,000
River otter — 30,000
Harbor seal — 60,000

0 50 100 150 200 250 300 350
Capacity
(in thousands of gallons)

54. Four students shared 6 boxes of markers equally. Each of the boxes had the same number of markers. Each student received 6 markers. How many markers were in each box?

55. The largest frog is the Goliath frog. With its legs stretched out, it is about 0.8 meter long. When its legs are not stretched out, its body is about 0.5 times that length. How long is its body?

Mixed Review and Test Prep

56. $7{,}981 + 6{,}909 + 2{,}574$ (p. 46)

57. Solve $87 + n = 147$. (p. 70)

58. ⭐ **TEST PREP** In which is eight thousandths written as a decimal? (p. 22)

 A 0.80   C 0.008
 B 0.08   D 0.0008

59. Solve $5 + (9 + 3) = (5 + n) + 3$. Name the addition property used. (p. 76)

60. ⭐ **TEST PREP** In which number does the digit 4 have the least value? (p. 22)

 F 7.0492   H 7.4902
 G 7.2049   J 7.9204

Problem Solving LINKUP... to Reading

STRATEGY • SUMMARIZE To *summarize,* you restate information in a shortened form. You include only the most important information.

Gwen runs her computer 8 hours each day, 5 days each week. How much does the electricity cost for 4 weeks?

ELECTRICITY COST (based on a 2001 average electric rate)	
Appliances	**Cost per hour**
Computer	$0.01
Lamp, 100 watt	$0.01
Refrigerator/freezer	$0.02
Hair dryer	$0.12
Television	$0.02
Water heater	$0.40

Summary	Solve
A. Electricity costs $0.01 per hour.	
B. The computer runs 8 hours a day.	$8 \times \$0.01 = \$0.08$
C. The computer runs 5 days a week.	$5 \times \$0.08 = \$0.40$
D. How much does it cost for 4 weeks?	$4 \times \$0.40 = \$1.60$

So, it costs Gwen $1.60.

USE DATA For 1–2, use the table.

1. Mr. Ramos' water heater is on a timer. It runs a total of 3 hours each day. How much does it cost to run his water heater each week?

2. A fluorescent lamp costs $0.003 per hour to run. How much more does it cost to run the 100-watt lamp for 10 hours than the fluorescent lamp for 10 hours?

5 Zeros in the Product

Quick Review

1. 1×0.4
2. 2×0.4
3. 10×0.4
4. 20×0.4
5. 125×0.5

 Learn

Sometimes when you multiply with decimals, there are zeros in the product.

SUPER ANT A *Formica japonica* worker ant weighs 0.004 gram. It can walk while holding in its mouth an object weighing 5 times as much as its own body. How many grams can a worker ant carry?

Find 5×0.004.

$$
\begin{array}{r}
0.004 \\
\times \quad 5 \\
\hline
0.020
\end{array}
$$
← Since there are 3 decimal places in the factors, you will need 3 decimal places in the product.
↑ Write a zero at the left in the product to place the decimal point.

So, a worker ant can carry 0.020, or 0.02, gram.

Examples

A Find $0.003 \times \$18$.

$$
\begin{array}{r}
\$18 \\
\times 0.003 \\
\hline
\$0.054
\end{array}
$$
↑

Since 3 decimal places are needed in the product, write a zero in this place.

B Find 0.09×0.07.

$$
\begin{array}{r}
0.07 \\
\times 0.09 \\
\hline
0.0063
\end{array}
$$
↑↑

Since 4 decimal places are needed in the product, write zeros in these places.

C Find 0.002×9.27.

$$
\begin{array}{r}
9.27 \\
\times 0.002 \\
\hline
0.01854
\end{array}
$$
↑

Since 5 decimal places are needed in the product, write a zero in this place.

D You can use a calculator to multiply decimals.

Find 0.06×0.34.

[.] [0] [6] [×] [.] [3] [4] [Enter =]

.06 × .34 =
0.0204

• In Example A, what is the product to the nearest cent?

MATH IDEA You may need to insert zeros at the left in the product to keep the same number of decimal places in the product as in the factors.

174

1. **Explain** how you know when to insert a zero in a product to place a decimal point.

Find the product.

2. 8×0.003
3. 0.04×0.4
4. 0.018×9
5. 6×0.0006

▶ **Practice and Problem Solving**   Extra Practice, page 178, Set D

Find the product.

6. 9×0.007
7. 0.02×2
8. 0.016×0.5
9. 0.8×0.03

10. $\begin{array}{r} 0.006 \\ \times\quad 9 \\ \hline \end{array}$

11. $\begin{array}{r} 0.08 \\ \times 0.02 \\ \hline \end{array}$

12. $\begin{array}{r} 0.004 \\ \times\quad 24 \\ \hline \end{array}$

13. $\begin{array}{r} 0.12 \\ \times 0.09 \\ \hline \end{array}$

14. $\begin{array}{r} 54.07 \\ \times\ 0.04 \\ \hline \end{array}$

15. $\begin{array}{r} 0.007 \\ \times\quad 8 \\ \hline \end{array}$

16. $\begin{array}{r} 0.032 \\ \times\quad 17 \\ \hline \end{array}$

17. $\begin{array}{r} 0.014 \\ \times\ 0.06 \\ \hline \end{array}$

Find the product. Round to the nearest cent.

18. $\$0.89 \times 0.08$
19. $\$0.95 \times 0.05$
20. $\$3.09 \times 0.05$
21. $\$5.05 \times 0.06$

Write <, >, or = for each ●.

22. 0.008×9 ● 0.009×8
23. 3×0.025 ● 3.01×0.02

24. **? What's the Question?** Eileen bought 2 gallons of milk at $3.02 per gallon and one loaf of bread at $0.99. The answer is $7.03.

25. ✎ **Write a problem** including this information: a dozen eggs costs $0.78, a loaf of bread costs $1.03, a pound of bananas costs $0.63.

26. You can draw a line 35 miles long with a standard pencil. That's 0.9 of the distance from Baltimore to Washington, D.C. How long a line can you draw with 3 pencils?

27. The price of an ant farm is $28.00. The computer multiplies the price by 1.07 to find your total cost including tax. What change would you get from two $20-bills?

28. ✎ **Write About It** To find 0.05×0.06, would you use a calculator, paper and pencil, or mental math? Explain.

Mixed Review and Test Prep

29. $9,126,543 - 3,972,645$ (p. 52)

30. $19,282,443 + 723,451$ (p. 52)

31. $456 - 309$ (p. 46)

32. $13 \times \$1.25$ (p. 170)

33. **TEST PREP** Round 2.2178 to the place of the blue digit. (p. 40)

   A 2 **B** 2.2 **C** 2.22 **D** 2.218

Problem Solving Skill
Make Decisions

UNDERSTAND ▶ PLAN ▶ SOLVE ▶ CHECK

Quick Review

Write <, >, or = for each ●.

1. $36.52 ● $36.25
2. 49¢ ● 51¢
3. $7.81 ● $7.84
4. $0.98 ● $0.89
5. 4 × $1.50 ● 6 × $1.25

ARTIST'S CHOICE   Suppose you are planning to take art lessons. You can sign up for either painting or sculpture. To help you make a decision on which to take, there are several things that you need to think about before you decide.

THINGS TO CONSIDER	PAINTING	SCULPTURE
Time	Wednesday, 4:00 P.M. to 6:00 P.M.	Saturday, 10 A.M. to 11:30 A.M.
Number of lessons	6	9
Cost per lesson	$12.75	$9.50
Cost of general supplies	$10	$25
Cost per project	$2.35 per canvas panel	$1.45 per 5-lb bag of clay

Use the information in the table to help you answer the following questions.

A. For each choice, how much will it cost for lessons and general supplies? Which costs less?

B. What is the difference in cost for general supplies for each choice?

C. How many total hours will each choice last? What is the difference in the amount of time?

D. You will complete a total of 4 painting projects or 6 sculpture projects. How much will you spend on project supplies for painting? for sculpture? In which project would supplies cost less?

Talk About It

• If you had to take the one that costs less, would you take painting or sculpture? Explain the reasons for your decision.

• Make a list of other things you may consider before deciding which to take.

⚡ **MATH IDEA**   To help you make a decision, compare facts and data.

Problem Solving Practice

USE DATA For 1–3, use the information in the table.

1. You have a coupon from Store A for $2.00 off if you purchase $10.00 worth of art supplies. You plan to buy 12 sheets of charcoal paper and 10 pastels. Would you spend more at Store A or Store B? How much more?

You are buying art supplies for a drawing class. You need 4 sticks of charcoal, 3 kneaded erasers, and 2 pastels. You do not have any store coupons.

WHICH STORE HAS THE BEST BUY?			
Items	Store A	Store B	Store C
Charcoal	2 for $0.75	$0.33 each	4 for $1.40
Kneaded eraser	$0.47 each	3 for $1.50	$0.51 each
Charcoal paper	3 for $1.89	$0.57 each	2 for $1.36
Pastels	$0.98 each	2 for $1.80	$0.92 each

2. You need to buy all the supplies from the same store. At which store would you spend the least?

A Store A

B Store B

C Store C

D The cost is the same at each store.

3. What if you could go to more than one store? What is the least amount you could spend?

F $4.53   H $4.77

G $4.62   J $4.87

Mixed Applications

4. On an average day, 450 cars pass through the toll plaza. Val says about 164,250 cars pass through the toll plaza in a year. Chuck says about 42,750 pass through the toll plaza in a year. Whose answer is reasonable? Explain.

5. ✏ Write a problem in which you need to make a decision that can be answered with information in the table above.

6. Use the diagram above. Al's balloon is not next to Maggie's. Clem's balloon is larger than Maggie's. Who has the striped balloon?

Extra Practice

Set A (pp. 166–167)

Multiply each number by 10, by 100, and by 1,000.

1. 0.7   **2.** 0.32   **3.** 0.003   **4.** 0.152

ALGEBRA Find the value of *n*.

5. $100 \times 0.1 = n$ **6.** $10 \times 5.643 = n$ **7.** $1{,}000 \times 0.9023 = n$

8. $10 \times n = 0.06$ **9.** $n \times 10 = 0.27$ **10.** $100 \times n = 0.45$

11. In 1910, it cost about $0.80 per week to educate a public school student in the United States. By 1920, the weekly cost had doubled. How much did it cost to educate a student for 1 week in 1920?

Set B (pp. 168–169)

Make a model to find the product.

1. 0.6×0.6 **2.** 0.1×0.8 **3.** 0.5×0.3 **4.** 0.7×0.3

Find the product.

5. 0.6×0.8 **6.** 0.3×0.8 **7.** 0.9×0.5 **8.** 0.4×0.9

9. 0.2×0.9 **10.** 0.5×0.4 **11.** 0.2×0.3 **12.** 0.2×0.2

Set C (pp. 170–173)

Find the product. Estimate to check.

1. 0.3×14 **2.** $0.5 \times 1{,}206$ **3.** 6.8×4.5 **4.** 7.25×3.8

5. 0.67×8 **6.** 3.94×0.04 **7.** 0.53×58 **8.** 5.06×28

9. Gustavo has a pumpkin with a mass of 4.8 kilograms. If 0.9 of its mass is water, how much of its mass is water? How much is not water?

10. Bernadette bought 2 loaves of bread at $0.97 each and a carton of milk for $1.18. How much did she spend?

Set D (pp. 174–175)

Find the product.

1. 8×0.006 **2.** 0.03×2 **3.** 0.02×4 **4.** 7×0.004

5. 0.7×0.07 **6.** 0.025×0.6 **7.** 0.075×0.9 **8.** 0.5×0.024

Review/Test

✓ CHECK VOCABULARY AND CONCEPTS

Choose the best term from the box.

greater than
less than
one tenth
one hundredth
one thousandth

1. 0.1 represents __?__. (p. 22)

2. The product of 9 and 0.65 is __?__ 9. (p. 164)

3. 0.01 represents __?__. (p. 22)

Make a model to find the product. (pp. 168–169)

4. 0.6×5 **5.** 0.51×3 **6.** 2×0.25 **7.** 0.82×4

✓ CHECK SKILLS

Multiply each number by 10, by 100, and by 1,000. (pp. 166–167)

8. 0.3   **9.** 0.64   **10.** 0.002   **11.** 0.0225

Copy each exercise. Place the decimal point in each product. (pp. 170–173)

12. $0.5 \times 0.5 = 25$ **13.** $1.6 \times 3.34 = 5344$ **14.** $0.152 \times 0.78 = 11856$

15. $0.28 \times 0.7 = 196$ **16.** $0.9 \times 2.186 = 19674$ **17.** $25.4 \times 0.92 = 23368$

Find the product. (pp. 174–175)

18. 6.50×0.8 **19.** 2.85×22 **20.** 4.15×0.6 **21.** 4.34×0.3

22. 0.62×0.07 **23.** 0.7×0.1 **24.** 0.4×0.5 **25.** 0.76×65

26. $\begin{array}{r} 0.96 \\ \times\ \ \ 5 \\ \hline \end{array}$ **27.** $\begin{array}{r} 7.62 \\ \times 0.08 \\ \hline \end{array}$ **28.** $\begin{array}{r} 0.9 \\ \times 0.09 \\ \hline \end{array}$ **29.** $\begin{array}{r} 3.96 \\ \times\ \ 28 \\ \hline \end{array}$

✓ CHECK PROBLEM SOLVING

For 30–31, use the table. (pp. 176–177)

30. Janet needs to mail a 1-oz letter. Today is Monday. What is the least amount she could spend and guarantee it will arrive by Wednesday?

31. Which service is the fastest? How much does it cost?

32. Jorge earns $24.65 a week. How much does he earn in 12 weeks? (pp. 170–173)

SERVICE	DELIVERY SCHEDULE	RATE (in 2002)
First-Class Mail	varies	$0.37 for the first ounce, $0.23 for each additional ounce
Priority Mail	2 days	$3.85
Express Mail	next day	$13.65

33. What is the value of 100 quarters? of 1,000 quarters? (pp. 166–167)

⭐Standardized Test Prep

⭐ NUMBER SENSE, CONCEPTS, AND OPERATIONS

1. Becky buys 10 one-way bus tickets each week to get to work and back home. How much does she spend each week on bus fare?

BUS TICKETS	
One-Way Ticket	$ 0.95
20-Trip Commuter Booklet	$16.00

A $95.00   **C** $9.50

B $10.95   **D** $0.95

> **TIP** **Decide on a plan.** See item 2. This problem involves more than one step, since you need to find the cost of 40 one-way tickets and the cost of two 20-trip commuter booklets.

2. Look at the sign in Problem 1. In one month Becky buys 40 one-way tickets. How much will Becky save each month by buying two 20-trip commuter booklets?

  F $3

  G $6

  H $32

  J $38

3. Explain It Marisa read that a blue whale weighs 4.9 times as much as a humpback whale. A humpback whale weighs 26.5 tons. About how much does a blue whale weigh? Explain how you would use estimation to solve the problem.

⭐ MEASUREMENT

4. A dipstick is used to check the oil level in a car. The distance between the two marks shown on the dipstick at the right represents 1 quart. How many cups of oil would be needed to increase the oil level from the ADD mark to the FULL mark?

  A 2 cups   **C** 6 cups

  B 4 cups   **D** 8 cups

5. Peter wants to frame the painting he just finished. What length of wood will he need for the frame?

12 inches

11 inches

  F 23 inches   **H** 46 inches

  G 36 inches   **J** 132 inches

6. Explain It Shane's goal was to pick 25 pounds of tomatoes from his garden last week. The table shows the number of pounds of tomatoes he picked.

TOMATOES PICKED					
Day	Mon	Tue	Wed	Thu	Fri
Weight (pounds)	5.2	2.5	3.1	3.8	5.3

Explain how to use estimation strategies to decide whether Shane reached his goal.

⭐ ALGEBRAIC THINKING

7. After writing this check, Mark had a balance of $85 in his account.

```
Mark Doe                          Check No. 171
123 Main St.
Anywhere, USA        Date  January 3, 2004

Pay to the Order of  U.S. Power        $15.00
Fifteen dollars and no/100---------

For  Electric bill        Mark Doe
```

If *b* equals Mark's balance before he wrote the check, which equation could be used to find Mark's balance before he wrote the check?

A $15b = 85$

B $b - 15 = 85$

C $15 - b = 85$

D $85 - b = 15$

8. Leigh put weights on the balance to solve the inequality $x + 5 > 9$.

Which weights could she have used for *x*?

F 1, 2, 3

G 1, 2, 3, 4

H 1, 2, 3, 4, 5, 6, 7, 8

J 5, 6, 7, 8

9. Explain It Cara baked some brownies. She gave away 10 brownies, and then ate 3 of the remaining brownies. Let *n* represent the number of brownies Cara baked. Write an expression using *n* to show this. Explain your answer.

⭐ GEOMETRY AND SPATIAL SENSE

10. Alana is making a symmetrical design on a grid. Which ordered pair names the point she should plot so she can complete the design?

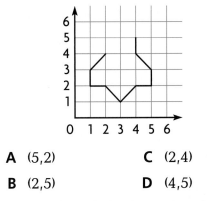

A (5,2)   **C** (2,4)

B (2,5)   **D** (4,5)

11. Which of the following pairs of figures appear to be congruent?

F

G

H

J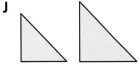

12. Explain It Fred drew a figure inside a circle. Name each radius he drew. Explain how you know.

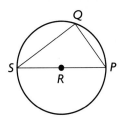

IT'S IN THE BAG

Multiplication Trail

PROJECT Make a board game to practice multiplication of whole numbers and decimals.

Materials

- 1 file folder
- Construction paper
- Markers or crayons
- Scissors, glue
- Card stock
- Spinner or number cube
- Game pieces

Directions

1. Choose a theme for your multiplication game. Decorate the front of a file folder to match the theme. *(Picture A)*

2. Cut strips for the game path out of construction paper, and glue onto the inside of the folder. Draw the playing spaces on the path, and write *Start* and *Finish* on the appropriate spaces. All spaces should be about the same size. Draw a $1\frac{1}{2}$-in. × 2-in. rectangle on the board to show where to place the cards. Decorate the folder around the path. *(Picture B)*

3. Cut $1\frac{1}{2}$-in. × 2-in. pieces of cardstock. On each card, write a multiplication problem using whole numbers or decimals. Place these cards face down on the rectangle you drew on the gameboard. *(Picture C)*

4. Write the directions for playing your game and glue them on the back of the file folder. Players can use paper and pencil to solve the problems and keep score.

Challenge

Lattice Multiplication

Lattice multiplication is another way to find products.

Multiply. 295 × 731

STEP 1

Draw a 3 × 3 lattice like the one shown. Write 295 across the top. Write 731 down the right side. Write an × above 731 as shown. Draw a diagonal line through each of the boxes.

```
  2  9  5  ×
 ┌──┬──┬──┐
 │╱ │╱ │╱ │ 7
 ├──┼──┼──┤
 │╱ │╱ │╱ │ 3
 ├──┼──┼──┤
 │╱ │╱ │╱ │ 1
 └──┴──┴──┘
```

STEP 2

For each box, multiply the number at the top of that column by the number at the right of that row. Write the digits of the product above and below the diagonal. If the product has only one digit, write a zero above the diagonal.

```
  2   9   5  ×
 ┌───┬───┬───┐
 │1╱6│6╱3│3╱5│ 7
 │ 4 │ 3 │ 5 │
 ├───┼───┼───┤
 │0╱2│2╱1│1╱5│ 3
 │ 6 │ 7 │ 5 │
 ├───┼───┼───┤
 │0╱0│0╱0│0╱5│ 1
 │ 2 │ 9 │ 5 │
 └───┴───┴───┘
```

STEP 3

Add along the diagonals. Start with the lower right corner. If needed, regroup to the next diagonal. Write the sums along the bottom and left side of the lattice.

```
    2₁  9₁  5₁  ×
   ┌───┬───┬───┐
 2 │1╱6│6╱3│3╱5│¹7
   │ 4 │ 3 │ 5 │
   ├───┼───┼───┤
 1 │0╱2│2╱1│1╱5│ 3
   │ 6 │ 7 │ 5 │
   ├───┼───┼───┤
 5 │0╱0│0╱0│0╱5│ 1
   │ 2 │ 9 │ 5 │
   └───┴───┴───┘
     6   4   5
```

STEP 4

Read the product by moving down the left side and across the bottom.

```
    2   9   5  ×
   ┌───┬───┬───┐
 2 │1╱6│6╱3│3╱5│ 7
   │ 4 │ 3 │ 5 │
   ├───┼───┼───┤
 1 │0╱2│2╱1│1╱5│ 3
   │ 6 │ 7 │ 5 │
   ├───┼───┼───┤
 5 │0╱0│0╱0│0╱5│ 1
   │ 2 │ 9 │ 5 │
   └───┴───┴───┘
     6   4   5
```

So, 295 × 731 = 215,645.

Try It

Use lattice multiplication to find the product.

1. 124 × 562   **2.** 552 × 601   **3.** 759 × 106   **4.** 324 × 651   **5.** 944 × 293

6.   783   **7.**   342   **8.**   427   **9.**   135   **10.**   246
      × 504   × 175   × 899   × 975   × 806

PROBLEM SOLVING ON LOCATION
in Tennessee

THE TENNESSEE AQUARIUM

The Tennessee Aquarium is the first and largest freshwater life center in the world. There you can see more than 9,000 animals swim, fly, and crawl in their re-created natural habitats.

1. Fish at the aquarium eat more than 1,200 pounds of seafood each month. How many pounds of seafood do they eat in a year?

2. Two barracuda were 14 inches long when the aquarium opened in 1992. Ten years later they were about 3.5 times this length. About how long were the barracuda 10 years later?

3. A sturgeon swims about 10 miles a day in a counterclockwise direction. How far has the sturgeon swum in the past 10 years?

For 4–6, use the table.

4. The Knights live in Knoxville. If they leave home at 10 A.M. and drive an average of 55 miles per hour, will they arrive at the Tennessee Aquarium by 12:30 P.M.? Explain.

| DISTANCES TO THE TENNESSEE AQUARIUM ||
City	Distance (in mi)
Cleveland, TN	32.7
Knoxville, TN	112.6
Columbia, TN	150.4
Nashville, TN	135.2
Manchester, TN	70.4

5. Jason drove round-trip from Nashville to the Tennessee Aquarium. Melissa drove from Columbia to the Tennessee Aquarium and then to Manchester. Who drove farther? How much farther?

6. Write a problem that can be solved using multiplication with the data in the table. Solve the problem.

▲ Cove Forest exhibit

SEAHORSES, SEADRAGONS, AND PIPEFISH

One of the most popular exhibits at the aquarium is *Seahorses: Beyond Imagination.* There you will find seahorses, seadragons, and pipefish. These fish are found in both warm tropic seas and chilly waters. They live in grass beds, in kelp forests, near mangroves, and around corals.

Weedy seadragon

◄ Leafy seadragon

1. Most leafy seadragons reach a length of about 30 cm. Weedy seadragons are larger and can grow to about 1.5 times the size of the leafy ones. About how long is an adult weedy seadragon?

2. Scientists have identified 2 species of seadragons and 32 species of seahorses. They have identified about 4.7 times the number of species of pipefish as seahorses. About how many species of pipefish have scientists identified?

3. In the wild, the number of seahorses that are born is about 200 times the number that survive to become adults. About how many are born for every 5 that become adults?

4. The smallest adult seahorses are about 2.5 centimeters long. The largest are about 14 times as long as the smallest. About how long are the largest seahorses?

5. To move in the water, seahorses beat their dorsal fins up to 35 times per second. At this rate, how many times would a seahorse beat its dorsal fins in 0.5 minute?

6. It has been reported that a two-week-old seahorse can eat at least 3,600 baby shrimp in one day. At this rate, how many baby shrimp can it eat in one week?

Blue catfish

Divide by 1-Digit Divisors

≡FAST FACT •

SOCIAL STUDIES

Since history was first recorded, beads have been used for trade, adornment, and decoration. Beads were also used in ceremonies and to confirm treaties.

PROBLEM SOLVING

The table shows the number of beads of various sizes that are needed to string a bracelet approximately 7 inches long. For each bead size, about how many beads are needed for 1 inch?

BEADS PER 7-INCH BRACELET	
Bead Size	**Number of Beads**
2 mm	91
3 mm	56
4 mm	42
6 mm	28
8 mm	21

CHECK WHAT YOU KNOW

Use this page to help you review and remember
important skills needed for Chapter 9.

ESTIMATE QUOTIENTS
Estimate the quotients.

1. $3\overline{)260}$ 2. $9\overline{)830}$ 3. $8\overline{)580}$ 4. $6\overline{)400}$

5. $6\overline{)290}$ 6. $7\overline{)450}$ 7. $4\overline{)340}$ 8. $8\overline{)650}$

9. $640 \div 7$ 10. $380 \div 9$ 11. $470 \div 3$ 12. $87 \div 9$

13. $270 \div 4$ 14. $58 \div 4$ 15. $190 \div 3$ 16. $510 \div 8$

DIVIDE 2-DIGIT NUMBERS
Divide.

17. $3\overline{)85}$ 18. $7\overline{)93}$ 19. $2\overline{)61}$ 20. $6\overline{)92}$ 21. $6\overline{)29}$

22. $4\overline{)83}$ 23. $8\overline{)54}$ 24. $3\overline{)81}$ 25. $9\overline{)95}$ 26. $8\overline{)36}$

27. $7\overline{)84}$ 28. $2\overline{)58}$ 29. $6\overline{)44}$ 30. $8\overline{)97}$ 31. $5\overline{)52}$

VOCABULARY POWER

REVIEW **PREVIEW**

quotient [kwō′shənt] *noun*

compatible numbers

A *quotient* is the answer in a division
problem. *Quotient* comes from the Latin
root word *quot,* which means "how many."
Find how many equal groups of 9 can
be made from 450.

www.harcourtschool.com/mathglossary

Estimate Quotients

VOCABULARY

compatible numbers

▶ Learn

CLOSE ENCOUNTERS Musa Manarov is a famous Soviet cosmonaut who spent a total of 541 days in space during two space flights. About how many weeks did Manarov spend in space?

Estimate.   541 ÷ 7 $7\overline{)541}$

Compatible numbers are numbers that are easy to compute mentally. Compatible numbers for 7 are multiples of 7, such as 14, 21, 28, 35, 42, 49, and 56.

Use 2 sets of compatible numbers to estimate 541 ÷ 7.

541 ÷ 7   or 541 ÷ 7
  ↓   ↓   ↓   ↓
490 ÷ 7 = 70   560 ÷ 7 = 80

Think: 541 is between 490 and 560. So, use 490 and 560 as dividends.

So, Manarov spent between 70 and 80 weeks in space.

▲ *Soyuz TM-4:* Cosmonauts Levchenko, Manarov, and Titov

MATH IDEA To estimate quotients, use compatible numbers.

Examples

A Estimate 4,126 ÷ 8.

Think: 40 is close to 41 and is a multiple of 8.

4,126 ÷ 8
  ↓   ↓
4,000 ÷ 8 = 500

So, 4,126 ÷ 8 is about 500.

B Estimate 23,078 ÷ 4.

Think: 24 is close to 23 and is a multiple of 4.

23,078 ÷ 4
  ↓   ↓
24,000 ÷ 4 = 6,000

So, 23,078 ÷ 4 is about 6,000.

C Estimate 462,028 ÷ 7.

Think: 49 is close to 46 and is a multiple of 7.

462,028 ÷ 7
  ↓   ↓
490,000 ÷ 7 = 70,000

So, 462,028 ÷ 7 is about 70,000.

- **What if** you use two sets of compatible numbers, 180 ÷ 6 and 240 ÷ 6, to estimate 239 ÷ 6? Which estimate will be closer to the exact answer? Explain.

Check

1. **Explain** how compatible numbers help you estimate quotients. Give an example.

Estimate the quotient. Tell what compatible numbers you used.

2. $5\overline{)263}$

3. $7\overline{)1,502}$

4. $8\overline{)1,389}$

5. $9\overline{)61,409}$

6. $11,583 \div 2$

7. $451,133 \div 9$

8. $337,028 \div 4$

9. $58,074 \div 8$

Practice and Problem Solving   Extra Practice, page 202, Set A

Estimate the quotient. Tell what compatible numbers you used.

10. $8\overline{)316}$

11. $9\overline{)5,536}$

12. $4\overline{)3,306}$

13. $7\overline{)34,072}$

14. $372 \div 6$

15. $125,703 \div 6$

16. $78,305 \div 7$

17. $2,500,823 \div 4$

Estimate the quotient, using two sets of compatible numbers.

18. $8,219 \div 9$

19. $25,316 \div 7$

20. $50,068 \div 4$

21. $172,388 \div 5$

22. $6,358 \div 8$

23. $71,269 \div 9$

24. $1,369,168 \div 5$

25. $800,625 \div 9$

USE DATA   For 26–28, use the table.

26. About how many Earth weeks does it take Mars to complete one revolution around the sun?

27. Estimate how many Earth weeks it takes Pluto to complete one revolution around the sun.

28. About how many times does Mercury revolve around the sun during one Earth revolution?

29. **REASONING**   When I am divided by 4, the quotient has two digits and the remainder is 0. When I am divided by 6, the quotient has one digit and the remainder is 0. My ones digit is 8. What number am I?

PLANET REVOLUTIONS AROUND THE SUN (based on Earth days)	
Planet	**Number of Days**
Mars	687
Mercury	88
Pluto	90,465

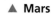
▲ Mars

Mixed Review and Test Prep

30. $71,053 \times 28$ (p. 154)

31. $192,550 \times 47$ (p. 154)

32. $7.3 + 8.9 + 2.7 + 4.2$ (p. 48)

33. Write 505.05 in word form. (p. 22)

34. **TEST PREP**   Which number is between 0.5 and 0.711? (p. 28)

   A 0.071   C 0.571

   B 0.157   D 0.750

2 Divide 3-Digit Dividends

Quick Review

1. 4×70 2. 8×90
3. 2×400 4. 3×300
5. 6×90

▶ **Learn**

WEIGHT LOSS The moon's weaker gravity causes things to weigh one-sixth as much on the moon as they weigh on Earth. Suppose some of the rocks brought back from the moon weigh 102 pounds on Earth. How much did they weigh on the moon?

◀ Between 1969 and 1972, Apollo missions brought back 382 kg (843 lb) of lunar rocks and soil from the moon's surface.

One Way Use estimation to place the first digit in the quotient.
Find $102 \div 6$.

STEP 1

Estimate.

Think: $\frac{10}{6\overline{)60}}$ or $\frac{20}{6\overline{)120}}$

$6\overline{)102}$ ■ So, place the first digit in the tens place.

STEP 2

Divide the 10 tens.

$\begin{array}{r} 1 \\ 6\overline{)102} \\ -6 \\ \hline 4 \end{array}$

Divide. $6\overline{)10}$
Multiply. 6×1
Subtract. $10 - 6$
Compare. $4 < 6$

STEP 3

Bring down the 2 ones.
Divide the 42 ones.

$\begin{array}{r} 17 \\ 6\overline{)102} \\ -6\downarrow \\ \hline 42 \\ -42 \\ \hline 0 \end{array}$

Divide. $6\overline{)42}$
Multiply. 6×7
Subtract. $42 - 42$
Compare. $0 < 6$

So, the rocks weighed 17 pounds on the moon.

Another Way Use place value to place the first digit.
Find $893 \div 9$.

STEP 1

Look at the hundreds.

$9\overline{)893}$ $8 < 9$, so look at the tens.

■

$9\overline{)893}$ $89 > 9$, so use 89 tens. Place the first digit in the tens place.

STEP 2

Divide the 89 tens.

$\begin{array}{r} 9 \\ 9\overline{)893} \\ -81 \\ \hline 8 \end{array}$

Divide.
Multiply.
Subtract.
Compare.

STEP 3

Bring down the 3 ones. Divide the 83 ones.

$\begin{array}{r} 99\ \text{r2} \\ 9\overline{)893} \\ -81\downarrow \\ \hline 83 \\ -81 \\ \hline 2 \end{array}$

Divide.
Multiply.
Subtract.
Compare.

CHECK ✓

Multiply the quotient by the divisor. Then add the remainder.

$\begin{array}{r} 99 \\ \times\ 9 \\ \hline 891 \\ +\ \ 2 \\ \hline 893 \end{array}$ ← dividend

1. **Explain** how you can tell without dividing whether the quotient of $539 \div 6$ will have 2 digits or 3.

Name the position of the first digit of the quotient.

2. $9\overline{)117}$ 3. $5\overline{)213}$ 4. $2\overline{)472}$ 5. $6\overline{)917}$ 6. $9\overline{)526}$

▷ **Practice and Problem Solving**   Extra Practice, page 202, Set B

Name the position of the first digit of the quotient.

7. $8\overline{)504}$ 8. $2\overline{)724}$ 9. $4\overline{)183}$ 10. $7\overline{)857}$ 11. $6\overline{)176}$

Divide.

12. $2\overline{)408}$ 13. $7\overline{)489}$ 14. $5\overline{)516}$ 15. $4\overline{)844}$ 16. $8\overline{)246}$

17. $8\overline{)113}$ 18. $9\overline{)912}$ 19. $3\overline{)607}$ 20. $2\overline{)526}$ 21. $4\overline{)223}$

22. $348 \div 8$ 23. $905 \div 5$ 24. $124 \div 6$ 25. $414 \div 5$ 26. $807 \div 4$

ALGEBRA   Find the value of *n*.

27. $357 \div 3 = n$ 28. $n \div 5 = 35$ r4   29. $n \div 7 = 47$ r3   30. $269 \div n = 134$ r1

USE DATA   For 31–32, use the table.

31. If there are 7 crew members, how many servings of each food type does each crew member receive? Copy and complete the table.

32. Which food type has the most servings per crew member?

SPACE FLIGHT FOOD (based on a standard 7-day shuttle menu)		
Food Type	**Number of Servings**	**Servings Per Crew Member**
Rehydratable Beverage	203	■
Fresh Food	175	■
Rehydratable Food	238	■

33. The weight allowed for food is 3.8 pounds per crew member per day. How does the weight of the food supply for 7 crew members for 6 days compare to the weight for 6 crew members for 7 days?

34. ≡**FAST FACT** • SCIENCE The diameter of the moon, 2,160 miles, is 2 times as great as the radius. Find the radius of the moon.

Mixed Review and Test Prep

35. $0.8 + 6.8$ (p. 48)

36. $6.16 - 3.47$ (p. 48)

37. Find the next number in the pattern: 24, 36, 48, 60, ... Describe the pattern.

38. 4×16.5 (p. 170)

39. **TEST PREP** Without multiplying, estimate which product is least. (p. 170)

A 0.9×10 C 0.9×0.1

B 0.9×1 D 0.9×0.01

Zeros in Division

Quick Review

1. 3)60   2. 2)80
3. 4)80   4. 9)90
5. 10)100

▶ **Learn**

LOONY TUNES Mr. Knowles owns 4 music stores. He ordered 432 kazoos. He wants each store to have the same number of kazoos. How many will each store receive?

Example

Divide. $432 \div 4$ 4)432

Estimate. $440 \div 4 = 110$ ← Use compatible numbers.

STEP 1

Divide the 4 hundreds.

Think: 4 hundreds can be divided by 4. So, place the first digit in the hundreds place in the quotient.

```
   1
4)432    Divide.
 -4      Multiply.
  0      Subtract.
         Compare. 0 < 4
```

STEP 2

Bring down the tens.
Divide the 3 tens.

Think: Since 4 > 3, write 0 in the quotient.

```
  10
4)432    Divide.
 -4↓     Multiply.
   3     Subtract.
  -0     Compare. 3 < 4
   3
```

STEP 3

Bring down the ones.
Divide the 32 ones.

Think: $32 \div 4 = 8$

```
  108
4)432    Divide.
 -4|     Multiply.
   3     Subtract.
  -0↓    Compare. 0 < 4
   32
  -32
    0
```

Since 108 is close to the estimate of 110, the answer is reasonable. So, each store will receive 108 kazoos.

- What happens to your answer if you forget to write the zero in the quotient?

MATH IDEA In division, if the divisor is greater than the number to be divided, place a zero in the quotient.

▶ **Check**

1. **Explain** how you decide when to write a zero in the quotient. Give an example.

Divide. Estimate to check.

2. $5\overline{)250}$ **3.** $7\overline{)73}$ **4.** $4\overline{)801}$

Practice and Problem Solving   Extra Practice, page 202, Set C

Divide. Estimate to check.

5. $9\overline{)87}$ **6.** $7\overline{)440}$ **7.** $4\overline{)82}$ **8.** $5\overline{)726}$ **9.** $6\overline{)91}$

10. $3\overline{)309}$ **11.** $5\overline{)54}$ **12.** $6\overline{)635}$ **13.** $4\overline{)816}$ **14.** $3\overline{)908}$

15. $6\overline{)612}$ **16.** $8\overline{)255}$ **17.** $5\overline{)525}$ **18.** $6\overline{)624}$ **19.** $7\overline{)745}$

20. $61 \div 2$ **21.** $528 \div 9$ **22.** $744 \div 8$ **23.** $606 \div 3$ **24.** $401 \div 5$

25. $122 \div 4$ **26.** $504 \div 5$ **27.** $824 \div 8$ **28.** $631 \div 6$ **29.** $801 \div 2$

ALGEBRA   **Find the value of n.**

30. $305 \div 5 = n$ **31.** $n \div 8 = 110 \text{ r}7$ **32.** $n \div 7 = 101 \text{ r}3$ **33.** $209 \div n = 104 \text{ r}1$

ALGEBRA   **Complete each table and write a division rule.**

34.

Input, n	49	107	239	564
Output	7	15 r2	■	■

35.

Input, n	83	■	404	412
Output	20 r3	24 r3	101	■

36. Felipe's family is planning to see a "Kazoo Band" show at a festival 306 miles away. It takes them 6 hours to drive there. On average, how many miles do they drive each hour?

37. At the "Kazoo Band" shows, everyone in the audience is given a kazoo for the grand finale. There were 357 adults and 529 children at the first show and 644 adults and 496 children at the second show. Did more adults or more children attend the shows? How many more?

38. **REASONING** Are there any zeros in the quotient $884 \div 4$? How can you tell without dividing?

39. **? What's the Error?** Jackie says $6 \div 6$ equals 1, so $606 \div 6$ equals 11. Find her error and write the correct division sentence.

Mixed Review and Test Prep

40. $\begin{array}{r} 100 \\ -\ 47 \\ \hline \end{array}$ (p. 46)   **41.** $\begin{array}{r} 500 \\ -176 \\ \hline \end{array}$ (p. 46)

42. $2{,}000 - 786$ (p. 46)

43. Write 246.975 in expanded form. (p. 22)

44. **TEST PREP** Choose an equivalent decimal for 0.04. (p. 26)

     A 4.0   **B** 0.4   **C** 0.040   **D** 0.004

Choose a Method

▶ **Learn**

DRAMATIC PARTS   The Sunrise Drama Club has 1,240 beads to make necklaces for the costumes for the school play. If there are 4 beads to an inch, how long would a single strand of all the beads be?

Use Mental Math   Divide. 1,240 ÷ 4

Think: 1,240 = 1,200 + 40
1,200 ÷ 4 = 300   40 ÷ 4 = 10   300 + 10 = 310

So, a single strand would be 310 inches long.

Suppose the beads are used to make 6 necklaces that are equal in length. How many beads will be in each necklace?

Use a Calculator   Divide. 1,240 ÷ 6

 1 2 4 0 ÷R 6 =   206 R4

So, each necklace will have 206 beads; there will be 4 beads left over.

▲ In the 1920s, women wore single strands of beads between 30 inches and 120 inches long.

Use Paper and Pencil   For 4-digit numbers, use the same steps that you used for dividing 3-digit numbers. Just repeat the steps for all the digits.

Example

STEP 1

The first digit will be in the hundreds place.

$$\begin{array}{r} 2 \\ 6\overline{)1,240} \\ -12 \\ \hline 0 \end{array}$$
Divide.
Multiply.
Subtract.
Compare.
0 < 6

STEP 2

Bring down the 4 tens. Divide the 4 tens.

$$\begin{array}{r} 20 \\ 6\overline{)1,240} \\ -12\downarrow \\ \hline 04 \\ -0 \\ \hline 4 \end{array}$$
Divide.
Multiply.
Subtract.
Compare.
4 < 6

STEP 3

Bring down the 0 ones. Divide the 40 ones.

$$\begin{array}{r} 206 \text{ r4} \\ 6\overline{)1,240} \\ -12 \\ \hline 04 \\ -0\downarrow \\ \hline 40 \\ -36 \\ \hline 4 \end{array}$$
Divide.
Multiply.
Subtract.
Compare.
4 < 6

☀ **MATH IDEA**   You can find a quotient by using mental math, paper and pencil, or a calculator. Choose the method that works best with the numbers in the problem.

Technology Link
More Practice: Harcourt
Mega Math The
Number Games,
Up, Up, & Array, Level O

1. **Explain** when you might choose mental math instead of paper and pencil to find a quotient.

Divide. Choose mental math, paper and pencil, or a calculator.

2. $3\overline{)2,424}$ 3. $8,100 \div 4$ 4. $2\overline{)8,345}$ 5. $19,145 \div 5$

▷ **Practice and Problem Solving**   Extra Practice, page 202, Set D

Divide. Choose mental math, paper and pencil, or a calculator.

6. $6\overline{)4,200}$ 7. $3\overline{)3,012}$ 8. $6\overline{)6,459}$ 9. $8\overline{)3,348}$

10. $8\overline{)4,762}$ 11. $2\overline{)3,760}$ 12. $4\overline{)11,286}$ 13. $7\overline{)700,000}$

14. $4,294 \div 3$ 15. $5,407 \div 7$ 16. $32,700 \div 4$ 17. $4,000,000 \div 5$

18. $9,088 \div 3$ 19. $12,422 \div 6$ 20. $45,090 \div 9$ 21. $74,608 \div 6$

USE DATA   For 22–23, use the circle graph.

22. The Booster Club donates money for costumes and props each year. If the Booster Club matches each dollar in the budget for costumes and props, how much money will the Sunrise Drama Club have for costumes and props?

23. The club members plan to print 28,620 programs. If they print an equal number for each of 4 plays, how many will they print for 1 play? How much money is budgeted per play for printing programs?

24. **?** **What's the Question?**   An embossing machine stamps 20 sheets of paper in one minute. The answer is 300 sheets.

SUNRISE DRAMA CLUB'S ANNUAL BUDGET OF $2,320

Costumes and Props

Rent and Utilities

Programs

25. **Vocabulary Power** The word *calculator* has the suffix *-or*. When this suffix is attached to a word, it means that a person (or thing) does something. What other words contain the suffix *-or*?

Mixed Review and Test Prep

26. Write the value of the blue digit in 7,543,229. (p. 4)

27. Evaluate $26 + n$ if $n = 20$. (p. 64)

28. Solve the equation $x - 7 = 52$. (p. 70)

29. Find $24,548 \times 4$. (p. 150)

30. **TEST PREP**   Find 0.4×0.8. (p. 168)

A 3.2   C 0.32

B 1.2   D 0.12

Problem Solving Skill
Interpret the Remainder

Quick Review

1. 29 ÷ 8   2. 39 ÷ 9
3. 60 ÷ 7   4. 22 ÷ 5
5. 25 ÷ 6

FIGURE IT OUT   Determine how the remainder was used to solve each of the problems below. The situation determines when to drop the remainder, round the quotient to the next greater number, or use the remainder as a part of the answer.

MATH IDEA   When you solve a division problem with a remainder, the way you interpret the remainder depends on the situation.

Examples

A

There are 1,853 athletes and parents signed up for a sports picnic. Each table will seat 6 people. How many tables will be needed?

$$\begin{array}{r} 308 \text{ r5} \\ 6\overline{)1,853} \\ -18 \\ \hline 05 \\ -0 \\ \hline 53 \\ -48 \\ \hline 5 \end{array}$$

Since 308 tables will not be enough to seat everyone, 309 tables will be needed.

B

Erik made punch with 3 ounces of lemon juice, 32 ounces of orange juice, 32 ounces of lemonade, and 64 ounces of ginger ale. How many 6-ounce servings did the punch recipe make?

$$\begin{array}{r} 3 \\ 32 \\ 32 \\ +64 \\ \hline 131 \end{array} \rightarrow \begin{array}{r} 21 \text{ r5} \\ 6\overline{)131} \\ -12 \\ \hline 11 \\ -6 \\ \hline 5 \end{array}$$

It made 21 six-ounce servings. The 5 ounces left over are not enough for another 6-ounce serving.

C

Mrs. Clarke brought a 145-inch rope to demonstrate tying knots. She divided the rope into 4 pieces of equal length. How long was each piece of rope?

Write the remainder as a fraction.

$$\begin{array}{r} 36\frac{1}{4} \\ 4\overline{)145} \\ -12 \\ \hline 25 \\ -24 \\ \hline 1 \end{array}$$ ← Use the remainder as the numerator and the divisor as the denominator.

So, each piece of rope was $36\frac{1}{4}$ inches long.

Talk About It

• Explain how the remainder was used to answer Examples A–C.

• Explain why a fractional remainder was appropriate for Example C, but not for Examples A or B.

Problem Solving Practice

Solve and then explain how you interpreted the remainder.

1. Jake has 172 books to display on 5 shelves in the bookstore. If Jake places an equal number of books on each shelf, what is the maximum number of books on each? How many books will be left over?

2. The nursery assistant has 124 roses to arrange in vases. There are 18 vases on the shelves. Will there be enough roses for each vase to have 7 roses in it?

USE DATA Use the table. At the concession stand, the popcorn machine pops 80 cups of popcorn at a time.

BAGS OF POPCORN	
Size	Amount per serving
Large	4 cups
Jumbo	6 cups

3. Marci calculated that she could fill 13 jumbo popcorn bags from one batch. Explain how she interpreted the remainder.

    A There is no remainder.
    B She dropped the remainder.
    C She rounded the quotient.
    D She used the remainder.

4. Marci sold 8 jumbo bags. Does she have enough popcorn left to fill 9 large popcorn bags? How many large bags can she fill?

    F no; 8 bags
    G no; 3 bags
    H yes; 10 bags
    J yes; 9 bags

Mixed Applications

5. Elena has a $20 bill. She buys 5 cookies for $2.00 each, a cup of tea for $1.50, and a sandwich for $2.35. How much change should she get?

6. Chiano bought a 50-page photo album. Each page holds 6 photos. She took 288 photos on her trip. Will the album hold all of her photos? Explain.

7. Mr. Jones is planning for buses for the school trip. A total of 105 students signed up. If each bus holds 42 students, will 2 buses be enough for the trip? Explain.

8. **PATTERNS** Carla is designing a necklace. She plans to repeat the pattern 1 red bead, 1 blue bead, and 1 green bead until she strings a total of 60 beads. What color will the 31st bead be?

9. Brian's model train track is 4 times as long as Mario's track. Brian's track is 1,247 inches long. How long is Mario's track?

10. Write three problems in which the remainder is used in three different ways.

Extra Practice

Set A (pp. 192–193)

Estimate the quotient. Tell what compatible numbers you used.

1. 8)902
2. 7)2,936
3. 9)1,989
4. 7)51,409
5. 7)313,084

Estimate the quotient, using two sets of compatible numbers.

6. 2,958 ÷ 3
7. 46,133 ÷ 5
8. 172,506 ÷ 8
9. 217,028 ÷ 2

10. Maria wants to put 468 stickers into a book. If each page gets 8 stickers, about how many pages will she need?

Set B (pp. 194–195)

Name the position of the first digit of the quotient.

1. 2)417
2. 5)213
3. 3)697
4. 6)489
5. 2)526

Divide.

6. 4)448
7. 5)615
8. 6)212
9. 7)488
10. 8)568

11. Bailey and his family went on a 108-mile hiking trip in the mountains. They hiked 9 miles each day. How many days did they hike?

Set C (pp. 196–197)

Divide. Estimate to check.

1. 7)714
2. 5)54
3. 9)936
4. 9)725
5. 8)167
6. 3)92
7. 2)815
8. 6)628
9. 8)105
10. 7)425

11. Tickets to the school basketball game cost $5. If the sale of tickets brought in $2,040, how many tickets were sold?

Set D (pp. 198–199)

Divide. Choose mental math, paper and pencil, or a calculator.

1. 7)4,900
2. 3)4,005
3. 8)32,880
4. 5)26,253
5. 6)36,305
6. 3)75,249
7. 2)3,269
8. 4)8,400,000

9. The Tropical Tour Company has 2,375 programs to distribute equally among its 7 resort hotels. How many programs will each resort receive?

Review/Test

✓ CHECK VOCABULARY AND CONCEPTS

Choose the best term from the box.

> compatible numbers
> place value
> remainder
> zero

1. To decide where to place the first digit in the quotient, you can estimate or use __?__. (p. 194)

2. Numbers that are close to the actual numbers and are easy to compute mentally are __?__. (p. 192)

3. The amount left over when you find a quotient is called the __?__. (p. 200)

✓ CHECK SKILLS

Estimate the quotient. Tell what compatible numbers you used. (pp. 192–193)

4. $3\overline{)3,296}$
5. $5\overline{)13,158}$
6. $2\overline{)23,498}$
7. $4\overline{)29,746}$

8. $7\overline{)4,387}$
9. $3\overline{)24,472}$
10. $8\overline{)56,703}$
11. $9\overline{)89,436}$

Divide. (pp. 194–199)

12. $9\overline{)504}$
13. $7\overline{)4,308}$
14. $8\overline{)998}$
15. $6\overline{)1,241}$

16. $5\overline{)421}$
17. $5\overline{)120,250}$
18. $4\overline{)2,872}$
19. $9\overline{)18,081}$

20. $6\overline{)704}$
21. $4\overline{)38,632}$
22. $8\overline{)105,687}$
23. $4\overline{)82,053}$

✓ CHECK PROBLEM SOLVING

Solve. Explain how you interpreted the remainder. (pp. 200–201)

24. A group of 123 students will take a swimming course. Each class can have 11 students. What is the least number of classes needed?

25. Mark has 300 miniature cars that he would like to display equally in 7 cases. Will 7 cases hold all of his collection? Explain.

Standardized Test Prep

⭐ NUMBER SENSE, CONCEPTS, AND OPERATIONS

1. Greg is putting his vacation photos into an album. He has 284 photos. If two sides of a sheet of paper in the album can hold 8 photos in all, how many sheets will he need?

   A 32

   B 35

   C 36

   D 71

2. The table shows the number of cans of food that students at Sandpiper Elementary School collected for a food drive.

FOOD DRIVE COLLECTION			
Grade	3	4	5
Number of Cans Collected	390	400	425

   What was the average number of cans collected per grade?

   F 405

   G 406

   H 450

   J 460

   > **TIP** **Eliminate choices.**
   > See item 2. You can eliminate choices H and J since the average number of cans collected per grade cannot be greater than 425.

3. **Explain It** Bottles of grape juice are on sale at 2 for $2.89. Tyler has $15.00. Can he buy 10 bottles of juice? ESTIMATE to solve. Explain your answer.

⭐ ALGEBRAIC THINKING

4. There are 18 apples in a bowl. Five of the apples are green, and the rest are red.

   Suppose *r* represents the number of red apples. Which equation can be used to find the number of red apples in the bowl?

   A $r + 5 = 18$

   B $r - 5 = 18$

   C $r - 18 = 5$

   D $r + 18 = 5$

5. Cara is building bridges with connecting cubes. If the pattern continues, how many cubes will be in Bridge 5?

   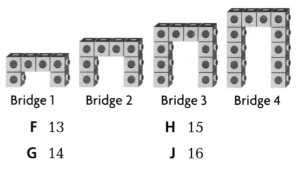

   Bridge 1   Bridge 2   Bridge 3   Bridge 4

   F 13   **H** 15

   G 14   **J** 16

6. **Explain It** Find a rule for the table below. Explain how you found the rule. Then use the rule to find the output when the input is 40.

INPUT	*x*	4	7	15	29
OUTPUT	*y*	21	24	32	46

★ DATA ANALYSIS AND PROBABILITY

7. The graph shows Miguel's practice times. On which day did Miguel practice 35 minutes more than he practiced on Friday?

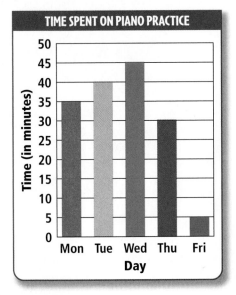

A Monday

B Tuesday

C Wednesday

D Thursday

8. Use the graph in Problem 7. For the week, what is the mean amount of time that Miguel practiced per day?

F 40 minutes

G 37.5 minutes

H 35 minutes

J 31 minutes

9. Explain It The Lake Bear basketball scores are shown below. Find the median of the five scores. Explain how to find the median, and tell what the median shows.

BASKETBALL SCORES					
Game	1	2	3	4	5
Points Scored	35	42	52	36	47

★ GEOMETRY AND SPATIAL SENSE

10. The Blakes are planting sod around their house and driveway. How many square feet of sod do they need?

A 5,000 square feet

B 3,500 square feet

C 3,150 square feet

D 350 square feet

11. What term **best** describes how the figure was moved?

F translation

G reflection

H rotation

J tessellation

12. Explain It Find the area and perimeter of the rectangle below. Then draw another figure that has the same area but a different perimeter. Explain how you found your answer.

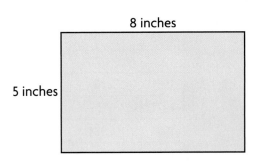

8 inches

5 inches

Divide by 2-Digit Divisors

≡FAST FACT • SOCIAL STUDIES Little League Baseball was founded in 1939 with 45 participants. A $35 donation purchased the uniforms for the first three teams. Today almost 3,000,000 children participate in Little League around the world. The table shows the number of Little League participants since its founding.

PROBLEM SOLVING Find the average number of players who participated in each league in 1948.

LITTLE LEAGUE PARTICIPANTS		
Year	Number of Leagues	Number of Participants
1939	1	45
1948	94	5,600
1951	775	46,600
1961	5,700	896,000
1971	6,552	1,447,200
1981	6,984	1,908,608
1991	7,056	2,534,355
2001	7,330	2,748,765

In 2001, the U.S. Champion team from Apopka, Florida, played the team from Japan in the 55th Little League World Series.

Use this page to help you review and remember important skills needed for Chapter 10.

MULTIPLY WHOLE NUMBERS

Find the product. Estimate to check.

1. 84
   ×22

2. 949
   × 16

3. 24
   ×19

4. 845
   × 67

5. 150
   × 74

6. 8,864
   × 14

7. 2,611
   × 69

8. 5,200
   × 45

COMPATIBLE NUMBERS

Estimate by using compatible numbers.

9. 9)660

10. 8)702

11. 4)122

12. 6)5,568

13. 359 ÷ 5

14. 2,662 ÷ 3

15. 820 ÷ 4

16. 9,074 ÷ 3

DIVIDE BY 1-DIGIT NUMBERS

Divide.

17. 3)85

18. 4)907

19. 8)47

20. 4)556

21. 806 ÷ 5

22. 75 ÷ 4

23. 882 ÷ 7

24. 3)624

VOCABULARY POWER

REVIEW

divide [di•vīd′] *verb*

In the word *divide*, the prefix, *di-*, means "through" or "apart." The root word *-videre* means "to separate." When you combine these you get "separated apart." Name other math words in which the prefix *di-* appears.

www.harcourtschool.com/mathglossary

Algebra: Patterns in Division

Quick Review
1. $(2 \times 4) \times 10$
2. $(3 \times 6) \times 20$
3. $(8 \times 5) \times 100$
4. $(6 \times 7) \times 100$
5. $(8 \times 8) \times 1,000$

Learn

ON THE ROAD AGAIN   Last summer, Emilie's family drove 6,000 miles round trip from Portland, OR, to Richmond, VA. On the trip, the car averaged 30 miles per gallon (mpg). How many gallons of gasoline did the car use?

Divide. $6,000 \div 30$ $30\overline{)6,000}$

Look for a pattern.

$6 \div 3 = 2$ ← **Think:** Use the basic fact.
$60 \div 30 = 2$
$600 \div 30 = 20$
$6,000 \div 30 = 200$

So, the car used 200 gallons of gasoline.

- What pattern do you see in $60 \div 30 = 2$, $600 \div 30 = 20$, and $6,000 \div 30 = 200$?

▲ The average American car got about 15 mpg in 1980 and about 24 mpg in 2003.

Examples

A
$8 \div 2 = 4$ ← basic
$80 \div 20 = 4$ fact
$800 \div 20 = 40$
$8,000 \div 20 = 400$
$80,000 \div 20 = 4,000$

B
$12 \div 6 = 2$ ← basic
$120 \div 60 = 2$ fact
$1,200 \div 60 = 20$
$12,000 \div 60 = 200$
$120,000 \div 60 = 2,000$

C
$30 \div 6 = 5$ ← basic
$300 \div 60 = 5$ fact
$3,000 \div 60 = 50$
$30,000 \div 60 = 500$
$300,000 \div 60 = 5,000$
$3,000,000 \div 60 = 50,000$

 MATH IDEA   Basic facts and patterns can help you divide mentally.

Check

1. **Compare** the basic facts and patterns in Examples B and C. How are they different?

Use mental math to complete. Write the basic fact you use.

2. $320 \div 40 = 8$
   $3,200 \div 40 = 80$
   $32,000 \div 40 = \blacksquare$

3. $420 \div 60 = 7$
   $4,200 \div 60 = 70$
   $42,000 \div 60 = \blacksquare$

4. $400 \div 50 = \blacksquare$
   $4,000 \div 50 = 80$
   $40,000 \div 50 = 800$

Use mental math to complete. Write the basic fact you use.

5. $90 \div 30 = \blacksquare$
$900 \div 30 = 30$
$9,000 \div 30 = 300$

6. $100 \div 50 = 2$
$1,000 \div 50 = 20$
$10,000 \div 50 = \blacksquare$

7. $450 \div 90 = 5$
$4,500 \div 90 = \blacksquare$
$45,000 \div 90 = \blacksquare$

ALGEBRA   **Use basic facts and patterns to solve for *n*.**

8. $90 \div 3 = n$
9. $160 \div 40 = n$
10. $280 \div 40 = n$
11. $360 \div 40 = n$

12. $540 \div 90 = n$
13. $3,000 \div 60 = n$
14. $7,200 \div 90 = n$
15. $36,000 \div 90 = n$

16. $n \div 80 = 30$
17. $1,000 \div n = 50$
18. $3,500 \div n = 70$
19. $18,000 \div n = 600$

20. $330,000 \div 10 = n$
21. $4,800,000 \div 80 = n$
22. $4,000,000 \div n = 50$

Compare. Use <, >, or = for the ●.

23. $400 \div 20$ ● $400 \div 200$
24. $5,600 \div 70$ ● $560 \div 7$
25. $80,000 \div 40$ ● $800 \div 4$

USE DATA   **For 26–27, use the map.**

26. Mr. Fiori's truck route is round trip from Charlotte to Asheville, 4 days a week. On his route, he drives an average of 60 miles per hour. How many hours does he drive each week on his route?

27. Ricky's delivery van averages 30 miles per gallon. How many gallons of gas does the van use on the route from Asheville to Charleston to Richmond to Charlotte and back to Asheville?

28. A typical person will walk about 70,000 miles between childhood and senior years. If a person lives 70 years, how many miles will he or she walk, on average, a year?

29. **? What's the Error?** Tina says the quotient of $200,000 \div 40$ has four zeros. Describe Tina's error and find the correct quotient.

Mixed Review and Test Prep

30. $596 \div 4$ (p. 194)
31. $434 \div 7$ (p. 194)

32. Find the value of *n*: $12 + n = 72$. (p. 80)

33. Write sixty million, five hundred two thousand, four in standard form. (p. 4)

34. **TEST PREP** The Chelsea Hotel has 225 rooms. If the hotel has 9 floors, what is the mean number of rooms on each floor of the hotel? (p. 100)

A 10   **C** 50
B 25   **D** 55

LESSON 2 · Estimate Quotients

▷ Learn

WILD BLUE YONDER In 1927 Charles Lindbergh was the first person to fly solo across the Atlantic Ocean. He flew the 3,610 miles from New York to Paris in about 34 hours. About how many miles did Lindbergh fly per hour?

MATH IDEA You can use compatible numbers to estimate quotients.

Estimate. $3{,}610 \div 34$
$$\begin{array}{cc} \downarrow & \downarrow \\ 3{,}400 \div 34 = 100 \leftarrow \end{array}$$ 3,400 and 34 are compatible numbers, since 34 ÷ 34 = 1.

So, Lindbergh flew about 100 miles per hour.

You can also estimate a quotient by using two sets of compatible numbers to find two different reasonable estimates.

Example

Estimate. $3{,}281 \div 52$

> **Think:** 3,281 is between 3,000 and 3,500. Use 3,000.
>
> $3{,}281 \div 52$
> $\downarrow \quad \downarrow$
> $3{,}000 \div 50 = 60 \leftarrow$ 3,000 and 50 are compatible numbers, since 30 ÷ 5 = 6.

> **Think:** 3,281 is between 3,000 and 3,500. Use 3,500.
>
> $3{,}281 \div 52$
> $\downarrow \quad \downarrow$
> $3{,}500 \div 50 = 70 \leftarrow$ 3,500 and 50 are compatible numbers, since 35 ÷ 5 = 7.

So, two reasonable estimates for $3{,}281 \div 52$ are 60 and 70.

- Will the quotient of $4{,}340 \div 62$ be greater than or less than 100? Explain how you know.

Lindbergh's flight helped make air travel popular. Between 1926 and 1930, the number of people traveling by plane each year grew from about 6,000 to about 400,000. ▼

▷ Check

1. **Show** two reasonable estimates for $2{,}652 \div 43$.

Write two pairs of compatible numbers for each.
Give two possible estimates.

2. $524 \div 68$ **3.** $329 \div 26$ **4.** $171 \div 34$ **5.** $2{,}548 \div 65$

Practice and Problem Solving Extra Practice, page 222, Set B

Write two pairs of compatible numbers for each.
Give two possible estimates.

6. $186 \div 62$ **7.** $1{,}275 \div 47$ **8.** $20{,}725 \div 49$

Estimate the quotient.

9. $42\overline{)508}$ **10.** $27\overline{)849}$ **11.** $64\overline{)532}$ **12.** $73\overline{)620}$ **13.** $86\overline{)743}$

14. $23\overline{)1{,}260}$ **15.** $47\overline{)3{,}524}$ **16.** $59\overline{)4{,}636}$ **17.** $77\overline{)8{,}199}$ **18.** $31\overline{)6{,}468}$

19. $81\overline{)2{,}417}$ **20.** $92\overline{)5{,}583}$ **21.** $34\overline{)27{,}925}$ **22.** $36\overline{)33{,}842}$ **23.** $53\overline{)48{,}574}$

Name the compatible numbers used to find the estimate.

24. $652 \div 18$
     estimate: 30

25. $423 \div 21$
     estimate: 20

26. $2{,}993 \div 75$
     estimate: 40

27. $37{,}642 \div 38$
     estimate: 900

USE DATA   For 28–30, copy and complete the table.
Estimate each flight speed.

	Year	Flight	Miles	Time (hours)	Speed (mph)
		HISTORIC FLIGHTS			
28.	1931	First Nonstop Trans-Pacific Flight	4,458	42	▪
29.	1932	First Woman's Trans-Atlantic Solo	2,026	15	▪
30.	1949	First Nonstop Round-the-World Flight	23,452	94	▪

31. REASONING A single-engine airplane can safely carry 5 people whose total weight is 857 pounds or less. Can the plane safely travel with 5 passengers if the average of their weights is 180 pounds? Explain.

▲ Amelia Earhart Putnam flew solo from Hawaii to California in a Wasp-powered Vega plane.

32. ✎ Write About It How do compatible numbers help you estimate quotients? Give an example.

Mixed Review and Test Prep

33. Order 36.9581, 36.5981, and 36.9851 from least to greatest. (p. 28)

34. Round 37,968,534 to the nearest hundred thousand. (p. 38)

35. $360 \div 90$ (p. 208)   **36.** $720 \div 80$ (p. 208)

37. TEST PREP   Nine more than half Amy's age is 17. How old is Amy? (p. 70)

A 6   **C** 10

B 8   **D** 16

Divide by 2-Digit Divisors

▶ **Learn**

TAKE ME OUT TO THE BALL GAME Henry Louis "Hank" Aaron is American baseball's all-time champion home-run hitter. In his 23-year Major League career, Aaron hit 755 home runs. How many home runs did he average per year?

Example

Divide. $755 \div 23$ $23\overline{)755}$

STEP 1

Estimate to place the first digit in the quotient.

Think:

$$\frac{30}{25\overline{)750}} \quad \text{or} \quad \frac{40}{20\overline{)800}}$$

$$\overset{\blacksquare}{23\overline{)755}}$$ So, place the first digit in the tens place.

STEP 2

Divide the 75 tens.

$$\begin{array}{r} 3 \\ 23\overline{)755} \\ -69 \\ \hline 6 \end{array}$$

Divide. $23\overline{)75}$
Multiply. 23×3
Subtract. $75 - 69$
Compare. $6 < 23$

STEP 3

Bring down the 5 ones. Divide the 65 ones.

$$\begin{array}{r} 32 \text{ r19} \\ 23\overline{)755} \\ -69\downarrow \\ \hline 65 \\ -46 \\ \hline 19 \end{array}$$

Divide. $23\overline{)65}$
Multiply. 23×2
Subtract. $65 - 46$
Compare. $19 < 23$

So, Hank Aaron averaged between 32 and 33 home runs per year.

- Explain how to use multiplication to check $755 \div 23 = 32$ r19.

MATH IDEA To divide by a 2-digit divisor, first estimate in order to place the first digit. Then follow the steps for division: divide, multiply, subtract, and compare. Repeat the steps until the remainder is zero or less than the divisor.

Hank Aaron entered the record books on April 8, 1974, by breaking Babe Ruth's record of 714 home runs. Aaron's lifetime batting average was .305. ▶

More Examples

Ⓐ
Divide.

$$\begin{array}{r} 95\ r15 \\ 16\overline{)1{,}535} \\ -1\ 44 \\ \hline 95 \\ -80 \\ \hline 15 \end{array}$$

Check ✓

$$\begin{array}{r} 95 \\ \times 16 \\ \hline 570 \\ +950 \\ \hline 1{,}520 \\ +\ \ \ 15 \\ \hline 1{,}535\ ✓ \end{array}$$

Ⓑ
Divide.

$$\begin{array}{r} 1{,}303\ r22 \\ 24\overline{)31{,}294} \\ -24 \\ \hline 72 \\ -72 \\ \hline 09 \\ -\ 0 \\ \hline 94 \\ -72 \\ \hline 22 \end{array}$$

Check ✓

$$\begin{array}{r} 1{,}303 \\ \times\ \ 24 \\ \hline 5\ 212 \\ +26\ 060 \\ \hline 31{,}272 \\ +\ \ \ \ 22 \\ \hline 31{,}294\ ✓ \end{array}$$

• In Example B, what does the zero in the quotient indicate?

Technology Link

More Practice: Harcourt Mega Math The Number Games, *Up, Up, and Array*, Levels R, S

▶ Check

1. Explain how you can use an estimate to help you divide.

Name the position of the first digit of the quotient.

2. $36\overline{)209}$ **3.** $14\overline{)1{,}624}$ **4.** $53\overline{)2{,}369}$ **5.** $47\overline{)7{,}395}$

6. $89\overline{)8{,}969}$ **7.** $43\overline{)205}$ **8.** $38\overline{)7{,}268}$ **9.** $13\overline{)24{,}613}$

Divide. Check by multiplying.

10. $831 \div 38$ **11.** $2{,}816 \div 56$ **12.** $3{,}974 \div 23$ **13.** $694 \div 81$

14. $42\overline{)365}$ **15.** $38\overline{)4{,}031}$ **16.** $74\overline{)3{,}568}$ **17.** $54\overline{)34{,}078}$

▶ Practice and Problem Solving Extra Practice, page 222, Set C

Name the position of the first digit of the quotient.

18. $47\overline{)310}$ **19.** $25\overline{)3{,}205}$ **20.** $63\overline{)1{,}824}$ **21.** $71\overline{)9{,}546}$

22. $42\overline{)42{,}785}$ **23.** $68\overline{)54{,}330}$ **24.** $21\overline{)458}$ **25.** $34\overline{)3{,}894}$

Divide. Check by multiplying.

26. $942 \div 49$ **27.** $5{,}690 \div 78$ **28.** $458 \div 45$ **29.** $10{,}675 \div 11$

30. $4{,}369 \div 74$ **31.** $12{,}362 \div 35$ **32.** $8{,}149 \div 41$ **33.** $30{,}362 \div 62$

LESSON CONTINUES

Divide.

34. $24\overline{)824}$ **35.** $50\overline{)545}$ **36.** $73\overline{)7,809}$ **37.** $29\overline{)6,932}$

38. $33\overline{)669}$ **39.** $43\overline{)759}$ **40.** $37\overline{)4,801}$ **41.** $58\overline{)9,286}$

42. $73\overline{)5,841}$ **43.** $29\overline{)31,803}$ **44.** $26\overline{)5,330}$ **45.** $37\overline{)3,363}$

46. $399 \div 26$ **47.** $2,904 \div 45$ **48.** $4,598 \div 61$ **49.** $35,718 \div 13$

Match each check with a division problem.

50. Check: $(66 \times 14) + 60 = 984$

51. Check: $(82 \times 108) + 71 = 8,927$

52. Check: $(98 \times 1,010) + 9 = 98,989$

53. Check: $(69 \times 115) + 47 = 7,982$

a. $7,982 \div 69 = 115 \text{ r}47$

b. $984 \div 66 = 14 \text{ r}60$

c. $8,927 \div 82 = 108 \text{ r}71$

d. $98,989 \div 98 = 1,010 \text{ r}9$

ALGEBRA For 54–57, find the missing digit that makes each equation true.

54. $1,288 \div 23 = 5\blacksquare$

55. $3,580 \div (\blacksquare \times 10) = 89 \text{ r}20$

56. $(456 - 18) \div 42 = 1\blacksquare \text{ r}18$

57. $452 \div 22 = 20 \text{ r}\blacksquare$

58. **? What's the Error?** In the student paper on the right, which is incorrect, the problem or the check? Describe and correct the error.

59. **REASONING** What is the greatest remainder you can have if you divide by 48? Explain.

60. **NUMBER SENSE** Two numbers have a sum of 64. The quotient is 7. What are the two numbers?

61. An adult ticket to the baseball game costs $9. A student ticket is $6. Anna paid a total of $153 for tickets to a game. She bought 11 adult tickets. How many student tickets did she buy?

$$
\begin{array}{r}
15 \text{ r}12 \\
18\overline{)282} \\
18 \\
\hline
102 \\
-90 \\
\hline
12
\end{array}
\qquad
\begin{array}{r}
\text{Check } \checkmark \\
15 \\
\times 12 \\
\hline
30 \\
+150 \\
\hline
180 \\
+ 18 \\
\hline
198
\end{array}
$$

USE DATA For 62–64, use the table.

62. Estimate how many games Cy Young won in an average season.

63. **? What's the Question?** The answer is Warren Spahn won 10 fewer games.

64. **REASONING** Who averaged more wins per season, Alexander or Spahn?

PITCHER WINS		
Pitcher	Seasons Pitched	Games Won
Cy Young	22	511
Walter Johnson	21	416
Christy Mathewson	17	373
Grover Alexander	20	373
Warren Spahn	21	363

Walter Johnson ▶

65. The Crestview School had an "Eat Apples" fund-raising activity and sold 2,485 apples. The apples were sold by 87 students. If an equal number of apples were sold by each student, about how many apples did each student sell?

66. Vocabulary Power Compatible numbers work easily together. The prefix *com-* in *compatible* means "with" or "together." Name other words you know that have the prefix *com-*.

Mixed Review and Test Prep

67. Find the mean.
85.7, 70.8, 34.1, 12 (p. 100)

68. Solve: $420 - t = 360$ (p. 70)

69. Round 0.605 to the nearest hundredth. (p. 40)

70. Find the missing number in the pattern 40, 36, 32, ■, 24.

71. 6.829 (p. 48)
+8.551

72. 19.05 (p. 48)
− 5.637

73. 265 ÷ 5 (p. 194) **74.** 299 ÷ 9 (p. 194)

75. TEST PREP How many zeros will be in the quotient of 72,000 ÷ 90? (p. 208)

A 1 zero **C** 3 zeros
B 2 zeros **D** 4 zeros

76. TEST PREP Pam had 7 bracelets and got 4 more for her birthday. Which expression models this situation? (p. 64)

F 7 − 4 **H** 7 + 4
G 7 ÷ 4 **J** 7 × 4

Problem Solving Thinker's Corner

REMAINDER SCOREBOARD

Materials: 5 blank number cubes

Getting Ready: Label 2 number cubes 0–5. Label 3 number cubes 4–9.

Let's Play!

• One player tosses all the cubes, using the results as digits to write a 3-digit by 2-digit division problem that has a high remainder. Then the player divides.

• The other players check the quotient and remainder. If both are correct, the player records the remainder as the score for that round. If both are incorrect, the remainder is not recorded.

• Players continue alternating turns, writing division problems, and adding the remainders (if correct) to their scores. The player with the highest score after ten rounds wins.

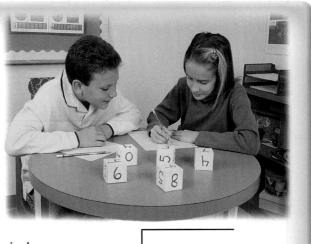

3 r76
90)346

(90 × 3) + 76 = 346

5 Practice Division

▶ **Learn**

ALL YOU CAN EAT An adult giant panda in the wild eats about 10,220 pounds of bamboo shoots and leaves a year. On average, how many pounds of bamboo does a giant panda eat each month?

◀ Bamboo makes up 99 percent of a giant panda's diet. A panda sometimes consumes as much as 80 pounds of fresh bamboo shoots per day.

Example

Divide. 10,220 ÷ 12   12)10,220

STEP 1	STEP 2	STEP 3	STEP 4
Estimate. **Think:** $\frac{800}{12)9,600}$ or $\frac{900}{12)10,800}$ $\frac{\blacksquare}{12)10,220}$ So, place the first digit in the hundreds place.	Divide the 102 hundreds. Use your lower estimate. $\begin{array}{r} 8 \\ 12)\overline{10,220} \\ -\underline{96} \\ 6 \end{array}$	Bring down the 2 tens. Divide the 62 tens. $\begin{array}{r} 85 \\ 12)\overline{10,220} \\ -\underline{96}\downarrow \\ 62 \\ -\underline{60} \\ 2 \end{array}$	Bring down the 0 ones. Divide the 20 ones. $\begin{array}{r} 851\ r8 \\ 12)\overline{10,220} \\ -\underline{96}\downarrow \\ 62 \\ -\underline{60}\downarrow \\ 20 \\ -\underline{12} \\ 8 \end{array}$

Express the remainder as a fraction. So, a giant panda eats an average of $851\frac{8}{12}$, or $851\frac{2}{3}$, pounds of bamboo each month.

More Examples

A

$$\begin{array}{r} 24\ r3\ or\ 24\frac{3}{35} \\ 35)\overline{843} \\ -\underline{70} \\ 143 \\ -\underline{140} \\ 3 \end{array}$$

Check ✓
$$\begin{array}{r} 24 \\ \times 35 \\ \hline 120 \\ +720 \\ \hline 840 \\ +\ \ 3 \\ \hline 843\checkmark \end{array}$$

B

$$\begin{array}{r} 61\ r17\ or\ 61\frac{17}{42} \\ 42)\overline{2,579} \\ -\underline{2\ 52} \\ 59 \\ -\underline{42} \\ 17 \end{array}$$

Check ✓
$$\begin{array}{r} 61 \\ \times 42 \\ \hline 122 \\ +2\ 440 \\ \hline 2,562 \\ +\ \ 17 \\ \hline 2,579\checkmark \end{array}$$

You can use a calculator to divide.

2 5 7 9 Int÷ 4 2 Enter   2579÷42=
                                        61r17

1. **Explain** how to express the remainder as a fraction in a division problem.

Divide. Check by multiplying.

2. $851 \div 15$

3. $93 \div 14$

4. $1,242 \div 48$

5. $84 \div 17$

6. $42\overline{)23,898}$

7. $61\overline{)36,182}$

8. $29\overline{)1,073}$

9. $28\overline{)5,016}$

▷ **Practice and Problem Solving**   Extra Practice, page 222, Set E

Divide.

10. $402 \div 65$

11. $4,161 \div 19$

12. $4,591 \div 37$

13. $89 \div 23$

14. $71\overline{)7,171}$

15. $33\overline{)1,877}$

16. $51\overline{)4,095}$

17. $92\overline{)46,235}$

18. $91\overline{)5,396}$

19. $69\overline{)2,109}$

20. $48\overline{)24,916}$

21. $42\overline{)23,911}$

22. $25\overline{)424,867}$

23. $32\overline{)306,452}$

24. $24\overline{)6,809}$

25. $76\overline{)3,965}$

ALGEBRA   For 26–31, find the missing digit that makes each equation true.

26. $4\blacksquare4 \div 23 = 18$

27. $1,065 \div \blacksquare1 = 15$

28. $7,\blacksquare22 \div 99 = 78$

29. $12,084 \div 76 = 15\blacksquare$

30. $(1,188 - 18) \div 90 = 1\blacksquare$

31. $1,860 \div (\blacksquare \times 15) = 62$

32. About 31,000 people visited the San Diego Zoo's website the day the live "Panda Cam" was launched. On average, how many people visited the website each hour?

33. **NUMBER SENSE**   What is the least 4-digit number that can be divided by 20 and have a remainder of 5?

34. **FAST FACT • SCIENCE**   A newborn panda is about the size of a stick of butter. An adult panda weighs about 200 lb, about 800 times as great as the weight of a newborn. Find the weight of a newborn. (16 oz = 1 lb)

Mixed Review and Test Prep

For 35–36, identify the addition property shown. (p. 76)

35. $10 + 7 = 7 + 10$

36. $(4 + 2) + 3 = 4 + (2 + 3)$

37. $24.18 - 16.09$
(p. 48)

38. $16.82 + 7.48$
(p. 48)

39. **TEST PREP**   A bag of popcorn sells for $2.75. If a teacher uses a $50 bill to buy 18 bags for his class, how much will he receive in change? (p. 170)

A $0.03   C $0.60

B $0.50   D $1.50

Problem Solving Strategy
Predict and Test

PROBLEM A collector has 158 world's fair souvenirs. He wants to sell them in equal groups with no more than 25 in each group. After he divides them into equal groups, there are 20 souvenirs left over that he will sell individually. How many groups was he able to make? How many souvenirs are in each group?

UNDERSTAND ▶

- What are you asked to find?
- What information will you use?

PLAN ▶

- What strategy can you use to solve the problem?

  Since you know the dividend is 158, you can use *predict and test* to find equal groups with no more than 25 souvenirs in each.

SOLVE ▶

- How can you use the strategy to solve the problem?

  Since there are 20 souvenirs left over, there must be more than 20 souvenirs in each group. So, start by predicting different divisors greater than 20. Then test each prediction to see if the remainder is 20.

Predict the number of souvenirs in each group.	Divide to find the number of groups.	Compare the remainder to 20.	Does the remainder equal 20?
21	$158 \div 21 = 7\ r11$	$11 < 20$	No
22	$158 \div 22 = 7\ r4$	$4 < 20$	No
23	$158 \div 23 = 6\ r20$	$20 = 20\ \sqrt{}$	Yes

So, the collector made 6 groups, each with 23 souvenirs.

CHECK ▶

- How can you decide if your answer is correct?

Problem Solving Practice

Predict and test to solve.

1. What if there were 18 souvenirs left over? How many groups would he be able to make? How many souvenirs would be in each group?

2. Tim spent $22.50 on souvenirs at the fair. He bought 2 souvenirs. One of them cost $4.50 more than the other. How much was each souvenir?

The fifth-grade students had 181 paintings to be displayed in equal groups on walls throughout the school. No more than 30 paintings would fit on each wall. After the paintings were placed, 20 were left over and were placed on the office wall.

3. How many groups were formed? How many paintings were in each group?

   A 6 groups of 30 paintings
   B 7 groups of 23 paintings
   C 8 groups of 21 paintings
   D 9 groups of 20 paintings

4. Which equation models this situation?

   F $181 \div 30 = 6\ r1$
   G $181 \div 20 = 9\ r1$
   H $181 \div 23 = 7\ r20$
   J $181 \div 7 = 25\ r6$

Strategies

Draw a Diagram or Picture
Make a Model or Act It Out
Make an Organized List
Find a Pattern
Make a Table or Graph
▶ **Predict and Test**
Work Backward
Solve a Simpler Problem
Write an Equation
Use Logical Reasoning

Problem Solving

Mixed Strategy Practice

USE DATA   For 5–6, use the table.

5. If a tour boat travels 19 miles per hour down the Colorado River and another tour boat travels 25 miles per hour down the Rio Grande, which tour boat will travel the length of its river first?

6. Suppose there are rescue stations every 35 miles along the Yenisey River. If the first station is located at the beginning of the river, how many stations are there in all?

7. Karen left her house and drove 35 miles north and then 15 miles west to the mall. When she left the mall, she drove 5 miles east and then 20 miles south to the library. How far north and west was Karen from her house?

8. **NUMBER SENSE**   The sum of two numbers is 36. Their product is 320. What are the two numbers?

9. ✎ Write a problem using the table above. Explain the strategy you would use to solve the problem.

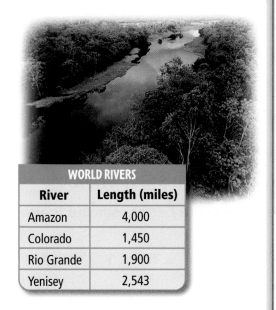

WORLD RIVERS	
River	**Length (miles)**
Amazon	4,000
Colorado	1,450
Rio Grande	1,900
Yenisey	2,543

Extra Practice

Set A (pp. 208–209)

Use mental math to complete. Write the basic fact you use.

1.
$200 \div 40 = 5$
$2,000 \div 40 = 50$
$20,000 \div 40 = \blacksquare$

2.
$160 \div 40 = 4$
$1,600 \div 40 = \blacksquare$
$16,000 \div 40 = 400$

3.
$180 \div 30 = \blacksquare$
$1,800 \div 30 = 60$
$18,000 \div 30 = \blacksquare$

4. A tour group traveled 6,000 miles in 30 days. How many miles a day did it average?

5. If you average 50 miles per hour for 550 miles, how many hours will you travel?

Set B (pp. 210–211)

Write two pairs of compatible numbers for each. Give two possible estimates.

1. $198 \div 28$

2. $336 \div 46$

3. $1,344 \div 87$

Estimate the quotient.

4. $22\overline{)215}$

5. $33\overline{)605}$

6. $42\overline{)1,378}$

7. $51\overline{)9,750}$

8. $41\overline{)8,261}$

Set C (pp. 212–215)

Divide.

1. $842 \div 27$

2. $2,946 \div 76$

3. $8,888 \div 62$

4. $15,432 \div 18$

5. $23\overline{)532}$

6. $31\overline{)8,461}$

7. $18\overline{)2,468}$

8. $27\overline{)16,798}$

9. $23\overline{)86,698}$

Set D (pp. 216–217)

Write *too high*, *too low*, or *just right* for each estimate.

1. $34\overline{)26,163}$ (800)

2. $41\overline{)325}$ (6)

3. $29\overline{)23,007}$ (800)

4. $69\overline{)698}$ (10)

5. $76\overline{)1,826}$ (20)

Choose the better estimate to use for the quotient. Write *a* or *b*.

6. $14\overline{)92}$ a. 6   b. 5

7. $18\overline{)138}$ a. 6   b. 7

8. $61\overline{)192}$ a. 3   b. 4

Set E (pp. 218–219)

Divide.

1. $12\overline{)58}$

2. $18\overline{)79}$

3. $24\overline{)9,168}$

4. $33\overline{)234}$

5. $84\overline{)31,164}$

6. $36\overline{)24,469}$

7. $21\overline{)6,954}$

8. $26\overline{)635,204}$

Review/Test

✔ CHECK VOCABULARY AND CONCEPTS

Choose the best term from the box.

> estimate
> multiples
> multiplication
> patterns

1. You can use basic facts and __?__ to divide mentally. (p. 208)

2. You can use compatible numbers to __?__ quotients. (p. 210)

3. You can use __?__ to check division. (p. 212)

✔ CHECK SKILLS

Use mental math to complete. Write the basic fact you use. (pp. 208–209)

4. $490 \div 70 = 7$
    $4{,}900 \div 70 = 70$
    $49{,}000 \div 70 = ■$

5. $640 \div 80 = 8$
    $6{,}400 \div 80 = ■$
    $64{,}000 \div 80 = 800$

6. $810 \div 90 = ■$
    $8{,}100 \div 90 = ■$
    $81{,}000 \div 90 = 900$

Write two pairs of compatible numbers for each. Give two possible estimates. (pp. 210–211)

7. $263 \div 43$

8. $1{,}456 \div 37$

9. $5{,}063 \div 81$

Write *too high*, *too low*, or *just right* for each estimate. (pp. 216–217)

10. $13\overline{)667}$ 40

11. $26\overline{)3{,}521}$ 90

12. $41\overline{)37{,}651}$ 900

13. $75\overline{)49{,}036}$ 700

Divide. (pp. 212–215 and pp. 218–219)

14. $17\overline{)64}$

15. $22\overline{)90}$

16. $36\overline{)184}$

17. $47\overline{)2{,}943}$

18. $34\overline{)3{,}294}$

19. $27\overline{)344}$

20. $36\overline{)645}$

21. $45\overline{)4{,}292}$

22. $42\overline{)8{,}325}$

23. $71\overline{)685{,}210}$

✔ CHECK PROBLEM SOLVING

Predict and test to solve. (pp. 220–221)

24. The Trader Card Store has 161 baseball cards. The store wants to sell the cards in equal groups, with no more than 30 cards in each group. There will be 17 cards left over that they will sell individually. How many equal groups can be made? How many cards will be in each group?

25. **NUMBER SENSE** The sum of two numbers is 35 and their difference is 7. What are the two numbers?

Standardized Test Prep

⭐ NUMBER SENSE, CONCEPTS, AND OPERATIONS

1. Last month Steve earned $378 mowing lawns. He has 7 customers, and he mowed each lawn 3 times during the month. How much money does Steve charge to mow one lawn?

   A $18

   B $21

   C $54

   D $126

2. Joan is buying the dining room set shown below.

   She will make a down payment of $225 and monthly payments of $75. How many monthly payments does Joan have to make to pay for the dining room set?

   F 7

   G 9

   H 24

   J 27

3. **Explain It** Sara's class sold pencils for 20¢ each as a fund-raising project. They collected $28.40. Is the total number of pencils they sold closer to 100, 150, 200, or 250? ESTIMATE to solve. Explain your estimate.

⭐ ALGEBRAIC THINKING

4. Jamie earned d dollars baby-sitting on Friday and $15 baby-sitting on Saturday. Which expression represents how much Jamie earned baby-sitting?

   A $d - 15$ **C** $d + 15$

   B $15 - d$ **D** $15d$

   > **TIP** **Understand the problem.** See item 5. The number of used books and total number of books are given. You do not know the number of new books.

5. Trevor sold 127 used books and some new books at a book sale. He sold 221 books in all.

   Suppose n represents the number of new books sold. Which equation could be used to find the number of new books sold?

   F $127 + n = 221$

   G $n + 221 = 127$

   H $221 + 127 = n$

   J $n - 221 = 127$

6. **Explain It** Janelle is 2 years younger than Hannah and 6 years older than Sal. Write two expressions with different variables to represent Janelle's age.

⭐ MEASUREMENT

7. Noah planted a bush that was 30 centimeters tall. Six months later, the bush was 1 meter tall. How much had the bush grown?

A 70 millimeters

B 7 centimeters

C 70 centimeters

D 700 centimeters

8. Briana went to the post office to mail the package shown below.

How many ounces did the package weigh?

F 18 ounces

G 22 ounces

H 26 ounces

J 34 ounces

9. **Explain It** To make a trail mix, Jeff bought 3 pounds of raisins at $2.15 per pound. He also bought 2 pounds of walnuts at $3.90 per pound. Did Jeff spend more on raisins or more on walnuts? ESTIMATE to find the answer. Explain your answer.

⭐ DATA ANALYSIS AND PROBABILITY

10. The graph shows the number of ice skating lessons offered at Jo's Ice Rink.

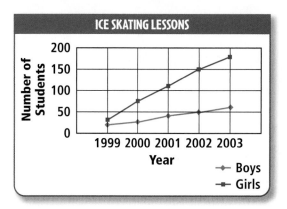

What conclusion can you make about the data?

A The number of lessons for boys decreased from 1999 to 2000.

B The number of lessons for girls decreased from 2001 to 2003.

C The number of students taking lessons stayed the same every year.

D More girls than boys took lessons each year from 1999 to 2003.

11. Parker's math quiz scores are 10, 8, 10, 9, and 10. Which of the following is true about his scores?

F The median equals the mode.

G The range equals the median.

H The mode equals the range.

J The mode, median, and range are all equal.

12. **Explain It** Evan is deciding what clothes to wear. He has a red shirt, a blue shirt, and a white shirt. He has black, brown, and blue pants. Draw a diagram to show how many choices he has. Explain the diagram.

Divide Decimals by Whole Numbers

≡FAST FACT • SOCIAL STUDIES In the 1800s, it took four hours to travel by horse and carriage to the top of Lookout Mountain in Chattanooga, Tennessee. Today it takes 10 minutes to travel by the Incline Railway to the same point.

PROBLEM SOLVING Between 350,000 and 450,000 passengers take the Incline Railway during an average year. The graph shows the fraction of passengers who ride from April to October. Write this fraction as a decimal.

THE INCLINE RAILWAY PASSENGER TRIPS
(in an average year)

Nov–Mar $\frac{1}{10}$

Apr–Oct $\frac{9}{10}$

The Incline Railway is the steepest and safest passenger incline in the world.

Use this page to help you review and remember
important skills needed for Chapter 11.

✓ DIVISION PATTERNS

Complete the pattern.

1. $350 \div 50 = 7$
    $3{,}500 \div 50 = 70$
    $35{,}000 \div 50 = n$

2. $180 \div 30 = 6$
    $1{,}800 \div 30 = n$
    $18{,}000 \div 30 = 600$

3. $360 \div 40 = n$
    $3{,}600 \div 40 = 90$
    $36{,}000 \div 40 = 900$

4. $300 \div 60 = 5$
    $3{,}000 \div 60 = 50$
    $n \div 60 = 500$

5. $320 \div 80 = 4$
    $n \div 80 = 40$
    $32{,}000 \div 80 = 400$

6. $400 \div 50 = 8$
    $4{,}000 \div n = 80$
    $40{,}000 \div 50 = 800$

✓ DIVIDE WHOLE NUMBERS

Divide.

7. $7\overline{)84}$
8. $4\overline{)92}$
9. $5\overline{)485}$
10. $9\overline{)207}$

11. $6\overline{)288}$
12. $4\overline{)824}$
13. $3\overline{)1{,}620}$
14. $8\overline{)3{,}248}$

15. $144 \div 16$
16. $832 \div 32$
17. $3{,}825 \div 45$
18. $1{,}365 \div 91$

✓ EQUIVALENT DECIMALS

Write two equivalent decimals for each.

19. 8
20. 0.25
21. 1.3
22. 2.60

VOCABULARY POWER

REVIEW

hundredth [hun′drədth] *adjective* or *noun*

One whole can be divided into 100 equal parts, or 100 hundredths.
One dollar can be divided into hundredths. What is another name for
one hundredth of one dollar?

www.harcourtschool.com/mathglossary

Algebra: Patterns in Decimal Division

Quick Review

1. 540 ÷ 9   2. 480 ÷ 8
3. 240 ÷ 4   4. 5,600 ÷ 8
5. 3,000 ÷ 6

▶ Learn

POP! POP! POP!   Roderic read that the average person in the United States eats about 16 gallons of popcorn each year. Roderic bought 4 cans of popcorn for $2. What is the cost for one can?

Find 2 ÷ 4.

Look for a pattern in these quotients.

200 ÷ 4 = 50   ← Pattern in the zeros
  20 ÷ 4 = 5   ← Basic fact
    2 ÷ 4 = 0.5   ← Decimal quotient

So, one can of popcorn costs $0.50.

Examples   Use a pattern to solve.

Ⓐ Find 2 ÷ 5.	**Ⓑ** Find 1.8 ÷ 6.	**Ⓒ** Find 3.2 ÷ 4.
200 ÷ 5 = 40	180 ÷ 6 = 30	320 ÷ 4 = 80
20 ÷ 5 = 4	18 ÷ 6 = 3	32 ÷ 4 = 8
2 ÷ 5 = 0.4	1.8 ÷ 6 = 0.3	3.2 ÷ 4 = 0.8

MATH IDEA   When the divisor is greater than the dividend, the quotient is a decimal less than 1.

▶ Check

1. **Explain** what happens to the quotient in Examples A–C as the dividend gets smaller.

Remember

In any whole number, a decimal point is to the right of the ones place.

50 = 50.
        ↑

Copy and complete each pattern.

2. 100 ÷ 5 = ■

   10 ÷ 5 = ■

   1 ÷ 5 = ■

3. 400 ÷ 8 = ■

   40 ÷ 8 = ■

   4 ÷ 8 = ■

4. 600 ÷ 8 = ■

   60 ÷ 8 = ■

   6 ÷ 8 = ■

Copy and complete each pattern.

5. $300 \div 5 = \blacksquare$
$30 \div 5 = \blacksquare$
$3 \div 5 = \blacksquare$

6. $160 \div 4 = \blacksquare$
$16 \div 4 = \blacksquare$
$1.6 \div 4 = \blacksquare$

7. $720 \div 8 = \blacksquare$
$72 \div 8 = \blacksquare$
$7.2 \div 8 = \blacksquare$

8. $400 \div 5 = \blacksquare$
$40 \div 5 = \blacksquare$
$4 \div 5 = \blacksquare$

9. $250 \div 5 = \blacksquare$
$25 \div 5 = \blacksquare$
$2.5 \div 5 = \blacksquare$

10. $630 \div 9 = \blacksquare$
$63 \div 9 = \blacksquare$
$6.3 \div 9 = \blacksquare$

ALGEBRA   **Copy and complete each table. Use patterns and mental math.**

11. Divide by 25.

Input	Output
10,000	▨
1,000	▨
100	▨
10	▨

12. Divide by 40.

Input	Output
28,000	▨
▨	70
▨	7
28	▨

13. Divide by 8.

Input	Output
2,000	▨
200	▨
▨	2.5
2	▨

Write the check for each division problem.

14. $10 \div 2 = 5$
$1 \div 2 = 0.5$

15. $5,000 \div 10 = 500$
$5 \div 10 = 0.5$

16. $360 \div 6 = 60$
$3.6 \div 6 = 0.6$

17. REASONING Continue the pattern until the quotient extends to the hundredths place:

$$560 \div 7 = 80$$
$$56 \div 7 = 8$$

18. Amy bought 5 bags of peanuts for $3.00. Did she pay more or less than $0.50 for each bag? Explain.

19. ✎ **Write About It** Show how a pattern beginning with $640 \div 8 = 80$ leads to a decimal quotient of 0.8.

20. A bus traveled 3,000 miles over 6 days. If it covered the same route every day, how long was the route?

21. Find values for ♦ and ▼ that make the equation true. $♦ \div ▼ = 0.5$

22. John boarded his dog at the kennel and paid $72. It costs $20 for the first day and $13 for each additional day. How many days did he board his dog?

Mixed Review and Test Prep

23. $152,073$ (p. 150)
$$\underline{\times \qquad 6}$$

24. $81,514 \times 28$ (p. 154)

25. $8,041 \div 48$ (p. 212)

26. Which addition property is illustrated in $306 + (28 + 4) = (306 + 28) + 4$? (p. 76)

27. TEST PREP Which is the quotient for $1,400 \div 7$? (p. 198)

A 2   C 200
B 20   D 2,000

Decimal Division

▶ **Explore**

You can make a model to find the quotient of a decimal divided by a whole number.

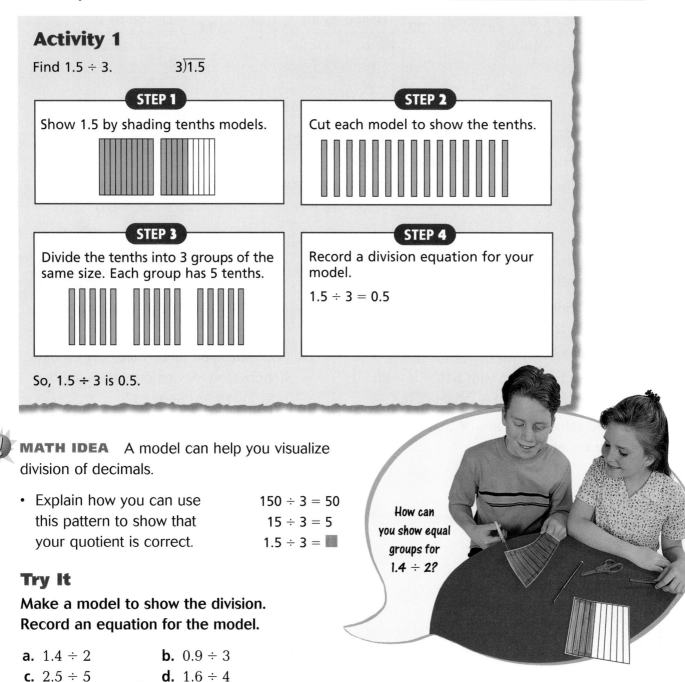

Activity 1

Find $1.5 \div 3$. $3\overline{)1.5}$

STEP 1

Show 1.5 by shading tenths models.

STEP 2

Cut each model to show the tenths.

STEP 3

Divide the tenths into 3 groups of the same size. Each group has 5 tenths.

STEP 4

Record a division equation for your model.

$1.5 \div 3 = 0.5$

So, $1.5 \div 3$ is 0.5.

⚠ **MATH IDEA**   A model can help you visualize division of decimals.

- Explain how you can use this pattern to show that your quotient is correct.

$150 \div 3 = 50$
$15 \div 3 = 5$
$1.5 \div 3 = \blacksquare$

How can you show equal groups for $1.4 \div 2$?

Try It

Make a model to show the division. Record an equation for the model.

a. $1.4 \div 2$ **b.** $0.9 \div 3$
c. $2.5 \div 5$ **d.** $1.6 \div 4$

▷ **Connect**

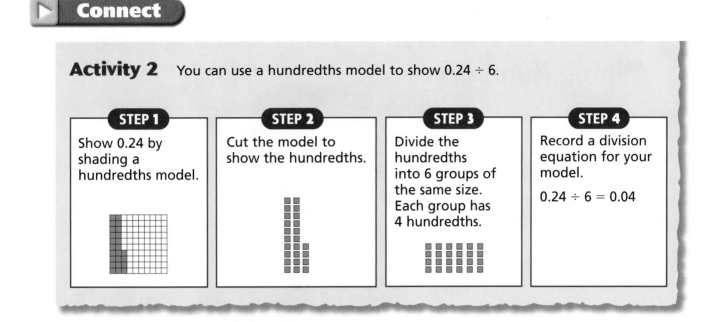

Activity 2 You can use a hundredths model to show 0.24 ÷ 6.

STEP 1	STEP 2	STEP 3	STEP 4
Show 0.24 by shading a hundredths model.	Cut the model to show the hundredths.	Divide the hundredths into 6 groups of the same size. Each group has 4 hundredths.	Record a division equation for your model. $0.24 \div 6 = 0.04$

▷ **Practice and Problem Solving**

Make a model and find the quotient.

1. $0.08 \div 2$ **2.** $\$0.24 \div 2$ **3.** $0.15 \div 3$

4. $1.2 \div 4$ **5.** $\$0.12 \div 4$ **6.** $3.5 \div 5$

7. $2.4 \div 3$ **8.** $0.08 \div 8$ **9.** $\$0.39 \div 3$

10. $\$0.44 \div 2$ **11.** $0.18 \div 9$ **12.** $0.18 \div 6$

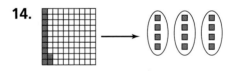

Technology Link

More Practice:
Harcourt Mega Math
The Number Games,
Tiny's Think Tank,
Level S
Buggy Bargains,
Levels N, O, and P

Use the model to find the value of *n*.

13.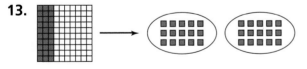

$0.30 \div 2 = n$

14.

$0.12 \div 3 = n$

15. Mario bought 4 pieces of wood for a total of $7.20. If two of the pieces together cost $4.20, and each of the other two pieces had the same cost, how much was each remaining piece?

16. ❓ **What's the Error?** Look at the model below for $0.16 \div 4$. Describe and correct the error.

Mixed Review and Test Prep

17. $\begin{array}{r} 5{,}000 \\ -3{,}436 \end{array}$ (p. 46)   **18.** $\begin{array}{r} 4.846 \\ +1.404 \end{array}$ (p. 48)

20. Write an equivalent decimal for 0.90. (p. 26)

19. Write four and one thousandth as a decimal. (p. 22)

21. **TEST PREP** Solve for *n*. $58 = n + 39$ (p. 70)

A $n = 9$ **C** $n = 20$
B $n = 19$ **D** $n = 90$

Divide Decimals by Whole Numbers

▶ **Learn**

UP, UP, AND AWAY Paulo and his friends are making 3 kites. To make the tails for the kites, they will cut a narrow piece of cloth that is 4.2 meters long into 3 equal lengths. How long will each piece of cloth be?

◀ **One of the largest kites ever flown had an area of 5,952 square feet.**

Example

Find 4.2 ÷ 3.
Estimate. 3 ÷ 3 = 1

One Way You can divide by using a model.

STEP 1	STEP 2
Shade decimal models to show 4.2.	Divide the models into 3 groups of the same size.

- Explain how you know how many wholes and how many tenths to put in each of the 3 equal groups.

Another Way You can divide by using paper and pencil.

STEP 1

Write the decimal point of the quotient above the decimal point of the dividend.

$$3\overline{)4.2}$$

STEP 2

Divide as you would divide whole numbers.

$$\begin{array}{r} 1.4 \\ 3\overline{)4.2} \\ -3 \\ \hline 12 \\ -12 \\ \hline 0 \end{array}$$

So, each piece of cloth will be 1.4 meters long. Since the answer is close to the estimate, the answer is reasonable.

More Examples

Ⓐ

Find 2.49 ÷ 3.

```
     0.83
  3)2.49
    -0
     24
    -24
     09
     -9
      0
```
← The divisor is greater than the dividend, so place a zero in the ones place.

You can multiply to check your answer.

Check ✓

```
   0.83
 ×    3
   2.49
```

Ⓑ

Find $18.45 ÷ 15.

```
      $1.23
  15)$18.45
     -15
      34
     -30
      45
     -45
       0
```
← When you divide money, remember to include a dollar sign in the quotient.

Check ✓

```
   $1.23
 ×    15
    615
  +123
  $18.45
```

Ⓒ

Find 5.628 ÷ 4.

```
      1.407
  4)5.628
    -4
     16
    -16
     02
     -0
      28
     -28
       0
```
← Since 4 > 2, place a zero in the hundredths place.

Check ✓

```
   1.407
 ×     4
   5.628
```

MATH IDEA When the dividend is a decimal and the divisor is a whole number, divide as with whole numbers. Line up the decimal point in the quotient with the decimal point in the dividend.

▶ Check

1. **Explain** where you place the decimal point in the quotient when you divide a decimal by a whole number.

Draw a picture to show the quotient.

2. 1.26 ÷ 3

3. 2.38 ÷ 7

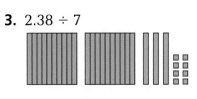

Copy the quotient and correctly place the decimal point.

4.
```
   0 5 3
 2)1.06
```

5.
```
   0 0 0 9
 5)0.045
```

6.
```
     7 0
 7)49.0
```

7.
```
    8 1 5
 4)32.60
```

Find the quotient. Check by multiplying.

8. 6)4.8

9. 9)$9.09

10. 4)12.04

11. 2)$1.04

12. 35.7 ÷ 7

13. $0.80 ÷ 5

14. 4.355 ÷ 5

15. 115.2 ÷ 24

LESSON CONTINUES

Copy the quotient and correctly place the decimal point.

16. 7)6.3
09

17. 4)8.08
202

18. 8)6.00
075

19. 15)4.05
027

20. 6)4.272
0712

21. 3)0.366
0122

22. 8)27.28
341

23. 5)61.80
1236

Find the quotient. Check by multiplying.

24. 8)74.4

25. 3)27.9

26. 5)$55.55

27. 2)19.64

28. 7)85.4

29. 70)854.0

30. 3)$93.66

31. 4)9.064

32. 8)$33.04

33. 4)21.56

34. 14)59.22

35. 19)$234.84

36. 12)39.0

37. 10)212.5

38. 9)343.89

39. 11)570.9

40. 24.6 ÷ 6

41. $2.46 ÷ 6

42. 0.93 ÷ 3

43. 8.05 ÷ 7

44. 0.54 ÷ 6

45. 5.04 ÷ 8

46. 72.64 ÷ 8

47. 48.6 ÷ 9

48. 48.3 ÷ 7

49. 18.5 ÷ 5

50. 21.6 ÷ 4

51. $4.24 ÷ 8

USE DATA For 52–55, use the data in the list.

52. How much did Blair pay for 1 paintbrush?

53. How much did Bryan pay for 2 yards of ribbon?

54. Ian bought 6 silk flowers and 2 glue sticks. How much did he spend?

55. ✎ Write a problem that uses data in the list and is solved by dividing a decimal. Solve your problem.

56. ▤*FAST FACT* • HISTORY The world record for the longest "kite fly" is 180 hours. How many days is 180 hours? Write the answer as a decimal. (HINT: 180 = 180.0)

57. **Vocabulary Power** The word *equation* comes from the Latin root word *aequus,* which means "level" or "equal." Write the equation that shows 8 wholes and 4 tenths divided into 2 equal groups.

Price List
Paintbrushes 3 for $7.47
Silk flowers $15.48 per dozen
Glue sticks 5 for $9.45
Ribbon $1.19 per yard

58. Tennis balls are 3 for $2.79 or $5.00 for a half dozen. Which is the better buy?

59. ❓ **What's the Question?** The difference between the prices of two bikes is $16. The sum of their prices is $232. The answer is $124.

Mixed Review and Test Prep

60. Divide 24,804 by 4. (p. 198)

61. $345 \div 2$ (p. 194)

62. Round 50,624 to the nearest thousand. (p. 38)

63. Write 213,675 in word form. (p. 4)

64. Compare 0.0989 and 0.989. Use <. (p. 28)

65. ⭐ **TEST PREP** Find y. $y + 42 = 80$ (p. 70)

    A $y = 38$ **C** $y = 118$
    B $y = 48$ **D** $y = 122$

66. Charlie recorded the daily high temperature for nine days: 79°F, 82°F, 74°F, 82°F, 78°F, 84°F, 76°F, 80°F, 82°F. What was the median temperature? (p. 102)

67. **TEST PREP** Janell bought 2 shirts for $11.98 each, a sweater for $18.98, and 3 pairs of socks for $2.05 a pair. How much did she spend in all? (p. 48)

    F $49.00   **H** $61.07
    G $49.09   **J** $140.05

Problem Solving Thinker's Corner 💡

REASONING Mr. Renard had $120 to buy supplies for his kite-making classes. After he finished shopping, he had $7.82 left. Mr. Renard lost his receipt and recorded what he remembered in the table below.

For 1–2, choose the best answer. Then copy and complete the table.

1. How can you find the total amount spent on all the supplies?

    A Find $17.88 + $25.50 + $14.80. Then subtract the sum from $120.00.

    B Subtract $7.82 from $120.00.

    C Add $120.00 and $7.82.

    D Add all the numbers in the table.

2. ✏️ **ALGEBRA** If b equals the cost per package for paintbrushes, which equation can you use to solve for b?

    F $b = \$14.80 \times 8$ **H** $b \div \$14.80 = 8$

    G $\$14.80 - b = 8$ **J** $\$14.80 \div 8 = b$

KITE-MAKING SUPPLIES			
Item Bought	Cost per Package	Number of Packages	Total Amount Spent
Kite fabric	$1.49	12	$17.88
Paints	$2.55	■	$25.50
Balsa wood	$3.00	■	■
Paintbrushes	■	8	$14.80
Total Spent →			■

Problem Solving Skill
Choose the Operation

UNDERSTAND ▷ PLAN ▷ SOLVE ▷ CHECK

"WEIGH OUT" IN SPACE   Beth used data she found on a class trip to the Space Museum to make this table. The table shows how much a 1-pound weight on Earth would weigh on other planets.

ONE EARTH POUND IN SPACE	
Planet	Weight (in pounds)
Mercury	0.38
Venus	0.91
Earth	1
Mars	0.38
Jupiter	2.53
Saturn	1.07
Uranus	0.90
Neptune	1.10
Pluto	0.07

MATH IDEA   The way numbers in a problem are related can help you choose the operation needed to solve the problem.

Add	To join groups.
Subtract	To take away or compare groups.
Multiply	To join equal-sized groups.
Divide	To separate into equal-sized groups. To find out how many in each group.

Decide how the numbers in the problem are related. Name the operation needed to solve the problem. Then solve.

A. A cocker spaniel weighs 35 pounds on Earth. To the nearest pound, how much would it weigh on Jupiter?

B. The 9 moon rocks on display at the museum weigh a total of 3.69 pounds. What is the average weight of one moon rock?

C. How much more would a kitten that weighs 1 pound on Earth weigh on Jupiter?

D. How much would 2 hamsters weigh on Mercury if they weigh 1 pound each on Earth?

Talk About It

- Explain how you decided which operation to use to solve each problem.

- **What if** the cocker spaniel in Problem A weighed 27.5 pounds on Earth? To the nearest pound, how much would it weigh on Jupiter?

Solve. Name the operation or operations you used.
For 1–2, use the table on page 236.

1. On Earth, an astronaut's suit weighed 65.2 pounds, and the life-support systems weighed 41.6 pounds. About how much weight would this be on Saturn?

2. If a blue whale weighs 286,600 pounds on Earth, how much would it weigh on Mars?

3. Suppose a polar bear weighs 1,323 pounds and a walrus weighs 1,503 pounds. How much more does the walrus weigh than the polar bear?

4. Suppose 3 giant pandas weigh a total of 1,056 pounds. What is the average weight of the pandas?

In 1999, the record was set for the most animals on a space mission. On board the space shuttle were 1,500 crickets, 18 mice, 152 rats, 135 snails, 4 oyster toadfish, and 229 swordtail fish.

◀ Laika, the first living creature in space, was launched aboard *Sputnik 2* in 1957.

5. What operation would you use to find the total number of creatures on the mission?
   A multiplication   C subtraction
   B division   D addition

6. How many more crickets were there than all other animals combined?
   F 538   H 962
   G 872   J 1,500

Mixed Applications

USE DATA   For 7–8, use the bar graph.

7. What is the difference in speed between the fastest and slowest fish on the graph?

8. How long would it take a marlin to travel 1,000 miles?

9. The sixth-fastest fish is the wahoo. It swims 66 kilometers per hour. How many miles per hour does it swim? (1 kilometer equals 0.62 mile)

10. Anthony has a total of 74 inches of string to wrap 6 boxes. He uses 12 inches of string for each of the boxes. Find how many inches of string Anthony will have left after wrapping 6 boxes.

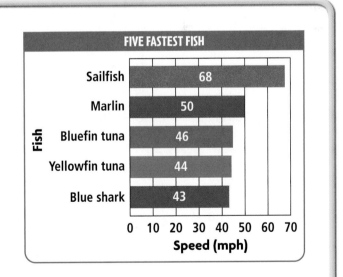

FIVE FASTEST FISH

Fish	Speed (mph)
Sailfish	68
Marlin	50
Bluefin tuna	46
Yellowfin tuna	44
Blue shark	43

0 10 20 30 40 50 60 70
Speed (mph)

11. ✍ Write a problem using the information in the graph above. Exchange problems with a classmate and solve.

5 Divide to Change a Fraction to a Decimal

► Learn

HAVING FUN! The students at Lakeville School are planning their school carnival. After school, $\frac{2}{5}$ of the students planned the game booths and $\frac{1}{4}$ of the students planned the food booths. Did more students plan the food or the game booths?

One way to compare fractions that have different denominators is to change the fractions to decimals.

MATH IDEA Change a fraction to an equivalent decimal by dividing the numerator by the denominator.

Example Compare $\frac{2}{5}$ and $\frac{1}{4}$.

STEP 1

Write each fraction as a division problem.

$$\frac{2}{5} \rightarrow 5\overline{)2}$$

$$\frac{1}{4} \rightarrow 4\overline{)1}$$

STEP 2

Divide as with whole numbers. Place a decimal point and zeros as needed in the dividend. Place a decimal point and a zero in the quotient.

$$\begin{array}{r} 0.4 \\ 5\overline{)2.0} \\ -2\,0 \\ \hline 0 \end{array}$$

$$\begin{array}{r} 0.25 \\ 4\overline{)1.00} \\ -8 \\ \hline 20 \\ -20 \\ \hline 0 \end{array}$$

Remember

$\frac{1}{4}$ can be read as one fourth, one quarter, one out of four, or one divided by four.

Since $0.4 > 0.25$, $\frac{2}{5} > \frac{1}{4}$. So, more students planned the games.

More Examples   Write the fraction as a decimal.

A

$$\frac{1}{5} \rightarrow \begin{array}{r} 0.2 \\ 5\overline{)1.0} \\ -1\,0 \\ \hline 0 \end{array}$$

B

$$\frac{3}{4} \rightarrow \begin{array}{r} 0.75 \\ 4\overline{)3.00} \\ -2\,8 \\ \hline 20 \\ -20 \\ \hline 0 \end{array}$$

C

$$\frac{7}{8} \rightarrow \begin{array}{r} 0.875 \\ 8\overline{)7.000} \\ -6\,4 \\ \hline 60 \\ -56 \\ \hline 40 \\ -40 \\ \hline 0 \end{array}$$

You can also use a calculator to change a fraction to a decimal.

$$\frac{2}{5} = \boxed{2} \div \boxed{5} = \boxed{0.4}$$

Check

1. Explain how you know that $\frac{1}{4}$ and 0.25 are equivalent.

Write as a decimal.

2. $\frac{2}{10}$ **3.** $\frac{3}{5}$ **4.** $\frac{3}{8}$ **5.** $\frac{4}{8}$ **6.** $\frac{6}{10}$ **7.** $\frac{3}{20}$

Practice and Problem Solving   (Extra Practice, page 240, Set C)

Write as a decimal.

8. $\frac{7}{10}$ **9.** $\frac{23}{25}$ **10.** $\frac{9}{12}$ **11.** $\frac{2}{5}$ **12.** $\frac{2}{4}$ **13.** $\frac{2}{8}$

14. $\frac{3}{10}$ **15.** $\frac{17}{20}$ **16.** $\frac{5}{8}$ **17.** $\frac{1}{8}$ **18.** $\frac{4}{5}$ **19.** $\frac{6}{8}$

USE DATA   For 20–22, use the circle graph.

20. Use a decimal to name the part of the money Jake's family spent on souvenirs.

21. Use a decimal to name the part of the money Jake's family spent on rides and games.

22. What if Jake's family had bought food for $15 and saved the extra money? Use a decimal to name the part of their money they would have saved.

23. Jenny ran $\frac{6}{25}$ mile. Greg ran 0.21 mile. Who ran farther? Explain how you know.

24. Write a fraction that has a decimal equivalent that is greater than 0.5 and less than 0.75.

HOW JAKE'S FAMILY SPENT $100 AT THE CARNIVAL

Rides $25
Food $40
Souvenirs $20
Games $15

Mixed Review and Test Prep

25. Order 6.010, 6.101, and 6.001 from least to greatest. (p. 28)

26. Ricki filled her car's gas tank. She pumped 18.8 gallons of gas at $1.45 per gallon. How much change will she receive from $30.00? (p. 170)

27.   6,213 (p. 152)
     $\times$ 52

28.   1,559 (p. 154)
     $\times$ 274

29. TEST PREP   Which is the quotient for $62,320 \div 82$? (p. 212)

A 82   **C** 7,691

B 760   **D** 70,196

Standardized Test Prep

NUMBER SENSE, CONCEPTS, AND OPERATIONS

1. A stack of 9 identical math textbooks is 30.6 centimeters tall. How thick is each book?

   A 0.34 centimeter

   B 3.4 centimeters

   C 34 centimeters

   D 275.4 centimeters

2. At the deli, Mrs. Dawson asked for $\frac{1}{4}$ pound of roast beef. The clerk weighed that amount and printed a label showing the weight as a decimal. Which of the following was shown on the label?

   F 0.75

   G 0.60

   H 0.50

   J 0.25

3. **Explain It** A small wedge of cheese costs $3.75. About how much does the whole wheel of cheese cost? Explain how you found your answer.

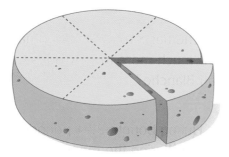

ALGEBRAIC THINKING

4. Brooke and Jamie each have a collection of troll dolls. Brooke has 8 more dolls than Jamie. If *d* represents the number of dolls that Jamie has, which expression describes the number of dolls that Brooke has?

   A $d - 8$

   B $8d$

   C $8 - d$

   D $d + 8$

5. Yuko is shorter than Sue. Sue is no more than 3 inches taller than Yuko. Sue is 51 inches tall. Which are the possible heights, in inches, for Yuko?

   F 48, 49, 50, 51

   G 49, 50, 51

   H 48, 49, 50

   J 47, 48, 49, 50

6. **Explain It** Name a rule for the table. Write the rule as an equation. Then copy and complete the table. Explain how you know your rule is correct.

n	p
21	6
33	18
15	■
47	■
59	44

MEASUREMENT

7. What is the volume of this toy box?

3 feet · TOYS · 2 feet · 6 feet

| Volume of rectangular prism = *l* × *w* × *h* |

- **A** 11 feet
- **B** 36 cubic feet
- **C** 36 square feet
- **D** 150 cubic feet

8. The area of a rectangular rug is 84 square feet. The width of the rug is 7 feet. What is the length of the rug?

7 feet · ?

| Area of rectangle = *l* × *w* |

- **F** 12 feet
- **G** 28 feet
- **H** 77 feet
- **J** 91 feet

9. Explain It ESTIMATE the area of the figure. Each square on the grid represents 1 square foot. Explain how you found your estimate.

DATA ANALYSIS AND PROBABILITY

TIP **Get the information you need.** See item 10. Look at the graph. Read the scale to determine the lengths of the bars. A bar halfway between 8 miles and 10 miles represents 9 miles.

10. The bar graph shows the results of the Annual Walk-a-Thon.

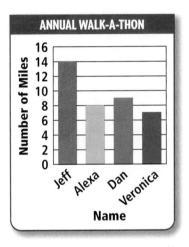

How many more miles did Jeff walk than Alexa?

- **A** 6 miles
- **C** 7.5 miles
- **B** 7 miles
- **D** 8.5 miles

11. Look at the graph in Problem 10. Suppose $2.00 is pledged for every mile walked. In all, how much money will the four friends raise?

- **F** $7.50
- **H** $76.00
- **G** $37.50
- **J** $750.00

12. Explain It Three fifth-grade students are running for class president. Ron wants to take a survey to predict the most likely winner of the election. Describe one way Ron can select a fair sample for his survey. Explain your choice.

Algebra: Use Multiplication and Division

≡FAST FACT • SOCIAL STUDIES
The largest flying flag in the United States is in Gastonia, NC. It covers 7,410 square feet, weighs 180 pounds, and takes at least 6 people to raise and lower it.

PROBLEM SOLVING   The flag is 65 feet wide. Write and solve an equation to find the length of the flag, using $A = l \times w$. See the table. Write and solve equations to find the missing dimensions for some United States flags.

DIMENSIONS OF SOME UNITED STATES FLAGS			
Flag	Length (*l*)	Width (*w*)	Area (*A*)
Gastonia, NC	■	65 ft	7,410 ft²
U.S. Capitol Building	8 ft	■	40 ft²
Betsy Ross Flag	3 ft	5 ft	■
Ft. McHenry Flag	42 ft	■	1,260 ft²

CHECK WHAT YOU KNOW

Use this page to help you review and remember
important skills needed for Chapter 12.

RELATE MULTIPLICATION AND DIVISION

Find the value of the variable. Write a related division equation.

1. $2 \times 6 = n$ **2.** $8 \times 4 = n$ **3.** $7 \times 9 = n$ **4.** $6 \times 8 = n$

5. $5 \times 6 = n$ **6.** $7 \times 8 = n$ **7.** $9 \times 6 = n$ **8.** $9 \times 9 = n$

USE PARENTHESES

Choose the expression that shows the given value.

9. 32
  a. $2 + (10 \times 3)$
  b. $(2 + 10) \times 3$

10. 0
  a. $15 - (3 \times 5)$
  b. $(15 - 3) \times 5$

11. 24
  a. $4 + (8 \times 2)$
  b. $(4 + 8) \times 2$

12. 12
  a. $12 + (0 \times 4)$
  b. $(12 + 0) \times 4$

MULTIPLICATION PROPERTIES

Write the letter of the multiplication property used
in each equation.

a. Order Property
b. Grouping Property
c. Identity Property
d. Zero Property

13. $8 \times 5 = 5 \times 8$

14. $(4 \times 2) \times 5 = 4 \times (2 \times 5)$

15. $(8 \times 2) \times 5 = 8 \times (2 \times 5)$

16. $25 \times 1 = 25$

17. $78 \times 0 = 0$

18. $4 \times 11 = 11 \times 4$

VOCABULARY POWER

REVIEW

algebra [al′ jə brə] *noun*

Algebra is a branch of mathematics
that deals with the relationships among
numbers. The word *algebra* comes from
an Arabic word meaning "the reunion of
broken parts, such as broken bones."
Explain how this definition relates to an
equation such as $4 + n + 8 = 15$.

PREVIEW

evaluate   Commutative Property

order of operations   Associative Property

function   Distributive Property

GO ON-LINE

www.harcourtschool.com/mathglossary

CHAPTER 13 Factors and Multiples

FAST FACT • SCIENCE Seed Savers Exchange in Decorah, Iowa, maintains 135 varieties of eggplant seeds. The exchange is an organization that gathers, grows, and distributes heirloom seeds. Heirloom seeds are rare vegetable, fruit, and flower seeds that have been passed down from generation to generation.

PROBLEM SOLVING How many packages of 50 seeds can be made from 1,500 heirloom eggplant seeds?

PACKAGES OF EGGPLANT SEEDS FROM 1,500 SEEDS	
Seeds per Package	**Complete Package? (Yes or No)**
20	■
30	Yes
40	No
50	■
60	■
70	No
80	■

Use this page to help you review and remember
important skills needed for Chapter 13.

FACT FAMILIES

Copy and complete each number sentence.

1. $4 \times 4 = \blacksquare$
$16 \div \blacksquare = 4$

2. $3 \times \blacksquare = 27$
$27 \div \blacksquare = 3$

3. $\blacksquare \times 5 = 40$
$40 \div \blacksquare = 5$

4. $6 \times \blacksquare = 42$
$42 \div \blacksquare = 6$

5. $8 \times 4 = \blacksquare$
$32 \div \blacksquare = 8$

6. $\blacksquare \times 9 = 45$
$\blacksquare \div 5 = 9$

7. $7 \times 2 = \blacksquare$
$\blacksquare \div 2 = 7$

8. $7 \times 8 = \blacksquare$
$56 \div \blacksquare = 8$

Write the fact family for each set of numbers.

9. 2, 3, 6

10. 2, 5, 10

11. 3, 7, 21

12. 3, 4, 12

13. 8, 11, 88

14. 4, 7, 28

15. 8, 9, 72

16. 7, 9, 63

17. 3, 6, 18

18. 6, 7, 42

19. 4, 8, 32

20. 5, 10, 50

MULTIPLES

Find the first six multiples of each number.

21. 4

22. 6

23. 5

24. 8

25. 9

26. 3

27. 7

28. 10

29. 11

30. 14

31. 12

32. 15

REVIEW

multiple [mul′tə•pəl] *noun*

Multiple is related to the Latin word
multiplicare and the concept of increasing.
Explain how this concept can be used to
describe the multiples of 7.

PREVIEW

divisible

greatest common factor (GCF)

common multiple

least common multiple (LCM)

 www.harcourtschool.com/mathglossary

Divisibility

▶ **Learn**

BRANCH OUT For the Arbor Day celebration, Duncan and Leila have 1,764 seedlings to divide evenly among some of the county schools. Can they divide the seedlings evenly among 2, 3, 4, 5, 6, 9, or 10 schools?

A number is **divisible** by another number when the quotient is a whole number and the remainder is zero.

Some numbers have a divisibility rule. Look at the divisibility rules below.

Quick Review

Find the quotient. Tell if the quotient is *even* or *odd*.
1. 54 ÷ 9   **2.** 48 ÷ 4
3. 93 ÷ 3   **4.** 180 ÷ 9
5. 153 ÷ 3

VOCABULARY

divisible

A number is divisible by		Divisible	Not Divisible
2	if the last digit is an even number.	324	753
3	if the sum of the digits is divisible by 3.	612	7,540
4	if the last two digits form a number divisible by 4.	6,028	861
5	if the last digit is 0 or 5.	5,875	654
6	if the number is divisible by 2 and 3.	3,132	982
9	if the sum of the digits is divisible by 9.	9,423	6,032
10	if the last digit is 0.	450	7,365

Example Use the divisibility rules to determine whether 1,764 is divisible by 2, 3, 4, 5, 6, 9, or 10.

STEP 1

Look at the last digit to check for divisibility by 2, 5, and 10.
The last digit is 4, so
• 1,764 is divisible by 2.
• 1,764 is not divisible by 5 or 10.

STEP 2

Find the sum of the digits to check for divisibility by 3 or 9.
The sum of the digits is
1 + 7 + 6 + 4, or 18, so
• 1,764 is divisible by 3 and 9.

STEP 3

Look at the last two digits to check for divisibility by 4.
The last two digits are 64, so
• 1,764 is divisible by 4.

STEP 4

Look to see if the number is divisible by 2 and 3 to check for divisibility by 6.
1,764 is divisible by 2 and 3, so
• 1,764 is divisible by 6.

So, the seedlings can be divided evenly among 2, 3, 4, 6, or 9 schools.
They cannot be divided evenly among 5 or 10 schools.

Check

1. **Explain** why a number that is divisible by 10 is also divisible by 2 and by 5.

Tell if each number is divisible by 2, 3, 4, 5, 6, 9, or 10.

2. 10   **3.** 18   **4.** 30   **5.** 56   **6.** 72

Practice and Problem Solving   Extra Practice, page 286, Set A

Tell if each number is divisible by 2, 3, 4, 5, 6, 9, or 10.

7. 24   **8.** 45   **9.** 108   **10.** 308   **11.** 519

12. 3,750   **13.** 2,604   **14.** 605   **15.** 1,896   **16.** 12,035

Leap years have 366 days. Every year whose number is divisible by 4 is a leap year, except years that end in two zeros. These years are leap years only when they are divisible by 400. Write *yes* or *no* to tell whether the year was a leap year.

Technology Link

More Practice:
Harcourt Mega
Math Ice Station
Exploration, *Arctic
Algebra*, Levels M, N

17. 1985   **18.** 2000   **19.** 1776   **20.** 1492

21. REASONING For what values of ■ is 2,3■1 divisible by 9? by 3?

22. Is the statement, "All numbers that are divisible by 3 are also divisible by 9" *true* or *false*? Explain.

USE DATA For 23–24, use the table.

23. The printer wants to package the "How to Care for a Tree" brochures into stacks with none left over. Can he put them in stacks of 6? stacks of 10?

24. The tree seedlings for the celebration come in trays of 28. If each tray costs $7, how much will be spent on seedlings?

ARBOR DAY CELEBRATION MATERIALS	
Item	**Number**
Tree Seedlings	1,764
Brochures	504
Shovels	9

25. Vocabulary Power The word *remainder* means "part left over." Explain how a remainder is used to determine divisibility.

26. ✎ **Write About It** What is the least number that is divisible by 2, 3, 5, and 10? Explain.

Mixed Review and Test Prep

27. 6.03 ÷ 9 (p. 232)   **28.** 0.12 ÷ 3 (p. 232)

29. Write $\frac{3}{4}$ as a decimal. (p. 238)

30. Write four million, four hundred twelve in standard form. (p. 4)

31. TEST PREP In which number does 6 have the greatest place value? (p. 4)

     A 4,346,470   **C** 387,650

     B 396,324   **D** 360,034

Greatest Common Factor

Quick Review

Name two multiplication facts for each product.

1. 6   **2.** 12
3. 24   **4.** 36
5. 45

VOCABULARY

greatest common factor (GCF)

▷ Learn

GREEN THUMB   Kevin and Celia are selling boxes of red petunia and pansy plants. Each box will have one type of plant, and all boxes will have the same number of plants. There are 12 red petunia plants and 18 pansy plants. What is the greatest number of plants Kevin and Celia can put in each box?

To find how many plants they can put in each box, Kevin and Celia found all the common factors of 12 and 18. Common factors for a set of numbers are factors of each number in the set.

Kevin listed the factors.   **Celia made a Venn diagram.**

Kevin

Factors of 12: 1, 2, 3, 4, 6, 12

Factors of 18: 1, 2, 3, 6, 9, 18

Common factors: 1, 2, 3, 6

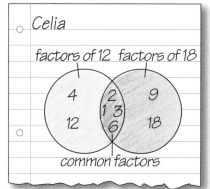

Celia

factors of 12   factors of 18

4   2   9
1 3
12   6   18

common factors

The greatest number of plants can be found by using the greatest common factor. The **greatest common factor**, or **GCF**, is the greatest factor that two or more numbers share. The greatest common factor of 12 and 18 is 6.

So, the greatest number of plants they can put in each box is 6 plants.

GCF of Three Numbers

What if there are 15 purple petunia plants to put into boxes? Now what is the greatest number of plants Kevin and Celia can put in each box?

Factors of 12: 1, 2, 3, 4, 6, 12
Factors of 18: 1, 2, 3, 6, 9, 18
Factors of 15: 1, 3, 5, 15

The GCF of 12, 18, and 15 is 3. So, they can put 3 plants in each box.

- **REASONING** Explain how you can tell if a number is a factor of another number.

MATH IDEA You can find the greatest common factor of two or more numbers by listing the factors and finding the greatest factor shared by all of the numbers.

Examples

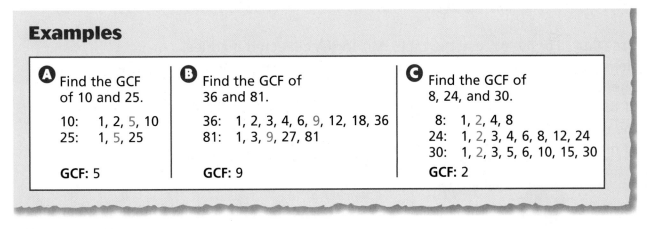

Ⓐ Find the GCF of 10 and 25.

10: 1, 2, 5, 10
25: 1, 5, 25

GCF: 5

Ⓑ Find the GCF of 36 and 81.

36: 1, 2, 3, 4, 6, 9, 12, 18, 36
81: 1, 3, 9, 27, 81

GCF: 9

Ⓒ Find the GCF of 8, 24, and 30.

8: 1, 2, 4, 8
24: 1, 2, 3, 4, 6, 8, 12, 24
30: 1, 2, 3, 5, 6, 10, 15, 30

GCF: 2

Check

1. **Explain** how divisibility rules can help you find common factors.

List the factors for each number.

2. 32	**3.** 55	**4.** 21	**5.** 17	**6.** 100
7. 37	**8.** 42	**9.** 56	**10.** 63	**11.** 77

Write the common factors for each set of numbers.

12. 6, 14	**13.** 8, 16	**14.** 30, 45	**15.** 18, 22	**16.** 5, 9, 18
17. 5, 25	**18.** 4, 24	**19.** 36, 54	**20.** 13, 19	**21.** 8, 12, 18

Write the greatest common factor for each set of numbers.

22. 4, 12   **23.** 5, 25   **24.** 3, 12, 18

LESSON CONTINUES

List the factors for each number.

25. 16   **26.** 20   **27.** 23   **28.** 28   **29.** 80

30. 15   **31.** 51   **32.** 31   **33.** 49   **34.** 50

Write the common factors for each set of numbers.

35. 2, 14   **36.** 11, 15   **37.** 30, 50   **38.** 13, 26   **39.** 5, 20, 45

40. 16, 20   **41.** 12, 14   **42.** 36, 45   **43.** 34, 51   **44.** 8, 16, 20

Write the greatest common factor for each set of numbers.

45. 6, 15   **46.** 12, 21   **47.** 7, 35   **48.** 18, 45   **49.** 6, 8, 12

50. 9, 15   **51.** 12, 36   **52.** 16, 24   **53.** 42, 49   **54.** 6, 50, 60

55. 14, 21   **56.** 12, 28   **57.** 8, 32   **58.** 21, 56   **59.** 4, 8, 16

USE DATA   For 60–61, use the table. Mr. Torres collected marbles. He is placing all the marbles in bags. Each bag will have only one kind of marble. All bags of the same color will have the same number of marbles.

MR. TORRES'S MARBLE COLLECTION				
Type	Swirl	Helmet Patch	Patch	Slag	Sunburst
Number	18	20	12	32	30

60. Mr. Torres is placing swirl and sunburst marbles in green bags. What is the greatest number of marbles he can put in a bag?

61. Mr. Torres is placing helmet patch, patch, and slag marbles in red bags. What is the greatest number of marbles he can put in a bag?

62. **? What's the Question?** Eva is making gift baskets. She has 18 ribbons, 36 barrettes, and 12 bracelets. All baskets must have the same number of each item with no items left over. Eva can make 6 baskets.

63. **REASONING**   I am thinking of two numbers. Each number is between 20 and 30. The greatest common factor of the numbers is 4. What are the numbers?

64. A total of 90 students were divided into 15 groups. In each group, there were 3 boys. How many girls were there in all?

65. **REASONING**   What is the greatest factor any number can have? What is the least factor any number can have?

66. **Write About It**   Explain how to find the greatest common factor of three numbers.

67. ▤ **FAST FACT • SCIENCE** Bamboo grows an average of 30 cm a day. Castor bean plants grow an average of 0.2125 cm an hour. Which grows more in an hour? Explain.

68. Four friends plan to hike a 102-mile section of the Appalachian Trail in 9 days. If they walk 10 miles each day, will they walk the length of the entire 102-mile section? If not, how many more miles will they have to walk?

Mixed Review and Test Prep

69.   2,901 (p. 150)
$$\begin{array}{r} 2,901 \\ \times \quad 9 \\ \hline \end{array}$$

70.   4,056 (p. 152)
$$\begin{array}{r} 4,056 \\ \times \quad 30 \\ \hline \end{array}$$

71. 9)320.58 (p. 232)

72. 11)7,524 (p. 212)

73. If a number is divisible by 4, what other number is it also divisible by? (p. 276)

74. Order 3.652, 3.562, and 3.256 from least to greatest. (p. 28)

75. **TEST PREP**   Find $(n - 6) \times 2$ if $n = 14$.
(p. 246)

  A 2   **B** 10   **C** 14   **D** 16

76. Round 56.754 to the nearest tenth. (p. 40)

77. Write six billion, five hundred six thousand, twenty-eight in standard form. (p. 4)

78. Write an equivalent decimal for 6.03. (p. 26)

79. **TEST PREP**   There are some rows with 25 seats in each row. Which expression models this situation? (p. 246)

  F $25 + n$ **H** $n \times 25$
  G $n \div 25$ **J** $25 \div n$

Problem Solving   LiNKUP . . . to History

Euclid, a Greek mathematician who lived more than 2,000 years ago, described another method for finding the greatest common factor in his book *Elements*. The method is now known as the **Euclidean algorithm**. He used division to find the GCF. Follow the steps to find the GCF of 220 and 60.

Example

STEP 1	**STEP 2**	**STEP 3**	**STEP 4**
Divide the greater number by the lesser number.	Divide the divisor, 60, by the remainder, 40.	Continue dividing the divisors by the remainders until the remainder is 0.	The divisor in the last division problem is the GCF.
$$\begin{array}{r} 3 \\ 60)\overline{220} \\ -180 \\ \hline 40 \end{array}$$	$$\begin{array}{r} 1 \\ 40)\overline{60} \\ -40 \\ \hline 20 \end{array}$$	$$\begin{array}{r} 2 \\ 20)\overline{40} \\ -40 \\ \hline 0 \end{array}$$	Since $40 \div 20$ has a remainder of 0, the GCF of 220 and 60 is 20.

Use the Euclidean algorithm to find the GCF for each pair of numbers.

1. 16, 60   **2.** 190, 36   **3.** 27, 40   **4.** 45, 330   **5.** 90, 105

Multiples and the Least Common Multiple

HANDS ON

Quick Review

Count by

1. fives from 5 to 30.
2. threes from 3 to 18.
3. fours from 4 to 24.
4. sixes from 6 to 36.
5. eights from 8 to 40.

VOCABULARY

common multiple
least common multiple (LCM)

MATERIALS

red and yellow counters

▶ **Explore**

A multiple is the product of two or more nonzero whole numbers.

When a number is a multiple of two or more numbers in a set, it is a **common multiple**.

The least number that is a common multiple of two or more numbers is the **least common multiple**, or **LCM**.

Activity

You can make a model to find the least common multiple of 3 and 5.

STEP 1

Place 3 red counters in a row. Place 5 yellow counters in a row directly below.

STEP 2

Continue placing groups of 3 red counters and groups of 5 yellow counters until both rows have the same number of counters. At that point, the number of counters in each row is the least common multiple, or LCM, of 3 and 5.

There are 15 counters in each row. So, the least common multiple of 3 and 5 is 15.

Try It

Use counters to find the least common multiple for each set of numbers.

What should you do next to find the LCM of 2 and 7?

a. 2, 7   b. 4, 5   c. 4, 8

d. 3, 4   e. 2, 3, 6   f. 2, 3, 9

▶ Connect

You can also find the LCM of two or more numbers by making a list or by using a number line.

Make a List	Use a Number Line
Multiples of 4: 4, 8, **12**, 16, 20, 24 Multiples of 6: 6, **12**, 18, 24, 30, 36 LCM of 4 and 6: 12	
Multiples of 3: 3, 6, 9, 12, 15, **18**, 21, 24 Multiples of 6: 6, 12, **18**, 24, 30, 36, 42 Multiples of 9: 9, **18**, 27, 36, 45, 54, 63 LCM of 3, 6, and 9: 18	

▶ Practice and Problem Solving

List the first six multiples of each number.

1. 4 **2.** 5 **3.** 6 **4.** 8 **5.** 9

Write the least common multiple for each set of numbers.

6. 2, 3 **7.** 3, 7 **8.** 16, 48 **9.** 4, 16, 96 **10.** 24, 27, 108

USE DATA For 11–12, use the graph.

11. What are the least numbers of packs of glass and ceramic beads you have to buy to have the same number of each type of bead?

12. What are the least numbers of packs of glass, wooden, and silver beads you have to buy to have the same number of each type of bead?

13. The LCM of two numbers is 24. Their GCF is 4. The numbers differ by 4. What are the numbers?

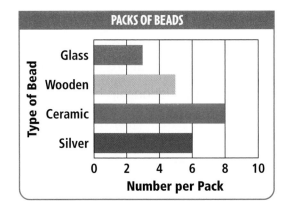

PACKS OF BEADS

⌐Mixed Review **and** Test Prep

14. 23.45 × 3.5 (p. 170) **15.** 3.85 ÷ 7 (p. 232)

16. Compare. Write <, >, or =.
67.031 ● 67.103 (p. 28)

17. Solve for *n*. 35 = *n* − 21 (p. 70)

18. **TEST PREP** After buying 3 markers for $1.25 each, Sarah had $3.45 left. How much did Sarah have before she made her purchases? (p. 236)

A $3.75 **B** $4.70 **C** $7.20 **D** $10.00

Problem Solving Skill
Identify Relationships

UNDERSTAND > PLAN > SOLVE > CHECK

THEY'RE RELATED!   When you test numbers for divisibility or find the least common multiple (LCM) or greatest common factor (GCF), you are *identifying relationships* between numbers.

Lynn and Lynda used this table to help them find relationships between two numbers and their LCM and GCF.

First Number, *a*	Second Number, *b*	*a* × *b*	GCF	LCM	GCF × LCM
2	3	6	1	6	6
4	6	24	2	12	24
5	10	50	5	10	50
7	3	21	1	21	21
9	3	27	3	9	27
60	3	180	3	60	180

Talk About It

* Look at 2 and 3 in the first row of the table. When 1 is the GCF of two numbers, what is the LCM?

* Look at 5 and 10. If the GCF of two numbers is one of the numbers, what is the LCM?

* Look at 9 and 3. If one number is divisible by the other number, what are the GCF and LCM?

* What is the relationship between the product of two numbers and the product of their GCF and LCM?

Examples

A
The GCF of 3 and another number is 1. The LCM is 15. What is the other number?

Think: When 1 is the GCF of two numbers, the LCM is the product of the numbers, *a* × *b*.

$3 × b = 15$ ← 3 times what number equals 15?

$b = 5$

So, the other number is 5.

B
The GCF of 4 and 20 is 4. What is the LCM of 4 and 20?

Think: When the GCF of two numbers is one of the numbers, the LCM is the other number.

So, the LCM is 20.

Use the relationships between the given numbers to find the missing number.

1. The GCF of 7 and another number is 1. The LCM is 28. What is the other number?

2. The GCF of 3 and 21 is 3. What is the LCM of 3 and 21?

3. The LCM of 25 and 75 is 75. What is the GCF of 25 and 75?

4. The LCM of 12 and 36 is 36. What is the GCF of 12 and 36?

5. Which statement describes a relationship between 14 and 17?

   A The GCF is 2.
   B The LCM is 238.
   C Both numbers are multiples of 2.
   D Both numbers are even.

6. Which statement does *not* describe a relationship between 8 and 14?

   F The GCF is 2.
   G The LCM is 112.
   H GCF × LCM = 112
   J Both numbers are even.

Mixed Applications

7. Carlos divided 60 by a number and got 2.5 for an answer. Is the number greater than or less than 70? Explain.

8. What is the number of pieces of string you can get by using 16 cuts to cut apart a straight piece of string?

9. How many angles are in 3 triangles, 4 squares, and 1 pentagon?

10. What is the average of all the numbers from 1 to 50 that are divisible by 4?

USE DATA For 11–12, use the table.

11. Find the range, mean, median, and mode for the data.

12. What if the membership of each club doubles? What are the range, mean, median, and mode for the new set of data?

13. Dave packed oranges into boxes, 36 oranges per box. He then packed the boxes into crates, 16 boxes per crate. When he finished, he had 4 crates, 11 boxes, and 23 loose oranges. How many oranges did he have when he started?

14. ✎ Write a problem about a relationship between a pair of numbers. Use the GCF or LCM.

MOTHERS OF TWINS AND TRIPLETS CLUBS

Club	Number of Members
1	27
2	35
3	32
4	25
5	27
6	34

Extra Practice

Set A (pp. 276–277)

Tell if each number is divisible by 2, 3, 4, 5, 6, 9, or 10.

1. 15   2. 26   3. 60   4. 132   5. 725

6. 1,410   7. 135   8. 109   9. 15,324   10. 378

11. 1,618   12. 16,836   13. 855   14. 740   15. 234

16. 489   17. 1,971   18. 2,538   19. 620   20. 396

Is the statement true or false? Explain.

21. All even numbers are divisible by 4.   22. All odd numbers are divisible by 3.

23. All numbers divisible by 6 are divisible by 3.   24. Some even numbers are divisible by 5.

Set B (pp. 278–281)

List the factors for each number.

1. 3   2. 17   3. 32   4. 75   5. 100

6. 36   7. 56   8. 120   9. 60   10. 132

Write the common factors for each set of numbers.

11. 17, 18   12. 12, 32   13. 10, 50   14. 35, 75   15. 60, 100

16. 18, 20   17. 15, 63   18. 25, 80   19. 6, 24   20. 27, 54

Write the greatest common factor for each set of numbers.

21. 2, 12   22. 6, 21   23. 14, 28   24. 30, 36   25. 9, 27

26. 16, 18   27. 27, 33   28. 48, 72   29. 24, 54   30. 20, 35

For 31–32, use the table.

31. Gina is making packages with toothbrushes and toothpaste. What is the greatest number of identical packages she can make without any items left over? How many of each item will be in each package?

32. Kevin is placing bandages and bars of soap in bags for his classmates. How many identical bags can he make, and how many of each item will be in each bag if none are left over?

HEALTH FAIR SAMPLES	
Item	Number
Toothbrushes	72
Toothpaste	48
Bars of soap	75
Adhesive bandages	100

Review/Test

✓ CHECK VOCABULARY AND CONCEPTS

Choose the best term from the box.

1. The least number that is a common multiple of two or more numbers is called the __?__. (p. 282)

2. Multiples of one number that are also multiples of another number are called __?__. (p. 282)

3. The number 45 is __?__ by 9 because the remainder is 0 when 45 is divided by 9. (p. 276)

4. The __?__ of 20 and 30 is 10. (p. 278)

> common multiples
>
> divisible
>
> greatest common factor (GCF)
>
> least common multiple (LCM)

✓ CHECK SKILLS

Tell if each number is divisible by 2, 3, 4, 5, 6, 9, or 10. (pp. 276–277)

5. 42	**6.** 48	**7.** 56	**8.** 63	**9.** 66
10. 90	**11.** 264	**12.** 681	**13.** 1,245	**14.** 6,460

Write the common factors for each set of numbers. (pp. 278–281)

15. 8, 14   **16.** 24, 28   **17.** 4, 12, 20   **18.** 8, 16, 32

Write the greatest common factor for each set of numbers. (pp. 278–281)

19. 6, 12   **20.** 18, 32   **21.** 3, 15, 30   **22.** 6, 12, 36

List the first six multiples of each number. (pp. 282–283)

23. 3   **24.** 7   **25.** 9   **26.** 12

Write the least common multiple for each set of numbers. (pp. 282–283)

27. 5, 30   **28.** 8, 36   **29.** 10, 24, 120   **30.** 8, 32, 160

✓ CHECK PROBLEM SOLVING

31. Baseball cards come in packs of 20; race car cards, packs of 40; and football cards, packs of 50. What is the least number of packs of each that will give you the same number of each kind of card? (pp. 278–281)

32. The GCF of 11 and another number is 1. The LCM is 99. What is the other number? (pp. 284–285)

33. The LCM of 7 and 14 is 14. What is the GCF of 7 and 14? (pp. 284–285)

Standardized Test Prep

⭐ NUMBER SENSE, CONCEPTS, AND OPERATIONS

1. Which of the following shows 0.125 written in expanded form?

  A 100 + 20 + 5

  B 1 + 2 + 5

  C 0.1 + 0.2 + 0.5

  D 0.1 + 0.02 + 0.005

> **TIP** **Get the information you need.**
> See item 2. To find the first day they will volunteer on the same day, find the least common multiple of 4 and 6.

2. Mel and Jo volunteer at the hospital in March. Mel volunteers every fourth day beginning on March 4. Jo volunteers every sixth day beginning on March 6. Which is the first day they will volunteer on the same day?

  F March 6   **H** March 10

  G March 8   **J** March 12

3. A group of 90 students went on a field trip. The students were put into groups, with an equal number of boys and an equal number of girls in each group. If 48 boys went on the field trip, how many groups were there?

  A 6   **C** 8

  B 7   **D** 9

4. Explain It Feather eats 4 pounds of dog food each week. The food is sold in 20-pound bags. ESTIMATE to determine whether it will take more than 9 bags to feed Feather for one year. Explain your answer.

⭐ MEASUREMENT

5. The Dolphins show lasts 45 minutes. At what time does it end?

ANIMAL REVIEW	SHOW	TIME
	Flying Friends	10:30 A.M.
	Dolphins	10:45 A.M.
	Amazing Animals	11:00 A.M.
	Monkeys	11:15 A.M.

  F 11:00 A.M.

  G 11:30 A.M.

  H 11:45 A.M.

  J 12:00 P.M.

6. Look at the schedule above. The Amazing Animals show starts in 20 minutes. What time is it now?

7. Explain It Randy estimates that the height of the classroom door is about 800 centimeters. Is this estimate reasonable? Explain how you know.

ALGEBRAIC THINKING

8. There were 9 people at a party. After some other people arrived, there were 15 people at the party. If n represents the number of people who arrived later, which equation can be used to find n?

F $9 + n = 15$

G $n - 9 = 15$

H $15 + n = 9$

J $9 - n = 15$

9. The number line below shows the value of x.

Which of the following number lines shows the value of $x + 25$?

A

B

C

D

10. **Explain It** What are the next two numbers in the pattern?

50, 43, 36, 29, ■, ■

Explain how you decided.

DATA ANALYSIS AND PROBABILITY

11. The graph below shows sources of energy used in the United States. Hydroelectric and nuclear energy are used half as much as which other energy source?

F coal

G natural gas

H petroleum

J other sources

12. Look at the graph above. Which shows the part of energy sources from petroleum and coal together?

A 0.22

B 0.38

C 0.50

D 0.60

13. **Explain It** The ages of seven people at a picnic are 10, 6, 13, 20, 9, 25, and 15. If the 10-year-old leaves the picnic and a 17-year-old arrives, how will the median age of the people at the picnic change? Explain your answer.

14 Exponents and Prime Numbers

View of Earth
from near the moon

FAST FACT • SCIENCE Our solar system consists of the sun and nine planets. Earth is 150 million kilometers, or about 93 million miles, from the sun.

PROBLEM SOLVING Numbers can be written in word form, standard form, and expanded form with or without exponents. The table shows the average distances, from the sun, of the other eight planets in our solar system. Write the average distances for Mercury and Mars using expanded form with exponents.

AVERAGE DISTANCE TO SUN	
Planet	**Average Distance to Sun (km)**
Mercury	58,000,000
Venus	108,000,000
Mars	228,000,000
Jupiter	778,000,000
Saturn	1,429,000,000
Uranus	2,871,000,000
Neptune	4,500,000,000
Pluto	5,900,000,000

CHECK WHAT YOU KNOW

Use this page to help you review and remember
important skills needed for Chapter 14.

MULTIPLICATION AND DIVISION FACTS

Find the product.

1. 3×5 **2.** 5×12 **3.** 7×2 **4.** 9×1

5. 2×0 **6.** 4×8 **7.** 6×7 **8.** 8×9

Find the quotient.

9. $16 \div 2$ **10.** $21 \div 7$ **11.** $36 \div 6$ **12.** $44 \div 11$

13. $108 \div 9$ **14.** $144 \div 12$ **15.** $80 \div 10$ **16.** $64 \div 8$

FACTORS

Write all the factors for each number.

17. 9   **18.** 12   **19.** 18   **20.** 21

21. 36   **22.** 32   **23.** 20   **24.** 24

VOCABULARY POWER

REVIEW

array [ə•rā′] *noun*

An array is an arrangement of objects in
rows and columns. Describe a real-life
example of an array.

PREVIEW

exponent   prime number
base   prime factorization
square number   factor tree
composite number   square root

GO
ON-LINE

www.harcourtschool.com/mathglossary

Introduction to Exponents

▶ **Learn**

VOCABULARY

exponent
base
square number

ONE, TWO, FOUR, EIGHT . . . An amoeba is a one-celled organism that reproduces by splitting. After 1 amoeba split 5 times, there were $2 \times 2 \times 2 \times 2 \times 2$, or 32 amoebas.

You can use words, pictures, and numerical expressions to represent a number. The following all represent the number 5.

| five | 5 | V | $4 + 1$ | $(12 - 10) + 3$ |

You can also represent a number by using an exponent and a base. An **exponent** shows how many times a number, called the **base**, is used as a factor.

$$
\underbrace{32 = 2 \times 2 \times 2 \times 2 \times 2}_{5 \text{ factors}} = 2^5
$$

exponent ↓   ↑ base

Read the expression 2^5 as "the fifth power of two."

So, 32 can be written as $2 \times 2 \times 2 \times 2 \times 2$, or 2^5.

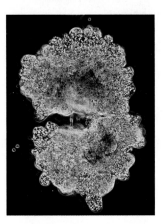

▲ Some freshwater amoebas travel between 0.5 and 3 microns per second. A micron is 0.001 millimeter. So, the fastest time for an amoeba 1-millimeter dash is about 5 minutes.

Examples

A Write 3×3 by using an exponent.
Think: 3 is used as a factor 2 times. The base is 3 and the exponent is 2.

So, $3 \times 3 = 3^2$.
Read: "the second power of 3," or "three squared."

B Find the value of 7^3.
$$
\begin{aligned}
7^3 &= 7 \times 7 \times 7 \\
&= (7 \times 7) \times 7 \\
&= 49 \times 7 \\
&= 343
\end{aligned}
$$

So, $7^3 = 343$.
Read: "the third power of 7," or "seven cubed."

C Find the value of 1^7.
$$
\begin{aligned}
1^7 &= 1 \times 1 \times 1 \times 1 \times 1 \times 1 \times 1 \\
&= 1
\end{aligned}
$$

So, $1^7 = 1$.
Read: "the seventh power of 1."

• Explain how you can use $4^3 = 64$ to find 4^4.

• What is the value of 1^3? of 1^5? of 1^9? Explain a rule for finding the value of any power of 1.

Square Numbers

A square number is the product of a number and itself. A **square number** can be expressed with the exponent 2.

Activity

MATERIALS: square tiles or grid paper

* Make a square array with 3 square tiles on each side. How many tiles did you use?

* Make a square array with 4 square tiles on each side. Continue to make square arrays, using tiles or grid paper, until you have a square array with 12 tiles on each side. Copy, complete, and continue the table to show arrays with 1 to 12 tiles on each side.

Model				
Equal Factors	1×1	2×2	3×3	■
Exponent Form	1^2	2^2	■	■
Standard Form	1	4	■	■

* Write a rule for the number of tiles in each array.

* Suppose you have a square array with n square tiles on each side. How many tiles would be in the square array?

You can use a calculator to find the value of a number with an exponent.

$13^2 \rightarrow$ (1) (3) ^ (2) (Enter =) | 13^2 = 169 |

Check

1. **Explain** how you would rewrite 3^4 as a multiplication problem. What is the value of 3^4?

2. **Explain** how 2^6 and 6^2 are different.

Write in exponent form. Then find the value.

3. 9 cubed

4. $6 \times 6 \times 6 \times 6$

5. $4 \times 4 \times 4 \times 4 \times 4 \times 4$

Find the value.

6. 9^2

7. 4^3

8. 10^2

9. 4^4

10. 7^2

11. 2^4

12. 2^7

13. 1^5

14. 3^3

15. 5^3

LESSON CONTINUES ▶

Write in exponent form. Then find the value.

16. seven squared

17. the sixth power of 2

18. 11 cubed

19. $7 \times 7 \times 7 \times 7$

20. $3 \times 3 \times 3 \times 3 \times 3 \times 3 \times 3$

21. 15×15

Find the value.

22. 3^2
23. 8^3
24. 1^4
25. 4^5
26. 9^4

27. 11^2
28. 10^6
29. 3^4
30. 6^3
31. 10^3

32. 2^3
33. 0^5
34. 7^5
35. 14^2
36. 5^4

37. Use the expressions in the box. Write three pairs of expressions that have the same value.

$$4^2 \quad 1^7 \quad 2^6 \quad 4^3 \quad 1^5 \quad 2^4$$

ALGEBRA Find the value of *n*.

38. $3^n = 81$
39. $n^5 = 32$
40. $10^n = 1,000$
41. $n^3 = 125$

42. $n^2 = 121$
43. $8^n = 64$
44. $10^n = 100,000$
45. $n^4 = 1$

For 46–49, match the word expression with its value.

46. four cubed

a. $4 \times 4 \times 4 \times 4 \times 4 = 4^5 = 1,024$

47. four squared

b. $4 \times 4 = 4^2 = 16$

48. the fifth power of four

c. $4 \times 4 \times 4 = 4^3 = 64$

49. the sixth power of four

d. $4 \times 4 \times 4 \times 4 \times 4 \times 4 = 4^6 = 4,096$

USE DATA **For 50–51, use the schedule.**

50. Class B is in the science lab for 45 minutes. What time does Class B leave the lab?

51. Class D spends 50 minutes in the lab. How much time is there between the time Class C leaves the lab and Class D enters the lab?

SCIENCE LAB SCHEDULE		
Class	**Start Time**	**End Time**
Class A	9:30 A.M.	10:15 A.M.
Class B	10:35 A.M.	■
Class C	12:15 P.M.	1:05 P.M.
Class D	■	2:15 P.M.

52. **REASONING** Maria thinks that $5^4 = 625$. How can she use division to check her work?

53. ✎ Write a problem involving a number pattern. Explain how to find the sixth number in the pattern.

54. **Vocabulary Power** Many words used in mathematics also have meanings outside mathematics. Write a mathematical definition and a nonmathematical definition for *power*.

55. A bacterium cell splits into 2 every hour. How many cells will there be in 4 hours? in 7 hours?

56. Jacob has 18.75 meters of fencing that he needs to cut into 3 equal sections. After he has cut off one section, how long is the remaining fencing?

57. REASONING How can you use what you know about exponents to find the values of $(1.2)^3$ and $(0.4)^2$?

Mixed Review and Test Prep

Write as a decimal. (p. 238)

58. $\frac{6}{8}$ **59.** $\frac{7}{14}$ **60.** $\frac{8}{10}$ **61.** $\frac{3}{8}$

62. TEST PREP Which number is divisible by 9? (p. 276)

A 5,684   **C** 38,654

B 22,691   **D** 1,096,353

63. TEST PREP What is the GCF of 12 and 15? (p. 278)

F 3   **G** 6   **H** 60   **J** 180

64. Write an equivalent decimal for 0.010. (p. 26)

USE DATA For 65–66, use the stem-and-leaf plot of points scored.

65. What is the range of points scored? (p. 96)

66. What is the median for the points scored? (p. 102)

Stem	Leaves
5	8
6	8 9
7	2 2 8
8	0 4 5 6 8

Problem Solving   Thinker's Corner

PATTERNS WITH EXPONENTS You can make models of cubes to help visualize numbers with an exponent of 3. Look at the cube at the right. You can write the volume of the cube as 4^3.

Copy and complete the table.

1.

Model	⬜	⬜	⬜	⬜	⬜	⬜
Equal Factors	1 × 1 × 1	2 × 2 × 2	3 × 3 × 3	■	■	■
Exponent Form	1^3	2^3	■	■	■	■
Standard Form	1	8	■	■	■	■

2. How many small cubes do you need to make a large cube that is 25 small cubes along each edge?

3. Describe a pattern in the models shown in the table.

4. What is the exponent form for the volume of a cube with 50 tiles on a side?

5. Suppose you have a large cube with n small cubes along each edge. How many small cubes would be in the large cube?

Exponents and Expanded Form

Quick Review

Find the value.

1. 2^6 **2.** 3^3

3. 5^4 **4.** 8^3

5. 7^2

▶ Learn

You have learned how to find the value of expressions such as 2^2, 2^4, 10^3, and 10^5 that have 2 or a greater number as an exponent. How can you find the value of expressions that have 1 or 0 as an exponent?

HANDS ON

Activity

Look at the patterns below. What are the values of 2^1, 2^0, 10^1, and 10^0?

$2^5 = 2 \times 2 \times 2 \times 2 \times 2 = 32$
$2^4 = 2 \times 2 \times 2 \times 2 \quad\quad = 16 = 32 \div 2$ **Think:** Divide by 2
$2^3 = 2 \times 2 \times 2 \quad\quad\quad = 8 = 16 \div 2$ each time.
$2^2 = 2 \times 2 \quad\quad\quad\quad = 4 = 8 \div 2$
$2^1 = 2 \quad\quad\quad\quad\quad = 2 = 4 \div 2$
$2^0 = 1 \quad\quad\quad\quad\quad = 1 = 2 \div 2$

$10^5 = 10 \times 10 \times 10 \times 10 \times 10 = 100,000$ **Think:** Divide by 10 each time.
$10^4 = 10 \times 10 \times 10 \times 10 \quad\quad = 10,000 = 100,000 \div 10$
$10^3 = 10 \times 10 \times 10 \quad\quad\quad = 1,000 = 10,000 \div 10$
$10^2 = 10 \times 10 \quad\quad\quad\quad = 100 = 1,000 \div 10$
$10^1 = 10 \quad\quad\quad\quad\quad\quad = 10 = 100 \div 10$
$10^0 = 1 \quad\quad\quad\quad\quad\quad = 1 = 10 \div 10$

- Explain how to use the values of 2^2 and 10^2 to find 2^1 and 2^0 and 10^1 and 10^0.

- Start with 3^5 and make a similar pattern to find 3^1 and 3^0.

- Predict the values of the first power and zero power of any number greater than zero.

You can use these rules to find the value of numbers with 0 or 1 as an exponent.

The zero power of any number, except 0, is 1.	The first power of any number equals that number.
$2^0 = 1$ $9^0 = 1$ $10^0 = 1$	$2^1 = 2$ $9^1 = 9$ $10^1 = 10$

Expanded Form

The continent of Antarctica has a land area of about 5,404,000 square miles and is bordered by the South Atlantic, Indian, and South Pacific Oceans.

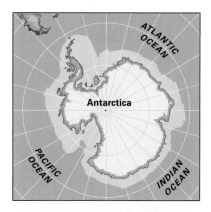

You can use powers of ten to show numbers in expanded form. The value of each digit in 5,404,000 can be expressed with or without an exponent. For example, the value of 5 can be written as 5,000,000, as $5 \times 1,000,000$, or as 5×10^6.

MILLIONS	THOUSANDS			ONES		
Ones	Hundreds	Tens	Ones	Hundreds	Tens	Ones
5,	4	0	4,	0	0	0
$5 \times 1,000,000$, or 5,000,000	$4 \times 100,000$, or 400,000	$0 \times 10,000$, or 0	$4 \times 1,000$, or 4,000	0×100, or 0	0×10, or 0	0×1, or 0
5×10^6	4×10^5	0×10^4	4×10^3	0×10^2	0×10^1	0×10^0

You do not need to write the value of a place with a zero digit. The land area of Antarctica can be written in expanded form with exponents as $(5 \times 10^6) + (4 \times 10^5) + (4 \times 10^3)$.

Examples

A Write 40,503 in expanded form with exponents.

$$40,000 = 4 \times 10^4$$
$$500 = 5 \times 10^2$$
$$40,503 \leftarrow 3 = 3 \times 10^0$$

$$40,503 = (4 \times 10^4) + (5 \times 10^2) + (3 \times 10^0)$$

B Write $(5 \times 10^5) + (6 \times 10^3) + (7 \times 10^2) + (8 \times 10^1) + (9 \times 10^0)$ in standard form.

Think:
$$(5 \times 10^5) = 5 \times 100,000 = 500,000$$
$$(6 \times 10^3) = 6 \times 1,000 = 6,000$$
$$(7 \times 10^2) = 7 \times 100 = 700$$
$$(8 \times 10^1) = 8 \times 10 = 80$$
$$(9 \times 10^0) = 9 \times 1 = 9$$

$$500,000 + 6,000 + 700 + 80 + 9 = 506,789$$

Check

1. **Explain** how you know the value of 5^1 and 5^0.

Find the value.

2. 3^0 3. 12^1 4. 10^1 5. 16^1 6. 7^0

7. Write 4,062,035 in expanded form with exponents.

8. Write $(2 \times 10^6) + (4 \times 10^5) + (7 \times 10^3) + (9 \times 10^1) + (5 \times 10^0)$ in standard form.

LESSON CONTINUES ▶

Find the value.

9. 8^1 **10.** 10^7 **11.** 2^0 **12.** 10^9 **13.** 12^0

14. 13^1 **15.** 5^6 **16.** 9^0 **17.** 10^1 **18.** 11^1

Write in expanded form with exponents.

19. 734,261   **20.** 15,934   **21.** 127,803   **22.** 25,000,005   **23.** 396,047

Write in standard form.

24. $(4 \times 10^6) + (5 \times 10^5) + (1 \times 10^3) + (2 \times 10^1) + (9 \times 10^0)$

25. $(1 \times 10^6) + (7 \times 10^4) + (4 \times 10^3) + (2 \times 10^0)$

26. $(2 \times 10^5) + (4 \times 10^4) + (9 \times 10^2)$

Copy and complete each table.

27.

Exponent Form	Standard Form
3^4	81
3^3	■
3^2	■
3^1	■
3^0	■

28.

Exponent Form	Standard Form
5^4	625
5^3	■
5^2	■
5^1	■
5^0	■

29.

Exponent Form	Standard Form
10^4	■
10^3	■
10^2	■
10^1	■
10^0	■

ALGEBRA Compare. Write <, >, or = for each ●.

30. 6^0 ● 2^0 **31.** 10^3 ● 2^{10} **32.** 1^7 ● 7^1

33. 10^2 ● 100^1 **34.** 1^0 ● 1^1 **35.** 8^0 ● 0^8

USE DATA For 36–37, use the graph.

36. Between which years did the population of Florida become greater than 10^7?

37. If the pattern continues, what is a reasonable estimate for the population of Florida in 2010?

38. Elianne earned $10 each week for 10 weeks of baby-sitting. Ricardo earned $17 each week for 6 weeks of mowing lawns. How much money did they earn altogether?

39. Cal puts 56 marbles into 7 bags so that each bag contains the same number of marbles. How many marbles are in 4 bags?

Population of Florida

40. ≡**FAST FACT** • SOCIAL STUDIES
Tallgrass prairie in North America once covered 142 million acres. Write the number of acres in standard form and in expanded form using exponents.

41. After Kelly paid $26.50 for books, $3.55 for paper, and $4.36 for pens, she had $5.98 left. How much money did she have to start?

Mixed Review and Test Prep

USE DATA For 42–43, use the table.

AVERAGE PRECIPITATION (IN.) OKLAHOMA CITY, OK					
Jan	Feb	Mar	Apr	May	Jun
1.1	1.6	2.7	2.8	5.2	4.3

42. **TEST PREP** What is the average monthly precipitation in Oklahoma City for the first three months of the year? (p. 232)

A 1.4 in. **C** 1.8 in.
B 1.6 in. **D** 2.7 in.

43. **TEST PREP** How much greater is the average precipitation in May than in April? (p. 48)

F 2.4 in. **H** 3.4 in.
G 2.6 in. **J** 3.6 in.

List the first six multiples. (p. 282)

44. 12 **45.** 8 **46.** 15 **47.** 16

Find the greatest common factor for each set of numbers. (p. 278)

48. 18, 45 **49.** 8, 10, 12

Problem Solving Thinker's Corner

ALGEBRA The binary, or base-two, number system uses only the digits 0 and 1.

decimal	0	1	2	3	4	5	6	7	8	9	10
binary	0	1	10	11	100	101	110	111	1000	1001	1010

In the decimal system, each place value is ten times the place value to the right. In the binary system, each place value is two times the place value to the right. You can use powers of 2 to find the decimal equivalent of a binary number.

$$10100_{two} = (1 \times 2^4) + (0 \times 2^3) + (1 \times 2^2) + (0 \times 2^1) + (0 \times 2^0)$$
$$= (1 \times 16) + (0 \times 8) + (1 \times 4) + (0 \times 2) + (0 \times 1)$$
$$= 16 + 0 + 4 + 0 + 0$$
$$= 20$$

Find the decimal equivalent of each binary number.

1. 1111_{two} **2.** 10001_{two} **3.** 11000_{two} **4.** 11111_{two} **5.** 101010_{two}

6. Explain the similarities and differences between the decimal number system and the binary number system.

HANDS ON Prime and Composite Numbers

VOCABULARY

composite number
prime number

MATERIALS
square tiles

▶ Explore

You can make rectangular arrays to find factors.

Activity 1
Show all the ways 6 tiles can be arranged in an array.

1
6
$1 \times 6 = 6$

6
$6 \times 1 = 6$

2
3
$2 \times 3 = 6$

You can show four arrays. So, the number 6 has four factors: 1, 2, 3, and 6.

3
2
$3 \times 2 = 6$

If a whole number has more than two factors, it is a **composite number**. So, 6 is a composite number.

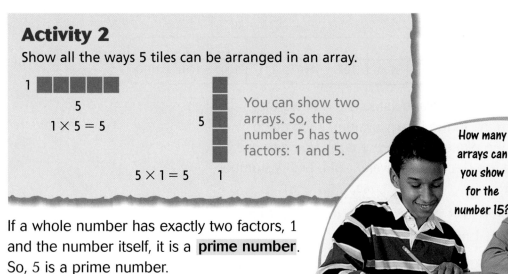

Activity 2
Show all the ways 5 tiles can be arranged in an array.

1
5
$1 \times 5 = 5$

5

$5 \times 1 = 5$ 1

You can show two arrays. So, the number 5 has two factors: 1 and 5.

How many arrays can you show for the number 15?

If a whole number has exactly two factors, 1 and the number itself, it is a **prime number**. So, 5 is a prime number.

Try It

Use tiles to show all the arrays for each number. Write *prime* or *composite*.

   a. 15   **b.** 9   **c.** 13   **d.** 7

▷ Connect

Use tiles to show all the rectangular arrays you can make for the numbers 2–12. Copy and complete the table below.

Number	Rows × Columns for Arrays	Factors	Prime or Composite?
2	1 × 2 2 × 1	1, 2	prime
3	1 × 3 3 × 1	1, 3	prime
4	1 × 4 ■ × ■ ■ × ■	■, ■, ■	?

⚡ **MATH IDEA** Every whole number greater than 1 is either prime or composite. The number 1 is neither prime nor composite.

- **REASONING** Explain why 2 is the only even prime number.

▷ Practice and Problem Solving

Use tiles to show all the rectangular arrays for each number. Write *prime* or *composite*.

1. 3   **2.** 10   **3.** 11   **4.** 12   **5.** 17

Write *prime* or *composite* for each number.

6. 7   **7.** 14   **8.** 21   **9.** 25   **10.** 23

11. 41   **12.** 32   **13.** 37   **14.** 49   **15.** 19

16. List all the prime numbers from 1 to 100.

17. List all the composite factors of 72.

18. Chris spent $24.00 at the pet store. He bought a toy for $4.50 and 2 bags of dog food. If the bags of food cost the same, how much did he spend on each bag?

19. ✏️ Write About It Explain the difference between a prime number and a composite number. Use examples in your explanation.

Mixed Review and Test Prep

20. Each child who visits the nature center is given 8 different leaves to help in tree identification. On Monday, 144 children visited the center. How many leaves were given out? (p. 150)

21. $8.4 - 1.69$ (p. 48)   **22.** 8×1.2 (p. 168)

23. Write $3,000,000 + 6,000 + 700 + 2$ in expanded form using exponents. (p. 296)

24. **TEST PREP** By which number is 612 NOT divisible? (p. 276)

   A 2   **B** 3   **C** 4   **D** 10

Prime Factors and Exponents

Quick Review

Write *prime* or *composite* for each.

1. 6   **2.** 5

3. 8   **4.** 12

5. 13

VOCABULARY

prime factorization

factor tree

square root

▶ **Learn**

PRIME TIME All composite numbers can be written as the product of prime factors. This is called the **prime factorization** of the number. To find the prime factorization of a number, you can use a diagram called a **factor tree**.

To use a factor tree to find the prime factorization of 36, first choose any two factors of 36. Continue factoring until only prime factors are left.

David and Luisa each made a factor tree.

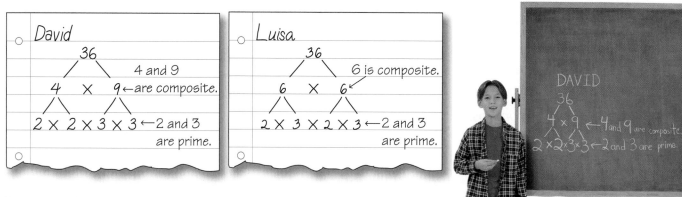

Because of the Commutative Property of Multiplication, $2 \times 2 \times 3 \times 3 = 2 \times 3 \times 2 \times 3$. Order the prime factors from least to greatest. So, the prime factorization of 36 is $2 \times 2 \times 3 \times 3$.

Examples

A What is the prime factorization of 40?

$$40$$
$$8 \times 5$$
$$4 \times 2$$
$$2 \times 2$$

So, $40 = 2 \times 2 \times 2 \times 5$.

B What is the prime factorization of 27?

$$27$$
$$9 \times 3$$
$$3 \times 3$$

So, $27 = 3 \times 3 \times 3$.

C What is the prime factorization of 630?

$$630$$
$$63 \times 10$$
$$9 \times 7 \times 2 \times 5$$
$$3 \times 3$$

So, $630 = 2 \times 3 \times 3 \times 5 \times 7$.

Exponents in Prime Factorizations

Sometimes you can use exponents to write the prime factorization of a number.

When a prime factor is repeated in a factorization, use the prime as the base and use the number of times it is repeated as the exponent.

$36 = \underline{2 \times 2} \times \underline{3 \times 3}$ ← 2 is a factor two times.
$\qquad\qquad\qquad\qquad$ 3 is a factor two times.

$36 = 2^2 \times 3^2$ ← So, use 2 for the exponents.

Examples D, E, and F show how you can write the prime factorization by using exponents for the numbers in Examples A, B, and C on page 302.

DAVID
$40 = \underline{2 \times 2 \times 2} \times 5$
$40 = 2^3 \times 5$

Examples

D $40 = \underline{2 \times 2 \times 2} \times 5$

$40 = 2^3 \times 5$

E $27 = \underline{3 \times 3 \times 3}$

$27 = 3^3$

F $630 = 2 \times \underline{3 \times 3} \times 5 \times 7$

$630 = 2 \times 3^2 \times 5 \times 7$

Notice in Examples D and F that exponents of 1 are not written.

Check

Technology Link
More Practice: Harcourt Mega Math Ice Station Exploration, *Arctic Algebra*, Levels O, W

1. **Explain** why you would not use the number 1 as a factor in a factor tree.

Copy and complete to find the prime factorization.

2. $5 \times 4 = 5 \times \blacksquare \times \blacksquare$

3. $6 \times 9 = \blacksquare \times 3 \times 3 \times 3$

4. $4 \times 4 = \blacksquare \times \blacksquare \times \blacksquare \times 2$

5. $2 \times 6 = 2 \times \blacksquare \times \blacksquare$

6. $35 \times 2 = \blacksquare \times \blacksquare \times 2$

7. $98 = \blacksquare \times \blacksquare \times \blacksquare$

Rewrite the prime factorization by using exponents.

8. $125 = 5 \times 5 \times 5$

9. $24 = 2 \times 2 \times 2 \times 3$

10. $100 = 2 \times 2 \times 5 \times 5$

11. $147 = 3 \times 7 \times 7$

12. $150 = 2 \times 3 \times 5 \times 5$

13. $5,929 = 7 \times 7 \times 11 \times 11$

Find the prime factorization of the number. Use exponents when possible.

14. 4

15. 21

16. 24

17. 19

18. 65

19. 10

20. 16

21. 28

22. 100

23. 155

LESSON CONTINUES

Copy and complete to find the prime factorization.

24. $3 \times 9 = 3 \times \blacksquare \times \blacksquare$ **25.** $5 \times 6 = 5 \times \blacksquare \times \blacksquare$ **26.** $8 \times 7 = \blacksquare \times \blacksquare \times \blacksquare \times 7$

27. $50 = 2 \times \blacksquare \times \blacksquare$ **28.** $6 \times 7 = \blacksquare \times \blacksquare \times 7$ **29.** $39 = \blacksquare \times \blacksquare$

Rewrite the prime factorization by using exponents.

30. $242 = 2 \times 11 \times 11$ **31.** $100 = 5 \times 2 \times 2 \times 5$ **32.** $338 = 2 \times 13 \times 13$

33. $275 = 11 \times 5 \times 5$ **34.** $220 = 2 \times 5 \times 2 \times 11$ **35.** $342 = 2 \times 3 \times 3 \times 19$

Find the prime factorization of the number. Use exponents when possible.

36. 18   **37.** 46   **38.** 22   **39.** 35   **40.** 243

41. 38   **42.** 44   **43.** 26   **44.** 196   **45.** 225

46. 125   **47.** 294   **48.** 135   **49.** 224   **50.** 686

ALGEBRA   **Complete the prime factorization. Find the value of the variable.**

51. $2 \times 2 \times 2 = 2^n$ **52.** $2^2 \times m = 28$ **53.** $3^s \times 5 = 45$

54. $3 \times 3 \times r = 3^3$ **55.** $5^n \times 11 = 275$ **56.** $5^2 \times s^2 = 1{,}225$

57. NUMBER SENSE What is the greatest square number that is a factor of 72 and a whole number?

58. Find the prime factorizations of all the composite numbers from 4 to 20. Use exponents when possible.

59. NUMBER SENSE The prime factors of a number are the first three prime numbers. No factor is repeated. What is the number?

60. REASONING Jen says the prime factorization of 24 is $2 \times 2 \times 2 \times 3$. Ralph says it is $2 \times 3 \times 2 \times 2$. Who is right? Explain.

61. Tamika spent $4.35, $14.15, and $19.45 at the mall. Did she spend more than $37? Explain.

62. Bill has to wait 98 days for his vacation. How many weeks does Bill have to wait?

For 63–64, use the factor tree.

63. **? What's the Error?** Tyler made this factor tree for 72. Describe and correct his error.

64. Make two other factor trees for 72.

65. Ohio has a population of about 11 million. Is the population greater than or less than 10^7?

66. Is 10^4 greater than, less than, or equal to $2^4 \times 5^4$? Explain.

67. Josh is shipping 4 cases of water. Each case holds 24 bottles. The 4 cases hold 1,536 ounces in all. How many ounces does each bottle hold?

68. Of 314 runners entered in a race, 29 were unable to finish. If those who finished ran a combined total of 2,280 km, how long was the race?

Mixed Review and Test Prep

USE DATA For 69–71, use the pictograph.

69. How many flowers are in Sue's garden? (p. 106)

FLOWERS IN SUE'S GARDEN	
Roses	🌸🌸🌸🌸🌸🌸
Tulips	🌸🌸🌸(
Carnations	🌸🌸🌸🌸🌸🌸🌸🌸🌸(
Daisies	🌸🌸🌸🌸🌸🌸🌸🌸🌸🌸🌸🌸

Each 🌸 = 10 flowers.

70. **TEST PREP** Sue wants to divide the roses equally among bouquets and do the same with the daisies. What is the greatest possible number of bouquets of roses and daisies without any roses or daisies left over? (p. 278)

  A 5 bouquets   **C** 10 bouquets
  B 8 bouquets   **D** 16 bouquets

71. **TEST PREP** Sue sells her carnations for $4.50 per box. Each box has 5 flowers. How much will she get for all the carnations? (p. 170)

  F $8.55   **H** $58.50
  G $19.00   **J** $85.50

72. 2,000 ÷ 5 = ■
    200 ÷ 5 = ■
    20 ÷ 5 = ■
    2 ÷ 5 = ■
    (p. 208)

73. 2,400 ÷ 8 = ■
    240 ÷ 8 = ■
    24 ÷ 8 = ■
    2.4 ÷ 8 = ■
    (p. 208)

74. What are the least common multiple and the greatest common factor of 24 and 36? (p. 284)

75. List all the numbers from 1 to 10 by which 48 is divisible. (p. 276)

Problem Solving LINKUP . . . to History

Ancient Egyptian mathematicians understood the idea of the square root. They used square roots to help solve geometric puzzles. Other cultures, including the Greeks, Chinese, and Babylonians, also studied square roots.

The **square root** of a number is a number that, when multiplied by itself, equals the original number.

Example

Find the square root of 9.
Think of the factors of 9: 9 × 1 and 3 × 3
You see that 3, when multiplied by itself, equals 9.
So, the square root of 9 is 3.

Find the square root of each number.

1. 16   **2.** 1   **3.** 100   **4.** 36   **5.** 144

Problem Solving Strategy
Make a Table

PROBLEM Liz is studying number patterns at school. For her project, she saves two pennies on Day 1, four pennies on Day 2, and eight pennies on Day 3. If she continues to double the number of pennies she saves each day for 10 days, how many pennies will she save on the tenth day? How much will she save in all?

UNDERSTAND

• What are you asked to find?

• What information will you use?

PLAN

• What strategy can you use to solve the problem?

You can make a table to organize the data. Then you can use the table to answer the questions.

SOLVE

• How can you organize the table?

Decide on a title and row labels. Find the daily amount represented by each number of pennies. Add the daily amounts to find the total amount Liz will save in 10 days.

AMOUNT OF MONEY SAVED										
Day	1	2	3	4	5	6	7	8	9	10
Number of Pennies	2	4	8	16	32	64	128	256	512	1024
Daily Amount	$0.02	$0.04	$0.08	$0.16	$0.32	$0.64	$1.28	$2.56	$5.12	$10.24
Total Amount	$0.02	$0.06	$0.14	$0.30	$0.62	$1.26	$2.54	$5.10	$10.22	$20.46

Next, use the table to answer the questions. Liz will save 1,024 pennies, or $10.24, on the tenth day. She will save $20.46 in all.

CHECK

• Look back at the problem. Do the answers make sense?

Problem Solving Practice

Strategies

Draw a Diagram or Picture
Make a Model or Act It Out
Make an Organized List
Find a Pattern
▶ **Make a Table or Graph**
Predict and Test
Work Backward
Solve a Simpler Problem
Write an Equation
Use Logical Reasoning

1. **What if** Liz continued saving pennies in the same way for 14 days? How much would she save in all?

2. Don saves $1 on Day 1 and continues to save one dollar more each day than the previous day for 14 days. How much will he save in all?

USE DATA Jane's mother buys her 4 sheets of stickers for every 5 days that Jane completes her chores. Copy and complete the table. Then use the table for questions 3–4.

STICKER SHEETS										
Days of Doing Chores	5	10	15	■	■	■	■	■	■	■
Total Number of Sheets	4	8	12	■	■	■	■	■	■	■

3. How many days will it take Jane to have 40 sheets of stickers?

   A 15   **B** 20   **C** 40   **D** 50

4. If there are 10 stickers on each sheet, in how many days could Jane earn 200 stickers?

   F 16   **G** 20   **H** 25   **J** 200

Mixed Strategy Practice

5. Sal walked 1.25 miles on Saturday, 1.75 miles on Sunday, and 1.75 miles on Monday. His goal was to walk a total of 5 miles. Did he reach his goal? How far did he walk in all?

6. **What's the Question?** Cheri wants to buy equal numbers of lemons and limes. Lemons are sold in packages of 4. Limes are sold in bags of 10. The answer is 20 lemons.

7. Ben's dad builds 3-legged stools and 4-legged tables. He used 60 legs to build 6 more stools than tables. How many stools and tables did he build?

8. Jack's family plans to cook 2 turkey burgers for every 3 people at a picnic. How many turkey burgers should they cook for 15 people?

9. Marshall is counting the number of people at the assembly. So far, he has counted 8 rows, with 8 people in each row, in each of 8 sections. How many people has he counted so far?

10. Les and his two brothers collect stamps. Les has twice as many stamps as his older brother, who has 42 stamps. Les has three times as many stamps as his younger brother. How many stamps do they have in all?

Extra Practice

Set A (pp. 292–295)

Write in exponent form. Then find the value.

1. $5 \times 5 \times 5 \times 5 \times 5$ **2.** 8 cubed   **3.** $10 \times 10 \times 10 \times 10$

4. $3 \times 3 \times 3 \times 3$ **5.** 4 squared   **6.** $4 \times 4 \times 4 \times 4$

Find the value.

7. 2^8 **8.** 4^6 **9.** 10^7 **10.** 7^4 **11.** 12^3

12. 1^7 **13.** 11^3 **14.** 9^4 **15.** 10^5 **16.** 3^5

17. 6^4 **18.** 10^8 **19.** 8^4 **20.** 3^6 **21.** 2^5

Set B (pp. 296–299)

Find the value.

1. 5^0 **2.** 4^1 **3.** 14^0 **4.** 8^0 **5.** 7^1

Write in standard form.

6. $(3 \times 10^6) + (2 \times 10^5) + (8 \times 10^2) + (1 \times 10^1) + (6 \times 10^0)$

7. $(9 \times 10^6) + (7 \times 10^5) + (4 \times 10^3) + (5 \times 10^0)$

8. $(1 \times 10^5) + (8 \times 10^3) + (2 \times 10^2)$

Write in expanded form with exponents.

9. 3,005   **10.** 5,120   **11.** 6,409   **12.** 7,158   **13.** 9,224

14. 12,504   **15.** 22,009   **16.** 18,030   **17.** 34,559   **18.** 80,003

Set C (pp. 302–305)

Rewrite the prime factorization by using exponents.

1. $45 = 3 \times 3 \times 5$ **2.** $150 = 2 \times 3 \times 5 \times 5$ **3.** $686 = 2 \times 7 \times 7 \times 7$

4. $882 = 2 \times 3 \times 3 \times 7 \times 7$ **5.** $120 = 2 \times 2 \times 2 \times 3 \times 5$ **6.** $825 = 3 \times 5 \times 5 \times 11$

Find the prime factorization of the number. Use exponents when possible.

7. 49   **8.** 54   **9.** 23   **10.** 36

11. 84   **12.** 25   **13.** 52   **14.** 60

Review/Test

✓ CHECK VOCABULARY AND CONCEPTS

Choose the best term from the box.

> base
> composite number
> exponent
> prime factorization
> prime number

1. The __?__ of a number is the number written as the product of prime numbers. (p. 302)

2. For 10^2, 10 is the __?__. (p. 292)

3. A number that has more than two factors is a __?__. (p. 300)

✓ CHECK SKILLS

Find the value. (pp. 292–295, 296–299)

4. 7^3 5. 15^0 6. 6^4 7. 10^2 8. 10^1

9. 12^2 10. 1^0 11. 9^3 12. 2^0 13. 5^4

14. 0^6 15. 13^1 16. 8^5 17. 4^6 18. 15^3

Write in expanded form with exponents. (pp. 296–299)

19. 16,741   20. 24,053   21. 340,204   22. 605,489   23. 701,039

Write *prime* or *composite* for each number. (pp. 300–301)

24. 13   25. 21   26. 101   27. 2   28. 57

29. 61   30. 85   31. 87   32. 47   33. 94

Find the prime factorization of the number. Use exponents when possible. (pp. 302–305)

34. 33   35. 30   36. 63   37. 42   38. 48

39. 72   40. 225   41. 150   42. 85   43. 96

44. 112   45. 166   46. 144   47. 210   48. 240

✓ CHECK PROBLEM SOLVING

49. Pam earns $6.50 an hour at a grocery store. Every six months, she will earn an increase of $0.50 an hour. What will her hourly pay be after 2 years? (pp. 306–307)

50. Kia has $15.00. If she saves $2.50 each week, how much money will she have after 8 weeks? (pp. 306–307)

Standardized Test Prep

⭐ NUMBER SENSE, CONCEPTS, AND OPERATIONS

1. The table shows packaging and price information about hot dogs and buns.

Item	Number per Package	Price per Package
Hot dogs	10	$2.75
Buns	8	$1.50

What is the **least** number of packages of hot dogs and buns Ted needs to buy to have as many hot dogs as buns?

A 4 packs of hot dogs and 5 packs of buns

B 5 packs of hot dogs and 6 packs of buns

C 7 packs of hot dogs and 9 packs of buns

D 8 packs of hot dogs and 10 packs of buns

> **TIP** **Decide on a plan.** Look at item 2. Using the strategy *work backward,* find the cost of the buns, and subtract it from the total cost. Then find how many packages of hot dogs were bought.

2. Look at the table above. Shana spent $14.25 on hot dogs and buns. If she bought 4 packages of buns, how many packages of hot dogs did she buy?

F 6	**H** 4
G 5	**J** 3

3. **Explain It** Explain how to ESTIMATE the number of students who will buy lunch at school in one week if 488 students bought lunch today.

⭐ GEOMETRY AND SPATIAL SENSE

4. Noah drew the figure shown below.

Which is Noah's figure after he flipped it vertically?

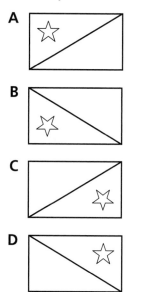

A

B

C

D

5. A band is marching due north. During the routine the band members make a 180° turn. In which direction are they marching now?

F north

G south

H east

J west

6. **Explain It** Evan has a rectangular patio with a perimeter of 20 feet. He knows that the width of the patio is 3 feet. Explain how he can find the length of the patio.

⭐ DATA ANALYSIS AND PROBABILITY

7. The graph shows the types of sports equipment sold during May.

SPORTS EQUIPMENT SOLD IN MAY

About how many pieces of equipment were sold in May?

A 24

B 60

C 80

D 90

8. Look at the graph above. Which type of sports equipment had the **most** sales in May?

F bats

G balls

H gloves

J helmets

9. **Explain It** Ariel has a spinner with 8 equal sections. Four of the sections are blue, 2 are yellow, and 2 are green. About how many times will Ariel have to spin the pointer of the spinner for it to stop on the blue section 5 times? Explain your answer.

⭐ ALGEBRAIC THINKING

10. Jean has $130 in her checking account. After making a deposit, she has $200 in the account. If d equals the amount of her deposit, which equation could be used to find the amount of the deposit?

A $$130d = \$200$$

B $\dfrac{\$200}{d} = \$130$

C $\$130 - d = \$200$

D $\$130 + d = \$200$

11. Mr. White challenged his class to find the missing number in this table.

Input	1	2	3	7
Output	1	4	9	■

If the pattern continues, which is the missing number?

F 49

G 16

H 14

J 13

12. **Explain It** Ivan and Irene were playing a number game that used a rule. Ivan called out a number, and Irene called out another number. The results are shown in the table.

Ivan	4	7	19	13
Irene	9	12	24	18

What is a rule for the game? Explain how you found it.

Fraction Concepts

In 1607, 104 passengers from 3 ships came ashore at Jamestown, Virginia. This was 13 years before the colony at Plymouth, Massachusetts, was established.

PROBLEM SOLVING Spoon bread was a favorite of some early Americans. Rewrite the list of ingredients so that the amounts are in order from least to greatest.

Students churn butter like the first settlers did in Jamestown, Virginia.

Spoon Bread

$1\frac{1}{2}$ cups water

2 cups milk

$1\frac{1}{2}$ cups cornmeal

$1\frac{1}{4}$ teaspoons salt

$1\frac{1}{2}$ teaspoons sugar

2 tablespoons butter

5 eggs (about $\frac{2}{3}$ cup)

1 tablespoon baking powder

CHECK WHAT YOU KNOW

Use this page to help you review and remember important skills needed for Chapter 15.

UNDERSTAND FRACTIONS

Write the fraction for the shaded part.

1. 2. 3. 4.

Write in words.

5. $\frac{2}{3}$ 6. $\frac{4}{5}$ 7. $\frac{1}{6}$ 8. $\frac{3}{8}$

COMPARE FRACTIONS

Compare the fractions. Write <, >, or = for each ●.

9. $\frac{5}{6}$ ● $\frac{1}{6}$

10. $\frac{2}{3}$ ● $\frac{3}{4}$

11. $\frac{5}{8}$ ● $\frac{3}{4}$

12. $\frac{5}{6}$ ● $\frac{5}{8}$

13. $\frac{1}{4}$ ● $\frac{1}{3}$

14. $\frac{2}{5}$ ● $\frac{3}{10}$

15. $\frac{3}{4}$ ● $\frac{3}{5}$

16. $\frac{3}{8}$ ● $\frac{2}{3}$

17. $\frac{5}{6}$ ● $\frac{7}{10}$

VOCABULARY POWER

REVIEW

denominator [di•nä′mə•nā•tər] *noun*

Denominator comes from the root *nomen,* for *name*. The bottom number of a fraction "names" the type of fraction being counted. What part of speech names a person, place, thing, or idea that can be described?

PREVIEW

equivalent fractions

simplest form

mixed number

GO ON-LINE

www.harcourtschool.com/mathglossary

Chapter 15 **313**

Equivalent Fractions

Quick Review

Tell the common factors.

1. 3 and 6   **2.** 4 and 8

3. 9 and 12   **4.** 12 and 15

5. 16 and 24

► Learn

SUB DIVISION! Sharonda bought two sub sandwiches. She cut one into halves and the other into fourths. She noticed that one half of a sub and two fourths of a sub are the same amount.

VOCABULARY

equivalent fractions

You can use a number line to represent a fraction. On the number lines, the fractions $\frac{1}{2}$ and $\frac{2}{4}$ name the same amount because they are the same distance from 0.

Fractions that name the same amount are called **equivalent fractions**. So, $\frac{1}{2} = \frac{2}{4}$.

MATH IDEA You can find equivalent fractions by multiplying or dividing both the numerator and denominator of a fraction by the same number.

Examples

A *Multiply* the numerator and the denominator by the same number.

$$\frac{4}{6} = \frac{4 \times 2}{6 \times 2} = \frac{8}{12}$$

B *Divide* the numerator and the denominator by the same common factor.

$$\frac{6}{18} = \frac{6 \div 3}{18 \div 3} = \frac{2}{6}$$

C Find a fraction equivalent to $\frac{5}{8}$.

$$\frac{5}{8} = \frac{5 \times 3}{8 \times 3} = \frac{15}{24}$$

D Find a fraction equivalent to $\frac{8}{12}$.

$$\frac{8}{12} = \frac{8 \div 4}{12 \div 4} = \frac{2}{3}$$

► Check

1. Explain how you could use number lines to show that $\frac{8}{12}$ and $\frac{2}{3}$ are equivalent.

Use the number lines to name an equivalent fraction for each.

2. $\frac{3}{4}$ **3.** $\frac{2}{8}$ **4.** $\frac{2}{4}$ **5.** $\frac{6}{8}$

Use the number lines to name an
equivalent fraction for each.

6. $\frac{1}{3}$ **7.** $\frac{2}{3}$ **8.** $\frac{3}{6}$ **9.** $\frac{2}{6}$

Write an equivalent fraction. Use
multiplication or division.

10. $\frac{2}{6}$ **11.** $\frac{2}{12}$ **12.** $\frac{1}{3}$ **13.** $\frac{4}{8}$ **14.** $\frac{5}{25}$ **15.** $\frac{9}{12}$

16. $\frac{2}{9}$ **17.** $\frac{5}{6}$ **18.** $\frac{3}{15}$ **19.** $\frac{7}{21}$ **20.** $\frac{2}{7}$ **21.** $\frac{4}{11}$

Which fraction is *not* equivalent to the given fraction?
Write *a*, *b*, or *c*.

22. $\frac{3}{4}$ **a.** $\frac{6}{8}$ **b.** $\frac{12}{16}$ **c.** $\frac{6}{12}$ **23.** $\frac{1}{2}$ **a.** $\frac{4}{8}$ **b.** $\frac{4}{7}$ **c.** $\frac{7}{14}$

24. $\frac{8}{12}$ **a.** $\frac{2}{3}$ **b.** $\frac{10}{18}$ **c.** $\frac{4}{6}$ **25.** $\frac{5}{15}$ **a.** $\frac{2}{3}$ **b.** $\frac{1}{3}$ **c.** $\frac{4}{12}$

Copy and complete to make a true statement.

26. $\frac{2}{7} = \frac{\blacksquare}{14}$ **27.** $\frac{7}{8} = \frac{\blacksquare}{24}$ **28.** $\frac{9}{12} = \frac{3}{\blacksquare}$ **29.** $\frac{3}{4} = \frac{6}{\blacksquare}$

30. $\frac{2}{\blacksquare} = \frac{6}{9}$ **31.** $\frac{10}{25} = \frac{\blacksquare}{5}$ **32.** $\frac{\blacksquare}{12} = \frac{1}{3}$ **33.** $\frac{1}{6} = \frac{3}{\blacksquare}$

USE DATA   For 34, use the table at the right.

34. Sayre has $7.50 to spend at the bakery.
She wants to buy 2 loaves of wheat
bread. Does she have enough money to
also buy one each of the other weekly
specials? Explain.

35. Mr. Florez had 10 cans of juice. He gave
3 cans to Greg and 5 cans to Meg. Write
two equivalent fractions to describe the
fraction of the cans that are left.

36. Describe the pattern. Then write the
next two numbers in the pattern.
$$\frac{2}{5}, \frac{4}{10}, \frac{6}{15}, \frac{8}{20}, \blacksquare, \blacksquare, \dots$$

37. ? **What's the Error?**   Rita used $\frac{2}{5}$ of
her pet-food supply last week. She said
that was the same as $\frac{4}{25}$. Describe and
correct her error.

Mixed Review and Test Prep

38.   23
        $\times 30$ (p. 152)

39.   9,541
        $\times$ 96 (p. 152)

40. $0.39 ÷ 3 (p. 230)   **41.** 4.355 ÷ 5 (p. 232)

42. **TEST PREP**   Which is equivalent to 0.05?
(p. 26)

A 5.0   **C** 0.050

B 0.5   **D** 0.005

Simplest Form

Quick Review

Find the greatest common factor, or GCF, for each set of numbers.

1. 6, 9   **2.** 12, 24

3. 3, 9, 15   **4.** 12, 16, 20

5. 6, 12, 18, 24

VOCABULARY

simplest form

▶ **Learn**

MUFFIN MAN! Andy increased a recipe for muffins and decided he needs $\frac{4}{8}$ cup of butter. He doesn't have a $\frac{1}{8}$-cup measure. What fraction can he use instead of $\frac{4}{8}$?

A fraction is in **simplest form** when the numerator and denominator have 1 as their only common factor.

Example 1

One Way You can divide by common factors to write $\frac{4}{8}$ in simplest form.

Divide both the numerator and the denominator by a common factor of 4 and 8.

Try 2. $\frac{4 \div 2}{8 \div 2} = \frac{2}{4}$ ← not in simplest form

Try 2 again. $\frac{2 \div 2}{4 \div 2} = \frac{1}{2}$ The numerator and denominator have 1 as their only common factor.

So, $\frac{4}{8}$ in simplest form is $\frac{1}{2}$. Andy needs $\frac{1}{2}$ cup of butter.

▲ Measuring cups used for cooking are often in sets of 1, $\frac{3}{4}$, $\frac{2}{3}$, $\frac{1}{2}$, $\frac{1}{3}$, and $\frac{1}{4}$ cup.

More Examples

A Write $\frac{6}{12}$ in simplest form.

$$\frac{6 \div 2}{12 \div 2} = \frac{3}{6}$$

$$\frac{3 \div 3}{6 \div 3} = \frac{1}{2}$$

So, $\frac{6}{12}$ in simplest form is $\frac{1}{2}$.

B Write $\frac{15}{18}$ in simplest form.

$$\frac{15 \div 3}{18 \div 3} = \frac{5}{6}$$

So, $\frac{15}{18}$ in simplest form is $\frac{5}{6}$.

C Write $\frac{30}{45}$ in simplest form.

$$\frac{30 \div 5}{45 \div 5} = \frac{6}{9}$$

$$\frac{6 \div 3}{9 \div 3} = \frac{2}{3}$$

So, $\frac{30}{45}$ in simplest form is $\frac{2}{3}$.

You can also use a calculator to find simplest form.

Example 2

Another Way You can use the greatest common factor, or GCF, to help you write a fraction in simplest form.

Write $\frac{12}{16}$ in simplest form.

STEP 1

List the factors of 12 and 16. Find the GCF.

Factors of 12: 1, 2, 3, 4, 6, 12
Factors of 16: 1, 2, 4, 8, 16
The GCF is 4.

STEP 2

Divide the numerator and the denominator of $\frac{12}{16}$ by the GCF.

$$\frac{12 \div 4}{16 \div 4} = \frac{3}{4}$$

So, $\frac{12}{16}$ in simplest form is $\frac{3}{4}$.

More Examples

A Write $\frac{9}{16}$ in simplest form.

$\frac{9}{16}$ 1 is the only common factor for 9 and 16.

So, $\frac{9}{16}$ is in simplest form.

B Write $\frac{21}{42}$ in simplest form.

$$\frac{21 \div 21}{42 \div 21} = \frac{1}{2}$$

So, $\frac{21}{42}$ in simplest form is $\frac{1}{2}$.

C Write $\frac{18}{45}$ in simplest form.

$$\frac{18 \div 9}{45 \div 9} = \frac{2}{5}$$

So, $\frac{18}{45}$ in simplest form is $\frac{2}{5}$.

MATH IDEA You can divide by using common factors until 1 is the only common factor, or you can divide by the GCF one time to write a fraction in simplest form.

Check

1. **Explain** how you would find the simplest form of $\frac{16}{24}$ by using both the common factor method and the GCF method.

Tell whether the fraction is in simplest form.
Write *yes* or *no*.

2. $\frac{2}{6}$ 3. $\frac{1}{10}$ 4. $\frac{5}{12}$ 5. $\frac{6}{18}$ 6. $\frac{8}{20}$ 7. $\frac{25}{32}$

Name the GCF of the numerator and the denominator.

8. $\frac{2}{6}$ 9. $\frac{8}{24}$ 10. $\frac{12}{15}$ 11. $\frac{15}{45}$ 12. $\frac{18}{30}$ 13. $\frac{50}{100}$

Write each fraction in simplest form.

14. $\frac{4}{10}$ 15. $\frac{8}{14}$ 16. $\frac{8}{20}$ 17. $\frac{12}{36}$ 18. $\frac{8}{8}$ 19. $\frac{24}{32}$

LESSON CONTINUES

Tell whether the fraction is in simplest form. Write *yes* or *no*.

20. $\frac{3}{8}$ **21.** $\frac{4}{10}$ **22.** $\frac{10}{32}$ **23.** $\frac{7}{15}$ **24.** $\frac{20}{45}$ **25.** $\frac{48}{50}$

Name the GCF of the numerator and the denominator.

26. $\frac{8}{22}$ **27.** $\frac{9}{30}$ **28.** $\frac{8}{12}$ **29.** $\frac{21}{33}$ **30.** $\frac{9}{54}$ **31.** $\frac{36}{60}$

Write each fraction in simplest form.

32. $\frac{6}{16}$ **33.** $\frac{14}{49}$ **34.** $\frac{40}{75}$ **35.** $\frac{24}{26}$ **36.** $\frac{15}{45}$ **37.** $\frac{8}{12}$

38. $\frac{27}{36}$ **39.** $\frac{4}{4}$ **40.** $\frac{8}{72}$ **41.** $\frac{48}{54}$ **42.** $\frac{30}{25}$ **43.** $\frac{60}{32}$

Complete.

44. $\frac{4}{16} = \frac{1}{\blacksquare}$ **45.** $\frac{21}{24} = \frac{\blacksquare}{8}$ **46.** $\frac{\blacksquare}{36} = \frac{1}{2}$

47. $\frac{15}{18} = \frac{\blacksquare}{6}$ **48.** $\frac{\blacksquare}{20} = \frac{3}{5}$ **49.** $\frac{7}{\blacksquare} = \frac{1}{8}$

USE DATA   Use the graph for 50–53. The graph shows the number of boxes of cookies four students have sold. Each student set a goal of selling 20 boxes of each kind of cookie.

50. What fraction of Carol's goal for the sale of chocolate chip cookies has she met? Write the fraction in simplest form.

51. What fraction of Luis's goal for the sale of peanut butter cookies has he *not* met? Write the fraction in simplest form.

COOKIE SALES

Chocolate Chip Cookies
Peanut Butter Cookies

52. How many more boxes of cookies does Marie need to sell to meet her goal for both kinds of cookies?

53. The cookies sell for $2.50 a box. How much money have the students collected so far?

54. **REASONING**   Colette looked at fractions in simplest form and said that any fraction that had both an odd and an even number was in simplest form. Do you agree with Colette? Explain.

55. Kyle earns $12.00 per week for baby-sitting. He saves $8.00 per week. Write the fraction, in simplest form, for the part he saves.

56. Hannah used $\frac{3}{4}$ cup of sugar, $\frac{2}{3}$ cup of cornmeal, and $\frac{1}{2}$ cup of flour for muffins. Of which ingredient did she use the greatest amount?

57. ✎ **Write About It**   Describe the way you would find the simplest form of $\frac{32}{40}$.

Write < , > , or = for each ⬤. (p. 10)

58. 5,650 ⬤ 5,650

59. 451,300 ⬤ 452,030

Write an equation for the problem. Use the variable *n* and state what *n* represents. (p. 68)

60. Walter has 12 pencils. There are 5 red, 3 green, and some blue. How many pencils are blue?

Find the product. (p. 154)

61.   2,118
      $\times\ \ 117$

62.   6,463
      $\times\ \ 213$

Complete each pattern. (p. 228)

63. $117 \div 3 = \blacksquare$
   $11.7 \div 3 = \blacksquare$
   $1.17 \div 3 = \blacksquare$

64. $280 \div 7 = \blacksquare$
   $28 \div 7 = \blacksquare$
   $2.8 \div 7 = \blacksquare$

Solve each equation. (p. 246)

65. TEST PREP $38 \times n = 152$

   A $n = 4$ **C** $n = 190$

   B $n = 114$ **D** $n = 5,776$

66. TEST PREP $24 \div n = 4$

   F $n = 6$ **H** $n = 28$

   G $n = 20$ **J** $n = 96$

Problem Solving Thinker's Corner

DATA AND GRAPHING You can show factors graphically and then use the graph to find the greatest common factor of two numbers.

MATERIALS: grid paper, ruler

Make a line graph. Show the numbers 1–20 on the horizontal axis and the factors 1–20 on the vertical axis. Use points to show all the factors of each number. The graph at the right shows the factors for 1–10. The factors for 4 are 1, 2, and 4.

1. Study your graph. Look up the vertical lines for 6 and 9. What factors have points in both lines? What is the greatest common factor?

2. Use your graph to find the greatest common factor for 8 and 20.

3. Explain how to use your graph to help you write $\frac{12}{18}$ in simplest form.

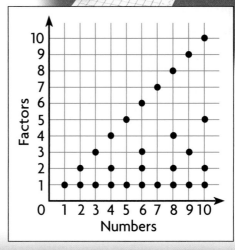

Understand Mixed Numbers

Quick Review

1. $(3 \times 9) + 2$
2. $(2 \times 8) + 1$
3. $14 \div 3$
4. $15 \div 2$
5. $24 \div 5$

▶ **Learn**

BAGEL MANIA A baker packages bagels in boxes that each hold one dozen. Stephanie bought one full box of bagels and 5 more bagels, or $1\frac{5}{12}$ dozen bagels.

A **mixed number** is made up of a whole number and a fraction.

Read: one and five twelfths   **Write:** $1\frac{5}{12}$

Use models and number lines to show mixed numbers.

VOCABULARY

mixed number

Examples

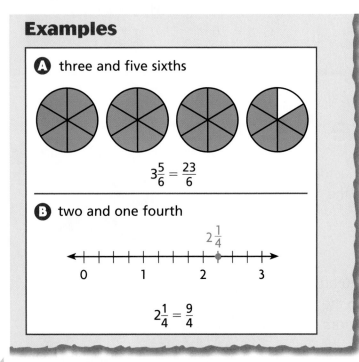

A three and five sixths

$$3\frac{5}{6} = \frac{23}{6}$$

B two and one fourth

$$2\frac{1}{4} = \frac{9}{4}$$

⚡ **MATH IDEA** A fraction that is greater than 1 can be renamed as a mixed number. A mixed number can be renamed as a fraction.

More Examples

C Rename $2\frac{3}{4}$ as a fraction.

$$2\frac{3}{4} = \frac{2 \times 4}{1 \times 4} + \frac{3}{4}$$
$$= \frac{8}{4} + \frac{3}{4}$$
$$= \frac{11}{4}$$

Write a fraction for the whole number by using the denominator, 4. Find the sum of the fractions.

D Rename $\frac{11}{4}$ as a mixed number.

$$4\overline{)11} \rightarrow 2\frac{3}{4}$$
$$\underline{-8}$$
$$3$$

Divide the numerator by the denominator. Use the remainder and the divisor to write a fraction.

A fraction greater than 1 is sometimes called an *improper fraction*.

320

Check

1. Explain how you can tell whether a fraction is greater than or less than 1.

Write a mixed number and a fraction for each.

2. four and three fourths

3. one and five eighths

Write each mixed number as a fraction. Write each fraction as a mixed number.

4. $4\frac{1}{4}$ **5.** $3\frac{2}{5}$ **6.** $2\frac{3}{7}$ **7.** $\frac{9}{8}$ **8.** $\frac{31}{6}$ **9.** $\frac{7}{3}$

Practice and Problem Solving

Extra Practice, page 332, Set C

Write a mixed number and a fraction for each.

10. three and two thirds

11. two and one fifth

Write each mixed number as a fraction.

12. $4\frac{1}{3}$ **13.** $6\frac{3}{5}$ **14.** $2\frac{7}{11}$ **15.** $9\frac{2}{9}$ **16.** $1\frac{11}{12}$ **17.** $5\frac{3}{4}$

Write each fraction as a mixed number.

18. $\frac{5}{2}$ **19.** $\frac{10}{3}$ **20.** $\frac{11}{6}$ **21.** $\frac{15}{4}$ **22.** $\frac{11}{8}$ **23.** $\frac{11}{5}$

24. Dan used $2\frac{1}{2}$ cups of flour to make bread. Write as a fraction the number of cups he used.

25. REASONING Ashley thinks $2\frac{1}{4} = \frac{7}{4}$. Is she correct? Explain by using a model and a number line.

26. Which of the fractions $\frac{13}{8}$, $\frac{16}{8}$, $\frac{8}{8}$, and $\frac{7}{8}$ is less than 1? Explain.

Mixed Review and Test Prep

27. 4.61 (p. 48)
-2.49

28. $3.16 - 2.78$ (p. 48)

Solve each equation for *n*. (p. 246)

29. $3n = 180$ **30.** $42 = 6n$

31. TEST PREP The Chows drove for 3 days, the same distance each day. If the odometer showed 24,260 miles at the beginning of the trip and 25,700 miles at the end of the trip, how many miles did they drive each day? (p. 198)

A 1,440   **B** 513   **C** 480   **D** 400

Chapter 15 **321**

Compare and Order Fractions and Mixed Numbers

Quick Review

Find the LCM for each set of numbers.

1. 3, 4   **2.** 2, 4
3. 2, 3, 6   **4.** 2, 3, 5
5. 6, 8

 Learn

WET PAINT! Joe and Ricardo are painting the walls of their clubhouse. By noon Joe had painted $\frac{5}{6}$ of his wall and Ricardo had painted $\frac{3}{4}$ of his wall. Who had painted more of his wall?

Example 1

One Way You can use fraction bars to compare.

| $\frac{1}{6}$ | $\frac{1}{6}$ | $\frac{1}{6}$ | $\frac{1}{6}$ | $\frac{1}{6}$ |

| $\frac{1}{4}$ | $\frac{1}{4}$ | $\frac{1}{4}$ |

$\frac{5}{6} > \frac{3}{4}$

Remember

To compare fractions with like denominators, compare the numerators.

Since $3 > 1$, $\frac{3}{4} > \frac{1}{4}$.

So, Joe had painted more of his wall.

Example 2

Another Way You can rename fractions with unlike denominators, such as $\frac{5}{6}$ and $\frac{3}{4}$, so they have like denominators for easy comparison.

STEP 1
Find the least common multiple, or LCM, of the denominators.

6: 6, 12, 18, 24
4: 4, 8, 12, 16

So, the LCM is 12.

STEP 2
Rename as equivalent fractions with denominators of 12.

$\frac{5 \times 2}{6 \times 2} = \frac{10}{12}$

$\frac{3 \times 3}{4 \times 3} = \frac{9}{12}$

STEP 3
Compare the numerators of the new fractions.

Since $10 > 9$, $\frac{10}{12} > \frac{9}{12}$.

So, $\frac{5}{6} > \frac{3}{4}$.

• Explain how to compare $1\frac{4}{5}$ and $1\frac{2}{3}$.

Order Fractions

By noon Mr. Banak had painted $\frac{5}{8}$ of his wall. Order the fractions $\frac{5}{6}$, $\frac{3}{4}$, and $\frac{5}{8}$ from least to greatest to find who painted the least amount.

When you have three or more fractions to order, rename the fractions so they have like denominators. Then put them in order.

Example 1

STEP 1

Find the LCM of 6, 4, and 8.

6: 6, 12, 18, 24, 30, 36

4: 4, 8, 12, 16, 20, 24, 28

8: 8, 16, 24, 32, 40, 48

The LCM is 24.

STEP 2

Rename as equivalent fractions with denominators of 24.

$$\frac{5 \times 4}{6 \times 4} = \frac{20}{24}$$

$$\frac{3 \times 6}{4 \times 6} = \frac{18}{24}$$

$$\frac{5 \times 3}{8 \times 3} = \frac{15}{24}$$

STEP 3

Compare the numerators. Put them in order from least to greatest.

Since 15 < 18 < 20,

$$\frac{15}{24} < \frac{18}{24} < \frac{20}{24}.$$

So, the order is $\frac{5}{8}$, $\frac{3}{4}$, and $\frac{5}{6}$.

So, Mr. Banak painted the least amount.

• Order the fractions above from greatest to least.

To order mixed numbers, compare the whole numbers. Then, compare the fractions.

Example 2

Order $3\frac{2}{3}$, $2\frac{7}{9}$, and $3\frac{5}{6}$ from least to greatest.

STEP 1

Compare the whole numbers.

$3\frac{2}{3}$ $2\frac{7}{9}$ $3\frac{5}{6}$

Since 2 < 3, $2\frac{7}{9}$ is the least.

STEP 2

Compare the other two fractions. Use equivalent fractions.

$3\frac{2}{3} = 3\frac{8}{12}$ $3\frac{5}{6} = 3\frac{10}{12}$

Since 8 < 10, $3\frac{8}{12} < 3\frac{10}{12}$.

The order is $2\frac{7}{9}$, $3\frac{2}{3}$, and $3\frac{5}{6}$.

 Check

1. **Describe** a situation in which the LCM of two numbers is one of the numbers.

LESSON CONTINUES

Compare the fractions. Write <, >, or = for each ●.

2. $\frac{5}{6}$ ● $\frac{7}{8}$

3. $\frac{3}{4}$ ● $\frac{2}{3}$

Write in order from least to greatest.

4. $\frac{3}{4}, \frac{3}{6}, \frac{3}{5}$

5. $\frac{1}{4}, \frac{5}{6}, \frac{5}{12}$

6. $4\frac{3}{4}, 4\frac{1}{6}, 3\frac{2}{3}$

7. $2\frac{1}{5}, 2\frac{1}{2}, 2\frac{3}{10}$

▶ **Practice and Problem Solving** Extra Practice, page 332, Set D

Compare. Write <, >, or = for each ●.

8. $\frac{3}{10}$ ● $\frac{1}{4}$

9. $\frac{2}{3}$ ● $\frac{3}{4}$

10. $\frac{4}{9}$ ● $\frac{2}{6}$

11. $\frac{1}{3}$ ● $\frac{3}{8}$

12. $\frac{4}{6}$ ● $\frac{8}{12}$

13. $\frac{7}{8}$ ● $\frac{3}{4}$

14. $3\frac{2}{7}$ ● $3\frac{5}{14}$

15. $6\frac{1}{4}$ ● $6\frac{2}{8}$

Write in order from least to greatest.

16. $\frac{1}{10}, \frac{3}{5}, \frac{1}{2}$

17. $\frac{2}{3}, \frac{3}{4}, \frac{7}{12}$

18. $2\frac{9}{14}, 3\frac{2}{4}, 2\frac{5}{7}$

19. $4\frac{4}{5}, 4\frac{7}{10}, 4\frac{1}{2}$

20. $\frac{2}{3}, \frac{5}{9}, \frac{1}{2}$

21. $\frac{1}{6}, 2\frac{1}{12}, 1\frac{1}{12}$

22. $5\frac{6}{10}, 5\frac{2}{5}, 5\frac{2}{7}$

23. $1\frac{2}{5}, \frac{3}{5}, 1\frac{1}{2}$

USE DATA For 24–25, use the table.

24. Order the fractions from greatest to least. On which day were the most rooms painted? On which day were the fewest rooms painted?

25. There are 20 classrooms in all, and 9 still need to be painted. What fraction of the total have been painted?

26. How can you compare fractions with *like* numerators and *unlike* denominators, such as $\frac{2}{3}$ and $\frac{2}{5}$, without renaming or using fraction strips?

27. Liza needs music for her gymnastics routine. The selection needs to be less than $3\frac{1}{2}$ min. *Changes* is $3\frac{2}{3}$ min, and *Dreaming* is $3\frac{2}{5}$ min. Which should she choose? Explain.

28. **VOCABULARY POWER** The word *order* comes from the Latin word *ordinem*, meaning "arrangement." List things other than numbers that you can order.

CLASSROOMS PAINTED	
Day	**Fraction of Total**
Monday	$\frac{1}{5}$
Tuesday	$\frac{1}{4}$
Wednesday	$\frac{1}{10}$

Write *equivalent* or *not equivalent* to describe each pair of decimals. (p. 26)

29. 1.034 and 1.0340

30. 0.1230 and 0.023

For 31–32, write an expression. (p. 246)

31. Chris ate two apples every day for ten days.

32. Maria shared fifteen cookies equally among five friends.

33. Sara has $23.50. She buys 12 party favors for $1.50 each and 2 door prizes for $1.75 each. How much change should she receive? (p. 170)

Write an equivalent decimal for each. (p. 26)

34. 0.4   **35.** 1.28   **36.** 0.07

USE DATA
For 37–38, use the circle graph.
(p. 106)

ANNA'S CD COLLECTION

Country

Classical   Rock

Blues

37. TEST PREP   Which fraction represents the part that is country music?

A $\frac{1}{5}$ B $\frac{5}{10}$ C $\frac{5}{8}$ D $\frac{5}{5}$

38. TEST PREP   Of which kind of music does Anna have the fewest CDs?

F Country   H Classical
G Rock   J Blues

Problem Solving   LiNKUP . . . to Reading

STRATEGY • COMPARE AND CONTRAST You can compare to see how things are alike. You can also contrast to see how they are different. Read the following problem.

A recipe for hot chocolate calls for $\frac{1}{2}$ cup of cocoa, $\frac{1}{8}$ cup of sugar, and $\frac{3}{4}$ cup of milk. List the ingredients in order from greatest amount to least amount.

Compare	Contrast
All the ingredients are measured in cups.	The amounts are not equal.
All the amounts are fractions less than 1.	The fractions have different denominators.

Order the fractions. Think: $\frac{3}{4} > \frac{1}{2} > \frac{1}{8}$

So, the ingredients in order are milk, cocoa, and sugar.

Compare and contrast the data to solve.

1. Latoya used $\frac{1}{2}$ cup of milk for icing, $\frac{7}{8}$ cup for a cake, and $\frac{3}{4}$ cup for hot chocolate. For which item did she use the most milk?

2. A recipe for apple pie calls for $\frac{5}{8}$ tsp of nutmeg. Kara has $\frac{1}{2}$ tsp of nutmeg. Does she have enough for the recipe? Explain.

Problem Solving Strategy
Make a Model

PROBLEM Minh made a table to record the number of miles he walked each day. On which day did Minh walk the greatest distance? On which day did he walk the least distance?

Day	Mon	Tue	Wed	Thu
Miles Walked	$2\frac{1}{2}$	$3\frac{1}{4}$	$2\frac{3}{4}$	$2\frac{3}{8}$

Quick Review

Compare. Write $<$, $>$, or $=$ for each ●.

1. $\frac{4}{4}$ ● $\frac{3}{4}$ **2.** $\frac{2}{4}$ ● $\frac{1}{2}$

3. $\frac{1}{2}$ ● $\frac{1}{3}$ **4.** $\frac{2}{3}$ ● $\frac{3}{4}$

5. $\frac{1}{4}$ ● $\frac{2}{9}$

UNDERSTAND

- What are you asked to find?

- What information will you use?

- Is there any information you will not use?

PLAN

- What strategy can you use to solve the problem?

  You can *make a model* with fraction bars.

SOLVE

- How can you use the strategy to solve the problem?

  You can use fraction bars to help you compare the numbers.

  First, look at the whole numbers: $2\frac{1}{2}$, $3\frac{1}{4}$, $2\frac{3}{4}$, $2\frac{3}{8}$. Since 3 is the greatest whole number, $3\frac{1}{4}$ miles is the greatest distance.

  Now use fraction bars to compare the fractional parts of $2\frac{1}{2}$, $2\frac{3}{4}$, and $2\frac{3}{8}$. Since $\frac{3}{8}$ is the shortest, $2\frac{3}{8}$ miles is the least distance.

  So, Minh walked the greatest distance on Tuesday and the least distance on Thursday.

CHECK

- What other strategy can you use?

Problem Solving Practice

Strategies

Draw a Diagram or Picture
▶ **Make a Model or Act It Out**
Make an Organized List
Find a Pattern
Make a Table or Graph
Predict and Test
Work Backward
Solve a Simpler Problem
Write an Equation
Use Logical Reasoning

Problem Solving

Make a model to solve.

1. **What if** Minh had walked only $2\frac{1}{4}$ miles on Tuesday? How would this change the answers?

2. The five planets closest to the sun are Earth, Venus, Mars, Mercury, and Jupiter. Earth is the only planet between Venus and Mars. Mercury is the only planet between Venus and the sun. Which of these planets is next to Jupiter?

USE DATA Use the table for 3 and 4.

3. How do you know that April had the most rainfall?

   A The greatest rainfall is always in April.

   B April has the greatest whole-number part.

   C April has the greatest fractional part.

   D April is the last month listed.

MONTHLY RAINFALL				
Month	Jan	Feb	Mar	Apr
Rainfall (in inches)	$3\frac{3}{8}$	$2\frac{2}{4}$	$3\frac{1}{2}$	$5\frac{7}{8}$

4. What is the order of the months from greatest rainfall to least rainfall?

   F Apr, Mar, Feb, Jan

   G Jan, Mar, Feb, Apr

   H Apr, Mar, Jan, Feb

   J Apr, Jan, Mar, Feb

Mixed Strategy Practice

5. **GEOMETRY** Alex is enclosing his pentagon-shaped garden with fencing. If each side is 8 meters long, how much fencing does he need?

6. If 2 people can be seated on each side of a square table, how many people can be seated at 12 square tables that are pushed together end to end to form a rectangle?

7. Aiko had $20.00 to buy candles. She returned 2 candles for which she had paid $4.75 each. Then she bought 3 candles for $3.50 each and 1 candle for $5.00. How much money did Aiko have then?

8. In Ted's class, students were asked to name their favorite sport. Football was the response of $\frac{1}{8}$ of them. If 3 students said football, how many students are in Ted's class?

6 Relate Fractions and Decimals

Quick Review

What fraction is shaded? What fraction is *not* shaded?

1.   2.
3. 4.
5.

 Learn

KICK OFF! At the World Cup soccer tournament, each match has two 45-minute halves. The times can be expressed as fractions, mixed numbers, or decimals.

	FRACTION	MIXED NUMBER	DECIMAL
First Half	$\frac{3}{4}$ hr		0.75 hr
Match	$\frac{3}{2}$ hr	$1\frac{1}{2}$ hr	1.50 hr

MATH IDEA The same number can be represented as a fraction or as a decimal. If the number is greater than 1, it can be represented as a mixed number, a fraction, or a decimal.

One way to show a number both ways is to use a number line.

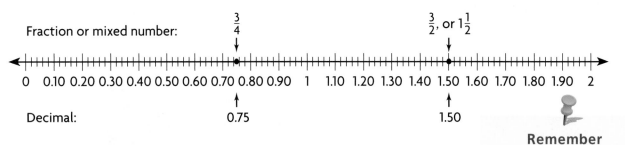

Fraction or mixed number: $\frac{3}{4}$ $\frac{3}{2}$, or $1\frac{1}{2}$

0   0.10 0.20 0.30 0.40 0.50 0.60 0.70 0.80 0.90 1 1.10 1.20 1.30 1.40 1.50 1.60 1.70 1.80 1.90 2

Decimal: 0.75   1.50

Another way to show numbers as fractions, mixed numbers, or decimals is to use grids.

Remember

There are three ways to think of a fraction. $\frac{3}{4}$ is three fourths, three out of four, or three divided by four.

Examples

A Write a fraction and a decimal for the model.

fraction
Three out of ten equal parts are shaded.

$\frac{3}{10}$, or three tenths, is shaded.

decimal
Three out of ten equal parts are shaded.

0.3, or three tenths, is shaded.

B Write a mixed number and a decimal for the model.

mixed number
One whole plus three out of four equal parts are shaded.

$1\frac{3}{4}$, or one and three-fourths, is shaded.

decimal
One whole plus seventy-five out of one hundred equal parts are shaded.

1.75, or one and seventy-five hundredths, is shaded.

Place Value and Division

Here are other ways you can change a decimal to a fraction or a fraction to a decimal.

Examples

Decimal to Fraction You can use place value to change a decimal to a fraction.

0.24   Identify the place value of the last digit. The 4 is in the hundredths place.

$\frac{24}{100}$ Use that place value for the denominator.

So, $0.24 = \frac{24}{100} = \frac{6}{25}$.

Fraction to Decimal You can use division to change a fraction to a decimal.

$\frac{2}{5}$ Divide the numerator by the denominator.

$$\begin{array}{r} 0.4 \\ 5\overline{)2.0} \\ -2\,0 \\ \hline 0 \end{array}$$

Place the decimal point. Since 5 does not divide into 2, place a zero. Then divide as with whole numbers.

So, $\frac{2}{5} = 0.4$.

More Examples

A Write 0.375 as a fraction in simplest form.

0.375   The 5 is in the thousandths place.

$0.375 = \frac{375}{1,000} = \frac{3}{8}$

So, $0.375 = \frac{3}{8}$.

B Write $\frac{3}{4}$ as a decimal.

$$\begin{array}{r} 0.75 \\ 4\overline{)3.00} \\ -2\,8 \\ \hline 20 \\ -20 \\ \hline 0 \end{array}$$

So, $\frac{3}{4} = 0.75$.

C Write $3\frac{5}{8}$ as a decimal.

$$\begin{array}{r} 0.625 \\ 8\overline{)5.000} \\ -4\,8 \\ \hline 20 \\ -16 \\ \hline 40 \\ -40 \\ \hline 0 \end{array}$$

Rename the fraction as a decimal. Then add the whole number to the decimal.

So, $3\frac{5}{8} = 3.625$.

Check

1. **Describe** two ways you can change a decimal to a fraction and two ways you can change a fraction to a decimal.

Identify a decimal and a fraction or mixed number for the point.

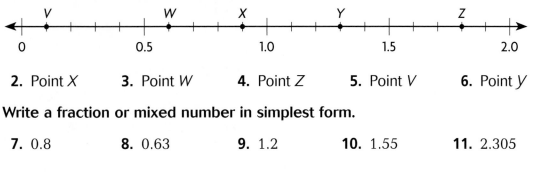

2. Point X 3. Point W 4. Point Z 5. Point V 6. Point Y

Write a fraction or mixed number in simplest form.

7. 0.8   8. 0.63   9. 1.2   10. 1.55   11. 2.305

LESSON CONTINUES

Write a decimal for each fraction or mixed number.

12. $\frac{1}{100}$ **13.** $\frac{3}{10}$ **14.** $\frac{1}{5}$ **15.** $1\frac{2}{4}$ **16.** $4\frac{3}{8}$

Practice and Problem Solving   Extra Practice, page 332, Set E

Identify a decimal and a fraction or mixed number for the point.

```
              K              H    F              G              E
◄──┼┼┼┼┼┼┼┼┼┼●┼┼┼┼┼┼┼┼┼┼┼┼┼┼●┼┼┼●┼┼┼┼┼┼┼┼┼┼┼┼┼┼●┼┼┼┼┼┼┼┼┼┼┼┼┼●┼┼┼┼┼┼┼┼►
   0  0.10 0.20 0.30 0.40 0.50 0.60 0.70 0.80 0.90  1  1.10 1.20 1.30 1.40 1.50 1.60 1.70 1.80 1.90  2
```

17. Point E **18.** Point F **19.** Point G **20.** Point H **21.** Point K

Write a fraction or mixed number in simplest form.

22. 0.8   **23.** 0.37   **24.** 0.90   **25.** 2.125   **26.** 1.33

Write a decimal for each fraction or mixed number.

27. $\frac{8}{100}$ **28.** $\frac{7}{10}$ **29.** $\frac{1}{4}$ **30.** $2\frac{4}{5}$ **31.** $3\frac{7}{8}$

Compare. Write <, >, or = for each ●.

32. $\frac{1}{2}$ ● 0.75   **33.** 0.25 ● $\frac{2}{8}$ **34.** $\frac{3}{5}$ ● 0.52   **35.** 0.65 ● $\frac{3}{4}$

36. $1\frac{1}{5}$ ● 1.23   **37.** $2\frac{7}{10}$ ● 1.75   **38.** $\frac{1}{4}$ ● 0.50   **39.** 2.30 ● $2\frac{3}{10}$

For 40–41, draw a number line and label points for the numbers described.

40. the number that is halfway between 0.2 and the number that is twice 0.2

41. the number $1\frac{7}{10}$ and the number that is 0.3 less than it

42. Order $\frac{5}{12}$, 1.60, 0.50, $1\frac{3}{4}$, $\frac{3}{8}$ from greatest to least.

43. **? What's the Error?** Harvey says $\frac{1}{4}$ is equivalent to 0.4 because they both have a 4. Explain and correct the error.

44. Kelly walks her dog 0.8 of a mile every day. Write as a fraction the number of miles Kelly walks her dog.

45. **FAST FACT • SCIENCE** The world's smallest vegetable is a snow pea, measuring about 0.25 inch in diameter. Write the diameter as a fraction.

46. Mariko hoped to sell a used book for $0.80 but accepted $\frac{3}{4}$ of a dollar for it. What is the difference in the two amounts?

47. ✍ **Write a problem** about someone who walks more than 1 mile. Express as both a mixed number and a decimal.

Mixed Review and Test Prep

Find the mean for each set of data. (p. 100)

48. 23, 53, 46, 75, 48   **49.** 0.8, 0.4, 0.2, 0.6

50. 16, 37, 68, 84, 95   **51.** 53, 68, 35, 60

Find the difference. (pp. 46, 48)

52. 62,459
      −31,157

53. 68,316
      −64,945

54. 3.75 − 1.29   **55.** 23.35 − 1.07

Copy and complete the pattern. (p. 208)

56. 21,000 ÷ 7 = ■
     2,100 ÷ 7 = ■
     210 ÷ 7 = ■
     21 ÷ 7 = ■

57. 18 ÷ 6 = ■
     180 ÷ 6 = ■
     1,800 ÷ 6 = ■
     18,000 ÷ 6 = ■

58. Daora is mailing 15 cases of cookies. Each case has 25 boxes of cookies. Each box contains 8 ounces of cookies. How many ounces do the cookies weigh altogether? (p. 152)

Solve for *n*. (pp. 70, 250)

59. **TEST PREP** $n − 12 = 30$

A $n = 18$ **C** $n = 32$
B $n = 22$ **D** $n = 42$

60. **TEST PREP** $(3 \times 10) − 2 = n$

F $n = 24$ **H** $n = 30$
G $n = 28$ **J** $n = 32$

Problem Solving Thinker's Corner

REASONING Think about the number of numbers that you can represent on a number line.

1. Are there numbers between 0 and 0.1? If so, name some of them.

2. Are there numbers between 0 and 0.01? If so, name some of them.

3. What are some numbers between 0.08 and 0.09? between 0.09 and 0.10?

4. How many numbers can be represented on a number line? Explain.

Extra Practice

Set A (pp. 314–315)

Write three equivalent fractions for each.

1. $\frac{2}{4}$ 2. $\frac{3}{8}$ 3. $\frac{4}{5}$ 4. $\frac{6}{9}$ 5. $\frac{12}{15}$ 6. $\frac{22}{33}$

7. $\frac{8}{24}$ 8. $\frac{2}{8}$ 9. $\frac{1}{2}$ 10. $\frac{6}{7}$ 11. $\frac{2}{12}$ 12. $\frac{2}{3}$

Set B (pp. 316–319)

Write each fraction in simplest form.

1. $\frac{4}{16}$ 2. $\frac{6}{18}$ 3. $\frac{12}{18}$ 4. $\frac{6}{10}$ 5. $\frac{6}{36}$ 6. $\frac{15}{20}$

7. $\frac{19}{38}$ 8. $\frac{8}{24}$ 9. $\frac{18}{72}$ 10. $\frac{18}{24}$ 11. $\frac{30}{45}$ 12. $\frac{25}{125}$

Set C (pp. 320–321)

Write each fraction as a mixed number. Write each mixed number as a fraction.

1. $\frac{9}{7}$ 2. $5\frac{2}{3}$ 3. $\frac{13}{4}$ 4. $6\frac{4}{5}$ 5. $\frac{16}{6}$ 6. $6\frac{3}{4}$

7. $4\frac{1}{2}$ 8. $\frac{8}{3}$ 9. $\frac{25}{8}$ 10. $5\frac{1}{4}$ 11. $\frac{8}{5}$ 12. $4\frac{2}{7}$

Set D (pp. 322–325)

Compare. Write <, >, or = for each ●.

1. $\frac{1}{2}$ ● $\frac{2}{6}$ 2. $\frac{2}{3}$ ● $\frac{4}{6}$ 3. $5\frac{5}{7}$ ● $6\frac{3}{5}$ 4. $2\frac{5}{6}$ ● $3\frac{2}{4}$ 5. $7\frac{4}{8}$ ● $7\frac{2}{4}$

Write in order from least to greatest.

6. $\frac{1}{6}, \frac{2}{5}, \frac{1}{3}$ 7. $\frac{4}{8}, \frac{2}{3}, \frac{1}{6}$ 8. $2\frac{1}{4}, 3\frac{2}{12}, 2\frac{4}{6}$ 9. $6\frac{4}{6}, 5\frac{9}{11}, 6\frac{7}{12}$ 10. $1\frac{8}{9}, \frac{2}{5}, 1\frac{12}{18}$

Set E (pp. 328–331)

Write a fraction or mixed number in simplest form.

1. 0.55   2. 0.7   3. 0.26   4. 11.751   5. 6.2   6. 8.305

Write a decimal for each fraction or mixed number.

7. $\frac{1}{4}$ 8. $\frac{17}{20}$ 9. $\frac{3}{8}$ 10. $4\frac{6}{10}$ 11. $2\frac{35}{100}$ 12. $7\frac{1}{8}$

Review/Test

✓ CHECK VOCABULARY AND CONCEPTS

Choose the best term from the box.

> equivalent fractions
> fraction
> mixed number
> simplest form

1. Fractions that name the same amount are called __?__. (p. 314)

2. A fraction is in __?__ when the greatest common factor of the numerator and denominator is 1. (p. 316)

3. A number, like $2\frac{1}{2}$, that has a whole-number part and a fraction part is a(n) __?__. (p. 320)

✓ CHECK SKILLS

Write an equivalent fraction. (pp. 314–315)

4. $\frac{1}{7}$ 5. $\frac{3}{9}$ 6. $\frac{6}{42}$ 7. $\frac{2}{9}$ 8. $\frac{21}{49}$

Write each fraction in simplest form. (pp. 316–319)

9. $\frac{4}{16}$ 10. $\frac{8}{12}$ 11. $\frac{20}{45}$ 12. $\frac{16}{56}$ 13. $\frac{63}{81}$

Write each fraction as a mixed number. Write each mixed number as a fraction. (pp. 320–321)

14. $\frac{9}{4}$ 15. $\frac{17}{8}$ 16. $\frac{13}{4}$ 17. $2\frac{1}{5}$ 18. $3\frac{3}{8}$

Compare. Write <, >, or = for each ●. (pp. 322–325)

19. $\frac{2}{4}$ ● $\frac{5}{8}$ 20. $\frac{3}{4}$ ● $\frac{6}{12}$ 21. $1\frac{7}{28}$ ● $1\frac{4}{7}$ 22. $2\frac{7}{8}$ ● $2\frac{14}{16}$

Write in order from least to greatest. (pp. 322–325)

23. $\frac{1}{6}, \frac{15}{18}, \frac{2}{3}$ 24. $\frac{3}{6}, \frac{1}{3}, \frac{8}{12}$ 25. $\frac{1}{4}, 1\frac{1}{3}, \frac{1}{2}$ 26. $3\frac{2}{5}, 3\frac{1}{2}, 3\frac{3}{4}$

Write a fraction or mixed number in simplest form for each decimal. Write a decimal for each fraction or mixed number. (pp. 328–331)

27. 0.4   28. $\frac{3}{5}$ 29. 0.042   30. $4\frac{3}{4}$ 31. 13.65

✓ CHECK PROBLEM SOLVING

Make a model to solve. (pp. 326–327)

32. Dave's practice swims were $1\frac{3}{8}$ miles, $1\frac{2}{6}$ miles, and $1\frac{3}{4}$ miles. Which was the greatest distance?

33. Rosa bought $1\frac{2}{5}$ lb of chocolate, $2\frac{1}{2}$ lb of fudge, and $1\frac{5}{8}$ lb of caramels. Of which candy did she buy the least amount?

⭐Standardized Test Prep

⭐ NUMBER SENSE, CONCEPTS, AND OPERATIONS

> **TIP** **Understand the problem.** See item 1. Each fraction represents a part of a pound of cheese. Compare and order the fractions to find the second greatest amount.

1. Mrs. Gold wants to buy $\frac{1}{3}$ pound of Muenster cheese, $\frac{1}{4}$ pound of American cheese, $\frac{1}{2}$ pound of Swiss cheese, and $\frac{1}{5}$ pound of Cheddar cheese.

   Of which cheese does she plan to buy the **second** greatest amount?

   A Swiss   **C** American

   B Muenster   **D** Cheddar

2. Look at the cheese list in Problem 1. Which statement is true about the cheeses in the list?

   F The amount of Cheddar cheese is greater than the amount of American cheese.

   G The amount of American cheese is greater than the amount of Muenster cheese.

   H The amount of Swiss cheese is greater than the amount of Cheddar cheese.

   J The amount of Cheddar cheese is greater than the amount of Muenster cheese.

3. **Explain It** Tim is making a circle graph to show how he spent his day yesterday. He worked for 8 hours. In the circle graph, should the fractional part for work be greater than or less than half of the circle? Explain how you know.

⭐ MEASUREMENT

4. According to the airline schedule, how long is the flight from Albany to Baltimore?

```
Albany, NY, to  Baltimore, MD
Leaves 10:05 A.M. Arrives 11:30 A.M.

Baltimore, MD, to  Miami, FL
Leaves 1:00 P.M. Arrives 3:35 P.M.
```

   A 1 hour 25 minutes

   B 1 hour 35 minutes

   C 2 hours 35 minutes

   D 5 hours 30 minutes

5. Use the table in Problem 4. How long is the layover in Baltimore before the plane takes off for Miami?

   F 10 hours 30 minutes

   G 2 hours 35 minutes

   H 2 hours 30 minutes

   J 1 hour 30 minutes

6. **Explain It** A professional soccer team left town on August 16 for a trip. The team returned on September 1. Was the team gone for more than or less than two weeks? Explain how you know.

August						
Sun	Mon	Tue	Wed	Thu	Fri	Sat
1	2	3	4	5	6	7
8	9	10	11	12	13	14
15	16	17	18	19	20	21
22	23	24	25	26	27	28
29	30	31				

GEOMETRY AND SPATIAL SENSE

7. The diagram shows Mitch's four vegetable gardens.

□ = 1 square foot

Which garden does NOT have the same area as the others?

A tomato

B pepper

C cucumber

D lettuce

8. Look at the diagram above. Which garden has the greatest perimeter?

F tomato

G pepper

H cucumber

J lettuce

9. Explain It Tyler drew this diagram of his new tent.

Tyler said the tent is shaped like a triangular pyramid. Mackenzie said the tent is shaped like a triangular prism. Who is correct? Explain how you know.

DATA ANALYSIS AND PROBABILITY

10. Lou made a circle graph to show the deductions taken out of his paycheck for each dollar he earns.

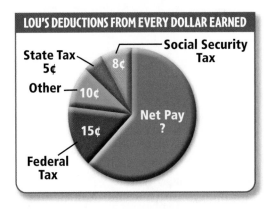

Out of every dollar Lou earns, how much is left after all the deductions?

A 38¢   **C** 62¢

B 48¢   **D** 72¢

11. Look at the circle graph above. Which two deductions make up $\frac{1}{4}$ of the whole circle?

F Social Security Tax and Other

G Social Security Tax and State Tax

H State Tax and Other

J Federal Tax and Other

12. Explain It A movie rental store wants to display the data below in a graph. What type of graph is best for displaying the data? Explain your choice.

DAILY RENTALS		
Day	DVDs Rented	Videos Rented
Monday	623	430
Tuesday	582	550
Wednesday	791	702
Thursday	807	598
Friday	1,045	825

IT'S IN THE BAG

Venn Diagrams

PROJECT Make a Venn diagram to show relationships among sets of numbers.

Materials

- 1 page protector cut in half
- $8\frac{1}{2}$-in. x $5\frac{1}{2}$-in. sheet of construction paper
- Permanent markers
- Stapler
- Venn diagram worksheet

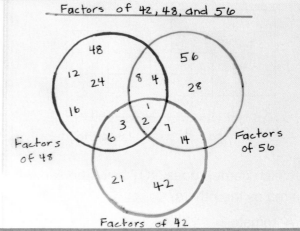

Factors of 42, 48, and 56

48
12 24 8 4 56
16   28
        1
      3 2 7
    6   14
Factors of 48   Factors of 56
    21   42
Factors of 42

Directions

1. For each half of the page protector, cut off the closed top or bottom edge, if present. Cut between the sheets, along the fold at the right edge of each half, separated to form a total of 4 sheets. *(Picture A)*

2. Place the sheet of construction paper on the table. Place both halves of the protector over the construction paper, with the hole-punched sides on the left. Staple along the left side. *(Picture B)*

3. Insert the Venn diagram worksheet underneath all 4 protector sheets. Trace a different circle onto each of the three bottom sheets. On the top sheet, trace the line for the title. *(Picture C)*

4. Using each description once, label the circles *Factors of 42, Factors of 48, Factors of 56*. Title the Venn diagram *Factors of 42, 48, and 56*. Write the factors of each number in the appropriate parts of the diagram.

Challenge

Scientific Notation

Today's biggest and fastest computers can perform more than 850,000,000,000 operations in 1 second. The number 850,000,000,000 is written in standard form. You can use **scientific notation** to write a large number like 850,000,000,000 more easily.

A number written in scientific notation is expressed as a product of two factors.

The first factor is a number that is at least 1 but less than 10.   The second factor is a power of 10.

$$8.5 \times 10^{11}$$

Follow these steps to write a number in scientific notation.

Example

STEP 1

Count the number of places the decimal point must be moved to the left to form a number that is at least 1 but less than 10.

$$850{,}000{,}000{,}000 \rightarrow 8.5$$
11 places

STEP 2

Since the decimal point moved 11 places, the exponent of 10 is 11. Write the number as the product of the two factors.

$$8.5 \times 10^{11}$$

So, $850{,}000{,}000{,}000 = 8.5 \times 10^{11}$.

More Examples

Ⓐ $5{,}470{,}000 = 5.47 \times 10^{6}$
6 places

Ⓑ $38{,}211{,}000{,}000 = 3.8211 \times 10^{10}$
10 places

Talk About It

• Tell why each of these numbers is not written in scientific notation: 12×10^{4}, 2.7×5^{4}, and $9.4 + 10^{4}$.

• **STRETCH YOUR THINKING** By 2002, more than 5.8×10^{8} people around the world were using the Internet. Explain how you can write 5.8×10^{8} in standard form.

Try It

Write the number in scientific notation.

1. 4,000,000

2. 73,000

3. 682,100,000

4. 100,000

5. 3,140,000

6. 9,502,000,000

Study Guide and Review

VOCABULARY

Choose the best term from the box.

1. A number that tells how many times the base is used as a factor is called a(n) __?__. (p. 292)

2. All composite numbers can be written as the product of __?__. (p. 302)

3. When a fraction's numerator and denominator have 1 as their only common factor, the fraction is in __?__. (p. 316)

> common multiples
> composite numbers
> exponent
> least common multiples
> prime factors
> simplest form

STUDY AND SOLVE

Chapter 13

Find the greatest common factor of two numbers.

> Find the GCF of 16 and 24.
> Factors of 16: 1, 2, 4, 8, 16
> Factors of 24: 1, 2, 3, 4, 6, 8, 12, 24
> So, the GCF is 8.

Write the GCF for each set of numbers. (pp. 278–281)

4. 14 and 28   5. 15 and 35

6. 18 and 42   7. 6, 12, and 45

8. 9 and 12   9. 7, 14, and 35

Find the least common multiple of two numbers.

> Find the LCM of 6 and 9.
> Multiples of 6: 6, 12, 18, 24, 30, 36, . . .
> Multiples of 9: 9, 18, 27, 36, 45, 54, . . .
> So, the LCM is 18.

Write the LCM for each set of numbers. (pp. 282–283)

10. 2 and 14   11. 6 and 32

12. 3 and 18   13. 3, 5, and 20

14. 5 and 6   15. 2, 7, and 14

Chapter 14

Write and evaluate exponents.

> exponent
> Base → $3^5 = 3 \times 3 \times 3 \times 3 \times 3 = 243$

Find the value. (pp. 292–299)

16. 10^3 17. 8^3 18. 2^2 19. 1^0

20. 4^3 21. 3^1 22. 5^2 23. 2^6

Find the prime factorization of a number.

> What is the prime factorization of 54?
> $54 = 2 \times 3 \times 3 \times 3$
> $54 = 2 \times 3^3$ ← Use 3 for the exponent.

Find the prime factorization of the number. Use exponents when possible. (pp. 302–305)

24. 30   25. 80

26. 33   27. 126

Chapter 15

Write equivalent fractions.

Multiply the numerator and the denominator by the same number. $\frac{4}{6} = \frac{4 \times 2}{6 \times 2} = \frac{8}{12}$	Divide the numerator and the denominator by a common factor. $\frac{8}{12} = \frac{8 \div 4}{12 \div 4} = \frac{2}{3}$

Write an equivalent fraction. (pp. 314–315)

28. $\frac{9}{21}$ 29. $\frac{10}{12}$

30. $\frac{2}{5}$ 31. $\frac{4}{7}$

32. $\frac{11}{12}$ 33. $\frac{16}{20}$

Write the fraction in simplest form.

Write $\frac{12}{16}$ in simplest form.

$\frac{12}{16} = \frac{12 \div 4}{16 \div 4} = \frac{3}{4}$ ← Divide the numerator and the denominator by the GCF.

So, $\frac{12}{16}$ in simplest form is $\frac{3}{4}$.

Write each fraction in simplest form. (pp. 316–319)

34. $\frac{9}{24}$ 35. $\frac{7}{49}$

36. $\frac{6}{24}$ 37. $\frac{15}{48}$

38. $\frac{10}{42}$ 39. $\frac{6}{28}$

Write fractions as decimals and decimals as fractions.

To write $\frac{2}{5}$ as a decimal, divide 2 by 5.

$2 \div 5 = 0.4$

To write 0.125 as a fraction, use place value.

$0.125 = \frac{125}{1,000} = \frac{1}{8}$

Write a fraction in simplest form for each decimal. (pp. 328–331)

40. 0.16   41. 0.5   42. 0.012

Write a decimal for each fraction. (pp. 328–331)

43. $\frac{3}{4}$ 44. $\frac{1}{5}$ 45. $\frac{5}{8}$

46. $\frac{2}{5}$ 47. $\frac{3}{8}$ 48. $\frac{1}{4}$

PROBLEM SOLVING PRACTICE

Solve. (pp. 284–285, 326–327)

49. The GCF of 8 and another number is 1. The LCM is 24. What is the other number?

50. Shawn rode his bike $\frac{5}{8}$ mi on Monday, $1\frac{2}{3}$ mi on Tuesday, $\frac{3}{2}$ mi on Wednesday, $2\frac{1}{9}$ mi on Thursday, and $\frac{7}{16}$ mi on Friday. On which day did he ride the least distance? the greatest distance?

PERFORMANCE ASSESSMENT

TASK A • BAKE SALE

Ariel, Brad, and Curt baked cookies for the school bake sale. The students want to put the cookies in bags. Each bag will contain all three kinds of cookies. All of the bags will have the same number of each kind of cookie.

Baker	Number of Cookies	Kind of Cookie
Ariel	24	Peanut
Brad	18	Raisin
Curt	12	Oatmeal

a. Find all the ways each kind of cookie can be divided so there is the same number in each bag.

b. What is the greatest number they can put in each bag? How many bags of cookies does this make?

c. Other students want to bring in cookies. Name two other numbers of cookies that can be divided in the same way.

TASK B • CLOWNING AROUND

Jolynn and her mother are making a clown costume for the class play. They found some pieces of fabric at a yard sale. Help them choose fabric pieces for the costume.

$1\frac{1}{4}$ yd $1\frac{1}{2}$ yd $2\frac{2}{8}$ yd $\frac{1}{2}$ yd

$2\frac{3}{4}$ yd $2\frac{1}{2}$ yd $1\frac{4}{8}$ yd

a. They can use the shortest piece of fabric for the hat. Which piece should they choose for the hat?

b. They need $2\frac{5}{8}$ yards for the top of the costume. Is there a piece large enough for the top? If so, which is it?

c. Decide what other pieces of fabric they might buy for the sleeves and the pants of the costume. The pants will take more fabric than the top or the sleeves.

Bases and Exponents

You can use a calculator to find the missing base or missing exponent in an equation.

On the Casio *fx-55* calculator, use x^y to evaluate equations with exponents.

Find the missing numbers. Use the strategy *predict and test*.

MISSING BASE

$$x^4 = 625$$

• Try $x = 6$.

| 6 | x^y | 4 | = | = | *1296* |

$1{,}296 > 625$
Try a lesser number for the base.

• Try $x = 5$.

| 5 | x^y | 4 | = | *625* |

$625 = 625$

So, $x = 5$. $5^4 = 625$.

MISSING EXPONENT

$$5^y = 15{,}625$$

• Try $y = 5$.

| 5 | x^y | 5 | = | = | *3125* |

$3{,}125 < 15{,}625$
Try a greater number for the exponent.

• Try $y = 6$.

| 5 | x^y | 6 | = | = | *15625* |

$15{,}625 = 15{,}625$

So, $y = 6$. $5^6 = 15{,}625$.

Practice and Problem Solving

Use the x^y key to find the missing exponent or base.

1. $b^5 = 1{,}024$ **2.** $y^4 = 2{,}401$ **3.** $n^6 = 46{,}656$ **4.** $a^8 = 65{,}536$

5. $w^7 = 128$ **6.** $x^9 = 19{,}683$ **7.** $3^q = 6{,}561$ **8.** $7^s = 16{,}807$

9. $8^r = 512$ **10.** $12^y = 20{,}736$ **11.** $15^x = 3{,}375$ **12.** $9^m = 59{,}049$

13. REASONING Find 10^{-x} on your calculator. What do you think this key is used to evaluate? Use the key to check your thinking.

GO ON-LINE

Multimedia Math Glossary www.harcourtschool.com/mathglossary
Vocabulary Power Look up *base* and *exponent* in the Multimedia Math Glossary. Write a sentence that uses *exponent* to explain *base*.

PROBLEM SOLVING ON LOCATION

in Oklahoma

UP, UP, AND AWAY!

Summer in Broken Arrow and in Oklahoma City means a sky full of color. Spectators watch 55 to 60 hot-air balloons soar overhead at festivals in each city.

1. During the 2002 Gatesway Balloon Festival in Broken Arrow, 60 balloons were launched. Seven of the balloons had special shapes. What fraction of the balloons did not have special shapes?

USE DATA For 2–4, use the table.

2. Arrange the activities from the least to the greatest amount of time that Alberto spent at them. Explain how you arrived at your answer.

3. What type of graph could you use to show the data in the table? Make the graph and explain why you chose it.

4. 📝 **Write a problem** that can be solved using the data in the table. Then solve your problem.

5. Fifty-five hot-air balloons were launched at the 2002 Balloon Fest in Oklahoma City. Is the number 55 prime or composite? Explain your answer.

6. There were 84 balloons—40 red, 22 white, 22 blue—in John Ninomiya's helium cluster balloon. The balloons ranged in diameter from 5 feet to 7 feet. Write fractions in simplest form for the numbers of red, white, and blue balloons in the cluster.

TIME ALBERTO SPENT AT THE FESTIVAL	
Activity	**Time Spent**
Quarter Carnival	$1\frac{1}{2}$ hr
Safari Joe's Zoological Park	$\frac{3}{4}$ hr
Clownz Around Tulsey Town	$\frac{1}{2}$ hr
Superplay Inflatables	$1\frac{1}{4}$ hr

The 2002 Balloon Fest in Oklahoma City featured a helium cluster balloon flown by John Ninomiya. ▶

BACK TO NATURE

For people who love the outdoors, Oklahoma offers 51 state parks. Lake Keystone State Park, near Tulsa, has 714 acres of land that visitors can use for hiking, camping, and biking. The 26,000-acre lake gives visitors a chance to go boating, waterskiing, swimming, or fishing.

1. Write the prime factorization of the number of acres of land in the park.

2. The fish in Lake Keystone include about equal numbers of bass, striper, walleye, and catfish. Sergio caught some catfish. What fraction of the fish in the lake are catfish?

VISITORS' ACTIVITIES

Watersking $\frac{3}{20}$

Boating $\frac{1}{5}$

Hiking $\frac{1}{4}$

Biking $\frac{2}{5}$

USE DATA Bob surveyed 60 visitors to the recreation area. His results are shown at the right. For 3–4, use the circle graph.

3. How would you label the circle graph to show the same information using decimals instead of fractions?

4. Which activity was the most popular? Explain.

5. Antelope and Buffalo Springs Trail in the Chickasaw National Recreation Area is 1.2 miles roundtrip. There are also 3 trail loops along the main trail that average about 0.6 mile each. About how long is the entire trail, including the three side trails?

6. There are over 300 species of mammals, amphibians, reptiles, fish, and birds in the Chickasaw National Recreation Area. Of the 58 reptile species, 13 are turtles. What fraction of the reptile species are turtles?

The Chickasaw National Recreation Area ▶ in Sulphur, Oklahoma, was the first Oklahoma state park.

Add and Subtract Fractions

A TYPICAL 24-HOUR DAY AT U.S. SPACE CAMP
HUNTSVILLE, ALABAMA

Lab Work $\frac{1}{12}$ day

Meals $\frac{1}{8}$ day

Training $\frac{1}{6}$ day

Sleep $\frac{5}{12}$ day

Educational Activities $\frac{5}{24}$ day

FAST FACT • SOCIAL STUDIES The White House began the Young Astronaut Program in 1984. Since then, more than 2,000,000 students worldwide have participated in programs developed by the Young Astronaut Council.

PROBLEM SOLVING   What part of a typical day at U.S. Space Camp is spent doing lab work and sleeping? Write the answer in simplest form.

Use this page to help you review and remember important skills needed for Chapter 16.

EQUIVALENT FRACTIONS

Write an equivalent fraction.

1. $\dfrac{15}{20}$ 2. $\dfrac{1}{3}$ 3. $\dfrac{5}{10}$ 4. $\dfrac{2}{6}$ 5. $\dfrac{9}{21}$

6. $\dfrac{2}{5}$ 7. $\dfrac{3}{12}$ 8. $\dfrac{3}{8}$ 9. $\dfrac{2}{3}$ 10. $\dfrac{5}{6}$

11. $\dfrac{7}{8}$ 12. $\dfrac{2}{9}$ 13. $\dfrac{3}{10}$ 14. $\dfrac{4}{12}$ 15. $\dfrac{1}{7}$

SIMPLEST FORM

Write each fraction in simplest form.

16. $\dfrac{6}{42}$ 17. $\dfrac{7}{56}$ 18. $\dfrac{10}{32}$ 19. $\dfrac{8}{12}$ 20. $\dfrac{4}{30}$

21. $\dfrac{5}{40}$ 22. $\dfrac{4}{28}$ 23. $\dfrac{16}{18}$ 24. $\dfrac{7}{35}$ 25. $\dfrac{9}{72}$

Tell whether the fraction is in simplest form. Write *yes* or *no*.

26. $\dfrac{5}{12}$ 27. $\dfrac{6}{18}$ 28. $\dfrac{8}{20}$ 29. $\dfrac{12}{15}$ 30. $\dfrac{12}{56}$

31. $\dfrac{2}{8}$ 32. $\dfrac{6}{7}$ 33. $\dfrac{9}{12}$ 34. $\dfrac{8}{11}$ 35. $\dfrac{9}{31}$

VOCABULARY POWER

REVIEW

numerator [nōō′mə•rā•tər] *noun*

Numerator is from the Latin word *enumerate*, "to count out." The top number of a fraction shows how many parts of the whole are being "counted." What other words come from the Latin *enumerate*?

PREVIEW

least common denominator (LCD)

www.harcourtschool.com/mathglossary

Add and Subtract Like Fractions

Learn

WHOOSH! Damon's basketball team practices each afternoon. The team works on free throws for $\frac{3}{8}$ hour and runs plays for $\frac{5}{8}$ hour. How long is the team practice?

Example 1 Add. $\frac{3}{8} + \frac{5}{8}$

One Way Use a model.

$$\frac{3}{8} + \frac{5}{8} = 1$$

Another Way Use paper and pencil.

$$\begin{array}{r} \frac{3}{8} \\ + \frac{5}{8} \\ \hline \frac{8}{8} = 1 \end{array}$$

- Add the numerators.
- Write the sum over the denominator.
- Write the sum in simplest form.

$$\frac{3}{8} + \frac{5}{8} = 1$$

Technology Link

More Practice: Harcourt Mega Math Fraction Action, *Fraction Flare-Up*, Levels G, H

On May 10, 1997, Karl Malone set a record for the most free throws made in a play-off game. He made 18 free throws without missing one! ▼

So, the team practice lasts 1 hour.

Example 2 How much more time does the team spend on plays than on free throws?

Subtract. $\frac{5}{8} - \frac{3}{8}$

One Way Use a model.

$$\frac{5}{8} - \frac{3}{8} = \frac{2}{8} = \frac{1}{4}$$

Another Way Use mental math.

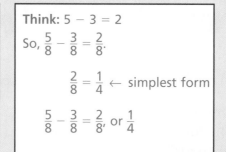

Think: $5 - 3 = 2$

So, $\frac{5}{8} - \frac{3}{8} = \frac{2}{8}$.

$\frac{2}{8} = \frac{1}{4}$ ← simplest form

$\frac{5}{8} - \frac{3}{8} = \frac{2}{8}$, or $\frac{1}{4}$

So, the team spends $\frac{1}{4}$ hour longer on plays than on free throws.

1. Explain what is true about the numerators of two like fractions with a sum of 1.

Find the sum or difference. Write it in simplest form.

2. $\frac{2}{3} + \frac{1}{3}$ **3.** $\frac{1}{4} + \frac{2}{4}$ **4.** $\frac{5}{10} + \frac{2}{10}$

5. $\frac{2}{3} - \frac{1}{3}$ **6.** $\frac{7}{8} - \frac{1}{8}$ **7.** $\frac{5}{6} - \frac{2}{6}$

▶ Practice and Problem Solving

Find the sum or difference. Write it in simplest form.

8. $\frac{1}{6} + \frac{3}{6}$ **9.** $\frac{3}{10} - \frac{1}{10}$ **10.** $\frac{5}{7} + \frac{2}{7}$

11. $\frac{4}{5} - \frac{1}{5}$ **12.** $\frac{7}{12} + \frac{1}{12}$ **13.** $\frac{4}{9} - \frac{1}{9}$

14. $\frac{2}{8} + \frac{3}{8}$ **15.** $\frac{5}{12} - \frac{2}{12}$ **16.** $\frac{1}{10} + \frac{4}{10}$

ALGEBRA **Find the value of *n*.**

17. $n + \frac{4}{9} = \frac{7}{9}$ **18.** $\frac{9}{10} - n = \frac{7}{10}$ **19.** $1 - n = \frac{8}{11}$

20. MEASUREMENT Karla is using $\frac{3}{8}$ yard of ribbon for one craft project and $\frac{5}{8}$ yard for another. How much ribbon is she using in all?

21. Sara and Matt each ordered a medium pizza. Sara ate $\frac{3}{8}$ of her pizza for lunch and $\frac{2}{8}$ for a snack. Matt ate $\frac{2}{4}$ of his pizza for lunch and $\frac{1}{4}$ for a snack. Who ate more pizza? Explain.

22. REASONING Pat made $\frac{3}{5}$ of her free throws in the basketball game. What part of her free throws did she not make?

23. ✎ **Write About It** When you add or subtract two like fractions, when does the final answer have a different denominator?

Mixed Review and Test Prep

24. Order 0.101, 0.011, and 0.111 from greatest to least. (p. 28)

25. $\begin{array}{r} 32,734 \\ +12,196 \end{array}$ (p. 46)   **26.** $\begin{array}{r} 6,213 \\ -4,789 \end{array}$ (p. 46)

27. $7 \times 213,645$ (p. 150)

28. **TEST PREP** Choose the mean for the following set of data. 123, 64, 76, 149 (p. 100)

A 99   **C** 102
B 101   **D** 103

Add and Subtract Unlike Fractions

▶ **Learn**

BEST FRIENDS FOREVER! At a crafts class, Liz and Whitney are making bracelets using beads and colored string. Liz is using $\frac{1}{2}$ cup of large red beads and $\frac{1}{4}$ cup of yellow beads. How many cups of beads is she using in all?

HANDS ON

Activity 1

Use fraction bars to add fractions with unlike denominators.

Add. $\frac{1}{2} + \frac{1}{4}$

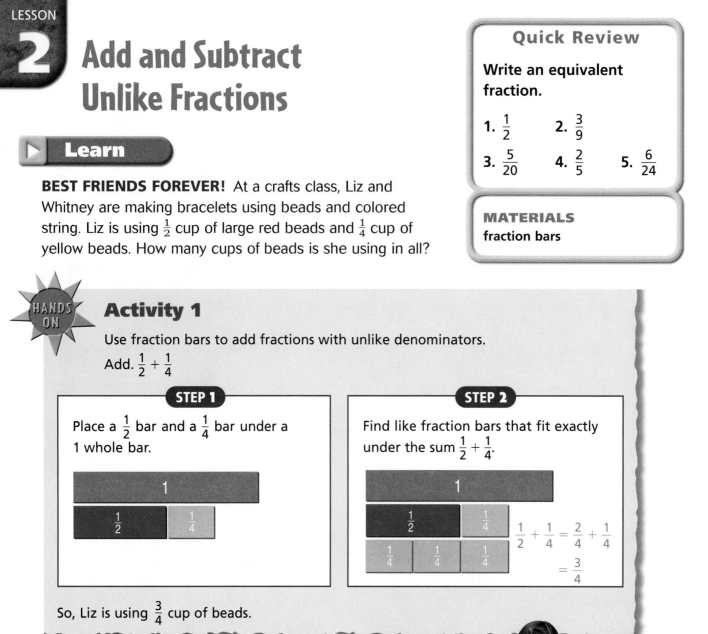

STEP 1

Place a $\frac{1}{2}$ bar and a $\frac{1}{4}$ bar under a 1 whole bar.

STEP 2

Find like fraction bars that fit exactly under the sum $\frac{1}{2} + \frac{1}{4}$.

$$\frac{1}{2} + \frac{1}{4} = \frac{2}{4} + \frac{1}{4}$$
$$= \frac{3}{4}$$

So, Liz is using $\frac{3}{4}$ cup of beads.

In the second step of your model, the $\frac{1}{2}$ bar was replaced with two $\frac{1}{4}$ bars. The fractions $\frac{2}{4}$ and $\frac{1}{4}$ have like denominators. To add fractions with unlike denominators, you need to find equivalent fractions with like denominators.

- What fraction bars can you use to show equivalent fractions for $\frac{1}{3}$ and $\frac{1}{2}$?

Subtract Unlike Fractions

Whitney cut colored string to make a bracelet.
A piece of blue string is $\frac{2}{3}$ yard long.
Whitney cut $\frac{1}{2}$ yard from it. How much string was left?

HANDS ON

Activity 2

Use fraction bars to subtract fractions with unlike denominators.

Subtract. $\frac{2}{3} - \frac{1}{2}$

STEP 1

Place two $\frac{1}{3}$ bars under a 1 whole bar. Then place one $\frac{1}{2}$ bar under the $\frac{1}{3}$ bars.

Compare the bars.

1

| $\frac{1}{3}$ | $\frac{1}{3}$ |

| $\frac{1}{2}$ | ? |

↑
difference

STEP 2

Find like fraction bars that fit exactly under the difference $\frac{2}{3} - \frac{1}{2}$.

| 1 |

| $\frac{1}{3}$ | $\frac{1}{3}$ |

| $\frac{1}{2}$ | ? |

| $\frac{1}{6}$ |

$\frac{2}{3} - \frac{1}{2} = \frac{1}{6}$

So, Whitney had $\frac{1}{6}$ yard of string left.

When you use fraction bars to subtract fractions with unlike denominators, you can think of equivalent fractions with like denominators.

Example   Subtract. $\frac{7}{8} - \frac{1}{2}$

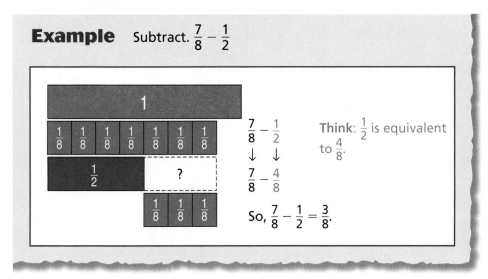

$\frac{7}{8} - \frac{1}{2}$
↓   ↓
$\frac{7}{8} - \frac{4}{8}$

Think: $\frac{1}{2}$ is equivalent to $\frac{4}{8}$.

So, $\frac{7}{8} - \frac{1}{2} = \frac{3}{8}$.

LESSON CONTINUES

1. **Explain** how to find $\frac{1}{3} + \frac{3}{6}$ using fraction bars.

2. **Explain** how to find $\frac{5}{6} - \frac{1}{2}$ using fraction bars.

Use fraction bars to find the sum.

3.

4. (fraction bars: $\frac{1}{5}$ $\frac{1}{10}$ $\frac{1}{10}$ $\frac{1}{10}$)

Use fraction bars to find the difference.

5.

6.

Practice and Problem Solving — Extra Practice, page 362, Set B

Use fraction bars to find the sum.

7. (fraction bars: $\frac{1}{2}$ $\frac{1}{6}$ $\frac{1}{6}$)

8. (fraction bars: $\frac{1}{10}$ $\frac{1}{10}$ $\frac{1}{2}$)

9. $\frac{1}{4} + \frac{1}{6}$

10. $\frac{2}{5} + \frac{3}{10}$

11. $\frac{5}{6} + \frac{1}{12}$

12. $\frac{3}{10} + \frac{1}{2}$

13. $\frac{1}{6} + \frac{2}{3}$

14. $\frac{4}{10} + \frac{1}{2}$

15. $\frac{2}{3} + \frac{1}{4}$

16. $\frac{1}{8} + \frac{3}{4}$

17. $\frac{1}{4} + \frac{1}{3}$

18. $\frac{1}{6} + \frac{1}{2}$

19. $\frac{3}{5} + \frac{1}{10}$

20. $\frac{1}{4} + \frac{3}{8}$

Use fraction bars to find the difference.

21.

22.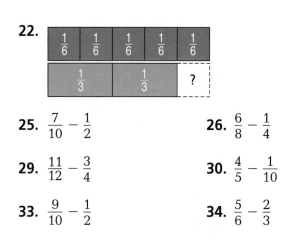

23. $\frac{4}{6} - \frac{1}{4}$

24. $\frac{5}{6} - \frac{1}{12}$

25. $\frac{7}{10} - \frac{1}{2}$

26. $\frac{6}{8} - \frac{1}{4}$

27. $\frac{2}{3} - \frac{1}{12}$

28. $\frac{1}{2} - \frac{1}{5}$

29. $\frac{11}{12} - \frac{3}{4}$

30. $\frac{4}{5} - \frac{1}{10}$

31. $\frac{5}{8} - \frac{1}{2}$

32. $\frac{2}{3} - \frac{1}{6}$

33. $\frac{9}{10} - \frac{1}{2}$

34. $\frac{5}{6} - \frac{2}{3}$

35. Amy is making a burrito dish that calls for $\frac{3}{4}$ cup of grated cheddar cheese. She has grated $\frac{1}{2}$ cup. How much more cheese does Amy have to grate?

36. Every week Tim spends $\frac{1}{2}$ of his allowance on entertainment and $\frac{1}{3}$ of it on snack food. What fraction of Tim's weekly allowance is this in all?

37. REASONING John has to mix $\frac{1}{2}$ cup of flour and $\frac{1}{4}$ cup of sugar. He has a container that holds $\frac{7}{8}$ cup. Can John mix the flour and sugar in the container? Explain.

38. ? **What's the Question?** Carl worked for $\frac{5}{6}$ hour. He tilled his garden for $\frac{1}{2}$ hour, planted seeds for $\frac{1}{6}$ hour, and watered for the rest of the time. The answer is $\frac{1}{6}$ hour.

Mixed Review and Test Prep

39. Order 31.019, 30.091, and 31.119 from least to greatest. (p. 28)

40. List the factors of 30. (p. 278)

41. 108,097 (p. 46)
     $+112,336$

42. 51,002 (p. 46)
     $-39,659$

43. TEST PREP Which fraction is between $\frac{1}{8}$ and $\frac{1}{2}$? (p. 326)

A $\frac{1}{10}$

B $\frac{1}{4}$

C $\frac{2}{3}$

D $\frac{3}{4}$

44. Find the value of n in $59 - 13 = n$. (p. 70)

45. Evaluate $81 + n$ if n is 19. (p. 64)

46. 90,116 (p. 46)
     $-83,909$

47. 79,210 (p. 46)
     $+92,885$

48. TEST PREP In which decimal does the digit 8 have the least value? (p. 22)

F 8.026

G 7.826

H 7.280

J 7.068

Problem Solving LINKUP... to History

The earliest known writing about fractions is called the Rhind Papyrus. It is a roll of papyrus paper 18 feet long and 1 foot high. The Rhind Papyrus was written 3,600 years ago by Egyptian mathematicians. In 1858 it was discovered by a Scottish man, Alexander Henry Rhind.

Egyptian fractions were expressed as sums of different "unit" fractions. A unit fraction is a fraction that has a 1 in the numerator. To write $\frac{3}{4}$, for example, the Egyptians would write $\frac{1}{2} + \frac{1}{4}$.

Find the fraction represented by the unit fractions.

1. $\frac{1}{2} + \frac{1}{5}$ **2.** $\frac{1}{3} + \frac{1}{4}$ **3.** $\frac{1}{5} + \frac{1}{10}$ **4.** $\frac{1}{8} + \frac{1}{4}$

5. Find Egyptian fractions for $\frac{2}{7}$ and $\frac{5}{6}$.

Estimate Sums and Differences

▶ **Learn**

HAPPY TRAILS   On a weekend camping trip, Ken, Eric, and their dad went for a 2-hour walk on the Woodland Trail to look for the trail markings. The first hour, they walked $\frac{3}{8}$ mile. The second hour, they walked $\frac{4}{5}$ mile. About how many miles did the boys and their dad walk?

MATH IDEA   Rounding fractions to benchmarks such as 0, $\frac{1}{2}$, or 1 on a number line can help you estimate sums and differences.

Example Estimate. $\frac{3}{8} + \frac{4}{5}$

STEP 1

The fraction $\frac{3}{8}$ is close to $\frac{1}{2}$. Round to $\frac{1}{2}$.

$$\frac{1}{8}\ \frac{2}{8}\ \frac{3}{8}\ \frac{4}{8}\ \frac{5}{8}\ \frac{6}{8}\ \frac{7}{8}$$

0    $\frac{1}{2}$ 1

STEP 2

The fraction $\frac{4}{5}$ is close to 1. Round to 1.

$$\frac{1}{5}\ \frac{2}{5}\ \frac{3}{5}\ \frac{4}{5}$$

0    $\frac{1}{2}$ 1

STEP 3

Add the rounded fractions.

$$\begin{aligned}\frac{3}{8} &\rightarrow \frac{1}{2}\\ +\frac{4}{5} &\rightarrow +1\\ \hline &\quad 1\frac{1}{2}\end{aligned}$$

So, Ken, Eric, and their dad walked about $1\frac{1}{2}$ miles.

More Examples

A Estimate. $\frac{2}{3} + \frac{4}{5}$

$$\frac{1}{5}\qquad \frac{2}{5}\qquad \frac{3}{5}\qquad \frac{4}{5}$$

0    $\frac{1}{3}$ $\frac{1}{2}$ $\frac{2}{3}$ 1

$\frac{2}{3} \rightarrow \frac{1}{2}$ $\frac{2}{3}$ is between $\frac{1}{2}$ and 1, but closer to $\frac{1}{2}$.

$+\frac{4}{5} \rightarrow +1$ $\frac{4}{5}$ is between $\frac{1}{2}$ and 1, but closer to 1.

$\phantom{+\frac{4}{5} \rightarrow} 1\frac{1}{2}$ The sum is greater than 1, but less than 2.

B Estimate. $\frac{3}{8} - \frac{1}{6}$

$$\frac{1}{6}\qquad \frac{2}{6}\qquad \frac{3}{6}\qquad \frac{4}{6}\qquad \frac{5}{6}$$

0   $\frac{1}{8}$ $\frac{2}{8}$ $\frac{3}{8}$ $\frac{1}{2}$ $\frac{5}{8}$ $\frac{6}{8}$ $\frac{7}{8}$ 1

$\frac{3}{8} \rightarrow \frac{1}{2}$ $\frac{3}{8}$ is between 0 and $\frac{1}{2}$, but closer to $\frac{1}{2}$.

$-\frac{1}{6} \rightarrow -0$ $\frac{1}{6}$ is between 0 and $\frac{1}{2}$, but closer to 0.

$\phantom{-\frac{1}{6} \rightarrow} \frac{1}{2}$ The difference is greater than 0, but less than $\frac{1}{2}$.

1. **Compare** the numerators and denominators of fractions that round to 1, such as $\frac{11}{12}, \frac{8}{9}, \frac{7}{8}$, and $\frac{8}{10}$. What do you notice?

Write whether the fraction is closest to 0, $\frac{1}{2}$, or 1. Use the number lines.

$\frac{0}{10}$ $\frac{1}{10}$ $\frac{2}{10}$ $\frac{3}{10}$ $\frac{4}{10}$ $\frac{5}{10}$ $\frac{6}{10}$ $\frac{7}{10}$ $\frac{8}{10}$ $\frac{9}{10}$ $\frac{10}{10}$

0        $\frac{1}{2}$ 1

$\frac{0}{12}$ $\frac{1}{12}$ $\frac{2}{12}$ $\frac{3}{12}$ $\frac{4}{12}$ $\frac{5}{12}$ $\frac{6}{12}$ $\frac{7}{12}$ $\frac{8}{12}$ $\frac{9}{12}$ $\frac{10}{12}$ $\frac{11}{12}$ $\frac{12}{12}$

0        $\frac{1}{2}$ 1

2. $\frac{7}{10}$ 3. $\frac{1}{12}$ 4. $\frac{3}{10}$ 5. $\frac{5}{12}$ 6. $\frac{9}{10}$ 7. $\frac{2}{10}$

▶ **Practice and Problem Solving**   Extra Practice, page 362, Set C

Write whether the fraction is closest to 0, $\frac{1}{2}$, or 1.

8. $\frac{4}{7}$ 9. $\frac{2}{9}$ 10. $\frac{6}{7}$ 11. $\frac{8}{9}$ 12. $\frac{3}{7}$ 13. $\frac{5}{6}$

Estimate each sum or difference.

14. $\frac{1}{9} + \frac{5}{6}$ 15. $\frac{2}{3} + \frac{5}{7}$ 16. $\frac{3}{8} - \frac{1}{5}$ 17. $\frac{9}{10} - \frac{3}{8}$ 18. $\frac{7}{12} + \frac{1}{7}$

19. $\frac{8}{10} - \frac{2}{3}$ 20. $\frac{6}{7} + \frac{3}{5}$ 21. $\frac{7}{9} - \frac{2}{6}$ 22. $\frac{7}{8} + \frac{2}{3}$ 23. $\frac{10}{12} - \frac{1}{10}$

Estimate to compare. Write < or > for each ●.

24. $\frac{6}{8} + \frac{2}{3}$ ● 1   25. $\frac{1}{2}$ ● $\frac{3}{5} - \frac{1}{3}$ 26. $\frac{2}{5} + \frac{1}{7}$ ● 1

27. **REASONING** The number ♣ is three times the number ♥. What is the fraction $\frac{♥}{♣}$ in simplest form?

28. 📓 **Write About It** Explain how you can estimate the sum of $\frac{4}{5}$ and $\frac{1}{10}$.

29. Yoko added $\frac{3}{4}$ cup cashews, $\frac{1}{2}$ cup pecans, $\frac{5}{6}$ cup banana chips, and $\frac{1}{3}$ cup peanuts to the trail mix. Did she add more nuts or more fruit?

Mixed Review and Test Prep

Find the value of *n*. (pp. 250 and 258)

30. $4 \times (6 \times n) = (4 \times 6) \times 8$

31. $(7 \times 3) \times n = 105$

32. Find the mean, median, and mode for the data set 90, 94, 89, 90, 92. (pp. 100 and 102)

33. $96.54 \div 6$ (p. 232)

34. **TEST PREP** What are the LCM and GCF of 4 and 50? (pp. 278 and 282)

A LCM: 150; GCF: 2
B LCM: 100; GCF: 4
C LCM: 100; GCF: 2
D LCM: 200; GCF: 4

Use Common Denominators

▶ **Learn**

GREEN THUMB Zach is planting a garden in his backyard. He planted daisies in $\frac{3}{8}$ of the garden and marigolds in $\frac{1}{2}$ of the garden. How much of the garden did Zach use?

To add or subtract unlike fractions, you need to rename them as like fractions with a common denominator.

Quick Review

Write the least common multiple for each pair.

1. 8 and 4   **2.** 6 and 4
3. 3 and 8   **4.** 7 and 4
5. 3 and 5

VOCABULARY

least common denominator (LCD)

Example Add. $\frac{3}{8} + \frac{1}{2}$

Estimate. $\frac{3}{8}$ is close to $\frac{1}{2}$, so the sum is close to 1.

One Way Use a common denominator.

Multiply the denominators to find a common denominator.

$8 \times 2 = 16 \leftarrow$ common denominator

Use the common denominator to write equivalent fractions. Then add.

$$\frac{3}{8} = \frac{6}{16}$$
$$+\frac{1}{2} = +\frac{8}{16}$$
$$\frac{14}{16} = \frac{7}{8} \leftarrow \text{simplest form}$$

Another Way Use the least common denominator.

The **least common denominator**, or **LCD**, is the least common multiple of two or more denominators. List multiples of each denominator. Then find the least common multiple of the denominators.

Multiples of 8: 8, 16, 32, 40, 48, 56
Multiples of 2: 2, 4, 6, 8, 10, 12

The LCM is 8. So, the LCD of $\frac{3}{8}$ and $\frac{1}{2}$ is 8. Write equivalent fractions. Then add.

$$\frac{3}{8} = \frac{3}{8}$$
$$+\frac{1}{2} = +\frac{1 \times 4}{2 \times 4} = +\frac{4}{8}$$
$$\frac{7}{8} \leftarrow \text{simplest form}$$

So, Zach used $\frac{7}{8}$ of the garden. The answer is close to the estimate, so the answer is reasonable.

• What would the least common denominator be for $\frac{3}{4} - \frac{2}{5}$? Explain.

MATH IDEA To add or subtract unlike fractions, write equivalent fractions with a common denominator.

1. Explain how you can use multiples to find the LCD for $\frac{2}{3} + \frac{3}{5}$.

Find the sum. Write it in simplest form.

2. $\frac{1}{5} + \frac{1}{10}$ **3.** $\frac{1}{4} + \frac{1}{3}$ **4.** $\frac{1}{3} + \frac{2}{9}$ **5.** $\frac{1}{6} + \frac{2}{4}$ **6.** $\frac{1}{5} + \frac{5}{10}$

Find the difference. Write it in simplest form.

7. $\frac{2}{3} - \frac{1}{2}$ **8.** $\frac{3}{4} - \frac{3}{8}$ **9.** $1 - \frac{1}{4}$ **10.** $\frac{11}{12} - \frac{1}{6}$ **11.** $\frac{7}{10} - \frac{1}{5}$

▷ **Practice and Problem Solving**   Extra Practice, page 362, Set D

Find the sum or difference. Write it in simplest form.

12. $\frac{1}{8} + \frac{3}{4}$ **13.** $\frac{1}{2} + \frac{2}{5}$ **14.** $\frac{5}{6} - \frac{3}{4}$ **15.** $1 - \frac{3}{5}$ **16.** $\frac{7}{8} + \frac{1}{4}$

17. $\frac{2}{3} + \frac{1}{6}$ **18.** $\frac{2}{3} - \frac{1}{9}$ **19.** $\frac{7}{8} - \frac{1}{2}$ **20.** $\frac{1}{4} + \frac{2}{3}$ **21.** $\frac{1}{4} + \frac{2}{8}$

22. $\frac{4}{5} + \frac{2}{10}$ **23.** $\frac{3}{12} - \frac{1}{6}$ **24.** $\frac{9}{10} - \frac{1}{2}$ **25.** $\frac{1}{4} + \frac{1}{12}$ **26.** $\frac{1}{4} - \frac{3}{16}$

ALGEBRA   **Find the value of *n*.**

27. $\frac{2}{10} + n = 1$ **28.** $n + \frac{1}{12} = \frac{7}{12}$ **29.** $\frac{5}{8} - n = \frac{3}{8}$ **30.** $\frac{9}{10} - n = \frac{1}{5}$

USE DATA   **For 31–32, use the table.**

31. Which type of plant grew more during the first week?

32. ✎ Write a problem that uses subtraction, using the data from the second week.

GARDEN PLANT GROWTH (in inches)		
	First Week	**Second Week**
Tulips	$\frac{7}{8}$	$\frac{3}{4}$
Daffodils	$\frac{1}{4}$	$\frac{1}{2}$

33. Dan wrote a report. He found $\frac{1}{8}$ of the information for the report on the Internet and $\frac{1}{2}$ at the library. How much of his information did he get from sources other than the Internet and the library?

Mixed Review and Test Prep

Use mental math to find each sum. (p. 52)

34. $125 + 80 + 20 + 75$

35. $35,200 + 4,800 + 10,000$

36. Round 3,950,964 to the nearest million.

(p. 38)

37. Find the value of *n* in $102 - n = 57$.

(p. 70)

38. **TEST PREP**   Which number is between 0.285 and 0.29? (p. 28)

A 0.128   **B** 0.278   **C** 0.289   **D** 0.291

5 Use the Least Common Denominator

▶ **Learn**

LIFT OFF! Kevin and Stuart are building a model rocket at U.S. Space Camp. The body tube is $\frac{1}{2}$ yard long and the nose cone is $\frac{1}{6}$ yard long. How tall will the rocket be when the parts are joined?

Example 1

Add. $\frac{1}{6} + \frac{1}{2}$

Estimate. $\frac{1}{6}$ is a little more than 0, so the sum is close to $\frac{1}{2}$.

STEP 1

The LCM of 2 and 6 is 6. So, the LCD of $\frac{1}{2}$ and $\frac{1}{6}$ is 6. Use the LCD to write like fractions.

$$\frac{1}{6} = \frac{1}{6}$$
$$+\frac{1 \times 3}{2 \times 3} = +\frac{3}{6}$$

STEP 2

Add the fractions. Write the answer in simplest form.

$$\frac{1}{6} = \frac{1}{6}$$
$$+\frac{1 \times 3}{2 \times 3} = +\frac{3}{6}$$
$$\frac{4}{6} = \frac{2}{3}$$

▲ **U.S. Space Camp is located in Huntsville, Alabama.**

So, the model rocket will be $\frac{2}{3}$ yard tall when the parts are joined. The exact answer is close to the estimate, so the answer is reasonable.

You can also use a calculator that operates with fractions.

`1` `b/c` `6` `+` `1` `b/c` `2` `=`   SIMP = $\frac{2}{3}$

Example 2

Subtract. $\frac{3}{4} - \frac{1}{6}$

Estimate. $\frac{3}{4}$ is halfway between $\frac{1}{2}$ and 1, and $\frac{1}{6}$ is a little more than 0, so the difference is close to $\frac{1}{2}$.

STEP 1

The LCM of 4 and 6 is 12. So, the LCD of $\frac{3}{4}$ and $\frac{1}{6}$ is 12. Use the LCD to change the fractions to like fractions.

$$\frac{3}{4} = \frac{3 \times 3}{4 \times 3} = \frac{9}{12}$$

$$-\frac{1}{6} = -\frac{1 \times 2}{6 \times 2} = -\frac{2}{12}$$

STEP 2

Subtract the fractions.
Write the answer in simplest form.

$$\frac{3}{4} = \frac{3 \times 3}{4 \times 3} = \frac{9}{12}$$

$$-\frac{1}{6} = -\frac{1 \times 2}{6 \times 2} = -\frac{2}{12}$$

$$\frac{7}{12} \leftarrow \text{simplest form}$$

More Examples

Ⓐ Find $\frac{3}{4} + \frac{5}{8}$.

$$\frac{3 \times 2}{4 \times 2} = \frac{6}{8}$$

$$+\frac{5}{8} = +\frac{5}{8}$$

$$\frac{11}{8}, \text{ or } 1\frac{3}{8}$$

Ⓑ Find $1 - \frac{2}{5}$.

$$\frac{1 \times 5}{1 \times 5} = \frac{5}{5}$$

$$-\frac{2}{5} = -\frac{2}{5}$$

$$\frac{3}{5}$$

> **MATH IDEA** To add or subtract unlike fractions, you need to find the least common denominator (LCD) to write equivalent fractions. Then add or subtract the numerators.

▶ Check

1. **Explain** what the least common denominator is.

Find the LCD. Then add or subtract.

2. $\frac{6}{12}$
    $-\frac{1}{3}$

3. $\frac{1}{5}$
    $+\frac{1}{2}$

4. $\frac{5}{7}$
    $-\frac{1}{2}$

5. $\frac{8}{9}$
    $-\frac{2}{3}$

6. $\frac{1}{2}$
    $+\frac{1}{3}$

Find the sum or difference. Write the answer in simplest form.

7. $\frac{2}{3} + \frac{1}{6}$

8. $\frac{2}{3} - \frac{1}{9}$

9. $\frac{7}{8} - \frac{1}{2}$

10. $\frac{1}{4} + \frac{2}{3}$

11. $\frac{1}{4} + \frac{2}{8}$

12. $\frac{7}{12} - \frac{1}{3}$

13. $\frac{3}{8} + \frac{3}{4}$

14. $1 - \frac{5}{6}$

15. $\frac{3}{9} + \frac{1}{3}$

16. $1 - \frac{7}{10}$

LESSON CONTINUES ▶

Find the LCD. Then add or subtract.

17. $\dfrac{1}{6}$
    $+\dfrac{1}{3}$

18. $\dfrac{7}{10}$
    $+\dfrac{1}{2}$

19. $\dfrac{5}{9}$
    $-\dfrac{1}{6}$

20. $\dfrac{2}{8}$
    $+\dfrac{3}{4}$

21. $\dfrac{2}{3}$
    $-\dfrac{1}{4}$

Find the sum or difference. Write it in simplest form.

22. $\dfrac{1}{8} + \dfrac{3}{4}$

23. $\dfrac{1}{2} + \dfrac{2}{5}$

24. $\dfrac{5}{6} - \dfrac{3}{4}$

25. $1 - \dfrac{3}{5}$

26. $\dfrac{2}{3} + \dfrac{1}{4}$

27. $1 - \dfrac{5}{7}$

28. $\dfrac{4}{5} + \dfrac{3}{10}$

29. $\dfrac{7}{8} - \dfrac{1}{2}$

30. $\dfrac{3}{4} + \dfrac{1}{12}$

31. $\dfrac{4}{5} + \dfrac{1}{10}$

32. $\dfrac{7}{14} - \dfrac{1}{7}$

33. $\dfrac{2}{5} + \dfrac{6}{10}$

34. $1 - \dfrac{8}{9}$

35. $\dfrac{4}{18} + \dfrac{2}{6}$

36. $\dfrac{6}{8} - \dfrac{1}{4}$

37. $\dfrac{1}{3} + \dfrac{5}{12}$

38. $\dfrac{2}{3} - \dfrac{5}{9}$

39. $\dfrac{1}{3} + \dfrac{2}{5}$

40. $\dfrac{5}{6} - \dfrac{1}{8}$

41. $\dfrac{4}{9} + \dfrac{1}{3}$

ALGEBRA **Compare. Write < or > for each ●.**

42. $\dfrac{1}{2} + \dfrac{2}{3}$ ● $\dfrac{1}{6} + \dfrac{1}{3}$

43. $\dfrac{2}{4} - \dfrac{2}{8}$ ● $\dfrac{1}{2} - \dfrac{1}{8}$

44. $\dfrac{7}{12} - \dfrac{1}{2}$ ● $\dfrac{4}{6} + \dfrac{1}{12}$

45. **REASONING** Jake and Libby both made streamers for the nose cones of their model rockets from the same piece of ribbon. Jake said he used $\dfrac{3}{8}$ of the ribbon, and Libby said she used $\dfrac{3}{4}$ of the ribbon. Was this possible? Explain.

46. **?** **What's the Error?** Ramon says $\dfrac{2}{3} - \dfrac{1}{2} = \dfrac{1}{1} = 1$. Describe his error. Write the correct answer.

For 47–50, use the drawing.

47. What fraction of the square is red?

48. What fraction of the square is green or orange?

49. What subtraction equation can you write to find the fraction of the square that is yellow? Solve the equation.

50. What fraction of the square is white, blue, or yellow?

51. **FAST FACT • SCIENCE** On the surface of the moon, gravity is only about $\dfrac{1}{6}$ of what it is on Earth because the moon is smaller than Earth. How much would a person weigh on the moon if he weighs 90 pounds on Earth?

52. **Vocabulary Power** Some words show a comparison when *-er* or *-est* is added to them. An example of this comparison is *simple, simpler,* and *simplest*. Write the comparison for the word *great*. Then use one form of *great* in a sentence that describes how numbers compare.

53. Edward says that if you add $\frac{2}{3}$ and $\frac{3}{4}$, the sum will be greater than 1. Is he correct? Explain.

54. Mitchell paid $94 for ten tickets to the concert. Adult tickets cost $15 each. Student tickets cost $8 each. How many of each kind of ticket did he buy?

Mixed Review and Test Prep

Find the mean, median, mode, and range for each set of data. (pp. 96–103)

55. 75, 29, 83, 45, 53

56. 2, 4, 8, 14

57. Solve. Explain how you interpreted the remainder. (p. 200)
Ken has 75 books. Each shelf holds 14 books. How many shelves will he use?

58. **TEST PREP** Which is the value of 8^4?
(p. 292)

   A 64   **C** 4,096

   B 512   **D** 32,768

Copy and complete each pattern. (p. 208)

59. $6,000 \div 4 = \blacksquare$
$600 \div 4 = \blacksquare$
$60 \div 4 = \blacksquare$
$6 \div 4 = \blacksquare$

60. $18,000 \div 3 = \blacksquare$
$1,800 \div 3 = \blacksquare$
$180 \div 3 = \blacksquare$
$18 \div 3 = \blacksquare$

61. **TEST PREP** What number is 10,000 more than 2,692,450? (p. 4)

   F 2,690,450

   G 2,693,450

   H 2,702,450

   J 2,720,450

Problem Solving Thinker's Corner

PATTERNS You can use models to help you look at patterns in fractions.

Examples   **MATERIALS:** fraction strips

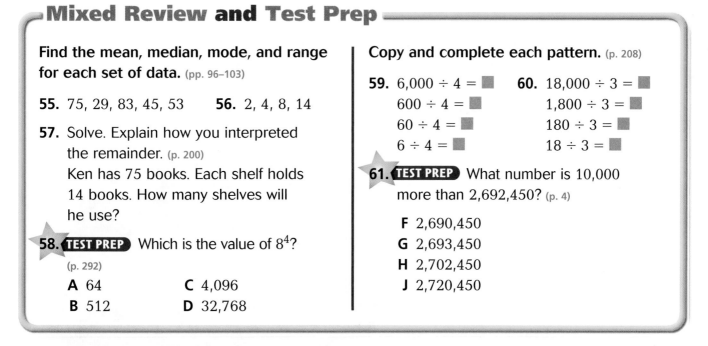

A How do the values of these fractions change as the denominators increase?

$$\frac{1}{2}, \frac{1}{3}, \frac{1}{4}, \frac{1}{5}, \frac{1}{6}$$

Use fraction strips to model the fractions.

As the denominators increase, the values of the fractions decrease.

B How do the values of these fractions change as the numerators increase?

$$\frac{3}{10}, \frac{4}{10}, \frac{5}{10}, \frac{6}{10}, \frac{7}{10}$$

Use fraction strips to model the fractions.

As the numerators increase, the values of the fractions increase.

Use fraction strips to model the fractions. Then describe how the values of the fractions change.

1. $\frac{8}{8}, \frac{7}{8}, \frac{6}{8}, \frac{5}{8}, \frac{4}{8}$

2. $\frac{1}{12}, \frac{1}{10}, \frac{1}{8}, \frac{1}{6}, \frac{1}{4}$

3. $\frac{3}{3}, \frac{3}{4}, \frac{3}{5}, \frac{3}{6}, \frac{3}{7}$

4. $\frac{1}{2}, \frac{2}{2}, \frac{3}{2}, \frac{4}{2}, \frac{5}{2}$

Problem Solving Strategy
Work Backward

Quick Review

1. $52 + 19 + 21$
2. $133 - 30 - 14$
3. $609 + 91 + 170$
4. $\frac{3}{4} - \frac{1}{6} - \frac{1}{12}$
5. $\frac{2}{3} + \frac{1}{6} + \frac{1}{9}$

PROBLEM Jessica built a tower out of building blocks for a craft fair. She worked on her tower for three weeks. After three weeks, the tower was $\frac{9}{10}$ meter tall. This was $\frac{1}{5}$ meter taller than it was after two weeks. The height at two weeks was $\frac{1}{2}$ meter taller than it was after the first week. How tall was Jessica's tower after the first week?

UNDERSTAND

- What are you asked to find?

- What information will you use?

PLAN

- What strategy can you use to solve this problem?

  You can *work backward* to find out how tall Jessica's tower was after the first week.

SOLVE

- How can you work backward to solve?

  The growth can be shown by this equation: $n + \frac{1}{2} + \frac{1}{5} = \frac{9}{10}$.

  To work backward, start with $\frac{9}{10}$ and subtract.

  $$\frac{9}{10} - \frac{1}{5} - \frac{1}{2} = n$$

  $$\frac{9}{10} - \frac{2}{10} - \frac{5}{10} = n \quad \text{Find a common denominator.}$$

  $$\frac{7}{10} - \frac{5}{10} = n \quad \text{Subtract.}$$

  $$\frac{2}{10} = n, \; or \; \frac{1}{5} = n$$

  So, Jessica's tower was $\frac{1}{5}$ meter tall after one week.

▲ Miniature model of Manhattan skyline

CHECK

- How can you determine if your answer is reasonable?

Problem Solving Practice

Problem Solving

Strategies

Draw a Diagram or Picture
Make a Model or Act It Out
Make an Organized List
Find a Pattern
Make a Table or Graph
Predict and Test
▶ **Work Backward**
Solve a Simpler Problem
Write an Equation
Use Logical Reasoning

Work backward to solve.

1. **What if** Jessica's tower was $\frac{11}{12}$ yard tall after 3 weeks? This was $\frac{1}{6}$ yard taller than it was after 2 weeks. The height at 2 weeks was $\frac{1}{4}$ yard taller than it was after the first week. How tall was the tower after the first week?

2. On Friday, Michael's plant was $\frac{5}{6}$ foot tall. It had grown $\frac{1}{3}$ foot from Wednesday to Friday. It had grown $\frac{3}{8}$ foot from Monday to Wednesday. How tall was Michael's plant on Monday?

3. Lisa came home from the toy store with $2.26. At the store she spent $7.38 on blocks, $4.17 on a book, and $8.55 on a science kit. She used a gift certificate worth $3.00 to help pay the bill. How much money did Lisa have before she went to the toy store?

USE DATA **Mrs. Balog's class raised money for a field trip. The circle graph shows the field trip expenses.**

FIELD TRIP EXPENSES

4. Which expression shows what fraction of the money was used for the bus and gas?

   A $\frac{3}{16} - \frac{1}{8}$ **B** $\frac{5}{16} + \frac{1}{8}$ **C** $\frac{3}{16} + \frac{3}{8}$ **D** $\frac{5}{16} - \frac{1}{8}$

5. What fraction of the money was not for the bus and gas?

   F $\frac{5}{16}$ **G** $\frac{3}{8}$ **H** $\frac{7}{16}$ **J** $\frac{9}{16}$

Mixed Strategy Practice

6. Charity gave 12 baseball cards to Rhonda and 18 to James. Then she traded 5 of her cards for 3 of Andy's cards. Charity now has 48 cards. How many cards did she have to start with?

7. A rectangular fence has a perimeter of 20 feet. If the width is 2 feet, what is the length?

8. Carlotta bought 9 packages of lemonade for $1.10 each and 2 packages of cups for $1.09 each. She sold 23 cups of lemonade every hour for 4 hours at $0.40 per cup. How much more money did Carlotta earn than she spent on supplies?

9. Sherwood earned $35 last week. He earned twice as much for baby-sitting as he did for mowing lawns. He earned twice as much for mowing lawns as he did for washing cars. How much did Sherwood earn for each job?

Extra Practice

Set A (pp. 346–347)

Find the sum or difference. Write it in simplest form.

1. $\frac{3}{6} + \frac{1}{6}$
2. $\frac{4}{10} + \frac{1}{10}$
3. $\frac{1}{3} + \frac{2}{3}$
4. $\frac{3}{8} + \frac{4}{8}$

5. $\frac{1}{4} + \frac{2}{4}$
6. $\frac{4}{5} - \frac{1}{5}$
7. $\frac{5}{8} - \frac{3}{8}$
8. $\frac{5}{12} + \frac{2}{12}$

Set B (pp. 348–351)

Use fraction bars to find the sum or difference.

1. $\frac{2}{5} + \frac{5}{10}$
2. $\frac{2}{4} + \frac{1}{6}$
3. $\frac{2}{8} + \frac{1}{4}$
4. $\frac{1}{6} + \frac{3}{9}$

5. $\frac{9}{10} - \frac{1}{2}$
6. $\frac{7}{8} - \frac{3}{4}$
7. $\frac{10}{12} - \frac{5}{6}$
8. $\frac{4}{5} - \frac{3}{10}$

Set C (pp. 352–353)

Estimate each sum or difference.

1. $\frac{5}{6} - \frac{1}{8}$
2. $\frac{3}{7} + \frac{7}{9}$
3. $\frac{10}{11} - \frac{2}{4}$
4. $\frac{2}{3} + \frac{7}{8}$
5. $\frac{6}{10} - \frac{1}{5}$

Estimate to compare. Write < or > for each ●.

6. $\frac{2}{3} + \frac{3}{4}$ ● $\frac{4}{5} + \frac{1}{10}$
7. $\frac{5}{8} - \frac{1}{9}$ ● $\frac{4}{10} + \frac{5}{12}$
8. $\frac{5}{6} - \frac{3}{7}$ ● 0

Set D (pp. 354–355)

Find the sum or difference. Write it in simplest form.

1. $\frac{1}{3} + \frac{1}{6}$
2. $\frac{1}{5} + \frac{4}{10}$
3. $\frac{7}{8} - \frac{1}{4}$
4. $\frac{2}{3} + \frac{1}{4}$

5. $\frac{1}{3} + \frac{1}{4}$
6. $\frac{5}{8} - \frac{1}{2}$
7. $\frac{8}{9} - \frac{1}{3}$
8. $\frac{4}{5} - \frac{3}{4}$

Set E (pp. 356–359)

Find the sum or difference. Write it in simplest form.

1. $\begin{array}{r} \frac{2}{3} \\ +\frac{2}{9} \\ \hline \end{array}$
2. $\begin{array}{r} \frac{1}{4} \\ +\frac{3}{8} \\ \hline \end{array}$
3. $\begin{array}{r} \frac{1}{3} \\ +\frac{2}{4} \\ \hline \end{array}$
4. $\begin{array}{r} \frac{4}{5} \\ -\frac{1}{2} \\ \hline \end{array}$
5. $\begin{array}{r} \frac{8}{9} \\ -\frac{2}{3} \\ \hline \end{array}$

6. Eva used $\frac{3}{4}$ yard, $\frac{7}{8}$ yard, and $\frac{1}{2}$ yard of ribbon to make a hair bow. How much ribbon did she use?

7. The sauce has $\frac{3}{4}$ teaspoon basil, $\frac{1}{2}$ teaspoon oregano, and $\frac{3}{4}$ teaspoon parsley. How many teaspoons of herbs does the sauce have in all?

Review/Test

✓ CHECK VOCABULARY AND CONCEPTS

Choose the best term from the box.

denominators
numerators
least common denominator (LCD)

1. The least common multiple of two or more denominators is the __?__. (p. 354)

2. When you add or subtract fractions with unlike denominators, first write equivalent fractions with like __?__. (p. 348)

✓ CHECK SKILLS

Estimate each sum or difference. (pp. 352–353)

3. $\frac{5}{6} - \frac{3}{8}$
4. $\frac{3}{9} + \frac{5}{8}$
5. $\frac{7}{8} - \frac{2}{3}$
6. $\frac{1}{3} + \frac{1}{5}$

Find the sum or difference. Write it in simplest form. (pp. 346–347, 348–351, 354–355, 356–359)

7. $\frac{2}{8} + \frac{4}{8}$
8. $\frac{7}{9} - \frac{4}{9}$
9. $\frac{4}{12} + \frac{2}{12}$
10. $\frac{5}{8} - \frac{1}{8}$

11. $\begin{array}{r} \frac{3}{4} \\ + \frac{2}{3} \\ \hline \end{array}$
12. $\begin{array}{r} \frac{3}{4} \\ - \frac{4}{6} \\ \hline \end{array}$
13. $\begin{array}{r} \frac{1}{2} \\ + \frac{4}{5} \\ \hline \end{array}$
14. $\begin{array}{r} \frac{2}{5} \\ - \frac{1}{3} \\ \hline \end{array}$

15. $\frac{1}{7} + \frac{1}{2}$
16. $\frac{4}{6} - \frac{1}{4}$
17. $1 - \frac{3}{8}$
18. $\frac{4}{5} - \frac{1}{4}$

19. $\frac{1}{4} + \frac{2}{3}$
20. $\frac{5}{8} - \frac{1}{3}$
21. $\frac{4}{5} + \frac{1}{3}$
22. $\frac{6}{7} - \frac{1}{3}$

✓ CHECK PROBLEM SOLVING (pp. 360–361)

23. On Friday, Kayla's bean plant was $\frac{7}{8}$ in. tall. It had grown $\frac{3}{8}$ in. from Wednesday to Friday. It had grown $\frac{1}{4}$ in. from Monday to Wednesday. How tall was the plant on Monday?

24. From 9 A.M. to 4 P.M., $\frac{1}{3}$ foot of snow fell on the mountain. At 8 P.M., the snow was $\frac{5}{6}$ foot deep, which was $\frac{1}{4}$ foot deeper than it was at 4 P.M. How much snow was on the ground at 9 A.M.?

25. Blaine has $2.05 left after going on a field trip. He spent $4.95 on lunch, $5.35 on a souvenir, and $12.65 on a T-shirt. How much money did Blaine have before he left for the field trip?

Standardized Test Prep

⭐ NUMBER SENSE, CONCEPTS, AND OPERATIONS

1. Carl went to the fair with $20.00. Admission to the fair was $4.50. While he was there, his friend Anna gave him $6.00. He spent $8.25 on food and rides. How much money did Carl have when he left the fair?

A $1.25

B $7.25

C $13.25

D $29.75

2. How long would it take the elevator of the Metropolitan Life Tower Building to go from the first floor to the top of the building if it moves 25 feet per second?

FAMOUS NEW YORK CITY BUILDINGS		
Building	**Number of Stories**	**Height (in feet)**
Park Row	30	386
Empire State	103	1,250
Metropolitan Life Tower	50	700
Chrysler	77	1,047

F   2 seconds

G   28 seconds

H   50 seconds

J   200 seconds

3. Explain It Use the table in Problem 2. About how tall is each story in the Park Row Building? Explain how you found your answer.

⭐ ALGEBRAIC THINKING

4. Haley created this pattern with triangles. If the pattern continues, how many triangles will be in the next figure?

A 12

B 13

C 14

D 15

> **TIP**   **Check your work.**
> See item 4. Draw the next figure in the pattern. Count the triangles in the figure to see if it matches your answer choice.

5. Suppose m represents the number of miles from Jay's house to the mall. Which expression represents the number of miles in a round trip from Jay's house to the mall?

F $m - 2$

G $2 \times m$

H $2 + m$

J $m \div 2$

6. Explain It Rosa paid $108 for 9 cans of paint. If each can costs the same amount, how much did she pay for each can of paint? Write an equation with a variable to solve. Explain what the variable represents and how you solved the equation.

⭐ DATA ANALYSIS AND PROBABILITY

7. The circle graph shows the results of a survey about the type of transportation families use when they travel on vacation.

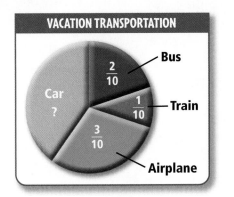

VACATION TRANSPORTATION

Which fraction of those surveyed travel by car?

A $\frac{3}{10}$

B $\frac{4}{10}$

C $\frac{6}{10}$

D $\frac{10}{10}$

8. There are 6 red marbles, 5 blue marbles, and 9 green marbles in a bag. What is the probability of drawing a marble that is NOT green?

F $\frac{9}{11}$

G $\frac{11}{20}$

H $\frac{9}{20}$

J $\frac{11}{9}$

9. Explain It Pete, Rose, and Sara are competing in the 50-yard dash. In how many different ways can they finish first, second, and third in the race? Explain your answer.

⭐ MEASUREMENT

10. The clock shows the time Wesley finished his homework. It took him 15 minutes to do his homework. At what time did Wesley begin his homework?

A 3:45 **C** 3:55

B 3:50 **D** 4:25

11. Jeff is not feeling well. Which tool would be **best** to measure his body temperature?

F **H**

G **J**

12. Explain It Yoriko drew this 2-inch line segment.

inches

ESTIMATE to determine whether the line segment is greater than or less than 8 centimeters. Explain how you know.

1 inch ≈ 2.5 centimeters

Add and Subtract Mixed Numbers

≡FAST FACT • HEALTH Every year between 2,000 and 3,000 hikers set off with the intention of completing the Appalachian Trail. However, only 200 to 300 hikers are successful because it takes the average person more than six months to complete it.

PROBLEM SOLVING   Look at the graph. How many more miles of the Appalachian Trail are in North Carolina than in Georgia?

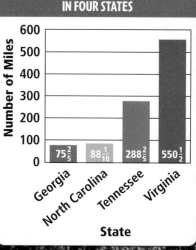

APPALACHIAN TRAIL IN FOUR STATES

Number of Miles

Georgia $75\frac{2}{5}$, North Carolina $88\frac{1}{10}$, Tennessee $288\frac{2}{5}$, Virginia $550\frac{1}{2}$

State

Use this page to help you review and remember
important skills needed for Chapter 17.

UNDERSTAND MIXED NUMBERS

Write a mixed number for each picture.

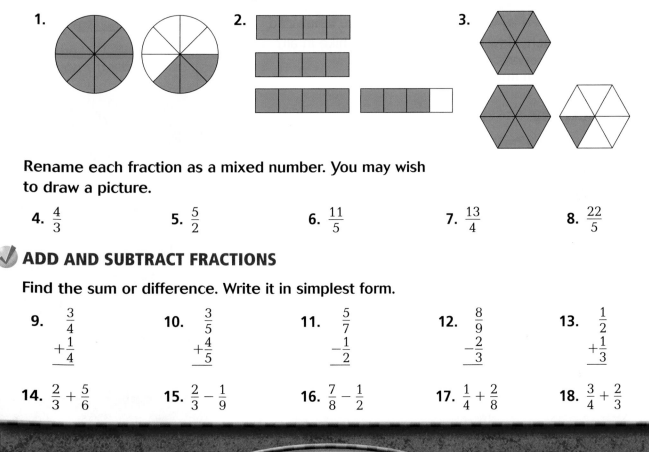

1.

2.

3.

Rename each fraction as a mixed number. You may wish
to draw a picture.

4. $\frac{4}{3}$ 5. $\frac{5}{2}$ 6. $\frac{11}{5}$ 7. $\frac{13}{4}$ 8. $\frac{22}{5}$

ADD AND SUBTRACT FRACTIONS

Find the sum or difference. Write it in simplest form.

9. $\begin{array}{r} \frac{3}{4} \\ +\frac{1}{4} \\ \hline \end{array}$ 10. $\begin{array}{r} \frac{3}{5} \\ +\frac{4}{5} \\ \hline \end{array}$ 11. $\begin{array}{r} \frac{5}{7} \\ -\frac{1}{2} \\ \hline \end{array}$ 12. $\begin{array}{r} \frac{8}{9} \\ -\frac{2}{3} \\ \hline \end{array}$ 13. $\begin{array}{r} \frac{1}{2} \\ +\frac{1}{3} \\ \hline \end{array}$

14. $\frac{2}{3} + \frac{5}{6}$ 15. $\frac{2}{3} - \frac{1}{9}$ 16. $\frac{7}{8} - \frac{1}{2}$ 17. $\frac{1}{4} + \frac{2}{8}$ 18. $\frac{3}{4} + \frac{2}{3}$

VOCABULARY POWER

REVIEW

mixed number [mikst num′bər] *noun*

A mixed number is the combination of two types of numbers: a whole
number and a fraction. Give an example of a situation in which mixed
numbers are used.

www.harcourtschool.com/mathglossary

ON-LINE

Multiply Fractions

Tomatoes | Corn | Squash
Green beans | Green peppers | Lettuce
Peas | Flowers

20 feet

20 feet

≡FAST FACT • SOCIAL STUDIES

In Ohio, more than 500 volunteer leaders helped begin and maintain 212 community gardens. Community and school gardens are becoming more and more popular. Gardeners are encouraged to share their harvest with a neighborhood family.

PROBLEM SOLVING   Look at the garden diagram. If $\frac{1}{4}$ of the garden is planted with tomatoes, how many square feet are planted with tomatoes?

Use this page to help you review and remember important skills needed for Chapter 18.

✓ PARTS OF A WHOLE

Write a fraction to represent the shaded part.

1.

2.

3.

4.

5.

6.

✓ RENAME FRACTIONS AND MIXED NUMBERS

Write the mixed number as a fraction. Write each fraction as a mixed number.

7. $1\frac{4}{5}$

8. $2\frac{1}{3}$

9. $\frac{17}{5}$

10. $5\frac{1}{2}$

11. $\frac{14}{3}$

12. $\frac{25}{4}$

13. $1\frac{9}{10}$

14. $8\frac{5}{6}$

15. $\frac{31}{8}$

16. $2\frac{5}{9}$

17. $7\frac{3}{4}$

18. $\frac{22}{3}$

19. $9\frac{6}{7}$

20. $13\frac{1}{2}$

21. $\frac{31}{9}$

VOCABULARY POWER

REVIEW

fraction [frak′ shən] *noun*

Fraction comes from the Latin word *frangere,* which means "to break." A fraction represents a broken part of a whole. Explain how this meaning applies to the fraction $\frac{1}{4}$.

www.harcourtschool.com/mathglossary

Multiply a Fraction by a Fraction

▶ **Learn**

HIGH-STRUNG   In an orchestra, $\frac{2}{3}$ of the musicians play stringed instruments. In the string section, $\frac{1}{4}$ of the musicians play the viola. What part of the orchestra plays the viola?

Example   Multiply. $\frac{1}{4} \times \frac{2}{3}$

One Way   You can make a model to find the product.

STEP 1

Fold a piece of paper vertically into 3 equal parts. Color 2 columns to represent $\frac{2}{3}$ of the whole.

$\frac{2}{3}$

STEP 2

Fold the paper horizontally into fourths so that each of the thirds is divided into 4 equal parts.

$\frac{1}{4}$

STEP 3

Use the other color to shade 1 of the fourths rows to represent $\frac{1}{4}$. The overlapped shading shows the product.

$\frac{2}{12}$

Since 2 of the 12 parts are shaded both colors, $\frac{1}{4}$ of $\frac{2}{3} = \frac{2}{12}$, or $\frac{1}{6}$.

- Look at the numerators and denominators of the factors and the product. What relationship do you see?

Another Way   You can compute the product $\frac{1}{4} \times \frac{2}{3}$.

STEP 1

Multiply the numerators. Then multiply the denominators.

$\frac{1}{4} \times \frac{2}{3} = \frac{1 \times 2}{4 \times 3} = \frac{2}{12}$

STEP 2

Write the product in simplest form.

$\frac{2 \div 2}{12 \div 2} = \frac{1}{6}$

So, $\frac{1}{6}$ of the musicians in the orchestra play the viola.

Some problems can be solved with mental math.

$\frac{2}{3} \times \frac{1}{5}$ Think: $2 \times 1 = 2$ and $3 \times 5 = 15$. So, $\frac{2}{3} \times \frac{1}{5} = \frac{2}{15}$.

MATH IDEA   To multiply a fraction by a fraction, multiply the numerators and then multiply the denominators. Write the product in simplest form.

1. **Explain** why the product of two fractions less than one is less than each of its factors.

Find the product. Write it in simplest form.

2. $\frac{1}{4} \times \frac{1}{3}$ 3. $\frac{2}{3} \times \frac{1}{3}$ 4. $\frac{1}{3} \times \frac{3}{4}$ 5. $\frac{1}{5} \times \frac{2}{5}$ 6. $\frac{1}{4} \times \frac{2}{5}$

▶ **Practice and Problem Solving**   Extra Practice, page 396, Set A

Find the product. Write it in simplest form.

7. $\frac{2}{3} \times \frac{1}{5}$ 8. $\frac{1}{5} \times \frac{1}{4}$ 9. $\frac{1}{3} \times \frac{3}{5}$ 10. $\frac{5}{6} \times \frac{3}{4}$ 11. $\frac{1}{4} \times \frac{3}{4}$

12. $\frac{3}{7} \times \frac{2}{3}$ 13. $\frac{8}{9} \times \frac{5}{6}$ 14. $\frac{4}{5} \times \frac{8}{11}$ 15. $\frac{7}{10} \times \frac{3}{8}$ 16. $\frac{6}{7} \times \frac{11}{18}$

17. $\frac{2}{3} \times \frac{3}{4}$ 18. $\frac{1}{5} \times \frac{3}{4}$ 19. $\frac{2}{7} \times \frac{1}{2}$ 20. $\frac{7}{8} \times \frac{4}{5}$ 21. $\frac{5}{6} \times \frac{1}{3}$

Write the number sentence each model represents.

22.   23.   24.   25.

26. ✏️ **Write About It**   Explain how to multiply $\frac{3}{8} \times \frac{1}{3} \times \frac{2}{3}$. Then find the product.

27. Of the 50 students in the school band, $\frac{2}{5}$ play woodwind instruments. In the woodwind section, $\frac{1}{2}$ of the students play the clarinet. How many students play the clarinet?

28. Mel ate $\frac{1}{3}$ of $\frac{1}{2}$ of the pizza. Sue ate $\frac{1}{2}$ of $\frac{1}{4}$ of the pizza. Who ate more pizza? Explain.

29. **Vocabulary Power** Some words have several meanings. Write a mathematical and a nonmathematical definition for *product*.

Mixed Review and Test Prep

Find the least common multiple. (p. 282)

30. 4 and 30   31. 15 and 40

32. Round 5.0699 to the nearest tenth.
    (p. 40)

33. Evaluate $n - 26$ if n is 50. (p. 64)

34. **TEST PREP**   Which illustrates the Distributive Property? (p. 260)
    A $5 \times 16 = 16 \times 5$
    B $5 \times (10 + 6) = (5 \times 10) + (5 \times 6)$
    C $5 \times (10 \times 6) = (5 \times 10) \times 6$
    D $5 \times 16 = (1 + 1 + 1 + 1 + 1) \times 16$

Multiply Fractions and Whole Numbers

Quick Review

Write as a mixed number or whole number.

1. $\frac{8}{4}$ 2. $\frac{12}{5}$

3. $\frac{10}{3}$ 4. $\frac{7}{1}$ 5. $\frac{9}{7}$

▶ **Learn**

BAKER'S DOZEN A chef is making 3 batches of doughnuts. The recipe calls for $\frac{3}{4}$ cup of sugar for each batch. How many cups of sugar does the chef need?

Example

Find $3 \times \frac{3}{4}$, or 3 groups of $\frac{3}{4}$.

One Way You can draw a picture.

STEP 1	STEP 2	STEP 3
Use circles to show 3 groups of $\frac{3}{4}$.	Count the shaded fourths.	Write the answer as a mixed number.
$\frac{3}{4}$ $\frac{3}{4}$ $\frac{3}{4}$	$\frac{3}{4} + \frac{3}{4} + \frac{3}{4} = \frac{9}{4}$	$\frac{9}{4} = 2\frac{1}{4}$

Another Way You can multiply.

STEP 1	STEP 2	STEP 3
Write the whole number as a fraction. Think: $3 = \frac{3}{1}$ $\frac{3}{1} \times \frac{3}{4}$	Multiply the numerators. Then multiply the denominators. $\frac{3 \times 3}{1 \times 4} = \frac{9}{4}$	Write the answer as a mixed number. $\frac{9}{4} = 2\frac{1}{4}$

So, the chef needs $2\frac{1}{4}$ cups of sugar.

More Examples

A
$$12 \times \frac{2}{3} = \frac{12}{1} \times \frac{2}{3}$$
$$= \frac{12 \times 2}{1 \times 3}$$
$$= \frac{24 \div \boxed{3}}{3 \div \boxed{3}} = \frac{8}{1} = 8$$

B
$$\frac{2}{5} \times 3 = \frac{2}{5} \times \frac{3}{1}$$
$$= \frac{2 \times 3}{5 \times 1}$$
$$= \frac{6}{5}, \text{ or } 1\frac{1}{5}$$

Technology Link

More Practice: Harcourt Mega Math Fraction Action, *Number Line Mine*, Level L

1. **Explain** how to draw a model to show the product $4 \times \frac{2}{3}$.

Write the multiplication number sentence each model represents.

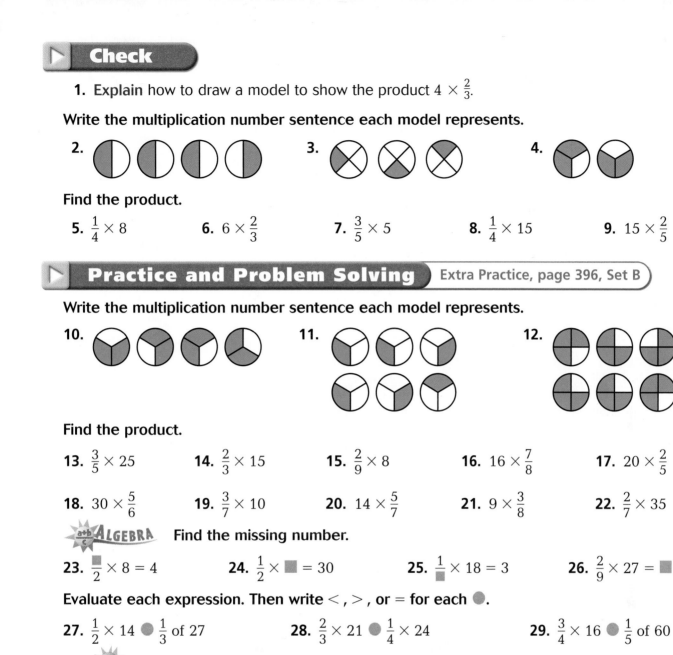

Find the product.

5. $\frac{1}{4} \times 8$ 6. $6 \times \frac{2}{3}$ 7. $\frac{3}{5} \times 5$ 8. $\frac{1}{4} \times 15$ 9. $15 \times \frac{2}{5}$

▶ **Practice and Problem Solving**   Extra Practice, page 396, Set B

Write the multiplication number sentence each model represents.

Find the product.

13. $\frac{3}{5} \times 25$ 14. $\frac{2}{3} \times 15$ 15. $\frac{2}{9} \times 8$ 16. $16 \times \frac{7}{8}$ 17. $20 \times \frac{2}{5}$

18. $30 \times \frac{5}{6}$ 19. $\frac{3}{7} \times 10$ 20. $14 \times \frac{5}{7}$ 21. $9 \times \frac{3}{8}$ 22. $\frac{2}{7} \times 35$

ALGEBRA   **Find the missing number.**

23. $\frac{\blacksquare}{2} \times 8 = 4$ 24. $\frac{1}{2} \times \blacksquare = 30$ 25. $\frac{1}{\blacksquare} \times 18 = 3$ 26. $\frac{2}{9} \times 27 = \blacksquare$

Evaluate each expression. Then write $<$, $>$, or $=$ for each ●.

27. $\frac{1}{2} \times 14$ ● $\frac{1}{3}$ of 27   28. $\frac{2}{3} \times 21$ ● $\frac{1}{4} \times 24$ 29. $\frac{3}{4} \times 16$ ● $\frac{1}{5}$ of 60

30. **? What's the Question?** Cyd saved $20 in quarters. The answer is 80 quarters.

31. Don is making 4 batches of fig bars and 3 batches of date bars. He needs $\frac{2}{3}$ c sugar for each batch. How much sugar does he need?

32. **REASONING** Will the product of a fraction less than one and a whole number be less than or greater than the whole number? Explain.

Mixed Review and Test Prep

33. $25.06 - 0.43$ (p. 48)

34. $93.056 - 1.8$ (p. 48)

35. Sarah has $5\frac{2}{3}$ cups of flour. She needs $2\frac{3}{4}$ cups per cake. Does she have enough flour for 2 cakes? (p. 368)

36. Write $\frac{4}{12}$ in simplest form. (p. 316)

37. **TEST PREP** Which represents this expression: a number, n, plus $\frac{2}{5}$? (p. 64)

A $\frac{2}{5} + n$ C $n \times \frac{2}{5}$

B $n \div \frac{2}{5}$ D $\frac{2}{5} \div n$

Multiply Fractions and Mixed Numbers

Quick Review

1. $3\frac{3}{5} = \frac{\blacksquare}{5}$ 2. $2\frac{4}{7} = \frac{\blacksquare}{7}$

3. $1\frac{2}{3} = \frac{\blacksquare}{3}$ 4. $5\frac{1}{6} = \frac{\blacksquare}{6}$

5. $6\frac{3}{4} = \frac{\blacksquare}{4}$

▶ **Learn**

CHEF'S GARDEN   Maria's parents run a bed-and-breakfast inn. They grow fresh produce in their garden, on $1\frac{1}{3}$ acres. They planted $\frac{1}{4}$ of the garden with herbs. How many acres of herbs did they plant?

Remember

You can write a mixed number as a fraction.

$2\frac{1}{3} = 2 + \frac{1}{3} = \frac{6}{3} + \frac{1}{3} = \frac{7}{3}$

Example

Multiply. $\frac{1}{4} \times 1\frac{1}{3}$

One Way   Use models to multiply fractions and mixed numbers.

STEP 1

Show 2 whole squares. Divide each square into thirds. Shade 1 whole square and $\frac{1}{3}$ of the other square yellow to show $1\frac{1}{3}$, or $\frac{4}{3}$.

STEP 2

Divide the squares into fourths the other way. Each of the squares is now divided into twelfths.

STEP 3

Shade $\frac{1}{4}$ of each whole square blue. The overlapped shading shows the product.

$\frac{3}{12} + \frac{1}{12} = \frac{4}{12}$, or $\frac{1}{3}$

Another Way   Compute the product $\frac{1}{4} \times 1\frac{1}{3}$.

STEP 1

Rename the mixed number as a fraction.

Think: $1\frac{1}{3} = \frac{4}{3}$

$\frac{1}{4} \times 1\frac{1}{3} = \frac{1}{4} \times \frac{4}{3}$

STEP 2

Multiply.

$\frac{1}{4} \times \frac{4}{3} = \frac{1 \times 4}{4 \times 3} = \frac{4}{12}$

STEP 3

Write the product in simplest form.

$\frac{4 \div 4}{12 \div 4} = \frac{1}{3}$

So, they planted $\frac{1}{3}$ acre of herbs.

More Examples

Ⓐ $1\frac{1}{2} \times \frac{3}{4} = \frac{3}{2} \times \frac{3}{4} = \frac{9}{8}$, or $1\frac{1}{8}$

Ⓑ $\frac{2}{3} \times 3\frac{2}{5} = \frac{2}{3} \times \frac{17}{5} = \frac{34}{15}$, or $2\frac{4}{15}$

1. **Explain** how multiplying a fraction and a mixed number is different from multiplying a fraction by a fraction.

Find the product. Draw fraction squares as needed.

2. $\frac{1}{3} \times 1\frac{1}{5}$ 3. $\frac{1}{2} \times 1\frac{2}{3}$ 4. $\frac{1}{2} \times 2\frac{2}{5}$ 5. $\frac{3}{5} \times 1\frac{1}{2}$ 6. $2\frac{1}{4} \times \frac{1}{6}$

▶ **Practice and Problem Solving**   Extra Practice, page 396, Set C

Find the product. Draw fraction squares as needed.

7. $\frac{3}{4} \times 1\frac{1}{6}$ 8. $\frac{2}{5} \times 3\frac{2}{3}$ 9. $3\frac{1}{5} \times \frac{1}{4}$ 10. $4\frac{1}{2} \times \frac{1}{9}$ 11. $\frac{1}{4} \times 2\frac{1}{5}$

12. $\frac{1}{3} \times 3\frac{5}{8}$ 13. $\frac{5}{12} \times 2\frac{2}{5}$ 14. $6\frac{1}{4} \times \frac{3}{8}$ 15. $5\frac{6}{7} \times \frac{1}{10}$ 16. $\frac{1}{9} \times 3\frac{1}{2}$

17. $\frac{1}{2} \times 5\frac{3}{5}$ 18. $1\frac{1}{8} \times \frac{2}{3}$ 19. $\frac{1}{4} \times 6\frac{2}{7}$ 20. $2\frac{5}{6} \times \frac{1}{9}$ 21. $\frac{2}{5} \times 5\frac{1}{3}$

22. $3\frac{3}{4} \times \frac{1}{5}$ 23. $4\frac{1}{6} \times \frac{1}{12}$ 24. $\frac{3}{8} \times 2\frac{5}{6}$ 25. $\frac{1}{3} \times 6\frac{3}{5}$ 26. $4\frac{1}{4} \times \frac{2}{3}$

27. $\frac{2}{5} \times 4\frac{3}{4}$ 28. $\frac{3}{7} \times 2\frac{1}{3}$ 29. $1\frac{3}{4} \times \frac{2}{9}$ 30. $3\frac{1}{5} \times \frac{1}{7}$ 31. $\frac{5}{6} \times 2\frac{1}{3}$

32. ▤**FAST FACT** • **SCIENCE** Strawberries are the only fruit with seeds on the outside. One strawberry has about 200 seeds! At the market, strawberries cost $3.00 a pound. If you paid for $1\frac{1}{4}$ pounds with a $5 bill, how much change would you receive?

33. Chef Leo bought $1\frac{1}{2}$ pints of strawberries. He used $\frac{3}{4}$ of the strawberries to make tarts. How many pints of strawberries does he have left?

34. ✎ Write a problem about finding a fractional part of $3\frac{1}{2}$ dozen apples. Solve the problem.

Mixed Review and Test Prep

For 35–36, use the data set 95, 87, 76, 95, and 82.

35. What is the mean? (p. 100)

36. What is the median? (p. 102)

37.   98,056 (p. 46)   38.   71,204 (p. 46)
    −32,569   −65,501

39. **TEST PREP** In which place would you write the first digit of the quotient for 1.2635 ÷ 4? (p. 232)

A ones

B tenths

C hundredths

D thousandths

Multiply with Mixed Numbers

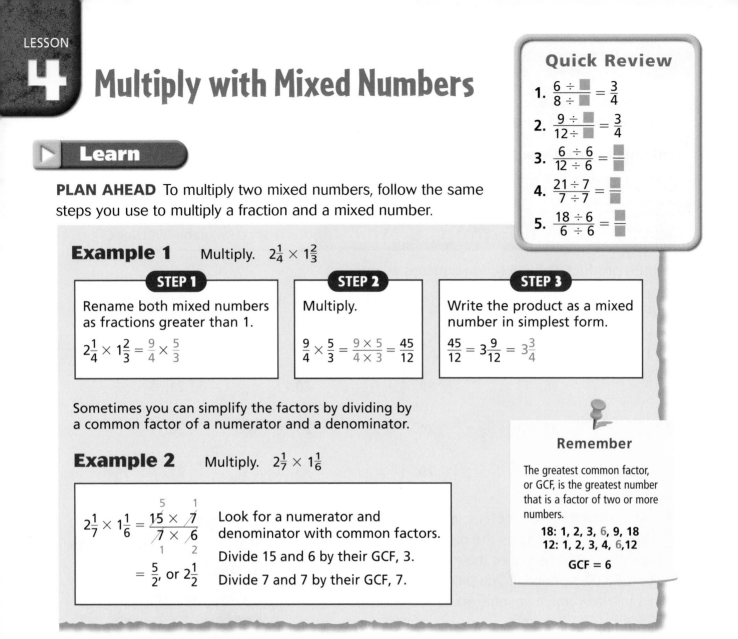

Quick Review

1. $\frac{6 \div \blacksquare}{8 \div \blacksquare} = \frac{3}{4}$

2. $\frac{9 \div \blacksquare}{12 \div \blacksquare} = \frac{3}{4}$

3. $\frac{6 \div 6}{12 \div 6} = \frac{\blacksquare}{\blacksquare}$

4. $\frac{21 \div 7}{7 \div 7} = \frac{\blacksquare}{\blacksquare}$

5. $\frac{18 \div 6}{6 \div 6} = \frac{\blacksquare}{\blacksquare}$

▶ **Learn**

PLAN AHEAD To multiply two mixed numbers, follow the same steps you use to multiply a fraction and a mixed number.

Example 1   Multiply. $2\frac{1}{4} \times 1\frac{2}{3}$

STEP 1

Rename both mixed numbers as fractions greater than 1.

$2\frac{1}{4} \times 1\frac{2}{3} = \frac{9}{4} \times \frac{5}{3}$

STEP 2

Multiply.

$\frac{9}{4} \times \frac{5}{3} = \frac{9 \times 5}{4 \times 3} = \frac{45}{12}$

STEP 3

Write the product as a mixed number in simplest form.

$\frac{45}{12} = 3\frac{9}{12} = 3\frac{3}{4}$

Sometimes you can simplify the factors by dividing by a common factor of a numerator and a denominator.

Example 2   Multiply. $2\frac{1}{7} \times 1\frac{1}{6}$

$2\frac{1}{7} \times 1\frac{1}{6} = \frac{\overset{5}{\cancel{15}} \times \overset{1}{\cancel{7}}}{\underset{1}{\cancel{7}} \times \underset{2}{\cancel{6}}}$ Look for a numerator and denominator with common factors.

$= \frac{5}{2}$, or $2\frac{1}{2}$ Divide 15 and 6 by their GCF, 3.
Divide 7 and 7 by their GCF, 7.

Remember

The greatest common factor, or GCF, is the greatest number that is a factor of two or more numbers.

18: 1, 2, 3, **6**, 9, 18
12: 1, 2, 3, 4, **6**, 12

GCF = 6

You can also use a calculator to multiply mixed numbers.
Find $7\frac{1}{4} \times 5\frac{3}{4}$.

7 | **a** | **1** | **b/c** | **4** | **×** | **5** | **a** | **3** | **b/c** | **4** | **=**   = $41\frac{11}{16}$

▶ **Check**

1. **Explain** how you can use division with a common factor before you compute to simplify $4 \times 5\frac{1}{4}$.

Copy and complete each problem. Show how to simplify before you multiply.

2. $4\frac{2}{3} \times 1\frac{3}{7} = \frac{14}{3} \times \frac{10}{7} = \frac{14 \times 10}{3 \times 7} = \blacksquare$

3. $2\frac{1}{2} \times 5\frac{1}{3} = \frac{5}{2} \times \frac{16}{3} = \frac{5 \times 16}{2 \times 3} = \blacksquare$

Multiply. Write the answer in simplest form.

4. $4\frac{1}{3} \times 2\frac{1}{2}$ **5.** $3\frac{3}{4} \times 1\frac{1}{10}$ **6.** $4\frac{1}{2} \times 1\frac{2}{3}$ **7.** $6 \times 3\frac{2}{3}$ **8.** $5\frac{1}{3} \times 3\frac{3}{4}$

Practice and Problem Solving   Extra Practice, page 396, Set D

Copy and complete each problem. Show how to simplify before you multiply.

9. $2\frac{1}{4} \times 3\frac{2}{3} = \frac{9}{4} \times \frac{11}{3} = \frac{9 \times 11}{4 \times 3} = \blacksquare$ **10.** $3\frac{1}{3} \times 2\frac{2}{5} = \frac{10}{3} \times \frac{12}{5} = \frac{10 \times 12}{3 \times 5} = \blacksquare$

Multiply. Write the answer in simplest form.

11. $4\frac{2}{3} \times 1\frac{1}{2}$ **12.** $3\frac{1}{3} \times 2\frac{2}{5}$ **13.** $2\frac{3}{8} \times 1\frac{2}{5}$ **14.** $\frac{1}{2} \times 2\frac{2}{3}$ **15.** $\frac{4}{5} \times \frac{5}{6}$

16. $\frac{3}{8} \times 24$ **17.** $1\frac{2}{3} \times \frac{1}{4}$ **18.** $1\frac{1}{4} \times \frac{5}{6}$ **19.** $1\frac{1}{6} \times 4\frac{2}{3}$ **20.** $14 \times \frac{3}{7}$

21. $4 \times 2\frac{1}{3} \times \frac{1}{2}$ **22.** $3\frac{1}{5} \times \frac{2}{3} \times \frac{1}{4}$ **23.** $\frac{1}{6} \times 2\frac{2}{3} \times 1\frac{1}{3}$ **24.** $7\frac{1}{4} \times \frac{1}{2} \times 2\frac{1}{2}$

Solve the equation. Identify the multiplication property used.

25. $1\frac{1}{2} \times 3\frac{3}{4} = 3\frac{3}{4} \times n$ **26.** $(6\frac{3}{8} \times 8\frac{1}{3}) \times 4 = 6\frac{3}{8} \times (n \times 4)$ **27.** $5\frac{1}{4} \times n = 0$

USE DATA For 28–30, use the circle graph.

28. If Bob spent $\frac{1}{5}$ of his time at school in art class, how long was his art class?

29. Bob spent a quarter of his free time surfing the Internet. How much free time did he have left for other things?

30. How much more sleep time did he have than free time?

BOB'S DAY

Sleep $8\frac{1}{4}$ hr

School $7\frac{1}{2}$ hr

Free time $4\frac{1}{6}$ hr

Homework $2\frac{1}{3}$ hr

Soccer practice $1\frac{3}{4}$ hr

31. **ALGEBRA** Find n if $\clubsuit = 2$, $\blacklozenge = 2 \times \clubsuit$, $\heartsuit = \blacklozenge \times 2$, and $\frac{\clubsuit}{\blacklozenge} = \frac{n}{\heartsuit}$.

32. **Write About It** How is multiplying fractions different from adding fractions?

Mixed Review and Test Prep

33. What is the least common denominator of $\frac{1}{12}$ and $\frac{7}{15}$? (p. 354)

34. Cards are sold in packs of 35 and envelopes in packs of 40. What is the least number of each pack you need to have an equal number of cards and envelopes with none left over? (p. 282)

35. What is $\frac{3}{8}$ of $\frac{4}{5}$? (p. 386)

36. What is $\frac{5}{7}$ of 6? (p. 388)

37. **TEST PREP** Which graph or plot would be best to display the number of students completing their projects on Monday, Tuesday, and Wednesday? (p. 130)

  A circle graph   **C** stem-and-leaf plot

  B bar graph   **D** double-bar graph

Problem Solving Skill
Sequence and Prioritize Information

Quick Review
1. $5 ÷ 2   2. $10 ÷ 10
3. $4.20 ÷ 4   4. $3.75 ÷ 3
5. $20 \times \frac{3}{4}$

UNDERSTAND ▶ **PLAN** ▶ **SOLVE** ▶ **CHECK**

BUDGET YOUR BUCKS! Ms. James saved $\frac{1}{4}$ of her paycheck in the bank. Then she paid bills with half of what was left. She used a third of her remaining cash for tickets to a concert. After she went grocery shopping, she had $30 left. Her paycheck was $300. How much did she spend on groceries?

MATH IDEA Sometimes to solve a problem, you need to put events in order of time and importance—you need to *sequence and prioritize information*.

First, prioritize your information: The answer depends on the fact that Ms. James's check was for $300.

Then you can make a list or a table to sequence the amounts she spent.

EXPENSE TABLE		
Event	Amount Used	Balance
1. She started with $300.	0	$300
2. She saved $\frac{1}{4}$ in bank.	$300 x $\frac{1}{4}$ = $75	$300 – $75 = $225
3. She paid bills with $\frac{1}{2}$ of what was left.	$225 x $\frac{1}{2}$ = $112.50	$225 – $112.50 = $112.50
4. She spent $\frac{1}{3}$ on concert tickets.	$112.50 x $\frac{1}{3}$ = $37.50	$112.50 – $37.50 = $75
5. She bought groceries.	■	$75 – ■ = $30
6. She had $30 left.	0	$30

Look at Event 5. $75 − $45 = $30

So, Ms. James spent $45 on groceries.

- **REASONING** Why is the check amount an important fact in the problem? Why can't you solve the problem without sequencing the events?

Sequence and prioritize information to solve.

1. **What if** Ms. James's paycheck had been for $350? How much would she have spent on groceries?

2. The United States produced 569 movies in one year. In the same year, England made $\frac{1}{2}$ the number of movies that France made and 499 fewer than the United States made. How many movies did France make that year?

The compact disc (CD) was invented 273 years after the piano. The tape recorder was invented in 1898. Thomas Edison invented the phonograph 21 years before the tape recorder and 95 years before the compact disc.

3. Which invention's date will you use to find the dates of all the others?

   A tape recorder
   B compact disc
   C piano
   D phonograph

4. Which list is in sequence from earliest invention to latest invention?

   F recorder, piano, phonograph, CD
   G piano, phonograph, CD, recorder
   H phonograph, piano, recorder, CD
   J piano, phonograph, recorder, CD

Mixed Applications

For 5–7, use the map.

5. Morgan left home and drove 127 miles north to Jacksonville. Then she continued 339 miles to Charlotte. In what city on the map does Morgan live?

6. Charlie drove from Nashville to Miami to attend college. About how many miles did he drive?

7. Lucy visits her grandparents in Asheville twice a year. If she lives in Savannah, about how many miles does she travel each year for these visits?

8. The Cineplex has 16 theaters. Each theater shows a different movie. Each movie is played 7 times a day on Saturdays and Sundays. How many shows are there in one weekend?

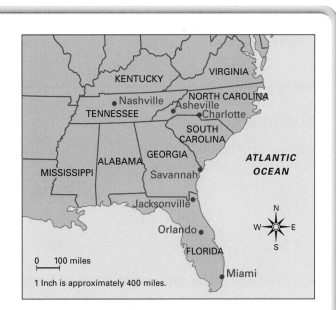

9. **NUMBER SENSE** Jim chose a number. Then he multiplied it by 3, added 5, and divided the sum by 2. After he subtracted 4 from the quotient, he got 6. What number did Jim choose?

Extra Practice

Set A (pp. 386–387)

Find the product. Write it in simplest form.

1. $\frac{3}{4} \times \frac{5}{6}$
2. $\frac{2}{3} \times \frac{4}{5}$
3. $\frac{3}{4} \times \frac{1}{3}$
4. $\frac{1}{3} \times \frac{3}{5}$
5. $\frac{3}{8} \times \frac{2}{3}$

6. $\frac{3}{10} \times \frac{1}{6}$
7. $\frac{1}{5} \times \frac{5}{12}$
8. $\frac{2}{3} \times \frac{5}{6}$
9. $\frac{5}{8} \times \frac{2}{5}$
10. $\frac{2}{3} \times \frac{3}{5}$

11. A muffin recipe calls for $\frac{3}{4}$ cup of flour. If you cut the recipe in half, how much flour do you need?

12. Julie bought $\frac{3}{4}$ yard of fabric. She used $\frac{1}{3}$ of it to make a doll dress. How much fabric does she have left?

Set B (pp. 388–389)

Find the product.

1. $\frac{2}{5} \times 10$
2. $\frac{1}{4} \times 12$
3. $15 \times \frac{3}{5}$
4. $\frac{4}{7} \times 28$
5. $32 \times \frac{5}{8}$

6. $30 \times \frac{5}{6}$
7. $\frac{7}{8} \times 16$
8. $\frac{3}{4} \times 20$
9. $\frac{1}{2} \times 22$
10. $24 \times \frac{1}{3}$

11. There are 15 cars in a parking lot. Of the 15 cars, $\frac{1}{3}$ are red. How many of the cars in the parking lot are red?

12. Mike has 22 baseball cards. Of the 22 cards, $\frac{1}{2}$ show rookie players. How many of the cards show rookie players?

Set C (pp. 390–391)

Find the product. Write it in simplest form.

1. $\frac{1}{2} \times 1\frac{1}{2}$
2. $2\frac{1}{3} \times \frac{1}{4}$
3. $\frac{4}{5} \times 2\frac{1}{6}$
4. $2\frac{1}{2} \times \frac{2}{3}$
5. $\frac{3}{4} \times 3\frac{1}{2}$

6. $\frac{3}{4} \times 1\frac{2}{3}$
7. $2\frac{1}{3} \times \frac{1}{5}$
8. $\frac{5}{6} \times 3\frac{1}{5}$
9. $1\frac{3}{4} \times \frac{4}{7}$
10. $2\frac{1}{2} \times \frac{5}{8}$

Set D (pp. 392–393)

Multiply. Write the answer in simplest form.

1. $2\frac{1}{4} \times 1\frac{2}{3}$
2. $3\frac{2}{3} \times 4\frac{1}{2}$
3. $1\frac{7}{8} \times 2\frac{2}{5}$
4. $2\frac{2}{3} \times 4\frac{1}{2}$
5. $4 \times 1\frac{7}{8}$

6. $3\frac{1}{2} \times 2\frac{3}{5}$
7. $1\frac{5}{7} \times 3\frac{1}{3}$
8. $4\frac{1}{3} \times 6\frac{3}{4}$
9. $5\frac{1}{4} \times 3\frac{2}{5}$
10. $2\frac{5}{8} \times 4\frac{2}{3}$

11. LaKeshia is training for a track meet. She walks $5\frac{3}{4}$ mi every day. How many miles does she walk in one week?

Review/Test

✓ CHECK CONCEPTS

Write the multiplication number sentence each model represents. (pp. 386–389)

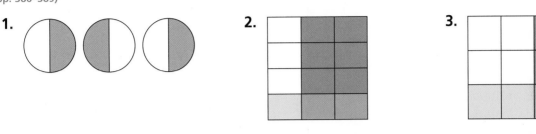

1. 2. 3.

✓ CHECK SKILLS

Find the product. Write it in simplest form. (pp. 386–393)

4. $\frac{2}{5} \times 50$

5. $6 \times \frac{4}{9}$

6. $\frac{3}{4} \times 16$

7. $2 \times \frac{3}{10}$

8. $\frac{1}{3} \times \frac{1}{4}$

9. $\frac{3}{4} \times \frac{1}{2}$

10. $\frac{1}{6} \times \frac{3}{5}$

11. $\frac{1}{7} \times \frac{2}{3}$

12. $\frac{1}{6} \times \frac{2}{7}$

13. $\frac{1}{2} \times \frac{3}{10}$

14. $\frac{3}{8} \times \frac{1}{4}$

15. $\frac{2}{9} \times \frac{1}{4}$

16. $\frac{1}{2} \times 2\frac{1}{5}$

17. $3\frac{3}{4} \times \frac{1}{3}$

18. $\frac{5}{6} \times 5\frac{1}{2}$

19. $4\frac{1}{2} \times \frac{3}{7}$

20. $1\frac{2}{3} \times 3\frac{1}{5}$

21. $4 \times 2\frac{5}{8}$

22. $3\frac{1}{4} \times 1\frac{3}{5}$

23. $2\frac{2}{5} \times 3\frac{3}{4}$

✓ CHECK PROBLEM SOLVING

Sequence and prioritize information to solve. (pp. 394–395)

24. Colin has 2 hours before dinner is ready. He does homework for $\frac{3}{4}$ hour, plays basketball for $\frac{3}{4}$ hour, and then plays a computer game until dinner. How long does he play the computer game?

25. Karen had 100 beads. She used $\frac{3}{5}$ of the beads to make necklaces. Then she used $\frac{1}{2}$ of the leftover beads to make earrings. She used the rest to make a bracelet. How many beads are on the bracelet?

Standardized Test Prep

NUMBER SENSE, CONCEPTS, AND OPERATIONS

TIP **Get the information you need.**
See item 1. To find the height of the can of tennis balls, you need the height of each ball. The height of the ball is the same as the diameter of the ball.

1. A tennis ball has a diameter of $2\frac{5}{8}$ inches. There are 3 tennis balls in a can. What is the least possible height for a can of tennis balls?

   A $5\frac{5}{8}$ inches   **C** $7\frac{5}{8}$ inches

   B $6\frac{7}{8}$ inches   **D** $7\frac{7}{8}$ inches

2. Use the data in the table. How much more does a tennis ball weigh than a golf ball?

WEIGHTS OF BALLS	
Ball	**Weight (in ounces)**
Baseball	$4\frac{4}{5}$
Tennis ball	2
Golf ball	$1\frac{3}{5}$

   F $1\frac{2}{5}$ ounces   **H** $\frac{2}{5}$ ounce

   G $1\frac{3}{5}$ ounces   **J** $\frac{3}{5}$ ounce

3. **Explain It** A bottle of cranberry juice that holds $40\frac{3}{4}$ ounces is $\frac{2}{3}$ full. Is there enough juice in the bottle to fill two 12-ounce glasses? Explain how you know.

ALGEBRAIC THINKING

4. The table shows how much Cindy will earn if she mows up to 5 lawns. How much will she earn if she mows 8 lawns?

AMOUNT EARNED MOWING LAWNS	
Number of Lawns	**Amount Earned**
1	$9
2	$18
3	$27
4	$36
5	$45

   A $54

   B $63

   C $72

   D $81

5. Suppose the number of students in a class is represented by x. Which expression shows the number of students present on Tuesday?

STUDENTS ABSENT					
Day	M	T	W	Th	F
Number Absent	1	4	3	2	5

   F $x + 4$

   G $x - 4$

   H $4 - x$

   J $4x$

6. **Explain It** Alex had 40¢. He bought a pencil and gave the cashier three of the same coin to pay for it. Then he had a quarter left. What coins did Alex give the cashier? Explain how you know.

★ GEOMETRY AND SPATIAL SENSE

7. Which line is perpendicular to $\overleftrightarrow{BE}$?

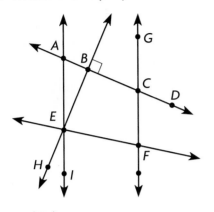

  A $\overleftrightarrow{AE}$

  B $\overleftrightarrow{FE}$

  C $\overleftrightarrow{AD}$

  D $\overleftrightarrow{AI}$

8. Use the drawing in Exercise 7. Which of these is an obtuse angle?

  F angle *ACG*

  G angle *HEF*

  H angle *CBE*

  J angle *DAI*

9. What part of the figure below does the letter *C* name?

  A a side

  B a vertex

  C a plane

  D a base

10. Explain It Rita said that Figure 2 shows a reflection of Figure 1. Did she name the transformation correctly? Explain your answer.

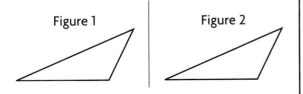

Figure 1   Figure 2

★ MEASUREMENT

11. The Johnsons marked Frank's height on the doorway every year on his birthday.

5 ft (2002)
57 in. (2001)

How much did Frank grow from 2001 to 2002?

  F 1 inch

  G 3 inches

  H 7 inches

  J 11 inches

12. How long is line segment *AB*?

  A 5 centimeters

  B 4 centimeters

  C 5 millimeters

  D 4 millimeters

13. Explain It Elena has solved the first three of the 20 math problems in her homework. To solve the problems, it took her $1\frac{1}{2}$ minutes, $1\frac{1}{4}$ minutes, and $1\frac{1}{2}$ minutes. If each of the remaining problems takes about the same amount of time, about how long will it take her to solve all 20 problems? Explain your answer.

Divide Fractions

FAST FACT • SOCIAL STUDIES
The explorers, Meriwether Lewis and William Clark, crossed into Idaho in August 1805. They traveled over mountains and took canoes down rock-strewn rapids on the Snake River.

PROBLEM SOLVING   Today people ride the same rapids as Lewis and Clark rode. With stops for resting and lunch, a team of rafters averages $\frac{3}{4}$ mile per hour down Milner Gorge. About how long will the trip take?

SNAKE RIVER WHITEWATER RUN

Length in Miles

45
40
35
30
25
20
15
10
5
0

South Fork
Milner Gorge
Wiley Reach
Murtaugh Canyon

Runs

Use this page to help you review and remember important skills needed for Chapter 19.

✔ RENAME FRACTIONS AND MIXED NUMBERS

Write each fraction as a mixed number. Write each mixed number or whole number as a fraction.

1. $\frac{13}{3}$ 2. $\frac{7}{4}$ 3. $\frac{46}{5}$ 4. $\frac{28}{8}$ 5. $\frac{17}{6}$

6. 3 7. $1\frac{1}{6}$ 8. 4 9. $7\frac{1}{2}$ 10. 7

11. $\frac{16}{5}$ 12. $4\frac{2}{3}$ 13. 6 14. $\frac{31}{8}$ 15. $2\frac{3}{5}$

✔ MULTIPLY FRACTIONS

Find the product. Write it in simplest form.

16. $\frac{1}{3} \times \frac{3}{4}$ 17. $\frac{2}{3} \times \frac{1}{6}$ 18. $\frac{2}{5} \times \frac{3}{8}$ 19. $\frac{1}{2} \times \frac{2}{6}$ 20. $\frac{7}{8} \times \frac{3}{5}$

21. $\frac{1}{8} \times \frac{3}{4}$ 22. $\frac{3}{5} \times \frac{1}{2}$ 23. $\frac{5}{6} \times \frac{1}{3}$ 24. $\frac{1}{9} \times \frac{3}{4}$ 25. $\frac{3}{8} \times \frac{2}{3}$

26. $\frac{5}{8} \times \frac{1}{5}$ 27. $\frac{1}{9} \times \frac{2}{5}$ 28. $\frac{1}{4} \times \frac{5}{6}$ 29. $\frac{6}{10} \times \frac{1}{5}$ 30. $\frac{3}{4} \times \frac{1}{12}$

VOCABULARY POWER

REVIEW

inverse [in′vərs] *adjective*

In math, *inverse* means "opposite." For example, two inverse operations that are opposites are addition and subtraction, since $5 + 8 = 13$ and $13 - 5 = 8$. Give an example to show that multiplication and division are inverse operations.

PREVIEW

reciprocal

www.harcourtschool.com/mathglossary

Explore Division of Fractions

Quick Review

1. $\frac{3}{9} + \frac{4}{9}$ 2. $\frac{5}{6} + \frac{1}{6}$

3. $\frac{1}{5} + \frac{2}{5}$ 4. $\frac{1}{7} + \frac{3}{7}$

5. $\frac{1}{4} + \frac{1}{2}$

MATERIALS
fraction bars

▶ Explore

Kari has 2 yards of ribbon to use for a craft project.
She needs to cut the ribbon into pieces that are $\frac{1}{3}$ yard long.
How many pieces of ribbon will Kari have?

Activity 1

Divide 2 by $\frac{1}{3}$. $2 \div \frac{1}{3}$

Use fraction bars to show how many thirds are in 2.

STEP 1

Model the bars for 2.
Model the bar for $\frac{1}{3}$.

STEP 2

See how many $\frac{1}{3}$ bars are equal to 2 whole bars.
So, six $\frac{1}{3}$ bars are equal to 2 whole bars.

STEP 3

Record a number sentence for the model.

$2 \div \frac{1}{3} = 6$

So, Kari will have 6 pieces of ribbon.

Try It

Write a number sentence for each model.

a.

b.

How many $\frac{1}{4}$ bars are equal to 1 whole bar?

Use fraction bars to find the quotient.

c. $1 \div \frac{1}{4}$ d. $3 \div \frac{1}{6}$ e. $5 \div \frac{1}{2}$

Technology Link

More Practice: Harcourt Mega Math
Fraction Action, *Fraction Flare Up*,
Level P

You can also use fraction bars to help you divide a fraction by a fraction.

Activity 2 Divide $\frac{1}{2}$ by $\frac{1}{8}$. $\frac{1}{2} \div \frac{1}{8}$

STEP 1

Model $\frac{1}{2}$ and $\frac{1}{8}$ with fraction bars.

STEP 2

See how many $\frac{1}{8}$ bars are equal to a $\frac{1}{2}$ bar.

So, four $\frac{1}{8}$ bars are equal to a $\frac{1}{2}$ bar.

STEP 3

Record a number sentence for the model.

$\frac{1}{2} \div \frac{1}{8} = 4$

Practice and Problem Solving

Write a division number sentence for each model.

1.

2.

3.

Use fraction bars to find the quotient.

4. $\frac{9}{10} \div \frac{1}{10}$ **5.** $1 \div \frac{1}{3}$ **6.** $\frac{3}{4} \div \frac{3}{12}$ **7.** $5 \div \frac{2}{4}$

8. $\frac{3}{4} \div \frac{1}{4}$ **9.** $3 \div \frac{2}{8}$ **10.** $\frac{1}{3} \div \frac{1}{6}$ **11.** $\frac{10}{2} \div \frac{1}{2}$

12. Cindy used $\frac{3}{4}$ yard of wire to make earrings. Each pair of earrings took $\frac{1}{12}$ yard of wire and sold for \$2.98. If she sold all the earrings, how much money would Cindy earn?

13. REASONING If you divide $\frac{1}{10}$ of a dollar into parts that are each $\frac{1}{100}$ of a dollar, how many parts are there? What are they called?

14. Compare the answers for **a** and **b**. What did you find?   **a.** $12 \times \frac{4}{3}$ **b.** $12 \div \frac{3}{4}$

Mixed Review and Test Prep

15. $\frac{7}{8} - \frac{3}{4}$ (p. 356)   **16.** $\frac{6}{7} - \frac{5}{14}$ (p. 356)

17. 47.04×6.1 (p. 170)

18. 82.03×2.8 (p. 170)

19. TEST PREP A bakery ships 24,480 loaves of bread to 60 different stores. The 30 stores in the city each receive twice as many loaves as each of the 30 suburban stores. How many loaves does each city store receive? (p. 212)

A 272   **B** 408   **C** 544   **D** 816

Quick Review

Write each whole number or mixed number as a fraction.

1. 6   2. $2\frac{2}{3}$

3. $1\frac{7}{10}$ 4. $4\frac{3}{8}$ 5. 2

▶ **Learn**

WORKING FOR PEANUTS!   Hanh and three friends visited the elephant exhibit at the zoo. Hanh divided a 4-pound bag of peanuts into four smaller bags. He put $\frac{1}{4}$ of the peanuts into each bag. How many pounds of peanuts did Hanh put into each bag?

Think: $\frac{1}{4}$ of $4 \rightarrow \frac{1}{4} \times 4 = \frac{1}{4} \times \frac{4}{1}$

$$= \frac{4}{4} = 1$$

So, Hanh put 1 pound of peanuts into each bag.

The product of a number and its **reciprocal** is 1. $\frac{1}{4}$ and 4 are reciprocals because $\frac{1}{4} \times 4 = 1$.

MATH IDEA   To write the reciprocal of a fraction, write a new fraction by exchanging the numerator and denominator.

VOCABULARY

reciprocal

Examples

A The reciprocal of $2\frac{2}{3}$, or $\frac{8}{3}$, is $\frac{3}{8}$.

$$\frac{8}{3} \times \frac{3}{8} = \frac{24}{24} = 1$$

B The reciprocal of 6, or $\frac{6}{1}$, is $\frac{1}{6}$.

$$\frac{6}{1} \times \frac{1}{6} = \frac{6}{6} = 1$$

C The reciprocal of $\frac{14}{7}$ is $\frac{7}{14}$.

$$\overset{1}{\underset{1}{\frac{14}{7}}} \times \overset{1}{\underset{1}{\frac{7}{14}}} = \frac{1}{1} = 1$$

▶ **Check**

1. **Explain** how to find the reciprocal of 3 and the reciprocal of $3\frac{5}{8}$.

Are the two numbers reciprocals? Write *yes* or *no*.

2. $\frac{5}{4}$ and $\frac{4}{5}$ 3. $\frac{1}{7}$ and $\frac{7}{3}$ 4. $\frac{1}{8}$ and 8   5. $\frac{5}{7}$ and $1\frac{2}{5}$ 6. $2\frac{3}{4}$ and $2\frac{4}{3}$

Are the two numbers reciprocals? Write *yes* or *no*.

7. $\frac{5}{9}$ and $\frac{9}{5}$ **8.** $\frac{3}{10}$ and $\frac{10}{3}$ **9.** 4 and $\frac{1}{4}$ **10.** $\frac{3}{4}$ and $3\frac{1}{3}$ **11.** $2\frac{1}{4}$ and $\frac{4}{9}$

Write the reciprocal of each number.

12. $\frac{3}{5}$ **13.** $1\frac{3}{4}$ **14.** $\frac{1}{9}$ **15.** $\frac{12}{7}$ **16.** 7

17. 12   **18.** $3\frac{1}{5}$ **19.** $\frac{23}{6}$ **20.** $\frac{1}{13}$ **21.** $\frac{2}{9}$

ALGEBRA Find the value of *n*.

22. $\frac{1}{8} \times \frac{n}{1} = 1$ **23.** $\frac{1}{n} \times \frac{6}{1} = 1$ **24.** $\frac{8}{9} \times \frac{n}{8} = 1$ **25.** $\frac{7}{n} \times \frac{4}{7} = 1$ **26.** $8 \times \frac{1}{n} = 1$

27. $5 \times \frac{1}{n} = 1$ **28.** $\frac{9}{28} \times 3\frac{1}{n} = 1$ **29.** $\frac{1}{n} \times \frac{n}{1} = 1$ **30.** $5\frac{2}{3} \times \frac{n}{17} = 1$ **31.** $\frac{2}{n} \times 3\frac{1}{2} = 1$

Multiply. Use the Associative and Commutative Properties to help you.

32. $\frac{1}{5} \times \frac{5}{1} \times \frac{2}{7}$ **33.** $\frac{7}{8} \times \frac{6}{1} \times \frac{8}{7}$ **34.** $\frac{2}{5} \times \frac{5}{6} \times \frac{5}{2}$

35. $\frac{1}{5} \times \frac{11}{4} \times \frac{4}{11} \times 5$ **36.** $\frac{3}{4} \times \frac{10}{3} \times \frac{3}{10} \times 8$ **37.** $\frac{3}{2} \times \frac{2}{3} \times \frac{2}{3} \times 9$

Which is greater, the number or its reciprocal?

38. $\frac{1}{5}$ **39.** 8   **40.** $\frac{4}{7}$ **41.** $1\frac{1}{2}$ **42.** $\frac{97}{98}$

43. **? What's the Error?** Blair said that the reciprocal of $3\frac{1}{3}$ is $\frac{3}{7}$. Describe and correct her error.

44. **? What's the Question?** Christy has $\frac{3}{4}$ pound of peanuts. Alex has $\frac{4}{3}$ pounds of peanuts. The answer is $\frac{7}{12}$. What is the question?

45. REASONING If a number is greater than 1, what can you say about its reciprocal?

46. Mr. Ross bought 1.5 pounds of tomatoes for spaghetti sauce and 8 ounces for salad. Tomatoes cost $2.49 a pound. How much did Mr. Ross pay for the tomatoes?

Mixed Review and Test Prep

Round to the nearest million.

47. 52,095,500 (p. 38)   **48.** 496,750,000 (p. 38)

49. Brian's batting average went up by .025 points this season. Last season his batting average was .228. What is his average now? (p. 48)

50. Multiply 49.084 by 0.7. (p. 170)

51. TEST PREP Which number is the greatest number less than the product of 28 and 734? (p. 152)

A 24,004   **C** 20,408

B 20,804   **D** 20,008

Divide Whole Numbers By Fractions

▶ **Learn**

SLOW MOTION   If a giant tortoise walks $\frac{1}{5}$ mile per hour, how many hours will it take the tortoise to walk 2 miles?

Example 1

Find $2 \div \frac{1}{5}$.   ←Think: How many $\frac{1}{5}$ miles are in 2 miles?

One Way   Use a model.

1	1

| $\frac{1}{5}$ | $\frac{1}{5}$ | $\frac{1}{5}$ | $\frac{1}{5}$ | $\frac{1}{5}$ | $\frac{1}{5}$ | $\frac{1}{5}$ | $\frac{1}{5}$ | $\frac{1}{5}$ | $\frac{1}{5}$ |

Another Way   Use patterns.

$2 \times \frac{1}{1} = 2$ $2 \div 1 = 2$

$2 \times \frac{2}{1} = 4$ $2 \div \frac{1}{2} = 4$

$2 \times \frac{3}{1} = 6$ $2 \div \frac{1}{3} = 6$

$2 \times \frac{4}{1} = 8$ $2 \div \frac{1}{4} = 8$

$2 \times \frac{5}{1} = 10$ $2 \div \frac{1}{5} = 10$

So, it will take a giant tortoise 10 hours.

You can also use a reciprocal to divide by a fraction. Look at the patterns at the right. The patterns show that dividing by a number is the same as multiplying by its reciprocal.

$6 \div 2 = 3$ $6 \times \frac{1}{2} = 3$

$6 \div 1 = 6$ $6 \times \frac{1}{1} = 6$

$6 \div \frac{1}{2} = 12$ $6 \times 2 = 12$

Example 2   Find $5 \div \frac{2}{3}$.

STEP 1

Write the whole number as a fraction.

$5 \div \frac{2}{3} = \frac{5}{1} \div \frac{2}{3}$

STEP 2

Use the reciprocal of the divisor to write a multiplication problem.

$\frac{5}{1} \div \frac{2}{3} = \frac{5}{1} \times \frac{3}{2}$

↑   ↑
reciprocals

STEP 3

Multiply.

$\frac{5}{1} \times \frac{3}{2} = \frac{15}{2}$, or $7\frac{1}{2}$

So, $5 \div \frac{2}{3} = \frac{15}{2}$, or $7\frac{1}{2}$.

MATH IDEA   To divide a whole number by a fraction, write the whole number as a fraction and then multiply it by the reciprocal of the divisor.

1. **Explain** two ways you can find $3 \div \frac{1}{6}$.

Use fraction bars, patterns, or reciprocals to divide.

2. $2 \div \frac{1}{4}$ 3. $3 \div \frac{1}{6}$ 4. $5 \div \frac{1}{3}$ 5. $1 \div \frac{1}{6}$ 6. $4 \div \frac{1}{3}$

Divide.

7. $8 \div \frac{1}{2}$ 8. $9 \div \frac{2}{5}$ 9. $7 \div \frac{3}{4}$ 10. $3 \div \frac{1}{5}$ 11. $5 \div \frac{3}{10}$

▷ **Practice and Problem Solving**   Extra Practice, page 414, Set B

Use fraction bars, patterns, or reciprocals to divide.

12. $5 \div \frac{1}{2}$ 13. $3 \div \frac{1}{3}$ 14. $8 \div \frac{2}{3}$ 15. $1 \div \frac{1}{8}$ 16. $7 \div \frac{1}{4}$

Divide. Write the answer in simplest form.

17. $9 \div \frac{3}{8}$ 18. $8 \div \frac{6}{7}$ 19. $4 \div \frac{4}{5}$ 20. $6 \div \frac{3}{4}$ 21. $1 \div \frac{2}{5}$

Find the missing number.

22. $4 \div \frac{2}{9} = \blacksquare$ 23. $\blacksquare \div \frac{1}{2} = 16$ 24. $5 \div \frac{1}{\blacksquare} = 30$ 25. $3 \div \frac{\blacksquare}{4} = 12$

26. How many halves are in 4?   27. How many thirds are in 5?

28. How many three-fourths are in 6?   29. How many twos are in 9?

30. **What if** a tortoise travels $\frac{2}{12}$ miles per hour? How many hours will it take the tortoise to walk 6 miles?

31. ✏ **Write a problem** that has a whole number divided by a fraction, with a quotient of 4.

32. 📖 **Write About It** Explain how you can use multiplication to solve $4 \div \frac{1}{2}$.

33. **Vocabulary Power** The origin of *reciprocal* is the Latin word *reciprocus*. It means "returning" or "alternating." Write the reciprocal for $\frac{7}{1}$. Explain how the digits in $\frac{7}{1}$ and its reciprocal alternate.

▲ **Giant tortoises have one of the longest life spans of any animal, sometimes more than 200 years.**

Mixed Review and Test Prep

34. $\frac{1}{4} + \frac{1}{3}$ (p. 356)   35. $\frac{3}{5} + \frac{7}{8}$ (p. 356)

36. $\frac{3}{4} - \frac{1}{2}$ (p. 356)   37. $\frac{9}{10} - \frac{2}{5}$ (p. 356)

38. **TEST PREP** Which is 0.45 written as a fraction? (p. 328)

A $\frac{5}{20}$ B $\frac{9}{20}$ C $\frac{11}{20}$ D $\frac{15}{20}$

LESSON 4

Divide Fractions

Learn

BUZZZY WORK!   If one honeybee makes $\frac{1}{12}$ teaspoon of honey during its lifetime, how many honeybees are needed to make $\frac{1}{2}$ teaspoon of honey?

Example 1

Find $\frac{1}{2} \div \frac{1}{12}$. ←Think: How many $\frac{1}{12}$ teaspoons are in $\frac{1}{2}$ teaspoon?

One Way You can use fraction bars to help you divide fractions by fractions.

> See how many $\frac{1}{12}$ bars are equal to a $\frac{1}{2}$ bar.
>
>

Another Way You can find the quotient of two fractions by using what you know about reciprocals.

STEP 1	STEP 2
Use the reciprocal of the divisor to write a multiplication problem. $\frac{1}{2} \div \frac{1}{12} = \frac{1}{2} \times \frac{12}{1}$ ↑ ↑ reciprocals	Multiply. Write the answer in simplest form. $\frac{1}{2} \times \frac{12}{1} = \frac{12}{2}$, or 6 So, $\frac{1}{2} \div \frac{1}{12} = 6$.

▲ A honeybee would have to visit over 2,000,000 flowers in order to collect enough nectar to produce 1 pound of honey.

So, 6 honeybees are needed to make $\frac{1}{2}$ teaspoon of honey.

• What multiplication problem could you write for $\frac{3}{5} \div \frac{1}{5}$? What is the quotient?

MATH IDEA   To find the quotient of two fractions, multiply the dividend by the reciprocal of the divisor.

408

Use Reciprocals to Divide

You can use reciprocals to divide mixed numbers by fractions and fractions by whole numbers.

Example 2

Find $2\frac{1}{4} \div \frac{1}{3}$.

STEP 1

Write the mixed number as a fraction.

$$2\frac{1}{4} \div \frac{1}{3} = \frac{9}{4} \div \frac{1}{3}$$

STEP 2

Use the reciprocal of the divisor to write a multiplication problem.

$$\frac{9}{4} \div \frac{1}{3} = \frac{9}{4} \times \frac{3}{1}$$
        ↑   ↑
      reciprocals

STEP 3

Multiply. Write the answer in simplest form if needed.

$$\frac{9}{4} \times \frac{3}{1} = \frac{27}{4}, \text{ or } 6\frac{3}{4}$$

So, $2\frac{1}{4} \div \frac{1}{3} = \frac{27}{4}$, or $6\frac{3}{4}$.

More Examples

A

Find $1\frac{2}{3} \div \frac{2}{5}$.

$$1\frac{2}{3} \div \frac{2}{5} = \frac{5}{3} \div \frac{2}{5} = \frac{5}{3} \times \frac{5}{2}$$

$$\frac{5}{3} \times \frac{5}{2} = \frac{25}{6}, \text{ or } 4\frac{1}{6}$$

B

Find $1\frac{1}{4} \div 2\frac{1}{3}$.

$$1\frac{1}{4} \div 2\frac{1}{3} = \frac{5}{4} \div \frac{7}{3} = \frac{5}{4} \times \frac{3}{7}$$

$$\frac{5}{4} \times \frac{3}{7} = \frac{15}{28}$$

C

Find $\frac{5}{6} \div 3$.

$$\frac{5}{6} \div 3 = \frac{5}{6} \times \frac{1}{3}$$

$$\frac{5}{6} \times \frac{1}{3} = \frac{5}{18}$$

▶ **Check**

1. **Explain** whether the dividend is greater than or less than the divisor in Examples A, B, and C. When is the quotient greater than 1?

Write a division sentence for each model.

2. 3. 4.

Use a reciprocal to write a multiplication problem for the division problem.

5. $\frac{3}{4} \div \frac{1}{3}$

6. $\frac{1}{3} \div \frac{1}{2}$

7. $2 \div \frac{2}{5}$

8. $3\frac{2}{3} \div \frac{3}{8}$

9. $2\frac{1}{5} \div 1\frac{1}{4}$

Divide. Write the answer in simplest form.

10. $\frac{1}{4} \div \frac{1}{2}$

11. $\frac{2}{5} \div \frac{1}{10}$

12. $\frac{1}{2} \div 2$

13. $1\frac{3}{4} \div \frac{1}{2}$

14. $1\frac{1}{3} \div 1\frac{1}{2}$

LESSON CONTINUES ▶

Write a division sentence for each model.

15.
| $\frac{1}{6}$ | $\frac{1}{6}$ | $\frac{1}{6}$ | $\frac{1}{6}$ |

| $\frac{1}{6}$ | $\frac{1}{6}$ |

16.
| $\frac{1}{10}$ | $\frac{1}{10}$ | $\frac{1}{10}$ | $\frac{1}{10}$ | $\frac{1}{10}$ | $\frac{1}{10}$ | $\frac{1}{10}$ | $\frac{1}{10}$ |

| $\frac{1}{5}$ | $\frac{1}{5}$ |

17.
| $\frac{1}{12}$ | $\frac{1}{12}$ | $\frac{1}{12}$ | $\frac{1}{12}$ | $\frac{1}{12}$ | $\frac{1}{12}$ | $\frac{1}{12}$ | $\frac{1}{12}$ | $\frac{1}{12}$ |

| $\frac{1}{4}$ |

Use a reciprocal to write a multiplication problem for the division problem.

18. $\frac{3}{8} \div \frac{1}{2}$

19. $\frac{7}{8} \div \frac{1}{3}$

20. $4 \div \frac{3}{8}$

21. $1\frac{2}{5} \div \frac{1}{4}$

22. $2\frac{2}{7} \div 1\frac{1}{5}$

Divide. Write the answer in simplest form.

23. $6 \div \frac{3}{8}$

24. $7 \div \frac{6}{7}$

25. $\frac{3}{5} \div \frac{1}{5}$

26. $\frac{4}{7} \div \frac{2}{3}$

27. $1\frac{1}{4} \div \frac{3}{4}$

28. $8 \div \frac{4}{5}$

29. $\frac{5}{6} \div \frac{1}{3}$

30. $\frac{7}{12} \div \frac{2}{3}$

31. $\frac{3}{4} \div \frac{1}{8}$

32. $\frac{3}{4} \div 2\frac{1}{4}$

33. $3\frac{7}{10} \div 2\frac{4}{5}$

34. $2\frac{3}{4} \div \frac{1}{8}$

35. $\frac{4}{5} \div 8$

36. $\frac{1}{3} \div 12$

37. $2\frac{4}{5} \div 1\frac{2}{3}$

⭐ **ALGEBRA** For 38–40, copy and complete each rule table.

38.
n	$n \div \frac{1}{3}$
$\frac{5}{6}$	■
$\frac{1}{2}$	■
$\frac{1}{9}$	■

39.
y	$y \div \frac{1}{4}$
$\frac{7}{8}$	■
■	2
■	$\frac{16}{5}$, or $3\frac{1}{5}$

40.
n	$n \div \frac{1}{2}$
■	$\frac{6}{8}$, or $\frac{3}{4}$
3	■
■	5

41. If a bee travels $\frac{1}{8}$ mile on each trip it makes to gather nectar, how many trips will the bee make to travel $\frac{1}{2}$ mile?

42. **REASONING** If $\frac{3}{4} \div \frac{n}{8} = \frac{3}{4} \times \frac{n}{8}$, what is the value of n? Explain.

43. How many more $1\frac{1}{2}$-ounce servings are in the large jar of honey on the right than in the small jar?

44. ⭐ **ALGEBRA** Find n if $a = 4$, $b = 6$, and $c = 4$.
$$\frac{a}{b} \div \frac{c}{n} = \frac{1}{2}$$

45. Mrs. Banak bought a $12\frac{1}{2}$-ounce box of honeycomb cereal for $3. How much does the cereal cost per ounce?

46. **≡FAST FACT** • **SOCIAL STUDIES**
On average, each person in the United States eats $1\frac{1}{10}$ pounds of honey every year. At this rate, how much honey do 5 people eat in a year?

47. Scott uses $2\frac{1}{4}$ ounces of honey to make a loaf of bread. How many loaves can he make from a 12-ounce jar of honey? How much honey will be left?

Mixed Review and Test Prep

USE DATA For 48–50, use the circle graph.

TODD'S VIDEO COLLECTION

Action
Drama
Comedy
Other

48. Todd has 24 videos. How many comedy videos does he own? (p. 106)

49. What fraction of Todd's collection is either action or drama videos? (p. 106)

50. If $\frac{1}{3}$ of Todd's "Other" videos are live concerts, what fraction of his collection is live concert videos? (p. 106)

51. Write 6.9054 in word form. (p. 22)

52. $\frac{3}{4} + \frac{1}{2} + \frac{1}{4}$ 53. 0.3×0.03
(p. 356)   (p. 174)

54. **TEST PREP** What is the least common multiple of 16 and 12? (p. 282)

   A 4   **B** 16   **C** 48   **D** 192

55. **TEST PREP** Tomas has 6 pounds of ground beef. How many quarter-pound hamburgers can he make? (p. 406)

   F $1\frac{1}{2}$ **G** 12   **H** 24   **J** 96

Problem Solving LiNKUP . . . to Reading

STRATEGY • IDENTIFY INFORMATION A careful reader must identify the details needed to solve a word problem. Read the following problem.

The average bee collects nectar for honey within 1 mile of its hive, makes up to 25 trips each day, and can carry a load of about 0.002 ounce—about half its weight. After the first half of their lives, bees eat only honey. In fact, for every pound of honey sold in stores, 8 pounds are used by the hive. About how much does a honeybee weigh?

1. What detail do you need to solve this problem?

2. Solve the problem.

For 3–4, use the paragraph above. Write the detail you need to solve each problem. Then solve.

3. If a bee visits 75 flowers during each nectar-collecting trip, about how many flowers does it visit each day?

4. For every $\frac{1}{4}$ pound of honey sold in stores, how many pounds are used by the hive?

Problem Solving Strategy
Solve a Simpler Problem

Quick Review

1. 120 ÷ 3   **2.** 140 ÷ 2

3. 250 ÷ 5   **4.** 720 ÷ 8

5. $9 \div \frac{2}{3}$

PROBLEM   The greatest weight ever recorded for a great white shark was about 7,000 pounds. This is $\frac{4}{25}$ the weight of the world's largest shark, the whale shark. How much does a whale shark weigh?

UNDERSTAND

• What are you asked to find?

• What information will you use?

PLAN

• What strategy can you use to solve the problem?

You can *solve a simpler problem* by using simpler numbers.

▲ Great whites are the largest meat-eating sharks. They have 3,000 teeth that are triangular, razor-sharp, and up to 3 inches long.

SOLVE

• How can you use the strategy to solve the problem?

Think: ■ $\times \frac{4}{25}$ = 7,000, so 7,000 $\div \frac{4}{25}$ = ■.

Use a simpler number instead of 7,000.
Since 7 × 1,000 = 7,000, use the simpler number 7 to represent the weight of the great white shark.

$$7 \div \frac{4}{25} = \frac{7}{1} \times \frac{25}{4} = \frac{175}{4}$$

To find the actual weight of a whale shark, multiply by 1,000.

$$\frac{175}{4} \times 1,000 = \frac{175,000}{4} = 43,750$$

So, a whale shark weighs about 43,750 pounds.

CHECK

• Look back at the problem. How can you decide if your answer is correct?

Strategies

Draw a Diagram or Picture
Make a Model or Act It Out
Make an Organized List
Find a Pattern
Make a Table or Graph
Predict and Test
Work Backward
▶ **Solve a Simpler Problem**
Write an Equation
Use Logical Reasoning

Problem Solving

Use a simpler problem to solve.

1. **What if** a whale shark is 1,500 centimeters long and a great white shark is $\frac{2}{5}$ as long? How long is the great white shark?

2. A Pacific gray whale can weigh 70,000 pounds. This is about $\frac{7}{30}$ the weight of a blue whale. How much does a blue whale weigh?

A whale shark is 600 inches long. The world's smallest shark, the smalleye pygmy shark, is $\frac{1}{75}$ the length of a whale shark.

3. Which equation can be used to find the length of a pygmy shark?

   A $600 \times \frac{1}{75} = n$

   B $600 \times n = \frac{1}{75}$

   C $600 \div \frac{1}{75} = n$

   D $600 - \frac{1}{75} = n$

4. How long is a smalleye pygmy shark in feet?

   F 80 feet   **G** 8 feet   **H** $1\frac{1}{2}$ feet   **J** $\frac{2}{3}$ foot

▲ **Whale shark**

Mixed Strategy Practice

5. Cole's dresser is $5\frac{1}{4}$ feet wide. His bookcase is $\frac{2}{3}$ as wide as his dresser. How wide is his bookcase?

6. Rachel has $4.75 in coins. She has 6 dimes and twice as many quarters. The rest are nickels. How many of each coin does she have?

7. The city bought 48,000 tulip bulbs. Workers planted $\frac{1}{8}$ in parks and $\frac{2}{3}$ along roads. How many bulbs do they have left?

8. Chloe made a square design. She colored $\frac{1}{4}$ of the square blue, $\frac{1}{8}$ yellow, and $\frac{1}{8}$ green. She left $\frac{1}{2}$ of the square white. What might her design look like?

9. **NUMBER SENSE** Oren chose a number and multiplied it by 3. Then he added 6, divided by 9, and subtracted 5. The answer was 4. What number did Oren choose?

10. **?** **What's the Error?** Of the 398 species of sharks in the world, 199 are less than 39 inches long. Joe says the other $\frac{1}{3}$ are 39 inches or longer. Describe and correct his error.

Extra Practice

Set A (pp. 404–405)

Are the two numbers reciprocals? Write *yes* or *no*.

1. $\frac{2}{3}$ and 3
2. $\frac{3}{4}$ and $1\frac{1}{3}$
3. $\frac{4}{7}$ and $1\frac{4}{7}$
4. $1\frac{2}{3}$ and $\frac{3}{5}$
5. $\frac{3}{4}$ and $1\frac{1}{4}$

Write the reciprocal of each number.

6. $\frac{1}{3}$
7. 10
8. $\frac{7}{2}$
9. $1\frac{3}{4}$
10. $2\frac{1}{3}$

11. $\frac{6}{9}$
12. $1\frac{1}{4}$
13. $\frac{7}{8}$
14. 6
15. $5\frac{2}{5}$

16. Jane writes the reciprocal of $\frac{7}{10}$. What number does she write?

17. Is the reciprocal of $1\frac{2}{5}$ greater than or less than 1?

Set B (pp. 406–407)

Divide. Write the answer in simplest form.

1. $9 \div \frac{3}{4}$
2. $4 \div \frac{1}{3}$
3. $2 \div \frac{4}{5}$
4. $7 \div \frac{2}{3}$
5. $10 \div \frac{1}{4}$

6. $3 \div \frac{3}{4}$
7. $8 \div \frac{1}{6}$
8. $6 \div \frac{3}{8}$
9. $1 \div \frac{5}{6}$
10. $15 \div \frac{2}{3}$

11. How many halves are in 7?

12. How many thirds are in 6?

13. There are 8 pounds of clay for projects. Each project uses $\frac{1}{2}$ pound of clay. How many projects can be made from the clay?

14. A pastry chef has 9 pounds of butter and uses $\frac{3}{4}$ pound for each batch of cookies. How many batches of cookies can he make?

Set C (pp. 408–411)

Use a reciprocal to write a multiplication problem for the division problem.

1. $\frac{3}{4} \div \frac{1}{5}$
2. $\frac{3}{5} \div \frac{6}{7}$
3. $\frac{1}{3} \div \frac{5}{9}$
4. $\frac{6}{7} \div \frac{1}{8}$
5. $\frac{5}{8} \div \frac{2}{3}$

Divide. Write the answer in simplest form.

6. $\frac{4}{7} \div \frac{3}{4}$
7. $\frac{7}{8} \div \frac{5}{6}$
8. $\frac{5}{7} \div \frac{5}{9}$
9. $\frac{1}{6} \div \frac{3}{7}$
10. $\frac{2}{7} \div \frac{1}{4}$

11. $\frac{2}{3} \div \frac{4}{7}$
12. $\frac{3}{10} \div 4$
13. $\frac{5}{8} \div 2\frac{1}{2}$
14. $3\frac{1}{3} \div \frac{2}{3}$
15. $2\frac{2}{3} \div 1\frac{1}{6}$

16. Chris wants to build a fence $8\frac{1}{3}$ yards long. How many $1\frac{2}{3}$-yard pieces of fence will he need?

17. Mr. Cook wants to fence his rectangular garden which covers 100 ft^2. The width of the garden is $7\frac{1}{2}$ ft. What is the length of the garden? How much fencing will Mr. Cook need?

Review/Test

✓ CHECK VOCABULARY AND CONCEPTS

Choose the best term from the box.

denominator
divisor
fraction
numerator
reciprocal

1. To find the quotient of two fractions, multiply the dividend by the reciprocal of the __?__. (p. 408)

2. To find the reciprocal of a mixed number, first rename the mixed number as a __?__. (p. 404)

3. To divide a whole number by a fraction, first write the whole number as a fraction with a __?__ of 1. (p. 406)

4. The product of a number and its __?__ is 1. (p. 404)

✓ CHECK SKILLS

Write the reciprocal of each number. (pp. 404–405)

5. $\frac{3}{10}$ 6. $8\frac{2}{3}$ 7. 14   8. $4\frac{2}{11}$ 9. $\frac{2}{5}$

Divide. Write the answer in simplest form. (pp. 406–411)

10. $12 \div \frac{2}{3}$ 11. $9 \div \frac{4}{5}$ 12. $\frac{4}{5} \div 4$ 13. $7 \div \frac{5}{9}$

14. $8 \div \frac{3}{7}$ 15. $\frac{8}{9} \div 11$ 16. $\frac{2}{7} \div \frac{2}{3}$ 17. $\frac{5}{6} \div 1\frac{1}{9}$

18. $\frac{3}{5} \div \frac{3}{10}$ 19. $1\frac{1}{2} \div \frac{1}{4}$ 20. $2\frac{5}{8} \div \frac{1}{4}$ 21. $2\frac{3}{4} \div 2\frac{1}{6}$

✓ CHECK PROBLEM SOLVING

Solve. (pp. 412–413)

22. The mustard factory has 20,000 ounces of mustard to put into small packets. If each packet holds $\frac{1}{4}$ ounce, how many packets can be filled?

23. Lydia needs $\frac{3}{4}$ cup of flour to make bread. She has only a $\frac{1}{8}$-cup measuring cup. How many times will she fill the $\frac{1}{8}$ cup to get the $\frac{3}{4}$ cup she needs?

24. The Sports Card Store has 200,000 cards. If $\frac{1}{10}$ of them are baseball cards, how many cards are *not* baseball cards?

25. Gretchen has 27 feet of ribbon. She needs to cut the ribbon into $\frac{3}{4}$-foot pieces. How many pieces of ribbon can she cut?

Standardized Test Prep

⭐ NUMBER SENSE, CONCEPTS, AND OPERATIONS

1. Theresa is thinking of a number. She wrote these clues for her number.

- The number has 5 digits.
- The sum of the digits is 19.
- The digit 0 is not used.
- All the digits are different.

What is the **greatest** number you can write using Theresa's clues?

A 98,765   **C** 95,320

B 98,761   **D** 94,321

2. The table shows the number of horses in four countries.

HORSE POPULATIONS	
Country	**Number of Horses**
Brazil	6,394,140
China	8,854,800
Mexico	6,250,000
United States	6,150,000

How many more horses are there in China than in the United States?

F 1,704,800   **H** 2,704,800

G 2,604,800   **J** 15,004,800

3. Explain It Use the table in Problem 2. ESTIMATE, to the nearest hundred thousand, the total horse population of the four countries. Explain how you found your answer.

⭐ DATA ANALYSIS AND PROBABILITY

4. Joseph's average for four bowling games was 135. If his bowling scores for the first three games were 127, 149, and 130, what was his score for the last game?

A 134   **C** 406

B 146   **D** 540

5. The graph shows flower sales at Gala Flowers.

What was the total number of arrangements sold in February?

F 125

G 155

H 180

J 210

6. Explain It Look at the graph above. Medium arrangements sell for $15. How much more did Gala Flowers make on sales of medium floral arrangements in February than in January? Explain how you solved the problem.

⭐ ALGEBRAIC THINKING

7. Four students each wrote an expression using the numbers 3, 4, 6, and 8. Who wrote the expression with the **greatest** value?

STUDENT EXPRESSIONS	
Debra	$(6 \div 3) \times (8 \div 4)$
Andrew	$(6 + 8) \div (3 + 4)$
Tomoko	$8 \times 3 \div 6 - 4$
Lacey	$(4 + 8) - 6 \div 3$

A Debra

B Andrew

C Tomoko

D Lacey

8. A camp group went to the aquarium. The table shows the relationship between the number of campers and the cost of admission.

AQUARIUM ADMISSION COSTS					
Number of Campers	1	2	3	4	5
Cost (in dollars)	6	12	18	24	30

What is the cost of admission for a camp group with 8 campers?

F $36

G $42

H $48

J $54

9. Explain It Write a rule for this pattern.

16, 8, 24, 12, 36, 18, 54, ■, ■

Then write the next two numbers in the pattern. Explain your answer.

⭐ GEOMETRY AND SPATIAL SENSE

10. Which figure does NOT have line symmetry?

> **TIP** **Look for important words.**
> See item 10. The term *line symmetry* is important. If a figure has line symmetry, it can be folded along a line so that the two parts match exactly.

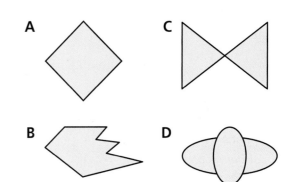

A   C

B   D

11. The perimeter of a square rug is 32 feet. What is the area of the rug?

F 16 square feet

G 24 square feet

H 48 square feet

J 64 square feet

12. Explain It Name a diameter of the circle.

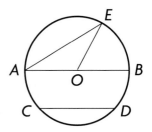

Explain how you know that the segment you named is a diameter.

IT'S IN THE BAG

Create-a-Meal Cookbook

PROJECT Make a cookbook to practice comparing fractions.

Materials

- 3 to 9 recipes
- 3 sheets of white paper
- 1 piece of fabric (11 in. × 9 in.)
- Glue stick
- Colored paper for title
- Markers
- Cookbook comparisons worksheet

CREATE-A-MEAL COOKBOOK

Directions

1. Make the cookbook pages. Fold a white sheet of paper in half and cut a window down the folded side that is about $6\frac{1}{2}$ in. long and $\frac{1}{2}$ in. wide. *(Picture A)*

2. Fold the other two white papers in half and cut slits of 1 in. on each end of the fold. Fold these papers lengthwise and put them through the "window". Open them so the slits are at the top and bottom to form the pages of the book. *(Picture B)*

3. Open the book and lay it on the reverse side of the fabric. Glue the first and last pages of the book to the fabric, forming the cover. Make a label with colored paper, write the title on it, and glue it to the front of the book cover. Glue the cookbook comparisons worksheet inside the front cover of the book. Choose 3 to 9 recipes for your favorite meals and copy them into the book. *(Picture C)*

4. Suppose you are having a party. How much of each ingredient would you need to serve 12 people? 16 people? 24 people? Explain.

Challenge

Explore Patterns with Fractions

A **pattern** of fractions follows a rule. When you know the rule for the pattern, you can figure out the next fraction in the sequence.

Example Find the next fraction in this pattern. $\frac{1}{2}, \frac{2}{4}, \frac{3}{6}, \frac{4}{8}, \ldots$

STEP 1

Look for a pattern to find a rule.

Think: What do I do to $\frac{1}{2}$ to get $\frac{2}{4}$?

$\frac{1 + 1}{2 + 2}$ $\begin{array}{l}\leftarrow\text{add 1}\\\leftarrow\text{add 2}\end{array} = \frac{2}{4}$

STEP 2

Test the rule for all the terms.

Rule: Add 1 to the numerator. Add 2 to the denominator.

$\frac{2 + 1}{4 + 2} = \frac{3}{6}, \frac{3 + 1}{6 + 2} = \frac{4}{8}$

STEP 3

Use the rule to find the next term.

$\frac{4}{8} \rightarrow \frac{4 + 1}{8 + 2} = \frac{5}{10}$

So, the next fraction in the pattern is $\frac{5}{10}$.

More Examples

A $\frac{1}{3}, \frac{2}{6}, \frac{3}{9}, \frac{4}{12}, \ldots$

Rule: Add 1 to the numerator. Add 3 to the denominator.

So, the next fraction in the pattern is $\frac{4 + 1}{12 + 3} = \frac{5}{15}$.

B $\frac{3}{6}, \frac{6}{12}, \frac{12}{24}, \frac{24}{48}, \ldots$

Rule: Multiply the numerator and the denominator by 2.

So, the next fraction in the pattern is $\frac{24 \times 2}{48 \times 2} = \frac{48}{96}$.

Talk About It

- What would you do if your rule in Step 1 did not work with the other fractions?

Try It

Write a rule. Find the next fraction in the pattern.

1. $\frac{3}{4}, \frac{9}{12}, \frac{27}{36}, \frac{81}{108}, \ldots$

2. $\frac{6}{7}, \frac{7}{8}, \frac{8}{9}, \frac{9}{10}, \ldots$

3. $\frac{1}{2}, \frac{3}{5}, \frac{5}{8}, \frac{7}{11}, \ldots$

Create a pattern for the rule. Start with any fraction.

4. **Rule:** Multiply the numerator by 2. Add 1 to the denominator.

5. **Rule:** Add 2 to the numerator. Add 1 to the denominator.

6. **Rule:** Add 2 to the numerator and the denominator.

Study Guide and Review

VOCABULARY

Choose the best term from the box.

equivalent fractions
greatest common factor
reciprocals
rename
least common denominator

1. The least common multiple of the denominators is the __?__ for the fractions. (p. 354)

2. Two numbers with a product of 1 are called __?__. (p. 404)

3. To simplify factors before you multiply them, you can divide by the __?__ of a numerator and a denominator. (p. 392)

STUDY AND SOLVE

Chapter 16

Add and subtract fractions.

Find $\frac{2}{3} + \frac{1}{4}$.

Use the LCD to write like fractions.

$$\frac{2}{3} = \frac{2 \times 4}{3 \times 4} = \frac{8}{12}$$

$$+ \frac{1}{4} = + \frac{1 \times 3}{4 \times 3} = + \frac{3}{12}$$

$$\frac{11}{12}$$

Add the numerators. Write the sum over the denominator.

Find the sum or difference. Write the answer in simplest form. (pp. 346–359)

4. $\frac{3}{5} + \frac{2}{5}$ 5. $\frac{5}{7} - \frac{3}{14}$

6. $\frac{7}{16} + \frac{3}{8}$ 7. $\frac{2}{3} - \frac{5}{9}$

8. $\frac{1}{4} - \frac{1}{12}$ 9. $\frac{1}{9} + \frac{5}{6}$

Chapter 17

Add and subtract mixed numbers.

$$2\frac{3}{8} = 2\frac{3}{8}$$

$$- 1\frac{1}{4} = - 1\frac{2}{8}$$

$$1\frac{1}{8}$$

Use the LCD to rename. Subtract the fractions. Then subtract the whole numbers. Simplify if possible.

Find the sum or difference. Write the answer in simplest form. (pp. 368–377)

10. $4\frac{7}{12} + 3\frac{1}{8}$ 11. $3\frac{4}{6} - 2\frac{1}{6}$

12. $6\frac{2}{5} - 5\frac{3}{5}$ 13. $6\frac{5}{8} + 7\frac{7}{8}$

Chapter 18

Multiply a fraction by a fraction.

Multiply. $\frac{3}{4} \times \frac{2}{5}$

$$\frac{3}{4} \times \frac{2}{5} = \frac{3 \times 2}{4 \times 5}$$

$$= \frac{6}{20} = \frac{3}{10}$$

Multiply the numerators. Multiply the denominators. Simplify if possible.

Find the product. Write the answer in simplest form. (pp. 386–389)

14. $\frac{1}{2} \times \frac{2}{7}$ 15. $\frac{1}{3} \times \frac{5}{9}$

16. $\frac{4}{9} \times \frac{6}{11}$ 17. $\frac{3}{8} \times \frac{1}{6}$

Multiply mixed numbers.

Multiply. $2\frac{2}{3} \times \frac{2}{3}$

$\frac{8}{3} \times \frac{2}{3} = \frac{16}{9}$, or $1\frac{7}{9}$ Rename the mixed number as a fraction. Multiply the fractions.

Find the product. Write the answer in simplest form. (pp. 390–393)

18. $\frac{5}{6} \times 3\frac{1}{2}$ **19.** $2\frac{1}{4} \times \frac{3}{8}$

20. $4\frac{3}{4} \times 1\frac{1}{2}$ **21.** $2\frac{2}{3} \times 3\frac{1}{4}$

22. $5\frac{1}{2} \times \frac{1}{4}$ **23.** $1\frac{5}{8} \times \frac{2}{3}$

Chapter 19

Write the reciprocal of a number.

Write the reciprocals of $\frac{2}{3}$ and $2\frac{3}{4}$.

Exchange the numerators and denominators.

$\frac{2}{3} \rightarrow \frac{3}{2}$, or $1\frac{1}{2}$ ← reciprocal

$2\frac{3}{4} = \frac{11}{4} \rightarrow \frac{4}{11}$ ← reciprocal

Write the reciprocal of each number.

(pp. 404–405)

24. 19   **25.** $2\frac{3}{7}$ **26.** $\frac{7}{12}$

27. $3\frac{2}{9}$ **28.** $\frac{14}{31}$ **29.** $4\frac{1}{3}$

Divide with fractions.

Divide. $4 \div \frac{2}{3}$

$\frac{4}{1} \div \frac{2}{3} = \frac{4}{1} \times \frac{3}{2}$ Write the whole number as a fraction. Multiply using the reciprocal of the divisor.

$= \frac{12}{2} = 6$ Write the answer in simplest form.

Find the quotient. Write the answer in simplest form. (pp. 406–411)

30. $5 \div \frac{2}{3}$ **31.** $\frac{9}{10} \div \frac{2}{5}$

32. $12 \div \frac{5}{6}$ **33.** $1\frac{3}{4} \div \frac{5}{8}$

PROBLEM SOLVING PRACTICE

Solve. (pp. 394–395, 412–413)

34. Mrs. Catalanello made 3 loaves of bread. The first loaf was $10\frac{7}{8}$ inches long, the second loaf was $3\frac{1}{2}$ inches shorter than the first, and the third was $1\frac{3}{4}$ inches longer than the second. How long was the third loaf?

35. In 1998, the populations of Los Angeles, San Francisco, and San Diego totalled about 5,500,000. The population of Los Angeles was $\frac{2}{3}$ of this total. What was the population of Los Angeles in 1998?

PERFORMANCE ASSESSMENT

TASK A • PIZZA TIME

Dan bought a pizza to share with Kenny. Each boy ate a different number of pieces. Dan ate the most. When the boys were finished, there was one piece left for Dan to give to his grandmother.

a. Draw a diagram of the pizza. Write fractions on the diagram to show the amounts Dan and Kenny ate.

b. If the boys ate the amounts you suggested, what fraction of the pizza was left for Dan's grandmother?

c. Dan baked four strawberry tarts to share with his grandmother and Kenny. Use mixed numbers to suggest a way they could have shared the tarts if Dan ate the most and his grandmother ate the least.

TASK B • ON THE JOB

A local grocery store has these part-time jobs available. Jon and Kate each want to apply for one of these jobs.

HELP WANTED

JOB A

Stock shelves after school for $2\frac{1}{2}$ hours per day, 4 days a week. Pays $6 per hour.

HELP WANTED

JOB B

Help at check-out counters for $3\frac{1}{2}$ hours every Friday and $5\frac{1}{2}$ hours every Saturday. Pays $6 per hour.

HELP WANTED

JOB C

Unload 3 delivery trucks every Saturday. Each truck requires about $2\frac{1}{2}$ hours to unload. Pays $20 per truck.

a. Jon wants to work 10 hours per week. Which job should he apply for?

b. Kate wants to work only on Saturdays to earn $100 as quickly as possible. Which job should she apply for?

c. Change the job descriptions so that Jon and Kate can choose between two part-time jobs.

Technology Linkup

Calculator • Operations with Fractions

You can use a calculator to extend number patterns involving operations with fractions.

Example The rule is add $\frac{2}{3}$. The first number in the pattern is $\frac{2}{3}$. Each fraction is expressed in simplest form. What are the next three numbers in the pattern?

Step 1 Enter the first fraction.

Step 2 Add $\frac{2}{3}$.
So, the second term is $\frac{4}{3}$, or $1\frac{1}{3}$.

Step 3 Add $\frac{2}{3}$.
Press **SIMP** until SIMP disappears from the display. So, the third term is $\frac{2}{1}$, or 2.

Step 4 Add $\frac{2}{3}$.
So, the fourth term is $\frac{8}{3}$, or $2\frac{2}{3}$.

So, the next three numbers in the pattern are $\frac{4}{3}$, 2, and $\frac{8}{3}$.

Practice and Problem Solving

Use a calculator to find the next three numbers in the pattern. Express all fractions in simplest form.

1. **rule:** subtract $\frac{1}{6}$
   first number: $\frac{19}{20}$

2. **rule:** mutiply by $\frac{3}{5}$
   first number: $\frac{7}{10}$

3. **rule:** divide by $\frac{1}{8}$
   first number: $\frac{1}{3}$

4. **REASONING** The first four terms in the pattern are 3, $4\frac{1}{2}$, $6\frac{3}{4}$, and $10\frac{1}{8}$. What is a rule for the pattern?

Multimedia Math Glossary www.harcourtschool.com/mathglossary
Vocabulary Power Find *least common denominator* in the Multimedia Math Glossary. Its definition contains words that are also math vocabulary words. Make a list of the words and definitions. Then draw a diagram to show how these words are related.

PROBLEM SOLVING ON LOCATION
in
Pretzel Country

VENDORS IN PHILADELPHIA

With food vendors selling pretzels at street corners, the people of Philadelphia can get pretzels far more easily than most Americans. Lititz, a city outside Lancaster, Pennsylvania, is the birthplace of the American pretzel.

1. Each year a typical person in the United States will eat $1\frac{1}{2}$ pounds of pretzels. A typical Philadelphian will eat about 12 times that amount! About how many pounds of pretzels does a Philadelphian eat each year?

2. Pretzels usually bake for about 10 minutes until they are golden brown. What fraction of an hour is 10 minutes?

USE DATA For 3–5, use the recipes.

3. What is the total amount of warm water needed for Recipe 1?

4. How much more flour is needed for Recipe 1 than for Recipe 2?

5. If you cut Recipe 1 in half, how much of each ingredient will you need?

Recipe 1

1 package active yeast

$\frac{1}{8}$ cup warm water (105°F) for yeast

$1\frac{1}{3}$ cups warm water

$\frac{1}{3}$ cup brown sugar

5 cups flour

Recipe 2

1 package active yeast

1 cup warm water

2 tbsp soft butter

$\frac{1}{2}$ tsp salt

1 tbsp sugar

5 tsp baking soda

coarse salt (if desired)

$2\frac{3}{4}$ cups bread flour

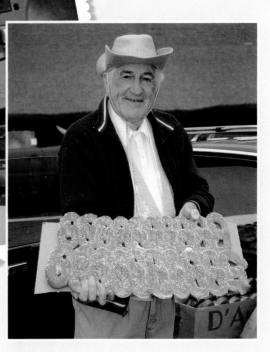

MUSTARD SPREADS FOR PRETZELS

Mustard, a popular spread for pretzels, is made from mustard seeds, vinegar, and other spices. In 1768, Benjamin Jackson produced the country's first mustard and sold it in glass bottles to fellow Philadelphians. Today there is a mustard museum in Mt. Horeb, Wisconsin, where about 3,000 different kinds of mustard are on display.

1. There are $1\frac{1}{2}$ grams of fat in 3 teaspoons of mustard. How many grams of fat are in twice as much mustard?

USE DATA For 3–5, use the recipe.

3. How much more Dijon mustard than honey is needed for the recipe?

4. If $\frac{1}{4}$ cup of mustard flour is put in a 1-cup measuring cup, how much of the cup is not filled?

5. If all the ingredients measured in cups were combined, would you have more than or less than 3 cups of ingredients? Explain.

2. A well-known mustard company produces 2,700 jars of mustard each hour. How many jars are produced in $\frac{2}{3}$ hour?

Honey Ginger Mustard

$\frac{1}{4}$ cup mustard flour

2 tbsp very cold water

$1\frac{1}{2}$ cups Dijon mustard

$\frac{2}{3}$ cup honey

$\frac{1}{2}$ cup candied ginger, very finely chopped

2 tsp grated fresh ginger

Geometric Figures

SHAPE	MESSAGE
STOP	Stop
YIELD	Yield
R X R	Railroad Warning
NO PASSING ZONE	No Passing Zone
PIER ENDS	Warning Signs
HANDICAPPED PARKING	Guide Signs
King Creek Falls	Recreational Area Signs

FAST FACT • SOCIAL STUDIES Traffic signs regulate the flow of traffic for motor vehicles, bicycles, and pedestrians. The signs give information through their shape, color, message, and placement. There are road signs to meet the special needs of handicapped people. For example, there are road signs in Braille for the blind and signs that designate handicapped parking.

PROBLEM SOLVING Look at the table. Name the shape of each type of sign.

Use this page to help you review and remember
important skills needed for Chapter 20.

✓ NAME POLYGONS

Name each polygon. Tell the number of sides and angles.

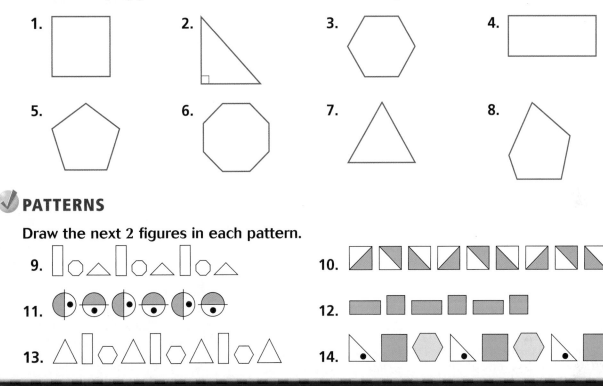

1.

2.

3.

4.

5.

6.

7.

8.

✓ PATTERNS

Draw the next 2 figures in each pattern.

9.

10.

11.

12.

13.

14.

VOCABULARY POWER ✓

REVIEW

geometry [jē am′ə trē] *noun*

The word *geometry* comes from *geo,* which
means "Earth," and *metry,* which means
"measure." So, *geometry* means "Earth
measure." Think of another word that has
geo or *metry* in it and explain what it
means.

PREVIEW

parallel lines	degree
intersecting lines	circle
perpendicular lines	radius
central angle	diameter
line symmetry	chord
rotational symmetry	similar
corresponding angles	congruent
corresponding sides	regular polygon

GO ON-LINE www.harcourtschool.com/mathglossary

Lines and Angles

▶ Learn

WHAT'S THE ANGLE? You can see basic geometric figures all around you. Some geometric figures have special names and symbols.

A **point** marks an exact location in space. Use a letter to name a point.	• A point *A*
A **line** is an endless straight path. It has no endpoints. Use two points on the line to name the line.	A ← → B line *AB* or $\overleftrightarrow{AB}$ or line *BA* or $\overleftrightarrow{BA}$
A **ray** is part of a line that has one endpoint and continues without end in one direction. Use an endpoint and one other point on the ray to name a ray.	K • ——— L → ray *KL* or $\overrightarrow{KL}$
A **line segment** is part of a line that includes two endpoints and all of the points between them. Use the two endpoints to name the line segment.	C • ——— • D line segment *CD* or $\overline{CD}$ or line segment *DC* or $\overline{DC}$
A **plane** is an endless flat surface. Use three points that are not on a line to name the plane.	F• •G •H plane *FGH*

▲ Vehicle Assembly Building, Kennedy Space Center

An **angle** is formed by two rays with the same endpoint. An angle can be named by three letters—a point from each side and the vertex as the middle letter. It can also be named by a single letter, its vertex.

ray *A*
vertex
B ← ray → *C*

∠*ABC*, ∠*CBA*, or ∠*B*

Angles can be different sizes. The unit of measure for an angle is called a **degree** (°).

A right angle measures 90°.	An acute angle is greater than 0° and less than 90°.	An obtuse angle is greater than 90° and less than 180°.	A straight angle measures 180°.

Line Relationships

Within a plane, lines can have different relationships.

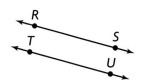

Lines in a plane that never intersect and are the same distance apart at every point are **parallel lines**. $\overleftrightarrow{RS} \parallel \overleftrightarrow{TU}$

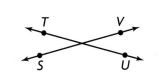

Lines that cross at one point are **intersecting lines**.

Lines that intersect to form four right angles are **perpendicular lines**. $\overleftrightarrow{AB} \perp \overleftrightarrow{CD}$

HINT: Remember that ∥ means "is parallel to" and ⊥ means "is perpendicular to."

• Are all intersecting lines perpendicular?

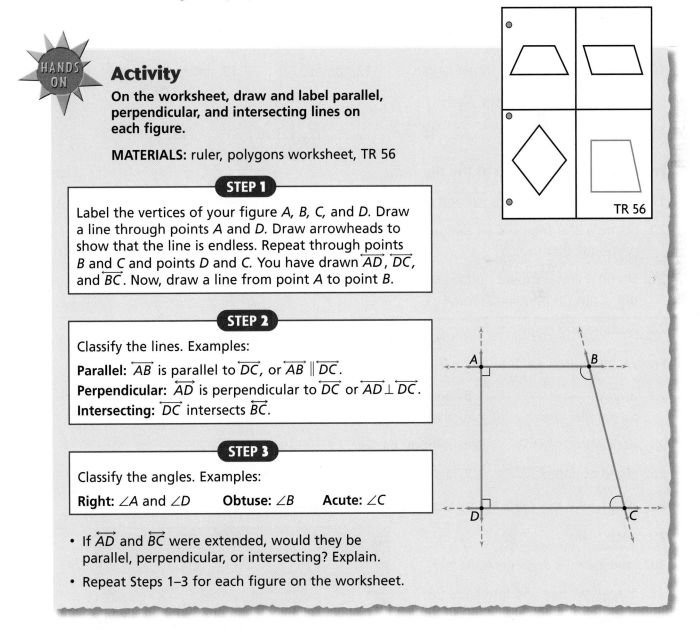

HANDS ON

Activity

On the worksheet, draw and label parallel, perpendicular, and intersecting lines on each figure.

MATERIALS: ruler, polygons worksheet, TR 56

TR 56

STEP 1

Label the vertices of your figure A, B, C, and D. Draw a line through points A and D. Draw arrowheads to show that the line is endless. Repeat through points B and C and points D and C. You have drawn $\overleftrightarrow{AD}$, $\overleftrightarrow{DC}$, and $\overleftrightarrow{BC}$. Now, draw a line from point A to point B.

STEP 2

Classify the lines. Examples:

Parallel: $\overleftrightarrow{AB}$ is parallel to $\overleftrightarrow{DC}$, or $\overleftrightarrow{AB} \parallel \overleftrightarrow{DC}$.
Perpendicular: $\overleftrightarrow{AD}$ is perpendicular to $\overleftrightarrow{DC}$ or $\overleftrightarrow{AD} \perp \overleftrightarrow{DC}$.
Intersecting: $\overleftrightarrow{DC}$ intersects $\overleftrightarrow{BC}$.

STEP 3

Classify the angles. Examples:

Right: ∠A and ∠D   **Obtuse:** ∠B   **Acute:** ∠C

• If $\overleftrightarrow{AD}$ and $\overleftrightarrow{BC}$ were extended, would they be parallel, perpendicular, or intersecting? Explain.

• Repeat Steps 1–3 for each figure on the worksheet.

LESSON CONTINUES

1. **Explain** the difference between a line and a line segment.

For 2–9, use the figure at the right. Name an example of each term.

2. acute angle

3. parallel line segments

4. line segment

5. plane

6. ray

7. line

8. right angle

9. perpendicular lines

▶ **Practice and Problem Solving** Extra Practice, page 450, Set A

For 10–13, use the figure above. Name an example of each.

10. straight angle

11. obtuse angle

12. point

13. intersecting lines

Draw and label a figure for each.

14. $\overline{LM}$

15. $\overrightarrow{CD}$

16. $\overleftrightarrow{AB}$

17. $\angle BDE$

18. point *P*

For 19–22, use the figure at the right.

19. Name the point where $\overline{AB}$ and $\overline{BC}$ intersect.

20. Name a line segment on plane *ABC* that is perpendicular to $\overline{AD}$.

21. Name a line segment on the plane that intersects but is not perpendicular to $\overline{DC}$.

22. Name a line segment that is parallel to $\overline{BC}$.

For 23–28, match each object with a term.

   a. ray   **b.** line segment   **c.** intersecting line segments
   d. parallel lines   **e.** plane   **f.** point

23. pencil tip

24. railroad tracks

25. the letter X

26. piece of paper

27. laser beam

28. flagpole

For 29–31, use the map. Name the geometric figure suggested by

29. each town.

30. Interstate 18 and Interstate 287.

31. Maple Avenue and Interstate 287.

32. ✎ **Write About It** Parallel lines never meet. Explain how you know.

33. Draw two rays that meet at a vertex. Label the rays, the vertex, the interior, and the exterior of the angle.

34. Mark one point on your paper. Label it *P*. How many lines can you draw through point *P*?

35. Sophia bought 5 packages of 8 hot dogs each and 3 packages of 12 buns each. Does she have enough buns for all the hot dogs? Explain.

36. Copy the points on your paper. Connect the points to make a closed figure. Find the perimeter and area of the figure.

Mixed Review and Test Prep

37. Name the addition property shown.
$(5 + 2) + 8 = 5 + (2 + 8)$ (p. 76)

38. Write the number that is 0.05 greater than 0.125. (p. 48)

39. $193{,}023 \times 24$ (p. 152)

40. $218{,}384 \times 13$ (p. 152)

41. **TEST PREP** Out of a total of 20 apples, oranges, and pears, $\frac{1}{2}$ are apples and $\frac{1}{5}$ are oranges. How many pears are there? (p. 388)

    A 4   **B** 6   **C** 8   **D** 10

USE DATA For 42–44, use the table.

WEEK'S SALES						
M	T	W	Th	F	Sa	Su
$150	$100	$160	$200	$250	$300	$275

42. What is the range of data? (p. 96)

43. Between which pairs of days did sales decrease? (p. 14)

44. **TEST PREP** Choose the kind of graph that would best display these data. (p. 130)

    F line graph   **H** circle graph
    G bar graph   **J** pictograph

Problem Solving   LiNKUP...to Science

Astronomers use star charts such as this one of the northern constellations to plot locations of stars.

1. What geometric figure represents each star?

2. What geometric figure represents the distance between two stars in a constellation?

3. Name an acute angle and an obtuse angle in Cepheus.

4. In the diagram of Cepheus, is $\overline{CD}$ parallel to $\overline{ED}$ or does it intersect $\overline{ED}$ at point *D*?

5. ✍ **Write a problem** using the star chart.

▲ To use the chart, face north soon after sunset and hold the chart in front of you with the current month at the top.

Measure and Draw Angles

HANDS ON

Quick Review

1. $(110 + 70) - 90$
2. $120 + 240$ 3. $270 - 180$
4. 4×90 5. $360 - 90$

VOCABULARY
protractor

MATERIALS
protractor

Explore

A **protractor** is a tool used for measuring or drawing angles. You can use a protractor to measure ∠ABC in degrees.

Activity 1

STEP 1

Place the center of the protractor on the vertex of the angle.

Extend the ray.

vertex

STEP 2

Line up the center point and the 0° mark on the protractor with one ray of the angle.

0° mark

ray

STEP 3

Read the measure of the angle where the other ray passes through the scale.

So, the measure of ∠ABC is 45°.

- If the rays are extended, will the angle measure change? Explain.

Try It

Trace each angle. Use a protractor to measure each angle.

a.

b.   c.

Which scale on the protractor do you read to find the measure of an angle?

You can use a protractor to draw a right angle. A right angle is 90°.

Activity 2

STEP 1

Draw and label a ray. Place the center point of the protractor on the endpoint of the ray. Then line up the ray with the 0° mark on the protractor.

A
endpoint
B

STEP 2

Find 90° on the protractor scale. Mark a point on your paper at 90°.

90° mark

A
B

STEP 3

Draw the ray connecting the endpoint and your 90° mark. Label one point on this ray.

C
This mark means 90°.

A
B

- A right angle measures 90°. What can you conclude about the measures of acute and obtuse angles?

▶ **Practice and Problem Solving**

For 1–8, use the figure at the right. Copy each angle. Then use a protractor to measure and classify each angle.

1. ∠AFB
2. ∠BFE
3. ∠AFE
4. ∠AFD
5. ∠AFC
6. ∠CFD
7. ∠DFE
8. ∠BFD

Use a protractor to draw each angle. Then write *acute,* *right,* **or** *obtuse* **for each angle.**

9. 40°
10. 90°
11. 120°
12. 15°
13. 95°

14. ❓ **What's the Error?** Ben measured a 50° angle as 130°. Explain how Ben made this error.

16. Draw a triangle with a 95° angle. Explain how you can find the measures of the other angles.

15. ▤*FAST FACT* • SCIENCE The fastest sailing vessel in the world can sail at 46 knots. One knot equals 1.15 miles per hour. How much faster or slower is 46 knots than 50 miles per hour?

Mixed Review **and Test Prep**

17. $5.09 + 9.106$ (p. 48)
18. $2.08 - 0.97$ (p. 48)
19. $\frac{3}{7} + \frac{1}{7}$ (p. 346)
20. $\frac{5}{8} - \frac{3}{8}$ (p. 346)

21. **TEST PREP** Which is $\frac{12}{48}$ in simplest form? (p. 316)

A $\frac{1}{6}$ B $\frac{1}{4}$ C $\frac{2}{8}$ D $\frac{2}{3}$

Angles and Polygons

▶ Learn

SIGNS OF THE TIMES   When you recognize a stop sign by its shape, you are classifying a polygon. A **polygon** is a closed plane figure formed by three or more line segments. Polygons are named by the number of their sides and angles. In a **regular polygon**, all sides have equal lengths and all angles have equal measures.

	Sides and angles	Regular polygon	Polygon that is not regular
Triangle	3	△	◺
Quadrilateral	4	▢	▭
Pentagon	5	⬠	⬠
Hexagon	6	⬡	⬦
Octagon	8	⯃	⯃
Decagon	10	⬡	⬡

Quick Review

Write *acute*, *obtuse*, or *right* for each angle.

1.

2.

3.

4.

5.

VOCABULARY

polygon
regular polygon

Remember

A polygon is two-dimensional. A two-dimensional figure is a plane figure measured in two directions such as length and width.

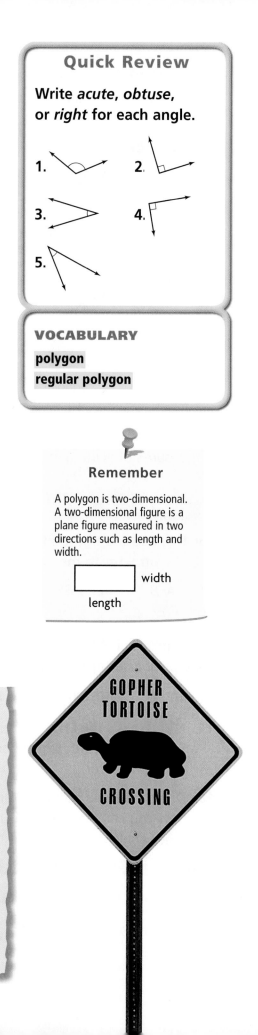

width

length

HANDS ON

Activity 1

MATERIALS: square and triangle dot paper, ruler

STEP 1	STEP 2
Draw a regular polygon.	Draw a polygon that is not regular.

• Now, use the triangular dot paper to draw two 6-sided polygons, one regular and one that is not regular. Name the figures and explain how they are alike and how they are different.

Angles of Polygons

A straight angle measures 180°. You can use this fact to find the sums of the angles of polygons.

180°

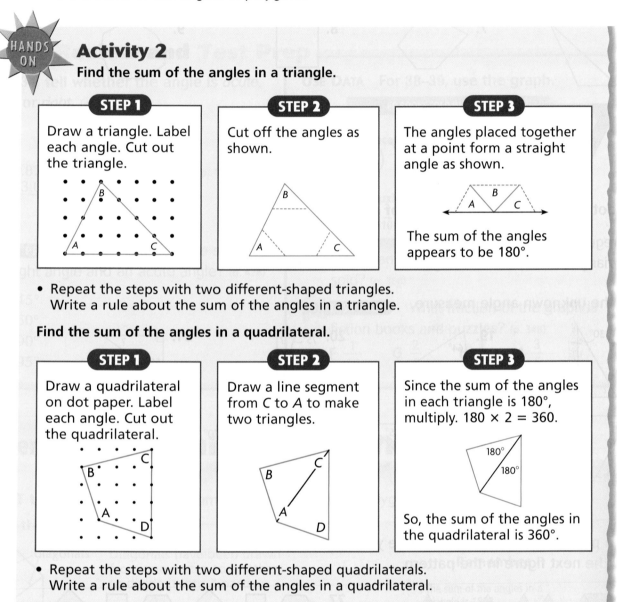

HANDS ON

Activity 2

Find the sum of the angles in a triangle.

STEP 1

Draw a triangle. Label each angle. Cut out the triangle.

STEP 2

Cut off the angles as shown.

STEP 3

The angles placed together at a point form a straight angle as shown.

The sum of the angles appears to be 180°.

• Repeat the steps with two different-shaped triangles. Write a rule about the sum of the angles in a triangle.

Find the sum of the angles in a quadrilateral.

STEP 1

Draw a quadrilateral on dot paper. Label each angle. Cut out the quadrilateral.

STEP 2

Draw a line segment from C to A to make two triangles.

STEP 3

Since the sum of the angles in each triangle is 180°, multiply. 180 × 2 = 360.

180°
180°

So, the sum of the angles in the quadrilateral is 360°.

• Repeat the steps with two different-shaped quadrilaterals. Write a rule about the sum of the angles in a quadrilateral.

MATH IDEA The sum of the angles in a triangle is 180°, and the sum of the angles in a quadrilateral is 360°.

▶ **Check**

1. **Explain** another way to show that the sum of the angles in a quadrilateral is 360°.

Name each polygon and tell if it is regular or not regular.

2.

3.

4.

5.

LESSON CONTINUES ▶

Standardized Test Prep

GEOMETRY AND SPATIAL SENSE

1. Which statement about these figures is true?

A They are congruent.

B They are similar.

C They are hexagons.

D They are regular pentagons.

2. Hans wants to pack marbles in boxes. Which box will hold the most marbles?

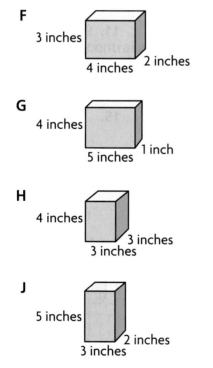

F 3 inches, 4 inches, 2 inches

G 4 inches, 5 inches, 1 inch

H 4 inches, 3 inches, 3 inches

J 5 inches, 3 inches, 2 inches

3. Explain It A quadrilateral has two right angles and one angle that measures 67°. What is the measure of the fourth angle? Explain how you found your answer.

DATA ANALYSIS AND PROBABILITY

4. In which country did the earthquake with the **greatest** magnitude occur?

STRENGTHS OF MAJOR EARTHQUAKES IN 2001

A El Salvador   C Japan

B India   D Peru

5. Look at the graph above. The strength of earthquakes is measured according to the Richter scale. Each whole number on the scale represents ground vibration 10 times as great as that represented by the next lower whole number. How many times as great was the strength of the earthquake in India than the earthquake in Japan?

F 1.5   G 15   H 150   J 1,500

6. Explain It Patti counted the number of peanuts in four mixed-nut snack packs.

MIXED-NUT PACKS				
Package	1	2	3	4
Number of Peanuts	12	15	16	13

Predict the number of peanuts Patti is likely to find in the fifth pack of mixed nuts. Explain your prediction.

⭐ NUMBER SENSE, CONCEPTS, AND OPERATIONS

7. The table shows the speeds of four insects.

INSECT SPEED	
Insect	**Speed (in feet per second)**
Honeybee	10.5
Hornet	19.6
Dragonfly	26.1
Horsefly	13.2

Which shows the insect speeds, in feet per second, in order from slowest to fastest?

A 10.5, 13.2, 19.6, 26.1

B 10.5, 13.2, 26.1, 19.6

C 26.1, 13.2, 19.6, 10.5

D 26.1, 19.6, 13.2, 10.5

8. Look at the table in Problem 7. How many feet can a dragonfly fly in 6 seconds?

F 156.6 feet

G 117.6 feet

H 79.2 feet

J 63 feet

9. Explain It Leslie recorded the number of minutes she spent solving four math problems.

TIME SOLVING PROBLEMS				
Problem	1	2	3	4
Time (in minutes)	$1\frac{1}{2}$	$2\frac{1}{2}$	$1\frac{3}{4}$	2

Leslie has 20 problems to solve in all. ESTIMATE to decide about how long it will take Leslie to solve all the problems. Explain how you found your answer.

⭐ ALGEBRAIC THINKING

> **TIP** **Decide on a plan.** See item 10. Look at each figure to see how it differs from the figure before it. Then, use the strategy *draw a diagram* to show the fourth figure in the pattern.

10. Dorothy drew a pattern with squares.

If the pattern continues, how many squares will be in the fourth figure?

A 15   **C** 25

B 20   **D** 28

11. The goal at Windward Elementary School was to collect 350 pounds of aluminum cans. The first week students collected 20 pounds. Each week they collected 10 pounds more than they had collected the previous week. How long did it take the students to reach their goal?

F 35 weeks   **H** 7.5 weeks

G 10 weeks   **J** 7 weeks

12. Explain It The sum along each side of this triangle is the same.

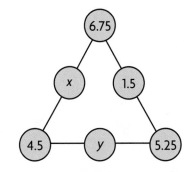

What are the values of *x* and *y*? Explain how you found your answer.

Classify Plane and Solid Figures

TYPES OF POLYGONS

Shape	Name
△	Triangle
▱	Quadrilateral
⬠	Pentagon
⬡	Hexagon

FAST FACT • SOCIAL STUDIES

The Sears Tower is the tallest building in Chicago, Illinois. On a clear day it is possible to see four states from the top of the building: Illinois, Indiana, Wisconsin, and Michigan.

PROBLEM SOLVING   Look at the photograph of the skyline of Chicago. Identify the polygon that is outlined in red. What other polygons can you see?

Use this page to help you review and remember
important skills needed for Chapter 21.

✓ CLASSIFY ANGLES

Classify the angle. Write *acute, right,* or *obtuse.*

1.

2.

3.

4.

✓ FACES OF SOLID FIGURES

Name the plane figure that is the shaded face of the solid figure.

5.

6.

7.

8.

9.

10.

11.

12.

VOCABULARY POWER ✓

REVIEW

congruent [kən•grōō′ənt] *adjective*
The word *congruent* is from the Latin
word *congruens,* which means "to come
together, correspond, or agree." Use some
of the words in the definition to explain
what it means to say that two triangles are
congruent.

PREVIEW

isosceles triangle
scalene triangle
equilateral
    triangle
hypotenuse
leg
figurate numbers

triangular
    numbers
trapezoid
parallelogram
rhombus
transformation
translation

reflection
rotation
tessellation
polyhedron
prism
base
pyramid

www.harcourtschool.com/mathglossary

Triangles

Learn

SIDE BY SIDE The crystal ball that was dropped in Times Square for New Year's Eve 2002 contained 504 equilateral triangular pieces. Why are the triangles called equilateral?

You can classify triangles by the lengths of their sides.

3 cm   3 cm

2 cm

A triangle with exactly two congruent sides is an **isosceles triangle**.

4 cm

2 cm

3 cm

A triangle with no congruent sides is a **scalene triangle**.

2 cm   2 cm

2 cm

A triangle with all sides congruent is an **equilateral triangle**.

So, the triangles of the crystal ball are called equilateral triangles because they each have three congruent sides.

• A regular polygon has congruent sides and angles. Which triangle is a regular polygon?

You can classify triangles by the measures of their angles.

hypotenuse

leg

leg

A triangle that has a right angle is a *right* triangle. The **hypotenuse** is the side opposite the right angle and is the longest side. The other sides are called **legs**.

A triangle that has three acute angles is an *acute* triangle.

A triangle that has one obtuse angle is an *obtuse* triangle.

• Without measuring the angles, how can you tell that the triangles on the crystal ball are acute?

▲ The crystal ball is 6 feet in diameter and contains 600 light bulbs, 96 strobe lights, and 90 pyramid mirrors.

Draw Triangles

HANDS ON

Activity

MATERIALS: ruler, protractor

Draw a triangle with angles measuring 30°, 60°, and 90°. Make the side between the 30° angle and the 60° angle 2 inches long.

Remember

The sum of the measures of the angles in a triangle is always 180°.

STEP 1 Use the protractor to draw a 30° angle. Label the vertex A.

STEP 2 Make a dot 2 inches from A along one of the rays. Label the point B.

STEP 3 Draw a 60° angle with its vertex at B.

STEP 4 Extend the rays until they intersect. Label the point of intersection C.

- What is the measure of ∠C? What kind of triangle is triangle ABC? Explain.

Technology Link

More Practice: Harcourt Mega Math Ice Station Exploration, *Polar Planes*, Levels E and F

▶ Check

1. **Explain** why the other two angles of a triangle must be acute if one angle is a right angle.

2. Name the legs and the hypotenuse of the right triangle in the Activity above.

Classify each triangle. Write *isosceles, scalene,* or *equilateral*.

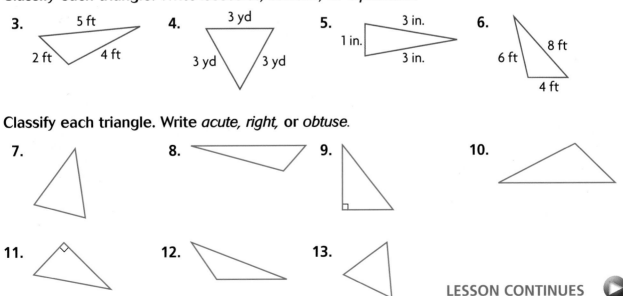

3. 5 ft, 2 ft, 4 ft

4. 3 yd, 3 yd, 3 yd

5. 3 in., 1 in., 3 in.

6. 8 ft, 6 ft, 4 ft

Classify each triangle. Write *acute, right,* or *obtuse*.

7.

8.

9.

10.

11.

12.

13.

LESSON CONTINUES ▶

Classify each triangle. Write *isosceles, scalene,* or *equilateral.*

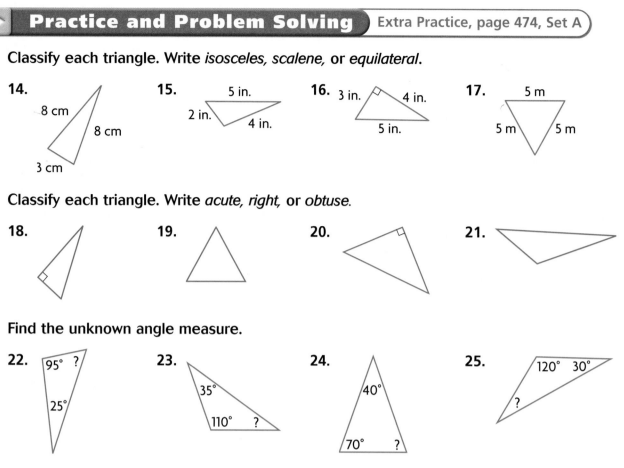

14. 8 cm 8 cm 3 cm

15. 5 in. 2 in. 4 in.

16. 3 in. 4 in. 5 in.

17. 5 m 5 m 5 m

Classify each triangle. Write *acute, right,* or *obtuse.*

18.

19.

20.

21.

Find the unknown angle measure.

22. 95° ? 25°

23. 35° 110° ?

24. 40° 70° ?

25. 120° 30° ?

Use a protractor and ruler to draw triangle *ABC* according to the given measurements. Then find the measure of the third angle. Classify the triangle by its sides and by its angles.

26. ∠A = 60°
∠B = 60°
$\overline{AB}$ = 2 in.

27. ∠C = 90°
∠B = 55°
$\overline{CB}$ = 3 in.

28. ∠A = 65°
∠C = 65°
$\overline{AC}$ = 4 in.

29. ∠C = 50°
∠B = 20°
$\overline{CB}$ = $2\frac{1}{2}$ in.

30. ? **What's the Question?** In a triangle, two angles measure 30° and 60°. The answer is right triangle.

31. ? **What's the Error?** Dan says he drew a triangle with two obtuse angles. Describe his error.

32. Copy this design onto your paper. See how many triangles congruent to this triangle you can draw within the square array, using only three dots.

33. Write About It Describe a relationship shown in this Venn diagram.

TRIANGLES
Acute Triangles
Equilateral Triangles

34. **FAST FACT** • SOCIAL STUDIES The first time a ball was lowered in Times Square to celebrate the new year was in 1907. How many months ago was that?

35. Keith drew an equilateral triangle. By drawing one line, how can he divide the triangle into two right triangles?

36. Draw a square and one of its diagonals. Classify the triangles by their angles and by their sides.

Mixed Review and Test Prep

USE DATA For 37–39, use the graph.

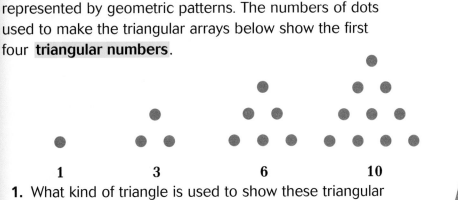

NUMBER OF SKYSCRAPERS IN SOME U.S. CITIES

37. Which cities have more than 20 skyscrapers? (p. 106)

38. Which cities have fewer than 15 skyscrapers? (p. 106)

39. What other kind of graph would be appropriate to display this data? (p. 130)

40. **TEST PREP** Which multiplication property is illustrated in $5 \times 1 = 5$? (p. 258)
   A Identity Property
   B Associative Property
   C Commutative Property
   D Distributive Property

41. **TEST PREP** Which shows the numbers ordered from greatest to least? (p. 28)
   F 0.25, 1.2, 1.5, 1.05, 2.5
   G 1.05, 2.5, 0.25, 1.5, 1.2
   H 2.5, 0.25, 1.5, 1.2, 1.05
   J 2.5, 1.5, 1.2, 1.05, 0.25

Problem Solving THINKER'S CORNER

ALGEBRA **Figurate numbers** are numbers that can be represented by geometric patterns. The numbers of dots used to make the triangular arrays below show the first four **triangular numbers**.

1   3   6   10

1. What kind of triangle is used to show these triangular numbers? Explain.

2. Draw the pattern of dots for the next three triangular numbers. How many dots did you draw for each triangular number?

3. **REASONING** Explain how the number of dots added for each new triangular number is related to the number of dots added to the triangular number just before it.

▲ More than 2,500 years ago, the Greek mathematician Pythagoras studied figurate numbers.

Quadrilaterals

Quick Review

Write the number of sides
for each polygon.
1. square   **2.** triangle
3. rectangle   **4.** pentagon
5. octagon

VOCABULARY

trapezoid   parallelogram
rhombus

▶ **Learn**

FOUR BY FOUR The faces of the Jacksonville, Florida, office building shown below are quadrilaterals because they have four sides and four angles. What types of quadrilaterals are suggested in the faces of this building?

Just as there are many types of triangles, there are many types of quadrilaterals.

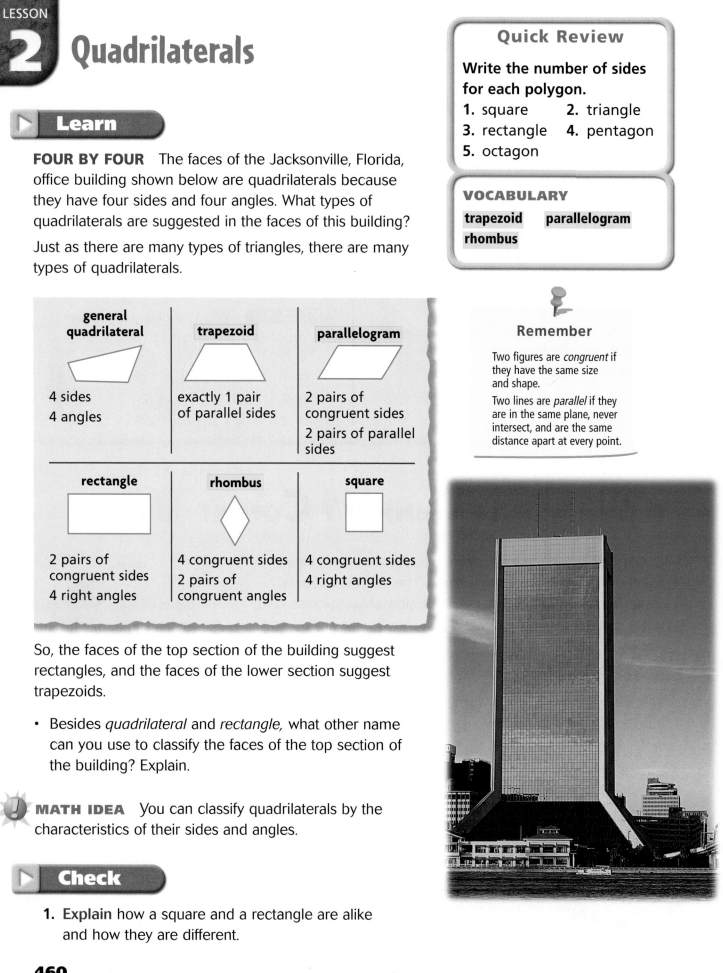

general quadrilateral

4 sides
4 angles

trapezoid

exactly 1 pair of parallel sides

parallelogram

2 pairs of congruent sides

2 pairs of parallel sides

rectangle

2 pairs of congruent sides
4 right angles

rhombus

4 congruent sides
2 pairs of congruent angles

square

4 congruent sides
4 right angles

Remember

Two figures are *congruent* if they have the same size and shape.

Two lines are *parallel* if they are in the same plane, never intersect, and are the same distance apart at every point.

So, the faces of the top section of the building suggest rectangles, and the faces of the lower section suggest trapezoids.

• Besides *quadrilateral* and *rectangle,* what other name can you use to classify the faces of the top section of the building? Explain.

MATH IDEA You can classify quadrilaterals by the characteristics of their sides and angles.

▶ **Check**

1. Explain how a square and a rectangle are alike and how they are different.

Classify each figure in as many ways as possible. Write *quadrilateral, parallelogram, square, rectangle, rhombus,* or *trapezoid.*

2.   **3.**   **4.**   **5.**

Practice and Problem Solving   Extra Practice, page 474, Set B

Classify each figure in as many ways as possible. Write *quadrilateral, parallelogram, square, rectangle, rhombus,* or *trapezoid.*

6.   **7.**   **8.**   **9.**

Write all of the names for each figure. Then write the names that do *not* name the figure. Choose from *trapezoid, parallelogram, rhombus, rectangle,* and *square.*

10.   **11.**   **12.**   **13.**

For 14–17, draw and classify each quadrilateral described.

14. a parallelogram that has all sides congruent

15. a parallelogram with 4 right angles

16. a figure that is both a rhombus and a rectangle

17. a figure that has only 1 pair of parallel sides

18. The building on page 460 has 37 stories and is 535 feet tall. To the nearest foot, how tall is each story?

19. REASONING Troy says that all parallelograms are rectangles. Do you agree? Explain.

20. I have 540 rectangles and trapezoids. I have 120 more trapezoids than rectangles. How many of each do I have?

21. Sam earns $6 per hour walking dogs. He worked 4 hours each day for 5 days. He put $\frac{1}{3}$ of his earnings into a savings account. How much did he have to spend?

Mixed Review and Test Prep

22. $654,821 \times 22$ (p. 152)

23. $78,975 \times 43$ (p. 152)

24. $\frac{2}{3} + \frac{7}{9}$ (p. 348)

25. $\frac{1}{5} + \frac{3}{8}$ (p. 348)

26. TEST PREP Two angles in a triangle measure 48° and 67°. What is the measure of the third angle? (p. 434)

A 48°   **B** 65°   **C** 67°   **D** 180°

Transformations and Tessellations

▶ **Learn**

MOVING ALONG A movement of a figure without changing the size or shape of the figure is called a rigid **transformation**.

VOCABULARY

transformation   translation
reflection   rotation
tessellation

Examples

A **translation**, or a slide, is the movement of a figure along a straight line.

A **reflection**, or a flip, is the movement of a figure by flipping it over a line.

A **rotation**, or a turn, is the movement of a figure by turning it around a point, or vertex.

90° clockwise

Technology Link

More Practice: Harcourt Mega Math Ice Station Exploration, *Polar Planes*, Level O

HANDS ON

Activity 1 Follow these steps to show a 90° counterclockwise rotation.

MATERIALS: dot paper, tracing paper, ruler

STEP 1
Draw this figure on a sheet of dot paper.

STEP 2
Draw a point of rotation. Trace the figure and the point of rotation.

STEP 3
Using the point of rotation, rotate the tracing counterclockwise 90°. Draw the figure in its new location on the dot paper.

• Draw the triangle in Step 1 on your dot paper. Using the same point of rotation, show a 270° clockwise rotation ($\frac{3}{4}$ turn). Compare this rotation with the rotation in Activity 1.

Tessellations

You can make a design by tracing a figure or figures and then translating, reflecting, or rotating the figures. When closed figures are arranged in a repeating pattern to cover a surface, with no gaps or overlaps, the pattern is called a **tessellation**.

Activity 2

MATERIALS: tracing paper, ruler, scissors

Follow these steps to make a tessellation.

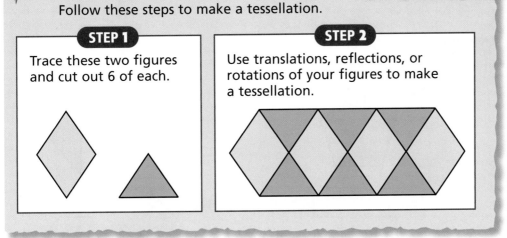

STEP 1
Trace these two figures and cut out 6 of each.

STEP 2
Use translations, reflections, or rotations of your figures to make a tessellation.

- What transformation or transformations did you use to make your tessellation?

Check

1. **Explain** how you move a figure to show a translation, to show a reflection, and to show a rotation.

2. **Explain** how you know if a figure can be used to form a tessellation.

Tell how the first figure was moved. Write *translation, reflection,* **or** *rotation.* **For a rotation, write** *clockwise* **or** *counterclockwise* **and** *90°, 180°,* **or** *270°.*

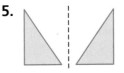

3.

4.

5.

Trace and cut out several of each figure. Tell if the figure or pair of figures will tessellate. Write *yes* **or** *no.*

6.

7.

8.

LESSON CONTINUES

Tell how the first figure was moved. Write *translation, reflection,* or *rotation.* For a rotation, write *clockwise* or *counterclockwise* and *90°, 180°,* or *270°.*

9.

10.

11.

Trace and cut out several of each figure. Tell if the figure or pair of figures will tessellate. Write *yes* or *no.*

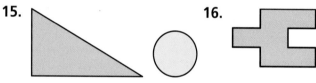

12.

13.

14.

15.

16.

17.

Tell what moves were made to transform each figure into its next position.

18.

19.

20. Draw a quadrilateral. Then draw a translation, a rotation, and a reflection of the quadrilateral. Label each transformation.

21. **VISUAL THINKING** Shelley's mom wants to cover her kitchen floor with square and regular octagon tiles. Draw what the design might look like.

22. Erica bought 3.4 pounds of oranges that were marked as $0.89 per pound. At the cash register, she was charged $0.99 per pound. Show how you can find how much Erica was overcharged for the oranges.

23. **Vocabulary Power** The root of the word *tessellation* is *tessera,* which means "four." Tessera describes square pieces of stone or glass that are used to form a mosaic. Research the history of mosaic.

24. Kay wants to lay floor tile in a kitchen that measures 12 feet by 15 feet and a hallway that measures 4 feet by 15 feet. What is the total area to be covered?

25. Leticia has pattern blocks that are equilateral triangles, squares, and hexagons. All blocks have sides that are 1 inch long. Which two of these blocks can be used together for a tessellation?

Mixed Review and Test Prep

Find the unknown angle measure. (p. 434)

26.   45° / 100°

27.   110° 45° / 70°

Write a rule and find the missing number. (p. 252)

28. 2.5, 3.5, 3.4, 4.4, 4.3, ▪, 5.2, 6.2

29. 8.0, 8.1, 8.3, ▪, 9.0, 9.5, 10.1, 10.8

Divide. Write the answer in simplest form. (p. 408)

30. $\frac{1}{2} \div 1\frac{1}{3}$

31. $8 \div \frac{4}{5}$

Evaluate each expression. Then write <, >, or = for each ●.

32. $\frac{3}{4} \times 8$ ● $9 \times \frac{2}{3}$ (p. 388)

33. $2\frac{4}{5} + 1\frac{3}{4}$ ● $5\frac{7}{8} - 1\frac{3}{4}$ (p. 376)

34. Marlo used $2\frac{3}{4}$ cups of berries for a pie and $1\frac{1}{2}$ cups for muffins. How many cups of berries did Marlo use in all? (p. 368)

A $3\frac{1}{4}$ **B** $3\frac{7}{8}$ **C** $4\frac{1}{4}$ **D** $4\frac{7}{8}$

35. Which of these angles is obtuse? (p. 428)

F 45°   **G** 90°   **H** 120°   **J** 180°

Problem Solving   LiNKUP... to Art

SYMMETRY AND ART   M. C. Escher, one of the world's most famous graphic artists, used tessellations in his work.

1. Trace one of the butterflies in *Symmetry Watercolor 70*. Move your tracing to cover other butterflies in the drawing. What transformations did you use?

2. Look at the point where the blue and yellow butterflies touch wings, shown by a black dot. How many blue butterflies and how many yellow butterflies rotate around this point?

▲ Symmetry Watercolor 70 by M. C. Escher

Solid Figures

Quick Review

Draw an example of each polygon.
1. rhombus
2. isosceles triangle
3. parallelogram
4. right triangle
5. trapezoid

▶ **Learn**

BOX, BALL, OR CAN? The design of the Rock and Roll Hall of Fame and Museum in Cleveland, Ohio, suggests several solid, or three-dimensional, figures.

A solid figure with flat faces that are polygons is called a **polyhedron**.

VOCABULARY

polyhedron	prism
base	pyramid

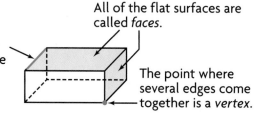

The line where two faces come together is an *edge*.

All of the flat surfaces are called *faces*.

The point where several edges come together is a *vertex*.

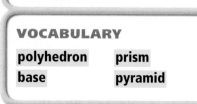

The main tower suggests a rectangular prism. A **prism** is a polyhedron that has two congruent polygons as **bases**. All other faces of a prism are rectangles. Prisms are named by the polygons that form their bases.

 — bases

triangular prism

rectangular prism

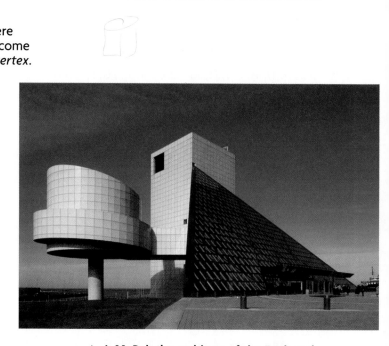

▲ I. M. Pei, the architect of the Rock and Roll Hall of Fame, is known for combining pyramids and other solids in his designs.

pentagonal prism

hexagonal prism

The glass structure next to the museum's tower suggests a triangular pyramid. A **pyramid** is a polyhedron with only one base. All other faces are triangles that meet at the same vertex.

 — base

triangular pyramid

square pyramid

pentagonal pyramid

hexagonal pyramid

Classify Solid Figures

Solids with curved surfaces are *not* polyhedrons.

cylinder
A cylinder has 2 flat circular bases and 1 curved surface.

cone
A cone has 1 flat circular base and 1 curved surface.

sphere
A sphere has no bases and 1 curved surface.

 MATH IDEA   Solid figures can be classified by the shape and number of their bases, faces, vertices, and edges.

Examples

Classify the solid figure suggested by each building. If the figure is a polyhedron, tell the number of faces, vertices, and edges it has.

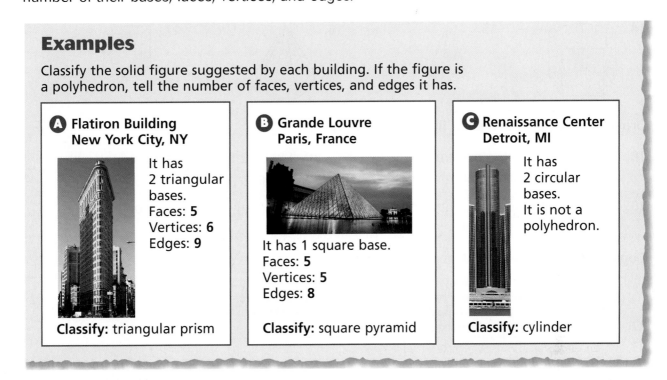

A Flatiron Building New York City, NY

It has 2 triangular bases.
Faces: **5**
Vertices: **6**
Edges: **9**

Classify: triangular prism

B Grande Louvre Paris, France

It has 1 square base.
Faces: **5**
Vertices: **5**
Edges: **8**

Classify: square pyramid

C Renaissance Center Detroit, MI

It has 2 circular bases. It is not a polyhedron.

Classify: cylinder

Check

1. **Explain** why a cylinder is *not* a polyhedron.

Classify each solid figure. Write *prism, pyramid, cone, cylinder,* or *sphere*.

2.

3.

4.

5.

Classify the solid figure. Then, write the number of faces, vertices, and edges.

6.

7.

8.

9.

LESSON CONTINUES ▶

Classify each solid figure. Write *prism, pyramid, cone, cylinder,* or *sphere.*

10.

11.

12.

13.

Classify the solid figure. Then, write the number of faces, vertices, and edges.

14.

15.

16.

17.

Draw and classify each solid figure described.

18. I have a base with 4 congruent sides. My other faces are 4 triangles.

19. I have 2 bases that are congruent circles.

20. I have 2 congruent triangles for bases and 3 rectangular faces.

21. All of my 4 faces are congruent triangles.

Copy and complete the table of solid figures.

	Name of Solid Figure	Number and Name of Bases	Number of Faces	Number of Vertices	Number of Edges
22.	rectangular prism	2 rectangles	6	■	■
23.	triangular pyramid	1 triangle	■	■	6
24.	pentagonal prism	■	7	10	■
25.	pentagonal pyramid	■	■	■	10

▼ Octagon House, Camillus, NY

For 26–28, use the picture at the right of the Octagon House in Camillus, NY.

26. What shape is the floor of the building?

27. What kind of angle does each corner of the building form?

28. When the Octagon House was built, each of its sides was 17 feet long. What was the perimeter of the house?

29. Which faces on a rectangular prism are parallel? Which faces are perpendicular and adjacent?

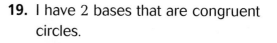

30. Yoko walked around the perimeter of a rectangular building. The length of the building was 110 ft and the width was 82 ft. How many yards did Yoko walk?

31. The Miller family spent 4 days on a camping trip. They spent $\frac{1}{6}$ of the time hiking. How many hours did they spend hiking?

Mixed Review and Test Prep

32. 6.25 (p. 170)
$\times$ 3.1

33. 106.54 (p. 170)
$\times$ 5.8

For 34–37, name the polygon with the given number of sides. (p. 434)

34. 5   **35.** 3   **36.** 8   **37.** 6

Evaluate. (p. 296)

38. 3^3 **39.** 5^2 **40.** 2^4 **41.** 10^3

42. **TEST PREP** What is the least common multiple of 15 and 20? (p. 282)

A 5   C 20
B 15   D 60

For 43–45, use the bar graph. (p. 106)

43. Which two names appear the same number of times?

44. What is the most common U.S. city name?

45. **TEST PREP** Which is the third most common U.S. city name?

F Fairview   H Oak Grove
G Midway   J Franklin

MOST COMMON CITY NAMES IN THE U.S.

City: Fairview, Midway, Oak Grove, Franklin, Riverside

Problem Solving Thinker's Corner

ALGEBRA EXPRESS! You can write and evaluate expressions to find the number of faces, vertices, and edges for prisms and pyramids.

Prisms	Pyramids
Let n = the number of sides on the base	Let n = the number of sides on the base
$n + 2$ = number of faces	$n + 1$ = number of faces
$n \times 2$ = number of vertices	$n + 1$ = number of vertices
$n \times 3$ = number of edges	$n \times 2$ = number of edges

hexagonal prism

The number of sides on the base is 6.
So, $n = 6$.
number of faces: $n + 2 = 6 + 2 = 8$
number of vertices: $n \times 2 = 6 \times 2 = 12$
number of edges: $n \times 3 = 6 \times 3 = 18$

▲ An 18th century mathematician, Leonhard Euler, showed that for both prisms and pyramids, the number of faces plus the number of vertices minus the number of edges is 2.

Tell how many faces, vertices, and edges each figure has.

1. triangular prism

2. hexagonal pyramid

3. octagonal prism

HANDS ON Draw Solid Figures from Different Views

Quick Review

Identify the solid that has the base or bases described.

1. 2 squares   **2.** 1 circle

3. 1 rectangle   **4.** 2 circles

5. 2 hexagons

MATERIALS
connecting cubes, grid paper

▶ Explore

You can use cubes to build a solid figure. Then you can use grid paper to draw the figure from different views.

How does the figure at the right look from the top, from the side, and from the front?

Activity

Use connecting cubes to build the solid above. Draw three pictures on grid paper to show how the figure looks from the top, from the side, and from the front.

Top View | **Side View** | **Front View**

Try It

Use cubes to build each figure. On grid paper, draw each figure from the top, from the side, and from the front.

a. 14 cubes

b. 10 cubes

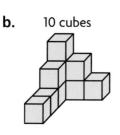

Which squares should I shade to show the front view?

c. 10 cubes

d. 11 cubes

You can identify some solids by the way they look from different views.

Technology Link

More Practice: Harcourt Mega Math Ice Station Exploration, *Frozen Solids,* **Level M**

Example Which solid figure is shown by these three views?

Top View	**Front View**	**Side View**
The top view shows that the base is a circle and that the top comes to a point.	From the front the figure looks like a triangle.	From the side the figure looks like a triangle.

So, a solid figure with these views is a cone.

• What solid figure has squares in the top, front, and side views?

Practice and Problem Solving

Use cubes to build each figure. On grid paper, draw each figure from the top, from the side, and from the front.

1. 2. 3. 4.

Identify the solid figure that has the given views.

5.
top   front   side

6.
top   front   side

7.
top   front   side

8. A side of a square measures 2 cm. A rectangle measures 1.5 cm by 2.1 cm. How much greater is the square's perimeter than the rectangle's?

9. Which solids have circles in some of their views?

Mixed Review and Test Prep

10. $\frac{3}{5} + \frac{1}{2}$ (p. 356)

11. $\frac{1}{3} + \frac{1}{7}$ (p. 356)

12. $3\overline{)6,852}$ (p. 198)

13. $6\overline{)22,692}$ (p. 198)

14. **TEST PREP** Which figure has 4 faces, 4 vertices, and 6 edges? (p. 466)

A cube
B sphere
C cone
D triangular pyramid

Problem Solving Strategy
Make a Model

PROBLEM For a math assignment, Tyler needs to draw the solid figure that has the top, side, and front views shown. How can Tyler determine what the solid figure looks like and find how many cubes he needs?

UNDERSTAND

- What are you asked to find?

- What information will you use?

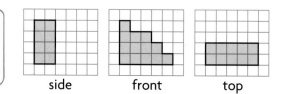

side   front   top

PLAN

- What strategy can you use to solve the problem?

  You can *make a model* of the figure with cubes.

SOLVE

- How can you use the strategy to solve the problem?

  Look at the drawings of the views to help you make the model with cubes. Then count the cubes you used.

  So, Tyler can see how the figure looks by observing his model. He used 26 cubes to make the model.

CHECK

- Look back at the drawings. Does your model match all of the drawings?

- To check the number of cubes, count the cubes in each layer and find the sum.

Problem Solving Practice

Strategies

Draw a Diagram or Picture
Make a Model or Act It Out
Make an Organized List
Find a Pattern
Make a Table or Graph
Predict and Test
Work Backward
Solve a Simpler Problem
Write an Equation
Use Logical Reasoning

Problem Solving

Make a model to solve.

1. **What if** Tyler decided to add to the figure another layer that is the same as the existing bottom layer? How many more cubes would he need?

2. Rachel is designing a tile mosaic for the top of her table. The shape she chooses for the tile must tessellate. Can she use the shape at the right? Explain.

Sara, Nicole, Dee, Brittney, and Jana are in line to buy lunch. Sara is between Nicole and Dee. Dee is next to Jana, who is first in line.

3. Who is last in line?

   A Sara
   B Nicole
   C Dee
   D Brittney

4. Suppose Sara leaves the line. Which of the following lists the remaining four students in order from first to last?

   F Jana, Dee, Nicole, Brittney
   G Jana, Nicole, Dee, Brittney
   H Jana, Brittney, Nicole, Dee
   J Jana, Nicole, Brittney, Dee

Mixed Strategy Practice

5. Kevin spent $20.00 at the mall. He bought a book for $12.50 and two hats that were the same price. How much did he pay for each hat?

6. Ray started at home. He walked 2 blocks north, 3 blocks east, 4 blocks south, and 3 blocks west. How far was Ray from home then?

7. The shelves in the bookcase are 1 foot apart. The bottom shelf is 1.5 feet from the floor. There are 6 shelves. How high is the bookcase?

8. Describe a relationship shown in this Venn diagram.

9. Jenna slept 9 hours, worked 8 hours, exercised 1 hour, read 2 hours, and shopped for 4 hours today. What type of graph should Jenna make to show how she spent her day? Explain.

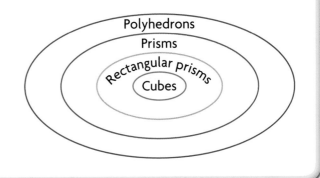

Polyhedrons
Prisms
Rectangular prisms
Cubes

Extra Practice

Set A (pp. 456–459)

Classify each triangle by its sides and angles. Write *isosceles, scalene, equilateral, right, acute,* or *obtuse.*

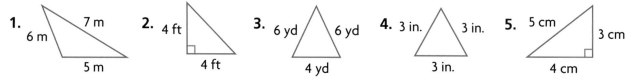

1. 7 m / 6 m / 5 m
2. 4 ft / 4 ft
3. 6 yd / 6 yd / 4 yd
4. 3 in. / 3 in. / 3 in.
5. 5 cm / 3 cm / 4 cm

6. The measures of two angles of a triangle are 30° and 60°. What is the measure of its third angle? Classify the triangle by its angles.

Set B (pp. 460–461)

Classify each figure in as many ways as possible. Write *quadrilateral, parallelogram, square, rectangle, rhombus,* or *trapezoid.*

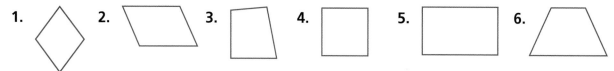

1. 2. 3. 4. 5. 6.

7. The measures of three angles of a quadrilateral are 60°, 120°, and 60°. What is the measure of the fourth angle? If all of its sides are congruent, what kind of quadrilateral is it?

Set C (pp. 462–465)

Tell how the first figure was moved. Write *translation, reflection,* or *rotation.* For a rotation, write *clockwise* or *counterclockwise* and *90°, 180°,* or *270°.*

1. 2. 3.

Set D (pp. 466–469)

Classify each solid figure. If it is a prism or pyramid, write the number of faces, vertices, and edges.

1. 2. 3. 4. 5. 6.

Review/Test

✓ CHECK VOCABULARY AND CONCEPTS

Choose the best term from the box.

rhombus
bases
prism
trapezoid

1. Prisms and pyramids are named by the polygons that form their __?__. (p. 466)

2. A quadrilateral with 4 congruent sides and 2 pairs of congruent angles is a __?__. (p. 460)

✓ CHECK SKILLS

Classify each triangle by its sides and angles. (pp. 456–459)

3. 3 ft, 3 ft, 2 ft

4. 5 in., 3 in., 6 in.

5. 2 cm, 2 cm, 2 cm

6. 6 yd, 10 yd, 8 yd

Classify each figure in as many ways as possible. Write *quadrilateral, parallelogram, square, rectangle, rhombus,* or *trapezoid*. (pp. 460–461)

7.

8.

Tell how the first figure was moved. Write *translation, reflection,* or *rotation*. For a rotation, write *90°, 180°,* or *270°* and *clockwise or counterclockwise*. (pp. 462–465)

9.

10.

Classify each solid figure. If it is a prism or pyramid, write the number of faces, vertices, and edges. (pp. 466–469)

11.

12.

13.

14.

Identify the solid figure that has the given views. (pp. 470–471)

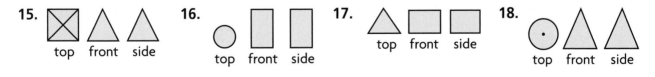

15. top front side

16. top front side

17. top front side

18. top front side

✓ CHECK PROBLEM SOLVING

Joe, Sue, Les, and Barb are in line to buy movie tickets. Barb is in front of Sue and behind Les. Joe is first in line. (pp. 472–473)

19. Who is in front of Barb?

20. Who is last in line?

Standardized Test Prep

⭐ GEOMETRY AND SPATIAL SENSE

1. Casey drew these diagrams of the top view, front view, and side view of a figure he built with blocks.

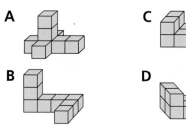

Top view   Front view   Side view

Which figure matches the diagrams?

A   C

B   D

2. Which figure is NOT a pyramid?

F   H

G   J

3. **Explain It** Evan drew a rectangle with a diagonal. He marked the measures of some of the angles.

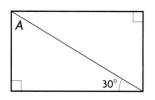

Explain how you can find the measure of angle *A*. Then write the measure of angle *A*.

⭐ NUMBER SENSE, CONCEPTS, AND OPERATIONS

4. How much longer than the Brooklyn-Battery Tunnel is the St. Gotthard Tunnel?

TUNNEL LENGTHS	
Tunnel and Location	**Length (in miles)**
St. Gotthard, Switzerland	$10\frac{1}{10}$
Brooklyn-Battery, New York	$1\frac{7}{10}$
Delaware Aqueduct, New York	85

A $8\frac{2}{5}$ miles

B $8\frac{3}{5}$ miles

C $9\frac{3}{5}$ miles

D $11\frac{4}{5}$ miles

5. Use the table in Problem 4. Suppose there are 425 equally-spaced lights in the Delaware Aqueduct. How many lights are in each mile?

F   0.5

G   5

H   50

J 36,125

6. **Explain It** Kenya has 24 math problems to do for homework. All the problems take about the same amount of time to solve. She finished 16 problems in $1\frac{1}{2}$ hours. Explain how you can ESTIMATE to decide whether Kenya should be able to finish the remaining problems in less than 40 minutes.

★ DATA ANALYSIS AND PROBABILITY

7. On which spinner is the probability of spinning a vowel $\frac{1}{2}$?

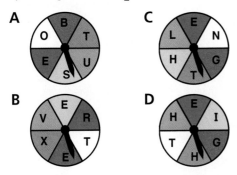

A

B

C

D

8. Penny rolled a 2 on a number cube labeled 1 to 6. She is going to roll the number cube again. What is the probability that the sum of her two rolls will be less than or equal to 5?

F $\frac{1}{2}$ **H** $\frac{1}{5}$

G $\frac{1}{3}$ **J** $\frac{1}{6}$

9. Explain It Jerry tried to make a graph to show the data in the table. Find the errors in his graph and explain how he can correct the errors.

JACKET SALES				
Color	Red	Yellow	Blue	Black
Number Sold	3	5	2	4

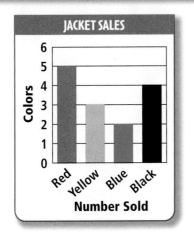

★ ALGEBRAIC THINKING

10. What are the next three figures in the pattern?

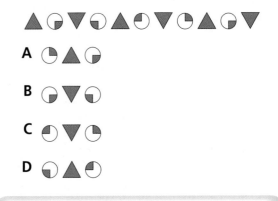

A ◐ ▲ ◑

B ◐ ▼ ◑

C ◐ ▼ ◐

D ◑ ▲ ◐

> **TIP** **Understand the problem.** See item 11. The equation states that $n + 9 = 15$. To find the value of n, you need to find a number that is 9 less than 15. Then, use the value of n to find the value of the expression $9 \times n$.

11. If $n + 9 = 15$, what is the value of $9 \times n$?

F 96

G 54

H 24

J 6

12. Explain It The table shows how many minutes it takes Heidi to read the pages in her book.

HEIDI'S READING PATTERN						
Number of Minutes	1	2	3	4	5	6
Number of Pages Read	1.5	3	4.5	6	■	■

How many pages can Heidi read in 6 minutes? Explain how the number of pages Heidi reads changes as the number of minutes changes.

CHAPTER 22

Algebra: Integers

FAST FACT • SPORTS At the age of 24, Tiger Woods became the first golfer to be under par in every PGA Tour event for an entire year. In golf, the object of the game is to get the ball into the hole in as few strokes (hits) as possible. The standard number of strokes to get the ball into the hole is called par. A golfer's score is sometimes shown as the number of strokes above (+) or below (−) par.

PROBLEM SOLVING Use the tournament scorecard to find the players whose scores were below par.

TOURNAMENT SCORECARD
82nd PGA CHAMPIONSHIP–LOUISVILLE, KENTUCKY

Player	Rounds				Total Score	Par
	1	2	3	4		
Sergio Garcia	74	69	73	69	285	−3
Phil Mickelson	70	70	69	70	279	−9
Loren Roberts	74	72	71	73	290	+2
Brian Watts	72	74	73	70	289	+1
Tiger Woods	66	67	70	67	270	−18

Tiger Woods

Use this page to help you review and remember
important skills needed for Chapter 22.

COMPARE WHOLE NUMBERS

Compare. Use <, >, or = for each ●.

1. 112 ● 111 **2.** 98 ● 99 **3.** 82 ● 87 **4.** 905 ● 950 **5.** 997 ● 999

6. 12 ● 10 **7.** 56 ● 65 **8.** 102 ● 120 **9.** 752 ● 725 **10.** 425 ● 424

11. 81 ● 88 **12.** 32 ● 320 **13.** 111 ● 101 **14.** 323 ● 423 **15.** 121 ● 120

READ A THERMOMETER

Write the Fahrenheit temperature reading for each.

16. **17.** **18.**

19. **20.** **21.**

VOCABULARY POWER

REVIEW

number [num'bər] *noun*

A number can have many names, such
as whole number, even number, or
prime number. Give an example and a
nonexample of a whole number, an even
number, and a prime number. Explain your
choices.

PREVIEW

integers opposites

negative integers absolute value

positive integers

GO ON-LINE www.harcourtschool.com/mathglossary

Understand Integers

▶ **Learn**

HIGHS AND LOWS The highest temperature in the United States, recorded in California, was $^+134°F$. The lowest temperature, recorded in Alaska, was $^-80°F$.

The numbers $^+134$ and $^-80$ are **integers**. You read $^+134$ as "positive one hundred thirty-four" and $^-80$ as "negative eighty."

Just as a thermometer shows temperatures above and below 0°, a number line shows numbers to the right and to the left of 0. Integers can be shown on a number line.

Integers less than 0 are **negative integers**. ← | → Integers greater than 0 are **positive integers**.

```
◄──┼───┼───┼───┼───┼───┼───┼───┼───┼───┼───┼───┼──►
  -6  -5  -4  -3  -2  -1   0  +1  +2  +3  +4  +5  +6
```

↑
The integer 0 is neither positive nor negative.

Positive and negative integers can be used to represent word situations.

Situation	Integer
Mt. McKinley, Alaska, the highest point in the United States, is 20,320 feet above sea level.	+20,320
Ken deposited $75 in his checking account.	+75
The Lions gained 6 yards for a first down.	+6
Death Valley, California, the lowest point in the United States, is 282 feet below sea level.	-282
Ken withdrew $25 from his checking account.	-25
The Bears lost 5 yards on the last play.	-5

The polar bear's body is designed to stay warm when the air is as cold as $^-49°F$. Under its fur, the bear has a layer of blubber 4 inches thick to help keep it warm. ▼

Opposites and Absolute Values

The opposite of going up 3 steps is going down 3 steps. In both cases the same distance is traveled, 3 steps.

Integers include all whole numbers and their opposites. For every positive integer, there is an opposite, negative integer. Integers that are **opposites** are the same distance from 0 on a number line, but in opposite directions.

The number line above has these opposites graphed:

$^-1$ and $^+1$ $^-3$ and $^+3$ $^-5$ and $^+5$

Technology Link

More Practice:
Harcourt Mega Math
The Number Games,
Tiny's Think Tank,
Level V

The **absolute value** of an integer is its distance from 0 on a number line.

3 units from 0   3 units from 0

Write: $|^-3| = 3$ **Read:** The absolute value of negative three is three.

Write: $|^+3| = 3$ **Read:** The absolute value of positive three is three.

Examples

A Name the opposite of $^-11$.

$^-11 \rightarrow {}^+11$

C Name the opposite of $^+14$.

$^+14 \rightarrow {}^-14$

B Use the number line to find $|^-4|$.

$|^-4| = 4$

D Use the number line to find $|^+9|$.

$|^+9| = 9$

Check

1. **Tell** how many total points you have if you win 10 points on your first turn and then lose 10 points on your second turn. Write the integers that represent what happens on each turn. Explain how these integers are related.

LESSON CONTINUES

Identify the integers graphed on the number line.

2.
-4 -3 -2 -1 0 +1 +2 +3 +4

3.
-6   -4   -2   0   +2

Write an integer to represent each situation.

4. a deposit of $30   5. 85 degrees above 0   6. a loss of 15 yards

Write the opposite of each integer.

7. $^+7$ 8. $^-9$ 9. $^-2$ 10. $^+8$ 11. 0

Practice and Problem Solving   Extra Practice, page 492, Set A

Identify the integers graphed on the number line.

12.
-1 0 +1 +2 +3 +4 +5 +6 +7 +8

13.
-2   0   +2   +4   +6

Write an integer to represent each situation.

14. three points ahead   15. a growth of 8 inches   16. 8 feet below sea level

17. a gain of 5 pounds   18. 15 feet underground   19. 4 seconds before liftoff

Write the opposite of each integer.

20. $^-3$ 21. $^+4$ 22. $^+16$ 23. $^-22$ 24. $^+41$

25. $^+54$ 26. $^-29$ 27. $^-73$ 28. $^+102$ 29. $^+2,314$

Write each integer's absolute value.

30. $|^+25|$ 31. $|^-10|$ 32. $|^+1,000|$ 33. $|^-1|$ 34. $|0|$

35. **ALGEBRA**   What values can n have if $|n| = 6$?

For 36–37, use the number line to locate each integer.

A B C D E F G H I J K
-5   0   +5

36. Write the letter for each integer.

  a. $^-3$ b. $^+4$ c. 0   d. $^-1$

37. Write the letter for the opposite of each integer.

  a. $^-2$ b. $^+3$ c. $^+4$ d. $^-3$

38. Which of the integers $^-7$, $^+4$, $^-13$, $^-4$, $^+2$, $^-2$, $^+7$, $^+13$ are positive? negative? Name the opposite pairs.

40. ✎ **Write About It** Describe a situation that uses positive and negative integers. Then write each integer and explain what each integer means.

39. **REASONING** If 0 stands for today, which integers stand for yesterday and tomorrow?

41. One week, Becka earned $2 on Sunday and $5 on each of the other days of the week. How much did she earn that week?

42. Vocabulary Power Many words used in mathematics have meanings outside of math. Write a mathematical and a nonmathematical definition for *opposite*.

Mixed Review and Test Prep

USE DATA For 43–44, use the graph.

AVERAGE DAILY TEMPERATURES

43. In which month was the temperature the highest? the lowest? (p. 106)

44. What is the mean temperature? (p. 100)

45. **TEST PREP** Mr. Lin found and sold a 0.175 ounce nugget of gold. If he sold the nugget for $320 per ounce, how much did he receive? (p. 170)

A $32   **B** $56   **C** $495   **D** $560

46. $1.05 + 0.509$ (p. 48)   **47.** $84 \times 1{,}504$ (p. 152)

48. 5.6×1.1 (p. 170)   **49.** 1.88×0.34 (p. 170)

50. **TEST PREP** Which is 0.13 written as a fraction? (p. 328)

F $1\frac{3}{10}$ **G** $\frac{13}{10}$ **H** $\frac{13}{100}$ **J** $\frac{13}{1{,}000}$

Problem Solving LiNKUP . . . to Reading

STRATEGY • USE CONTEXT To *use context,* look for words and phrases that help you understand the meanings of words, sentences, paragraphs, and situations. The words below can help you decide if an integer is negative, zero, or positive.

Negative	Zero	Positive
withdraw, loss, spend, lose, lost	no change, break even	deposit, profit, earn, gain, win
below, below sea level, down	sea level	above, above sea level, up
drop, behind	even	rise, ahead
before	now	after

Write an integer to represent what happens in each situation. Then write the word or phrase that helps you decide whether the integer is positive, negative, or zero.

1. Karen deposited $20 in her savings account on Monday.

2. Between ages 16 and 17, Antoine did not change in height.

3. When the cold front moved in, the temperature dropped five degrees.

Compare and Order Integers

▶ **Learn**

IN THE DEEP   In 1718, the pirate Blackbeard's flagship, *Queen Anne's Revenge (QAR),* sank at Beaufort Inlet, North Carolina. In 1996, divers discovered a shipwreck believed to be the *QAR.* The ship's cannons were found 21 feet below the water's surface, and its bell was found 20 feet below the surface. Which was closer to the surface, the cannons or the bell?

Use a number line to compare. On a number line, a number to the right is always greater than a number to the left.

Example 1

STEP 1

Name the integers that represent each situation.
  cannons 21 feet below the surface: ⁻21
  bell 20 feet below the surface: ⁻20
  water's surface: 0

STEP 2

Graph the integers ⁻21, ⁻20, and 0 on a number line.

cannons bell   water's surface: sea level

-22 -20 -18 -16 -14 -12 -10 -8 -6 -4 -2 0 +2

To find the integer closer to sea level, or 0, find the greater integer.

⁻20 is to the right of ⁻21. ⁻20 > ⁻21
So, the bell was closer to the surface than the cannons.

▲ A diver examines an anchor fluke at the QAR site. Excavation is done in 10-foot square units.

Technology Link

More Practice: Harcourt Mega Math Fraction Action, *Number Line Mine,* Level T

Use a number line to order integers.

Example 2

Use a number line to order ⁺5, ⁻2, ⁻4, ⁺1, and ⁻5 from least to greatest.

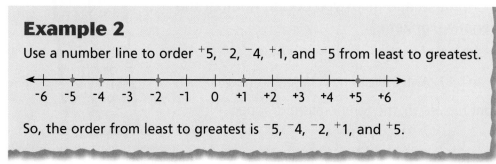

-6 -5 -4 -3 -2 -1 0 +1 +2 +3 +4 +5 +6

So, the order from least to greatest is ⁻5, ⁻4, ⁻2, ⁺1, and ⁺5.

1. **Explain** why integers are easier to compare when they are graphed on a number line.

Compare. Write <, >, or = for each ●.

2. $^{+}5$ ● $^{+}4$ 3. $^{-}6$ ● $^{-}3$ 4. $^{+}2$ ● $^{-}5$ 5. $^{-}1$ ● 0 6. $\left|^{-}2\right|$ ● $^{-}2$

▶ **Practice and Problem Solving**   Extra Practice, page 492, Set B

Compare. Write <, >, or = for each ●.

7. 0 ● $^{+}1$ 8. $^{-}8$ ● $^{-}9$ 9. $^{-}2$ ● $^{+}4$ 10. $\left|^{-}3\right|$ ● $^{-}6$ 11. $\left|^{-}4\right|$ ● $^{+}4$

Draw a number line to order each set of integers from greatest to least.

12. $^{+}1, ^{-}2, 0, ^{-}3$ 13. $^{-}4, ^{+}3, ^{-}2, ^{+}1$ 14. $^{+}5, ^{-}6, ^{+}7, ^{-}8$ 15. $^{-}10, ^{+}10, ^{+}8, ^{-}7$

ALGEBRA   Name the integer that is 1 less.

16. $^{+}8$ 17. $^{-}4$ 18. $^{-}1$ 19. 0 20. $^{+}3$

ALGEBRA   Name the integer that is 1 more.

21. $^{-}4$ 22. $^{-}1$ 23. $^{+}6$ 24. $^{-}8$ 25. $^{-}10$

USE DATA   For 26–27 and 30, use the table.

26. One mile is 5,280 feet. Which ocean is less than 1 mile deep?

27. Mt. Fuji in Japan is 12,388 feet tall. Which ocean's depth is closest to being the opposite of Mt. Fuji's height?

28. **REASONING**   Oarfish live at $^{-}3,000$ feet. Below $^{-}2,300$ feet, light cannot reach through water. Do oarfish live in the dark? Explain.

30. ✎ Write a problem that uses the table and requires comparing or ordering integers.

AVERAGE DEPTHS OF OCEANS	
Ocean	Depth in feet
Atlantic	12,880
Indian	13,002
Arctic	3,953
Pacific	13,215

29. **≡FAST FACT • SCIENCE** The most valuable shipwreck was found off Key West, Florida. The ship carried 21 tons of gold and 15 tons of silver. Was that more than or less than 50,000 pounds? Explain.

Mixed Review and Test Prep

31. $5\overline{)2,455}$ (p. 198)   32. $3\overline{)15.36}$ (p. 232)

33. Is 458 divisible by 2, 3, 4, 5, or 9? (p. 276)

34. Write $\frac{4}{5}$ as a decimal. (p. 328)

35. **TEST PREP** Which integer represents a loss of six pounds? (p. 480)

  A $^{-}6$ **B** $^{-}0.6$ **C** $^{+}0.6$ **D** $^{+}6$

Addition and Subtraction of Integers

Quick Review

1. 8 + 3   2. 15 − 8
3. 6 + 5   4. 11 − 6
5. 8 − 2

MATERIALS
two-color counters

▶ Learn

UNDER PAR In golf, *par* is the number of strokes needed to get the ball into a hole. The number of strokes it takes a golfer to do this is compared to par. ⁻1 means 1 stroke less than par or one under par.

In Round 4 of the 2002 Masters Tournament, Tiger Woods was ⁻2 for Holes 1 through 9 and ⁺1 for Holes 10 through 18. So in Round 4, Tiger was ⁻2 + ⁺1.

You can use two-color counters to add integers. Find ⁻2 + ⁺1.

◀ Tiger Woods won his third Masters Tournament in 2002. His final score was 276, which was ⁻12, or 12 strokes under par.

HANDS ON

Activity 1 Find ⁻2 + ⁺1.

STEP 1
Use yellow counters to represent positive integers and red counters to represent negative integers.

= ⁻2
= ⁺1

STEP 2
Make as many opposite pairs of one yellow and one red counter as possible. The sum of each opposite pair is 0, so take away each opposite pair.

STEP 3
The number and color of unpaired counters represent the sum.

= ⁻1

There is 1 red counter left, so ⁻2 + ⁺1 = ⁻1.

So, Tiger was ⁻1 for Round 4.

Examples

A Find ⁻3 + ⁻2.

= ⁻5

So, ⁻3 + ⁻2 = ⁻5.

B Find ⁺4 + ⁻3.

= ⁺1

So, ⁺4 + ⁻3 = ⁺1.

Subtract Integers

You can also use two-color counters to subtract integers.

HANDS ON

Activity 2 Find $^-4 - {}^-1$.

STEP 1
Make a row of 4 red counters to show $^-4$.

⬤ ⬤ ⬤ ⬤ = $^-4$

STEP 2
To subtract $^-1$, take away 1 red counter.

⬤ ⬤ ⬤ ⬤

STEP 3
The number and the color of counters left represent the difference.

⬤ ⬤ ⬤ = $^-3$

There are 3 red counters left, so $^-4 - {}^-1 = {}^-3$.

At 10:00 A.M., the temperature in Barrow, AL, was $^+3$°F. By midnight, it had fallen 5 degrees. What was the temperature at midnight?

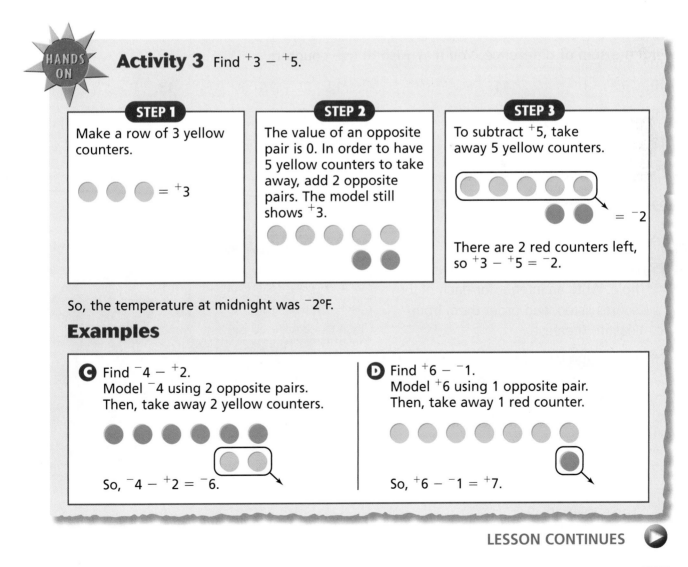

HANDS ON

Activity 3 Find $^+3 - {}^+5$.

STEP 1
Make a row of 3 yellow counters.

⬤ ⬤ ⬤ = $^+3$

STEP 2
The value of an opposite pair is 0. In order to have 5 yellow counters to take away, add 2 opposite pairs. The model still shows $^+3$.

⬤ ⬤ ⬤ ⬤ ⬤
      ⬤ ⬤

STEP 3
To subtract $^+5$, take away 5 yellow counters.

⬤ ⬤ ⬤ ⬤ ⬤
      ⬤ ⬤ = $^-2$

There are 2 red counters left, so $^+3 - {}^+5 = {}^-2$.

So, the temperature at midnight was $^-2$°F.

Examples

C Find $^-4 - {}^+2$.
Model $^-4$ using 2 opposite pairs.
Then, take away 2 yellow counters.

⬤ ⬤ ⬤ ⬤ ⬤ ⬤

So, $^-4 - {}^+2 = {}^-6$.

D Find $^+6 - {}^-1$.
Model $^+6$ using 1 opposite pair.
Then, take away 1 red counter.

⬤ ⬤ ⬤ ⬤ ⬤ ⬤ ⬤

So, $^+6 - {}^-1 = {}^+7$.

LESSON CONTINUES ▶

1. **Explain** how to make a model of $^+5 - {}^-2$. Tell how you decided the number of opposite pairs to add. Then, find $^+5 - {}^-2$.

Copy and complete the number sentence.

2. $^+5 + {}^-3 = \blacksquare$

3. $^-3 - {}^+4 = \blacksquare$

Find the sum or difference. You may wish to use counters.

4. $^+2 + {}^-3$ 5. $^+2 - {}^-3$ 6. $^-2 - {}^+3$ 7. $^+7 + {}^-3$

Copy and complete the number sentence.

8. $^-3 + {}^+1 = \blacksquare$

9. $^-6 - {}^-2 = \blacksquare$

Find the sum or difference. You may wish to use counters.

10. $^+6 - {}^+3$ 11. $^-8 - {}^+3$ 12. $^-7 + {}^+5$ 13. $^+9 + {}^+4$

14. $^+5 + {}^-2$ 15. $^-6 + {}^+5$ 16. $^-4 - {}^+9$ 17. $^+1 - {}^-8$

18. $^+6 + {}^-7$ 19. $0 - {}^+12$ 20. $^-5 + {}^-3 + 0$ 21. $^+4 + {}^-4 + {}^+4$

Compare. Write <, >, or = for each ▨.

22. $^-4 + {}^-5$ ▨ $^-1$ 23. $^+7 + {}^-4$ ▨ $^-3$ 24. $^+17 + {}^-3$ ▨ $^-20$

USE DATA For 25–26, use the chart.

25. Suppose 0 represents even par for a hole. Write an integer for each of the scores listed, and order them from least to greatest.

26. In golf, the lowest score is the best. On the fifth hole, Jenny made an eagle and Paul made a double bogey. Write an integer to represent each player's score. Who won the hole?

27. ☀ **What's the Question?** There are 6 red counters and 4 yellow counters. The answer is $^-2$.

GOLF TERMS

Bogey = 1 stroke over par

Double Bogey = 2 strokes over par

Birdie = 1 stroke under par

Eagle = 2 strokes under par

28. Pontchartrain Park in New Orleans, Louisiana is 5 feet below sea level. Write this elevation as an integer.

29. ? **What's the Error?** Correct the error in this model of $^-3 - {^+3}$.

Mixed Review and Test Prep

For 30–32, use the data set 88, 64, 72, 98, 88, 58.

30. What are the median and mode? (p. 102)

31. What is the range? (p. 96)

32. What is the mean? (p. 100)

33. The Emperor penguin can dive 1,000 feet underwater. Name the integer that describes this situation. (p. 480)

34. **TEST PREP** In which place would you write the first nonzero digit of the quotient $5.426 \div 6$? (p. 232)
  A ones
  B tenths
  C hundredths
  D thousandths

35. Find the greatest common factor of 12 and 50. (p. 278)

36. What is the least common denominator of $\frac{3}{4}$ and $\frac{5}{10}$? (p. 354)

37. Alexi cut a 3-foot sub sandwich into 3-inch slices. How many slices will he have? (p. 378)

38. What is $\frac{3}{4}$ and $\frac{1}{2}$? (p. 348)

39. **TEST PREP** Jaime is 7 years older than Lyle. If Lyle is 27 years old, how old is Jaime?
  F 20 years old
  G 24 years old
  H 30 years old
  J 34 years old

Problem Solving LiNKUP . . . to Science

The inner planets are Mercury, Venus, Earth, and Mars. The outer planets are Jupiter, Saturn, Uranus, Neptune, and Pluto. Scientists measure the surface temperatures of Mercury, Venus, Earth, Mars, and Pluto. Since Jupiter, Saturn, Uranus, and Neptune are gas and have no surface, scientists measure the temperature of the highest layer of clouds.

USE DATA Use the tables.

1. Which are the coldest and hottest inner planets?

2. Which are the coldest and hottest outer planets?

3. Order the planets from coldest to hottest.

TEMPERATURE AT CLOUD TOPS	
Planet	**Temperature**
Jupiter	$^-160°F$
Saturn	$^-220°F$
Uranus	$^-323°F$
Neptune	$^-330°F$

AVERAGE SURFACE TEMPERATURE	
Planet	**Temperature**
Mercury	$333°F$
Venus	$865°F$
Earth	$45°F$
Mars	$^-80°F$
Pluto	$^-382°F$

Problem Solving Strategy
Draw a Diagram

PROBLEM   Carson parked in the deepest underground parking garage in London, the Aldersgate Car Park. It has 14 floors for 670 cars. After a long day of sightseeing, he returned to the parking garage to find his car. He forgot where he had parked. So, he entered the elevator on the ground floor and took the elevator down 8 floors and looked. Then he went up 2 floors, down 5 floors, and up another 4 floors before he found his car. His car was parked on which floor?

UNDERSTAND

• What are you asked to find?

• What information will you use?

• Is there any information you will not use?

PLAN

• What strategy can you use to solve the problem?

You can *draw a diagram* of the underground floors.

GROUND
FLOOR
-1 FLOOR
-2 FLOOR
-3 FLOOR
-4 FLOOR
-5 FLOOR
-6 FLOOR   +2 floors
-7 FLOOR   +4 floors
-8 FLOOR
-9 FLOOR -8 floors
-10 FLOOR
-11 FLOOR
-12 FLOOR   -5 floors
-13 FLOOR
-14 FLOOR

First Second Third Fourth
Look   Look   Look   Look

SOLVE

• How can you use this strategy to solve the problem?

Draw a vertical number line to represent the parking garage's levels. Start at the ground floor and model Carson's movements.

So, Carson found his car parked 7 floors underground, or on the $^-7$ floor.

CHECK

• How can you decide if your answer is correct?

Strategies

▶ **Draw a Diagram or Picture**
Make a Model or Act It Out
Make an Organized List
Find a Pattern
Make a Table or Graph
Predict and Test
Work Backward
Solve a Simpler Problem
Write an Equation
Use Logical Reasoning

Draw a diagram to solve.

1. **What if** Carson entered the elevator on the ground floor and took the elevator down 6 floors and looked? Then he went up 3 floors, down 7 floors, and up another 5 floors before he found his car. His car was parked on which floor?

2. At 7:00 A.M., the temperature was ⁻3°F. At 1:00 P.M., the temperature had risen by 11 degrees. By 11:00 P.M., it had dropped 15 degrees. What was the temperature at 11:00 P.M.?

3. A scuba diver descended to 14 feet below sea level. She then ascended 4 feet and swam 10 feet ahead. She then descended 6 feet. At what depth is she now?

4. Starting on their own 40-yard line, the Tigers gained 5 yards on their first play. Then they lost 15 yards in a penalty. What yard line are they on now?

Mixed Strategy Practice

USE DATA For 5–8, use the table. The table shows the same time in each time zone from the West coast to the East coast.

TIME ZONES IN THE UNITED STATES					
Hawaii-Aleutian	Alaska	Pacific	Mountain	Central	Eastern
2 P.M.	3 P.M.	4 P.M.	5 P.M.	6 P.M.	7 P.M.

5. What integer represents the change from Eastern time to Pacific time?

6. Describe the time pattern as you travel west across the time zones.

7. Suppose a pilot left the Mountain time zone at 6 P.M., flew west for 2 hours, and landed in the Pacific time zone. What time did he land?

   A 6 P.M.   **B** 7 P.M.   **C** 8 P.M.   **D** 9 P.M.

8. Suppose a pilot left the Pacific time zone at 3 P.M., flew east for 3 hours, and landed in the Central time zone. What time did she land?

   F 6 P.M.   **G** 7 P.M.   **H** 8 P.M.   **J** 9 P.M.

9. On May 6, 1992, a U.S. diver went underwater in a module and stayed there for a record 69 days. On what date did he come up?

10. ✏ **Write a problem** using integers that you can solve by drawing a diagram. Draw your diagram.

Standardized Test Prep

⭐ NUMBER SENSE, CONCEPTS, AND OPERATIONS

1. The diagram shows distances between several locations.

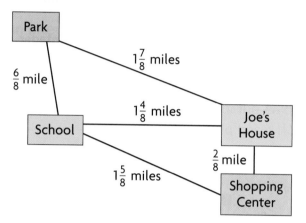

Park

$\frac{6}{8}$ mile

$1\frac{7}{8}$ miles

School

$1\frac{4}{8}$ miles

Joe's House

$1\frac{5}{8}$ miles

$\frac{2}{8}$ mile

Shopping Center

How many miles would Joe walk if he went from his house to school, then to the park, and then straight home from the park?

A $2\frac{17}{24}$ miles   **C** $4\frac{1}{8}$ miles

B $3\frac{7}{8}$ miles   **D** $21\frac{7}{8}$ miles

2. Look at the diagram above. How much farther is it from Joe's house to the park than from his house to the school?

F $\frac{3}{8}$ mile

G $1\frac{3}{8}$ miles

H $2\frac{3}{8}$ miles

J $3\frac{3}{8}$ miles

3. Explain It Joe likes to walk between 3 and 4 miles each evening after dinner. Look at the diagram and suggest a route he could take that begins and ends at his home. Explain how you chose your route.

⭐ DATA ANALYSIS AND PROBABILITY

4. The table shows the lengths of four of the largest snails.

LARGEST SNAILS	
Snail	**Length (in inches)**
California Sea Hare	30
Apple	20
Trumpet	15
African Land	10

Which graph or table is **most** appropriate to display the snail data?

A bar graph

B frequency table

C line graph

D circle graph

5. Look at the table above. Which is the **most** reasonable interval for graphing the snail data?

F 5

G 20

H 50

J 100

6. Explain It Fong is drawing a graph that shows how the United States population has changed over the past 50 years. Lena is drawing a graph that shows how her school enrollment has changed over the past 50 years. Explain what type of graph they should each draw, and tell why the scales for the two graphs would be different.

⭐ GEOMETRY AND SPATIAL SENSE

7. Mia drew two squares. The sides of Square B are 2 times the length of the sides of Square A. How does the area of Square B compare to the area of Square A?

A The area of Square B is equal to the area of Square A.

B The area of Square B is 2 times the area of Square A.

C The area of Square B is 3 times the area of Square A.

D The area of Square B is 4 times the area of Square A.

8. The letter E is shown below.

E

Which of the following is a reflection of the letter E?

F ⨆   H Ǝ

G ⊓   J (rotated E)

> **TIP** **Decide on a plan.** See item 9. Use the strategy *draw a diagram or picture.*

9. Explain It Mr. Thomas has a solid figure with 5 faces. He shows the class one face that is a triangle and another face that is a rectangle. What are the possible solid figures that Mr. Thomas has? Explain your answer.

⭐ MEASUREMENT

10. Deana cut a pizza into 4 pieces. She took the piece with the largest acute angle. Which piece did she eat?

A Piece 1

B Piece 2

C Piece 3

D Piece 4

11. Erin weighed a bunch of grapes on the scale at the supermarket.

How much do the grapes weigh to the nearest ounce?

F 1 pound 4 ounces

G 1 pound 8 ounces

H 1 pound 14 ounces

J 2 pounds

12. Explain It Jason started his homework at 4 P.M. He spent $\frac{1}{2}$ hour doing math problems, $\frac{3}{4}$ hour writing a book report, and $1\frac{1}{4}$ hours finding data for a science report. ESTIMATE to find out if Jason finished his homework before 6 P.M. Explain how you know.

CHAPTER 23

Geometry and the Coordinate Plane

≡FAST FACT • SOCIAL STUDIES When a city is planned, a grid is sometimes used to lay out the streets. The first city in the United States to be laid out in a grid was central Philadelphia, by William Penn in 1682. Every street was laid out at right angles with another except one, Dock Street.

PROBLEM SOLVING   Use the map grid to find the landmark, Independence Hall. Where is it located?

PHILADELPHIA HISTORIC DISTRICT

Independence Hall, known as the birthplace of the United States, is where the Declaration of Independence and the Constitution of the United States were adopted.

Use this page to help you review and remember
important skills needed for Chapter 23.

✅ IDENTIFY POINTS ON A GRID

Use the ordered pairs to name each point on the grid.

1. (5,3)   **2.** (1,1)   **3.** (7,6)

4. (1,7)   **5.** (2,9)   **6.** (7,1)

7. (6,5)   **8.** (7,9)   **9.** (4,2)

10. (4,10)   **11.** (4,6)   **12.** (3,3)

13. (10,8)   **14.** (8,10)   **15.** (9,2)

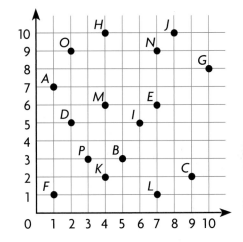

✅ TRANSFORMATIONS

Tell how each figure was moved. Write *translation, reflection,* or *rotation.*

16.

17.

18.

19.

20.

21.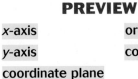

VOCABULARY POWER

REVIEW

ordered pair [ôr′dərd pâr] *noun*

When things are ordered, they are
arranged in a certain way for a reason.
Explain how this applies to the numbers in
the ordered pair (3,5).

PREVIEW

x-axis   origin

y-axis   coordinates

coordinate plane

GO ON-LINE   www.harcourtschool.com/mathglossary

Algebra: Graph Relationships

▶ Learn

PRISM PATTERNS Karen is making models of prisms. She uses gumdrops for the vertices and straws for the edges. She made a table and a graph to show the relationship between the number of sides on the prism's base and the number of vertices on the prism. On the graph, the horizontal number line is the **x-axis** and the vertical number line is the **y-axis**. Each point on the graph can be represented by an ordered pair, (*x,y*).

Number of Sides on Base, *x*	3	4	5	6
Number of Vertices, *y*	6	8	10	12

On this graph, the first number in an ordered pair tells the number of sides for the base of the prism. The second number tells the number of vertices in the prism. So, (5,10) means that a prism with 5 sides on its base has 10 vertices.

⚠ **MATH IDEA** To graph a relationship shown in a table, write the data as ordered pairs and then graph the ordered pairs.

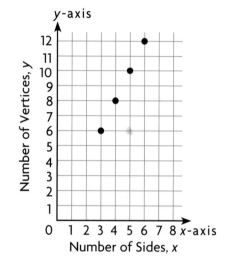

Example

Graph the relationship shown in the table.

Number of Sides on Base, *x*	3	4	5	6
Number of Faces, *y*	5	6	7	8

- Write ordered pairs for the data.

  (3,5), (4,6), (5,7), (6,8)

- Graph the ordered pairs.

1. **Explain** what the point (5,7) means in the second graph on page 498.

Write the ordered pairs. Then graph them.

2.
Input, x	1	2	3	4
Output, y	3	6	9	12

3.
Input, x	4	5	6	7
Output, y	2	3	4	5

 Practice and Problem Solving | Extra Practice, page 508, Set A

Write the ordered pairs. Then graph them.

4.
Input, x	0	1	2	3
Output, y	3	4	5	6

5.
Input, x	7	8	9	10
Output, y	3	4	5	6

6.
Input, x	1	2	3	4
Output, y	4	8	12	16

7.
Input, x	1	2	3	4
Output, y	2	4	6	8

USE DATA For 8–10, use the table.

Number of Sides on Base, x	3	4	5	6
Number of Vertices on Pyramid, y	4	5	6	7

8. Write the ordered pairs. Then graph them. What does (4,5) mean?

9. ✎ **Write About It** What kind of pyramid is represented by the ordered pair (5,6)? Explain.

10. **REASONING** How can you use your graph to find the number of vertices in an octagonal pyramid?

11. **Vocabulary Power** *Vertices* is the plural form of *vertex*. Write the plural form of *prism, face,* and *axis*.

12. A triangle has a perimeter of 27 cm. One side is 7 cm long and a second side is 9 cm long. Find the length of the third side.

Mixed Review and Test Prep

Find each value if n = 11. (p. 64)

13. $(39 + n) - 7$ 14. $20 + (17 - n)$

15. Find the mean of the data set 28, 35, 67, 29, 31. (p. 100)

16. Write 3,869,472 in word form. (p. 4)

17. **TEST PREP** Brad is making a bookcase. He has 2 pieces of lumber that are 4.5 ft each and 5 pieces that are 42 in. each. How many feet of lumber does Brad have? (p. 170)

A 26.5 ft   C 27.5 ft
B 26.8 ft   D 28.0 ft

Algebra: Graph Integers on the Coordinate Plane

▶ **Learn**

MAPPING HISTORY Archaeologists record the locations of artifacts and features that they find in a dig site by graphing them on a coordinate plane.

VOCABULARY

coordinate plane   origin
coordinates

A **coordinate plane** is formed by two intersecting and perpendicular number lines called axes. The point where the two lines intersect is called the **origin**, or (0,0).

The numbers to the left of the origin on the *x*-axis and below the origin on the *y*-axis are negative.

Start at the origin. Move 4 units to the left on the *x*-axis and 2 units up on the *y*-axis. The **coordinates**, or numbers in the ordered pair, are (⁻4,⁺2).

▲ Christopher Wolfe, at the age of 7, co-discovered the oldest horned ceratopsian dinosaur.

HANDS ON

Activity

MATERIALS: coordinate plane

- Graph the ordered pair (⁺4,⁻5). Start at the origin. Move **right** 4 units and then **down** 5 units. Plot and label the point, *A*.

- Graph the ordered pair (⁻3,⁻2). Start at the origin. Move **left** 3 units and then **down** 2 units. Plot and label the point, *B*.

- In which direction and how far would you move to graph (⁻4,⁺5)?

⚠ **MATH IDEA** The coordinates of a point tell you how far and in which direction to move first horizontally and then vertically on the coordinate plane.

Graphing Ordered Pairs

Examples

A To graph (⁻2,⁺3), start at the origin. Move 2 units to the *left* and 3 units *up.*

B To graph (⁺5,⁻4), start at the origin. Move 5 units to the *right* and 4 units *down.*

▶ **Check**

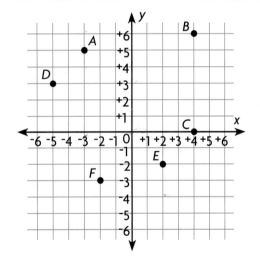

1. **Explain** how to graph (⁺4,⁺2) on a coordinate plane.

For 2–7, identify the ordered pair for each point.

2. point *A*
3. point *B*
4. point *C*
5. point *D*
6. point *E*
7. point *F*

Graph and label the ordered pairs on a coordinate plane.

8. *A* (⁻5,⁺8)
9. *B* (⁻7,⁻4)
10. *C* (⁺4,⁺4)
11. *D* (⁺1,⁻2)
12. *E* (⁻6,⁺5)
13. *F* (⁻2,⁺8)
14. *G* (⁺2,⁺6)
15. *H* (⁺3,⁻3)

Name the ordered pair that is described.

16. Start at the origin. Move 2 units to the right and 3 units down.

17. Start at the origin. Move 3 units to the left and 6 units up.

18. Start at the origin. Move 5 units to the left and 5 units down.

19. Start at the origin. Move 1 unit to the right and 3 units up.

20. Start at the origin. Move 3 units up.

21. Start at the origin. Move 4 units to the left.

LESSON CONTINUES

For 22–31, identify the ordered pair for each point.

22. point A

23. point B

24. point C

25. point D

26. point E

27. point F

28. point G

29. point H

30. point I

31. point J

Graph and label the ordered pairs on a coordinate plane.

32. A ($^-$1,$^+$3)

33. B ($^-$3,$^-$7)

34. C ($^+$6,$^+$7)

35. D ($^+$1,$^-$5)

36. E (0,$^+$8)

37. F ($^+$2,$^+$3)

38. G ($^+$9,$^-$2)

39. H ($^-$3,$^+$3)

For 40–45, name the ordered pair that is described.

40. Start at the origin. Move 8 units to the left and 7 units up.

41. Start at the origin. Move 3 units to the right and 9 units up.

42. Start at the origin. Move 6 units up.

43. Start at the origin. Move 5 units down.

44. Start at the origin. Move 4 units to the right and 6 units down.

45. Start at the origin. Move 5 units to the left and 6 units down.

For 46–51, use the archaeology grid.

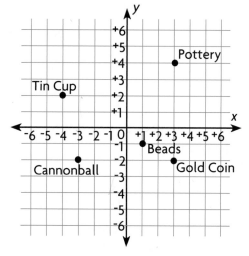

46. Which artifact is 3 units to the right of the origin and 4 units up from the origin?

47. Which two artifacts have negative x-coordinates?

48. Which two artifacts have opposite x-coordinates and the same y-coordinates?

49. What are the coordinates for the gold coin?

50. ✎ Write a problem that uses the archaeology grid to solve.

51. ❓ **What's the Error?** Tamara says the location of the beads is ($^-$1,$^+$1). Describe and correct her error.

52. ▤ **FAST FACT** • SCIENCE The Triceratops was a dinosaur that was 3 meters high and had a mass of 5,500 kilograms. If the Triceratops was three times as long as it was high, how long was it?

Technology Link

More Practice:
Harcourt Mega Math
The Number Games,
Arachna Graph, Level H

53. **? What's the Question?** Mark placed a coordinate grid over a map of his neighborhood. He labeled his house point *H*. The answer is (⁺4,⁻3).

54. The temperature at 6 P.M. was 12°F. It fell 17° during the night, then rose 4° by 6 A.M. What was the temperature at 6 A.M.?

Mixed Review and Test Prep

For 55–57, write the integer that is 1 more than the given integer. (p. 484)

55. ⁺5   **56.** ⁻3   **57.** ⁻1

58. 90,875 (p. 46)   **59.** 80,301 (p. 46)
    −89,286   −54,692

60. TEST PREP Which is the sum ⁻7 + ⁺2? (p. 486)

  A ⁻9   C ⁺5
  B ⁻5   D ⁺9

For 61–63, write the opposite of each integer. (p. 480)

61. ⁻32   **62.** ⁻83   **63.** ⁺101

64. TEST PREP A movie ticket cost $7 for adults and $5 for students. Mr. Chang spent $285 for tickets for his classes. He bought 5 adult tickets. How many student tickets did he buy? (p. 194)

  F 35   H 52
  G 50   J 60

Problem Solving   LiNKUP...to Geometry

You can draw geometric figures by locating and connecting points on the coordinate plane.

• Look at the coordinate plane at the right. What ordered pair tells the location of the fourth point that would make the figure a square?

Locate and connect the points in order on a coordinate plane. Then name the geometric figure that you drew.

1. (⁺2,⁺4) (⁺2,⁺6) (⁻3,⁺6) (⁻3,⁺4)

2. (⁺3,⁺2) (⁺3,⁻4) (⁻4,⁻4)

3. (0,⁺4) (⁺3,⁺2) (⁺3,⁻5) (⁻3,⁻4) (⁻3,⁺1)

4. (⁺4,⁻2) (⁺4,⁺6) (⁻4,⁺6) (⁻4,⁻2)

Transformations on the Coordinate Plane

▶ **Explore**

Explore rigid transformations by moving a figure on the coordinate plane. Place the figure so that its vertices can be named by ordered pairs. Then transform it.

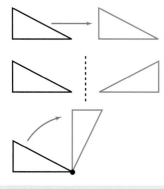

Sliding a figure in a straight line is called a *translation*.

Flipping a figure over a line is called a *reflection*.

Turning a figure around a point or vertex is called a *rotation*.

Technology Link

More Practice:
Harcourt Mega Math,
Ice Station Exploration,
Polar Planes, Level T

Activity

Graph a triangle with vertices ($^+$1,$^+$2), ($^+$4,$^+$2), and ($^+$4,$^+$6). Trace a copy, color it, and cut it out. Place the tracing over the original triangle on the coordinate plane. Transform the triangle. Name the ordered pairs for the new vertices.

Reflection
Reflect the triangle across the *y*-axis.

New ordered pairs:
($^-$1,$^+$2), ($^-$4,$^+$2), ($^-$4,$^+$6)

Rotation
Rotate the triangle 90° around the origin.

New ordered pairs:
($^-$2,$^+$1), ($^-$2,$^+$4), ($^-$6,$^+$4)

Translation
Translate each vertex 2 units left and 1 unit down.

New ordered pairs:
($^-$1,$^+$1), ($^+$2,$^+$1), ($^+$2,$^+$5)

Try It

Graph the triangle with vertices (1,1), (3,1), and (1,4). Then transform the triangle to the new given vertices. Write *translation, reflection,* or *rotation* to describe the move.

a. (3,3), (3,1), and (6,3)   **b.** (4,$^-$1), (6,$^-$1), and (4,2)

Connect

SPATIAL THINKING You can predict the effect of a translation, reflection, or rotation of a given figure.

Use the triangles on the coordinate plane to make predictions.

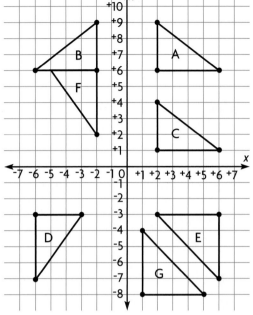

- Predict which figure could result from a translation of Triangle A.

- Predict which figure could result from a reflection of Triangle A.

- Predict which figure could result from a rotation of Triangle B.

- Predict which figure could result from a reflection of Triangle E.

MATH IDEA A rigid transformation, or movement of a figure, does not change its size or shape.

Practice and Problem Solving

Graph a triangle with vertices (2,2), (2,4), and (6,2). Then transform the triangle to the new given vertices. Write *translation, reflection,* or *rotation* to describe the move.

1. (4,0), (4,2), and (8,0) **2.** (6,6), (8,6), and (6,2) **3.** (2,2), (2,4), and ($^-$2,2)

For 4, graph a triangle with vertices (1,2), (5,2), and (1,4).

4. Translate the triangle 4 spaces to the right and 1 space up. What are the ordered pairs for the vertices of the triangle's new location?

5. Look at the coordinate plane above. Predict what two transformations would move Triangle A to Triangle D. Check your predictions.

Mixed Review and Test Prep

6. $\frac{3}{5} - \frac{1}{8}$ (p. 356) **7.** $\frac{4}{5} - \frac{1}{4}$ (p. 356)

8. What quadrilateral has 4 congruent sides and 2 pairs of congruent angles? (p. 460)

9. Write 3.695 in word form. (p. 22)

10. **TEST PREP** Will ordered 2 sandwiches for $1.39 each, potato sticks for $0.59, and a milk for $0.89. If he gives the cashier a five-dollar bill, how much change will he receive? (p. 170)

A $4.26 **B** $2.13 **C** $0.84 **D** $0.74

Problem Solving Skill
Relevant or Irrelevant Information

Quick Review

Name the *x*- or *y*-coordinate that is given by each direction from the origin.
1. 2 units up
2. 1 unit left
3. 4 units down
4. 3 units right
5. 2 units left

UNDERSTAND > **PLAN** > **SOLVE** > **CHECK**

TREASURE HUNT Jeff found this old map with instructions for finding a buried treasure. Where is the treasure?

The x-coordinate of the treasure is 2 times the cave's x-coordinate. The Lagoon is southwest of the cave. The Lagoon and the treasure have the same y-coordinate.

Sometimes a problem contains more information than you need to answer the question. You must decide which information is relevant, or needed, to solve the problem.

Read each fact and decide whether it is relevant or irrelevant to solving the problem.	• The *x*-coordinate of the treasure is 2 times the cave's *x*-coordinate.	relevant
	• The lagoon is southwest of the cave.	irrelevant
	• The lagoon and the treasure have the same *y*-coordinate.	relevant
Use the relevant information to solve the problem.	• Cave: ($^+$2, $^+$3). The treasure's *x*-coordinate is 2 × 2 = 4.	
	• Lagoon: ($^-$6, $^-$1). The treasure's *y*-coordinate is $^-$1.	

So, the coordinates of the treasure are ($^+$4, $^-$1).

Talk About It

• Which of the locations on the map are irrelevant to finding the treasure?

Problem Solving Practice

For 1–2, use the map. Tell the relevant information and solve.

1. The park and the library have the same *x*-coordinate. The library is 5 units left and 6 units up from the post office. The *y*-coordinate of the school is 3 more than the park's *y*-coordinate. Where is the park?

2. The Mall is south of the school and east of City Hall. If you go down 3 units and right 4 units from the library, you will find the Mall. Where is the Mall?

At 1 P.M., Amy left her house and rode her bike north 3 miles to Jeb's house. Next she rode east 2 miles and then turned south and rode 3 miles to Ann's house, where they had lunch. From there, she rode west back to her house. What shape did her trip make?

3. Which information is irrelevant to solving the problem?

   A Amy rode north to Jeb's house.
   B Amy and Ann had lunch at Ann's house.
   C Amy rode east and then south from Jeb's house to Ann's house.
   D Amy rode west back home.

4. Which question cannot be answered with the given information?

   F In what direction did Amy ride to Jeb's house?
   G What shape did her trip make?
   H How long did it take Amy to get to Ann's house?
   J How far is it from Amy's house to Ann's house?

Mixed Applications

5. The most valuable violin in the world is the Kreutzer, made in Italy in 1727. It was sold at auction for $1,516,000 in England in 1998. How old was the violin when it was sold?

6. Dante received $25.50 for his birthday. He bought a hat that cost $14.85 and a comic book. He has $7.70 left. How much did he spend on the comic book?

7. Kenya has two dogs. The sum of their ages is 7 years, and the difference in their ages is 3 years. How old are her two dogs?

8. **Patterns** Draw the next figure in this sequence.

9. **What's the Question?** Sue's triangle has vertices (1,2) and (1,5). The answer is (⁻2,⁻2).

10. Write a problem that includes relevant and irrelevant information. Exchange problems with a partner. Identify the relevant and irrelevant information and solve.

PERFORMANCE ASSESSMENT

TASK A • THE WINNING DESIGN

The math club is having a poster contest. The winning design will be used on posters to advertise the Spring Art Fair. These are the rules for the design:

1. The design should fit on a 24-inch by 24-inch poster.

2. Only a ruler, compass, protractor, and pencil may be used to create the design.

3. A circle must be the first figure drawn.

4. There must be some rotational symmetry in the design.

5. There must be similar and congruent figures in the design.

a. Create a design for the poster. Then write descriptions of shapes and sizes in the design so that someone else could make the same design.

b. The rules ask you to show rotational symmetry in your design. What did you draw?

c. Identify the figures in your design that are congruent.

TASK B • NAMING ORDERED PAIRS

The map shows where some of the furniture in Mrs. Henderson's classroom is located. She has asked her students to draw a new arrangement for the furniture.

a. Write the ordered pairs to show the locations for the corners of the bookshelf, the desk, and the table as they appear on the map.

b. Draw the new location for each piece of furniture on the grid.

c. Give the ordered pairs to show the new locations of the bookshelf, the desk, and the table.

Congruence and Similarity

You can use the drawing toolbar and *AutoShapes* in a word processing software program to draw congruent and similar figures. The figures in *AutoShapes* include triangles, rectangles, parallelograms, trapezoids, pentagons, and octagons.

Draw two congruent right triangles.

- Open the drawing toolbar and Click *AutoShapes*. Then click *Basic Shapes* and select the right triangle.

- Go to the place on the page where you want to place the figure and click.

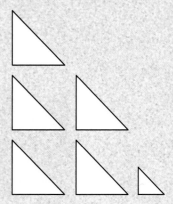

- To change the size or shape of the figure, move the cursor over the dots along the border of the figure until you see a vertical or horizontal arrow. Click and drag vertically to lengthen the figure. Click and drag horizontally to widen the figure.

- To draw a congruent figure, place the cursor inside the figure and click. Click *Edit* from the main menu and select *Copy*. This will make a copy of the figure. Then click *Edit* and select *Paste*. A congruent figure will appear slightly offset from the original figure. Click the middle of the new figure and drag it to a new location.

- To draw a similar figure, first draw a figure congruent to the first figure. Move the cursor over one of the dots that appear in the corners until you see the diagonal arrow. Click and drag along the diagonal away from the figure to enlarge the figure, or inside the figure to reduce it.

Practice and Problem Solving

Use drawing tools. Draw a congruent figure and a similar figure.

1. rectangle
2. pentagon
3. parallelogram

GO ON-LINE

Multimedia Math Glossary www.harcourtschool.com/mathglossary

Vocabulary Power Choose five new vocabulary words from Chapters 20 through 23 that are related. Locate them in the Multimedia Math Glossary. Write five sentences that each contain at least one of these words.

PROBLEM SOLVING ON LOCATION *in* *Maryland*

THE NATIONAL AQUARIUM BUILDING

Baltimore Inner Harbor has been an important United States seaport since the seventeenth century. Today it is the home of the National Aquarium and the *USS Constellation,* the last all-sail ship built by the U.S. Navy. The photograph below is of the National Aquarium in the Seaport.

USE DATA For 1–3, use the photograph.

1. Name some different polygons you can see in the faces of the National Aquarium Building.

2. Look at the two triangular faces at the top of the building. Do they appear to be congruent or similar? Explain how you decided.

3. The triangular face at the top of the building has two angles that measure 90° and 60°. What is the measure of the third angle?

4. The *USS Constellation* was built in 1854. About how many decades ago was that? (1 decade = 10 years)

THE SHOT TOWER

Located near the entrance to the Inner Harbor is the Shot Tower, which was constructed in 1828 and was originally used to manufacture gunshot. Molten lead was dropped from the top of the building into a vat of water at the bottom. During the fall, the lead took the shape of a sphere. When the lead hit the water, it cooled and became rifle shot. The Tower was in use until 1894. Now it is a museum.

The Shot Tower is 234 feet tall. If lead were dropped from the top of the Tower, the table shows approximately where the lead would be at each second of its fall.

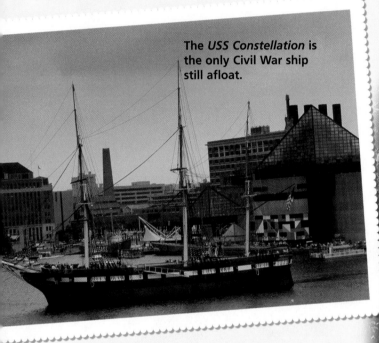

The *USS Constellation* is the only Civil War ship still afloat.

USE DATA For 1–3, suppose the Tower is a number line and street level is 0.

Seconds of Fall	Distance above Street Level
1	218 ft
2	170 ft
3	90 ft
3.8	0 ft

▲ Until the Washington Monument was built after the Civil War, the Shot Tower was the tallest building in the United States.

1. What integer names the location of the lead when it has fallen for 2 seconds? when it has fallen for 3.8 seconds?

2. The Tower extends 17 feet below street level. If the shot fell into a vat at the bottom of the Tower, what integer names the place where the vat is located?

3. If the shot fell from the top of the Tower to the bottom, about how many feet did it fall? Explain.

4. **STRETCH YOUR THINKING** If the year the Tower closed for business is 0 on a number line, what integer represents the year the tower was built? Explain.

Customary and Metric Systems

≡FAST FACT • SCIENCE Most of the United States has a *temperate* climate with warm summers and cool-to-cold winters. Florida's climate is *subtropical moist* with warm-to-hot summers and cool winters.

PROBLEM SOLVING The graph below shows the average July temperatures for five U.S. cities. Which city's average July temperature is higher than 76°F and lower than 85°F?

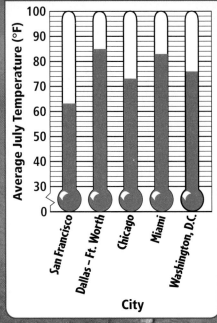

JULY TEMPERATURES IN FIVE CITIES

Average July Temperature (°F)

100
90
80
70
60
50
40
30
0

San Francisco
Dallas – Ft. Worth
Chicago
Miami
Washington, D.C.

City

Miami Beach, Florida

CHECK WHAT YOU KNOW

Use this page to help you review and remember
important skills needed for Chapter 24.

✔ CUSTOMARY UNITS AND TOOLS

Choose the tool you would use to
measure each.

1. the length of the chalkboard
2. the amount of flour needed to make a cake
3. the weight of a stapler

a.

b.

c.

Choose the unit you would use to measure each.

4. length of your foot
   inches or **yards**

5. weight of a truck
   pounds or **tons**

6. water in a pool
   quarts or **gallons**

✔ METRIC UNITS AND TOOLS

Choose the tool you would use to measure each.

7. the temperature outside
8. the mass of a bracelet
9. the distance across the classroom

a.

b.

c.

Choose the unit you would use to measure each.

10. distance run in a race
    centimeters or **kilometers**

11. mass of a big dog
    grams or **kilograms**

12. large bottle of soda
    liters or **milliliters**

VOCABULARY POWER

REVIEW

unit [yoo′nət] *noun*

A unit is a quantity used as a measure.
Customary and metric units are *standard
units*. Explain what you think a *nonstandard
unit* might be. Give some examples.

PREVIEW

precision   centimeter (cm)
millimeter (mm)   meter (m)
kilometer (km)   Celsius (°C)
Fahrenheit (°F)

GO ON-LINE   www.harcourtschool.com/mathglossary

Customary Length

Quick Review

Compare. Write $<$, $>$, or $=$ for each ●.

1. $\frac{2}{16}$ ● $\frac{3}{16}$ 2. $\frac{1}{4}$ ● $\frac{4}{16}$

3. $\frac{5}{16}$ ● $\frac{1}{2}$ 4. $\frac{8}{16}$ ● $\frac{1}{2}$

5. $\frac{3}{4}$ ● $\frac{15}{16}$

VOCABULARY

precision

MATERIALS

paper clips, string, customary measuring tools

CHOICES! CHOICES! Lengths are often measured in the customary system using *standard units* such as inches, feet, or yards. You can also use *nonstandard units* such as the length of a paper clip or a piece of string.

Activity 1

Measure and compare lengths using nonstandard units.

• Use a paper clip to measure the width of a table or desk. Record the width of the object in paper clips.

• Use a piece of string to measure the width of the same table or desk. Record the width in string lengths.

• Which unit is longer, a paper clip or a string length?

• Which unit would be more appropriate for measuring the width of a room—paper clips or pieces of string? Explain.

CUSTOMARY UNITS OF LENGTH

12 inches (in.) = 1 foot (ft)
3 feet = 1 yard (yd)
5,280 feet = 1 mile (mi)
1,760 yards = 1 mile

When you measure an object, you need to choose the appropriate unit and tool.

Activity 2

Estimate and then measure the length of your classroom using an appropriate standard unit and measuring tool.

• Which unit is best for measuring the length of your classroom—inches, feet, yards, or miles? Explain.

• Choose a tool to make the measurement. Why did you choose that tool?

• Measure the length and record the measurement.

• Was your estimate close to the actual measurement?

• Which unit is best for measuring the distance from New Orleans, Louisiana, to Charleston, West Virginia? Explain.

Precision

The **precision** of a measurement is related to the unit of measure you choose. The smaller the unit, the more precise the measurement will be.

$\frac{1}{8}$-in. mark

?

To the nearest inch, the crayon's length is 4 inches.
A more precise measurement is $3\frac{7}{8}$ inches.

HANDS ON

Activity 3   Estimate and measure the length of each object.

STEP 1

Copy the table.

Object	Estimate (nearest inch)	Measurement (nearest $\frac{1}{4}$ inch)	Measurement (nearest $\frac{1}{8}$ inch)
marker			
paper clip			
pencil			

STEP 2

Estimate the length of each object to the nearest inch. Record your estimate in the table.

STEP 3

Use a ruler. Measure the length of each object to the nearest $\frac{1}{4}$ inch and to the nearest $\frac{1}{8}$ inch. Record your measurements in the table.

• Why is measuring to the nearest $\frac{1}{8}$ inch more precise than measuring to the nearest $\frac{1}{4}$ inch?

• Carlos said that his desk is 2 feet $1\frac{1}{2}$ inches wide. How many inches wide is his desk?

▷ Check

1. **Explain** which unit would be the most appropriate for measuring the width of a postage stamp: inches, feet, yards, or miles.

Tell the best unit and tool for measuring each.

2. width of a shoe   3. height of the room   4. distance from school to your home

LESSON CONTINUES ▶

Tell which measurement is more precise.

5. 1 foot or 13 inches

6. 2 miles or 10,565 feet

7. 5 feet or 2 yards

8. 34 inches or 1 yard

9. $12\frac{1}{4}$ feet or $12\frac{1}{8}$ feet

10. $35\frac{3}{8}$ inches or 3 feet

Estimate the length of the marker in inches. Then measure the length

11. to the nearest inch.

12. to the nearest $\frac{1}{2}$ inch.

13. to the nearest $\frac{1}{8}$ inch.

14. In Exercises 11–13, which measurement is most precise? Explain.

▶ Practice and Problem Solving ⟨ Extra Practice, page 542, Set A ⟩

Tell the best unit and tool for measuring each.

15. length of a pen

16. distance from Miami to Orlando

17. length of the classroom

Tell which measurement is more precise.

18. 2 miles or 3,526 yards

19. 4 yards or 13 feet

20. 26,300 feet or 5 miles

21. $5\frac{7}{8}$ feet or 2 yards

22. $2\frac{1}{2}$ miles or 13,000 feet

23. 1 foot or $11\frac{3}{8}$ inches

Measure the length of the pencil

24. to the nearest foot.

25. to the nearest inch.

26. to the nearest $\frac{1}{8}$ inch.

Estimate the length in inches. Then measure to the nearest $\frac{1}{8}$ inch.

27.

28.

29. Joel measured the length of his garden in feet and in yards. Which was greater, the number of feet in the measurement or the number of yards? Explain.

30. Measure the width of the door to your classroom. Then measure the width of a door at home. Compare the widths and tell which door is wider. How much wider is it?

31. ✎ **Write About It** Explain how you would measure your pencil to the nearest $\frac{1}{8}$ inch.

32. Trenton's ruler has only $\frac{1}{4}$-inch marks. Explain how he can measure $3\frac{6}{8}$ inches of string.

33. On Monday, Tara drove 52.6 mi to Ocala and then 75.8 mi farther to Orlando. On Tuesday, she drove 167.8 mi. To the nearest $\frac{1}{2}$ mile, how much farther did Tara drive on Tuesday than on Monday?

34. The sum of Jason's and Elton's ages is 30 years. Jason is 8 years older than Elton. How old is Elton?

Mixed Review and Test Prep

Write each fraction as a decimal. (p. 328)

35. $\frac{7}{8}$ **36.** $\frac{3}{40}$ **37.** $\frac{11}{25}$

38. List the prime numbers between 5 and 30. (p. 300)

39. **TEST PREP** Which number is the product of 35 and 2.58? (p. 170)

A 90.03   C 90.33

B 90.3   D 93.0

Write each decimal as a fraction. (p. 328)

40. 0.57   **41.** 0.625   **42.** 0.35

43. Find the mean for this set of data. 13.4, 11.3, 16.8, 12, 14.5 (p. 100)

44. **TEST PREP** What is the value of the blue digit in 2.079? (p. 22)

F 9 tenths   H 9 thousandths

G 9 hundredths   J 9 ten-thousandths

Problem Solving LINKUP ... to Science

Echoes can be used to measure distances. Weather forecasters send sound waves toward weather systems such as tornadoes or hurricanes. They time how long it takes the waves to reach a system, "bounce off" it, and return. This method of measuring distances is called **sonar.**

Solve.

1. A ship was in a heavy fog. The navigator knew there was an iceberg nearby, and he sounded a horn. Four seconds later he heard an echo returning from the iceberg. Sound travels about 1,100 feet per second in air. About how far was the iceberg from the ship?

2. Sound travels about 1 mile per second in water. Suppose a ship's sonar emits a loud sound under water. Four miles away there is a submarine. How long will it be before the echo reaches the ship?

3. ✏ Write a problem about using echoes to measure distances. Have a classmate solve your problem.

HANDS ON — Metric Length

VOCABULARY

millimeter (mm)
centimeter (cm)
meter (m)
kilometer (km)

MATERIALS

metric measuring tools, paper clips

▶ Explore

You can use standard metric units to measure length or distance.

A **millimeter (mm)** is a very small unit. It is about the thickness of a spoke on a bicycle wheel.

A **centimeter (cm)** is about the thickness of a bicycle pedal.

A **meter (m)** is about the height of a bicycle.

A **kilometer (km)** is how far you can ride a bicycle in a few minutes.

Height

Spoke   Pedal

METRIC UNITS OF LENGTH

10 millimeters (mm) = 1 centimeter (cm)
100 centimeters = 1 meter (m)
1,000 meters = 1 kilometer (km)

Activity

Estimate and measure the length of one of your textbooks.

• Make a table to record your estimated length and your measurement.

• Choose an appropriate metric unit for measuring the book.

• Estimate the length of the book in your chosen unit. Record your estimate.

• Choose an appropriate tool for measuring the book. Measure and record the length of the book.

• Which unit and tool did you choose? Explain your choice.

Is the desktop longer or shorter than a meter?

Try It

Estimate and measure each. Record your data.

a. length of your desk

b. distance from your desk to the door

Connect

You can find the length or height of something that you cannot reach.

> Find the height of the building in the picture.
> The height of one floor in the building is 14.5 meters. Count the number of floors in the building. Multiply the number of floors by the height of one floor to find the height of the building.
>
> $$14.5 \times 8 = 116$$
>
> So, the building is about 116 meters tall.

• **What if** the height of one floor in the building were 12.25 meters? Explain how to find the height of the building.

Practice and Problem Solving

Write the appropriate metric unit for measuring each.

1. height of your school

2. thickness of a book

3. distance from New York to Los Angeles

Estimate and measure each.

4.

5.

6.

7. your height

8. width of your pencil

9. length of your little finger

Find the measurement of each.

10. the length of a road 12 blocks long if 1 block is 0.125 km long

11. the height of a building 12 stories high if 1 story is 13 m high

12. the length of a floor 92 tiles long if 1 tile is 30 cm long

13. **Write About It** Find the height of a building or an object you cannot reach. Draw a picture to explain your method.

14. **GEOMETRY** A rectangular frame has a perimeter of 50.6 cm. If the length is 8.3 cm, what is the width?

15. **NUMBER SENSE** Anne says 0.2 cm is the same as 2 mm. Do you agree? Explain.

Mixed Review and Test Prep

Write each in simplest form. (p. 316)

16. $\frac{3}{12}$

17. $\frac{16}{24}$

18. $\frac{15}{35}$

19. $\frac{6}{18}$

20. **TEST PREP** Find $\frac{3}{8}$ of 16. (p. 388)

A $\frac{3}{16}$

C 6

B $\frac{48}{128}$

D 16

Change Linear Units

Quick Review

1. 2×12 2. $60 \div 5$
3. $84 \div 3$ 4. $1{,}760 \times 2$
5. 25×3

▶ **Learn**

CUSTOM TOWELS   Jenna is making personalized beach towels for each member of her family. She needs 30 feet of fabric. Since fabric is sold by the yard, how many yards of fabric does Jenna need?

Think: 30 feet = ■ yards

To change smaller units to larger units, divide.

number ÷ of feet	number of feet in 1 yard	= total yards
↓	↓	↓
30 ÷	3	= 10

So, Jenna needs 10 yards of fabric.

CUSTOMARY UNITS OF LENGTH

12 inches (in.) = 1 foot (ft)
3 feet = 1 yard (yd)
5,280 feet = 1 mile (mi)
1,760 yards = 1 mile

METRIC UNITS OF LENGTH

10 millimeters (mm) = 1 centimeter (cm)
100 centimeters = 1 meter (m)
1,000 meters = 1 kilometer (km)

Examples

A How many millimeters are in 230 centimeters?

Think: 230 cm = ■ mm

To change larger units to smaller units, multiply.

number of cm	×	number of mm in 1 cm	=	number of mm
↓		↓		↓
230	×	10	=	2,300 mm

There are 2,300 millimeters in 230 centimeters.

B How many feet are in 168 inches?

Think: 168 inches = ■ feet

To change smaller units to larger units, divide.

number of inches	÷	number of inches in 1 foot	=	number of feet
↓		↓		↓
168	÷	12	=	14

There are 14 feet in 168 inches.

You can also use a calculator to change linear units.

7,200 ft = ■ mi

`7 2 0 0 ÷ 5 2 8 0 =` = 1.3636363

So, 7,200 ft is approximately equal to 1.4 mi.

Add and Subtract Measurements

You may need to change units to add and subtract measurements.

Example 1

Jenna needs 5 feet 7 inches of fabric for her mother's towel and 4 feet 6 inches for her little brother's towel. How much fabric does she need for both towels?

Find 5 ft 7 in. + 4 ft 6 in.

STEP 1

Add each kind of unit.

```
  5 ft   7 in.
+ 4 ft   6 in.
  9 ft  13 in.
```

STEP 2

Think: 12 in. = 1 ft
Since 13 in. is more than 1 ft, rename 13 in. as 1 ft + 1 in.

9 ft 13 in. = 9 ft + (1 ft + 1 in.)

STEP 3

Combine like units.
9 ft + (1 ft + 1 in.) = (9 ft + 1 ft) + 1 in. = 10 ft 1 in.

So, she needs 10 feet 1 inch of fabric.

Example 2

Mary made a towel bar with a piece of wooden dowel that was 1 m long. If she used 48.9 cm of the dowel, how much of it remained?

Find 1 m − 48.9 cm.

STEP 1

Think: 1 m = 100 cm
Use 100 cm for 1 m.

```
  100
−  48.9
```

STEP 2

Place a zero to show an equivalent decimal.

```
  100.0
−  48.9
```

STEP 3

Subtract.

```
    9 9
  0 10 10 10
  1 0 0.0
−   4 8.9
    5 1.1
```

So, 51.1 cm of wooden dowel was left.

▶ Check

1. **Explain** how you would rename units to subtract 4 feet 6 inches from 7 feet 2 inches.

Change the unit.

2. 3 ft = ■ in.

3. 5 yd = ■ ft

4. 60 in. = ■ ft

5. 24 ft = ■ yd

6. 5 m = ■ cm

7. 20 mm = ■ cm

8. 2 km = ■ m

9. 4,000 m = ■ km

Complete.

10. 4 ft 3 in. = 3 ft ■ in.

11. 5,360 ft = 1 mi ■ ft

12. 10 yd 1 ft = 9 yd ■ ft

LESSON CONTINUES ▶

Change the unit.

13. 24 in. = ■ ft   **14.** 30 ft = ■ yd   **15.** 13 yd = ■ ft   **16.** 8 ft = ■ in.

17. 4 mi = ■ yd   **18.** 48 in. = ■ ft   **19.** 6 m = ■ cm   **20.** 50 mm = ■ cm

21. 7 km = ■ m   **22.** 65 cm = ■ mm   **23.** 8 m = ■ cm   **24.** 700 cm = ■ m

25. 4 yd = ■ in.   **26.** 10,560 ft = ■ mi   **27.** 3 m = ■ mm   **28.** 6,000 m = ■ km

Complete.

29. 235 cm = ■ m 35 cm   **30.** 25 ft 12 in. = ■ yd 2 ft   **31.** 3 cm 25 mm = ■ mm

32. 7 mi 250 ft = ■ ft   **33.** 2 km 50 m = ■ cm   **34.** 62 m = 6,150 cm ■ mm

35. 2 ft = 1 ft ■ in.   **36.** 12 yd 2 ft = 11 yd ■ ft   **37.** 3 mi 27 ft = 2 mi ■ ft

Find the sum or difference.

38.   2 ft 2 in.
    +3 ft 7 in.

39.   3 yd 2 ft
    +8 yd 1 ft

40.   7 ft 4 in.
    −5 ft 1 in.

41.   14 yd
    − 5 yd 2 ft

42.   15 ft 4 in.
    +12 ft 6 in.

43.   3 mi 345 ft
    +1 mi   39 ft

44.   8 ft   6 in.
    −3 ft 10 in.

45.   12 yd 2 ft   3 in.
    − 3 yd 1 ft 11 in.

46. 88 cm − 69 cm   **47.** 50 km + 6.8 km   **48.** 830 mm − 4.6 cm

49. 13.4 km − 2.8 km   **50.** 10.3 cm + 7.8 cm   **51.** 15.6 cm − 6.4 cm

52. ⭐ **What's the Error?** Jason had 14 yd of string. He used 5 yd 8 in. for a string art project. He said that he had 8 yd 2 in. left. Describe his error and give the correct amount of string that was left.

53. ESTIMATION Estimate how many yards long your classroom is. Then use a yardstick to check. Record your estimate and the actual measurement.

54. NUMBER SENSE Describe how you could find the number of centimeters in a kilometer.

55. NUMBER SENSE Joel says that 40 cm is the same as 0.4 m. Do you agree? Explain your thinking.

56. Mr. Gomez had 15 ft of cable. He used 12 ft 6 in. to hook up his television. How long was the remaining piece?

57. Grace has 13 feet of fabric. Her pattern calls for $4\frac{1}{4}$ yards of fabric. Does she have enough? Explain.

58. Use the diagram on the right. By car, how many kilometers is it from Bill's house to the library following the path shown?

Bill's House

Library

1 cm = 2 km

59. Write the reciprocal. $\frac{7}{12}$ (p. 404)

For 60–61, round to the hundredths place. (p. 40)

60. 55.073

61. 172.6053

62. **TEST PREP** Which number is the product of 28 and 163? (p. 152)

    A 4,564   **C** 3,352

    B 4,453   **D** 3,176

63. $6\overline{)3.6}$ (p. 232)   **64.** $5\overline{)4.0}$ (p. 232)

65. Solve for *n*. $n \times 15 = 105$ (p. 246)

66. An angle that is less than 90° is called an ___?___ angle. (p. 428)

67. **TEST PREP** Multiply $\frac{4}{12} \times \frac{1}{3}$. (p. 386)

    F $\frac{1}{8}$ **H** $\frac{5}{36}$

    G $\frac{1}{9}$ **J** $\frac{1}{3}$

Problem Solving   Thinker's Corner

RELATING SYSTEMS You can use the comparisons below to explore the relationship between some customary and metric units of measure.

One yard is slightly shorter than 1 meter.
One mile is slightly longer than 1.5 kilometers.
One gallon is about 3.75 liters.
One pound is about 0.5 kilogram.

If a kilometer is about 6 city blocks long, about how many city blocks long is one mile?

There are about 6 city blocks in 1 kilometer, so 0.5 kilometer is about 3 city blocks. Since a mile is about 1.5 kilometers, one mile is about 6 + 3, or 9 city blocks long.

▲ **Miracle Mile is a popular shopping area in Coral Gables, Florida.**

1. Carmen's poodle Tinkerbell weighs 8 kilograms. Does Tinkerbell weigh more than 10 pounds? Explain.

2. A football field is 120 yards long, including the end zones. Is a football field shorter or longer than 120 meters?

3. Liam's fish tank holds 80 liters of water. Liam's new fish needs to be in a tank that holds at least 30 gallons of water. Does Liam's tank hold enough water? Explain.

4. Marlys is running in two 5K, or 5 kilometer, races this month. She is running in a 10K race next month. Will Marlys run more or less than 10 miles in all? Explain.

Customary Capacity and Weight

▶ **Learn**

ALL SHOOK UP! Al's Deli uses 1 pint of milk in each milkshake. There are 15 milkshakes ordered. If Al has 8 quarts of milk, does he have enough for all the milkshakes?

Think: 8 quarts = ■ pints

To change larger units to smaller units, multiply:

$$
\begin{array}{ccccc}
\text{number of} & & \text{number of pints} & & \text{total} \\
\text{quarts} & \times & \text{in 1 quart} & = & \text{pints} \\
\downarrow & & \downarrow & & \downarrow \\
8 & \times & 2 & = & 16
\end{array}
$$

There are 16 pints in 8 quarts. Since $15 < 16$, there is enough milk for 15 milkshakes.

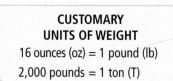

**CUSTOMARY
UNITS OF CAPACITY**

8 fluid ounces (fl oz) = 1 cup (c)

2 cups = 1 pint (pt)

2 pints = 1 quart (qt)

4 cups = 1 quart

4 quarts = 1 gallon (gal)

**CUSTOMARY
UNITS OF WEIGHT**

16 ounces (oz) = 1 pound (lb)

2,000 pounds = 1 ton (T)

Example

Al uses 2 ounces of cheese for each sandwich. If he makes 40 sandwiches, how many pounds of cheese does he use?

STEP 1

Find how many ounces of cheese are used in 40 sandwiches.

Think: 40 sandwiches = ■ ounces of cheese

$$
\begin{array}{ccccc}
\text{number of} & & \text{number of ounces} & & \text{total} \\
\text{sandwiches} & \times & \text{in 1 sandwich} & = & \text{ounces} \\
\downarrow & & \downarrow & & \downarrow \\
40 & \times & 2 & = & 80
\end{array}
$$

STEP 2

Find how many pounds are in 80 ounces.

Think: 80 ounces = ■ pounds

$$
\begin{array}{ccccc}
\text{number of} & & \text{number of ounces} & & \text{total} \\
\text{ounces} & \div & \text{in 1 pound} & = & \text{pounds} \\
\downarrow & & \downarrow & & \downarrow \\
80 & \div & 16 & = & 5
\end{array}
$$

So, he uses 5 pounds of cheese to make 40 sandwiches.

1. **Explain** how you could find the number of pounds in 160 ounces.

Change the unit.

2. 3 gal = ■ qt   **3.** 32 c = ■ qt   **4.** 4 gal = ■ c   **5.** 2 pt = ■ c

6. 48 oz = ■ lb   **7.** 2 lb = ■ oz   **8.** 1 T = ■ oz   **9.** 8,000 lb = ■ T

► **Practice and Problem Solving** — Extra Practice, page 542, Set C

Change the unit.

10. 10 pt = ■ qt   **11.** 5 c = ■ fl oz   **12.** 3 gal = ■ pt   **13.** 16 fl oz = ■ pt

14. 2 T = ■ lb   **15.** 6 lb = ■ oz   **16.** 112 oz = ■ lb   **17.** 1.5 T = ■ lb

Choose the best tool to measure each.

18. a cat's weight

19. amount of water in a bathtub

20. amount of juice in a glass

21. outside temperature

22. **What if** Al had 23 milkshake orders and 3 gallons of milk? Would he have enough milk for 1 pint in each milkshake? Explain.

23. Use the Frosty Freeze ad. Toby needs 1 gallon of ice cream for a party. What is the better buy? Explain.

24. **FAST FACT** • **HEALTH** You should not carry a backpack that weighs more than $\frac{1}{5}$ of your weight. Weigh each item in your backpack to the nearest ounce, and find the total weight. Is your backpack under the weight limit? Explain.

FROSTY FREEZE
ICE CREAM SALE!
Two 1-quart containers for $1.00!
1 gallon for $3.79!

25. **Write About It** Describe three items that are measured by capacity. Describe three items that are measured by weight.

Mixed Review and Test Prep

26. A 90° angle is called a __?__ angle. (p. 428)

27. A 120° angle is called an __?__ angle. (p. 428)

28. 56.3 × 2.1 (p. 170)   **29.** 18.1 × 0.5 (p. 170)

30. **TEST PREP** In which set are all numbers factors of 180? (p. 278)

A 2, 5, 7   C 2, 3, 5
B 2, 3, 5, 13   D 2, 3, 5, 7

Metric Capacity and Mass

▶ Learn

PUNCH LINE Ms. Allison needs 4 liters of juice to make fruit punch. The cafeteria sends her 12 metric cups of juice. Is this enough juice to make the punch?

Think: 12 metric cups = ▇ liters

To change smaller units to larger units, divide.

number of metric cups	÷	number of metric cups in 1 liter	=	total liters
↓		↓		↓
12	÷	4	=	3

There are 3 liters in 12 metric cups.

Since 3 < 4, Ms. Allison does not have enough juice.

Example

Ms. Allison needs to make 50 sandwiches for the fifth grade. If she uses two 1-kilogram jars of peanut butter, how many grams of peanut butter will she use for each sandwich?

STEP 1

Find how many grams are in 2 kilograms.

Think: 2 kilograms = ▇ grams

To change larger units to smaller units, multiply.

number of kilograms	×	number of grams in 1 kilogram	=	total grams
↓		↓		↓
2	×	1,000	=	2,000

So, there are 2,000 grams in 2 kilograms.

STEP 2

To find how many grams will be used for each sandwich, divide 2,000 grams into 50 equal groups.

number of grams	÷	number of sandwiches	=	grams per sandwich
↓		↓		↓
2,000	÷	50	=	40

So, Ms. Allison will use 40 grams of peanut butter for each sandwich.

250 milliliters (mL), or 1 metric cup

1 liter

METRIC UNITS OF CAPACITY

1,000 milliliters (mL) = 1 liter (L)

250 milliliters = 1 metric cup

4 metric cups = 1 liter

1,000 liters = 1 kiloliter (kL)

A large paper clip is about 1 gram.

A large container of peanut butter is about 1 kilogram.

METRIC UNITS OF MASS

1,000 milligrams (mg) = 1 gram (g)

1,000 grams = 1 kilogram (kg)

Technology Link
More Practice: Harcourt
Mega Math The Number
Games, *Tiny's Think
Tank*, Level Q

1. **Explain** whether you multiply or divide to find how many milliliters are in 5 liters.

Change the unit.

2. 4,000 L = ■ kL   3. 8 metric cups = ■ L   4. 6 kg = ■ g   5. 2,000 mg = ■ g

Measure each. Explain your method.

6. mass of a box of crayons   7. capacity of water in a bottle

▶ **Practice and Problem Solving**   ⟨ Extra Practice, page 542, Set D ⟩

Change the unit.

8. 1.5 kg = ■ g   9. 8 kL = ■ L   10. 5 L = ■ mL   11. 3 g = ■ mg

Measure each. Explain your method.

12. capacity of water in a sink   13. mass of a straight pin

Compare. Write <, >, or = for each ●.

14. 6 L ● 16 metric cups   15. 4,000 mg ● 4 g   16. 5 kg ● 15,000 g

Choose the best estimate.

17. the mass of a strawberry is
    a. 6 mg
    b. 6 g
    c. 6 kg

18. the dropper holds
    a. 3 mL
    b. 3 L
    c. 3 kL

19. the mass of a cat is
    a. 6 mg
    b. 6 g
    c. 6 kg

20. the bottle of soda holds
    a. 1 mL
    b. 1 L
    c. 1 kL

21. Four lawn care workers drank a total of 2 L of water. If each drank an equal amount, how many milliliters did each worker drink?

22. A can of soda holds 355 mL. Which holds more, a 2-L bottle of soda or a 6-pack of soda cans? Explain.

23. **? What's the Question?**   Monique had a 1-kg jar of peanut butter for sandwiches. She used 750 g of peanut butter in one week. The answer is 250 g.

24. Sometimes you can use a nonstandard measure, like a *handful*. How many handfuls of sand will fill a small plastic bag?

Mixed Review and Test Prep

25. Divide 345 by 20. (p. 212)

26. Find 4.30 − 1.32. (p. 48)

27. 37.5 ÷ 5 (p. 232)   28. 3.6 ÷ 9 (p. 230)

29. **TEST PREP**   Which shows the simplest form of $\frac{12}{32}$? (p. 316)

A $\frac{3}{8}$ B $\frac{8}{32}$ C $\frac{24}{64}$ D $\frac{2}{3}$

Time and Temperature

Learn

BEAT THE CLOCK   Naomi wants to run 5 miles in less than $1\frac{3}{4}$ hours. If she starts her run at 10:47 A.M. and runs 5 miles by 12:26 P.M., has she reached her goal?

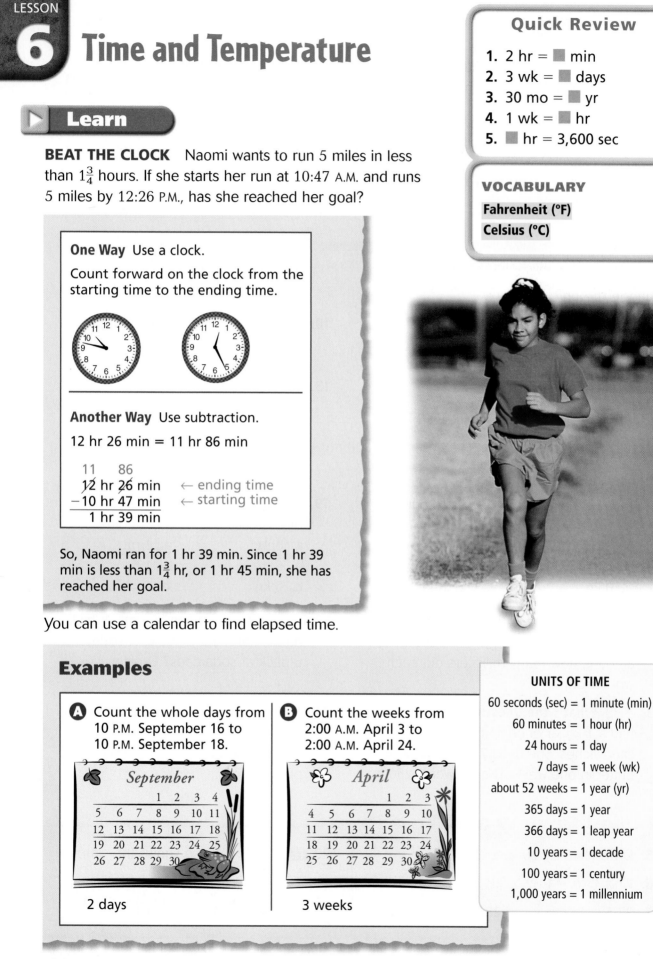

One Way Use a clock.

Count forward on the clock from the starting time to the ending time.

Another Way Use subtraction.

12 hr 26 min = 11 hr 86 min

```
      11    86
     12 hr 26 min    ← ending time
   − 10 hr 47 min    ← starting time
      1 hr 39 min
```

So, Naomi ran for 1 hr 39 min. Since 1 hr 39 min is less than $1\frac{3}{4}$ hr, or 1 hr 45 min, she has reached her goal.

You can use a calendar to find elapsed time.

Examples

A Count the whole days from 10 P.M. September 16 to 10 P.M. September 18.

September						
			1	2	3	4
5	6	7	8	9	10	11
12	13	14	15	16	17	18
19	20	21	22	23	24	25
26	27	28	29	30		

2 days

B Count the weeks from 2:00 A.M. April 3 to 2:00 A.M. April 24.

April						
				1	2	3
4	5	6	7	8	9	10
11	12	13	14	15	16	17
18	19	20	21	22	23	24
25	26	27	28	29	30	

3 weeks

UNITS OF TIME

60 seconds (sec) = 1 minute (min)

60 minutes = 1 hour (hr)

24 hours = 1 day

7 days = 1 week (wk)

about 52 weeks = 1 year (yr)

365 days = 1 year

366 days = 1 leap year

10 years = 1 decade

100 years = 1 century

1,000 years = 1 millennium

Measuring Temperature

Temperature is measured in degrees **Fahrenheit** (°F) in the customary system and in degrees **Celsius** (°C) in the metric system.

When Naomi began her run, the Fahrenheit thermometer outside her house read 65°F. She ended her run at the library, where a Celsius thermometer read 20°C. By how many degrees Fahrenheit had the temperature changed?

You can find the change by comparing the temperatures on the two thermometers. The Celsius reading of 20°C is about 70°F. From 65°F to 70°F is 5 degrees. So, the temperature changed by 5 degrees Fahrenheit.

▷ **Check**

1. **Explain** how to use a clock to find the elapsed time between 3:00 P.M. Wednesday and 1:00 A.M. Thursday.

2. **Explain** how you know whether 0°F or 0°C is colder.

Write the time for each.

3. Start: 4:30 P.M.
   45 min elapsed time
   End: ■

4. Start: ■
   25 min elapsed time
   End: 8:00 P.M.

5. Start: June 11, 9:00 P.M.
   ■ time has elapsed.
   End: June 16, 5:30 A.M.

Add or subtract.

6.   5 hr 10 min
   +2 hr 45 min

7.   8 hr 11 min
   −3 hr 24 min

8.   5 hr 15 min
   −3 hr 35 min

9.   1 hr 50 min
   +3 hr 22 min

Choose the temperature that is the better estimate.

10. a glass of ice water

    34°F or 34°C

11. a classroom

    23°F or 23°C

12. a bowl of hot stew

    80°F or 80°C

Use the thermometers above to find the change in temperature.

13. 25°F to 41°F

14. ⁻5°C to ⁻20°C

15. 45°F to 20°C

LESSON CONTINUES

Extra Practice

Set A (pp. 522–525)

Estimate the length in inches. Then measure to the nearest $\frac{1}{8}$ inch.

1.

2.

Tell the unit and tool to measure each.

3. width of a door

4. distance from New York to Boston

5. length of the kitchen

Set B (pp. 528–531)

Change the unit.

1. 15 ft = ■ yd

2. 72 in. = ■ ft

3. 100 mm = ■ cm

Find the sum or difference.

4. 3.9 cm + 4.8 cm

5. 6.1 cm − 5.2 cm

6. 5 ft 1 in. − 2 ft 9 in.

Set C (pp. 532–533)

Change the unit.

1. 3 gal = ■ c

2. 32 pt = ■ qt

3. 6 T = ■ lb

4. $\frac{1}{2}$ lb = ■ oz

5. Jane bought five 3-lb bags of apples to make apple pies. How many ounces of apples did she buy?

6. The Chungs ordered 500 gallons of juice for their restaurant. How many quarts of juice did they order?

Set D (pp. 534–535)

Change the unit.

1. 1,000 g = ■ kg

2. 3.5 kg = ■ g

3. 1.5 L = ■ mL

4. 1 kL = ■ L

5. Juan bought ten 1-L sodas. How many mL of soda did he buy?

6. Bob ate 10 g of fat at breakfast, 15 g at lunch, and 5 g at dinner. How many mg of fat did he eat?

Set E (pp. 536–539)

Write the time for each.

1. Start: noon
   6 hr 26 min
      elapsed time
   End: ■

2. Start: midnight
   ■ elapsed time
   End: 11:45 P.M.

3. Start: Jan. 10, 3:05 A.M.
   6 days 4 hr 16 min
      elapsed time
   End: ■

4. It is a warm, sunny day in June. Which would be a better estimate of the temperature, 80°C or 80°F?

Review/Test

✓ CHECK VOCABULARY AND CONCEPTS

Choose the correct term from the box.

| centimeter |
| liters |
| millimeters |

1. There are 10 __?__ in 1 centimeter. (p. 526)

2. A __?__ is about the thickness of a bicycle pedal. (p. 526)

✓ CHECK SKILLS

Estimate the length in inches. Then measure
to the nearest $\frac{1}{8}$ inch. (pp. 522–525)

3.

4.

Choose the appropriate tool to measure each. (pp. 522–539)

5. a pencil
   ruler or odometer

6. soda in a bottle
   liter or kilometer

7. your height
   paper clip or string

8. your weight
   thermometer or scale

Change the unit. (pp. 528–535)

9. 2 mi = ■ yd

10. 900 yd = ■ ft

11. 200 cm = ■ m

12. 20 mm = ■ cm

13. 5 T = ■ lb

14. 8 pt = ■ gal

15. 15 g = ■ mg

16. 20 metric cups = ■ L

17. 2.5 kg = ■ g

Find the sum or difference. (pp. 528–531)

18. 8 yd 2 ft
    −5 yd 1 ft

19. 67 m + 29 cm

20. 4 ft 6 in.
    −2 ft 7 in.

21. 3.6 cm − 19 mm

Write the time for each. (pp. 536–539)

22. Start: March 18, 10:05 A.M.
    5 days 5 hr 40 min elapsed time
    End: ■

23. Start: 5:10 A.M.
    ■ time has elapsed.
    End: 12:49 P.M.

Decide whether you need an estimate or an actual measurement.
Then solve. (pp. 540–541)

24. Rick needs 16.5 pounds of soil for
    a science project. If he has one
    12-pound bag, how much more soil
    does he need?

25. Jenna is painting the walls of the game
    room, which is 22 ft by 18 ft and 9 ft high.
    A gallon of paint covers about 350 ft^2.
    How many gallons of paint should she buy?

Standardized Test Prep

⭐ MEASUREMENT

1. A Fahrenheit thermometer inside a greenhouse read 90°F. A Celsius thermometer outside read 20°C. About how much warmer, in degrees Celsius, is the temperature inside the greenhouse than outside?

A 70°C **C** 30°C

B 50°C **D** 10°C

2. The weight of the people and goods in an elevator is 550 pounds. How much more weight can the elevator hold?

$$1 \text{ ton} = 2{,}000 \text{ pounds}$$

F 450 pounds **H** 2,450 pounds

G 1,450 pounds **J** 2,550 pounds

3. Explain It Alan's goal is to run a 26.2-mile marathon in less than 5 hours. If he runs at an average rate of 4.8 miles per hour, will he reach his goal? ESTIMATE to solve. Explain your answer.

⭐ ALGEBRAIC THINKING

4. Jillian is making a tile pattern. If she continues the pattern, how many tiles will be in the next group?

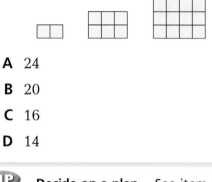

A 24

B 20

C 16

D 14

> **TIP** **Decide on a plan.** See item 5. Use the strategy *draw a diagram* to sketch the diagrams in the answer choices. Then write numbers on the diagrams as you count the places where people will sit.

5. A restaurant is setting up square tables for a party. Which arrangement will seat the **most** people?

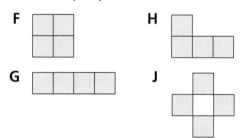

6. Explain It Eric forgot to fill in one of the numbers in this table.

Input	2	9	⬛	4
Output	12	54	42	24

What is the missing number? Explain how you know.

⭐ DATA ANALYSIS AND PROBABILITY

7. Which mountain is about twice the height of Mt. Rogers?

A Mt. Mitchell

B Mt. Whitney

C Mt. Harney

D Mt. Hood

8. This stem-and-leaf plot shows the number of hours that some students watched television for a week.

Stem	Leaves
0	3 8 9
1	0 1 1 2 2 3 5 6 6 7 7 7 7 8 9
2	0 1 3

What was the median number of hours of television watched?

F 15.5   **H** 16.5

G 16   **J** 17

9. Explain It Explain how line graphs and bar graphs are similar. How are they different?

⭐ NUMBER SENSE, CONCEPTS, AND OPERATIONS

10. Four students each wrote a number on a card.

Which shows the numbers in order from **least** to **greatest**?

A $0.45, \frac{3}{4}, \frac{4}{5}, 0.09$

B $0.45, \frac{3}{4}, 0.09, \frac{4}{5}$

C $0.09, \frac{4}{5}, 0.45, \frac{3}{4}$

D $0.09, 0.45, \frac{3}{4}, \frac{4}{5}$

11. Four people plan to rent a fishing boat for 2 hours. They will share the cost equally.

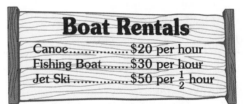

How much will each person save if they can find a fifth person to share the cost?

F $3.00

G $7.50

H $12.00

J $15.00

12. Explain It Marie's salary this year is $36,000. She says that if next year she gets a raise of $100 per month, she will earn $48,000. Is her answer reasonable? Explain how you know.

Perimeter

FAST FACT • SOCIAL STUDIES Tryon Palace, in New Bern, North Carolina, was built in 1770. After the Revolutionary War, Tryon Palace was the first state capitol building. In the 1950s, the palace and its gardens were reconstructed and restored to their original conditions.

PROBLEM SOLVING The diagram below shows the palace with part of its grounds. Find the perimeter of Tryon Palace.

82 ft
Tryon Palace 59 ft

Use this page to help you review and remember
important skills needed for Chapter 25.

✓ PERIMETER

Find the perimeter of each figure.

1.

2.

3.

4.

5.
13 m
7 m

6.
5 yd
8 yd

7. 2 cm
8 cm

8.
3 cm
1 cm

✓ MULTIPLY DECIMALS BY WHOLE NUMBERS

Find the product.

9. 0.5
× 5

10. 0.75
× 4

11. 0.25
× 8

12. 2.6
× 3

13. 4.8
× 4

14. 8.5
× 6

15. 0.10
× 10

16. 1.5
× 6

VOCABULARY POWER

REVIEW

polygon [pä′lē•gän] *noun*

Polygon comes from the Greek root words
poly- and *gonia*, which mean "many" and
"angle." Use these meanings to write your
own definition of *polygon*.

PREVIEW

perimeter
circumference

www.harcourtschool.com/mathglossary

Estimate Perimeter

Quick Review

Estimate by rounding to the nearest whole number.

1. 2.7 + 9.1 **2.** 8.12 + 4.83
3. 8 × 4.8   **4.** 5 × 12.21
5. 5.5 + 6.2 + 8.9 + 1.1

VOCABULARY

perimeter

MATERIALS
metric and customary rulers, string

ALABAMA

GEORGIA

★ Tallahassee   Jacksonville

Orlando

Tampa FLORIDA

Miami

ATLANTIC OCEAN

GULF OF MEXICO

1 cm = 50 mi

▶ Explore

The map shows that Florida's border touches Alabama, Georgia, the Atlantic Ocean, and the Gulf of Mexico. How can you estimate the perimeter of Florida?

The **perimeter** is the distance around a figure.

One way to estimate the perimeter of Florida is by using a map, a length of string, and a ruler.

Activity

Follow the steps to estimate the perimeter of Florida.

STEP 1

On the map, lay a piece of string around the state of Florida. Mark the string where it meets itself.

STEP 2

Use a ruler to measure the marked section of the string in centimeters.

STEP 3

Use the map scale. For this map, to estimate the perimeter in miles, multiply your measurement in centimeters by 50. Suppose the string measures 33 cm.

50 × 33 = 1,650

So, the estimated perimeter of Florida is 1,650 miles.

Talk About It

• What does a map scale tell you?

You can also use a string to estimate the perimeter of polygons.

A Estimate the perimeter in inches.

The perimeter is about 5 in.

B Estimate the perimeter in centimeters.

The perimeter is about 9 cm.

▷ **Practice and Problem Solving**

For 1–2, use the map of Virginia.

1 cm = 70 mi

1. Use string and a metric ruler. Estimate the perimeter of the state of Virginia on the map in centimeters.

2. Use the scale. What is an estimated perimeter of Virginia in miles?

Estimate the perimeter of the polygon in centimeters.

3.   **4.**   **5.**   **6.**

7. On a sheet of paper, trace the outline of your hand with your fingers closed. Then, use string and a ruler to estimate the perimeter in inches.

8. Using string and a ruler, estimate the perimeter of your desktop in inches.

Mixed Review and Test Prep

9. 8×0.017 (p. 174)

10. $24.6 \div 6$ (p. 232)

Find the value of *n*. (p. 292)

11. $n^2 = 100$ **12.** $3^n = 81$

13. **TEST PREP** Derek had $20. He bought 2 muffins for $1.25 each and a drink for $1.75. How much money did he have left? (p. 378)

A $3.00   **C** $15.75
B $4.25   **D** $16.75

Algebra: Find Perimeter

▶ **Learn**

IT ALL ADDS UP!   Dan drew a diagram of the playing field at Wrigley Field in Chicago. What is the perimeter of the playing field?

⚡ **MATH IDEA**   You can find the perimeter of any polygon by adding the lengths of its sides.

Estimate by rounding.

$400 + 400 + 200 + 0 + 200 + 200 = 1,400$

$$a + b + c + d + e + f = P$$
$$\downarrow \quad \downarrow \quad \downarrow \quad \downarrow \quad \downarrow \quad \downarrow \quad \downarrow$$

Find the sum. $390 + 377 + 246 + 25 + 232 + 155 = 1,425$

So, the perimeter of the playing field is 1,425 ft. The answer is close to the estimate, so the answer is reasonable.

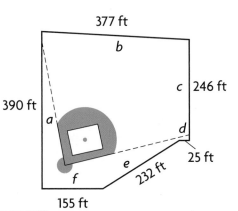

HANDS ON

Activity

MATERIALS: metric ruler

- Draw a square, a rectangle, a trapezoid, and a parallelogram. Make a table for your data.

FIGURE	SIDE 1	SIDE 2	SIDE 3	SIDE 4	P	FORMULA
Square						

- Measure and record the lengths of the sides of each quadrilateral. Then record each perimeter.

- For each quadrilateral, describe the relationship between the lengths of the sides and the perimeter. Then generate a formula for finding the perimeter and record it.

- Draw and measure another square, rectangle, trapezoid, and parallelogram. Use your formulas to find the perimeters.

▲ **Built in 1914, Wrigley Field is an old-fashioned baseball park.**

You can use the following formulas to find perimeter.

Rectangles
l = length w = width
$P = (2 \times l) + (2 \times w)$
$P = (2 \times 12) + (2 \times 8)$
$P = 40$
Perimeter: 40 cm

12 cm

8 cm

Regular Polygons
s = side
P = (number of sides) $\times s$
$P = 6 \times s$
$P = 6 \times 2$
$P = 12$
Perimeter: 12 ft

2 ft

Check

1. **Write** three formulas you could use to find the perimeter of a square park measuring 150 ft by 150 ft.

Find the perimeter of each polygon.

2. 12 in. / 12 in. (square)

3. 4 cm, 5 cm, 3 cm (triangle)

4. 3 ft, 6 ft, 6 ft, 5 ft (trapezoid)

5. 5 m, 4 m, 3 m, 2 m, 2 m, 2 m

Practice and Problem Solving ⟩ Extra Practice, page 556, Set A

Find the perimeter of each polygon.

6. 10 cm, 3.5 cm (rectangle)

7. 6 in., 6 in., 6 in. (triangle)

8. 12 ft, 12 ft, 12 ft, 12 ft, 12 ft (pentagon)

9. 18 m, 12 m, 12 m, 6 m, 6 m, 6 m, 6 m

10. 4.5 ft, 4.5 ft, 3.6 ft, 7 ft, 2.2 ft

11. 5 yd, 9 yd (parallelogram)

12. 6 in., 6 in., 12 in., 10 in., 2 in., 2 in.

13. $3\frac{1}{2}$ ft, $4\frac{3}{4}$ ft, $2\frac{1}{6}$ ft

USE DATA   For 14, use the figures.

14. Compare the shapes of Figures 1 and 2. Then compare the perimeter of Figure 1 to the total perimeter of *A* and *B* in Figure 2. Which perimeter is greater?

15. ✎ **Write About It** The perimeter of a triangle is 30 cm, and two of its sides are 10 cm and 7 cm long. Explain how to find the length of its third side.

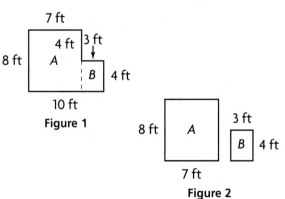

7 ft
4 ft, 3 ft
8 ft, *A*
B, 4 ft
10 ft
Figure 1

8 ft, *A*, 3 ft
B, 4 ft
7 ft
Figure 2

Mixed Review and Test Prep

Find the sum or difference. (p. 46)

16. 65,361
       +22,842

17. 25,605
       − 4,627

18. Sam drove 225 miles at an average speed of 54 miles per hour. Did he drive less than 4 hours? (p. 212)

19. Write $\frac{4}{5}$ as a decimal. (p. 328)

20. **TEST PREP**   Joan has half a pizza. If she gives $\frac{1}{5}$ of it to Bob, what fraction of the pizza will she have left? (p. 356)

   A $\frac{9}{10}$ **B** $\frac{4}{5}$ **C** $\frac{2}{5}$ **D** $\frac{1}{10}$

Problem Solving Skill
Make Generalizations

UNDERSTAND ▷ PLAN ▷ SOLVE ▷ CHECK ▷

Quick Review

Find the perimeter of
each regular polygon.

1. 6 cm   **2.** 3 yd

3. 4 ft   **4.** 2 cm

5. 5 m

GENERALLY SPEAKING . . .   The Luxor Hotel in Nevada
and the Great Pyramid in Egypt are the same shape. The
Great Pyramid is a square pyramid. Each side of its base is
756 feet long. The perimeter of the base of the hotel is
600 feet less than the perimeter of the base of the Great
Pyramid. What is the perimeter of the base of the hotel?

Sometimes you need to *make generalizations* to solve a
problem. When you generalize, you make a statement that
is true about a whole group of similar situations or objects.

▲ **The Great Pyramid in Giza, Egypt**

▲ **The Luxor Hotel in Nevada**

What You Know	Generalization	Conclusion
The Great Pyramid is a square pyramid. The Luxor Hotel is the same shape.	Square pyramids have square bases.	The hotel has a square base.
Each side of the base of the Great Pyramid is 756 feet long.	The perimeter of a square is 4 × length of one side.	The perimeter of the base of the Great Pyramid is 4 × 756 ft, or 3,024 ft.
The perimeter of the base of the hotel is 600 feet less than the perimeter of the base of the Great Pyramid.	To find an amount less than a given amount, you subtract.	The perimeter of the base of the hotel is 3,024 ft − 600 ft, or 2,424 ft.

So, the perimeter of the base of the hotel is 2,424 feet.

Talk About It

• What are some generalizations you can make about a building that
is the same shape as the model at the right?

Make generalizations to solve.

1. Two brands of juice are packaged in congruent cylinders. The first brand contains 12 ounces of juice in each can. How many ounces are in a 6-pack of the second brand?

2. The Pyramid of Khafre is the second largest pyramid in Giza. It is the same shape as the Great Pyramid. The perimeter of its base is 2,816 feet. How long is each side of its base?

A plane figure has 4 congruent sides.

3. The perimeter of the figure is 6 centimeters. What is the length of each side?

   A 24 cm   C 3 cm
   B 12 cm   D 1.5 cm

4. One of the angles of the figure has a measure of 110°. What is the shape of the figure?

   F rectangle   H circle
   G square   J rhombus

Mixed Applications

USE DATA For 5–7, use the bar graph.

5. What is the difference in length between the longest leg bone and longest arm bone?

6. **REASONING** This bone's length has a 1 in the tens place and a 9 in the tenths place. It is not the second-longest bone. Which bone is it?

7. What is the range of the data displayed on the graph?

LONGEST BONES IN THE HUMAN BODY

Femur (thighbone) 19.88
Tibia (shinbone) 16.94
Fibula (outer lower leg) 15.94
Humerus (upper arm) 14.35
Ulna (inner lower arm) 11.10

Type of Bone

Length (in inches)

8. **FAST FACT • SOCIAL STUDIES** About 2,300,000 stone blocks were used to build the Great Pyramid. If each block weighed 2.5 tons, about how much did they weigh in all?

9. **REASONING** Keyshawn's tree house is 5 feet by 7 feet. His circular table has a radius of 3 feet. Will the table fit in his tree house? Explain.

10. I have a circular base. From the side I look like a rectangle. What figure am I?

11. My two parallel bases are congruent. I have 3 other faces. What figure am I?

12. **? What's the Question?** The printer estimated it would cost $0.14 per brochure to print 1,000 one-color brochures. The answer is $140.

13. Write a problem using the data in the bar graph above.

LESSON 4

HANDS ON

Algebra: Circumference

Quick Review

1. $1.2 \div 3$
2. $2.4 \div 8$
3. $3.5 \div 7$
4. $0.81 \div 9$
5. $0.56 \div 8$

VOCABULARY

circumference

MATERIALS
metric ruler, string, cans

▶ **Explore**

Carla wants to find the distance around a can for a crafts project. The distance around a circular object is its **circumference**.

Find the circumference and diameter of the can. Round your measurements to the nearest tenth of a centimeter.

← diameter

Activity

STEP 1

Wrap the string around a can.

STEP 2

Use the ruler to measure the length of the string. This is the circumference (*C*) of the can.

STEP 3

Trace the base of the can, and measure the diameter (*d*) of the circle.

- Divide the circumference by the diameter. How many times as long as the diameter is the circumference?

Try It

Use three different size cans. Follow the steps above. Copy and complete the table. Round each quotient to the nearest hundredth of a centimeter.

Circle	Circumference (C)	Diameter (d)	c ÷ d
Example	15.7 cm	5 cm	
A			
B			

What do you do next to find the relationship between the circumference and the diameter?

- Use your results to describe the ratio between the circumference and the diameter of a circle.

554

Connect

The ratio of the circumference to the diameter of a circle, $C : d$, is called pi (π). The approximate decimal value of π is 3.14.

So, when you know the diameter, use the formula at the right to find the circumference.

$$C = \pi \times d$$

circumference $\approx$ 3.14 $\times$ diameter

$\approx$ means "is approximately equal to"

Examples Find the circumference to the nearest tenth.

A

4 in.

$C = \pi \times d$
$C \approx 3.14 \times 4$
$C \approx 12.56$
The circumference is about 12.6 in.

B

12.5 cm

$C = \pi \times d$
$C \approx 3.14 \times 12.5$
$C \approx 39.35$
The circumference is about 39.3 cm.

Practice and Problem Solving

For 1–3, complete the table.

	Object	C	d	C ÷ d
1.	spool	9.4 cm	3 cm	▪
2.	mug	28.3 cm	▪	3.14
3.	CD	▪	12 cm	3.14

4. Marta is putting lace trim around a can for her project. The diameter of the can is 7.5 cm. How many centimeters of lace trim does she need?

To the nearest tenth, find the circumference of a circle that has

5. a diameter of 10 cm.

6. a diameter of 17.8 ft.

7. a radius of 6 in.

8. The diameter of Bobby's cup is 8 cm. He wants to put two rows of red tape around the cup. How many centimeters of tape does he need?

9. Vocabulary Power The Greek word parts *dia-* and *metron* mean "across" and "to measure." What math word comes from the combination of these word parts?

10. **? What's the Error?** Madeleine says that to find the circumference of a quarter, you multiply pi by the radius. Is she correct? Explain.

11. REASONING The radius of the Earth is about 3,960 miles. About how long is the equator?

Mixed Review and Test Prep

12. $68,561 + 26,692$ (p. 46)

13. $10,008 - 8,976$ (p. 46)

14. Write $3\frac{10}{32}$ in simplest form. (p. 316)

15. Aaron has seventeen quarters. Express this in dollars and cents. (p. 164)

16. **TEST PREP** Which expression models this statement? Mrs. Ray took 2 vitamins 3 times a day for a week. (p. 246)

A $2 + 3$ **C** 2×3

B $2 \times 3 \times 7$ **D** $2 + 3 + 7$

≡FAST FACT • SCIENCE
Central Park, located in the center of Manhattan Island, New York, is home to 275 of the more than 800 species of birds found in the United States.

PROBLEM SOLVING   The park is shaped like a rectangle that is 2.5 miles by 0.5 mile. What are the perimeter and area of Central Park? How does the area of Central Park compare to the areas of the parks in the graph?

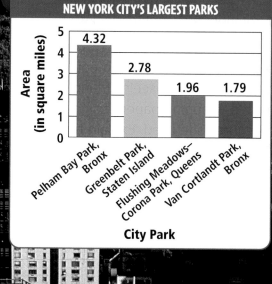

NEW YORK CITY'S LARGEST PARKS

Area (in square miles)

- Pelham Bay Park, Bronx — 4.32
- Greenbelt Park, Staten Island — 2.78
- Flushing Meadows–Corona Park, Queens — 1.96
- Van Cortlandt Park, Bronx — 1.79

City Park

Use this page to help you review and remember
important skills needed for Chapter 26.

✓ AREA

Find the area of each figure in square units.

1.

2.

3.

4.

5.

6.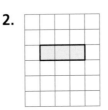

7.

8.

✓ MULTIPLICATION

Find the product.

9. $\begin{array}{r} 12 \\ \times\ 5 \\ \hline \end{array}$

10. $\begin{array}{r} 19 \\ \times\ 6 \\ \hline \end{array}$

11. $\begin{array}{r} 29 \\ \times 12 \\ \hline \end{array}$

12. $\begin{array}{r} 35 \\ \times 21 \\ \hline \end{array}$

13. $\begin{array}{r} 1.29 \\ \times\ \ 6 \\ \hline \end{array}$

14. $\begin{array}{r} 2.35 \\ \times\ \ 8 \\ \hline \end{array}$

15. $\begin{array}{r} 4.6 \\ \times 1.5 \\ \hline \end{array}$

16. $\begin{array}{r} 2.8 \\ \times 2.8 \\ \hline \end{array}$

17. $\begin{array}{r} 3.24 \\ \times\ 12 \\ \hline \end{array}$

18. $\begin{array}{r} 4.12 \\ \times\ 1.4 \\ \hline \end{array}$

VOCABULARY POWER ✓

REVIEW

perimeter [pə•ri′mə•tər] *noun*

The word *perimeter* comes from the Greek root words *peri,* meaning "around," and *metron,* meaning "measure." Explain how the root words help you understand the meaning of *perimeter.*

PREVIEW

area
base
height

 GO ON-LINE   www.harcourtschool.com/mathglossary

Estimate Area

Quick Review

1. 14 + 12   2. 16 + 6
3. 19 + 4   4. 13 + 8.5
5. 9 + 7.5

VOCABULARY

area

▶ **Learn**

BEAR CROSSING   A biologist drew a diagram showing the territory of a black bear in the Appalachian Mountains of Tennessee. How can you use the diagram to estimate the area of the bear's territory?

The **area** of a figure is the number of square units needed to cover it.

Activity

MATERIALS: grid paper

Copy the diagram of the territory, shown at the right. Each square on the grid is one square mile.

STEP 1

Count the number of full squares. There are 8 full squares.

STEP 2

Count the number of squares that are half or more than half full. There are 4. Do not count the squares that are less than half full.

STEP 3

Add the number of squares you counted.
8 + 4 = 12

So, the area of the bear's territory is about 12 sq mi, or 12 mi².

• Why is your answer an estimate, rather than the actual answer?

Example Estimate the area of the figure. Each square on the grid is 1 square yard.

There are 21 full blue squares.

There are 11 almost-full red squares.

There are 7 almost half-full yellow squares. Combine them to make $3\frac{1}{2}$ full squares.

Find the sum of the squares counted.
$$21 + 11 + 3\frac{1}{2} = 35\frac{1}{2}$$
So, the area of the figure is about $35\frac{1}{2}$ yd².

Check

1. **Explain** how to estimate the area of the figure.

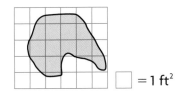

☐ = 1 ft²

Estimate the area of the shaded figure. Each square on the grid is 1 cm².

2.

3.

Practice and Problem Solving   Extra Practice, page 582, Set A

Estimate the area of the shaded figure. Each square on the grid is 1 yd².

4.

5.

6.

Estimate the area of the shaded figure. Each square on the grid is 1 cm².

7.

8.

9.

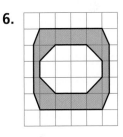

10. In the diagram of Heather's two flower-garden designs, each grid square represents 1 square foot. Estimate the total area of Heather's two gardens.

Mixed Review and Test Prep

11. $23.03 - 6.65$
(p. 48)

12. $5.2 + 4.88$
(p. 48)

13. 4.82×0.23
(p. 170)

14. 3.6×0.04
(p. 170)

15. **TEST PREP** Which is NOT equivalent to 0.75? (p. 328)

A $\frac{3}{4}$ B $\frac{9}{12}$ C $\frac{2}{3}$ D $\frac{6}{8}$

Algebra: Area of Squares and Rectangles

▶ **Learn**

MAKING PLANS!   In art class, Holly and Jake are designing floor plans for a house. In her floor plan, Holly designs her room to be 10 feet by 8 feet. In Jake's floor plan, his room is 9 feet by 9 feet. The rooms have the same perimeters. Are the areas the same?

You can make models to find the area of squares and rectangles.

HANDS ON

Activity

MATERIALS: grid paper
Let each square on the grid be 1 square foot.

STEP 1

Draw a rectangle 8 squares by 10 squares and shade it. Count the number of shaded grid squares.

STEP 2

Draw a square 9 squares by 9 squares and shade it. Count the number of shaded grid squares.

STEP 3

Compare the areas of the two rooms.

Area of Holly's room = 80 ft^2
Area of Jake's room = 81 ft^2
80 ft^2 < 81 ft^2

Technology Link

More Practice: Harcourt Mega Math Ice Station Exploration, *Polar Planes*, Level R

So, the areas of the rooms are not the same. Jake's room has the greater area.

• For each figure, look at the relationship between its area and its length and width. Write a formula you could use to find the areas.

Formulas

You can also use formulas to find the areas of rectangles and squares.

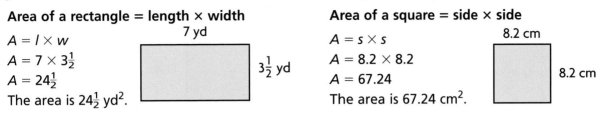

Area of a rectangle = length × width

$A = l \times w$

$A = 7 \times 3\frac{1}{2}$

$A = 24\frac{1}{2}$

The area is $24\frac{1}{2}$ yd².

7 yd

$3\frac{1}{2}$ yd

Area of a square = side × side

$A = s \times s$

$A = 8.2 \times 8.2$

$A = 67.24$

The area is 67.24 cm².

8.2 cm

8.2 cm

- Write a formula for the area of a square by using exponents.

You can find the area of some polygons by separating them into two or more different polygons.

Look at the drawing of Mr. Kelly's farm. It is divided into a square and a rectangle. How does the area of the combined field compare with the sum of the areas of the divided fields?

1 km

0.6 km

0.8 km

0.6 km

0.6 km

| COMBINED FIELD | DIVIDED FIELDS | |
	Rectangle	Square
Area	**Area**	**Area**
$A = (1 \times 0.8) + (0.6 \times 0.6)$	$A = (1 \times 0.8)$	$A = (0.6 \times 0.6)$
$A = 0.8 + 0.36 = 1.16$	$A = 0.8$	$A = 0.36$
The area is 1.16 km².	The area is 0.8 km².	The area is 0.36 km².

Sum of the areas: 0.8 km² + 0.36 km² = 1.16 km²

The area of the combined field is equal to the sum of the areas of the divided fields.

- Find the perimeters of the combined field and both of the divided fields. How does the perimeter of the combined field compare to the sum of the perimeters of the divided fields? If the perimeters are different, explain why.

 Check

1. **Explain** how the formula for the area of a rectangle can be used to find the area of a square.

Find the area of each figure.

2. 6 in.

6 in.

3. 13 m

8.5 m

4. 4 cm

6 cm

6 cm

12 cm

6 cm

10 cm

5. 8 ft

8 ft

4 ft

12 ft

LESSON CONTINUES ▶

Find the area of each figure.

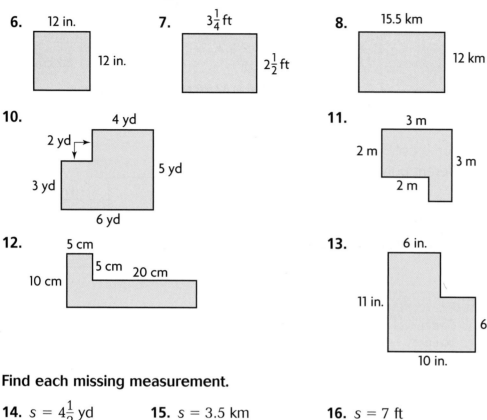

6. 12 in. / 12 in.

7. $3\frac{1}{4}$ ft / $2\frac{1}{2}$ ft

8. 15.5 km / 12 km

9. 32 mi / 32 mi

10. 4 yd / 2 yd / 5 yd / 3 yd / 6 yd

11. 3 m / 2 m / 3 m / 2 m

12. 5 cm / 5 cm / 20 cm / 10 cm

13. 6 in. / 11 in. / 6 in. / 10 in.

Find each missing measurement.

14. $s = 4\frac{1}{2}$ yd
$A = \blacksquare$

15. $s = 3.5$ km
$A = \blacksquare$

16. $s = 7$ ft
$A = \blacksquare$

17. $s = 1.25$ m
$A = \blacksquare$

18. $l = 3.2$ m
$w = 4$ m
$A = \blacksquare$

19. $l = \blacksquare$
$w = 7.2$ cm
$A = 28.8$ cm^2

20. $l = 2\frac{2}{3}$ ft
$w = 4\frac{1}{4}$ ft
$A = \blacksquare$

21. $P = 24$ yd
$l = 8$ yd
$w = \blacksquare$

$A = \blacksquare$

Use a centimeter ruler to measure each figure. Find the area and perimeter.

22.

23.

24. ✎ **Write About It** How can the formula for the area of a square be used to find the area of a rectangle that is 12 ft by 24 ft? Explain.

25. REASONING If you double the length of a rectangle, how does that affect its area? **What if** you double the width and the length?

26. How many 1-ft^2 tiles are needed to cover a 15 ft $\times$ 25 ft patio?

27. REASONING If you double the length of a square, how does that affect its area?

28. Jan's living room wall is 10 ft wide. She wants to buy 3 bookcases that are each 48 in. wide. Can all of the bookcases be placed against the wall? Explain.

29. Pam has a board that is 7 ft long. She needs to cut the board into $1\frac{3}{4}$-ft sections. How many cuts will she have to make?

Mixed Review and Test Prep

30. 7.3 (p. 170)
$$\times 4.8$$

31. 4.8 (p. 170)
$$\times 6.3$$

32. What are the factors of 56? (p. 278)

33. Order $^+3$, $^-4$, $^+7$, $^-7$ from least to greatest. (p. 484)

34. Penny needs $\frac{3}{4}$ yd of ribbon to make a costume. She has $\frac{3}{8}$ yd. How much more ribbon does she need? (p. 356)

35. $5\frac{2}{5} + 6\frac{4}{5}$ (p. 368)

36. Round 7.35 to the nearest tenth. (p. 40)

37. **TEST PREP** What is $4\frac{3}{4}$ written as a decimal? (p. 328)

A 4.25   **C** 4.50
B 4.34   **D** 4.75

38. **TEST PREP** Which are the least and the greatest fractions in this list? (p. 322)

$$\frac{7}{4}, \frac{8}{7}, \frac{6}{3}, \frac{11}{9}, \frac{5}{5}, \frac{7}{2}, \frac{2}{8}, \frac{9}{6}$$

F $\frac{2}{8}$; $\frac{7}{2}$ **H** $\frac{2}{8}$; $\frac{8}{7}$
G $\frac{6}{3}$; $\frac{11}{9}$ **J** $\frac{2}{8}$; $\frac{9}{6}$

Problem Solving   Thinker's Corner

COMPARE THE SQUARES   You can use the strategy *draw a diagram* to compare units of area within the customary system. How many square feet are there in 1 square yard?

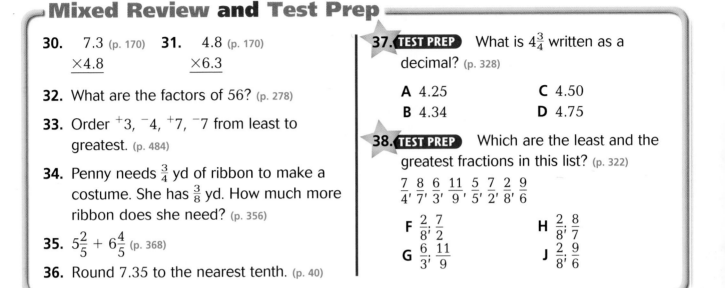

STEP 1
Draw a square with sides labeled 1 yard.

1 yd
1 yd

STEP 2
Divide the square into 3 rows of 3 squares to represent each side in feet. (Remember: 1 yd = 3 ft)

3 ft
3 ft

STEP 3
Count the squares.

3 ft
1	2	3
4	5	6
7	8	9
3 ft

So, there are 9 square feet in 1 square yard.

1. Draw a diagram to find the number of square inches in 1 square foot. Explain your thinking.

2. How many square centimeters are there in 1 square meter?

3. Which measurement gives a better idea about the area of a football field, 8,294,400 in.^{2} or 6,400 yd^2? Explain.

4. Ken needs to carpet a total of 414 ft^2 of his house. How many square yards of carpeting are needed?

Relate Perimeter and Area

Quick Review

Find the area of each rectangle.

1. 3 in. × 4 in.
2. 2 ft × 8 ft
3. 6 cm × 6 cm
4. 9 in. × 5 in.
5. 7 m × 11 m

▶ **Learn**

FRAME UP The students at Park School want to make a rectangular mosaic mural with the greatest possible area. If 12 ft of framing material is used, find the length and width of the mural.

HANDS ON

Activity 1 Make models to find the greatest possible area.

MATERIALS: geoboard, string

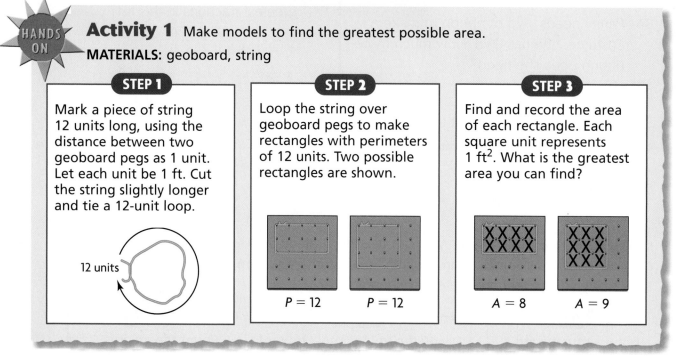

STEP 1	STEP 2	STEP 3
Mark a piece of string 12 units long, using the distance between two geoboard pegs as 1 unit. Let each unit be 1 ft. Cut the string slightly longer and tie a 12-unit loop.	Loop the string over geoboard pegs to make rectangles with perimeters of 12 units. Two possible rectangles are shown.	Find and record the area of each rectangle. Each square unit represents 1 ft². What is the greatest area you can find?

So, to have the greatest area, the mural should be a square with 3-ft sides. The area will be 3 ft × 3 ft, or 9 ft².

Example For a perimeter of 14 cm, find the length and width of the rectangle with the greatest area. Use whole numbers only.

Draw different rectangles with perimeters of 14 cm.

The greatest area is 12 cm². The length is 4 cm and the width is 3 cm.

MATH IDEA For a given perimeter, a square has the greatest area of all possible rectangles.

- If you could use the length 3.5 cm in the Example, what would the width be? What shape would the rectangle be?

The Least Perimeter

Now find the least perimeter of a rectangle with an area of 36 ft².

Activity 2

MATERIALS: square tiles

- Use square tiles to make different rectangles with areas of 36 ft². Let each tile be 1 ft².

- Copy and complete the table with your results. (HINT: To find all of the possible lengths and widths, find all the factors of 36.)

- As the rectangle gets closer to being a square, what happens to its perimeter?

Length ft	Width ft	Perimeter	Area
1	36	■	36 ft²
2	■	■	36 ft²
3	■	■	36 ft²
■	■	■	36 ft²
■	■	■	36 ft²

So, the least perimeter is 24 ft. The rectangle should be a square with sides of 6 ft.

MATH IDEA For a given area, a square has the least perimeter of all possible rectangles.

Examples

For the given area, find the length and width of the rectangle with the least perimeter. Use whole numbers only.

A Area: 49 in.²
You can make a square.

7 in.

7 in.   7 in. $P = 28$

7 in.

The perimeter is 28 in. The length and width are each 7 in.

B Area: 18 cm²

Make a table. Use factors of 18 as lengths and widths.

LENGTH	WIDTH	PERIMETER	AREA
18 cm	1 cm	38 cm	18 cm²
9 cm	2 cm	22 cm	18 cm²
6 cm	3 cm	18 cm	18 cm²

The least perimeter is 18 cm. The length is 6 cm and the width is 3 cm.

Check

1. **Explain** what happens to the area of a rectangle with a given perimeter as it gets closer to being a square.

For the given perimeter, find the length and width of the rectangle with the greatest area. Use whole numbers only.

2. 32 cm   **3.** 26 in.   **4.** 18 yd   **5.** 44 m   **6.** 60 cm

LESSON CONTINUES

For the given area, find the length and width of the rectangle with the least perimeter. Use whole numbers only.

7. 9 m^2 **8.** 20 ft^2 **9.** 12 cm^2 **10.** 64 in.^{2} **11.** 100 cm^2

Practice and Problem Solving   Extra Practice, page 582, Set C

For the given perimeter, find the length and width of the rectangle with the greatest area. Use whole numbers only.

12. 10 cm   **13.** 20 m   **14.** 22 in.   **15.** 42 ft   **16.** 30 yd

For the given area, find the length and width of the rectangle with the least perimeter. Use whole numbers only.

17. 8 cm^2 **18.** 30 m^2 **19.** 40 yd^2 **20.** 15 in.^{2} **21.** 81 ft^2

22. ALGEBRA Copy and complete the table. The perimeter is 8 m. Describe any pattern you see.

Length (in m)	0.5	1	1.5	2	2.5	3	3.5
Width (in m)	■	■	■	■	■	■	■
Area (in m^2)	■	■	■	■	■	■	■

23. REASONING If you increase the length of a rectangle with a perimeter of 20 ft, what has to happen to its width to keep the perimeter the same?

24. ? What's the Error? Bud says that with a given perimeter, the rectangle with the greatest length has the greatest area. Describe his error.

25. Using 48 feet of fencing, what is the greatest area that can be fenced? the least area? (Use whole numbers.)

26. Write a problem about a soccer field with dimensions of 110 m by 75 m.

USE DATA For 27–28, use the bar graph.

27. A pheasant flies 9 miles per hour slower than a common crane. How fast does a pheasant fly?

28. How long would it take a mallard to travel 100 mi?

29. FAST FACT • SCIENCE The eighth fastest bird is the oystercatcher. It can fly 58 km per hour. About how many miles per hour can it fly? (HINT: 1 km is about 0.62 mi.)

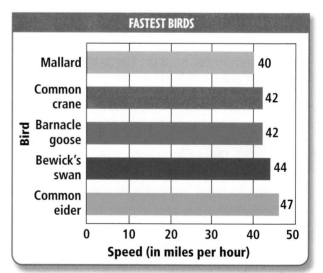

FASTEST BIRDS

Bird	Speed (in miles per hour)
Mallard	40
Common crane	42
Barnacle goose	42
Bewick's swan	44
Common eider	47

30. Emily's dad sells eggs at the Farmer's Market. He had 1,680 eggs. He sold $\frac{2}{5}$ of the eggs on Saturday and $\frac{1}{4}$ of the remainder on Sunday. How many eggs did he sell? How many dozens is that?

31. A playground has a perimeter of 100 m. It has the greatest possible area for a playground with that perimeter. What are the length and width of the playground?

Mixed Review and Test Prep

32. $4)\overline{3.68}$ (p. 232)　**33.** $8)\overline{8.64}$ (p. 232)

34. What kind of angle measures greater than 90 degrees and less than 180 degrees? (p. 428)

35. $\frac{1}{3} + \frac{3}{8}$ (p. 356)

36. **TEST PREP** Which of the following is NOT a measurement of length?

(pp. 522, 526, 534)

A meter

B liter

C foot

D kilometer

USE DATA For 37–38, use the table.

JIM'S BOWLING SCORES					
Game	1	2	3	4	5
Score	88	96	81	74	77

37. What is Jim's mean score? (p. 100)

38. What are the range and median for his scores? (pp. 96, 102)

39. **TEST PREP** Nan bought an 11.5 pound watermelon that cost $0.50 per pound. How much did she pay? (p. 170)

F $5.55　　**H** $5.85

G $5.75　　**J** $12.00

Problem Solving Thinker's Corner

You can use grid paper to show how the perimeter and area of a rectangle change when its length and width are doubled or halved.

Rectangle 1

STEP 1 Copy Rectangle 1. Draw a rectangle with sides twice as long as Rectangle 1. Label it Rectangle 2.

STEP 2 Draw a rectangle with sides half as long as Rectangle 1. Label it Rectangle 3.

STEP 3 Record the perimeter and area of each rectangle.

1. Compare the perimeters of Rectangle 2 and Rectangle 1. How do the areas compare?

2. Compare the perimeters of Rectangle 3 and Rectangle 1. How do the areas compare?

3. **ALGEBRA** The formula $A = 2l \times 2w$ shows how the area of a rectangle changes when the length and width are doubled. Write a formula to show the change when the length and width are halved.

Algebra: Area of Triangles

▶ **Learn**

SURF THE WIND

Dion is a windsurfer. He is making a model of his sailboard. The sail will have a base of 5 cm and a height of 10 cm. How much fabric does he need for the sail?

Find the *area* of the triangular sail.

The **height** is the length of a line segment perpendicular to the **base** of the triangle.

HANDS ON

Activity 1

MATERIALS: centimeter grid paper

Use grid paper and what you know about the area of a rectangle to find the area of a triangle.

STEP 1	STEP 2	STEP 3
Draw and shade a model of the triangular sail on grid paper.	Draw a rectangle around the triangle as shown. Find the area of the rectangle.	Cut out the rectangle. Cut it in half to make two triangles. Notice that they are congruent.

STEP 2

Rectangle:
$A = b \text{ (base)} \times h \text{ (height)}$
$A = 5 \times 10$
$A = 50$

STEP 3

So, the area of the triangle is half the area of the rectangle.

Triangle:
$A = \frac{1}{2} \times (b \times h)$
$A = \frac{1}{2} \times 50$
$A = 25$

The area of the triangle is 25 cm².

So, Dion needs 25 cm² of fabric to make the sail.

• How do the base and height of the sail relate to the length and width of the rectangle in Step 2?

Other Triangles

Activity 2

MATERIALS: grid paper

Some triangles are not right triangles. Find the area of the triangle below.

STEP 1	**STEP 2**	**STEP 3**
Draw and shade a model of the triangle inside a rectangle.	Cut out the rectangle and then the shaded triangle.	The unshaded parts of the rectangle fit exactly over the shaded triangle.

So, the area of the triangle is half the area of the rectangle.

MATH IDEA You can use the formula $A = \frac{1}{2} \times (b \times h)$ to find the area of any triangle.

Example

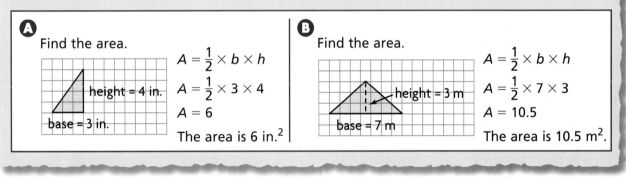

A

Find the area.

height = 4 in.
base = 3 in.

$A = \frac{1}{2} \times b \times h$
$A = \frac{1}{2} \times 3 \times 4$
$A = 6$

The area is 6 in.^{2}

B

Find the area.

height = 3 m
base = 7 m

$A = \frac{1}{2} \times b \times h$
$A = \frac{1}{2} \times 7 \times 3$
$A = 10.5$

The area is 10.5 m^2.

Check

1. **Explain** the relationship in Activity 1 between the area of the rectangle and the area of the triangle.

Find the area of each triangle.

2.

3.

4.

LESSON CONTINUES ▶

Find the area of each triangle.

5.

6.

7.

Find the area of each triangle.

8. 8 ft / 12 ft

9. 4 cm / 5 cm

10. 14 in. / 5 in.

Using the given measures, draw a right triangle and a triangle that is not a right triangle on grid paper. Then find the area.

11. base *(b)* = 10 cm

height *(h)* = 4 cm

Area *(A)* = ■

12. base *(b)* = 6 m

height *(h)* = 6 m

Area *(A)* = ■

13. base *(b)* = 7 yd

height *(h)* = 11 yd

Area *(A)* = ■

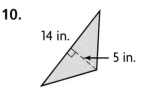 **ALGEBRA**   **Find the missing measurement for the triangle.**

14. $b = 2.6$ cm

$h = 4.7$ cm

$A = $ ■

15. $b = $ ■

$h = 10$ in.

$A = 40$ in.^{2}

16. $b = 5$ ft

$h = $ ■

$A = 15$ ft^2

17. $b = 3\frac{1}{2}$ yd

$h = 2$ yd

$A = $ ■

For 18–20, use the diagram of the Bermuda Triangle.

18. What is the perimeter of the Bermuda Triangle?

19. What are the base and height of the Bermuda Triangle?

20. What is the area of the Bermuda Triangle on the map?

21. ☀ **? What's the Error?**   A triangle has a base of 4 feet and a height of 7 feet. Barbara says its area is 28 ft^2. Describe and correct her error.

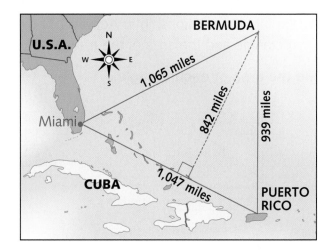

22. ✎ **Write About It** Explain the difference between an inch and a square inch. Draw an example of each.

23. REASONING Find the area of the figure.

3 cm

6 cm

6 cm

Mixed Review and Test Prep

For 24–26, use the bar graph. (p. 106)

24. How many people chose vanilla?

25. How many more people chose chocolate than strawberry?

26. TEST PREP How many more people chose chocolate than chose the other flavors?

   A 1 more   **C** 3 more

   B 2 more   **D** 4 more

FAVORITE ICE CREAM

Flavors: Chocolate, Strawberry, Vanilla

0 2 4 6 8 10 12 14 16
People

For 27–28, find the perimeter and area of each rectangle. (pp. 550, 564)

27. $s = 2.5$ ft

28. $l = \frac{1}{2}$ in.; $w = 3\frac{1}{2}$ in.

29. What is $\frac{2}{3}$ of 4? (p. 388)

30. TEST PREP The distance around a circle is called the ___?___ . (p. 554)

   F area   **H** circumference

   G diameter   **J** radius

Problem Solving Thinker's Corner

MATERIALS: tangram pattern

VISUAL THINKING As early as 4,000 years ago, the Chinese were playing with this math puzzle, called a *tangram*. The seven pieces, called *tans*, fit together to make hundreds of different shapes.

Cut out the tans from your pattern. Arrange them to make these shapes. Use all seven tans to form each shape.

1.

2.

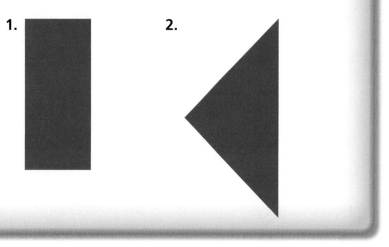

Algebra: Area of Parallelograms

Quick Review

Find the area of each figure.

1. 7 ft / 7 ft
2. 10 in. / 12 in.
3. 12 ft / 12 ft
4. 4 in. / 3 in.
5. 2 cm / 5 cm

▶ **Learn**

CATCH THE SUN Mecha is making a model of a stained-glass window out of colored tissue paper. How much paper does she need for each small parallelogram?

The lengths of the base and height are shown below. Find the area of one parallelogram.

height = 5 cm

base = 11 cm

Remember

A *parallelogram* is a quadrilateral with parallel and congruent opposite sides.

A *rhombus* is a parallelogram with all sides congruent.

HANDS ON

Activity

MATERIALS: centimeter grid paper, scissors

Use grid paper and what you know about the area of a rectangle to find the area of a parallelogram.

STEP 1

Copy the parallelogram and cut it out. Draw a line segment to form a right triangle as shown.

STEP 2

Cut out the right triangle on the left, and move it to the right of the parallelogram to form a rectangle.

STEP 3

The rectangle has the same area as the parallelogram. Count the grid squares to find its area.

5 cm

11 cm

There are 5 rows of 11 squares, or 55 squares.

So, Mecha needs 55 cm² of tissue paper to make each small parallelogram.

• How do the base and height of the parallelogram in Step 1 relate to the length and width of the rectangle in Step 3?

Use a Formula

MATH IDEA The area of a parallelogram is equal to the area of a rectangle with the same base (length) and height (width).

Area of a rectangle = length × width $A = l \times w$

Area of a parallelogram = base × height $A = b \times h$

Examples

A Find the area.

$A = b \times h$

$A = 9 \times 6$

$A = 54$

The area is 54 cm².

B Find the area.

$A = b \times h$

$A = 7.3 \times 3.5$

$A = 25.55$

The area is 25.55 m².

▶ Check

1. **Compare** the areas of a rectangle with a length of 6 cm and a width of 4 cm and a parallelogram with a base of 6 cm and a height of 4 cm.

Write the base and the height of each figure.

2.

3.

4.

ALGEBRA Find the missing dimension for each parallelogram. Use grid paper if necessary.

5. base *(b)* = ■ cm

    height *(h)* = 5 cm

    Area *(A)* = 20 cm²

6. base *(b)* = 11 ft

    height *(h)* = ■ ft

    Area *(A)* = 88 ft²

7. base *(b)* = ■ in.

    height *(h)* = 12 in.

    Area *(A)* = 36 in.²

Find the area of each parallelogram.

8.

3 ft

4 ft

9.

3 m

8 m

10.

5 in.

5 in.

LESSON CONTINUES

Write the base and the height of each figure.

11.

12.

13.

Find the area of each parallelogram.

14.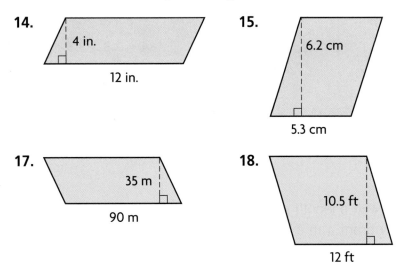
4 in.
12 in.

15.
6.2 cm
5.3 cm

16.
$4\frac{1}{2}$ ft
$2\frac{1}{2}$ ft

17.
35 m
90 m

18.
10.5 ft
12 ft

19.
$2\frac{1}{4}$ in.
$\frac{3}{4}$ in.

Find the missing dimension for each parallelogram.
Use grid paper if necessary.

20. base (b) = 3.5 cm

height (h) = 8.2 cm

Area (A) = ■

21. base (b) = ■

height (h) = 12 in.

Area (A) = 24 in.²

22. base (b) = 4 ft

height (h) = ■

Area (A) = 28 ft²

23. **? What's the Error?** The base of a parallelogram is 7 cm and the height is 6 cm. Tom says the area is 21 cm².

24. **? What's the Question?** The base of a parallelogram is 8 ft. The area is 32 ft². The answer is 4 ft.

25. **REASONING** Can you find the area of this parallelogram with the given measurements? Explain.

6 in.
3 in.   3 in.
6 in.

26. Write About It Describe the relationships shown in this Venn diagram.

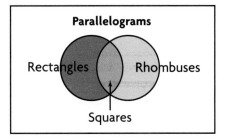
Parallelograms
Rectangles   Rhombuses
Squares

27. **REASONING** The base of a parallelogram is two times its height. If the base is 10 in., what is the area?

28. Vocabulary Power A dimension of a figure can be its length, width, or height. A line segment is a figure with one dimension, length. List examples of figures with two and three dimensions. Name the dimensions of each figure.

29. Lin's stained-glass model is a rectangle that is 18 in. by 12 in. She divides the model into four congruent triangles. How many square inches of tissue paper does she need for each triangle?

Mixed Review and Test Prep

For 30–32, use the pictograph. (p. 106)

WEEKLY MEDIA USE IN THE UNITED STATES

Television	
Radio	
Internet	
Newspapers and Magazines	

Each ▦ = 2 hours.

30. How many hours are spent listening to a radio each week?

31. How many more hours are spent watching television than reading newspapers and magazines?

32. **TEST PREP** Which is the number of hours spent listening to a radio in 6 weeks?

  A 12 hr   **B** 18 hr   **C** 60 hr   **D** 72 hr

For 33–34, find the area of each triangle. (p. 572)

33. base = 4 cm; height = 3 cm

34. base = $\frac{1}{2}$ in.; height = $\frac{1}{2}$ in.

35. Round 1.999 to the nearest tenth. (p. 40)

36. $5\overline{)0.875}$ (p. 232)

37. **TEST PREP** The distance around a square is called the __?__. (p. 548)

  F area   **H** diameter
  G perimeter   **J** side

Problem Solving Thinker's Corner

DOUBLE IT You can use the area of a triangle to find the area of a parallelogram.

• Draw this parallelogram on grid paper.

• Cut the parallelogram on a diagonal to form 2 congruent triangles.

1. Find the area of one triangle.

2. How is the area of the triangle related to the area of the parallelogram?

3. Write a formula for the area of a parallelogram.

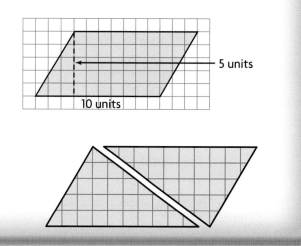

5 units

10 units

Problem Solving Strategy
Solve a Simpler Problem

PROBLEM Mike and Stephanie are designing a flat backdrop for their school play. How many square feet of backdrop will they use to make the house shown at the right?

UNDERSTAND

• What are you asked to find?

• What information will you use?

• Is there any information you will not use? Explain.

PLAN

• What strategy can you use to solve the problem?

You can *solve a simpler problem* by breaking the diagram of the house into simpler figures.

SOLVE

• How can you use the strategy to solve the problem?

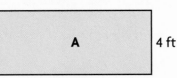

10 ft
Area = $l \times w$

6 ft
Area = $b \times h$

4 ft
Area = $\frac{1}{2} \times b \times h$

Find the area of each figure in the house. Then add all the areas.

Area of A (rectangle) $10 \times 4 = 40$
Area of C (parallelogram) $6 \times 3 = 18$
Area of D (triangle) $\frac{1}{2} \times (4 \times 3) = \underline{+\ 6}$
64

So, they need 64 ft² of backdrop to make the house.

CHECK

• How can you estimate to check your answer?

Problem Solving Practice

Strategies

Draw a Diagram or Picture
Make a Model or Act It Out
Make an Organized List
Find a Pattern
Make a Table or Graph
Predict and Test
Work Backward
Solve a Simpler Problem
Write an Equation
Use Logical Reasoning

Use a simpler problem to solve.

1. **What if** Mike cuts a 1 ft by 3 ft window from the house? What will the remaining area be?

2. Antoine made this design by wrapping string around nails on a piece of wood. How much string did he use?

3. The cartons of computer parts are labeled on the top and the front of each carton. How many labels are showing if there are 8 horizontal rows of 3 boxes each?

   A 24   **C** 32
   B 27   **D** 36

4. What is the area of the figure?

   F 28 sq units
   G 30 sq units
   H 32 sq units
   J 36 sq units

Mixed Strategy Practice

5. Mr. Bell's rectangular garden is 15 ft by 10 ft. Fencing costs $2.50 a foot. How much will he spend to fence in his entire garden?

6. Each can of paint covers 50 ft². How many cans does Vince need to paint a 12 ft by 16 ft backdrop for the play?

7. The diameter of the moon is about 3,500 kilometers. The diameter of the sun is 400 times the diameter of the moon. What is the circumference of the sun? the moon? (Use $\pi = 3.14$.)

8. Mr. Kelly shopped for art supplies. He bought 3 canvases for $10.98 each, a box of brushes for $6.50, and 8 bottles of paint for $5.69 each. He paid with five $20 bills. How much change did he receive?

9. Two equilateral triangles are put together to form a quadrilateral. Draw a diagram to find what kind of quadrilateral is formed.

10. Describe one way you could break apart a pentagon to find its area.

Extra Practice

Set A (pp. 562–563)

Estimate the area of the shaded figure. Each square is 1 cm².

1.

2.

Set B (pp. 564–567)

Find the area of each figure.

1. 4.3 cm, 6.25 cm

2. 8 ft, 8 ft

3. 3 ft, 12 ft, 6 ft, 10 ft, 3 ft

4. $3\frac{1}{3}$ yd, $3\frac{1}{3}$ yd

Set C (pp. 568–571)

For the given perimeter, find the length and width of the rectangle with the greatest area. Use whole numbers only.

1. 28 m   **2.** 16 yd   **3.** 12 cm   **4.** 8 ft   **5.** 36 in.   **6.** 46 yd

Set D (pp. 572–575)

Find the area of each triangle.

1. 13 ft, 7 ft

2. 7 in., 8 in.

3. 23 cm, 9 cm

Set E (pp. 576–579)

Find the area of each parallelogram.

1.

 7 yd, 10 yd

2.

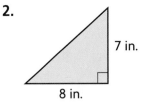 3 in., 8 in.

3.

 7 cm, 4 cm

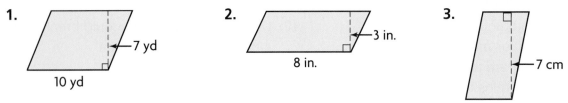

Review/Test

✓ CHECK VOCABULARY AND CONCEPTS

Choose the best term from the box.

> area
> base
> height
> perimeter

1. To find the area of a parallelogram, multiply its __?__ by its __?__. (p. 576)

2. The number of square units needed to cover the surface of an object is the __?__. (p. 562)

✓ CHECK SKILLS

Find the area of each figure. (pp. 564–567)

3. 9 m / 4.5 m

4. 13 yd / 13 yd

5. 25.8 cm / 12 cm

6. 22 mi / 22 mi

For the given area, find the length and width of the rectangle with the least perimeter. Use whole numbers only. (pp. 568–571)

7. 56 cm^2

8. 63 yd^2

9. 121 ft^2

10. 130 m^2

Find the area of each figure. (pp. 562–563, 572–579)

11. 3 in. / $3\frac{1}{2}$ in.

12. 6 m / 15 m

13. $\square = 1 \text{ cm}^2$

✓ CHECK PROBLEM SOLVING

Use a simpler problem to solve. (pp. 580–581)

14. By drawing 1 vertical line and 1 horizontal line, you can divide a sheet of paper into 4 sections. Into how many sections can you divide a sheet of paper by drawing 6 vertical and 6 horizontal lines?

1	2
3	4

15. Bill's Sign Shop makes road signs in this shape. What is the area of each sign?

12 m
4 m→
18 m

⭐Standardized Test Prep

⭐ GEOMETRY AND SPATIAL SENSE

> **TIP** **Decide on a plan.** See item 1. Use the strategy *solve a simpler problem*. Break the deck into a rectangle and a square and find the area of each.

1. Mr. Imanis is building a deck on the back of the house. This is the design.

What is the area of the deck?

A 72 square feet

B 265 square feet

C 415 square feet

D 420 square feet

2. Look at the diagram above. Mr. Imanis will put up a railing around the deck. To order enough wood for the railing, he needs to know the perimeter of the deck. Which is the perimeter of the deck?

F 36 feet **H** 72 feet

G 67 feet **J** 82 feet

3. **Explain It** There are 2 right triangles on the grid. Find the area of each. Explain how you found the area.

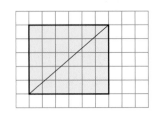

⭐ NUMBER SENSE, CONCEPTS, AND OPERATIONS

4. Art had 7 quarters, 3 dimes, 2 nickels, and 4 pennies in his pocket. This was the exact amount needed to buy which of the following items?

A 4-pack of lightbulbs, $1.99

B 6.4-oz toothpaste, $1.89

C 24-exposure film, $2.19

D 5 pens, $2.29

5. Matthew's mother sent him to the grocery store to buy these items.

64-oz bottle of apple juice: $1.79
Corn Crispies cereal: $2.89
Cleanz detergent: $5.49

If she gave him one bill to pay for the items, which is the smallest bill she could have given him?

F $1 **H** $10

G $5 **J** $20

6. **Explain It** Teri collects shells and uses them to decorate frames for mirrors. So far, she has used 15 shells on this frame.

ESTIMATE the total number of shells she will need for the whole frame. Explain your estimate.

⭐ ALGEBRAIC THINKING

7. Brian is reading a book that has 35 chapters. He read 2 chapters on Monday, 3 chapters on Tuesday, and 4 chapters on Wednesday. If he continues this reading pattern, on which day of the week will he finish the book?

A Thursday

B Friday

C Saturday

D Sunday

8. Martin made a pattern with toothpicks.

If he continues the pattern, how many toothpicks will he need to make 5 triangles?

F 13

G 11

H 9

J 8

9. When the bus arrived at the station, 37 people got off the bus and 29 remained on board. Which equation could be used to find p, the number of people on the bus before some people got off?

A $37 - 29 = p$

B $37 - p = 29$

C $p - 37 = 29$

D $29 + p = 37$

10. Explain It Explain why $x = 8$ is a solution of the inequality $x + 7 \leq 15$, but $x = 9$ is NOT a solution.

⭐ DATA ANALYSIS AND PROBABILITY

11. The stem-and-leaf plot below gives the number of games won by each of the National Basketball Association teams in the Eastern Conference for 2000–2001.

Stem	Leaves
1	5 9
2	5 6
3	0 2 6
4	1 3 6 7 8
5	0 2 6

2|5 means 25.

Which is the range of the number of games won?

F 41   **H** 35

G 37   **J** 31

12. Look at the stem-and-leaf plot above. Which is the median number of games won?

A 37.7

B 38.5

C 41

D 42

13. Explain It The table shows the number of students who walked to school and the number of students who rode to school for 3 days.

Day	1	2	3	4
Walked	6	3	6	■
Rode	20	24	19	■

Based on these data, predict the numbers of students who will walk and ride to school on Day 4. Explain how you made your predictions.

Surface Area and Volume

PROBLEM SOLVING Based on the measurements shown in the table, which tank has the smallest viewing window?

TANK DIMENSIONS			
Exhibit	Length (feet)	Width (feet)	Depth (feet)
Atlantic Shelf	$8\frac{3}{4}$	$6\frac{1}{2}$*	$7\frac{2}{3}$
Seahorse	3	$1\frac{1}{2}$*	$1\frac{1}{2}$*
Pacific Coral Reef	$9\frac{1}{6}$	$8\frac{3}{4}$	$7\frac{1}{2}$

*estimated measure

CHECK WHAT YOU KNOW

Use this page to help you review and remember important skills needed for Chapter 27.

✔ FACES, EDGES, AND VERTICES

Copy and complete the following table.

		Name of Figure	Number of Faces	Number of Edges	Number of Vertices
		Cube	6	12	8
1.		_?_	■	■	■
2.		_?_	■	■	■
3.		_?_	■	■	■
4.		_?_	■	■	■

✔ MULTIPLYING WITH THREE FACTORS

5. $4 \times 4 \times 4$ **6.** $(3 \times 5) \times 1$ **7.** $8 \times (5 \times 2)$ **8.** $10 \times 10 \times 10$

9. $7 \times (5 \times 4)$ **10.** $2 \times 5 \times 20$ **11.** $(3 \times 3) \times 9$ **12.** $6 \times (2 \times 15)$

13. $6 \times (4 \times 2)$ **14.** $3 \times 6 \times 2$ **15.** $7 \times 12 \times 4$ **16.** $(15 \times 3) \times 4$

VOCABULARY POWER

REVIEW

polyhedron [pol•i•hē′drən] *noun*

Polyhedron comes from the Greek root words *poli,* meaning "many," and *hedros,* meaning "face." Use this information to write your own definition of a polyhedron.

PREVIEW

net

surface area

volume

www.harcourtschool.com/mathglossary

Nets for Solid Figures

Quick Review

Name each polygon.

1. 2.

3. 4. 5.

VOCABULARY

net

▶ Learn

BOXED IN Boxes that contain products you buy in stores are made from patterns, or nets. A **net** is a two-dimensional pattern that can be folded into a three-dimensional polyhedron.

Here is one net for a cube-shaped box. A cube is formed by 6 congruent square faces: 1 for the top, 1 for the bottom, and 4 for the sides.

Top

4 sides

Bottom

Activity

HANDS ON

MATERIALS: 1-inch grid paper, scissors, tape

Use the net to make a cube-shaped box.

STEP 1

Copy the net onto grid paper and cut it out.

4 sides   Top →

Bottom →

STEP 2

Fold on the dashed lines.

STEP 3

Tape the edges together. Be sure there are no gaps and that none of the sides overlap.

Examples

A

base   base

6 faces

rectangular prism

B

5 faces

base

square pyramid

• How are the faces of a triangular prism and a triangular pyramid different?

Check

1. **Explain** why a cube is a prism.

Match each solid figure with its net. Write *a, b, c,* or *d.*

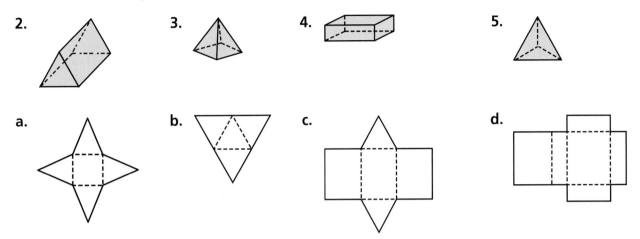

2. 3. 4. 5.

a. b. c. d.

Practice and Problem Solving   Extra Practice, page 600, Set A

Match each solid figure with its net. Write *a, b, c,* or *d.*

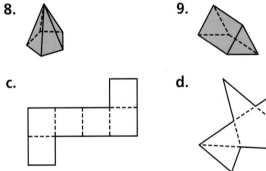

6. 7. 8. 9.

a. b. c. d.

10. Draw two different nets for a cube. Cut out the nets. Fold and tape the nets to form cubes.

11. Brittani had a piece of string $4\frac{1}{9}$ yards long. She cut it into $9\frac{1}{4}$-inch pieces. How many pieces did she get?

12. Find the area of one of the 5-in. × 7-in. bases of a rectangular prism.

13. ✎ **Write About It**   Explain how to make a net for a square pyramid.

Mixed Review and Test Prep

14. $3 \times \frac{1}{3}$ (p. 388)   15. $2\frac{2}{3} \times \frac{1}{2}$ (p. 390)

16. Evaluate 3^4. (p. 292)

17. What is the least common denominator of $\frac{1}{3}$ and $\frac{3}{4}$? (p. 354)

18. **TEST PREP**   Which is the value for *n* if $3\frac{1}{2} + n = 6$? (p. 368)

   A $n = 3\frac{1}{2}$ **C** $n = 2\frac{1}{2}$

   B $n = 2\frac{4}{5}$ **D** $n = 1\frac{1}{2}$

Surface Area

Learn

WRAPPED UP! You can use what you know about finding the area of a rectangle to find the surface area of a rectangular prism.

Surface area is the sum of the areas of the faces of a solid figure. Because surface area is a measurement of two dimensions, it is expressed in square units.

HANDS ON

Activity

MATERIALS: 1-centimeter grid paper, scissors, tape

To find the surface area of a rectangular prism, use its net.

STEP 1

Copy the net onto centimeter grid paper. Label the faces A–F as shown.

STEP 2

Cut out the net and fold on the lines to make the rectangular prism.

STEP 3

Unfold the prism and lay it flat. Find the area of each face, A–F. Record the areas in a table.

Face	Length	Width	Area = $l \times w$
A	5 cm	3 cm	15 cm²
B	■	■	■
C	■	■	■
D	■	■	■
E	■	■	■
F	■	■	■

STEP 4

Add the areas of the faces to find the surface area.

15 + 24 + 40 + 24 + 40 + 15 = 158

So, the surface area is 158 cm².

• Which faces have the same area? Why?

Check

1. Explain how you would find the surface area of a cube.

Use the net to find the area of each face. Then find the surface area of the prism.

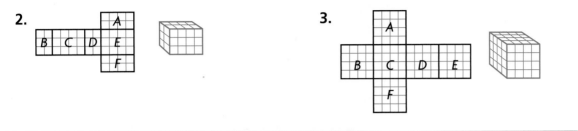

2.

3.

Practice and Problem Solving (Extra Practice, page 600, Set B)

Use the net to find the area of each face. Then find the surface area of the prism.

4.

5.

Find the surface area in cm². You may want to make the net.

6.

7.

8.

9. What is the surface area of a box 5 feet long, 3 feet wide, and 7 feet high?

10. What is the surface area of a box 11 cm long, 10 cm wide, and 12 cm high?

11. Ellie and Jon each wrapped a package that was a rectangular prism. Ellie's package was 2 ft by 3 ft by 4 ft. Jon's package was 3 ft by 3 ft by 3 ft. Whose package had the greater surface area? Explain how you know.

12. ESTIMATION Edward is painting a room that is $11\frac{3}{4}$ ft long, $10\frac{1}{2}$ ft wide, and 10 ft high. He will not paint the ceiling or the floor. If one can of paint covers 350 ft², will 2 cans of paint be enough? Use estimation to explain.

Mixed Review and Test Prep

13. 6×0.5 (p. 164) **14.** $\frac{4}{5} \div \frac{2}{5}$ (p. 408)

15. Write a decimal equivalent to 0.40. (p. 26)

16. Evaluate 2^3 and 3^2. (p. 292)

17. TEST PREP Which fraction is equivalent to $\frac{3}{4}$? (p. 314)

A $\frac{6}{9}$ **B** $\frac{6}{8}$ **C** $\frac{9}{10}$ **D** $\frac{10}{12}$

Algebra: Estimate and Find Volume

Quick Review

Find the area of each rectangle in square inches.
1. $l = 3$, $w = 4$
2. $l = 4$, $w = 5$
3. $l = 5$, $w = 5$
4. $l = 3$, $w = 6$
5. $l = 10$, $w = 9$

VOCABULARY
volume

▶ **Learn**

YO-YO FUN Alex is putting yo-yo boxes into a carton. By thinking about volume, he estimates that 60 yo-yo boxes will fit in the carton.

Volume is the amount of space a solid figure occupies. Volume is measured in *cubic units*. You can estimate the volume of a prism by visualizing how many cubes will fill it.

About 5 cubes fit along the length and about 3 cubes fit along the width. The bottom layer has about 15 cubes. There are about 4 layers of about 15 cubes each.

4 layers × 15 cubes = 60 cubes

So, about 60 yo-yo boxes will fit in the carton.

You can use cubes to find the volume of a rectangular prism.

HANDS ON

Activity

MATERIALS: centimeter cubes

1 cubic centimeter (cm³)

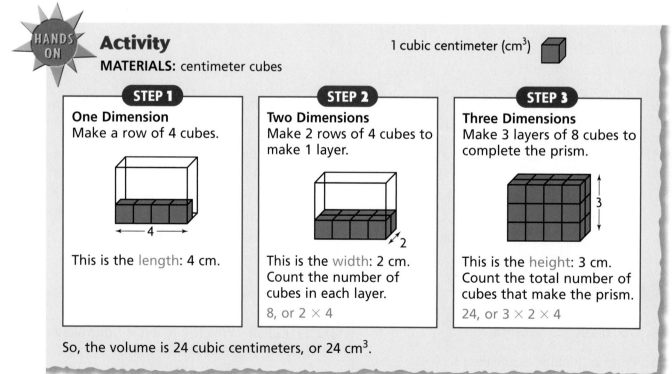

STEP 1

One Dimension
Make a row of 4 cubes.

This is the length: 4 cm.

STEP 2

Two Dimensions
Make 2 rows of 4 cubes to make 1 layer.

This is the width: 2 cm.
Count the number of cubes in each layer.
8, or 2 × 4

STEP 3

Three Dimensions
Make 3 layers of 8 cubes to complete the prism.

This is the height: 3 cm.
Count the total number of cubes that make the prism.
24, or 3 × 2 × 4

So, the volume is 24 cubic centimeters, or 24 cm³.

• Look at the dimensions of the rectangular prism. Write a formula you can use to find its volume.

Use a Formula

Instead of counting cubes, you can use a formula to find the volume of a rectangular prism:

Volume = length × width × height, or *V* = *l* × *w* × *h*

Technology Link

More Practice: Harcourt
Mega Math Ice Station
Explorations, *Frozen
Solids*, Level J

Examples

A

$V = l \times w \times h$
$V = 3 \times 2 \times 2$
$V = 12$

Volume is 12 units³.

B

10 in.
10 in.
10 in.

$V = l \times w \times h$
$V = 10 \times 10 \times 10$
$V = 1,000$

Volume is 1,000 in.³

C

You can use a calculator to compute volume.

5 cm
3 cm
6 cm

6 × 3 × 5 = 90

Volume is 90 cm³.

• Explain how to use rounding to estimate the volume of a prism that is 5.8 cm long, 4.2 cm wide, and 1.9 cm high.

If you know the volume of a rectangular prism and two of its dimensions, you can use the formula to find the unknown dimension.

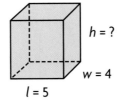

$h = ?$
$w = 4$
$l = 5$

Volume: 120 in.³

$V = l \times w \times h$
$120 = 5 \times 4 \times h$
$120 = 20 \times h$
$\dfrac{120}{20} = h$ The inverse of multiplication is division, so divide.
$6 = h$ The height is 6 in.

▶ Check

1. **Explain** how to estimate the volume of a cereal box in cubic inches.

Find the volume of each rectangular prism.

2.

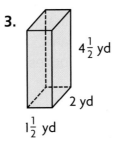

3.

$4\frac{1}{2}$ yd

2 yd

$1\frac{1}{2}$ yd

4.

3.5 cm

3.5 cm

3.5 cm

LESSON CONTINUES ▶

Find the volume of each rectangular prism.

5.

6.

7.

8.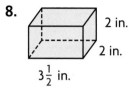
2 in.
2 in.
$3\frac{1}{2}$ in.

9.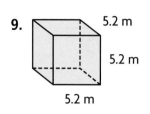
5.2 m
5.2 m
5.2 m

10.
10 ft
15 ft
11 ft

ALGEBRA Find the unknown measure.

11. $V = 60$ ft^3
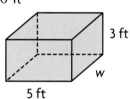
3 ft
w
5 ft

12. $V = 64$ m^3
8 m
2 m
l

13. $V = 144$ in.^{3}
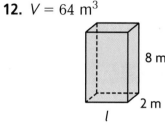
h
6 in.
12 in.

14. $l = 3$ in.
$w = 2$ in.
$h = 10$ in.
$V = $ ■

15. $l = 6$ yd
$w = 4$ yd
$h = $ ■
$V = 48$ yd^3

16. $l = 12$ ft
$w = $ ■
$h = 2$ ft
$V = 192$ ft^3

17. $l = $ ■
$w = 7$ m
$h = 5$ m
$V = 350$ m^3

For 18–20, use the drawings.

18. What is the volume of the small refrigerator? the height of the larger one?

19. How much area of the floor does each refrigerator cover?

20. Alan bought 2 small refrigerators. What is the difference between their combined volume and the volume of 1 large refrigerator?

20 in.
18 in.
19 in.
h
11,286 in.^{3}
18 in.
19 in.

21. **≡FAST FACT • SCIENCE** The total capacity of your lungs is about the same as the volume of a 10 in. × 6 in. × 5 in. box. What is the total capacity of your lungs?

22. Maria is packing boxes into a carton that is 4 in. × 6 in. × 3 in. The boxes are 2 in. × 1 in. × 1 in. How many boxes will fit in the carton?

23. A packing crate is $5\frac{1}{4}$ ft × $2\frac{7}{8}$ ft × $2\frac{1}{4}$ ft. Estimate the volume of the crate.

24. **Write a problem** that requires finding volume to solve.

25. REASONING Explain the difference between an inch, a square inch, and a cubic inch. Make a model of each.

26. Vocabulary Power A dimension of a figure is a measure of either length, width, or height. Draw an example of a one-, a two-, and a three-dimensional figure and explain each choice.

Mixed Review and Test Prep

USE DATA For 27–29, use the graph. (p. 106)

27. On which day was the lowest temperature recorded?

28. TEST PREP What was the low temperature on Wednesday?

    A 6°F   **C** 0°F

    B 5°F   **D** ⁻5°F

29. What was the difference between the low temperature on Monday and the low temperature on Tuesday?

30. $\frac{1}{4} + \frac{5}{6} + \frac{3}{8}$ (p. 356)

31. Write and evaluate an expression for this situation: Joe had 20 pens. He gave 2 students 3 pens each. How many pens are left? (p. 246)

32. TEST PREP A triangle with only two congruent sides is __?__. (p. 456)

    F isosceles   **H** parallel

    G scalene   **J** equilateral

Problem Solving Thinker's Corner

VISUAL THINKING Look at the models of a cubic inch and a cubic centimeter. You can think about models to help you compare different units of volume.

A cubic inch is larger than a cubic centimeter.

The volume of this marble box is 4 in. × 3 in. × 2 in., or 24 in.^{3}

Is the volume of the box greater than or less than 24 cm^3?

Since a cubic inch is greater than a cubic centimeter, 24 in.^{3} must be greater than 24 cm^3.

cubic inch   cubic centimeter

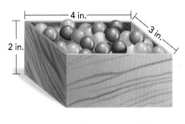

Choose the greater volume.

  1. 12 in.^{3} or 12 cm^3 **2.** 8 yd^3 or 8 m^3 **3.** 6 ft^3 or 6 yd^3

Measure Perimeter, Area, and Volume

Quick Review

1. 24 in. = ■ ft

2. 27 ft^2 = ■ yd^2

3. 2 yd = ■ in.

4. 3 m = ■ cm

5. 35 cm = ■ m

Learn

ANOTHER DIMENSION Geometric figures can be measured in one, two, or three dimensions. The unit you choose depends upon the number of dimensions being used.

Perimeter is the distance around a figure.	*Area* is the measure of the flat surface of a figure.	*Volume* is the measure of the space a figure occupies.
Its measure is in one dimension, *length*. Use linear units, such as in., ft, yd, mi, cm, m, or km.	Its measure is in two dimensions, *length* and *width*. Use square units, such as in.^{2}, ft^2, yd^2, mi^2, cm^2, m^2, or km^2.	Its measure is in three dimensions, *length*, *width*, and *height*. Use cubic units, such as in.^{3}, ft^3, yd^3, mi^3, cm^3, m^3, or km^3.

Activity

MATERIALS: 1-centimeter grid paper, centimeter ruler, centimeter cubes

STEP 1

On grid paper, draw a rectangle that is 3 cm by 4 cm. Measure or count to find the perimeter of the rectangle.

The perimeter, measured in linear units, is 14 cm.

STEP 2

Shade the squares to show the area of the rectangle.

The area, measured in square units, is 12 cm^2.

STEP 3

Use centimeter cubes to build a 3-layer prism on the rectangle. Find the volume of the prism.

The volume, measured in cubic units, is 36 cm^3.

• Explain how the units used to measure perimeter, area, and volume are different.

Check

1. **Describe** real-life situations in which you might need to find perimeter, area, and volume.

Tell the appropriate units for measuring each. Write *linear*, *square*, or *cubic*.

2. surface area   3. volume   4. perimeter   5. area

Tell the appropriate units for measuring each. Write *linear*, *square*, or *cubic*.

6. fence for a garden

7. tile for a floor

8. paper to cover a box

9. space in a refrigerator

Write the units you would use to measure each.

10. area of this rectangle

11. volume of this prism

12. perimeter of this figure

13. surface area of this figure

14. wood for an 8-in. by 10-in. picture frame

15. fabric covering a box, 5 cm × 3 cm × 2 cm

16. a 9-ft by 10-ft rug

17. space inside a box, 2 ft × 8 ft × 4 ft

Tom and his dad are making a toy box for Tom's little sister. Use the picture for 18–20.

18. Tom used tape to put two stripes around the toy box. What did he measure to find out how much tape he needed? How much tape did Tom use?

19. Tom said his dad's goal was for the toy box to have less than 25 ft^3 of space. What should Tom measure to see if they met the goal? How much space does the box have?

20. Tom painted the top, bottom, and sides of the outside of the toy box. A can of paint covers 20 ft^2. How many cans of paint did Tom need to paint the toy box? Explain.

21. **?** **What's the Error?** Joe's lunchbox is 10 in. long, 8 in. wide, and 3 in. high. He estimates the volume to be 240 in.^{2} Explain his error.

Mixed Review and Test Prep

22. Find the sum. 3.01 + 4.15 (p. 48)

23. 84 (p. 152)
×37

24. 209 (p. 152)
× 43

25. $7\frac{5}{6} - 3\frac{2}{3}$ (p. 372)

26. **TEST PREP** Evaluate $n \div 25$ if $n = 750$. (p. 246)

  A 20   **B** 25   **C** 30   **D** 35

Problem Solving Skill
Use a Formula

UNDERSTAND ▸ PLAN ▸ SOLVE ▸ CHECK

FILL IT UP! Mr. Lee plans to build a sandbox in his backyard that is 5 feet long, 4 feet wide, and $\frac{1}{2}$ foot high.

Use this table to help you decide which formula to use to solve each problem below.

RECTANGLE FORMULAS		
Want To Know	Find	Formula
Distance around an object	Perimeter	$P = (2 \times l) + (2 \times w)$
Number of square units needed to cover a flat surface	Area	$A = l \times w$
Space occupied by a solid figure	Volume	$V = l \times w \times h$

MATH IDEA To use a formula to solve a problem, first decide what you want to know. Then put your information in the formula and do the calculations.

Examples

A What length of 6-in. boards will Mr. Lee need to **surround** the sandbox?

He needs to find the *perimeter* of the sandbox.

Use a formula:

$P = (2 \times l) + (2 \times w)$

$P = (2 \times 5) + (2 \times 4)$

$P = 10 + 8 = 18$

He needs 18 feet of 6-in. boards to make the sides of the sandbox.

B How much of his yard will the sandbox **cover**?

He needs to find the *area* of the sandbox.

Use a formula:

$A = l \times w$

$A = 5 \times 4$

$A = 20$

The sandbox will cover 20 square feet of his yard.

C How much sand will he need to **fill** $\frac{3}{5}$ of the sandbox?

He needs to find $\frac{3}{5}$ of the *volume* of the sandbox.

Use a formula:

$V = l \times w \times h$

$V = 5 \times 4 \times \frac{1}{2}$

$V = 10$

Find $\frac{3}{5}$ of 10:

$\frac{3}{5} \times 10 = 6$

He needs 6 cubic feet of sand to fill $\frac{3}{5}$ of the sandbox.

• If you did not use formulas, how could you answer Examples *A–C*?

Problem Solving Practice

Use a formula to solve.

1. **What if** Mr. Lee decides to make the sandbox $\frac{3}{4}$ foot deep? How much sand will he need to fill $\frac{3}{5}$ of the sandbox?

2. Rachel's bedroom is 15 ft long and 12 ft wide. She is having wall-to-wall carpet installed. How many square yards of carpet does she need?

3. A playground area that is 66 ft long and 42 ft wide needs to be fenced. How much fencing will be needed?

4. Mrs. Lopez wants to store some boxes of winter clothes in a cabinet with inside dimensions slightly greater than 5 ft by 2 ft by 6 ft. Each box is 1 ft × 2 ft × 2 ft. How many boxes can she fit into the cabinet?

A regulation American football field is 120 yards long, including the end zones, and $53\frac{1}{3}$ yards wide. Each end zone is 10 yards deep and $53\frac{1}{3}$ yards wide.

5. What is the perimeter of the field?

    A $5,033\frac{1}{3}$ yd^2 **C** $346\frac{2}{3}$ yd^2

    B $5,033\frac{1}{3}$ yd   **D** $346\frac{2}{3}$ yd

6. What is the area of each end zone?

    F $306\frac{2}{3}$ yd^2 **H** $5,033\frac{1}{3}$ yd

    G $533\frac{1}{3}$ yd^2 **J** $53,033\frac{2}{3}$ yd^2

Mixed Applications

7. The veterinarian puts bird seed in a bin 15 in. × 5 in. × 6 in. How much bird seed can the bin hold?

8. A bag of fertilizer will cover an area of 100 ft^2. Will 4 bags be enough to cover a garden 25 ft × 18 ft?

9. Janine's book shelf is $4\frac{2}{3}$ ft tall. Her desk is $\frac{3}{4}$ as high as the book shelf. How high is Janine's desk?

10. **Write About It** Explain how you know whether to use the perimeter formula or the area formula in a problem.

11. **? What's the Question?** Mr. Lyle needs 66 yd^2 of ceiling tile for his basement. Each box of tiles contains 30 yd^2 of tile. The answer is 3 boxes.

12. Mr. Chu is unpacking some books from a box. There are 4 layers of books. Each layer has 3 rows with 3 books in each row. How many books are in the box?

Extra Practice

Set A (pp. 588–589)

Match each solid figure with its net. Write *a, b, c,* or *d.*

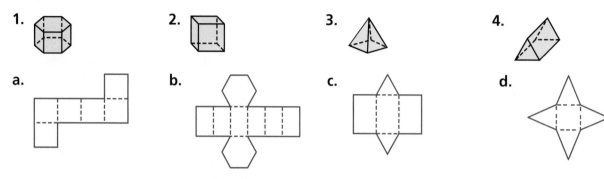

1.   **2.**   **3.**   **4.**

a.   **b.**   **c.**   **d.**

5. Which solid has more faces: a triangular pyramid or a square pyramid? Explain.

Set B (pp. 590–591)

Find the surface area in cm².

1.   **2.**   **3.**

4. How many square inches of paper are needed to cover a box that is 4 inches long, 10 inches wide, and 3 inches high?

Set C (pp. 592–595)

Find the unknown measure.

1. length = 8 ft
width = 2 ft
height = 3 ft
volume = ■

2. length = ■
width = 10 ft
height = 10 ft
volume = 1,000 ft³

3. length = 5.5 in.
width = 2 in.
height = 3 in.
volume = ■

4. Rick's fish tank has 10,640 cm³ of water in it. If the length is 38 cm and the width is 28 cm, what is the height of the water?

Set D (pp. 596–597)

Tell the appropriate units for measuring each. Write *linear, square,* or *cubic.*

1. room inside a space shuttle

2. fence for a play yard

3. carpet for a room

4. paper to cover a box

Review/Test

✓ CHECK VOCABULARY AND CONCEPTS

Choose the best term from the box.

| net |
| base |
| surface area |
| volume |

1. The measure of the space a solid figure occupies is __?__. (p. 592)

2. A two-dimensional pattern for a three-dimensional prism or pyramid is a __?__. (p. 588)

3. The sum of the areas of the faces of a solid figure is the __?__. (p. 590)

Match each solid figure with its net. Write *a*, *b*, or *c*. (pp. 588–589)

4.

5.

6.

a.

b.

c.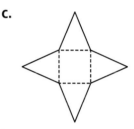

✓ CHECK SKILLS

Find the surface area in cm². (pp. 590–591)

7.

8.

Find the unknown measure. (pp. 592–595)

9. length = 3 yd
   width = 10 yd
   height = 17 yd
   volume = ■

10. length = 9 ft
    width = ■
    height = 8 ft
    volume = 504 ft³

Tell the appropriate units for measuring each. Write *linear*, *square*, or *cubic*. (pp. 596–597)

11. wood for a picture frame

12. fabric to cover a triangular prism

13. space in a closet

✓ CHECK PROBLEM SOLVING

Solve. (pp. 598–599)

14. The stereo packaging box is 3 ft long and 2.5 ft wide. What is the area of the base of the box?

15. The storage locker is 5 yd long, 3.5 yd high, and 6 yd wide. How much space is in the locker?

Standardized Test Prep

MEASUREMENT

1. The average length of a giraffe's tongue is 53.34 centimeters. What is the average length in millimeters?

  A   5.334 millimeters

  B   533.4 millimeters

  C   5,334 millimeters

  D   53,340 millimeters

> **TIP** **Decide on a plan.** See item 2. First find the dimensions of the area that includes the pool and the deck.

2. A deck surrounds a rectangular-shaped pool. The pool is 16 feet wide and 32 feet long. The deck is 4 feet wide. What is the area covered by the deck?

  F 208 square feet

  G 256 square feet

  H 448 square feet

  J 512 square feet

3. **Explain It** Mel has two boxes that are shaped like cubes. Box A has sides with lengths of 1 inch. Box B has sides with lengths of 2 inches. About 5 marbles fit in Box A. About how many marbles will fit in Box B? Explain how you know.

GEOMETRY AND SPATIAL SENSE

4. Which figure can be made from this net?

  A triangular pyramid

  B triangular prism

  C square pyramid

  D pentagonal prism

5. This drawing could be the top view of which solid?

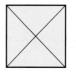

  F hexagonal prism

  G triangular prism

  H triangular pyramid

  J square pyramid

6. **Explain It** On a grid, graph the points (1,1), (4,1), (6,4) and (1,4). Connect the points in the order given and then connect (1,4) to (1,1). Classify the figure in as many ways as you can. Explain how you know how to classify the figure.

⭐ DATA ANALYSIS AND PROBABILITY

7. A post office clerk recorded these weights for some packages.

PACKAGE WEIGHTS						
Package	A	B	C	D	E	F
Weight (in ounces)	5	7	12	17	9	4

What is the mean weight of the packages?

A 6 ounces

B 8 ounces

C 9 ounces

D 13 ounces

8. A builder made a pictograph showing the number of new homes sold from April to June.

NEW HOME SALES

April	🏠 🏠 🏠
May	🏠 🏠
June	🏠 🏠 🏠 🏠

Key: Each 🏠 = 10 homes.

How many more houses were sold in June than in April?

F 40   **H** 20

G 25   **J** 15

9. Explain It Before an election for class president, you survey 50 boys and 50 girls in the fifth grade to find out which candidate each group plans to vote for. What kind of graph or plot would you choose to display the data you collect? Explain your choice.

⭐ ALGEBRAIC THINKING

10. The table shows how much Noelle earned baby-sitting and how much she saved each month for 4 months.

NOELLE'S EARNINGS AND SAVINGS				
	Jan	Feb	Mar	Apr
Earnings	$114	$96	$144	$156
Savings	$38	$32	$48	$52

If s represents Noelle's savings, which expression represents Noelle's earnings?

A $3 \times s$

B $s \div 3$

C $s + 76$

D $38 + s$

11. Ramon's dog is missing. He wants to make photocopies of a flyer to help find his dog. Copies cost $0.07 each for the first 100 copies and $0.04 for each additional copy. Which expression shows the cost for 150 copies of the flyer?

F $0.07 + (50 \times 0.04)$

G $150 \times (0.07 + 0.04)$

H $100 + (50 \times 0.04)$

J $(100 \times 0.07) + (50 \times 0.04)$

12. Explain It Describe this pattern.

1, 2, 2, 4, 8, 32 . . . .

Then write the next number in the pattern.

IT'S IN THE BAG

From Net to Solid

PROJECT Make a solid figure from a two-dimensional pattern.

Materials

- Box pattern
- Tagboard or large side of a cereal box
- Scissors
- Markers

Directions

1. Cut out the pattern. Place the pattern on the tagboard, and trace it. Cut out the tracing. *(Picture A)*

2. On the tagboard, use your scissors to carefully cut slits down the flap as shown. *(Picture B)*

3. Fold the rectangular flaps in toward the center, joining them at the slits. Then fold in the other flaps and secure them. *(Picture C)*

4. Measure the dimensions of the top, sides, and bottom of your solid figure.

5. Make other patterns for solid figures. Exchange the patterns with your classmates, and make the solid figures. Talk about how the figures are alike and different.

A

B

C

Challenge

Area of a Circle

To find the area of a circle, use the formula $A = \pi \times r^2$. The r in the formula represents the length of the radius of the circle. The approximate decimal value of π (pi) is 3.14.

To find the area of the circle, replace r with 5 and π with 3.14.

$A = \pi \times r^2 \qquad r = 5$

$A \approx 3.14 \times (5)^2$

$A \approx 3.14 \times 25$

$A \approx 78.5$ in.^{2}

The answer is expressed in square units because area is measured in square units.

Examples

A $\quad A = \pi \times r^2 \quad r = 7$

$A \approx 3.14 \times (7)^2$

$A \approx 3.14 \times 49$

$A \approx 153.86$

The area is about 154 cm^2.

7 cm

B $\quad A = \pi \times r^2 \quad r = 9$

$A \approx 3.14 \times (9)^2$

$A \approx 3.14 \times 81$

$A \approx 254.34$

The area is about 254 yd^2.

9 yd

Talk About It

• How do you determine what unit to use to express the area of a circle?

Try It

Find the area of the circle with the given radius. Use $\pi = 3.14$.

1. 4 in.
2. 6 cm
3. 8.5 ft
4. 10 mi

Find the radius of the circle with the given area.

5. 28.26 ft^2
6. 19.625 m^2
7. 254.34 in.^{2}
8. 379.94 cm^2

Study Guide and Review

VOCABULARY

Choose the best term from the box.

circumference
net
volume
radius
area

1. The distance around a circle is the __?__ . (p. 554)

2. A two-dimensional pattern that can be folded into a three-dimensional prism or pyramid is a __?__ . (p. 588)

3. The amount of space a solid figure occupies is its __?__ . (p. 592)

STUDY AND SOLVE

Chapter 24

Change linear units.

To change smaller units to larger units, divide.
200 cm = ■ m
200 ÷ 100 = 2 ← 100 cm = 1 m
So, 200 cm = 2 m.
To change larger units to smaller units, multiply.
3 ft = ■ in.
3 × 12 = 36 ← 1 ft = 12 in.
So, 3 ft = 36 in.

Change the unit. (pp. 528–531)

4. 5 ft = ■ in.

5. 15 yd = ■ ft

6. 6,160 yd = ■ mi

7. 7 m = ■ cm

8. 2.5 km = ■ m

9. 45 mm = ■ cm

Change units of capacity and mass.

To change smaller units to larger units, divide.
8 qt = ■ gal
8 ÷ 4 = 2 ← 4 qt = 1 gal
So, 8 qt = 2 gal.
To change larger units to smaller units, multiply.
2 kg = ■ g
2 × 1,000 = 2,000 ← 1 kg = 1,000 g
So, 2 kg = 2,000 g.

Change the unit. (pp. 532–535)

10. 7 kL = ■ L

11. 5 qt = ■ pt

12. 64 oz = ■ lb

13. 4 kg = ■ g

14. 300 mL = ■ L

15. 6 qt = ■ gal

Chapter 25

Find the perimeter of a polygon.

Find the perimeter.
$P = (2 \times l) + (2 \times w)$
$P = (2 \times 5.6) + (2 \times 3)$
$P = 11.2 + 6$
$P = 17.2$ Perimeter: 17.2 cm

3 cm
5.6 cm

Find the perimeter of each polygon.

(pp. 550–551)

16.

$4\frac{1}{2}$ ft

$2\frac{1}{2}$ ft

17.   5 m   5 m

5 m   5 m

5 m

Chapter 26

Find the area of a polygon.

Find the area.

$A = l \times w$
$A = 6.4 \times 4.5$
$A = 28.8$

4.5 cm

6.4 cm

So, the area is 28.8 cm².

Find the area of each figure. (pp. 564–579)

18. 6 in.
6 in.

19. 5.7 cm
3.3 cm

20. 10 yd
3 yd

21. 14 ft
3 ft

Chapter 27

Find the surface area.

Surface area is the sum of the areas of the faces of a solid figure.

Find the surface area.

$2 \times (3 \times 4) = 24$
$2 \times (2 \times 3) = 12$
$2 \times (2 \times 4) = 16$
$24 + 12 + 16 = 52$

So, the surface area is 52 units².

Find the surface area in cm². You may want to make the net. (pp. 590–591)

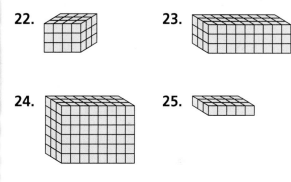

22.

23.

24.

25.

Find the volume of a rectangular prism.

Find the volume.

$V = l \times w \times h$
$V = 6 \times 2 \times 10$
$V = 120$

10 in.
2 in.
6 in.

So, the volume is 120 in.³

Find the volume of each rectangular prism. (pp. 592–597)

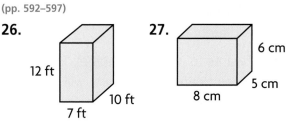

26. 12 ft
7 ft
10 ft

27. 6 cm
5 cm
8 cm

PROBLEM SOLVING PRACTICE

Solve. (pp. 580–581, 598–599)

28. The fish market sold 10,000 pounds of salmon on Friday. This was $\frac{2}{5}$ as much as the amount sold on Saturday. How many pounds of salmon were sold on Saturday?

29. Marie is using construction paper to cover a box 1 ft long, 3 ft wide, and 2 ft high. How much construction paper does she need?

PERFORMANCE ASSESSMENT

TASK A • WOODWORKING

MATERIALS: centimeter grid paper

Mr. Leon makes wooden jewelry boxes. On the tops of the boxes, he uses different kinds of wood to create geometric designs with triangles and quadrilaterals.

a. Draw a figure that is less than 15 centimeters by 15 centimeters. In the figure, design a box top that includes triangles, rectangles, and parallelograms.

b. Use a centimeter ruler to measure the dimensions of the largest triangle and rectangle in your design. Write the dimensions on the diagram. Then find the areas of those figures.

c. Mr. Leon charges $0.25 per square centimeter to make his box tops. How much would he charge for the top you designed?

TASK B • STORAGE CABINET

Jason and his mother are designing a cabinet to store his sports equipment. They want the cabinet to have about 50 cubic feet of space.

a. Jason wants the cabinet to be 5 feet wide. Decide what dimensions for the depth and height of the cabinet you would use for a volume of about 50 cubic feet.

b. Jason wants to paint the cabinet. He reads on the paint can that the paint will cover 100 square feet. Does he have enough paint to cover the back, sides, and the top of the cabinet?

c. Suppose Jason decides to put a wooden ledge around the top of the cabinet. How many feet of trim will he need?

Technology Linkup

Finding Volume

The table shows the length, width, and height of different packing boxes. You can use a spreadsheet to find the volume of each box.

BOX	LENGTH	WIDTH	HEIGHT
1	24 in.	18 in.	6 in.
2	12 in.	12 in.	12 in.
3	36.5 in.	6.25 in.	6.25 in.

You can find the volume of a rectangular prism by using the formula volume = length × width × height, or $V = l \times w \times h$.

• Enter the headings length, width, height, and volume into Columns A1 to D1 in the spreadsheet.

• Enter the data from the table into the appropriate cells.

• Click cell D2. Type = (A2*B2*C2). Then press *Enter*. Multiply cell A2 × cell B2 × cell C2. Use *Fill Down* and enter the formula in cells D3 and D4.

So, the volume of each box is: Box 1: 2,592 in.^{3}; Box 2: 1,728 in.^{3}; Box 3: 1,425.8 in.^{3}

◇	A	B	C	D
1	length	width	height	volume
2	24	18	6	2592.0
3	12	12	12	1728.0
4	36.5	6.25	6.25	1425.8

Practice and Problem Solving

Use a spreadsheet to solve the following problems.

1. $l = 4$ in.
   $w = 3$ in.
   $h = $ ■
   $V = 72$ in.^{3}

2. $l = 7$ m
   $w = $ ■
   $h = 10$ m
   $V = 350$ m^3

3. $l = 5$ yd
   $w = 6$ yd
   $h = $ ■
   $V = 270$ yd^3

4. $l = $ ■
   $w = 3$ ft
   $h = 4$ ft
   $V = 96$ ft^3

5. $l = 4.5$ cm
   $w = 2.5$ cm
   $h = 6$ cm
   $V = $ ■

6. $l = $ ■
   $w = 3$ m
   $h = 8\frac{1}{2}$ m
   $V = 153$ m^3

7. **REASONING** Explain how the volume changes when 1, 2, and 3 dimensions of a rectangular prism are doubled.

GO ON-LINE **Multimedia Math Glossary** www.harcourtschool.com/mathglossary
Vocabulary Power Compare the definitions in the Multimedia Math Glossary of *surface area* and *volume* of a rectangular prism. What dimensions do you need to find each? What units do you use to measure each?

PROBLEM SOLVING ON LOCATION

in

Washington, D.C.

THE ORANGUTANS

Nine orangutans at the National Zoo are involved in a study of how they think. The animals, which live in the Great Ape House, swing along cables to get to the Think Tank. In the Think Tank, the orangutans interact with members of the zoo staff and visitors. Here the orangutans learn a symbol language and develop social skills.

The distance between the Great Ape House and the Think Tank is about 500 feet. A square platform about 12 feet on each side is available partway across for the orangutans to rest on.

1. What is the perimeter of the platform?

2. What is the area of the platform?

3. What if the length of the platform were doubled but the width remained the same? What would be the dimensions and shape of the platform? How would the area be affected?

The Think Tank room is 10 feet long, 5 feet wide, and 10 feet high.

4. What is the area of the Think Tank floor?

5. What is the volume of the Think Tank?

▲ Orangutan

6. What if the length of the Think Tank were doubled? How would the volume change?

▲ Cheetah

Elephants ▶

THE CHEETAHS

Cheetahs at the National Zoo are also part of an important study. Zoo biologists want to learn more about these animals to help save them from extinction.

1. An adult cheetah's body can be as long as 56 inches. Is the adult cheetah's body length more than or less than 2 yards? Explain.

2. The adult cheetah's tail is about half as long as the length of its body. What is the cheetah's total length in feet? Explain how you found your answer.

3. The word *cheetah* means "spotted one." The black round or oval spots of an adult cheetah measure about 3.75 centimeters across. What is this measurement in millimeters?

4. The cheetah is built for speed. Other cats can sprint 200 meters, but the cheetah can sprint 27.5 times that distance. How far can a cheetah sprint? Compare this distance with the length of one side of your school.

CHAPTER 28 Ratio

≡**FAST FACT** • SPORTS

Ice hockey players use a special stick to drive a puck forward at speeds that can exceed 100 miles per hour. The table lists the results of four ice hockey games.

PROBLEM SOLVING What is the ratio of the number of goals the Sharks made to the number of goals the Otters made?

ICE HOCKEY GAME RESULTS

Team	Goals	Team	Goals
Badgers	2	Pelicans	0
Ducks	4	Eagles	2
Bears	5	Penguins	1
Sharks	4	Otters	3

Use this page to help you review and remember
important skills needed for Chapter 28.

✓ PARTS OF A GROUP

Write a fraction for the following.

1. ▲ ▲ ▲   ▲ ▲

What fraction of the
triangles are red?

2. ● ●   ● ●

What fraction of the
circles are blue?

3. ■ ■   ■ ■   ■

What fraction of the
squares are *not* red?

4. ● ● ●

What fraction of the
circles are red?

5. ■ ■   ■ ■

What fraction of the
squares are red?

6. ▲ ▲ △   ▲ ▲ △

What fraction of the
triangles are either
red or blue?

✓ EQUIVALENT FRACTIONS

Write an equivalent fraction for each.

7. $\frac{3}{6}$ **8.** $\frac{2}{5}$ **9.** $\frac{50}{100}$ **10.** $\frac{6}{16}$ **11.** $\frac{8}{15}$

✓ SIMPLEST FORM

Write each fraction in simplest form.

12. $\frac{5}{15}$ **13.** $\frac{4}{20}$ **14.** $\frac{14}{63}$ **15.** $\frac{6}{36}$ **16.** $\frac{10}{14}$

17. $\frac{8}{12}$ **18.** $\frac{7}{7}$ **19.** $\frac{25}{45}$ **20.** $\frac{11}{44}$ **21.** $\frac{6}{18}$

VOCABULARY POWER ✓

REVIEW

simplest form [sim′pləst] *noun*

The root word of *simplest* is *simple,* which
means "easy to do, solve, or understand."
Write a sentence to explain how this
definition can be applied to writing a
fraction in simplest form.

PREVIEW

ratio   equivalent ratios

proportion   scale drawing

map scale

GO
ON-LINE   www.harcourtschool.com/mathglossary

Understand Ratios

HANDS ON

▶ **Explore**

A **ratio** is a comparison of two quantities. For example, when you compare the number of red counters to the number of yellow counters, the ratio is 2 to 3.

VOCABULARY
ratio

MATERIALS
two-color counters

Activity

In a group of 10 students, 4 are boys and 6 are girls. Find the ratio of the number of boys to the number of girls.

STEP 1

Use the yellow side to represent all 10 students in the group. Each counter represents one student.

STEP 2

Turn the red side up to represent the number of students who are boys.

The ratio of boys to girls is the same as the ratio of red counters to yellow counters, 4 to 6.

How many counters do you turn red side up to represent the ratio 4 baseballs to 3 basketballs?

Try It

Use two-color counters to represent 4 baseballs and 3 basketballs. Write each ratio.

  a. baseballs to basketballs

  b. basketballs to all balls

  c. baseballs to all balls

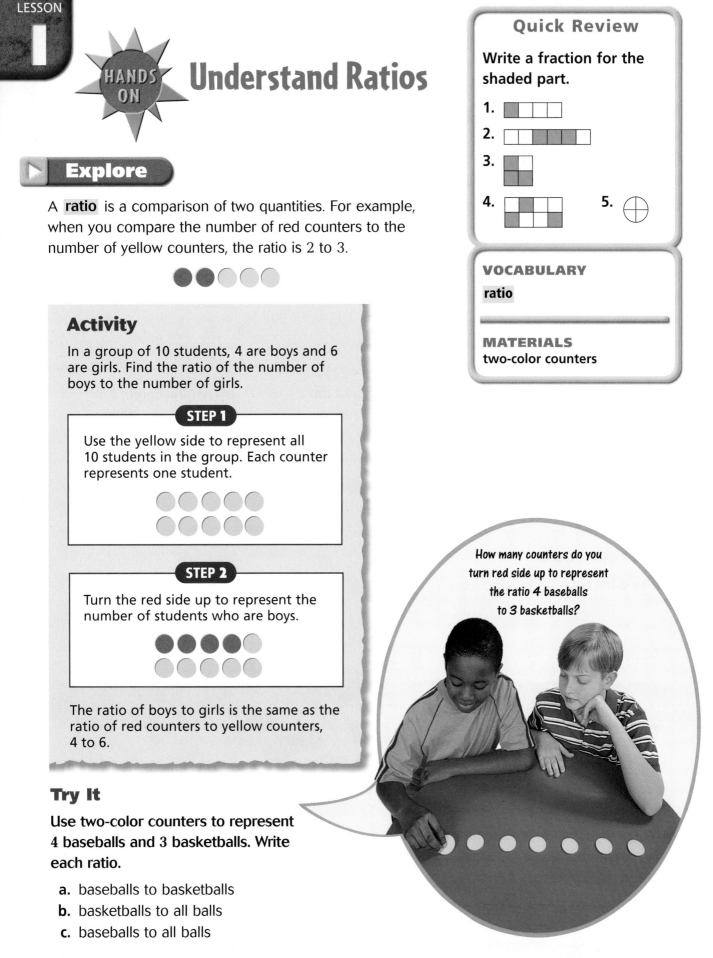

You can use a ratio to compare two numbers in *three ways:* whole to part, part to whole, and part to part. Sumi has 6 yellow counters and 3 red counters. Here are three examples of ratios that she can form.

Compare	Ratio	Type of Ratio
all counters to yellow counters	9 to 6	whole to part
red counters to all counters	3 to 9	part to whole
red counters to yellow counters	3 to 6	part to part

- Which type of ratio has the same meaning as a fraction?

▷ Practice and Problem Solving

Use two-color counters. Write each ratio and name the type of ratio.

1. Tennis is played by 3 out of 7 students.

2. There were 2 rainy and 5 sunny days.

3. There were 5 dogs and 6 cats in the room.

Write each ratio.

4.

wheels to skate

5. baseballs to players

6.

tires to bicycles

7. What is the ratio of vowels to consonants in the word PARALLELOGRAM? What kind of ratio is this?

8. Michelle packed 20 more boxes of books than Emily. Lisa packed 20 fewer boxes than Michelle. Emily packed 15 boxes of books. How many boxes of books did Michelle and Lisa pack?

9. ✷ **What's the Error?** Jordan has 3 goldfish, 2 turtles, and 1 snail. He says that the ratio of turtles to the total number of animals is 2 to 5. Find and correct Jordan's error.

10. **GEOMETRY** What is the ratio of number of sides of a triangle to number of sides of an octagon?

Mixed Review and Test Prep

11. Write $\frac{8}{12}$ in simplest form. (p. 316)

12. Write the LCM of 6 and 8. (p. 282)

13. Find the mean, median, and mode. 43, 64, 51, 64, 78 (pp. 100 and 102)

14. 62.16 ÷ 7 (p. 232)

15. **TEST PREP** Solve for *n*.
$8 + (7 + 9) = (n + 7) + 9$ (p. 76)
A $n = 8$ **B** $n = 7$ **C** $n = 6$ **D** $n = 4$

Express Ratios

▶ **Learn**

READING RATIOS At the library, 5 out of 8 books Loren checked out are about dogs. The other 3 books are about cats. The ratio of dog books to the total number of books he checked out is part to whole.

Write: 5 to 8   5:8 $\frac{5}{8}$

Read: "five to eight"

Find other ratios by considering the number of cat books Loren checked out.

Ⓐ cat books:all books
3 to 8, 3:8, $\frac{3}{8}$
part to whole

Ⓑ all books:cat books
8 to 3, 8:3, $\frac{8}{3}$
whole to part

Ⓒ cat books:dog books
3 to 5, 3:5, $\frac{3}{5}$
part to part

MATH IDEA You can use ratios to express the relationships between sets. The relationships of part to whole, whole to part, and part to part can be written in three ways.

▶ **Check**

1. **Explain** why the order in which you write a ratio is important.

Write each ratio in three ways. Then name the type of ratio.

2. circles to squares

3. all figures to red

4. circles to all figures

5. blue to red

6. all figures to squares

7. green to all figures

Write each ratio in three ways. Then name the type of ratio. Use the circles, squares, and stars on page 616.

8. squares to stars   **9.** red to green   **10.** stars to all figures

Write *a* or *b* to show which fraction represents each ratio.

11. 5 to 2
   a. $\frac{2}{5}$ **b.** $\frac{5}{2}$

12. 5:9
   a. $\frac{9}{5}$ **b.** $\frac{5}{9}$

13. 8 to 4
   a. $\frac{8}{4}$ **b.** $\frac{4}{8}$

14. 1:20
   a. $\frac{20}{1}$ **b.** $\frac{1}{20}$

USE DATA   For 15–17, use the circle graph. Write each ratio in three ways.

15. What is the ratio of mystery books to biography books?

16. What is the ratio of all books to biography books?

17. What is the ratio of travel books to all books?

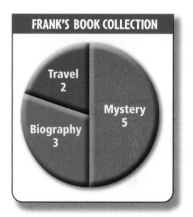

FRANK'S BOOK COLLECTION

Travel 2

Mystery 5

Biography 3

USE DATA   For 18–21, use this information: Out of every 60 people in the world, 12 live in China, 10 live in India, and 3 live in the United States. Match each ratio with its comparison.

   a. 60:3   **b.** 10:60   **c.** 12:10   **d.** 3:12

18. India:world   **19.** U.S.:China   **20.** world:U.S.   **21.** China:India

22. REASONING   If the ratio of games won to games lost is 3:2, what is the ratio of games won to the total number of games played?

23. **ALGEBRA**   Find the value of *n*.
$$\frac{5}{7} = \frac{(5 \times n)}{56}$$

24. **FAST FACT** • SOCIAL STUDIES
The Floating Garden Observatory atop Umeda Sky City in Osaka, Japan, is 54 meters by 54 meters. What is the area in square yards? (HINT: $1m^2 \approx 1.2$ yd^2)

25. Write About It Last month, 2 out of every 4 dogs adopted were Dalmatians. Explain why you can compare the number of Dalmatians to the total number with the ratio $\frac{1}{2}$.

Mixed Review and Test Prep

26. What is the greatest common factor of 24 and 60? (p. 278)

27. $90,211 \times 34$ (p. 152)

28. $358,976 \times 25$ (p. 152)

29. Evaluate $4n^2 - (3 \times n)$ if $n = 5$. (p. 292)

30. **TEST PREP**   Which number is between 2.011 and 2.022? (p. 28)
   A 2.150   **C** 2.015
   B 2.033   **D** 2.010

Ratios and Proportions

▶ **Learn**

POWER PLAY   Last year Lisa's ice-hockey team won 8 out of a total of 10 games. This year's team will play 20 games. The players hope to have the same ratio of games won to games played as last year. How many games must they win?

Find **equivalent ratios** in the same way you find equivalent fractions.

$$\frac{8}{10} = \frac{n}{20} \quad \begin{array}{l} \leftarrow \text{games won} \\ \leftarrow \text{games played} \end{array}$$

$$\frac{8 \times \boxed{2}}{10 \times \boxed{2}} = \frac{16}{20} \quad \textbf{Think: } 10 \times 2 = 20, \text{ so } 8 \times 2 = 16.$$

$$n = 16$$

So, $\frac{8}{10}$ and $\frac{16}{20}$ are equivalent ratios. Lisa's team must win 16 games this year.

VOCABULARY

equivalent ratios
proportion

⚡ **MATH IDEA**   To find an equivalent ratio, first express the ratio as a fraction, then multiply or divide the numerator and the denominator by the same number, using a fraction equal to 1.

Example 1 Write an equivalent ratio.

Ⓐ $\frac{3}{5}$

$$\frac{3 \times \boxed{3}}{5 \times \boxed{3}} = \frac{9}{15}$$

So, $\frac{9}{15}$ is equivalent to $\frac{3}{5}$.

Ⓑ 10:24

$$10:24 = \frac{10}{24} \quad \frac{10 \div \boxed{2}}{24 \div \boxed{2}} = \frac{5}{12}, \text{ or } 5:12$$

So, 5:12 is equivalent to 10:24.

Example 2 Tell whether the ratios are equivalent.

Ⓒ $\frac{20}{16}$ and $\frac{5}{4}$

$$\frac{20 \div \boxed{4}}{16 \div \boxed{4}} = \frac{5}{4}$$

So, $\frac{20}{16}$ and $\frac{5}{4}$ are equivalent ratios.

Ⓓ 3:8 and 5:16

$$3:8 = \frac{3}{8} \qquad 5:16 = \frac{5}{16}$$

$$\frac{3 \times \boxed{2}}{8 \times \boxed{2}} = \frac{6}{16} \qquad \frac{5}{16} < \frac{6}{16}$$

So, 3:8 and 5:16 are NOT equivalent ratios.

Proportions

Each container of hockey pucks holds 4 game pucks and 10 practice pucks. The ratio of game pucks to practice pucks in one container is $\frac{4}{10}$. Three containers would have 12 game pucks and 30 practice pucks, which is three times as many as are in one container. The two ratios $\frac{4}{10}$ and $\frac{12}{30}$ are equivalent ratios.

A **proportion** is an equation that shows two equivalent ratios.

$$\frac{4}{10} = \frac{12}{30} \leftarrow \text{proportion}$$

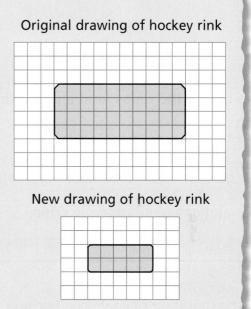

Example 3

Builders use ratios and proportions in reducing and enlarging drawings. The dimensions in this drawing of a hockey rink need to be reduced to half size. Write a proportion to show the old and new lengths and widths.

The ratio of length to width in units is $\frac{10}{4}$. Divide both 10 and 4 by 2.

Original drawing of hockey rink

$$\frac{10 \div 2}{4 \div 2} = \frac{5}{2}$$ The new ratio of length to width is $\frac{5}{2}$.

$\frac{10}{4}$ and $\frac{5}{2}$ are equivalent ratios. $\frac{10}{4} = \frac{5}{2}$

So, $\frac{10}{4} = \frac{5}{2}$ is a proportion that shows the old and new lengths and widths.

New drawing of hockey rink

- Suppose that the dimensions of the new drawing are twice those of the original drawing. Write a proportion to show the old and new lengths and widths.

1. Explain whether the ratios $\frac{5}{4}$ and $\frac{10}{8}$ form a proportion.

Write three ratios that are equivalent to the given ratio.

2. 3:1   **3.** $\frac{3}{5}$ **4.** 1 to 4   **5.** 2:7

Tell whether the ratios are equivalent. Write *yes* or *no*.

6. $\frac{2}{4}$ and $\frac{6}{12}$ **7.** 2:5 and 5:10   **8.** 4 to 12 and 1 to 3

LESSON CONTINUES

Tell whether the ratios are equivalent. Write *yes* or *no*.

9. $\frac{3}{4}$ and $\frac{12}{20}$

10. 5:10 and 1:2

11. 1 to 4 and 25 to 100

12. 3:9 and 9:27

13. 4 to 9 and 6 to 18

14. $\frac{5}{8}$ and $\frac{20}{32}$

Write three ratios that are equivalent to the given ratio.

15. 10 to 1

16. $\frac{1}{7}$

17. 9 to 3

18. 26:36

19. $\frac{1}{5}$

20. 50:100

21. $\frac{2}{2}$

22. 100 to 1

⭐**ALGEBRA**   **Find the unknown value.**

23. $\frac{4}{5} = \frac{x}{20}$

24. $\frac{n}{2} = \frac{21}{14}$

25. $\frac{8}{9} = \frac{8}{p}$

26. $\frac{9}{h} = \frac{3}{9}$

27. $\frac{12}{10} = \frac{y}{5}$

28. $\frac{c}{3} = \frac{10}{15}$

29. $\frac{36}{8} = \frac{9}{k}$

30. $\frac{20}{y} = \frac{4}{3}$

Tell whether the ratios form a proportion. Write *yes* or *no*.

31. $\frac{2}{4}$ and $\frac{6}{12}$

32. $\frac{1}{6}$ and $\frac{3}{15}$

33. $\frac{12}{5}$ and $\frac{24}{10}$

34. $\frac{12}{15}$ and $\frac{16}{20}$

35. $\frac{9}{6}$ and $\frac{15}{9}$

36. $\frac{3}{8}$ and $\frac{9}{25}$

37. $\frac{20}{15}$ and $\frac{15}{10}$

38. $\frac{6}{15}$ and $\frac{4}{10}$

Copy and complete the ratio table.

39.

Number of Apples	3	■	■	■
Cups of Apple Cider	1	3	9	27

40.

Number of Canoes	1	4	7	10
Number of People	3	■	■	■

41. REASONING During the ice hockey game, 3 of the 20 shots were goals. What is the ratio of shots made to all shots taken and shots made to shots missed? Do these two ratios make a proportion?

42. NUMBER SENSE Find the missing numbers in the pattern of equivalent ratios: $\frac{2}{■}, \frac{4}{10}, \frac{8}{■}, \frac{■}{40}$. Describe the pattern.

For 43–44, use the ratio of 4 oranges to 1 glass of juice.

43. How many oranges will Bryce need to make 3 glasses of orange juice?

44. Write three ratios equivalent to the ratio of oranges to glasses of orange juice.

45. On grid paper, make a drawing of a hockey puck with dimensions that are half the size of the drawing to the right. Write a proportion to show the old and new lengths and widths.

Hockey Puck, side view

620

46. On average, 2 of every 50 CDs in a shipment were defective. Mrs. Snyder bought 600 of the CDs for her store. How many would she expect to be defective?

47. Vocabulary Power A fraction names a part of a whole or part of a group. How is a ratio like a fraction? How is it different?

Mixed Review and Test Prep

48. Attendance at the last three games was 325, 410, and 465. What was the average attendance for those three games? (p. 100)

49. Write $\frac{3}{4}$ as a decimal. (p. 328)

50. **TEST PREP** Find the difference: $^-7 - {}^+6$. (p. 486)

   A $^-13$ **B** $^-1$ **C** $^+1$ **D** $^+13$

51. The diameter of the small apple pie is about half that of the large pie. The large pie has a circumference of 28 in. Find the diameter of the small pie. (p. 554)

52. How many grams are in 8.5 kilograms? (p. 534)

Write each ratio in two other ways. (p. 616)

53. 5 games to 7 games

54. 9 green to 4 red marbles

55. **TEST PREP** Which is the GCF of 18 and 45? (p. 278)

   F 3   **H** 6
   G 5   **J** 9

Problem Solving — LiNKuP...to Art

The Greeks experimented with the use of triangles and rectangles in their architecture. The length-to-width or length-to-height ratio of rectangular shapes in some buildings is called a Golden Ratio. A **Golden Ratio** is any ratio equivalent to the value of about 1.6.

Example Does Rectangle *A* show a Golden Ratio?

$\frac{l}{w} = \frac{8}{5}$ Write the length-to-width ratio for the rectangle.

$\frac{8}{5} = 1.6$ Write the equivalent decimal for the ratio.

So, Rectangle *A* shows a Golden Ratio.

1. The Parthenon was constructed around 450 B.C. in Athens, Greece. The front of the Parthenon has a length of 101 feet and a height of 60 feet. Does the front show a Golden Ratio? Explain.

2. Measure the length and width of the cover of your math book. Is the ratio of the measures a Golden Ratio?

Scale Drawings

Learn

GO THE DISTANCE! A **scale drawing** shows a real object smaller than (a reduction) or larger than (an enlargement) the real object. A map is a scale drawing. The ratio that compares the distance on a map to the actual distance is the **map scale**.

Example

You can use the scale to compute the distance from Asheboro to Greensboro.

Read the map scale.	The map shows a scale of 1 cm = 12 km, or $\frac{1 \text{ cm}}{12 \text{ km}}$.
Use a centimeter ruler to measure the distance from Asheboro to Greensboro on the map.	The distance is 3.5 cm on the map.
Use equivalent ratios to find the actual distance.	$\frac{1}{12} = \frac{3.5}{n}$ $\frac{1 \times 3.5}{12 \times 3.5} = \frac{3.5}{42}$ $n = 42$

So, the distance is 42 kilometers.

MATH IDEA You can use scale drawings and map scales to determine actual sizes and actual distances.

Quick Review

Find *n* to make the ratios equivalent.

1. $\frac{7}{14} = \frac{n}{28}$ 2. $\frac{8}{n} = \frac{16}{32}$

3. $\frac{5}{25} = \frac{n}{75}$ 4. $\frac{3}{100} = \frac{30}{n}$

5. $\frac{36}{42} = \frac{n}{7}$

VOCABULARY

scale drawing   map scale

Check

1. **Explain** how to find the distance from Liberty to Asheboro.

Copy and complete the map scale ratio table.

2.

Map Distance (inches)	1	■	2.6	■	7.8
Actual Distance (miles)	100	150	■	680	■

Copy and complete the ratio table.

3.

Scale Length (in.)	1	■	3.5	■	■
Actual Length (ft)	10	30	■	50	60

4.

Scale Distance (cm)	1	3	■	8	■
Actual Distance (m)	7.5	■	37.5	■	75

5.

Scale Length (in.)	1	2	4	■	■
Actual Length (ft)	12	■	■	60	72

6.

Scale Distance (cm)	1	2.6	■	7.6	■
Actual Distance (m)	75	■	375	■	600

7.

Scale Length (in.)	1	■	4	4.4	5
Actual Length (ft)	200	500	■	■	■

8.

Scale Distance (cm)	3	6	■	12	■
Actual Distance (m)	150	■	450	■	750

For 9–11, use the map and map scale to find the distance to the nearest mile.

9. Cincinnati to Columbus

10. Toledo to Columbus

11. Columbus to Akron

12. ✎ **Write a problem** about driving between two cities that are less than 100 miles apart. Use the map of Ohio.

13. A rectangular garden is 48 ft long and 42 ft wide. Fencing for the garden costs $12 for each foot. How much will it cost to fence in the garden?

14. Choose a scale for this drawing. Then use it to find the actual length and width of the cabin.

15. Maura has a dollhouse with a scale of 1 inch to 1.5 ft. The dimensions of the living room are 10 in. by 12 in. What would be the dimensions of this room in an actual house?

16. **REASONING**   Joy planned a scale drawing with a scale of 1 in. = 4 ft. She found that her drawing would not fit on her paper. How should she change the ratio to make the drawing fit? Explain.

Mixed Review and Test Prep

17. List the prime numbers between 30 and 40. (p. 300)

18. Write three ratios equivalent to 3:2. (p. 618)

19. Solve for n. $17 = 4n - 3$ (p. 246)

20. $23.574 - 13.221$ (p. 48)

21. **TEST PREP**   Which of the following is NOT equivalent to 1.5? (p. 328)

   A $1\frac{1}{2}$ C $1\frac{5}{10}$

   B 1.50   D 1.05

Problem Solving Skill
Too Much/Too Little Information

UNDERSTAND > PLAN > SOLVE > CHECK

CAN YOU SOLVE IT? Yoko found these people-to-pet ratios on the Internet. For her report she wants to know the ratio of pet dogs in the United States to pet cats.

Sometimes you have too much or too little information to solve a problem. If there is too much, you have to decide what to use. If there is too little, you can't solve the problem.

To decide, read the problem carefully and then ask yourself these questions:

1. **What do I want to know?**
   pet dogs:pet cats

2. **What do I know?**
   people:pet dogs = 30:6
   people:pet cats = 30:7

3. **What information is unnecessary?**
   people-to-bird ratios

4. **What necessary information is missing?**
   none

U.S. Populations
People to pets
People:cats 30:7
People:dogs 30:6
People:parakeets 300:15
People:parrots 3,000:15

Since the number of people compared to dogs and cats is the same, you can compare dogs to cats.

So, the ratio of pet dogs to pet cats is 6:7.

Talk About It

• How can you decide what information is necessary to solve a problem?

USE DATA For 1–4, use the chart on page 624. Write whether each problem has *too much* or *too little* information. Then solve if possible, or describe the additional information needed.

1. How many people are there in the U.S. for every one pet dog?

2. How many people are there in the U.S. for every one Siamese cat?

3. Which is the more popular pet in the U.S., a parrot or a goldfish?

4. How many pet parakeets are there for every 3,000 people in the U.S.?

Tomás needs to walk the dog, do the dishes, and finish his homework. It will take him 15 minutes to walk the dog, 30 minutes to do the dishes, and 1 hour 10 minutes to finish his homework. Does he have enough time to complete all three tasks?

5. What other information do you need to solve the problem?
   A the name of Tomás's dog
   B how much time Tomás has
   C how many dishes are dirty
   D what homework he needs to do

6. What is the least amount of time Tomás needs to complete all three tasks?
   F 2 hours
   G 1 hour 55 minutes
   H 1 hour 45 minutes
   J 1 hour 35 minutes

Mixed Applications

USE DATA For 7–8, use the table.

7. What is the weight difference between the largest and smallest dogs?

8. Which dog was bigger, the mastiff or the Great Dane?

9. The first year of a dog's life equals 15 "human years." The second year equals 10 human years. Every year thereafter equals 3 human years. Use this formula to find a 6-year-old dog's age in human years.

10. **? What's the Question?** An African gray parrot named Prudle was found in 1958. From then until 1977, it learned nearly 1,000 words. The answer is about 50.

11. ✏ **Write a problem** that has too little information to be solved. Then write one that includes information that is not needed to solve the problem.

WORLD DOG RECORDS		
Record	Breed	Measurement
Largest	Old English Mastiff	343 pounds
Tallest	Great Dane	3.5 feet
Smallest	Yorkshire Terrier	4 ounces

Extra Practice

Set A (pp. 616–617)

Write *a* or *b* to show which fraction represents the ratio.

1. 5 to 3

a. $\frac{3}{5}$ **b.** $\frac{5}{3}$

2. 4:9

a. $\frac{4}{9}$ **b.** $\frac{9}{4}$

3. 5 to 5

a. $\frac{5}{5}$ **b.** $\frac{1}{5}$

4. 7:2

a. $\frac{7}{1}$ **b.** $\frac{7}{2}$

5. 1 to 6

a. $\frac{1}{6}$ **b.** $\frac{6}{1}$

For 6–8, use the graph.

6. What is the ratio of guards to forwards in the league?

7. What is the ratio of forwards to the total number of players in the league?

8. If 2 more guards join the league, what will be the ratio of guards to total players in the league?

BASKETBALL LEAGUE PLAYERS

Centers, Forwards, Guards

🏀 = 2 players

Set B (pp. 618–621)

Tell whether the ratios form a proportion. Write *yes* or *no*.

1. $\frac{8}{12}$ and $\frac{12}{24}$

2. $\frac{6}{6}$ and $\frac{8}{8}$

3. $\frac{2}{4}$ and $\frac{5}{10}$

4. $\frac{7}{6}$ and $\frac{6}{5}$

5. $\frac{3}{5}$ and $\frac{6}{10}$

6. $\frac{4}{8}$ and $\frac{16}{24}$

Write three ratios that are equivalent to the given ratio.

7. 1 to 3

8. 4:5

9. $\frac{10}{7}$

10. 1 to 1

11. Twelve members of the drama club acted in the school play, and the remaining 19 members were stagehands. What is the ratio of actors to the total club membership?

12. The science club has 40 members, but only 30 members went on the trip to the aquarium. What is the ratio of members who went on the trip to those who did not?

Set C (pp. 622–623)

Copy and complete the map scale ratio table.

1.

Scale Length	1 in.	▓ in.	5 in.	▓ in.
Actual Length	5 mi	15 mi	▓ mi	35 mi

2.

Scale Length	1 cm	8 cm	▓ cm	12 cm
Actual Length	4.5 km	▓ km	45 km	▓ km

Review/Test

✓ CHECK VOCABULARY AND CONCEPTS

Choose the best term from the box.

| equivalent ratios |
| map scale |
| ratio |
| scale drawing |

1. You can use a __?__ to compare two quantities. (p. 614)

2. A ratio that compares the distance on a map to the actual distance is called the __?__. (p. 622)

3. Ratios that describe the same comparison of quantities are called __?__. (p. 618)

✓ CHECK SKILLS

For 4–6, use the letters in the word MULTIPLICATION to write each ratio. (pp. 614–615)

4. consonants to total letters   5. consonants to vowels   6. total letters to vowels

Write *a* or *b* to show which fraction represents each ratio. (pp. 616–617)

7. 5 to 1   8. 9 to 5   9. 12:36   10. 25:100   11. 1 to 50

a. $\frac{1}{5}$ b. $\frac{5}{1}$ a. $\frac{9}{5}$ b. $\frac{5}{9}$ a. $\frac{1}{3}$ b. $\frac{3}{1}$ a. $\frac{4}{1}$ b. $\frac{1}{4}$ a. $\frac{1}{50}$ b. $\frac{50}{1}$

Write three ratios that are equivalent to the given ratio. (pp. 618–621)

12. 6 to 8   13. 3:7   14. 9:5

Tell whether the ratios form a proportion. Write *yes* or *no*. (pp. 618–621)

15. $\frac{3}{21}$ and $\frac{1}{7}$ 16. $\frac{4}{6}$ and $\frac{2}{4}$

Copy and complete the map scale ratio table. (pp. 622–623)

17.

Scale Length (in.)	1	4	■	8
Actual Length (ft)	50	■	300	■

18.

Scale Length (cm)	1	■	4	■
Actual Length (m)	2.5	5	■	15

✓ CHECK PROBLEM SOLVING

Write whether each problem has *too much* or *too little* information. Then solve if possible, or describe the additional information needed. (pp. 624–625)

19. At Jerry's Market a gallon of chocolate milk costs $2.15, a half gallon costs $1.20, and a gallon of skim milk costs $1.75. How much will 2 gallons of chocolate milk cost?

20. The music store is having a CD sale. If you buy two CDs, you get one free. How much will three CDs cost?

Standardized Test Prep

⭐ MEASUREMENT

1. What is the perimeter of the *Mona Lisa*?

SIZES OF FAMOUS PAINTINGS		
Title	**Artist**	**Dimensions (in inches)**
Mona Lisa	da Vinci	30 × 21
Water Lily Pond	Monet	35 × 36
Apples and Oranges	Cézanne	29 × 37
Dancers in Blue	Degas	34 × 30

A 51 inches   **C** 102 inches

B 81 inches   **D** 630 inches

2. Look at the table in Problem 1. Which painting has the greatest area?

F *Mona Lisa*

G *Water Lily Pond*

H *Apples and Oranges*

J *Dancers in Blue*

3. **Explain It** Julie wants to buy ribbon to decorate the perimeter of a picture frame. She measured part of the perimeter. ESTIMATE to determine about how many centimeters of ribbon she needs. Explain how you found your estimate.

5.8 centimeters

⭐ NUMBER SENSE, CONCEPTS, AND OPERATIONS

4. The table shows the countries with the most movie theaters.

COUNTRIES WITH THE MOST MOVIE THEATERS	
Country	**Number of Theaters**
India	8,975
United States	23,662
China	4,364
Ukraine	14,960

Suppose a film is shown in half of all the theaters in the United States and in half of all the theaters in China. In how many theaters is the film shown?

A 1,413

B 2,182

C 11,831

D 14,013

5. Look at the table in Problem 4. How many more theaters are there in the United States than in China and Ukraine combined?

F 42,986

G 23,662

H 8,702

J 4,338

6. **Explain It** Jacob sleeps for about $8\frac{1}{6}$ hours each night. ESTIMATE to determine about how many hours he sleeps in a month. Explain how you found your answer.

⭐ ALGEBRAIC THINKING

7. After 6 students left the debate team to join the yearbook staff, there were 20 students on the team. Which equation can be used to find *n,* the number of people who were on the team before some left?

  A $20 + n = 6$

  B $20 - 6 = n$

  C $6 + n = 20$

  D $n - 6 = 20$

> **TIP** **Check your work.** See item 7. Express the equation that you chose in words. Check to make sure that the words make sense and match the problem.

8. A grocery store is putting up a display of cans. The bottom row has 47 cans, the second row from the bottom has 39 cans, and the third row from the bottom has 31 cans. If this pattern continues, how many cans will be in the sixth row from the bottom?

  F 1

  G 7

  H 8

  J 15

9. Explain It What are the missing numbers in this pattern of fractions?

$$\frac{3}{5}, \frac{6}{10}, \frac{9}{15}, \frac{12}{\blacksquare}, \frac{\blacksquare}{25}, \frac{18}{\blacksquare}$$

Explain how the fractions are related.

⭐ DATA ANALYSIS AND PROBABILITY

10. A jar contains 20 pink, 15 green, 12 blue, and 2 purple jelly beans. Which color jelly bean are you **least likely** to pull from the jar?

  A pink   **C** blue

  B green   **D** purple

11. What is the probability that the pointer on the spinner below will land on an odd number?

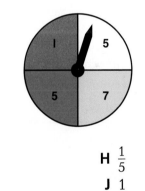

  F 0   **H** $\frac{1}{5}$

  G $\frac{1}{7}$ **J** 1

12. Explain It Colleen gathered this data on the high temperature outdoors for five days last week.

AVERAGE HIGH TEMPERATURE (IN DEGREES F)				
Mon	Tue	Wed	Thu	Fri
75	82	85	74	75

Which type of graph is most appropriate for displaying the data? Explain your choice. Then make a graph of the data.

Percent

≡FAST FACT • SOCIAL STUDIES The United States government owns 632.7 million acres of land. The National Park System is part of that land. The largest park is Wrangell-St. Elias National Park and Preserve in Alaska. It covers 13,200,000 acres. The smallest park is the Thaddeus Kosciuszko National Memorial in Pennsylvania. It is only 0.02 acre.

PROBLEM SOLVING Look at the circle graph. Of the acres that are owned by the government, how many acres are in the National Park System?

NATIONWIDE ACREAGE
(Owned and Managed by U.S. Federal Agencies)

Bureau of Land Management 43%

U.S. Forest Service 30%

National Park System 13%

Fish and Wildlife Service 14%

Denali National Park, Alaska

Use this page to help you review and remember
important skills needed for Chapter 29.

MULTIPLY DECIMALS BY WHOLE NUMBERS

Find the product.

1. 0.07
    × 5

2. 0.29
    × 7

3. 0.65
    × 4

4. 0.06
    × 3

5. $0.69
    × 8

6. $0.19
    × 5

7. $0.55
    × 9

8. $0.48
    × 2

RELATE FRACTIONS AND DECIMALS

Write a decimal and a fraction for the shaded part.

9. 10. 11.

Write as a decimal.

12. $\frac{54}{100}$

13. $\frac{36}{100}$

14. $\frac{3}{4}$

15. $\frac{19}{1,000}$

16. $\frac{4}{5}$

Write as a fraction.

17. 0.25

18. 0.9

19. 0.5

20. 0.63

21. 1.2

VOCABULARY POWER

REVIEW

PREVIEW

percent

ratio [rā′shē•ō] *noun*

A ratio is the comparison of two numbers.
The word rate is similar in meaning to *ratio*.
A rate is a ratio of two quantities, such as
miles and hours for rate of speed. Name
some ratios or rates that are used in
everyday life.

ON-LINE

www.harcourtschool.com/mathglossary

HANDS ON

Understand Percent

Quick Review

1. $\frac{1}{2}$ of 100

2. $\frac{1}{4}$ of 100

3. $\frac{1}{5}$ of 100

4. $\frac{1}{10}$ of 100

5. $\frac{3}{4}$ of 100

▶ **Explore**

Did you know that fifty percent of the Earth's species live in rain forests? **Percent** means "per hundred." A percent is a ratio of a number to 100. The symbol for percent is %. 1% means "1 out of 100." So, "50% of the Earth's species" means that 50 out of every 100, or $\frac{50}{100}$, species on Earth live in rain forests.

VOCABULARY

percent

MATERIALS
10 × 10 grid paper, colored pencils

Activity

Use a grid with 100 squares to model percents.

Out of every 100 known bird species on Earth, 30 live in rain forests. What percent of known bird species live in rain forests?

STEP 1

Let each grid square represent 1 bird species. To show 30 bird species out of 100, shade 30 squares.

STEP 2

Write the ratio of shaded squares to the total squares. Then write the percent.

$$\frac{\text{shaded squares}}{\text{total squares}} = \frac{30}{100} = 30\%$$

So, 30% of all known bird species live in rain forests.

• The unshaded squares represent the bird species that do not live in rain forests. What percent of known bird species do not live in rain forests?

Try It

Model each ratio on grid paper. Then write the percent.

a. 42 ducks out of 100 birds

b. 50 lions out of 100 cats

c. 25 puppies out of 100 pets

What model can I make to show 42 ducks out of 100 birds?

▶ Connect

Remember, a ratio is a comparison of two numbers. A percent is a special ratio because it always compares a part to 100. Percent is often used with money.

One dollar has 100 parts, or cents. Look at the 10 × 10 grid. There is 1 cent, or penny, in each of 100 squares, or a total of $1.00.

1% of $1.00 is 1 penny, or $0.01.

$$100\% = \frac{100}{100} = 1$$

Talk About It

- What is 50% of $1.00? 10% of $1.00? 76% of $1.00?

- What part of a dollar do you have if you have 0% of it? 100% of it?

- **REASONING** What does 200% of a number mean?

▶ Practice and Problem Solving

Model each ratio on grid paper. Then write the percent.

1. 31 tigers out of 100 animals

2. 100 red balls out of 100 balls

3. 4 dimes out of $1.00

4. 5 blue pens out of 100 pens

Write a percent to describe the shaded part.

5.   **6.**   **7.**   **8.**

Choose the more reasonable percent. Write *a* or *b*.

9. *"Almost everyone* passed the test," Mrs. Philips said with pride.
   a. 95% passed.   **b.** 15% passed.

10. *"Very few* children like spicy foods," said the chef.
   a. 40% like them.   **b.** 8% like them.

11. REASONING A few months ago, Van had 100 days to wait until his birthday. His wait is 98% over. Today is Monday. What day of the week is Van's birthday?

12. Vocabulary Power The *cent* in *percent* means "100." Write a list of words that contain *cent*, and explain how their definitions relate to 100.

Mixed Review and Test Prep

13. What is the greatest common factor of 12 and 15? (p. 278)

14. Write two ratios that are equivalent to 7:8. (p. 618)

15. 0.5 × 11 (p. 164)   **16.** 11.34 ÷ 7 (p. 232)

17. TEST PREP Write $\frac{23}{1,000}$ as a decimal. (p. 22)

   A 23   **B** 2.3   **C** 0.23   **D** 0.023

Relate Decimals and Percents

▶ **Learn**

MONEY, MONEY, MONEY!   A quarter of a dollar can be written as the decimal $0.25.

⚡ **MATH IDEA**   You can write a decimal as a percent.

What percent of a dollar is $0.25?

Write: 0.25

Read: twenty-five hundredths

Ratio: 25 out of 100, or $\frac{25}{100}$

Percent: 25%

So, $0.25 is 25% of a dollar.

Examples

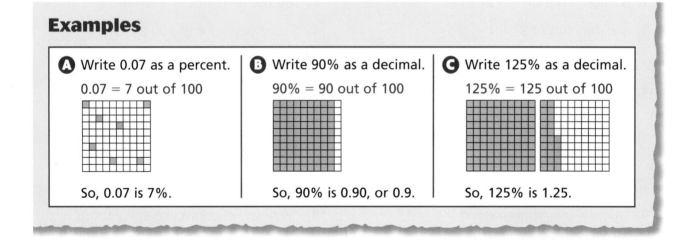

A Write 0.07 as a percent.

0.07 = 7 out of 100

So, 0.07 is 7%.

B Write 90% as a decimal.

90% = 90 out of 100

So, 90% is 0.90, or 0.9.

C Write 125% as a decimal.

125% = 125 out of 100

So, 125% is 1.25.

▶ **Check**

1. **Explain** why you can write the decimal in Example B as 0.90 and as 0.9 but you can't write 90% as 9%.

For 2–4, write a decimal and a percent to describe each shaded part of the model.

2. purple squares
3. yellow and blue squares
4. all the shaded squares

The Federal Reserve estimates that $395 million could be saved annually by replacing bills with coins like the Golden Dollar. ▶

USE DATA   For 5–7, use the circle graph. Write a decimal and a percent to describe each.

HAIR COLORS IN THE U.S.

70% Brown

15% Blond

10% Black

5% Red

5. What part of the population has either brown or black hair?

6. What part of the population does not have red hair?

7. Fifteen hundredths of the population has the same color hair as I do. What color is my hair?

Write the number as a decimal and a percent.

8. eighty-one hundredths

9. twelve hundredths

10. thirty-seven hundredths

11. four hundredths

Write each decimal as a percent.

12. 0.78   13. 0.99   14. 0.06   15. 0.2   16. 1.2

Write each percent as a decimal.

17. 35%   18. 100%   19. 2%   20. 60%   21. 104%

REASONING   Write the greater number of each pair.

22. 0.5, 5%   23. 0.14, 140%   24. 0.08, 80%   25. 1.9, 19%   26. 2, 2%

27. Out of 100 students in the spelling bee, 23 girls and 28 boys misspelled *aardvark*. What percent of the students spelled the word correctly?

28. **REASONING**   Jeb read that 10% of people are left-handed. If he surveys 200 people, about how many left-handers should he expect to find?

29. ▤*FAST FACT* • SOCIAL STUDIES
In early 2000, a poll found that 75 out of every 100 Americans opposed eliminating the $1 bill and using a $1 coin. What percent was this?

30. 📕 Write About It What pattern do you see in the placement of the decimal point when you write a decimal as a percent? a percent as a decimal?

Mixed Review **and Test Prep**

31. Write the ratio 13:4 as a fraction. (p. 616)

32. Find the value of 4^3. (p. 292)

33. 22.44 ÷ 4 (p. 232)

34. 3,005 × 18 (p. 152)

35. **TEST PREP**   Solve for *n*. $5 \times (n + 3) = 50$
(p. 70)

A $n = 5$ C $n = 10$

B $n = 7$ D $n = 50$

Fractions, Decimals, and Percents

▶ **Learn**

DON'T BUG ME! There are more beetles on Earth than any other animals. One out of four, or $\frac{1}{4}$, of all animals are beetles. What percent of the animals on Earth are beetles?

You can write a ratio that is in fraction form as a percent.

One Way Write an equivalent fraction with a denominator of 100. Then write the fraction as a percent.

$$\frac{1}{4} = \frac{1 \times 25}{4 \times 25} = \frac{25}{100}$$

$$\frac{25}{100} = 25\%$$

Another Way Divide the numerator by the denominator. Then write the decimal as a percent.

$$\frac{1}{4} \rightarrow 4\overline{)1.00}^{\,0.25}$$

$$0.25 = 25\%$$

So, 25% of all animals on Earth are beetles.

Examples

Write each fraction as a percent.

A

$$\frac{7}{20} = \frac{7 \times 5}{20 \times 5} = \frac{35}{100}$$

$$\frac{35}{100} = 35\%$$

B

$$\frac{4}{5} \rightarrow 5\overline{)4.00}^{\,0.80}$$

$$0.80 = 80\%$$

C

$$\frac{3}{40} \rightarrow 40\overline{)3.000}^{\,0.075}$$

$$0.075 = 7.5\%$$

- **REASONING** Which way would you use to write $\frac{1}{8}$ as a percent? Explain your choice.

Percents as Fractions

Scientists estimate that ants make up 10% of the Earth's biomass, the amount of living matter. What fraction of the Earth's biomass are ants?

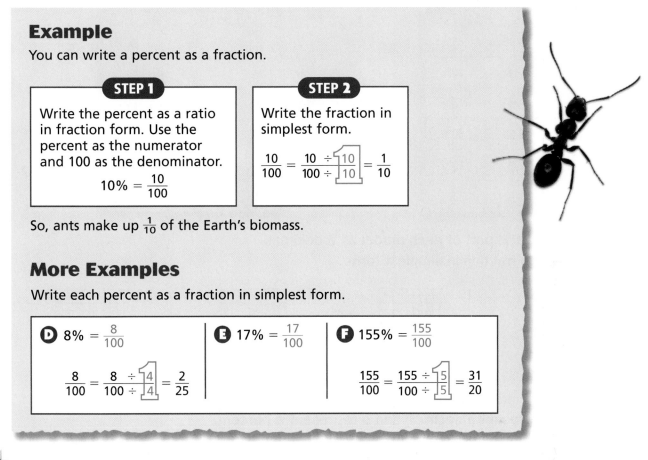

Example

You can write a percent as a fraction.

STEP 1

Write the percent as a ratio in fraction form. Use the percent as the numerator and 100 as the denominator.

$$10\% = \frac{10}{100}$$

STEP 2

Write the fraction in simplest form.

$$\frac{10}{100} = \frac{10 \div 10}{100 \div 10} = \frac{1}{10}$$

So, ants make up $\frac{1}{10}$ of the Earth's biomass.

More Examples

Write each percent as a fraction in simplest form.

D $8\% = \frac{8}{100}$

$$\frac{8}{100} = \frac{8 \div 4}{100 \div 4} = \frac{2}{25}$$

E $17\% = \frac{17}{100}$

F $155\% = \frac{155}{100}$

$$\frac{155}{100} = \frac{155 \div 5}{100 \div 5} = \frac{31}{20}$$

MATH IDEA To show a comparison, you can write a ratio as a fraction, as a decimal, or as a percent.

Ratio	Fraction	Decimal	Percent
25 to 100	$\frac{25}{100}$, or $\frac{1}{4}$	0.25	25%

▶ Check

1. **Explain** how a fraction, a decimal, and a percent are related. Write $\frac{12}{25}$ as a decimal. Then rewrite your answer as a percent.

Copy and complete the tables. Write each fraction in simplest form.

2. / 4.

Fraction	Decimal	Percent
$\frac{8}{25}$	■	■
■	0.80	80%

3. / 5.

Fraction	Decimal	Percent
■	0.04	■
$\frac{147}{100}$	■	147%

LESSON CONTINUES

Copy and complete the tables. Write each fraction in simplest form.

	Fraction	Decimal	Percent
6.	■	0.35	35%
8.	■	■	20%
10.	$\frac{1}{20}$	■	■
12.	■	0.60	60%
14.	$\frac{4}{25}$	■	16%
16.	$\frac{1}{40}$	■	2.5%

	Fraction	Decimal	Percent
7.	$\frac{29}{100}$	■	■
9.	$\frac{3}{50}$	■	■
11.	■	0.11	■
13.	■	2.0	■
15.	$\frac{117}{100}$	■	117%
17.	$\frac{3}{8}$	■	■

Express the shaded part of each model as a decimal,
a percent, and a fraction in simplest form.

18. **19.** **20.** **21.**

 Find the value of each variable. Let *f* represent
a fraction, *d* represent a decimal, and *p* represent a percent.

22. $f = 0.20 = 20\%$ **23.** $\frac{1}{4} = d = 25\%$ **24.** $f = 0.4 = 40\%$ **25.** $\frac{1}{2} = d = p$

26. $f = 75\% = d$ **27.** $p = \frac{9}{20} = d$ **28.** $f = p = 0.13$ **29.** $d = \frac{9}{10} = p$

Tell whether each fraction or decimal is greater than
100% or between 1% and 100%. Write *greater* or *between*.

30. 0.64   **31.** $\frac{24}{50}$ **32.** 2.50   **33.** $\frac{300}{100}$ **34.** $\frac{1}{5}$

35. 0.72   **36.** 3.0   **37.** $\frac{35}{50}$ **38.** $\frac{1}{4}$ **39.** $\frac{125}{100}$

40. NUMBER SENSE Ted scored 85% on his
spelling test. Kenya spelled 4 out of 5
words correctly. Rosa scored $\frac{16}{20}$ on the
test. Who got the highest test score?

41. At the concert, 100 students performed.
Out of that group, 35% played the flute.
How many students played a different
instrument?

42. Sophie misspelled 2 out of 20 words
on her spelling test. What percent of
the words did she spell correctly?

43. Zack spent $0.37 for a stamp. Write that
amount as a fraction and a percent of a
dollar.

44. Write About It How is writing a percent as a fraction like
writing a decimal as a fraction?

45. Mrs. Simms drove 240 miles on Monday and 85% of that distance on Tuesday. How many miles in all did she drive on those two days? Explain your thinking.

46. Bill's car uses 0.875 of a tank of gas each week. His car has a 20-gallon tank. Gas costs $1.40 per gallon. How much does he spend each week for gas?

Mixed Review and Test Prep

Write each ratio. Then write *part to whole, whole to part,* or *part to part* to describe the ratio. (p. 614)

47. Out of 15 students, 6 wear glasses.

48. There are 3 silver cars to 4 white cars parked on the street.

Write an equivalent fraction. (p. 328)

49. 0.45   **50.** 1.03

51. **TEST PREP**   Find 3,068 × 400. (p. 154)

A 12,272   **C** 1,224,200
B 122,720   **D** 1,227,200

52. **TEST PREP**   What is the range for the data set $80.00, $82.50, $75.00, $76.50? (p. 96)

F $5.00   **H** $78.50
G $7.50   **J** $79.50

Problem Solving   LiNKUP... to Science

The Earth's outside layer is called the crust, or lithosphere. The name comes from the Greek word *lithos,* meaning "rock." There are different kinds of rocks on the surface, made up of a variety of elements. The graph shows the most common elements in the crust.

The title tells you the subject of the graph.

The whole circle represents the whole crust.

MAIN COMPONENTS OF THE EARTH'S CRUST

47% Oxygen
28% Silicon
17% Other Elements
8% Aluminum

Each section of the circle represents one part of the crust. The label for each section names the element that makes up the part of the crust. The size of the section tells you how many parts of the whole it makes up.

Use the circle graph to solve each problem.

1. Which element composes about $\frac{1}{4}$ of the Earth's crust?

2. What fraction of the Earth's crust is composed of aluminum?

3. What percent of the Earth's crust is composed of oxygen or silicon?

4. The percent of oxygen in Earth's crust is about 2.25 times as great as in the air we breathe. About what percent of the air we breathe is composed of oxygen?

Compare Fractions, Decimals, and Percents

▶ **Learn**

FIELDER'S CHOICE Numbers can be written as fractions, decimals, and percents. Whatever their form, they can be compared and ordered.

Compare the fraction $\frac{19}{20}$ with the percent 90%.

One Way Write both numbers as fractions with denominators of 100. Then compare the numerators.

$$\frac{19}{20} = \frac{19 \times 5}{20 \times 5} = \frac{95}{100}$$
$$90\% = \frac{90}{100}$$

Since 90 < 95, then $90\% < \frac{19}{20}$.

Another Way Write both the fraction and the percent as decimals. Then compare the decimal values.

$$\frac{19}{20} = 19 \div 20 = 0.95$$
$$90\% = \frac{90}{100} = 0.90$$

Since 0.90 < 0.95, then $90\% < \frac{19}{20}$.

Example

Mike, Marty, and Meg are Florida Marlins fans. Their team has won 24 games and lost 23 games. So, the team's record of wins is just over 50%. The three friends report this record in three different ways.

Mike:	51%	percent
Marty:	$\frac{24}{47}$	fraction
Meg:	0.511	decimal

Order these numbers from least to greatest.

Express the percent and the fraction as decimals.

$$51\% = \frac{51}{100} = 0.51 \qquad \frac{24}{47} = 24 \div 47 \approx 0.5106 \qquad \begin{array}{r} 0.5106 \\ 47\overline{)24.0000} \end{array}$$

Compare and then order by using the decimal values.

$$0.51 < 0.5106 < 0.511 \qquad \text{So, } 51\% < \frac{24}{47} < 0.511.$$

These same three numbers can be ordered using a number line.

1. **Explain** two different methods for comparing $\frac{7}{20}$ and 36%.

Compare. Write <, >, or = for each ●.

2. 20% ● 0.02

3. $\frac{4}{5}$ ● 60%

4. 25% ● $\frac{1}{3}$

5. $\frac{3}{2}$ ● 150%

▶ **Practice and Problem Solving**   (Extra Practice, page 648, Set C)

Compare. Write <, >, or = for each ●.

6. 30% ● 0.30

7. $\frac{3}{10}$ ● 40%

8. 175% ● $\frac{7}{4}$

9. $\frac{6}{10}$ ● 80%

10. 104% ● $\frac{4}{4}$

11. 0.077 ● 77%

12. $\frac{10}{3}$ ● 305%

13. 40% ● $\frac{8}{25}$

14. 1.05 ● 105%

15. 35% ● $\frac{2}{5}$

16. 225% ● 2.025

17. $\frac{5}{8}$ ● 0.625

Order from least to greatest. You may use a number line.

18. 65%, 0.59, $\frac{3}{5}$

19. 1.20, 125%, $\frac{3}{4}$

20. 58%, $\frac{5}{8}$, 5.8

21. 3%, 0.003, $\frac{3}{10}$

22. 0.25, $\frac{3}{8}$, 23%

23. $\frac{10}{3}$, 3.20, 325%

24. 16%, 0.6, $\frac{1}{6}$

25. 4.26, $\frac{18}{4}$, 440%

26. **? What's the Error?** 50% of the 120 sixth graders and $\frac{3}{8}$ of the 120 fifth graders walk to school. Bob says the number of students who walk to school is the same for both grades. Find and correct Bob's error.

27. The math test had 25 problems. Beau got 88% of the problems correct, and Sandy got $\frac{23}{25}$ correct. How many more problems did Sandy answer correctly than Beau?

28. **Write About It** Explain how to order $\frac{9}{4}$, 35%, 0.3, and $2\frac{1}{2}$.

30. **REASONING** Andre has $10 more than Cassie, and Cassie has $5 more than Avery. Altogether they have $50. What percent of the money does Cassie have?

29. Kiley wanted to leave 15% of the cost of the meal for the tip. Joe said to leave $\frac{1}{5}$ of the cost and Kim said to leave 0.18 of the cost. Who wants to leave the greatest tip? Explain.

Mixed Review and Test Prep

31. Write the ratio 3:4 as a fraction. (p. 616)

32. Evaluate. $2^2 + 2^3 + 2^4$ (p. 296)

33. $3\frac{3}{4} + 3\frac{1}{2}$ (p. 376)

34. $675 \div 25$ (p. 212)

35. **TEST PREP** Evaluate. $2 \times (n + 25)$, if $n = 125$ (p. 260)

   A 152   B 200   C 275   D 300

Find a Percent of a Number

► Learn

ZZZZZ . . . The students in Andrew's science class hope 5,000 people visit their *Sleeptime* home page by the end of the school year. According to the latest tracking report, they have reached 30% of their goal. How many people have visited the home page? What is 30% of 5,000?

★ **HANDS ON**

Activity

Make a model to find 30% of 5,000.
MATERIALS: index cards

STEP 1

Let each card represent 10% of the number of visitors. Put down 10 cards to represent 100%, or 5,000. Each 10% represents 500 since 10 × 500 = 5,000.

◄────── 5,000 ──────►

| 10% | 10% | 10% | 10% | 10% | 10% | 10% | 10% | 10% | 10% |
| 500 | 500 | 500 | 500 | 500 | 500 | 500 | 500 | 500 | 500 |

STEP 2

Now separate 3 cards to show 3 × 10%, or 30%.

| 10% | 10% | 10% | | 10% | 10% | 10% | 10% | 10% | 10% | 10% |
| 500 | 500 | 500 |

Since each card represents 500, the 3 cards that make up 30% represent 3 × 500, or 1,500.

So far, 1,500 people have visited the *Sleeptime* home page.

- How many cards show 50% of 5,000? 80% of 5,000?

Quick Review

Write each percent as a decimal.

1. 70%   **2.** 55%
3. 4%   **4.** 99%
5. 100%

Change the Percent and Multiply

When asleep, the average person dreams about 25% of the time. If you sleep for 9 hours, for how long do you dream?

You can find a percent of a number by changing the percent to a decimal or a fraction and multiplying.

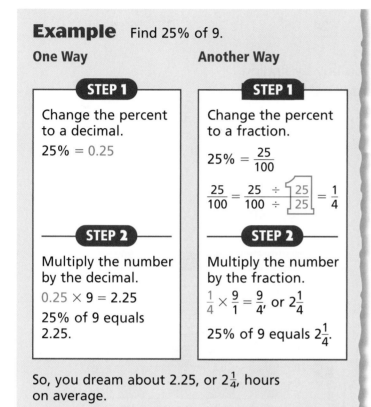

Example Find 25% of 9.

One Way

STEP 1

Change the percent to a decimal.

25% = 0.25

STEP 2

Multiply the number by the decimal.

$0.25 \times 9 = 2.25$

25% of 9 equals 2.25.

Another Way

STEP 1

Change the percent to a fraction.

$25\% = \frac{25}{100}$

$\frac{25}{100} = \frac{25 \div 25}{100 \div 25} = \frac{1}{4}$

STEP 2

Multiply the number by the fraction.

$\frac{1}{4} \times \frac{9}{1} = \frac{9}{4}$, or $2\frac{1}{4}$

25% of 9 equals $2\frac{1}{4}$.

So, you dream about 2.25, or $2\frac{1}{4}$, hours on average.

▲ Since everyone dreams for about a quarter of his or her nightly sleep, the total world dream time per night is one million years!

You can also find a percent of a number by using a calculator.

About 12% of people snore. Out of 600 people, how many of them snore?

Find 12% of 600.

So, about 72 out of 600 people snore.

 Check

1. **Explain** how to find a percent of a number.

Find the percent of the number.

2. 5% of 80   **3.** 25% of 64   **4.** 15% of 120   **5.** 50% of 92

6. 40% of 60   **7.** 75% of 120   **8.** 35% of 39   **9.** 150% of 400

LESSON CONTINUES

Find the percent of the number.

10. 30% of 130

11. 15% of 40

12. 8% of 44

13. 35% of 160

14. 90% of 64

15. 100% of 15

16. 23% of 175

17. 200% of 190

18. 65% of 100

19. 70% of 210

20. 40% of 20

21. 15% of 60

22. 2% of 37

23. 60% of 60

24. 85% of 42

25. 150% of 14

You can find the sales tax for any item you buy by finding a percent of the price. Find the sales tax for each price to the nearest cent.

26. price: $25.00
tax rate: 5%

27. price: $8.50
tax rate: 4%

28. price: $0.99
tax rate: 7%

29. price: $198.23
tax rate: 9%

30. price: $32.00
tax rate: 7.5%

31. price: $1.79
tax rate: 6%

32. price: $45.00
tax rate: 8.25%

33. price: $79.80
tax rate: 8.5%

USE DATA   For 34–37, use the graph.

34. On average, how many hours a day does a child sleep?

35. On average, how many more hours a day does an infant sleep than an adult over 65?

36. On average, how many hours does an adult sleep in a year?

37. Write a problem using the information in the graph.

HOW MUCH DO PEOPLE SLEEP?

Average Total Sleep Time (% of 24 hours)

Infant 67% • Child 40% • Adult 33% • Adult Over 65 23%

Age

38. **What's the Question?** Karen scored 85% on the test. The test had 20 questions. The answer is 3 questions.

39. **REASONING** Eduardo showed Jim 50% of his card collection. If he showed him 25 cards, how many cards does Eduardo have in all?

40. **NUMBER SENSE** Tom says that when you find any percent of a number, the answer is always less than the number. Do you agree? Explain.

41. On average, a cat sleeps 15.1 hours a day, a dog sleeps 10.6 hours a day, and a guppy sleeps 7.0 hours a day. Order the animals from the smallest percent of the day they sleep to greatest percent they sleep.

42. Huang is stringing 8-mm beads for a garland. There are about 3.25 beads per inch. How many beads will he need to make a garland 48 inches long?

43. Anya won 40% of her 20 games. Linda won 60% of her 15 games. Who won more games?

Mixed Review **and Test Prep**

44. Identify the property used.
$4 \times (20 + 3) = (4 \times 20) + (4 \times 3)$ (p. 260)

45. Find the value of m. $m + 25 = 76$ (p. 70)

46. Round 2,912 to the nearest hundred. (p. 38)

47. **TEST PREP** Which number is NOT evenly divisible by 4? (p. 276)

    A 119,022   **C** 137,032
    B 119,444   **D** 331,728

48. $2,567 \times 84$ (p. 152)

49. Write $\frac{3}{8}$ as a decimal. (p. 328)

50. Round 0.2374 to the nearest tenth. (p. 40)

51. **TEST PREP** Rita's school has a student-to-teacher ratio of 20:1. If there are 300 students in the school, how many teachers are there? (p. 618)

    F 5   **G** 10   **H** 15   **J** 20

Problem Solving　THINKER'S CORNER

SALE PRICE　Now that you know how to find a percent of a number, you can find the sale price of any item. Follow these steps to find the sale price of a sleeping bag.

Camping Gear Sale
REGULAR PRICE $159.75
Now 30% off

STEP 1

Change the percent to a decimal.

30% = 0.30

STEP 2

Multiply the regular price by the decimal.

$159.75 × 0.30 = $47.925
$47.93 ← Round to the nearest cent.

STEP 3

Subtract the discount from the regular price.

$159.75 − $47.93 = $111.82

So, the sale price is $111.82.

Find the sale price to the nearest cent.

1. Regular price: $15.00

20% OFF

2. Regular price: $17.50

Nighty-Night Lullabies

$\frac{1}{2}$ OFF

3. Regular price: $24.89

The Dreamer

SAVE 75%

4. Describe another way to find the sales price in Exercise 3.

Problem Solving Strategy
Make a Graph

Quick Review

1. 100×33.45
2. 10×0.78
3. 100×3.59
4. 10×0.06
5. 10×1.05

PROBLEM Sonya surveyed 200 students in her school to find out their favorite type of music. She wants to display her data to show how the votes for each type of music relate to the total number of votes. What is the best way to display her data?

UNDERSTAND

- What are you asked to find?
- What information will you use?

PLAN

- What strategy can you use to solve the problem?

  You can *make a graph* to display the data, showing the percent of students who prefer each type of music.

SOLVE

- What graph would be the best to make?

  Since Sonya wants to show how the parts relate to the whole, a circle graph is best. Divide a circle into ten equal parts. Each part represents 10% of the 200 students. Find the percent of total votes for each type of music.

WHAT TYPE OF MUSIC IS YOUR FAVORITE?	
Music	**Student votes**
Pop Rock	60
Jazz	20
Classical	20
Rap	20
Country	80

  Pop Rock   Jazz, Classical, Rap   Country

  $\frac{60}{200} = 30\%$ $\frac{20}{200} = 10\%$ each $\frac{80}{200} = 40\%$

  Shade the parts to represent each percent. Label and title the graph.

CHECK

- Why is this the best way to display the data?
- What is the sum of the percents that represents the whole, or 200 students?

WHAT TYPE OF MUSIC IS YOUR FAVORITE?

40% Country 30% Pop Rock 10% Jazz 10% Classical 10% Rap

Strategies

Draw a Diagram or Picture
Make a Model or Act It Out
Make an Organized List
Find a Pattern
▶ **Make a Table or Graph**
Predict and Test
Work Backward
Solve a Simpler Problem
Write an Equation
Use Logical Reasoning

Make a graph to solve.

1. **What if** 80 of the students liked pop rock, 40 liked country, 20 liked jazz, 40 liked classical, and 20 liked rap? What percent of the vote would pop rock receive? What percent of the vote would all the other types of music receive?

2. Out of $100 for the class trip, Kim spent $\frac{1}{10}$ for food, 20% for museum tickets, $\frac{3}{10}$ for souvenirs, and 40% for the bus ride. Which section of your graph is the largest? How much money does it represent?

USE DATA Use the circle graph. Each year people in the United States throw away more than 180 million tons of trash.

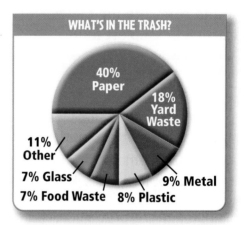

3. What fills $\frac{2}{25}$ of the trash?
   A paper   C yard waste
   B plastic   D other

4. How much paper goes in the trash in an average month?
   F 1 million tons H 6 million tons
   G 3 million tons J 72 million tons

Mixed Strategy Practice

USE DATA For 5–8, use the table to make a circle graph. There are 50 musicians in the school orchestra.

WHO PLAYS WHAT INSTRUMENT IN THE SCHOOL ORCHESTRA?

Section	Percent
Strings	60%
Percussion	10%
Brass	10%
Woodwind	20%

5. How many musicians play woodwind instruments?

6. How many more musicians play stringed instruments than brass instruments?

7. How many fewer musicians play woodwind instruments than stringed instruments?

8. **What if** there were 100 musicians in the orchestra. How many would play stringed instruments?

9. There are 56 teachers at Sunridge Elementary. Of the teachers, $\frac{1}{4}$ have no pets. Some teachers have one pet, and twice as many teachers have two or more. How many have two or more pets?

10. ✏ **Write About It** Out of 50 students surveyed on favorite national parks, 30 chose Yellowstone, 10 chose Everglades, and 10 Death Valley. Explain how you would display this data.

Extra Practice

Set A (pp. 634–635)

Write the number as a decimal and a percent.

1. six tenths   **2.** two hundredths   **3.** nineteen hundredths

Write each decimal as a percent.

4. 0.22   **5.** 0.37   **6.** 1.21   **7.** 2.08   **8.** 0.75

Write each percent as a decimal.

9. 64%   **10.** 25%   **11.** 250%   **12.** 50%   **13.** 10%

Set B (pp. 636–639)

For 1–4, copy and complete the tables.
Write each fraction in simplest form.

	FRACTION	DECIMAL	PERCENT
1.	$\frac{3}{5}$	■	60%
3.	■	■	10%

	FRACTION	DECIMAL	PERCENT
2.	■	■	40%
4.	$\frac{1}{20}$	■	■

5. Shawn scored 30% of the points. Mike scored 30 points out of 100. Jeff scored $\frac{2}{5}$ of the points. Who scored the most points?

Set C (pp. 640–641)

Compare. Write <, >, or = for each ●.

1. 60% ● 0.50   **2.** $\frac{4}{6}$ ● 60%   **3.** $\frac{4}{3}$ ● 135%   **4.** $\frac{7}{10}$ ● 70%

5. 95% ● $\frac{9}{10}$ **6.** 0.045 ● 45%   **7.** $\frac{5}{2}$ ● 250%   **8.** 24% ● $\frac{1}{4}$

Order from least to greatest. You may use a number line.

9. 25%, 0.23, $\frac{1}{5}$ **10.** 0.40, 39%, $\frac{3}{5}$ **11.** 105%, $\frac{6}{5}$, 1.5   **12.** 2%, 0.20, $\frac{1}{10}$

13. 0.75, $\frac{4}{5}$, 70%   **14.** $\frac{12}{5}$, 2.50, 205%   **15.** 12%, 0.20, $\frac{11}{100}$ **16.** 3.25, $\frac{14}{4}$, 320%

Set D (pp. 642–645)

Find the percent of the number.

1. 10% of 10   **2.** 12% of 75   **3.** 150% of 130   **4.** 70% of 65

5. 20% of 50   **6.** 100% of 97   **7.** 25% of 300   **8.** 40% of 80

9. Mark got 70% out of 80 questions correct and Richard got 80% out of 70 questions correct. Who got more correct?

10. Julie found a quarter, 2 dimes, and 4 pennies in her coat pocket. What percent of a dollar did she find?

Review/Test

✓ CHECK VOCABULARY AND CONCEPTS

Choose the best term from the box.

decimal
percent
product
ratio

1. You can write a __?__ as a fraction, a decimal, or a percent. (p. 636)

2. A ratio of a number to 100 is a __?__. (p. 632)

3. You can find a percent of a number by changing a percent to a __?__ and multiplying. (p. 643)

Model each ratio on grid paper. Then write the percent.

(pp. 632–633)

4. 27 tiles out of 100 tiles

5. 8 bats out of 100 bats

6. 49 balls out of 100 balls

✓ CHECK SKILLS

Write each decimal as a percent. (pp. 634–635)

7. 0.35

8. 0.75

9. 0.49

10. 1.23

Copy and complete the tables. Write each fraction in simplest form. (pp. 636–639)

11.

Fraction	Decimal	Percent
■	0.20	■

12.

Fraction	Decimal	Percent
■	■	43%

Compare. Write <, >, or = for each ●. (pp. 640–641)

13. 10% ● 0.01

14. $\frac{3}{4}$ ● 80%

15. 125% ● $1\frac{1}{3}$

16. 2.09 ● 209%

Order from least to greatest. You may use a number line. (pp. 640–641)

17. 0.25, 24%, $\frac{3}{8}$

18. 60%, $\frac{2}{3}$, 0.62

19. $\frac{5}{2}$, 248%, 2.6

Find the percent of the number. (pp. 642–645)

20. 6% of 50

21. 200% of 75

22. 15% of 345

23. 99% of 99

✓ CHECK PROBLEM SOLVING

For 24–25, make a circle graph to solve. 120 students were surveyed. (pp. 646–647)

FAVORITE BEVERAGES				
Beverage	Water	Milk	Soda	Juice
Student votes	12	36	48	24

24. What percent of the students liked soda the best?

25. What percent of the students liked milk the best?

Standardized Test Prep

⭐ NUMBER SENSE, CONCEPTS, AND OPERATIONS

> **TIP** **Get the information you need.**
> See item 1. You need to find what part of the total number of students is studying Italian. Write a fraction to represent this.

1. Brendan made a chart to show the languages that the 24 students in his fifth-grade class are studying.

LANGUAGE STUDY	
Language	**Number of Students**
Spanish	12
French	8
Italian	4

What fraction of the students in his class study Italian?

A $\frac{1}{6}$ **C** $\frac{1}{3}$

B $\frac{1}{4}$ **D** $\frac{1}{2}$

2. About 70% of the students at Jamie's school ride a bus to school. Which of the following is NOT equivalent to 70%?

F 0.07

G 0.7

H $\frac{70}{100}$

J $\frac{7}{10}$

3. **Explain It** Kelly's lunch bill was $9.89. She wants to leave a 15% tip. ESTIMATE to determine how much she should leave for a tip. Explain how you found your estimate.

⭐ DATA ANALYSIS AND PROBABILITY

4. What percent of the United States budget for 2002 was spent on health and Social Security?

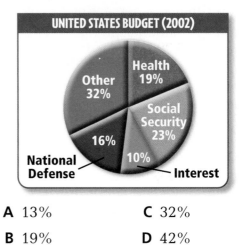

UNITED STATES BUDGET (2002)

Health 19%
Other 32%
Social Security 23%
16%
National Defense
10%
Interest

A 13%   **C** 32%

B 19%   **D** 42%

5. Use the circle graph in Problem 4. What percent of the budget is NOT spent on national defense?

F 84%   **H** 70%

G 75%   **J** 67%

6. **Explain It** The table shows the results of a survey of 100 travelers who were asked to name a continent they have visited.

SURVEY OF TRAVELERS	
Continent	**Number of Travelers**
Africa	10
Asia	20
Australia	10
Europe	40
South America	20

What type of graph would be best to display this data? Explain your choice and how you would make the graph.

⭐ ALGEBRAIC THINKING

7. Marcy made a pattern with dots.

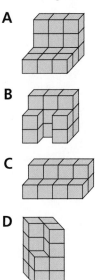

If the pattern continues, how many dots should she draw below the line if there are 6 dots above the line?

A 6

B 12

C 18

D 24

8. A bus stops at the corner of Main Street and First Avenue every 20 minutes.

If the first bus stops at 7:00 A.M., at what time does the seventh bus stop?

F 7:20 A.M.

G 8:40 A.M.

H 9:00 A.M.

J 9:20 A.M.

9. Explain It Carlton wrote a pattern of numbers.

3, 6, 4, 7, 5, 8, 6, 9, ▮

What is a rule for the pattern? What could be the next number in the pattern? Explain how you found your rule.

⭐ MEASUREMENT

10. Which figure has the greatest volume?

A

B

C

D

11. The diagram below shows the actual size of a large paper clip. Which of the following best describes the length of this paper clip?

F 5 kilometers

G 5 meters

H 5 centimeters

J 5 millimeters

12. Explain It Scott is putting boxes that each hold a baseball into a carton. ESTIMATE to determine how many boxes will fit in the carton. Explain how you found your estimate.

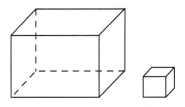

Probability

≡FAST FACT · SOCIAL STUDIES Pachisi is a game of chance that is the national game of India. The players toss cowrie shells and move pieces around a gameboard according to how the shells land.

PROBLEM SOLVING Sometimes winning a game depends on chance, and sometimes it depends on skill and strategy. Look at the games in the photos. Tell whether each is a game of chance or one of skill and strategy.

4000 B.C. — Babylonian board game played that was ancestor of chess and checkers

3000 B.C. — Backgammon played in ancient Sumeria

2000 B.C. — Egyptians played game like modern-day checkers

1000 B.C. —

B.C.
A.D.

— Pachisi played in India
— Mah-Jongg first played in China

A.D. 1000

— A modern version of Pachisi first played in 1959

A.D. 2000 — Computer games first played in 1970's

Use this page to help you review and remember
important skills needed for Chapter 30.

✓ IMPOSSIBLE, CERTAIN, LIKELY, UNLIKELY

Classify each event as *certain, impossible, likely,* or *unlikely.*

1. pulling a red counter from a bag containing only blue counters

2. pulling a yellow marble from a bag of 9 yellow and 2 green marbles

3. becoming warmer in front of a fire

4. going to the planet Jupiter on a family vacation

5. tossing a 3 on a cube labeled 1, 1, 1, 2, 2, 3

6. spinning an odd number on a spinner labeled 1, 3, 5, and 7

7. pulling a blue or red marble from a bag of 3 blue, 5 red, and 2 green marbles

8. spinning an even number on a spinner with equal sections labeled 1, 3, 5, 6, 7, and 9

✓ PARTS OF A WHOLE

Write a fraction that names the shaded part.

9.

10.

11.

12.

13.

14.

REVIEW

unlikely [un•līk′lē] *adverb*

The prefix *im-* or *un-* can be used to form a new word by adding "not" to the meaning of a word.

im + possible = impossible, which means "not possible"

Write a sentence with *likely.* Then write a sentence with *unlikely.*

PREVIEW

probability

possible outcomes

sample space

theoretical probability

equally likely

experimental probability

tree diagram

arrangement

combination

GO ON-LINE   www.harcourtschool.com/mathglossary

Probability Experiments

Quick Review

Write the fraction of each circle that is shaded.

1.

2.

3.

4.

5.

▶ **Explore**

Mark conducted an experiment. He put 5 red, 3 green, and 2 yellow tiles into a bag and pulled samples without looking. He predicted that half of his pulls would be red.

Probability is the chance that an event will happen. In Mark's experiment, the events are the colors. The three different events are red, green, yellow.

In his experiment, Mark pulled a tile from the bag 10 times, replacing the tile after each pull. He pulled 6 red tiles in 10 tries. Based on these results, the probability of pulling a red tile would be 6 out of 10.

Conduct the same experiment as Mark. Place 5 red, 3 green, and 2 yellow tiles in the bag.

- Make a table like the one shown.
- Pull a tile without looking. Record your pull in the table with a tally mark. Repeat 10 times. Replace the tile after each pull. Total your tally marks in the table.
- Based upon your results, what would you predict for the probability of pulling a red tile? Explain.

Try It

Use a bag with 6 blue, 2 red, and 2 yellow tiles.

a. If you pull 1 tile from the bag, what color do you think it will be?

b. Make a prediction about the probability of pulling a yellow tile.

c. Make your own table. Pull, record, and replace a tile 10 times. How do your results compare with your prediction above?

VOCABULARY

probability

MATERIALS

color tiles, paper bag

COLOR-TILE EXPERIMENT			
Event	Yellow	Red	Green
Frequency			
Total			

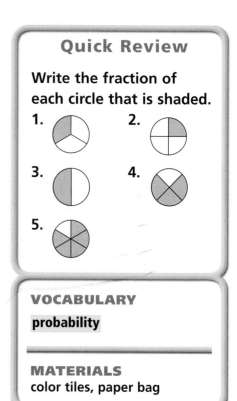

If you pull out 1 tile, what color do you think it will be?

Look back at Mark's experiment. Predict how many times out of 100 he would pull red. Since half of the tiles are red, a good prediction is 50 pulls.

Mark and nine other students recorded their results.

Technology Link

More Practice: Harcourt Mega Math Fraction Action, *Last Chance Canyon*, Level I

COLOR-TILE EXPERIMENT (100 Pulls)											
Students	A	B	C	D	E	F	G	H	I	J	Total
Red Pulls	4	6	4	7	5	4	6	7	5	4	52
Yellow Pulls	2	2	3	1	2	2	1	1	3	2	19
Green Pulls	4	2	3	2	3	4	3	2	2	4	29

With nine other classmates, make a table for 10 pulls each, and find the totals.

- How do your group's actual results compare to the prediction for pulling red? To the results of other groups?

Practice and Problem Solving

1. Justin pulls a marble from a bag of marbles 20 times. He pulls 7 blue marbles. Predict the probability of pulling a blue marble.

2. Kristin pulls a tile from a bag of tiles 15 times. She pulls 10 red tiles. Predict the probability of pulling a tile that is not red.

3. Half of the marbles in Jackson's bag are his favorite color, orange. If he pulls 12 marbles, how many do you predict will be orange?

4. Jonathan has a bag with 25 tiles. Fifteen of the tiles are red. Predict the probability of Jonathan pulling a red tile.

5. **USE DATA** Kyla pulls a tile from a bag 30 different times. Based on these results, what are the chances that neither the most likely nor the least likely color is pulled?

EVENT	RED	GREEN	YELLOW
Number of pulls	卌 III	卌 II	卌 卌 卌
Total	8	7	15

6. Ben is making a sandbox for his brother. He has 12 ft of wood for the sides. He wants the sandbox to have the greatest area possible. What will be the dimensions and area of the sandbox?

Mixed Review and Test Prep

7. $0.072 \div 8$ (p. 232)

8. Of the 50 cars in the parking lot, 18% are blue, 26% are red, and 24% are white. How many cars are a color other than blue, red, or white? (p. 642)

9. $13\overline{)78}$ (p. 212)   10. 9×21 (p. 150)

11. **TEST PREP** Which is a prime number? (p. 300)

   A 39   C 53

   B 45   D 76

Probability Expressed as a Fraction

▶ **Learn**

SPINNER WINNER! Ami draws a card and spins the pointer on the spinner below. She wins if the pointer stops on a number that matches what is shown on the card. What is the probability that the pointer stops on a number greater than 5?

There are 8 **possible outcomes**, or results. The **sample space**, or set of all possible outcomes, is 1, 2, 3, 4, 5, 6, 7, 8.

Three outcomes, 6, 7, 8, are greater than 5.

The **theoretical probability** of an event is a comparison of the number of favorable outcomes to the number of possible, equally likely outcomes. **Equally likely** outcomes have the same chance of happening. You can write theoretical probability as a fraction.

$$\text{Probability of an event} = \frac{\text{number of favorable outcomes}}{\text{number of possible, equally likely outcomes}}$$

$$\text{Probability of a win} = \frac{\text{number of choices greater than 5}}{\text{number of choices on the spinner}} = \frac{3}{8}$$

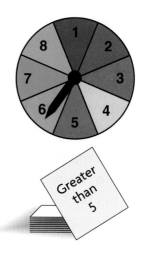

So, the probability that the pointer stops on a number greater than 5 is $\frac{3}{8}$.

The probability of an event can always be expressed as 0, 1, or a fraction between 0 and 1.

Examples Find the probability of each event. Use Ami's spinner.

A | 2, 3, 5, or 7

4 out of 8 — Express the probability using words.

$\frac{4}{8}$, or $\frac{1}{2}$ — Express the probability as a fraction.

B | an integer

1, 2, 3, 4, 5, 6, 7, 8 — List the integers.

8 out of 8 — Express the probability using words and as a fraction.

$\frac{8}{8}$, or 1

▶ Check

1. **Explain** how to use this spinner to find the probability that the event is a multiple of 3.

Use the spinner above to write a fraction for the probability of each event.

2. less than 4   3. greater than $\frac{1}{2}$ 4. factor of 28   5. prime number

▶ Practice and Problem Solving   (Extra Practice, page 666, Set A)

Use the spinner at the right to write a fraction for the probability of each event.

6. less than 40   7. a prime number   8. a factor of 100

9. between 10 and 30   10. a composite number   11. an integer greater than 40

Write a fraction for the probability of each event with a number cube labeled 1 to 6.

12. 2 or 3   13. 0 or 1   14. a prime number   15. not 6

16. **Vocabulary Power** In mathematics, an *outcome* is a possible result. Name two ways the word *outcome* is used outside of mathematics.

17. Write the sample space for tossing a number cube labeled 1 to 6.

18. Without looking, Jo pulled a marble from the bag at the right. Using a number line from 0 to 1, order the events *red, yellow or blue, not green, orange* by their probabilities.

19. ✎ **Write a problem** involving probability and a spinner with six equal-size sections. Three sections are red, two sections are blue, and one section is green.

⎯ Mixed Review and Test Prep ⎯

20. Write an equivalent decimal for 0.70.
   (p. 26)

21. Round 0.2134 to the nearest thousandth.
   (p. 40)

22. 3,159 ÷ 81 (p. 212)

23. Write the reciprocal of $7\frac{1}{7}$. (p. 404)

24. **TEST PREP**   The sum of two numbers is 49. Their difference is less than 10. Which is a possible pair? (p. 68)

   A 30 and 19
   B 24 and 25
   C 40 and 9
   D 35 and 14

Probability and Predictions

Quick Review

Find the product.

1. $\frac{1}{2} \times 36$ **2.** $\frac{2}{3} \times 24$

3. $\frac{5}{8} \times 40$ **4.** $\frac{3}{5} \times 60$

5. $\frac{3}{4} \times 300$

VOCABULARY

experimental probability

▶ **Learn**

FRACTION ACTION Vicki has a favorite video game. She won 7 of the first 10 games she played. Use a fraction to predict her chances of winning the next game.

Based on these results, Vicki's chances of winning the next game are 7 out of 10, or $\frac{7}{10}$. As she plays more games, she might get better at winning, so this probability may change.

The **experimental probability** of an event can be found by conducting repeated trials. Compare the number of times a certain event actually occurs to the total number of trials, or times you repeat the activity.

$$\text{Experimental probability} = \frac{\text{number of times event occurs}}{\text{total number of trials}}$$

You can use experimental probability to predict future events.

Example

Vicki's sister, Becky, won 2 of the first 5 video games she played. Based on these results, how many times can Becky expect to win in her next 20 games?

$\dfrac{\text{Probability of}}{\text{winning}} = \dfrac{\text{number of wins}}{\text{total number of games}} = \dfrac{2}{5}$	Find the experimental probability based on the games already played.
$\dfrac{2}{5} \times \dfrac{20}{1} = \dfrac{40}{5}$, or 8.	Multiply by 20, the number of new games to be played.

So, Becky can expect to win 8 of her next 20 games.

▶ **Check**

Technology Link

More Practice: Harcourt Mega Math Fraction Action, *Last Chance Canyon*, Level J

1. Explain how to predict the number of wins in 100 games if the experimental probability of winning is $\frac{3}{10}$.

Express the experimental probability as a fraction. Use it to predict the same event in future trials.

2. 5 wins in 6 games
   12 more games

3. 4 heads in 7 tosses
   14 more tosses

4. 8 red tiles in 12 pulls
   6 more pulls

The probability of winning is $\frac{9}{20}$. Predict the number of wins.

5. in 60 games

6. in 100 games

7. in 240 games

8. in 120 games

9. in 180 games

10. in 360 games

Express the experimental probability as a fraction. Use it to predict the same event in future trials.

11. 3 wins in 4 games
8 more games

12. 2 heads in 6 tosses
12 more tosses

13. 4 red tiles in 5 pulls
25 more pulls

14. 3 losses in 6 games
10 more games

15. 4 tails in 12 tosses
6 more tosses

16. 8 blue tiles in 12 pulls
3 more pulls

17. USE DATA Use the coin toss table at the right to find the experimental probability of tossing heads. How does it compare with the theoretical probability of $\frac{1}{2}$?

COIN TOSS EXPERIMENT	
Outcome	Times Tossed
Heads	47
Tails	53

Ken searches through the first 100 letters in a newspaper article and finds 13 *e*'s. Use this information for Exercises 18–20.

18. Find the experimental probability that a randomly chosen letter is an *e*.

19. How many *e*'s would you predict in the first 800 letters of this article?

20. REASONING The entire newspaper article contains 916 words. Each word has an average of 5 letters. Predict the total number of *e*'s in the entire article.

21. Nancy has $23.75 in quarters and Lynn has $5.85 in nickels. Who has more coins? Explain.

22. Holly takes $\frac{1}{2}$ hour to walk to school. She spends $\frac{1}{2}$ of that time walking down her street. What part of an hour does Holly spend walking down her street? How many minutes is this?

23. **? What's the Question?** In a random survey of 100 students at Holt School, 30 students chose cats as their favorite pet. There are 500 students at Holt School. The answer is 150.

Mixed Review and Test Prep

24. Order 23,546; 24,546; 23,456; and 23,564 from least to greatest. (p. 10)

25. $3{,}456 \times 24$ (p. 152)

26. $2{,}891 \times 58$ (p. 152)

27. Write 0.25 as a fraction. (p. 328)

28. TEST PREP A bag has 5 red, 3 blue, and 7 green tiles. Bob pulls one without looking. What is the probability it is not green? (p. 656)

A $\frac{7}{8}$

B $\frac{8}{12}$

C $\frac{7}{15}$

D $\frac{8}{15}$

▶ **Learn**

TEXT TYPE Nadine needs to choose a type font and size for her poster notes. The 3 fonts she has are Courier, Helvetica, and Times. The 4 sizes are 9 point, 10 point, 12 point, and 14 point. How many choices of fonts and sizes combined does she have?

One Way You can use a **tree diagram** to organize and show all possible choices or outcomes.

Fonts	Sizes	Choices
Courier	9 pt	Courier font in 9 point
	10 pt	Courier font in 10 point
	12 pt	Courier font in 12 point
	14 pt	Courier font in 14 point
Helvetica	9 pt	Helvetica font in 9 point
	10 pt	Helvetica font in 10 point
	12 pt	Helvetica font in 12 point
	14 pt	Helvetica font in 14 point
Times	9 pt	Times font in 9 point
	10 pt	Times font in 10 point
	12 pt	Times font in 12 point
	14 pt	Times font in 14 point

Count the number of choices. Nadine has 12 different font-and-size choices.

Another Way You can find the number of choices or outcomes by multiplying.

Number of type fonts		Number of type sizes		Number of choices
↓		↓		↓
3	×	4	=	12

• Would the number of outcomes be different if you listed size first and font second?

MATH IDEA You can use a tree diagram to organize and show a list of all possible choices. You can multiply to find the number of choices.

1. **Explain** how the outcomes would change if Nadine could choose from 5 type fonts but only 3 type sizes.

For 2–3, make a tree diagram to show the possible choices.

2. **School Outfits**
   Pants: tan, blue, black
   Shirts: white, brown, blue

3. **Room Decorating Choices**
   Paint: white, blue, pink
   Borders: wallpaper, stencils
   Windows: blinds, curtains

Practice and Problem Solving Extra Practice, page 666, Set C

For 4–5, make a tree diagram to show the possible choices.

4. **Summer School Classes**
   Subject: art, math, music, computers
   Session: first, second

5. **Sandwich Selections**
   Peanut Butter: smooth, chunky
   Jelly: grape, peach, apricot
   Bread: white, whole wheat

6. Ben can buy only one book. His choices are mystery, biography, or science fiction. He can choose hardback or paperback. How many choices does Ben have?

7. Chris has packed 4 shirts and 3 pairs of shorts for his trip. How many more shirt-and-shorts choices will he have if he packs another shirt and another pair of shorts?

8. Milo and Jill are playing a game. Milo chooses one letter from the word COMPUTER and one from MOUSE. How many choices does he have?

9. Jill chooses one letter from the word MATH and one from MUSIC. How many choices does she have? How many do not contain M?

10. For her notes, Nadine can choose single or double spacing and plain, bold, or italic type. How many choices of spacing and type does Nadine have?

11. **ALGEBRA** The numbers of different choices for shirts and slacks are x and y. Write an expression to show how many shirt-and-slacks outfits can be made.

Mixed Review and Test Prep

12. 3,289 (p. 152)
    $\times$ 43

13. 2,439 (p. 152)
    $\times$ 82

Round to the nearest hundred thousand.
(p. 38)

14. 7,809,432

15. 57,355,987

16. **TEST PREP** Which is the product $\frac{3}{4} \times \frac{2}{3}$?
    (p. 386)

    A $\frac{5}{12}$

    C $\frac{5}{7}$

    B $\frac{1}{2}$

    D $\frac{6}{7}$

Arrangements and Combinations

Quick Review

Find the product.

1. $1 \times 2 \times 3$
2. $1 \times 2 \times 3 \times 4 \times 5$
3. $1 \times 2 \times 3 \times 4$
4. $1 \times 3 \times 5 \times 7 \times 9$
5. $2 \times 4 \times 6 \times 8$

VOCABULARY

arrangement
combination

▶ **Learn**

BUG BITES Jon is making a poster for a science report on bugs. He wants to have three pictures in a row, showing a fly, a bee, and a mosquito. How many different arrangements are possible?

In this problem, the order of the pictures is important. An **arrangement** is an ordering of items.

One Way Make an organized list of all possible arrangements.

This list is organized in alphabetical order using the first letter of the name of each bug.

BFM   BMF   FBM   FMB   MBF   MFB

Another Way Multiply to find the total number of arrangements.

Think: What choices are available for the three positions?

3 choices for the first picture	2 choices remain for the second	1 choice left for the third

$$3 \quad \times \quad 2 \quad \times \quad 1 \quad = 6$$

So, there are 6 possible arrangements.

A **combination** is a choice in which the order of the items does not matter.

Example

In his report, Jon has time to talk about only 2 of the bugs. How many combinations of 2 bugs are possible?

Make an organized list of all possible combinations. Do not include pairs that reverse the ones already listed.

bee and fly
bee and mosquito
fly and mosquito

Think: The pairs "bee and fly" and "fly and bee" represent the same combination.

So, Jon has 3 possible combinations of 2 bugs.

1. **Explain** how to find the number of arrangements possible if Jonathan puts 4 different pictures in a row instead of 3.

For 2–3, use the letters L, E, G.

2. List the 6 two-letter arrangements that are possible.

3. List the 3 combinations, or choices, of two letters that are possible.

▶ **Practice and Problem Solving** (Extra Practice, page 666, Set D)

For 4–5, use the digits in 9,631.

4. List the 12 two-digit arrangements that are possible.

5. List the 6 combinations, or choices, of two digits that are possible.

6. In how many different ways can a penny, nickel, and dime be stacked, face-up, one on top of the other?

7. List the combinations, or choices, of two letters that are possible using the letters in the word METRIC.

Each card has a different arrangement of the letters in the word BUG. One card is chosen at random. Find the probability of each event.

8. The letters are in alphabetical order.

9. The letter U is the middle letter.

10. The letters B and G are together.

11. The letter B comes before the letter G.

12. **≡FAST FACT • SCIENCE** There are about 248,000 different kinds of plants. About 9 out of every 10 are flowering plants. About how many non-flowering plants are there?

13. **? What's the Error?** June has a bag of 99 blue tiles and 1 red tile. June says that it is certain she will pull a blue tile from the bag. Describe her error and write the correct answer.

Mixed Review and Test Prep

14. Order 3.241, 3.421, 3.412, and 3.142 from greatest to least. (p. 28)

15. 8.216×32 (p. 170)

16. 7.23×6.2 (p. 170)

17. Write 30% as a fraction in simplest form and as a decimal. (p. 636)

18. **TEST PREP** Find the probability that a number cube labeled 1–6 shows a prime number when rolled. (p. 656)

 A $\frac{1}{6}$ C $\frac{1}{3}$

 B $\frac{1}{4}$ D $\frac{1}{2}$

6 Problem Solving Strategy
Make an Organized List

PROBLEM Selena likes number games. She designed this game using a number cube and a coin.

A player tosses a number cube and a coin. The score is determined by using these rules. If the coin lands heads up, multiply the number by itself. If the coin lands tails up, add the number to itself. A winning result is a score of 10 or more. What is the probability of winning Selena's game?

Quick Review

Write each probability as a fraction.

1. 2 out of 7 **2.** 4 out of 9
3. 1 out of 6 **4.** 2 out of 8
5. 3 out of 5

UNDERSTAND

• What are you asked to find?

• What information will you use?

PLAN

• What strategy can you use to solve the problem?

You can *make an organized list* of all the possible outcomes.

SOLVE

• How can you use the strategy to solve the problem?

You can make a tree diagram to list all the possible outcomes.

There are 12 possible outcomes. Only 5 of these outcomes result in a score of 10 or more. So, the probability of winning is 5 out of 12, or $\frac{5}{12}$.

Cube Coin Score Result

$1 <$ H $1\times1=1$ loss / T $1+1=2$ loss

$2 <$ H $2\times2=4$ loss / T $2+2=4$ loss

$3 <$ H $3\times3=9$ loss / T $3+3=6$ loss

$4 <$ H $4\times4=16$ win / T $4+4=8$ loss

$5 <$ H $5\times5=25$ win / T $5+5=10$ win

$6 <$ H $6\times6=36$ win / T $6+6=12$ win

CHECK

• How can you check your answer?

Problem Solving Practice

Strategies

Draw a Diagram or Picture
Make a Model or Act It Out
▶ **Make an Organized List**
Find a Pattern
Make a Table or Graph
Predict and Test
Work Backward
Solve a Simpler Problem
Write an Equation
Use Logical Reasoning

Problem Solving

Make an organized list to solve.

1. **What if** Selena's rules were changed so that you won if the score was a multiple of 3? How would the probability change? Would you be more or less likely to win?

2. Pauline plays Selena's game with a number cube labeled 2 to 7. What is the probability of winning with this new number cube?

Marcus is conducting a probability experiment by tossing a coin and taking 1 marble from the bag below. Marcus will replace the marble after each turn.

3. How many possible outcomes are there for this experiment?

   A 4   **B** 6   **C** 8   **D** 16

4. What is the probability that Marcus will choose a red marble and toss heads?

   F $\frac{1}{2}$ **G** $\frac{1}{4}$ **H** $\frac{1}{6}$ **J** $\frac{1}{8}$

Mixed Strategy Practice

5. After school, Li rode his bike to the library. The ride took 10 minutes. He stayed there for 2 hours and 10 minutes. Riding home took another 35 minutes. If Li got home at 5:15 P.M., at what time did he leave school?

6. Sam stacks 4 cubes, one on top of another, to make a plant stand. He paints the outside of the stand blue, but not the bottom. How many faces of the original cubes are painted?

7. Alexandra has $0.30 more than Barbara. Together they have $4.50. How much money does each girl have?

8. Marshall has 15¢. How many combinations of coins could he have? What are they?

9. The drawing shows 1-square-foot tiles around a fish pond. What is the area that will be tiled?

   Let 1 square = 1 ft²

10. **REASONING** How many arrangements of the letters in the word FLORIDA start with an F and end with an A? Explain.

Extra Practice

Set A (pp. 656–657)

Write a fraction for the probability of the pointer landing on each color.

1. green
2. purple or yellow
3. white
4. purple, green, or yellow

5. Mark has a bag of fruit candy. Of the candies, 5 are strawberry, 4 are grape, and 1 is apple. What is the probability that Mark will pick grape?

6. If you toss one coin and roll one number cube, how many outcomes are possible? What is the probability that the result will include heads?

Set B (pp. 658–659)

Express the experimental probability as a fraction. Use it to predict the same event in future trials.

1. 6 wins in 8 games
   4 more games
2. 4 heads in 8 tosses
   6 more tosses
3. 3 red tiles in 5 pulls
   10 more pulls

The probability of winning is $\frac{2}{5}$. Predict the number of wins.

4. in 20 games
5. in 75 games
6. in 100 games

Set C (pp. 660–661)

For 1–2, make a tree diagram to show the possible choices.

1. **Lunch Menu**

   Entree: sandwich, hot dog, or hamburger

   Side: pretzel, apple, or pudding

2. **School Trips**

   Place: zoo, museum, or planetarium

   Day: Monday, Tuesday, Wednesday, Thursday, or Friday

3. Sarah needs a new television. She can buy one with a 13, 20, or 25 inch screen. She can buy each one with or without a VCR. How many choices does she have?

4. Maurice has to go to the store. He can go through the park or around the park. He can either walk or run. How many choices does he have?

Set D (pp. 662–663)

For 1–2, use the letters A, R, and M.

1. List the 6 two-letter arrangements that are possible.

2. List the 3 two-letter combinations that are possible.

3. Larry is ordering dinner. He has a choice of salad or soup. Then he has a choice of meatloaf, steak, spaghetti, or salmon. How many dinner choices does he have?

4. In how many different ways can Pete, Pat, and Paul stand in a row?

Review/Test

✔ CHECK VOCABULARY AND CONCEPTS

Choose the best term from the box.

1. A choice in which the order of the items does not matter is a(n) __?__. (p. 662)

2. You can use a __?__ to show all the possible outcomes of an event. (p. 660)

3. All the results that have an equal chance of happening are __?__. (p. 656)

> equally likely
> possible outcomes
> probability
> tree diagram
> arrangement
> combination

✔ CHECK SKILLS

For 4–6, write a fraction for the probability of each event with a number cube labeled 1 to 6. (pp. 656–657)

4. a 5
5. either 1 or 6
6. an even number

The experimental probability of winning is $\frac{2}{3}$. Predict the number of wins. (pp. 658–659)

7. in 9 games
8. in 18 games
9. in 15 games

Find the number of choices. (pp. 660–661)

10. **Music Class Choices**
    Class: band, choir, orchestra
    Teacher: Mr. Gibson, Ms. Garcia

11. **Pizza Choices** (1 topping)
    Crust: thick, thin
    Toppings: mushrooms, pepperoni, onions, anchovies

For 12–13, use the cards shown. (pp. 662–663)

12. List the 6 different ways the cards can be arranged in a row.

13. List the 3 combinations of 2 cards that can be chosen.

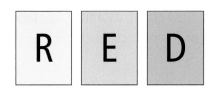

✔ CHECK PROBLEM SOLVING

Solve. (pp. 664–665)

14. Ben has 25¢, but he does not have any pennies. Find the possible choices of coins he has.

15. Adam tosses 2 coins. What are the possible outcomes? Determine the probability of tossing exactly 2 heads.

Standardized Test Prep

★ DATA ANALYSIS AND PROBABILITY

1. Cards numbered 2, 7, 13, 20, 37, and 52 are placed face down.

If you choose one of these cards, which outcome is most likely?

A The number is greater than 20.

B The number is less than 20.

C The number is a one-digit number.

D The number is a two-digit number.

2. The line graph shows the number of movies seen by Nan each month.

In how many months did Nan watch 3 or fewer movies?

F 2

G 3

H 4

J 5

3. Explain It Of the 20 equal sections on a spinner, $\frac{1}{2}$ are orange, $\frac{2}{5}$ are blue, and the rest are white. Explain how to find the probability of the pointer landing on white.

★ GEOMETRY AND SPATIAL SENSE

4. Brooke is gift-wrapping a present that is inside the box shown below.

Which is the volume of the box?

A 23 cubic inches

B 77 cubic inches

C 334 cubic inches

D 385 cubic inches

5. Peter made this diagram of a top he wants to make for a wooden box.

Which is the area of the figure he drew?

F 48 square inches

G 66 square inches

H 84 square inches

J 144 square inches

6. Explain It Which of these figures is NOT a parallelogram? Explain how you know.

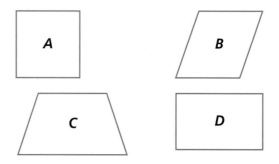

MEASUREMENT

7. Ariana is planning to put a wallpaper border around her bedroom where the walls meet the ceiling. The bedroom ceiling is square and has an area of 144 square feet. How many feet of wallpaper border does Ariana need?

A 12 feet   **C** 48 feet

B 24 feet   **D** 144 feet

8. Which of the following would be **best** to measure the number of degrees in an angle?

F compass

G ruler

H protractor

J balance scale

9. Explain It Jeremy knows that 50 trading cards have a mass of 50 grams. He has a stack of trading cards that has a mass of 0.4 kilogram. ESTIMATE whether there are more than or fewer than 500 cards in his stack. Explain how you know.

NUMBER SENSE, CONCEPTS, AND OPERATIONS

10. Four different stores at the mall have the same shirt on sale. If the original price of the shirt at each store is the same, which store is selling the shirt for the **least** price?

A Sale Store A Pay **75%** of the regular price.

C Sale Store C Pay $\frac{4}{5}$ of the regular price.

B Sale Store B Take $\frac{1}{3}$ **off** the regular price.

D Sale Store D Take 35% **off** the regular price.

TIP **Choose the answer.** See item 11. You need to calculate the weight of the water in the aquarium (8.3 × 20). If your answer doesn't match one of the answer choices, check your computation and the placement of the decimal point.

11. Mark's aquarium holds 20 gallons of water. If a gallon of water weighs 8.3 pounds, how much does the water in the aquarium weigh?

F 166 pounds   **H** 160.6 pounds

G 163 pounds   **J** 28.3 pounds

12. Explain It Three bags of apples weigh 3.5 pounds, 2.8 pounds, and 4.7 pounds. Matt says that the apples weigh about 9 pounds in all. Eve says that the apples weigh about 12 pounds in all. Which estimate is closer to the actual weight? Explain how you know.

Chapter 30 669

IT'S IN THE BAG

Flying Carpets

PROJECT Make a carpet to practice modeling percents.

Materials

- 10 x 10 piece of 1-cm graph paper
- Construction paper
- Fringe materials (yarn, raffia, ribbon)
- Glue
- Colored pencils
- Scissors
- Hole punch

Directions

1. Make a design for your carpet. Color the squares on the graph paper using the percents shown:

50% – purple	10% – red
10% – yellow	10% – black
10% – blue	10% – green

2. Cut a piece of construction paper 11 cm × 17 cm. Glue the graph paper in the center of the construction paper. (Picture A)

3. Punch the same number of holes along each of the short edges of the construction paper. (Picture B)

4. Add fringe materials to the holes along the edges as shown in the photograph. (Picture C)

5. Share your "flying carpet" with your classmates to show the percents of color used. Compare the patterns on the carpets.

Challenge

Fairness

Number Fun is a two-player game played with a number cube labeled 1 to 6. Each player scores a point when his or her type of number is rolled.

> **Rules**
>
> Player 1 scores 1 point if the number is even.
>
> Player 2 scores 1 point if the number is a multiple of 3.

Is this game fair?

You can use what you know about probability to see if this game is fair. A game is **fair** if each player has the same chance of winning.

Example

Player 1 scores if the number is even.	Player 2 scores if the number is a multiple of 3.
Even numbers on the number cube are 2, 4, and 6.	Multiples of 3 on the number cube are 3 and 6.
Probability of tossing an even number $= \frac{3}{6}$.	Probability of tossing a multiple of 3 $= \frac{2}{6}$.

Since $\frac{3}{6} > \frac{2}{6}$, the game is unfair. Player 1's chances of winning are greater than Player 2's.

Talk About It

- In order for a game to be fair, how should the probabilities of winning compare?

Try It

Use the same number cube but different rules. Tell whether the game is *fair* or *unfair*. Explain your answer.

1. Player 1 wins if the number is even.
   Player 2 wins if the number is odd.

2. Player 1 wins if the number is a multiple of 4.
   Player 2 wins if the number is prime.

PERFORMANCE ASSESSMENT

TASK A • SALE TIME

The Sports Shop is having a sale on soccer clothes and equipment.

a. Copy and complete the table for the sale items.

Soccer Item	Regular Price	Percent Off	Discount	Sale Price
ball	$12.00	40%	$4.80	$7.20
shorts	$18.00	25%		
knee pads	$10.00	40%		
shirt	$15.00	25%		
shoes	$45.00	40%		

b. Justin has $50.00. He plans to spend 75% of his money on soccer sale items. Suggest some items he could buy. Tell how much he will spend and how much money he will have left.

c. On the last day of the sale, the three soccer balls that were left were sold for 60% off. The regular prices for the balls were $15.00, $22.00, and $30.00. Sara has $10.00. Which soccer balls can she buy? Explain how you know.

TASK B • PROBABILITY SPINS

Suppose you are designing a spinner like the one below to use in an experiment.

a. Use at least 2 different numbers or colors to design your spinner. List the possible outcomes of your spinner. Is each outcome equally likely? Explain.

b. Describe a probability experiment using your spinner. Conduct your experiment and record your results in a table.

c. Misha designed the spinner at the right.

What is the probability of the pointer landing on each number on Misha's spinner? Which has a greater probability using Misha's spinner, the pointer landing on an odd number or on an even number? Explain.

Use a Calculator to Find Percent

The Warren family went out for dinner. The total bill was $37.45. Mr. Warren wants to leave a 22% tip. How much will the tip be? What is the total cost of dinner including the tip?

Use a calculator, such as the TI-15, to solve this problem.

- Since the problem involves money, you want to round to the nearest cent. So, press **Fix** **0.01** to set the calculator to round numbers to the hundredths place. You will see *Fix* appear at the top of the display.

- Put the cost of the dinner into memory.

```
Fix M
37.45 = 37.45
```

- Multiply by 22% to find the amount of the tip.

```
Fix M
37.45 X 22% =
        8.24
```

The tip will be $8.24.

- Use the **MR/MC** key to add the cost for the dinner to the tip and find the total cost.

```
Fix M
8.239 + 37.45
=        45.69
```

The total cost will be $45.69.

Practice and Problem Solving

Use a calculator to solve. Remember to clear the memory each time. On the TI-15, press **MR/MC** twice to reset the memory.

1. Three friends go out for dinner. Their bill is $42.78. They want to leave a 17% tip. How much will the tip be? What will be the total cost for dinner?

2. **REASONING** Julia and Timothy go out for lunch. Their bill is $14.28. They want to leave a 15% tip. How much should each person pay if they split the total cost equally? Explain.

GO ON-LINE

Multimedia Math Glossary www.harcourtschool.com/mathglossary
Vocabulary Power Look up *ratio*, *percent*, *probability*, and *prediction* in the Multimedia Math Glossary to see how they are related. Write a description of what each word means.

PROBLEM SOLVING ON LOCATION

in
Michigan Museums

THE NEW DETROIT SCIENCE CENTER

The Detroit Science Center was opened in the late 1970's. Its goal was to give children and their families the opportunity to learn and appreciate science through hands-on explorations. Now, after a $30 million renovation in 2001, it is a leading center for science education.

Laboratories	Theaters	Classrooms
Matter & Energy	IMAX® Dome Theatre	Applied Sciences
Waves & Vibrations	Digital Dome Planetarium	Space Sciences
Dow Foundation Life Sciences	Daimler Chrysler Science Stage	Physical Sciences
GM Motion	DTE Energy Sparks Theater	Life Sciences
SBC Ameritech Children's Gallery		Earth Sciences

USE DATA For 1–4, use the table and the photos.

1. What is the ratio of theaters to laboratories in the New Detroit Science Center? Show your answer in 3 different ways.

2. Gerry's class went to the Center on a class trip. They had time to visit only the Matter & Energy Laboratory and the GM Motion Laboratory. What percent of laboratories did they visit? Explain.

3. **REASONING** Suppose you want to make a scale drawing of the IMAX Dome which has a diameter of $67\frac{1}{2}$ feet. What is a reasonable scale to use to show the diameter of the dome? How long will you make the diameter in your drawing?

4. Make a tally table to show the number of laboratories, theaters, and classrooms at the Center. Then show the data in a graph. Explain why you chose the graph you did.

MUSEUM OF AFRICAN AMERICAN HISTORY

In 1965, Dr. Charles Wright created Detroit's first International Afro-American Museum. The museum would outgrow its facilities several times over the next 30 years. The latest version, renamed the Museum of African American History, opened in 1997. The table shows the funds raised each time the museum was added to or rebuilt.

▼ This 120,000-square-foot museum is the largest African American historical museum in the world.

USE DATA For 1–3, use the data from the table and the photos.

1. The Detroit Public School students raised $80,000 of the total funds raised in 1978. About what percent of the funds was raised by people other than the students?

2. Write an equation to show how much less was raised in 1985 than in 1996. Solve the equation.

Year	Funds Raised
1978	$380,000
1985	$3,500,000
1996	$10,000,000

3. The core exhibition gallery covers 16,000 square feet of the museum. What fraction of the total area of the museum is this? Explain how to convert this fraction to a percent.

4. **STRETCH YOUR THINKING** The *Of the People* exhibit consists of 8 different sections. Suppose you labeled each of 10 slips of paper with one of the sections A to H. How would you label the slips so that the probability of picking Section A, the African Memory, would be 1 to 5? Explain your method.

5. In 1996, 18 out of 25 voters in Detroit voted to approve the funds to complete the new Museum of African American History. What percent of the voters approved funds for the new museum?

The tips and the problems on the following pages will help you succeed on the SOL test.

Tips for Success on the SOL H2

Before working on the Getting Ready for the SOL problems and before taking the SOL test, sharpen your test-taking skills by reviewing these pages. Here you can find tips such as how to get ready for the test, how to understand the directions, and how to keep track of time.

Getting Ready for the SOL H6

The problems in this section cover the six mathematics strands of the Virginia Mathematics Standards of Learning. Use these problems to build your test-taking skills and to prepare for success.

Other Resources

Review addition, subtraction, multiplication, and division facts by taking the basic facts tests throughout the year to improve your memorization skills.

All the important measures used in this book are in this table. If you've forgotten exactly how many feet are in a mile, this table will help you.

This glossary will help you speak and write the language of mathematics. Use the glossary to check the definitions of important terms.

Use the index when you want to review a topic. It lists the page numbers where the topic is taught.

Being a good test-taker is like being a good problem solver. When you answer test questions, you are solving problems. Remember to **UNDERSTAND, PLAN, SOLVE,** and **CHECK.**

UNDERSTAND

Read the problem.

- Look for math terms and recall their meanings.
- Reread the problem and think about the question.
- Use the details in the problem and the question.

1. Tony is 10 years younger than Bill. Amber is 5 years older than Tony. Iris is 3 years younger than Amber. Bill is 15 years old. How old is Iris?

A 7   **C** 13

B 12   **D** 27

TIP! Understand the problem.
The critical information is that Bill is 15 years old. List all the given relationships and express them as equations. Use Bill's age to begin solving the equations. Be sure to answer the question asked. The answer is **A.**

- Each word is important. Missing a word or reading it incorrectly could cause you to get the wrong answer.
- Is there information given that you do not need?
- Pay attention to words that are in *italic* type.

2. Paul drew a line that is 1 inch long. Which is *closest* to 1 inch?

   F 25 meters

   G 2.5 meters

   H 25 centimeters

   J 2.5 centimeters

TIP! Look for important words.
The words *closest* to are important words. They tell you that you do not need to look for an exact answer. Since 1 centimeter is a little less than $\frac{1}{2}$ inch, 2 centimeters are a little less than 1 inch. The answer is **J.**

Think about how you can solve the problem.

- Can you solve the problem with the information given?
- Pictures, charts, tables, and graphs may have the information you need.
- You may need to recall information not given.
- The answer choices may have information you need.

3. Which of the following is the greatest common factor of 27, 33, and 63?

A 1
B 2
C 3
D 9

 Get the information you need.
The greatest common factor is the greatest number that is a factor of all the given numbers. Make a list of the factors of each number and look for the common factors. The greatest of these common factors is the answer. The answer is **C**.

- You may need to write a number sentence and solve it to answer the question.
- Some problems have two or more steps.
- In some problems you need to look at relationships instead of computing an answer.
- If the path to the solution isn't clear, choose a problem solving strategy and use it to solve the problem.

4. A gravel path surrounds a rectangular grass field. The field is 60 feet long and 40 feet wide. The path is 3 feet wide. What is the area covered by the path?

F 300 square feet
G 309 square feet
H 600 square feet
J 636 square feet

Decide on a plan.
Using the strategy *draw a diagram* will help you find the dimensions of the larger rectangle so you can find the area. Match the description in the problem and label your diagram. First find the combined area of the field and the path. Then subtract the area of the field. The answer is **J**.

Follow your plan, working logically and carefully.

- Estimate your answer. Are any answer choices unreasonable?
- Use reasoning to find the most likely choices.
- Make sure you solved all steps needed to answer the problem.
- If your answer does not match any of the answer choices, check the numbers you used. Then check your computation.

---

5. A point located at (2,4) on a coordinate plane was translated to (5,10). Which statement describes how the point was translated?

A 3 units up and 6 units to the right

B 3 units up and 6 units to the left

C 3 units to the right and 6 units up

D 3 units to the right and 6 units down

 Eliminate choices.

Thinking about the location of the point (5,10), you know it is to the right and up from the point (2,4). You can eliminate choices B and D because they say left or down. Now decide which of choices A or C is correct. When you subtract 2 from 5 and 4 from 10, you see that the point (5,10) is 3 units to the right and 6 units up from (2,4). The answer is **C**.

- If your answer still does not match one of the choices, look for another form of the number, such as a decimal instead of a fraction.
- If answer choices are given as pictures, look at each one by itself while you cover the other three.
- If answer choices are statements, relate each one to the problem.
- Change your plan if it isn't working. Try a different strategy.

---

6. Eduardo needs to find the total weight of a package he is mailing in order to calculate the postage needed. The package contains 15 copies of a document that weighs 2.5 ounces. The mailing envelope weighs 0.25 ounce. What is the total weight of the package?

F 17.5 ounces   **H** 37.5 ounces

G 17.75 ounces   **J** 37.75 ounces

Choose the answer.

You need to calculate the weight of all the copies of the document (15 × 2.5) and then add the weight of the envelope. If your answer doesn't match one of the answer choices, check your computation and the placement of the decimal point. The answer is **J**.

Take time to catch your mistakes.

- Be sure you answered the question asked.
- Check that your answer fits the information in the problem.
- Check for important words you might have missed.
- Be sure you used all the information you needed.
- Check your computation by using a different method.
- Draw a picture when you are unsure of your answer.

7. The distance from Todd's home to the soccer field is $\frac{3}{8}$ mile. The distance from Mia's home to the field is $\frac{2}{3}$ as great as Todd's distance. How far is it from Mia's home to the soccer field?

A $\frac{5}{11}$ mile

C $\frac{7}{24}$ mile

B $\frac{1}{3}$ mile

D $\frac{1}{4}$ mile

Check your work.

Since Mia's distance is $\frac{2}{3}$ of Todd's distance, it must be less than Todd's. To check your multiplication, draw a square. Divide the square into 8 equal columns and 3 equal rows. Shade the amounts given. Count the overlapping parts that are shaded and write the fraction that names that part. Be sure your fraction is in simplest form. The answer is **D**.

Don't Forget!

Before the test

- Listen to the teacher's directions and read the instructions.
- Write down the ending time of the test.
- Know where and how to mark your answers.
- Know whether you should write on the test page or use scratch paper.
- Ask any questions you may have before the test begins.

During the test

- Work quickly but carefully. If you are unsure how to answer a question, leave it blank and return to it later.
- If you cannot finish on time, look over the questions that are left. Answer the easiest ones first. Then go back to answer the others.
- Fill in each answer space carefully. Erase completely if you change an answer. Erase any stray marks.
- Check that the answer number matches the question number, especially if you skip a question.

✔ NUMBER AND NUMBER SENSE

1 Which shows $\frac{3}{5}$ as a decimal?

A 0.3

B 0.35

C 0.6

D 1.66

2 Which number does this show?

F 0.14

G 1.04

H 1.4

J 2.04

3 Mr. Yu buys $1\frac{3}{4}$ pounds of ham, $1\frac{5}{8}$ pounds of cheese, $1\frac{1}{2}$ pounds of turkey, and $1\frac{1}{3}$ pounds of salami. Of which does he buy the least?

A Turkey

B Salami

C Cheese

D Ham

4 Matthew walked 0.75 mile to get to the carnival. If Amy walked the same distance, what fraction of a mile did she walk?

F $\frac{1}{3}$ mile

G $\frac{3}{8}$ mile

H $\frac{1}{2}$ mile

J $\frac{3}{4}$ mile

5 Which digit is in the thousandths place in the number 4.786?

A 8

B 7

C 6

D 4

Study and Review	
Item	**Lesson Pages**
1	238–239
2	22–25
3	322–325
4	238–239
5	22–25

NUMBER AND NUMBER SENSE

6 Which statement is true?

    F $5.26 > 5.62$

    G $0.134 > 0.135$

    H $12.307 < 12.370$

    J $99.899 = 99.998$

7 Which shows the mixed numbers in order from greatest to least?

    A $5\frac{2}{3}, 5\frac{7}{8}, 5\frac{11}{12}$

    B $3\frac{1}{3}, 3\frac{3}{8}, 3\frac{1}{10}$

    C $6\frac{2}{9}, 6\frac{5}{6}, 6\frac{3}{7}$

    D $4\frac{7}{8}, 4\frac{1}{2}, 4\frac{5}{12}$

8 The figure below is shaded to represent a fraction.

Which shows the same value as the fraction represented above?

    F 0.80

    G 0.75

    H 0.70

    J 0.08

9 Nancy has $4.12, Allison has $4.22, Kim has $2.44, and Rashanda has $4.42. Which girl has the most money?

    A Rashanda

    B Allison

    C Kim

    D Nancy

10 Which number has a 7 in the thousandths place?

    F 345.274

    G 1,072.78

    H 3,023.837

    J 7,345.620

11 Which fraction is equivalent to 0.25?

    A $\frac{1}{2}$

    B $\frac{1}{3}$

    C $\frac{1}{4}$

    D $\frac{1}{5}$

Study and Review	
Item	Lesson Pages
6	28–29
7	322–325
8	238–239
9	28–29
10	22–25
11	238–239

✅ NUMBER AND NUMBER SENSE

12 Which shows 1.734 rounded to its hundredths place?

F 1.7

G 1.73

H 1.74

J 1.8

13 Which shows the fraction represented below as a decimal?

A 0.46

B 0.625

C 0.85

D 1.35

14 The elodea is a common aquarium plant. An epidermal cell of the elodea measures 0.065 mm. Which of the following has a value greater than 0.065?

F 0.005

G 0.006

H 0.06

J 0.66

15 Which number can be written as 10 + 6 + 0.3 + 0.02?

A 16.5

B 16.32

C 16.302

D 16.23

16 Which is 0.656 rounded to the nearest tenth?

F 0.65

G 0.656

H 0.66

J 0.7

17 In which of the following does the digit 6 have the least value?

A 16.398

B 23.645

C 34.567

D 95.786

Study and Review	
Item	**Lesson Pages**
12	40–41
13	238–239
14	28–29
15	22–25
16	40–41
17	28–29

✓ NUMBER AND NUMBER SENSE

18 Which shows 0.30 as a fraction?

F $\frac{1}{4}$

G $\frac{3}{10}$

H $\frac{2}{5}$

J $\frac{4}{8}$

19 Mrs. Wilson's class had a pizza party, and John, Melissa, and Rico shared a pizza. If John ate $\frac{1}{4}$, Melissa ate $\frac{1}{3}$, and Rico ate $\frac{5}{12}$ of the pizza, who ate the most pizza?

A Melissa

B Rico

C John

D They all ate the same amount.

20 Which shows 6.928 rounded to the place of the underlined digit?

F 6.0

G 6.9

H 6.93

J 7.0

21 Which shows 24.568 rounded to the place of the underlined digit?

A 24.56

B 24.57

C 24.6

D 25

22 Which is read "two and twenty-three hundredths"?

F 223

G 22.3

H 2.23

J 0.223

Study and Review	
Item	Lesson Pages
18	238–239
19	322–325
20	22–25
21	40–41
22	22–25

✔️ **NUMBER AND NUMBER SENSE**

23 Which is the least number?

A 54,677.33

B 54,677.23

C 54,667.32

D 54,667.23

24 Which number can be written as **1,000 + 0.001?**

F 1,000.001

G 1,000.1

H 1,000.01

J 1,001.1

25 Which shows the numbers in order from greatest to least?

A 0.16, 1.6, 0.016, 16

B 0.016, 1.6, 0.16, 16

C 16, 0.16, 1.6, 0.016

D 16, 1.6, 0.16, 0.016

26 Which shows **64.368** rounded to the nearest hundredth?

F 64.3

G 64.36

H 64.37

J 64.4

27 Which is a true statement?

A $76.465 > 76.645$

B $76.465 < 76.645$

C $76.546 = 76.544$

D $76.5 < 76.445$

28 Jack's family wants to plant a garden on **0.50** acre of their land. Which fraction is equivalent to **0.50?**

F $\frac{5}{12}$

G $\frac{4}{8}$

H $\frac{2}{3}$

J $\frac{3}{4}$

Study and Review	
Item	**Lesson Pages**
23	28–29
24	22–25
25	28–29
26	40–41
27	28–29
28	238–239

COMPUTATION AND ESTIMATION

Use the table below to answer questions 1 and 2.

The table shows the populations of five cities in Virginia.

| POPULATIONS OF VIRGINIA CITIES ||
City	Population
Alexandria	130,804
Charlottesville	43,833
Newport News	180,272
Petersburg	33,115
Richmond	197,456

1 What is the combined population of Charlottesville and Petersburg?

A 33,115

B 43,833

C 76,948

D 241,289

2 Compare the populations of Newport News and Alexandria. Which is the best estimate of how many more people live in Newport News than live in Alexandria?

F 5,000

G 20,000

H 50,000

J 80,000

3 $3.6 \div 3 =$

A 12

B 1.2

C 0.12

D 0.012

4 If Stephanie exercises for 55 minutes every day, how many minutes will she exercise in 24 days?

F 1,220 minutes

G 1,300 minutes

H 1,320 minutes

J 1,340 minutes

5 If Lucie works $3\frac{3}{4}$ hours on Monday and $2\frac{1}{2}$ hours on Tuesday, how many hours does she work in all?

A $5\frac{1}{4}$ hours

B $5\frac{2}{3}$ hours

C $6\frac{1}{4}$ hours

D $6\frac{2}{3}$ hours

| Study and Review ||
Item	Lesson Pages
1	46–47
2	42–45
3	230–231
4	152–153
5	368–371

✔ COMPUTATION AND ESTIMATION

6 $83.554 - 75.82 =$

F 18.734

G 17.734

H 12.734

J 7.734

7 The table below shows the amounts that Julian earned each day mowing lawns.

JULIAN'S DAILY EARNINGS	
Day	Amount
Monday	$21.50
Tuesday	$15.25
Wednesday	$8.75
Thursday	$17.75
Friday	$23.00

He earned the greatest amounts on Monday and Friday. Which is his total earnings for those days?

A $44.50

B $54.50

C $63.75

D $75.25

8 $7.26 \times 3.9 =$

F 29.6

G 28.314

H 21.18

J 2.83

9 Joan wants to buy an apple for each of her 6 friends. How much money will she need?

Apples $0.32 each

A $0.98

B $1.82

C $1.88

D $1.92

10 $820 \div 4 =$

F 25

G 200

H 205

J 250

Study and Review	
Item	Lesson Pages
6	48–51
7	52–53
8	170–173
9	164–165
10	198–199

✅ COMPUTATION AND ESTIMATION

11
$$3.2$$
$$\times 0.8$$

A 256

B 25.6

C 2.56

D 0.256

12 Terry's basketball team is buying new uniforms. The uniforms cost $166.50 in all. There are 9 boys on the team. If each uniform costs the same amount, how much does each uniform cost?

   F $19.50

   G $18.50

   H $18.05

   J $18.00

13
$$764 \div 9 =$$

   A 83 R7

   B 84 R5

   C 84 R8

   D 85 R1

14 Which is $\frac{2}{3} - \frac{1}{9}$ written in simplest form?

   F $\frac{1}{6}$

   G $\frac{1}{3}$

   H $\frac{4}{9}$

   J $\frac{5}{9}$

15 Olivia wants to make two types of cookies. She needs $\frac{1}{4}$ cup sugar for chocolate chip cookies and $\frac{3}{4}$ cup sugar for snickerdoodles. How much sugar does she need in all?

   A 1 cup

   B $\frac{3}{4}$ cup

   C $\frac{4}{8}$ cup

   D $\frac{3}{8}$ cup

Study and Review	
Item	**Lesson Pages**
11	170–173
12	232–235
13	194–195
14	354–355
15	346–347

COMPUTATION AND ESTIMATION

16 Which is the value of the expression $(14 + 5) + 3$?

  F 12

  G 14

  H 16

  J 22

17 Which is true?

  A $358 \div 58 = 7$ R10

  B $358 \div 58 = 6$ R10

  C $358 \div 58 = 6$ R8

  D $358 \div 58 = 5$ R13

18 Which multiplication sentence is shown?

  F 0.3×0.2

  G 0.3×0.4

  H 0.7×0.4

  J 0.7×0.6

19 Which is the value of the expression $15 - (3 \times 4) \div 3$?

  A 17

  B 16

  C 14

  D 11

20 Mr. Jackson bought 34 bicycles for his store. Each bicycle cost $236. Which is the best estimate of 34×236?

  F 6,000

  G 8,000

  H 9,000

  J 12,000

21 $32.775 + 73.791 =$

  A 105.466

  B 105.566

  C 106.556

  D 106.566

Study and Review	
Item	Lesson Pages
16	76–79
17	212–215
18	168–169
19	250–251
20	148–149
21	48–51

✓ COMPUTATION AND ESTIMATION

22 Which is true?

    F 579 ÷ 72 = 8 R3

    G 579 ÷ 72 = 8

    H 579 ÷ 72 = 7

    J 579 ÷ 72 = 6 R8

23 $12\overline{)3,816}$ =

    A 300

    B 310

    C 315

    D 318

24 Ellen, Maria, Kelvin, and Raul want to buy their teacher a small dish garden. If the dish garden costs $15.12, how much does each student pay if they want to share the cost equally?

    F $5.40

    G $5.04

    H $3.98

    J $3.78

25   1.06 × 3.4 =

    A 5.44

    B 4.8

    C 3.86

    D 3.604

26   9 × 0.008 =

    F 0.072

    G 0.72

    H 7.2

    J 720

27 There are 144 students in the fifth grade at Morris Elementary School. If there are a total of 6 fifth-grade classes with 11 girls in each class, how many boys are in the fifth grade?

    A 13

    B 66

    C 78

    D 133

Study and Review	
Item	**Lesson Pages**
22	212–215
23	212–215
24	232–235
25	170–173
26	174–175
27	150–151

✓ COMPUTATION AND ESTIMATION

28 Sarah makes fruit baskets. She puts 3 apples and 4 pears in each basket. She decides later to add bananas to the baskets. If she makes 5 baskets with a total of 10 pieces of fruit in each basket, how many bananas does she need in all?

  F 15

  G 17

  H 30

  J 50

29 Patty and Todd shared a pizza. Patty ate $\frac{1}{4}$ of the pizza and Todd ate $\frac{2}{3}$ of the pizza. How much of the pizza was left?

  A $\frac{11}{12}$

  B $\frac{3}{7}$

  C $\frac{1}{4}$

  D $\frac{1}{12}$

30 Nina has 273 beads to make 7 necklaces for the school play. If she uses the same number of beads to make each necklace, how many beads will be left over?

  F 0

  G 2

  H 4

  J 6

31 $8{,}923 + 7{,}489 =$

  A 15,402

  B 15,412

  C 16,402

  D 16,412

32 $8\frac{5}{6} - 5\frac{1}{3} =$

  F $3\frac{2}{3}$

  G $3\frac{5}{9}$

  H $3\frac{1}{2}$

  J $3\frac{4}{9}$

Study and Review	
Item	Lesson Pages
28	126–127
29	348–351
30	194–195
31	46–47
32	372–373

✓ COMPUTATION AND ESTIMATION

33 Andi spent $12.50 on a ticket to the ballet. She also spent $21.37 on bus fare and dinner. How much did she spend in all?

A $44.87

B $34.87

C $33.87

D $23.87

34 Danny runs $4\frac{1}{4}$ miles. James runs $2\frac{3}{8}$ miles. How much farther does Danny run?

F $2\frac{1}{2}$

G $2\frac{1}{4}$

H $1\frac{7}{8}$

J $1\frac{1}{2}$

35 $8.455 \div 5 =$

A 1.691

B 16.91

C 169.1

D 1,691.0

36 The Beacon Restaurant uses 2,675 pounds of potatoes each week to make its famous fries. Which of the following could be used to find the number of potatoes the restaurant will use in 7 weeks?

F $2,675 + 7 = ?$

G $2,675 \div 7 = ?$

H $2,675 \times 7 = ?$

J $2,675 - 7 = ?$

37 $0.07 \times 0.6 =$

A 0.0024

B 0.0042

C 0.042

D 0.42

Study and Review	
Item	Lesson Pages
33	52–55
34	374–375
35	232–235
36	236–237
37	174–175

✓ **MEASUREMENT**

1 Which is the measure of the length of the crayon below?

A 2 inches

B $2\frac{1}{2}$ inches

C 3 inches

D $3\frac{1}{2}$ inches

2 Bo wants to draw a 45° angle. Which tool should he use?

F Inch ruler

G Thermometer

H Compass

J Protractor

3 What is the area of the triangle below?

4 meters

16 meters

A 16 square meters

B 32 square meters

C 40 square meters

D 64 square meters

4 Jacob, Emily, and their father went winter camping by a lake. When they went to bed, it was 48°F. During the night the temperature dropped just enough for the lake to begin to freeze. What must the temperature have been during the night?

F About 0°F

G About 32°C

H About 0°C

J About 54°F

5 Which formula would you use to find the amount of tile needed to cover a rectangular kitchen floor?

A $l \times w$

B $l \times w \times h$

C $(2 \times l) + (2 \times w)$

D $\frac{1}{2}b \times h$

Study and Review	
Item	Lesson Pages
1	522–525
2	432–433
3	572–575
4	536–539
5	598–599

✔ MEASUREMENT

6 Alex left school at 2:30 P.M. He spent 30 minutes riding the bus, 20 minutes having a snack, 45 minutes doing his homework, and 1 hour playing outside. Then he came inside for dinner. What time was it when Alex came inside?

  F 4:35 P.M.

  G 4:45 P.M.

  H 4:50 P.M.

  J 5:05 P.M.

7 Which statement is true?

  A 4 liters are equal to 400 milliliters.

  B 1 liter is equal to 1,000 milliliters.

  C 1 kiloliter is equal to 1,000 milliliters.

  D 1 liter is about 10 kiloliters.

8 If each bag of popcorn kernels weighs exactly 8 ounces, how many bags can Pete fill if he has 4 pounds of popcorn kernels?

  F 1

  G 2

  H 4

  J 8

9 Chris puts grass seed on his front lawn. The lawn is 40 feet wide and 55 feet long. If each bag of seed covers 500 square feet, how many bags will Chris need?

  A 4

  B 5

  C 6

  D 7

10 What is the perimeter of the polygon below?

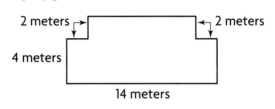

  F 40 meters

  G 35 meters

  H 32 meters

  J 26 meters

Study and Review	
Item	Lesson Pages
6	536–539
7	534–535
8	532–533
9	596–597
10	550–551

✓ MEASUREMENT

11 If the radius of a circle measures 3.4 centimeters, which is the length of the diameter of the circle?

    A 34 centimeters

    B 6.8 centimeters

    C 3.4 centimeters

    D 1.7 centimeters

12 Which is a reasonable amount of lemonade for a pitcher to hold?

    F 6 fluid ounces

    G 1 cup

    H 2 quarts

    J 3 gallons

13 Fred builds a square pen for his rabbits that is 6 feet on each side. Which is the area of the pen?

    A 36 square feet

    B 24 square feet

    C 12 square feet

    D 6 square feet

14 3,400 milligrams = _____ grams

    F 0.34

    G 3.4

    H 34

    J 340

15 Which measurement would be best to use to find how much grain would fill a container?

    A Volume

    B Surface area

    C Perimeter

    D Area

16 What is the perimeter of the rectangle below?

5 centimeters

12 centimeters

    F 17 centimeters

    G 29 centimeters

    H 34 centimeters

    J 60 centimeters

Study and Review	
Item	**Lesson Pages**
11	438–441
12	532–533
13	564–567
14	534–535
15	596–597
16	550–551

✓ MEASUREMENT

17 Which is the best unit to use to measure the length of a ladybug?

A Millimeter

B Inch

C Foot

D Meter

18 Angie drew diagrams of her flower garden and vegetable garden.

10 feet

12 feet

5 feet

9 feet

What is the total area of the two gardens?

F 72 square feet

G 130 square feet

H 142 square feet

J 165 square feet

19 Which is the area of the shaded figure? Each square on the grid is 1 square centimeter.

A 10 square centimeters

B 15 square centimeters

C 20 square centimeters

D 23 square centimeters

20 Which is a diameter of the circle shown below?

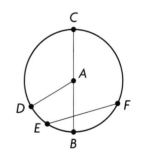

F $\overline{AB}$

G $\overline{EF}$

H $\overline{BC}$

J $\overline{AD}$

Study and Review	
Item	**Lesson Pages**
17	526–527
18	564–567
19	564–567
20	554–555

GEOMETRY

1 Which letter has 2 lines of symmetry?

A A

B H

C M

D Y

2 Which figure has no lines of symmetry?

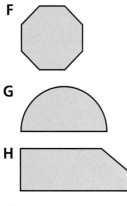

F

G

H

J

3 Which describes the figures below?

A Similar

B Congruent but not similar

C Both similar and congruent

D Neither similar nor congruent

4 Which set of ordered pairs shows a translation of the triangle?

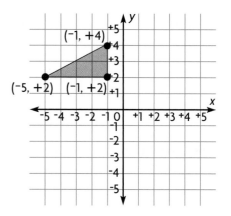

F (1,2), (1,4), (5,2)

G (⁻1,⁻2), (⁻1,⁻4), (⁻5,⁻2)

H (1,2), (1,4), (5,2)

J (⁻1,⁻2), (⁻1,⁻4), (⁻5,⁻4)

5 In a math trivia game, David is asked to draw a solid figure that has 6 faces, 12 edges, and 8 vertices. Which figure should David draw?

A Triangular prism

B Sphere

C Square pyramid

D Rectangular prism

Study and Review	
Item	Lesson Pages
1	446–447
2	446–447
3	442–445
4	504–505
5	466–467

GEOMETRY

6 Which of the following classifies the triangle below by the measures of its angles?

F Acute

G Obtuse

H Right

J Isosceles

7 Which figures are similar but not congruent?

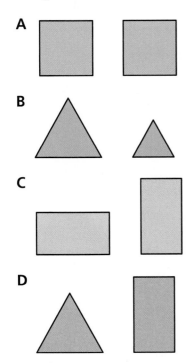

8 Which can be classified as an acute angle?

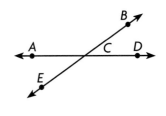

F ∠ACE

G ∠ACB

H ∠ACD

J ∠ECD

9 Which solid figure has six congruent faces?

A Square pyramid

B Cube

C Cylinder

D Cone

10 Bonnie wants to draw a quadrilateral that has exactly one pair of parallel sides. Which figure should she draw?

F Parallelogram

G Rhombus

H Rectangle

J Trapezoid

Study and Review	
Item	**Lesson Pages**
6	456–459
7	442–445
8	432–433
9	466–469
10	460–461

✓ GEOMETRY

11 Julie drew this angle in her math notebook. Which describes angle *CLB*?

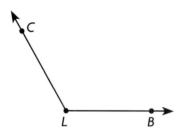

A Acute

B Straight

C Obtuse

D Right

12 Which movement would make the figure on the left look like the figure on the right?

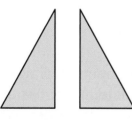

F Reflection

G Rotation

H Coordination

J Translation

13 Which solid figure is shown below?

A Triangular prism

B Triangular pyramid

C Square pyramid

D Cone

14 Which of the following is a property of a square?

F Exactly 1 pair of parallel sides

G 1 pair of acute angles

H 4 congruent sides

J 3 sides

Study and Review	
Item	**Lesson Pages**
11	428–431
12	462–465
13	588–589
14	460–461

✓ PROBABILITY AND STATISTICS

1 The table shows the colors of paper and markers available to students for their project. Each student will use one sheet of paper and one marker.

MATERIALS	
Paper	**Marker**
Yellow	Blue
White	Red
	Green

Which tree diagram shows all the combinations of one color of paper and one color of marker?

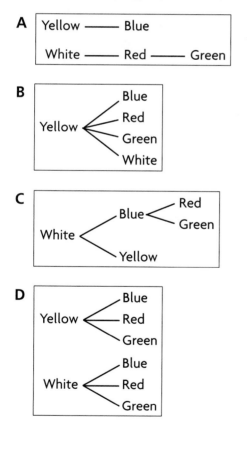

A
Yellow ——— Blue
White ——— Red ——— Green

B
Yellow ⟨ Blue
Red
Green
White

C
White ⟨ Blue ⟨ Red
Green
Yellow

D
Yellow ⟨ Blue
Red
Green
White ⟨ Blue
Red
Green

2 The table shows Alicia's scores on her first six quizzes.

QUIZ SCORES	
Date	**Score**
January 7	87
January 10	92
January 14	93
January 16	93
January 21	83
January 24	98

What was the mean (average) of Alicia's first six quizzes?

F 87

G 91

H 93

J 98

3 Based on previous results, the probability of Matt's team winning its hockey game is $\frac{7}{10}$. Predict the number of times his team will win if it plays 20 more games.

A 10

B 12

C 14

D 16

Study and Review	
Item	**Lesson Pages**
1	660–661
2	100–101
3	658–659

PROBABILITY AND STATISTICS

4 The stem-and-leaf plot shows Carol's math quiz grades. In which interval does she score the most frequently?

Stem	Leaves
9	0 2 8 9
8	0 1 1 6 7 7 9
7	3 5 6
6	7 9 9

Carol's Math Quiz Scores

F 90–100

G 80–89

H 70–79

J below 70

5 Look at the graph below. Which month has an average temperature *closest* to 60°?

AVERAGE MONTHLY TEMPERATURE IN NORFOLK, VA

A October

B July

C April

D January

6 Gina grew a sunflower as part of her science project. At the end of each week, she recorded its height. During which week did her plant grow the most?

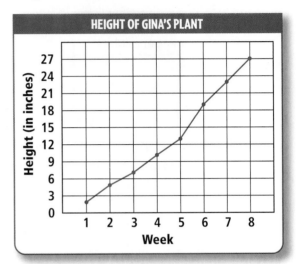

HEIGHT OF GINA'S PLANT

F Week 3

G Week 4

H Week 5

J Week 6

Study and Review	
Item	Lesson Pages
4	104–105
5	106–107
6	122–125

✓ PROBABILITY AND STATISTICS

7 Mrs. Harmon's students took a survey about their favorite ice cream flavors and made a table. How many students were surveyed?

ICE CREAM SURVEY	
Flavor	**Students**
Chocolate	11
Vanilla	4
Strawberry	5
Chocolate Chip	3
Other	2

A 11   **C** 25

B 20   **D** 27

8 Look at the spinner.

Which of the following questions about the spinner could you solve using probability?

F How many more sections of the spinner have an even number than an odd number?

G How many sections of the spinner have a number greater than 2?

H Into how many sections is the spinner divided?

J Is the arrow more likely to stop on a number greater than 4 or an odd number?

9 What is the probability of spinning a number greater than 2 using the spinner below?

A $\frac{1}{6}$

B $\frac{1}{3}$

C $\frac{1}{2}$

D $\frac{2}{3}$

10 Paul is making a graph of the data below. Which scale and interval should he use?

125, 208, 360, 420, 588, 675

F Scale: 0–700, interval: 10

G Scale: 125–675, interval: 25

H Scale: 0–700, interval: 100

J Scale: 125–675, interval: 100

Study and Review	
Item	**Lesson Pages**
7	96–99
8	656–657
9	656–657
10	116–119

PROBABILITY AND STATISTICS

11 Alicia wants to keep track of her science quiz scores so she can see how she improves over time. Which is the best type of graph for her to use?

SCIENCE QUIZ SCORES	
Date	**Score**
October 1	80
October 8	85
October 15	85
October 22	90

A Bar graph

B Circle graph

C Stem-and-leaf plot

D Line graph

12 Juan has a bag of marbles. There are 6 blue marbles, 10 red marbles, and 4 yellow marbles in the bag. He asks his friend to choose a marble. What is the probability that the marble will be yellow?

F $\frac{1}{5}$

G $\frac{3}{10}$

H $\frac{4}{10}$

J $\frac{9}{20}$

13 If each fifth grade class at Mann Elementary School has 24 students, how many boys are there in Miss Yelton's class?

A 17

B 16

C 12

D 7

14 Which is the mode for these data?

6, 8, 9, 3, 4, 7, 7, 3, 5, 7, 8, 5

F 3

G 5

H 7

J 8

Study and Review	
Item	**Lesson Pages**
11	130–133
12	656–657
13	106–109
14	102–103

✓ PROBABILITY AND STATISTICS

15 Robbie is taking a survey about pets. Which would be the best survey question for him to ask?

    A Is your favorite pet a dog or a cat?

    B Do you like fish best?

    C What is your favorite pet?

    D Aren't cats better than birds?

16 For her school uniform, Cindy can choose a white, blue, or red top and a blue or red skirt. How many possible uniform choices does Cindy have?

Tops: white, blue, red
Skirts: blue, red

    F 3

    G 4

    H 5

    J 6

17 Gary's baseball team won 4 of its first 6 games. If the team plays 12 more games, how many of those games can it expect to win?

    A 8

    B 7

    C 6

    D 5

18 Terrell plays on the school basketball team. In the first 7 games, he scored 12, 7, 9, 11, 21, 9, and 14 points. Which is the median number of points Terrell scored in the first 7 games?

    F 9

    G 11

    H 12

    J 14

19 Maria is waiting to ride the bumper cars at a festival. Each person in line is randomly assigned to one of 20 cars. There are 4 red, 8 yellow, 3 blue, and 5 green bumper cars. What is the probability that Maria is assigned to a yellow bumper car?

    A $\frac{1}{10}$

    B $\frac{3}{20}$

    C $\frac{1}{5}$

    D $\frac{2}{5}$

Study and Review	
Item	Lesson Pages
15	96–99
16	660–661
17	658–659
18	102–103
19	656–657

PATTERNS, FUNCTIONS, AND ALGEBRA

1 Kelly is arranging stickers to form a border for a sticker album.

If the pattern continues, what will be the next sticker?

A

B

C

D

2 Mr. Lopez is driving from Norfolk to Charlottesville, a distance of 164 miles. He stopped for gas after driving 125 miles.

Which of the following could be represented by the variable *m* in the equation below?

$$125 + m = 164$$

F The number of gallons of gas he bought

G The number of miles the car got per gallon

H The number of miles he still had to drive

J The number of minutes he stopped

3 Liz and Ken were running around the track. Ken ran 3 times as many laps as Liz ran. Let *t* represent the number of laps that Ken ran. Which expression represents the number of laps that Liz ran?

A $t + 3$

B $t - 3$

C $3 \times t$

D $t \div 3$

4 Julie had $25. She bought a ticket to the movie for $7 and then bought some dinner. She had $10 left over. How much did Julie spend on dinner?

Which of the following could be used to solve this problem?

F $25 + 7 + 10 = n$

G $25 - 7 - n = 10$

H $25 + 7 - n = 10$

J $25 + 7 + n = 10$

Study and Review	
Item	**Lesson Pages**
1	448–449
2	68–69
3	246–249
4	68–69

PATTERNS, FUNCTIONS, AND ALGEBRA

5 Gerald has 51 CDs. If Gerald had 1 fewer CD, he would have twice the number of CDs that Charles has. Let d represent the number of CDs that Charles has. Which of the following could be used to find the number of CDs that Charles has?

A $2d - 1 = 51$

B $2d = 51$

C $2d = 50$

D $2 + d = 50$

6 There are 4 times as many rabbits as hamsters in a pet store. Let h represent the number of hamsters. Which expression represents the total number of rabbits?

F $4 + h$

G $4 \times h$

H $4 - h$

J $4 \div h$

7 Which describes a rule for the pattern below?

23, 26, 20, 23, 17, 20, 14

A Add 3

B Add 6, then subtract 3

C Add 3, then subtract 6

D Add 6

8 Jen had some carrot sticks in her lunch. She gave 6 to Jordan. If c represents the number of carrot sticks Jen had, which expression represents how many Jen has left?

F $c + 6$

G $6 + c$

H $c - 6$

J $6 - c$

9 At Big John's Shell Shop, a conch shell costs $9. Peter spent $36 on conch shells. Let s represent the number of conch shells he bought. Which of the following could be used to find the number of conch shells Peter bought?

A $\$36 + s = \$9$

B $\$36 - s = \$9$

C $\$36 \times s = \$9$

D $\$36 \div s = \$9$

10 Which number is missing in the number pattern below?

48, 39, 30, _____, 12, 3

F 21

G 20

H 19

J 18

Study and Review	
Item	Lesson Pages
5	246–249
6	246–249
7	252–253
8	64–67
9	246–249
10	252–253

PATTERNS, FUNCTIONS, AND ALGEBRA

11 Which number is missing in the number pattern below?

24, 21, 18, ____, 12, 9

A 16

B 15

C 14

D 13

12 Which of the following can be solved using the equation below?

$$c \times 3 = 81$$

F Jim had a collection of 81 miniature cars. He bought 3 more cars today. How many miniature cars does he have now?

G Carol has 81 stamps. She has three times as many stamps as her sister. How many stamps does Carol's sister have?

H Hank had 81 coins in his coin collection. He gave his brother 3 coins. How many coins does he have left?

J Patty sold 3 quilts in her shop today. If each quilt sold for $81, how much did she make in all for the 3 quilts?

13 In the morning, Clive planted 8 rows of flowers in his garden. He planted some more rows later that afternoon. Mandy wrote the expression $8 + m$ to represent the total number of rows. What does m represent?

A The number of flowers in one row

B The number of rows of flowers planted in the morning

C The number of rows of flowers planted in the afternoon

D The total number of rows planted that day

14 Which number comes next in the pattern below?

$$\frac{1}{2}, \frac{3}{5}, \frac{5}{8}, \frac{7}{11}, \text{____}$$

F $\frac{8}{13}$

G $\frac{9}{14}$

H $\frac{9}{12}$

J $\frac{10}{13}$

Study and Review	
Item	Lesson Pages
11	252–253
12	246–249
13	64–67
14	418–419

15 Nancy wrote this pattern in her notebook.

3, 12, 48, 192, 768

Which describes a rule for the pattern above?

A Add 9

B Multiply by 4

C Multiply by 9

D Add 36

16 Which describes a rule for this pattern?

$$\frac{9}{10}, \frac{7}{9}, \frac{5}{8}, \frac{3}{7}, \frac{1}{6}$$

F Add 2 to the numerator, then add 1 to the denominator

G Subtract 1 from the numerator, then subtract 1 from the denominator

H Subtract 2 from the numerator, then subtract 1 from the denominator

J Add 1 to the numerator, then add 1 to the denominator

17 Renee had 20 trading cards. She gave Alex some of her cards. If *t* is the number of cards that Renee gave to Alex, which expression represents how many cards she has now?

A $t + 20$

B $20 - t$

C $t - 20$

D $t \times 20$

18 Glenn made this pattern of dots.

How many dots will there be in the fifth figure of this pattern?

F 8

G 11

H 12

J 13

✔ PATTERNS, FUNCTIONS, AND ALGEBRA

19 Look at the pattern below.

If this pattern continues, what will be the next figure?

A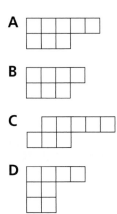

B

C

D

20 Peter had some pencils. He let a friend borrow 14 pencils. If *n* is the number of pencils Peter had, which expression shows how many he has left?

　F $n + 14$

　G $14 - n$

　H $n - 14$

　J $14 \times n$

21 If the rule for the pattern below is subtract 4 and then multiply by 2, which number is next in this pattern?

　　14, 10, 20, 16, 32, 28, 56, _____

　A 52

　B 62

　C 100

　D 104

22 Which of the following can be represented using the expression $12 - n$?

　F Jo had 12 crayons. Then she gave Fred some crayons.

　G Jo had 12 crayons. Fred gave her 6 crayons.

　H Jo had some crayons. After cleaning her room, she found 12 more crayons.

　J Jo had 6 crayons. Fred gave her 12 more.

23 Antwon caught 4 fish and Devon also caught some fish. Together they caught 14 fish. How many fish did Devon catch?

Which of the following could be used to solve this problem?

　A $4 + 14 = x$

　B $x - 14 = 4$

　C $4 + x = 14$

　D $4x = 14$

Study and Review	
Item	**Lesson Pages**
19	448–449
20	64–67
21	252–253
22	64–67
23	68–69

✔ PATTERNS, FUNCTIONS, AND ALGEBRA

24 A student in Mrs. Reid's class collected leaves for a project. She collected 4 on Monday and more on Tuesday. If she collected 15 in all, how many did she collect on Tuesday?

Which of the following could be used to solve this problem?

F $4 + 15 = n$

G $4 + n = 15$

H $15 = n \times 4$

J $15 \times 4 = n$

25 Which number is missing in the number pattern below?

88, 102, 116, _____, 144, 158

A 120

B 129

C 130

D 140

26 Franco's grandmother gave him a penny on the first day of the week. Each day after that, she gave him twice the amount that she had given him the day before. How much money did he have at the end of the first week?

F $0.28

G $0.60

H $1.27

J $2.55

27 Sara made designs by shading squares as shown below.

Design 1

Design 2

Design 3

If she continues the pattern, how many squares should she shade in Design 4?

A 8

B 10

C 12

D 14

Study and Review	
Item	Lesson Pages
24	80–81
25	252–253
26	64–67
27	448–449

ADDITION AND SUBTRACTION FACTS TEST

	K	L	M	N	O	P	Q	R
A	5 +6	9 −3	8 +6	10 − 7	18 − 9	7 +9	11 − 4	0 +9
B	12 − 4	9 +9	14 − 5	8 −5	9 +4	11 − 6	5 +3	16 − 9
C	6 +5	0 +8	9 −6	4 +4	13 − 6	3 +6	12 − 3	7 +4
D	6 +3	14 − 6	8 +8	7 −7	13 − 5	5 +8	9 +7	11 − 8
E	4 +6	17 − 9	10 − 5	6 +6	8 −4	1 +9	8 +7	12 − 9
F	8 +5	4 +7	11 − 3	3 +7	10 − 2	9 +0	12 − 8	7 +2
G	5 +7	13 − 4	6 +8	20 −10	8 −0	6 +9	14 − 7	4 +8
H	6 +7	11 − 7	9 −9	9 +8	16 − 8	8 +10	17 −10	7 −3
I	13 − 7	14 − 9	5 +5	9 +10	10 − 6	3 +9	9 −7	7 +6
J	11 − 2	9 +5	15 − 7	10 +10	13 − 9	7 +8	11 − 5	8 +4

	K	L	M	N	O	P	Q	R
A	4 ×8	5 ×4	8 ×9	6 ×2	9 ×5	12 × 8	3 ×9	1 ×5
B	7 ×1	6 ×3	5 ×3	3 ×8	5 ×5	3 ×3	0 ×8	8 ×5
C	5 ×7	9 ×6	6 ×4	3 ×4	8 ×6	7 ×3	11 × 7	4 ×2
D	3 ×2	9 ×8	1 ×6	7 ×2	4 ×6	7 ×5	12 ×12	4 ×7
E	7 ×8	2 ×4	5 ×9	12 ×10	7 ×6	6 ×9	6 ×0	4 ×4
F	1 ×9	7 ×7	12 × 5	9 ×3	8 ×11	6 ×6	2 ×9	11 ×11
G	3 ×7	4 ×3	9 ×9	7 ×4	6 ×10	9 ×7	2 ×5	6 ×8
H	12 × 3	11 × 5	8 ×3	12 × 7	10 × 4	4 ×5	10 ×10	9 ×4
I	3 ×5	9 ×12	12 ×11	12 × 6	11 ×10	8 ×8	11 × 3	5 ×12
J	7 ×9	4 ×12	9 ×11	3 ×10	9 ×10	12 × 2	8 ×12	6 ×12

DIVISION FACTS TEST

	K	L	M	N	O	P	Q	R
A	2)8̄	9)5̄4̄	7)2̄1̄	4)1̄6̄	3)1̄8̄	7)0̄	4)3̄2̄	6)4̄8̄
B	4)8̄	8)4̄0̄	1)4̄	5)3̄5̄	2)1̄2̄	5)1̄0̄	7)5̄6̄	6)3̄0̄
C	8)6̄4̄	7)4̄2̄	6)1̄8̄	9)2̄7̄	12)9̄6̄	6)5̄4̄	4)2̄0̄	7)4̄9̄
D	8)4̄8̄	9)7̄2̄	5)6̄0̄	7)2̄8̄	4)2̄4̄	5)4̄0̄	3)2̄7̄	9)3̄6̄
E	7)1̄4̄	8)2̄4̄	3)9̄	11)9̄9̄	5)2̄0̄	3)6̄	2)1̄4̄	4)1̄2̄
F	6)3̄6̄	4)2̄8̄	6)7̄2̄	12)6̄0̄	2)1̄0̄	8)0̄	5)4̄5̄	9)8̄1̄
G	2)1̄6̄	3)1̄5̄	3)2̄1̄	5)3̄0̄	9)6̄3̄	8)3̄2̄	9)9̄	3)3̄3̄
H	9)1̄8̄	6)2̄4̄	10)7̄0̄	3)1̄2̄	12)1̄2̄0̄	11)6̄6̄	5)2̄5̄	11)7̄7̄
I	8)7̄2̄	11)2̄2̄	12)3̄6̄	7)8̄4̄	11)5̄5̄	10)1̄0̄0̄	4)3̄6̄	8)8̄0̄
J	11)1̄2̄1̄	10)9̄0̄	7)6̄3̄	12)1̄0̄8̄	2)2̄4̄	10)1̄1̄0̄	12)1̄4̄4̄	11)1̄3̄2̄

MULTIPLICATION AND DIVISION FACTS TEST

	K	L	M	N	O	P	Q	R
A	$2\overline{)18}$	$\begin{array}{r}8\\\times4\end{array}$	$5\overline{)15}$	$\begin{array}{r}10\\\times\ 6\end{array}$	$\begin{array}{r}8\\\times1\end{array}$	$3\overline{)24}$	$6\overline{)12}$	$\begin{array}{r}5\\\times8\end{array}$
B	$\begin{array}{r}8\\\times2\end{array}$	$7\overline{)77}$	$9\overline{)81}$	$\begin{array}{r}4\\\times10\end{array}$	$\begin{array}{r}7\\\times12\end{array}$	$1\overline{)6}$	$8\overline{)80}$	$\begin{array}{r}4\\\times9\end{array}$
C	$12\overline{)36}$	$\begin{array}{r}11\\\times\ 5\end{array}$	$\begin{array}{r}7\\\times7\end{array}$	$10\overline{)90}$	$5\overline{)45}$	$\begin{array}{r}6\\\times7\end{array}$	$8\overline{)16}$	$\begin{array}{r}9\\\times9\end{array}$
D	$\begin{array}{r}10\\\times\ 2\end{array}$	$4\overline{)32}$	$9\overline{)99}$	$\begin{array}{r}7\\\times8\end{array}$	$\begin{array}{r}12\\\times\ 3\end{array}$	$9\overline{)108}$	$11\overline{)88}$	$\begin{array}{r}12\\\times\ 4\end{array}$
E	$\begin{array}{r}8\\\times10\end{array}$	$\begin{array}{r}12\\\times\ 9\end{array}$	$12\overline{)84}$	$2\overline{)20}$	$\begin{array}{r}9\\\times0\end{array}$	$\begin{array}{r}10\\\times11\end{array}$	$3\overline{)36}$	$10\overline{)100}$
F	$4\overline{)44}$	$12\overline{)72}$	$\begin{array}{r}7\\\times11\end{array}$	$\begin{array}{r}12\\\times\ 6\end{array}$	$7\overline{)56}$	$9\overline{)45}$	$\begin{array}{r}10\\\times\ 3\end{array}$	$\begin{array}{r}9\\\times7\end{array}$
G	$12\overline{)144}$	$6\overline{)60}$	$\begin{array}{r}9\\\times2\end{array}$	$\begin{array}{r}8\\\times12\end{array}$	$12\overline{)108}$	$11\overline{)44}$	$\begin{array}{r}5\\\times10\end{array}$	$7\overline{)84}$
H	$\begin{array}{r}6\\\times5\end{array}$	$\begin{array}{r}8\\\times8\end{array}$	$11\overline{)33}$	$5\overline{)55}$	$\begin{array}{r}6\\\times11\end{array}$	$\begin{array}{r}12\\\times\ 5\end{array}$	$11\overline{)132}$	$6\overline{)42}$
I	$8\overline{)96}$	$10\overline{)120}$	$\begin{array}{r}11\\\times\ 8\end{array}$	$\begin{array}{r}10\\\times\ 9\end{array}$	$5\overline{)60}$	$\begin{array}{r}11\\\times\ 4\end{array}$	$\begin{array}{r}10\\\times10\end{array}$	$10\overline{)80}$
J	$\begin{array}{r}11\\\times\ 6\end{array}$	$\begin{array}{r}12\\\times11\end{array}$	$4\overline{)40}$	$7\overline{)35}$	$\begin{array}{r}3\\\times6\end{array}$	$8\overline{)56}$	$\begin{array}{r}9\\\times8\end{array}$	$\begin{array}{r}12\\\times12\end{array}$

ADDITION FACTS TEST

1. $\square + 9 = 16$	**2.** $7 + \square = 12$	**3.** $\square + 8 = 12$	**4.** $7 + \square = 10$	**5.** $\square + 5 = 13$
6. $\square + 5 = 10$	**7.** $6 + \square = 14$	**8.** $\square + 9 = 18$	**9.** $3 + \square = 9$	**10.** $\square + 9 = 13$
11. $\square + 6 = 12$	**12.** $7 + \square = 14$	**13.** $\square + 9 = 15$	**14.** $7 + \square = 11$	**15.** $\square + 9 = 17$
16. $\square + 5 = 11$	**17.** $2 + \square = 11$	**18.** $\square + 0 = 9$	**19.** $4 + \square = 14$	**20.** $\square + 4 = 12$
21. $\square + 10 = 20$	**22.** $3 + \square = 8$	**23.** $\square + 3 = 12$	**24.** $4 + \square = 10$	**25.** $\square + 9 = 14$
26. $\square + 6 = 13$	**27.** $5 + \square = 9$	**28.** $\square + 8 = 10$	**29.** $3 + \square = 15$	**30.** $\square + 7 = 9$

MULTIPLICATION FACTS TEST

31. $\square \times 9 = 81$	**32.** $3 \times \square = 24$	**33.** $\square \times 4 = 12$	**34.** $5 \times \square = 30$	**35.** $\square \times 7 = 21$
36. $\square \times 3 = 15$	**37.** $4 \times \square = 24$	**38.** $\square \times 4 = 28$	**39.** $5 \times \square = 60$	**40.** $\square \times 3 = 27$
41. $\square \times 5 = 25$	**42.** $6 \times \square = 6$	**43.** $\square \times 8 = 88$	**44.** $5 \times \square = 20$	**45.** $\square \times 2 = 24$
46. $\square \times 10 = 60$	**47.** $5 \times \square = 45$	**48.** $\square \times 7 = 56$	**49.** $9 \times \square = 54$	**50.** $\square \times 5 = 55$
51. $\square \times 5 = 35$	**52.** $12 \times \square = 144$	**53.** $\square \times 8 = 72$	**54.** $4 \times \square = 32$	**55.** $\square \times 8 = 48$
56. $\square \times 3 = 36$	**57.** $8 \times \square = 8$	**58.** $\square \times 4 = 36$	**59.** $9 \times \square = 108$	**60.** $\square \times 10 = 100$

METRIC	CUSTOMARY
Length	
1 centimeter (cm) = 10 millimeters (mm)	1 foot (ft) = 12 inches (in.)
1 meter (m) = 1,000 millimeters	1 yard (yd) = 3 feet, or 36 inches
1 meter = 100 centimeters (cm)	1 mile (mi) = 1,760 yards,
1 meter = 10 decimeters (dm)	or 5,280 feet
1 kilometer (km) = 1,000 meters	
Capacity	
1 liter (L) = 1,000 milliliters (mL)	1 tablespoon (tbsp) = 3 teaspoons (tsp)
1 metric cup = 250 milliliters	1 cup (c) = 8 fluid ounces (fl oz)
1 liter = 4 metric cups	1 pint (pt) = 2 cups
1 kiloliter (kL) = 1,000 liters	1 quart (qt) = 2 pints
	1 quart = 4 cups
	1 gallon (gal) = 4 quarts
Mass/Weight	
1 gram (g) = 1,000 milligrams (mg)	1 pound (lb) = 16 ounces (oz)
1 kilogram (kg) = 1,000 grams	1 ton (T) = 2,000 pounds

TIME
1 minute (min) = 60 seconds (sec)
1 hour (hr) = 60 minutes
1 day = 24 hours
1 week (wk) = 7 days
1 year (yr) = 12 months (mo), or about 52 weeks
1 year = 365 days
1 leap year = 366 days
1 decade = 10 years
1 century = 100 years
1 millennium = 1,000 years

TABLE OF MEASURES

SYMBOLS

$=$	is equal to	%	percent
$\neq$	is not equal to	$\approx$	is approximately equal to
$>$	is greater than	$\perp$	is perpendicular to
$<$	is less than	$\parallel$	is parallel to
$\geq$	is greater than or equal to	$\overleftrightarrow{AB}$	line AB
$\leq$	is less than or equal to	$\overrightarrow{AB}$	ray AB
$\lvert 4 \rvert$	the absolute value of 4	$\overline{AB}$	line segment AB
2^3	the third power of 2	$\angle ABC$	angle ABC
10^2	ten squared	$\triangle ABC$	triangle ABC
10^3	ten cubed	π	pi (about 3.14)
10^4	the fourth power of 10	$^{\circ}$	degree
$(2,3)$	ordered pair (x,y)	$^{\circ}$C	degrees Celsius
$1:3$	ratio of 1 to 3	$^{\circ}$F	degrees Fahrenheit

FORMULAS

Perimeter		Area	
Polygon	$P =$ sum of the lengths of the sides	Rectangle	$A = l \times w$
		Square	$A = s^2$
Rectangle	$P = (2 \times l) + (2 \times w)$	Parallelogram	$A = b \times h$
Square	$P = 4 \times s$	Triangle	$A = \frac{1}{2} \times b \times h$
		Circle	$A = \pi \times r^2$

Circumference		Volume	
Circle	$C = \pi \times d$	Rectangular prism	$V = l \times w \times h$

Pronunciation Key

a	add, map	f	fit, half	n	nice, tin	p	pit, stop	yo͞o	fuse, few
ā	ace, rate	g	go, log	ng	ring, song	r	run, poor	v	vain, eve
â(r)	care, air	h	hope, hate	o	odd, hot	s	see, pass	w	win, away
ä	palm, father	i	it, give	ō	open, so	sh	sure, rush	y	yet, yearn
b	bat, rub	ī	ice, write	ô	order, jaw	t	talk, sit	z	zest, muse
ch	check, catch	j	joy, ledge	oi	oil, boy	th	thin, both	zh	vision,
d	dog, rod	k	cool, take	ou	pout, now	t͟h	this, bathe		pleasure
e	end, pet	l	look, rule	o͝o	took, full	u	up, done		
ē	equal, tree	m	move, seem	o͞o	pool, food	û(r)	burn, term		

ə   the schwa, an unstressed vowel representing the sound spelled *a* in above, *e* in sick**e**n, *i* in poss**i**ble, *o* in mel**o**n, *u* in circus

Other symbols:
• separates words into syllables
′ indicates stress on a syllable

A

absolute value [ab•sə•lo͞ot′ val′yo͞o] The distance of a number from zero on a number line (p. 481)

acute angle [ə•kyo͞ot′ ang′gəl] An angle that has a measure less than a right angle (less than 90°) (p. 428)
Example:

Word History

The Latin word for needle is *acus*. This means "pointed" or "sharp." You will recognize the root in the words acid (sharp taste), acumen (mentally sharp), and *acute* , which describes a sharp or pointed angle.

acute triangle [ə•kyo͞ot′ tri′ang•gəl] A triangle that has three acute angles (p. 456)

addends [ad′endz] Numbers that are added in an addition problem (p. 45)

addition [ə•dish′en] The process of finding the total number of items when two or more groups of items are joined; the opposite of subtraction

angle [ang′gəl] A figure formed by two rays that meet at a common endpoint (p. 428)
Example:

area [âr′ē•ə] The number of square units needed to cover a surface (p. 562)

arrangement [ə′ranj•mənt] An ordering of items (p. 662)

array [ə•rā′] An arrangement of objects in rows and columns (p. 300)
Example:

column ↓

row →

3 × 4 = 12

Associative Property of Addition [ə•sō′shē•ə•tiv prä′pər•tē əv ə•di′shən] The property that states that when the grouping of addends is changed, the sum is the same (p. 76)
Example: (5 + 8) + 4 = 5 + (8 + 4)

Associative Property of Multiplication [ə•sō′shē•ə•tiv prä′pər•tē əv mul•tə•plə•kā′shən] The property that states that the way factors are grouped does not change the product (p. 258)
Example: (2 × 3) × 4 = 2 × (3 × 4)

average [av′rij] See *mean.* (p. 100)

axis [ak′səs] The horizontal or vertical number line used in a graph or coordinate plane (p. 498)

B

bar graph [bär graf] A graph that uses horizontal or vertical bars to display countable data (p. 106) *Example:*

base [bās] A number used as a repeated factor (p. 292) *Example:* $8^3 = 8 \times 8 \times 8$. The base is 8.

base [bās] A polygon's side or a solid figure's face by which the figure is measured or named (pp. 466, 572) *Examples:*

benchmark [bench′märk] A familiar number used as a point of reference (p. 8)

billion [bil′yən] One thousand million; written as 1,000,000,000 (p. 5)

C

capacity [kə•pa′sə•tē] The amount a container can hold (p. 532)

Celsius (°C) [səl′sē•us] A metric scale for measuring temperature (p. 537)

centimeter (cm) [sen′tə•mē•tər] A unit for measuring length in the metric system; 0.01 meter = 1 centimeter

central angle [sen′trəl ang′gəl] The angle formed by two radii of a circle that meet at its center (p. 439)

certain [sur′tən] Sure to happen; will always happen (p. 656)

chord [kôrd] A line segment with endpoints on a circle (p. 438) *Example:*

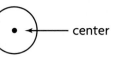

$\overline{AB}$ is a chord.

circle [sər′kəl] A closed figure with all points on the figure the same distance from the center point (p. 438) *Example:*

center

circle graph [sər′kəl graf] A graph that shows how parts of the data are related to the whole and to each other (p. 107) *Example:*

circumference [sər•kum′fər•əns] The distance around a circle (p. 554)

Word History

One of the oldest words in math is *circumference*. The Latin roots of this word are *circum* (around) and *ferre* (to carry). When you combine these roots, you get "to carry around." Think of a compass whose pencil is carried around a certain distance to trace a circle's perimeter.

combination [kam•bə•nā′•shən] A choice in which the order of items does not matter (p. 662)

common factor [kä′mən fak′tər] A number that is a factor of two or more numbers (p. 278)

common multiple [kä′mən mul′tə•pəl] A number that is a multiple of two or more numbers (p. 282)

Commutative Property of Addition [kə•myo͞o′tə•tiv prä′pər•tē əv ə•di′shən] The property that states that when the order of two addends is changed, the sum is the same (p. 76) *Example:* 4 + 5 = 5 + 4

Commutative Property of Multiplication
[kə•myōō′tə•tiv prä′pər•tē əv mul•tə•plə•kā′shən] The property that states that when the order of two factors is changed, the product is the same (p. 258)
Example: $4 \times 5 = 5 \times 4$

compass [kum′pəs] A tool used to construct circles and arcs (p. 438)

compatible numbers [kəm•pa′tə•bəl num′bərz] Numbers that are easy to compute mentally (pp. 55, 192)

compensation [kam•pən•sa′shən] An estimation strategy in which you change one addend to a multiple of ten and then adjust the other addend to keep the balance (p. 77)

composite number [käm•pä′zət num′bər] A number having more than two factors (p. 300)
Example: 6 is a composite number, since its factors are 1, 2, 3, and 6.

cone [kōn] A solid figure that has a flat, circular base and one vertex (p. 467)
Example:

congruent [kən•grōō′ənt] Having the same size and shape (p. 442)

coordinate plane [kō•ôr′də•nət plān] A plane formed by two intersecting and perpendicular number lines called axes (p. 500)
Example:

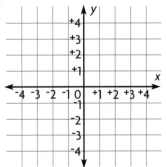

coordinates [kō•ôr′də•nəts] The numbers in an ordered pair (p. 500)

corresponding angles [kôr•ə•span′ding ang′gəlz] Angles that are in the same position in similar figures (p. 443)
Example:

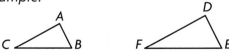

∠A and ∠D are corresponding angles.

corresponding sides [kôr•ə•span′ding sidz] Sides that are in the same position in similar figures (p. 443)
Example:

$\overline{CA}$ and $\overline{FD}$ are corresponding sides.

cube [kyōōb] A solid figure with six congruent square faces (p. 588)
Example:

cubic unit [kyōō′bik yōō′nət] A unit of volume with dimensions 1 unit × 1 unit × 1 unit (p. 592)

cumulative frequency [kyōō′myə•lə•tiv frē′kwən•sē] A running total of data (p. 97)

cylinder [si′lən•dər] A solid figure that has two parallel bases that are congruent circles (p. 467)
Example:

D

data [dā′tə] Information collected about people or things, often to draw conclusions about them (p. 95)

decimal [de′sə•məl] A number with one or more digits to the right of the decimal point (p. 22)

decimal point [de′sə•məl point] A symbol used to separate dollars from cents in money, and the ones place from the tenths place in decimal numbers (p. 26)

decimal system [de′sə•məl sis′təm] A system of computation based on the number 10 (p. 299)

decimeter (dm) [de′sə•mē•tər] A unit of length in the metric system; 10 decimeters = 1 meter

degree (°) [di•grē′] A unit for measuring angles or for measuring temperature (pp. 428, 537)

denominator [di•nä′mə•nā•tər] The number below the bar in a fraction that tells how many equal parts are in the whole (p. 314)

Example: $\frac{3}{4}$ ←denominator

diameter [di•am′ə•tər] A line segment that passes through the center of a circle and has its endpoints on the circle (p. 438)
Example:

difference [dif′ər•əns] The answer to a subtraction problem

digit [di′jit] Any one of the ten symbols 0, 1, 2, 3, 4, 5, 6, 7, 8, 9 used to write numbers

dimension [də•men′shən] A measure in one direction (p. 596)

Distributive Property of Multiplication
[di•strib′yə•tiv prä′pər•tē əv mul•tə•plə•kā′shən] The property that states that multiplying a sum by a number is the same as multiplying each addend in the sum by the number and then adding the products (p. 260)
Example: 3 × (4 + 2) = (3 × 4) + (3 × 2)
3 × 6 = 12 + 6
18 = 18

dividend [di′və•dend] The number that is to be divided in a division problem
Example: 36 ÷ 6; 6)36 The dividend is 36.

divisible [də•vi′zi•bəl] A number is divisible by another number if the quotient is a whole number and the remainder is zero. (p. 276)
Example: 21 is divisible by 3.

division [də•vi′zhən] The process of sharing a number of items to find how many groups can be made or how many items will be in a group; the operation that is the opposite of multiplication

divisor [də•vi′zər] The number that divides the dividend
Example: 15 ÷ 3; 3)15 The divisor is 3.

double-bar graph [du′bəl bär graf] A graph used to compare two similar kinds of data (p. 130)
Example:

E

edge [ej] The line made where two or more faces of a solid figure meet (p. 466)
Example:

elapsed time [i•lapst′ tīm] The time that passes between the start of an activity and the end of that activity (p. 536)

equally likely [ē′kwəl•lē lī′klē] Having the same chance of occurring (p. 656)

equation [i•kwā′zhən] An algebraic or numerical sentence that shows that two quantities are equal (p. 68)

equilateral triangle [ē•kwə•la′tə•rəl trī′ang•gəl] A triangle with three congruent sides (p. 456)
Example:

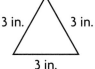

equivalent [ē •kwiv′ə•lənt] Having the same value

equivalent decimals [ē•kwiv′ə•lənt de′sə•məlz] Decimals that name the same number or amount (p. 26) *Example:* 0.4 = 0.40 = 0.400

equivalent fractions [ē•kwiv′ə•lənt frak′shənz] Fractions that name the same number or amount (p. 314) *Example:* $\frac{3}{4} = \frac{6}{8}$

equivalent ratios [ē•kwiv′ə•lənt rā′shē•ōz] Ratios that make the same comparison (p. 618)

estimate [es′tə•mət] *noun* A number close to an exact amount (p. 42)

estimate [es′tə•māt] *verb* To find a number that is close to an exact amount (p. 42)

evaluate [i•val′yə•wāt] To find the value of a numerical or algebraic expression (p. 246)

event [i•vent′] A set of outcomes (p. 654)

expanded form [ik•spand′id fôrm] A way to write numbers by showing the value of each digit (p. 2)
Example: 832 = 800 + 30 + 2

experimental probability [ik•sper•ə•men′tal prä•ba•bil′ə•tē] The ratio of the number of times the event occurs to the total number of trials or times the activity is performed (p. 658)

exponent [ek′spō•nənt] A number that shows how many times the base is used as a factor (p. 292)
Example: $10^3 = 10 \times 10 \times 10$;
3 is the exponent.

Word History

Exponent is the combination of the Latin roots *exo* (out of) + *ponere* (place). In the 17th century, mathematicians began to use complicated quantities. The idea of positioning a number by raising it "out of place" is traced to Descartes.

expression [ik•spre′shən] A mathematical phrase or the part of a number sentence that combines numbers, operation signs, and sometimes variables, but doesn't have an equal sign (p. 64)

F

face [fās] A polygon that is a flat surface of a solid figure (p. 466)
Example:

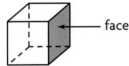
face

factor [fak′tər] A number multiplied by another number to find a product

factor tree [fak′tər trē] A diagram that shows the prime factors of a number (p. 302)

Fahrenheit (°F) [fâr′ən•hīt] A customary scale for measuring temperature (p. 537)

figurate numbers [fi′gyə•rət num′bərz] Numbers that can be represented by geometric figures (p. 459)
Example:

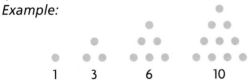

1   3   6   10

foot (ft) [fŏŏt] A unit of length in the customary system; 1 foot = 12 inches

formula [fôr′myə•lə] A set of symbols that expresses a mathematical rule (p. 598)
Example: $A = l \times w$

fraction [frak′shən] A number that names a part of a whole or a part of a group

frequency table [frē′kwen•sē tā′bəl] A table that uses numbers to record data about how often something happens (p. 95)

front-end estimation [frunt end es•tə•mā′shən] A method of estimating sums or differences by using the value of the front digits of the numbers (p. 43)
Example:

245		200
+386	→	+300
		500

function [funk′shən] A relationship between two quantities in which one quantity depends on the other (p. 254)

function table [funk′shən tā′bəl] A table that matches each input value with an output value. The output values are determined by the function. (p. 254)

G

gallon (gal) [ga′lən] A customary unit for measuring capacity; 4 quarts = 1 gallon

gram (g) [gram] A metric unit for measuring mass; 1,000 grams = 1 kilogram

greater than (>) [grā′tər ~~th~~an] A symbol used to compare two numbers, with the greater number given first
Example: $6 > 4$

greatest common factor (GCF) [grā′təst kä′mən fak′tər] The greatest factor that two or more numbers have in common (p. 278)
Example: 6 is the GCF of 18 and 30.

H

height [hīt] The length of a perpendicular from the base to the top of a plane figure or solid figure (p. 572)
Example:
height ⟶

hexagon [hek′sə•gän] A polygon with six sides and six angles (p. 434)

histogram [his′tə•gram] A bar graph that shows the number of times data occur within intervals (p. 128)

hundredth [hun′drədth] One of one hundred equal parts (p. 22)
Examples: 0.56 fifty-six hundredths
$\frac{45}{100}$ forty-five hundredths

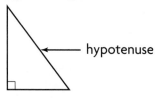

hypotenuse [hi•pot′ə•n(y)o͞os] In a right triangle, the side opposite the right angle; the longest side in a right triangle (p. 456)

hypotenuse

Word History

The *hypotenuse* of a right triangle looks like it is a line segment that is s-t-r-e-t-c-h-e-d. The prefix for "under" is *hypo* + the Greek word for "stretch" is *tenuse* (as in tension). So, hypotenuse is the line segment stretched under the right angle of the triangle.

I

Identity Property of Addition [i•den′tə•tē prä′pər•tē əv ə•di′shen] The property that states that when you add zero to a number, the result is that number (p. 76)

Identity Property of Multiplication [i•den′tə•tē prä′pər•tē əv mul•te•plə•kā′shen] The property that states that the product of any number and 1 is that number (p. 258)

impossible [im•pä′sə•bəl] Not able to happen; can never happen (p. 656)

inch (in.) [inch] A customary unit for measuring length or distance; 12 inches = 1 foot

inequality [in•i•kwä′lə•tē] A number sentence that contains the symbols <, >, ≤, ≥, or ≠ (p. 74)

integers [in′ti•jərz] The set of whole numbers and their opposites (p. 480)

intersecting lines [in•tər•sek′ting līnz] Lines that cross each other at exactly one point (p. 429)
Example:

interval [in′tər•vəl] The difference between one number and the next on the scale of a graph (p. 116)

inverse operations [in′vərs ä•pə•rā′shənz] Operations that undo each other, like addition and subtraction or multiplication and division (p. 247)

isosceles triangle [ī•sä′sə•lēz trī′ang•gəl] A triangle with exactly two congruent sides (p. 456)
Example:

10 in.   10 in.

7 in.

K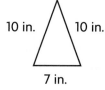

kilogram (kg) [ki′lə•gram] A metric unit that is used to measure mass; 1,000 grams = 1 kilogram

kiloliter (kL) [ki′lə•lē•tər] A metric unit that is used to measure capacity; 1,000 liters = 1 kiloliter

kilometer (km) [kə•lä′mə•tər] A metric unit that is used to measure length or distance; 1,000 meters = 1 kilometer

L

least common denominator (LCD) [lēst kä′mən di•nä′mə•nā•tər] The least common multiple of two or more denominators (p. 354)
Example: The LCD for $\frac{1}{4}$ and $\frac{5}{6}$ is 12.

least common multiple (LCM) [lēst kä′mən mul′tə•pəl] The least number, other than zero, that is a common multiple of two or more numbers (p. 282)

leg [leg] In a right triangle, either of the two sides that form the right angle (p. 456)

less than (<) [less ~~than~~] A symbol used to compare two numbers, with the lesser number given first
Example: 4 < 6

like fractions [līk frak′shənz] Fractions that have the same denominator (p. 346)
Example: $\frac{2}{5}$ and $\frac{4}{5}$ are like fractions.

line [līn] A straight path in a plane, extending in both directions with no endpoints (p. 428)
Example:

⟷

linear unit [li′nē•ər yo͞o′nət] A measure of length, width, height, or distance (p. 528)

line graph [līn graf] A graph that uses a line to show how data change over time (p. 107)

line plot [līn plät] A graph that shows frequency of data along a number line (p. 97)
Example:

Miles Jogged

line segment [līn seg′mənt] A part of a line between two endpoints (p. 428)

line symmetry [līn si′mə•trē] A figure has line symmetry if a line can separate the figure into two congruent parts (p. 446)

liter (L) [lē′tər] A metric unit for measuring capacity; 1 liter = 1,000 milliliters

map scale [map skāl] A ratio that compares distance on a map with actual distance (p. 622)

mass [mas] The amount of matter in an object

mean [mēn] The average of a set of numbers, found by dividing the sum of the set by the number of addends (p. 100)

median [mē′dē•ən] The middle number in a set of data that are arranged in order (p. 102)

meter (m) [mē′tər] A metric unit for measuring length or distance; 1 meter = 100 centimeters

mile (mi) [mīl] A customary unit for measuring length or distance; 5,280 feet = 1 mile

milligram (mg) [mil′ə•gram] A metric unit for measuring mass; 1,000 milligrams = 1 gram

milliliter (mL) [mi′lə•lē•tər] A metric unit for measuring capacity; 1,000 milliliters = 1 liter

millimeter (mm) [mi′lə•mē•tər] A metric unit for measuring length or distance; 1 millimeter = 0.001 meter

million [mil′yən] 1,000 thousands; written as 1,000,000 (p. 4)

mixed number [mikst num′bər] A number that is made up of a whole number and a fraction (p. 320) *Example:* $1\frac{5}{8}$

mode [mōd] The number or item that occurs most often in a set of data (p. 102)

multiple [mul′tə•pəl] The product of a given whole number and another whole number (p. 148)

multiplication [mul•tə•plə•kā′shən] A process to find the total number of items made up of equal-sized groups, or to find the total number of items in a given number of groups. It is the opposite operation of division.

multistep problems [mul′ti•stəp prä′bləmz] Problems requiring more than one step to solve (p. 378)

negative integer [ne′gə•tiv in′ti•jər] Any integer less than zero (p. 480)
Examples: ⁻4, ⁻5, and ⁻6 are negative integers.

net [net] A two-dimensional pattern that can be folded into a three-dimensional polyhedron (p. 588)
Example:

number line [num′bər līn] A line with equally spaced tick marks named by numbers. A number line does not always start at 0. (p. 10)
Example:

numerator [noo′mə•rā•tər] The number above the bar in a fraction that tells how many equal parts of the whole are being considered (p. 314)
Example: $\frac{3}{4}$ ←numerator

obtuse angle [äb•toos′ ang′gəl] An angle whose measure is greater than 90° and less than 180° (p. 428)
Example:

obtuse triangle [äb•toos′ tri′ang•gəl] A triangle that has one obtuse angle (p. 456)

octagon [äk′tə•gän] A polygon with eight sides and eight angles (p. 434)
Example:

opposites [ä′pə•zəts] Two numbers that are the same distance, but in opposite directions, from zero on a number line (p. 481)

ordered pair [ôr′dərd pâr] A pair of numbers used to locate a point on a grid. The first number tells the left-right position and the second number tells the up-down position. (p. 120)

order of operations [ôr′dər əv ä•pə•rā′shənz] Rules for performing operations in expressions with more than one operation (p. 250)

origin [ôr′ə•jən] The point where the two axes of a coordinate plane intersect, (0,0) (p. 500)

ounce (oz) [ouns] A customary unit used to measure weight

outcome [out′kum] A possible result of an experiment (p. 656)

outlier [out′li•ər] A value separated from the rest of the data (p. 97)

parallel lines [par′ə•lel līnz] Lines in a plane that do not intersect (p. 429)
Example:

parallelogram [pâ•rə•lel′ə•gram] A quadrilateral whose opposite sides are parallel and congruent (p. 460)
Example:

parentheses [pə•ren′thə•sēz] The symbols used to show which operation or operations in an expression should be done first

pentagon [pen′tə•gän] A polygon with five sides and five angles (p. 434)
Example:

percent [pər•sent′] A ratio of a number to 100 (p. 632)

perimeter [pə•rim′ə•tər] The distance around a closed plane figure (p. 548)

period [pir′ē•əd] Each group of three digits in a large number (p. 2)

perpendicular lines [pər•pen•dik′yə•lər līnz] Two lines that intersect to form right angles (p. 429)
Example:

pi (π) [pī] The ratio of the circumference to the diameter of a circle; an approximate decimal value of pi is 3.14. (p. 555)

pictograph [pik′tə•graf] A graph that displays countable data with symbols or pictures (p. 106) *Example:*

HOW WE GET TO SCHOOL	
Walk	✳ ✳ ✳
Ride a Bike	✳ ✳ ✳ ✳
Ride a Bus	✳ ✳ ✳ ✳ ✳ ✳
Ride in a Car	✳ ✳

Key: Each ✳ = 10 students

pint (pt) [pīnt] A customary unit for measuring capacity; 2 cups = 1 pint

place value [plās val′yōō] The value of a place, such as ones or tens, in a number (p. 2)

plane [plān] A flat surface that extends without end in all directions (p. 428)
Example:

plane figure [plān fig′yər] A figure that lies in a plane (p. 434)

point [point] An exact location in space, usually represented by a dot (p. 428)

polygon [pol′•i•gon] A closed plane figure formed by three or more line segments (p. 434)
Examples:

polyhedron [pol•i•hē′drən] A solid figure with faces that are polygons (p. 466)
Examples:

population [pä•pyə•lā′shən] The entire group of objects or individuals considered for a survey (p. 96)

positive integer [pä′zə•tiv in′ti•jər] Any integer greater than zero (p. 480)

possible outcomes [pä′sə•bəl out′kumz] The events that have a chance of happening in an experiment (p. 656)

pound (lb) [pound] A customary unit used to measure weight

precision [pri•sizh′ən] A property of measurement that is related to the unit of measure used; the smaller the unit of measure used, the more precise the measurement is (p. 523)

prediction [pri•dik′shən] A reasonable guess as to the outcome of an event (p. 220)

prime factorization [prīm fak•tə•ri•zā′shən] A number written as the product of all its prime factors (p. 302)

prime number [prīm num′bər] A number that has exactly two factors: 1 and itself (p. 300)
Examples: 5, 7, 11, 13, 17, and 19 are prime numbers.

prioritize [pri•or′ə•tīz] To put events in order of importance (p. 394)

prism [priz′əm] A solid figure that has two congruent, polygon-shaped bases, and other faces that are all rectangles (p. 466)
Examples:

rectangular prism

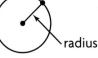
triangular prism

probability [prä•bə•bil′ə•tē] The likelihood that an event will happen (p. 654)

product [prä′dəkt] The answer to a multiplication problem

proportion [prə por′shən] An equation that shows that two ratios are equal (p. 619)
Example: $\frac{1}{3} = \frac{3}{9}$

protractor [prō′trak•tər] A tool used for measuring or drawing angles (p. 432)

pyramid [pir′ə•mid] A solid figure with a polygon base and all other faces triangles that meet at a common vertex (p. 466)
Example:

Word History

A fire is sometimes in the shape of a pyramid, with a point at the top and a wider base. This may be how *pyramid* got its name. The Greek word for fire was *pura,* which may have been combined with the Egyptian word *mer.*

Q

quadrilateral [kwäd•rə•lat′ə•rəl] A polygon with four sides (p. 434)
Example:

quart (qt) [kwôrt] A customary unit for measuring capacity; 2 pints = 1 quart

quotient [kwō′shənt] The number, not including the remainder, that results from dividing
Example: 8 ÷ 4 = 2. The quotient is 2.

R

radius [rā′dē•əs] A line segment with one endpoint at the center of a circle and the other endpoint on the circle (p. 438)
Example:

radius

random sample [ran′dəm sam′pəl] A sample in which each subject in the population has an equal chance of being chosen (p. 96)

range [rānj] The difference between the greatest number and the least number in a set of data (p. 96)
Example: 2, 2, 3, 5, 7, 7, 8, 9
The range is 9 − 2 = 7.

ratio [rā′shē•ō] The comparison of two quantities (p. 614)

ray [rā] A part of a line; it begins at one endpoint and extends forever in one direction. (p. 428)
Example:

reciprocal [ri•sip′rə•kəl] One of two numbers whose product is 1 (p. 404)
Example: 8 and $\frac{1}{8}$ are reciprocals since $8 \times \frac{1}{8} = 1$.

rectangle [rek′tang•gəl] A parallelogram with four right angles (p. 460)
Example:

rectangular prism [rek•tang′gyə•lər pri′zəm] A solid figure in which all six faces are rectangles (p. 466)
Example:

reflection [ri•flek′shən] A movement of a figure to a new position by flipping it over a line; a flip (p. 462)
Example:

regular polygon [re′gyə•lər pä′lē•gän] A polygon in which all sides are congruent and all angles are congruent (p. 434)

rhombus [räm′bəs] A parallelogram with four congruent sides (p. 460)
Example:

Word History

Rhombus is almost identical to its Greek origin, *rhombos*. The original meaning is "spinning top" or "magic wheel," which is easy to imagine when you look at a rhombus, an equilateral parallelogram.

right angle [rīt ang′gəl] A special angle formed by perpendicular lines and equal to 90° (p. 428)
Example:

90°

right triangle [rīt trī′ang•gəl] A triangle that has a right angle (p. 456)
Example:

rotation [rō•tā′shən] A movement of a figure to a new position by turning it around a vertex or point of rotation; a turn (p. 462)
Example:

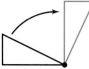

rotational symmetry [rō•tā′shən•əl si′mə•trē] A property of a figure that, when rotated less than 360° about a central point or a point of rotation, still matches the original figure (p. 446)

rounding [round′ing] Replacing a number with one that tells about how many or how much (p. 38)

sample [sam′pəl] A part of a population (p. 96)

sample space [sam′pəl spās] The set of all possible outcomes (p. 656)

scale [skāl] A series of numbers starting at zero and placed at fixed distances on a graph to help label the graph (p. 116)

scale drawing [skāl drô′ing] A reduced or enlarged drawing whose shape is the same as an actual object and whose size is determined by the scale (p. 622)

scalene triangle [skā′lēn trī′ang•gəl] A triangle with no congruent sides (p. 456)
Example:

30 cm
13 cm
18 cm

schedule [skej′oo•əl] A table that lists activities or events and the times they happen

similar [si′mə•lər] Having the same shape, but not necessarily the same size (p. 442)
Example:

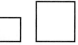

simplest form [sim′pləst fôrm] A fraction is in simplest form when the numerator and denominator have only 1 as their common factor. (p. 316)

solid figure [sä′ləd fig′yər] A three-dimensional figure (p. 466)

solution [sə•loo′shən] A value that, when substituted for the variable, makes an equation true (p. 70)

sphere [sfir] A round object whose curved surface is the same distance from the center to all its points (p. 467)
Example:

square [skwâr] A polygon with four equal sides (p. 460)

square number [skwâr num′bər] The product of a number and itself (p. 293)
Example: $4^2 = 16$; 16 is a square number.

square pyramid [skwâr pir′ə•mid] A solid figure with a square base and with four triangular faces that have a common point (p. 466)
Example:

square root [skwâr rōōt] One of two equal factors of a number (p. 305)

square unit [skwâr yōō′nət] A unit of area with dimensions 1 unit × 1 unit (p. 562)

standard form [stan′dərd fôrm] A way to write numbers by using the digits 0-9, with each digit having a place value (p. 2)
Example: 456 ←standard form

stem-and-leaf plot [stem and lēf plot] A table that shows groups of data arranged by place value (p. 104)
Example:

Stem	Leaves			
1	1	2	4	
2	0	3	4	5
3	4	5	7	
4	0	0	1	2

Number of Tickets Sold

subtraction [səb•trak′shən] The process of finding how many are left when a number of items are taken away from a group of items; the process of finding the difference when two groups are compared; the opposite of addition

sum [sum] The answer to an addition problem

surface area [sûr′fəs âr′ē•ə] The sum of the areas of all the faces, or surfaces, of a solid figure (p. 590)

survey [sûr′vā] A method of gathering information about a group (p. 96)

ten-thousandth [ten thou′zəndth] One of ten thousand equal parts (p. 23)
Example: 0.5784 = five thousand, seven hundred eighty-four ten-thousandths

tenth [tenth] One of ten equal parts (p. 22)
Example: 0.7 = seven tenths

tessellation [tes•ə•lā′shən] A repeating pattern of closed figures that covers a surface with no gaps and no overlaps (p. 463)
Example:

theoretical probability [thē•ə•re′ti•kəl prä•bə•bil′ə•tē] A comparison of the number of favorable outcomes to the number of possible equally likely outcomes (p. 656)

thousandth [thou′zəndth] One of one thousand equal parts (p. 23)
Example: 0.006 = six thousandths

ton (T) [tun] A customary unit used to measure weight; 2,000 pounds = 1 ton

transformation [trans•fər•mā′shən] A movement of a figure to a new position by a translation, reflection, or rotation (p. 462)

translation [trans•lā′shən] A movement of a figure to a new position along a straight line; a slide (p. 462)
Example:

trapezoid [tra′pə•zoid] A quadrilateral with exactly one pair of parallel sides (p. 460)
Example:

tree diagram [trē dī′ə•gram] An organized list that shows all possible outcomes for an event (p. 660)

trend [trend] A pattern over time, in all or part of a graph, where the data increase, decrease, or stay the same (p. 107)

triangle [tri′ang•gəl] A polygon with three sides (p. 434)
Example:

triangular numbers [trī•ang′gyə•lər num′bərz] Numbers that can be represented by triangular figures (p. 459)
Example:

1   3   6   10

unlike fractions [un•līk′ frak′shənz] Fractions that have different denominators (p. 348)

Example: $\frac{3}{4}$ and $\frac{2}{5}$ are unlike fractions.

unlikely [un•līk′lē] Having a less-than-even chance of happening (p. 653)

variable [vâr′ē•ə•bəl] A letter or symbol that stands for one or more numbers (p. 64)

Venn diagram [ven dī′ə•gram] A diagram that shows relationships among sets of things (p. 126)
Example:

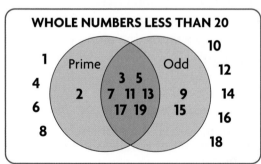

WHOLE NUMBERS LESS THAN 20

vertex [vûr′teks] The point where two or more rays meet; the point of intersection of two sides of a polygon; the point of intersection of three or more edges of a solid figure; the top point of a cone; the plural of vertex is vertices (pp. 428, 466)
Examples:

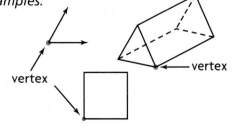

vertex
vertex

The Latin word *vertere* means to turn and also relates to highest. You can turn a figure around a point or *vertex*.

volume [väl′yəm] The measure of the space a solid figure occupies (p. 592)

whole number [hōl num′bər] One of the numbers 0, 1, 2, 3, 4, ... The set of whole numbers goes on without end.

word form [wurd fôrm] A way to write numbers in standard English (p. 2)
Example: 4,829 = four thousand, eight hundred twenty-nine

X

x-axis [eks•ak′səs] The horizontal number line on a coordinate plane (p. 498)

x-coordinate [eks•kō•ôr′də•nət] The first number in an ordered pair, which tells the distance to move right or left from (0,0) (p. 500)

Y

y-axis [wī•ak′səs] The vertical number line on a coordinate plane (p. 498)

y-coordinate [wī•kō•ôr′də•nət] The second number in an ordered pair, which tells the distance to move up or down from (0,0) (p. 500)

Zero Property of Multiplication [zē′rō prä′pər•tē əv mul•tə•plə•kā′shən] The property that states that when you multiply by zero, the product is zero (p. 258)

A

Absolute value, 481–482
Activities, 4, 70, 74, 96, 102, 122, 128–129, 164–165, 230–231,
   260, 282–283, 293, 296, 300–301, 348, 349, 368, 374–375,
   402–403, 429, 432–433, 434, 435, 438, 439, 443, 446, 457, 462,
   463, 470–471, 486, 487, 500, 504–505, 522, 523, 526–527,
   548–549, 550, 554–555, 562, 564, 568, 569, 572, 573, 576, 588,
   590, 592, 596, 614–615, 632–633, 642, 654–655
Acute angles, 428–431
Acute triangles, 456–459
Addends. *See* Addition
Addition
   basic facts tests, H36, H40
   of decimals, 42–45, 48–51, 53–55
   equations, 68–73, 78, 80–81
   estimating sums, 42–51, 54, 352–353, 369–370, 376–377
   of fractions
      like denominators, 346–347, 423
      unlike denominators, 348–351, 354–361, 423
   of integers, 486–489
   mental math strategies, 52–55, 76–79, 355
   of mixed numbers, 368–371, 373, 376–379
   modeling, 67, 346, 348–349, 368, 486–488
   properties of
      Associative, 76–79
      Commutative, 76–78
      Identity, 76–78
   of three addends, 76–79, 360
   of units of measure, 529–530
   of units of time, 536–538
   of whole numbers, xxvi, 42–47, 52–55, 64–81, H36, H40
Algebra, 62–83, 166–167, 208–209, 228–229, 244–263, 478–493,
   550–551, 564–567, 572–575, 576–579, 592–595
   coordinate grid, 115, 120–121, 498–499
   coordinate plane
      graphing integers, 500–507
      graphing ordered pairs in any quadrant, 500–507
      graphing relationships, 139, 498–499, 513
      graphing simple linear equations, 513
      transformations on, 504–505
   equations
      addition, 68–73, 78, 80–81
      division, 245, 247–248
      with exponents, 294, 304
      graphing simple linear, 513
      multiplication, 245, 247–249, 258–259
      solving, 70–72, 79, 244, 247–249, 258–259
      subtraction, 68–72, 80–81
      variables in, 68–76, 79–81, 247–249, 254–255, 258–259
      writing, 62, 68–72, 80–81, 247–249, 254–255, 258–259
   exponents, 292–299
   expressions, 64
      algebraic, 64–67, 73, 246, 248–249, 260–261
      evaluating, 65–67, 73, 246, 248, 250–251, 260–261
      with exponents, 296–299
      writing, 64–67, 246, 248–249
   finding a rule, 252–253
   formulas, using, 244, 550–551, 565–567, 572–579, 592–595,
      598–599
   function tables, 66, 254–255, 498–499
   functions, 254–255, 498–499
   in geometric calculations, 550–551, 554–555, 564–567,
      572–579, 592–596
   inequalities, 73–75
   input/output patterns, 66, 254–255, 499
   linear functions, 254–255, 513
   order of operations, 250–251, 271
   parentheses, 250–251, 499
   properties
      Associative, 76–79, 258–259

   Commutative, 76–79, 258–259
   Distributive, 260–261
   Identity
      of Addition, 76–79
      of Multiplication, 258–259
   Zero, 258–259
   proportions, 619–621
   variables, 64, 83
      equations with, 68–76, 79, 80–81, 247–249, 254–255,
         258–259
      expressions with, 64–67, 246, 248–249, 260–261
      inequalities with, 73, 74–75
Algebraic equations. *See* Equations
Algebraic expressions. *See* Expressions
Analyze data. *See* Data
Angles, 428–433
   acute, 428–431
   central, 439–441
   classifying, 428–431
   congruent, 442–444
   degrees in, 432–433, 435–437
   measuring and drawing, 432–433
   obtuse, 428–431
   in polygons, 434–437˜
   right, 428–431, 433
   straight, 428–431
   sum of
      in a quadrilateral, 435–437
      in a triangle, 435–437
Area, 562–579
   of circles, 605
   deriving formula for, 564–565, 576–577
   estimating, 562–563
   of irregular figures, 562–563
   modeling, 568
   of parallelograms, 576–579
   of rectangles, 564–567, 568–571, 596–599
   relating to perimeter, 568–571, 596–597
   surface, of a solid, 590–591, 596–597
   of triangles, 572–575
   units of measurement for, 596–597
Arrangements, 662–663
Arrays, 293, 300–301
Assessment
   Chapter Review/Test, 17, 33, 59, 83, 111, 135, 159, 179, 203,
      223, 241, 263, 287, 309, 333, 363, 381, 397, 415, 451, 475,
      493, 509, 543, 557, 583, 601, 627, 649, 667
   Check What You Know, 1, 21, 37, 63, 95, 115, 147, 163, 191,
      207, 227, 245, 275, 291, 313, 345, 367, 385, 401, 427, 455,
      479, 497, 521, 547, 561, 587, 613, 631, 653
   Cumulative Review. *See* Mixed Applications, Mixed Review
      and Test Prep, Mixed Strategy Practice, Performance
      Assessment, *and* Standardized Test Prep
   Mixed Review and Test Prep, 3, 7, 9, 13, 25, 27, 29, 39, 41, 45,
      47, 51, 55, 67, 69, 73, 75, 79, 99, 101, 103, 109, 119, 121, 125,
      129, 133, 149, 151, 153, 155, 165, 167, 169, 173, 175, 193,
      195, 197, 199, 209, 211, 215, 217, 219, 229, 231, 235, 239,
      249, 251, 253, 255, 259, 261, 277, 281, 283, 295, 299, 301,
      305, 315, 319, 321, 325, 331, 347, 351, 353, 355, 359, 371,
      373, 375, 377, 387, 389, 391, 393, 403, 405, 407, 411, 431,
      433, 437, 441, 445, 447, 459, 461, 465, 469, 471, 483, 485,
      489, 499, 503, 505, 525, 527, 531, 533, 535, 539, 549, 551,
      555, 563, 567, 571, 575, 579, 589, 591, 595, 597, 615, 617,
      621, 623, 633, 635, 639, 641, 645, 655, 657, 659, 661, 663
   Performance Assessment, 90, 142, 186, 270, 340, 422, 516,
      608, 674
   Standardized Test Prep, 18–19, 34–35, 60–61, 84–85, 112–113,
      136–137, 160–161, 180–181, 204–205, 224–225, 242–243,
      264–265, 288–289, 310–311, 334–335, 364–365, 382–383,

Student Handbook   H55

Page Placement Key: (t)- top, (c)-center, (b)-bottom, (l)-left, (r)-right, (bg)-background

iv Gloria H. Chomica/Masterfile; v (t) Todd Warshaw/Allsport USA; v (b) Rod Planck/Dembinsky Photo Associates; viii Duomo Photography; xi Latent Image Photography; xi Tom & Dee Ann McCarthy/The Stock Market; xv (t) Ron Scherl/StageImage; xv (b) Tui De Roy/Bruce Coleman, Inc.; xvi Tony Freeman/PhotoEdit.; xvii NASA; xx Davies & Starr/Stone; xxvii (b) Ron Kimball; 0 Earth Imaging/Stone; 2 David Barnes/Stone; 3 Mark Newman/New England Stock Photo; 4 (t)Leonard McCombe/TimePix; 4 (b) Corbis Digital Stock; 5 NASA; 6 Telegraph Colour Library/FPG International; 8 Mary Eleanor Browning/Photo Researchers; 10 Michael Hubrich/Dembinsky Photo Associates; 13 (t) Telegraph Colour Library/FPG International; 16 W. Metzen/H. Armstrong Roberts; 16 (inset 1) Dr. Dennis Kunkel/Phototake; 16 (inset 2) Grant Heilman/Grant Heilman Photography; 16 (inset 3) Ed Reschke/Peter Arnold Inc.; 16 (inset 4) Larry Lefever/Grant Heilman Photography; 16 (inset 5) E. F. Anderson/Visuals Unlimited; 16 (inset 6) S Lowry/Univ. Ulster/Stone; 16 (inset 7) G. Shih-R. Kessel/Visuals Unlimited; 18 Richard Shiell/Dembinsky Photo Associates; 20 Dennis O'Clair/Stone; 22 Gloria H. Chomica/Masterfile; 23 Shin Yoshino/ Minden Pictures; 24 Mike Powell/Allsport USA; 26 Jeff Foott/Bruce Coleman, Inc.; 27 John Warden/Stone; 30 Stephen J. Krasemann/DRK; 32 Todd Warshaw/Allsport USA; 36 Steve Kaufman/DRK; 38 Al Bello/Allsport Photography; 44 Julia Patriarche/ www.chalkdust.net; 46 Rod Planck/Dembinsky Photo Associates; 48 Julia Patriarche/www. chalkdust.net; 49 Duomo Photography; 53 Index Stock Photography; 55 Duomo Photography; 56 Index Stock Photography; 65A-65B Tom Till/Tom Till Photography; 65A Superstock; 61 Robert Essel/The Stock Market; 65B (l) Cosmo Condina/Stone; 65B (b) Barbara P. Williams/Bruce Coleman Collection; 66 S. Nielsen/Bruce Coleman, Inc.; 68 Carl Roessler/ Bruce Coleman, Inc.; 72 R. Andrew Odum/Peter Arnold, Inc.; 74 Mark J. Thomas/Dembinsky Photo Associates; 75 John Giustina/FPG International; 76 Ken Scott/Dembinsky Photo Associates; 78 Robert E. Daemmrich/Stone; 80 Bill Losh/FPG International; 81 Peter Gridley/FPG International; 84 (inset) Domino arrangement by: Scott Suko/Event organized by: EXPO Children's Museum; Gainesville, FL; 84 Henry Blackham/The Stock Market; 86 Photo courtesy of Ralf Laue; 92 AP Photo/Wide World; 97 E.R. Degginger/Dembinsky Photo Associates; 100 Todd Warshaw/Allsport; 106 (b) The Granger Collection; 106 (tl) Corbis; 110 Richard M. Smith/FPG International; 111 Duomo Photography; 114,115 (t) Ron Kimball; 115 (b) Frank Hecker/OKAPIA/Photo Researchers; 118 Stocktrek Corp/The Stock Market; 120 Gerry Ellis/Minden Pictures; 121 Konrad Wothe/Minden Pictures; 122 Tom McHugh/Steinhart Aquarium/Photo Researchers; 123 Robert Torrez/ Stone; 126 Dean Conger/Corbis; 128 Jimmy Rudnick/The Stock Market; 129 Chie Nishio/Omni-Photo Communications; 130 Rafael Macia/ Photo Researchers; 131 Ken Cole/Animals Animals; 137 John K. Gates/Glimpses by Gates; 145A (t) Ty Smedes Nature Photography; 145A (b) Tom Bean Photography; 145B (l) Robert Holmes/Corbis; 145B (r) Marc Muench/Corbis; 146 David Nunuk/Science Photo Library/Photo Researchers; 146 (inset) Stephen Agricola/Stock, Boston; 148 NASA; 150 Art Wolfe/Photo Researchers; 151 David Madison/Bruce Coleman, Inc.; 152 Duomo Photography; 153 Anup Shah/Animals Animals; 154 Richard J. Wainscoat/Peter Arnold, Inc.; 155 Monkmeyer/Rogers; 156 Michael Hubrich/Photo Researchers, Inc.; 157 Spencer Jones/FPG International; 160 Robert A. Tyrrell Photography; 164 M. Lammertink; 166 Robert A. Tyrrell Photography; 167 Rod Planck/Photo Researchers; 168 (fg) E. R. Degginger/Dembinsky Photo Associates; 169 John Mitchell/Photo Researchers; 172 Hans Pfletschinger/Peter Arnold, Inc.; 173 Runk/Schoenberger/Grant Heilman Photography; 182 (c) Rob Tringali Jr./SportsChrome; 183A (t) John Elk III; 183A-183B (both) Randall Hyman; 183B William Iseminger/Cahokia Mounds State Historic Site; 184 Suzanne Murphy-Larronde/Picture Quest; 186 ITAR-TASS/Sovfoto; 187 Philip James (University of Toledo), Steven Lee (University of Colorado) NASA; 188 NASA; 189 NASA; 191 Kazoobie, Inc.; 192 Archive Photos; 193 Ron Scherl/StageImage; 195 (t) Archive Photos; 195 (b) The Granger Collection, New York; 196 U.S. Postal Service; 197 Gemma Dickmann; 198 Ed Bock/The Stock Market; 199 Tony Freeman/PhotoEdit; 202 Damian Strohmeyer/Sports Illustrated; 206 (br) Hulton Getty/Liaison International; 207 (c) Corbis; 208 Herb Scharfman/Sports Illustrated/Time; 210 APA/Archive Photos; 212 Associated Press/Wide World Photos; 213 Frank Atura/Asolo Theatre Company; 214 John Cancalosi/DRK; 215 AFP/Corbis; 216 Steinouer Photography; 217 Claudia Parks/ The Stock Market; 220 Wolfgang Kaehler Photography; 222 Tom & Dee Ann McCarthy/The Stock Market; 226 Jay Syverson/CORBIS; 227 Tony Freeman/PhotoEdit; 229 Jose L. Pelaez/The Stock Market; 230 Latent Image Photography; 231 Mark E. Gibson Photograohy; 232 Tony Freeman/PhotoEdit; 233 Mark E. Gibson Photography; 242 Foodpix; 246 Wesley Bocxe/Photo Researchers; 247 Sovfoto/Eastfoto; 251 Index Stock Photography; 255A (t) James M. Mejuto Photography; 255A (b) E.R.Degginger/Color-Pic, Inc.; 255A-255B Joseph Sohm/Corbis; 255B Gail Mooney/Corbis; 256 David Cavagnaro; 258 Bill Aron/Photo Researchers; 265 The Granger Collection, New York; 270 AP Wirephoto/Wide World Photos; 272 Biophoto Associates/Photo Researchers; 274 A. B. Dowsett/Science Photo Library/Photo Researchers; 279 Wolfgang Kaehler Photography; 282 Rosenfeld Images Ltd./Science Photo Library/ Photo Researchers; 286 Myreen Ferguson/PhotoEdit; 301 D. Young-Wolff/PhotoEdit; 305 Hank Morgan/Rainbow/ Picture Quest; 309A-309B W. Metzen/H. Armstrong Roberts, Inc.; 309B (inset) Fred J. Eckert/Eckert Images; 309B Bob Krist/Corbis; 312 Duomo Photography; 313 David Madison; 318 Paul Harris/Stone; 321 S. Nielsen/Bruce Coleman, Inc.; 326 Dave G. Houser/Corbis; 330 Nigel Francis/the Stock Market; 330 (inset) Brian Brake/Photo Researhers; 332 Central Florida Council Boy Scouts of America; 334 (l) Federal Clipart/One Mile Up, Inc.; 334 (r) Federal Clipart/One Mile Up, Inc.; 335 Index Stock Photography; 336 Robert Holmes/Corbis; 337 Mark Greenberg/FPG International; 340 Grant Heilman, Inc.; 342 Scott Barrow, Inc.; 346 Kevin R. Morris/Stone; 350 Ron Scherl/StageImage; 351 Myrleen Ferguson/PhotoEdit; 352 Larry Lefever/Grant Heilman Photography; 353 Carlyn Iverson/Photo Researchers; 360 Larry Evans/Black Star/Harcourt; 364 Tony Freeman/PhotoEdit; 367 Tui De Roy/Bruce Coleman, Inc.; 368 E.R. Degginger/Photo Researchers; 371 Konrad Wothe/Minden Pictures; 372 Marty Snyderman/Waterhouse Stock Photo; 373 F. Stuart Westmorland/Photo Researchers; 377 Index Stock Photography; 381A Jodi Jacobson; 381A-381B Jodi Jacobson; 381B (inset) Jodi Jacobson; 382 Michael Zito/ SportsChrome; 384 Mark J. Thomas/Dembinsky Photo Associates; 387 Johnny Johnson/Animals Animals; 388 Julep Gillman-Bryan, N.C. Division of Archives and History; 389 Karen Kasmauski/Woodfin Camp & Associates; 390 David Cannon/Allsport Photography; 392 Steve Hix/FPG International; 396 Danielle Hayes/Bruce Coleman, Inc.; 398 WORLDSAT International, Inc./Photo Researchers; 399 Lynette Cook/Science Photo Library/Photo Researchers; 404 Lance Nelson/The Stock Market; 408 Hazel & Douglas Wolfe; 412 NASA; 416 Index Stock Imagery; 420 Paraskevas Photography; 420 (inset 1) Alan Schein/The Stock Market; 420 (inset 2) Bob Daemmrich/Stock, Boston; 420 (inset 3) Aneal Vohra/unicorn Stock Photos; 420 (inset 4) Bill Gallery/Stock, Boston; 420 (inset 5) Alan Schein/The Stock Market; 420 (inset 6) Shaun van Steyn/Pictor; 422 J. Messerschmidt/Bruce Coleman, Inc.; 428 L. West/Bruce Coleman, Inc.; 430 (l) Steve Solum/Bruce Coleman, Inc.; 430 (cl) Ken Straiton/The Stock Market; 430 (cr) Jeff Greenberg/PhotoEdit; 430 (r) Alan Schein/The Stock Market; 432 (t) Reuters/HO/Archive Photos; 433 AFP/Corbis; 436 (bg) Richard Dunoff/The Stock Market; 438 Mark Scott/FPG International; 444 Layne Kennedy; 446 Reuters Newsmedia, Inc./Corbis; 449 SEF/Art Resource, NY; 450 Phil Degginger/Bruce Coleman, Inc.; 454 Bill Ross/Corbis; 455 (l) Rafael Macia/Photo Researchers; 455 (c) Fergus O'Brien/FPG International; 455 (r) Vito Palmisano/Panoramic Images; 456 James M. Mejuto; 457 The Granger Collection, NY; 460 (l) Will & Deni McIntyre/Photo Researchers; 460 (r) David Ball/The Stock Market; 469A (t) Kevin R. Morris/Corbis; 469A (b) Kevin R. Morris/Stone; 469B (t) William Strode/Woodfin Camp & Associates; 469B (b) T. Wiewandt/Visions of America; 470 Craig Tuttle/The Stock Market; 474 (c) E.R. Degginger/Bruce Coleman, Inc.; 479 Mark E. Gibson/Dembinsky Photo Associates; 480 Ostentoski & Zoda/Envision; 483 (cr) Barbara Reed/Animals Animals; 484 Bob Daemmrich/The Image Works; 487 Greg Ryan/Sally Beyer; 490 David Ball/The Stock Market; 492 Lee Balterman/FPG International; 500 Jamie Squire/Allsport; 504 Art Resource, New York; 511 John W. Bova/Photo Researchers; 514 Richard T. Nowitz; 529 Comstock; 533 Bill Foley/Bruce Coleman, Inc.; 537A Henry Diltz/Corbis; 537A-537B John Skowronski/Folio; 537B (t) Lynda Richardson/Corbis; 537B (b) Lelia Hendrea/Folio; 538 William R. Sallaz/Duomo Photography; 544 Allsport Photography (USA); 547 Robert Frerck/Woodfin Camp & Associates; 551 (l) Yann Arthus-Bertrand/Corbis; 551 (r) Ron Kimball; 554 Roy Corral/Stone; 560 (tl) Davies & Starr/Stone; 560 (tr) Bruce Coleman, Inc; 560 (bl) Kjell B. Sandved/Bruce Coleman, Inc.; 560 (br) Davies & Starr/Stone; 561 (t) Raymond A. Mendez/Animals Animals; 561 (b) J.C. Carton/Bruce Coleman, Inc.; 563 Richard Reid/Earth Scenes; 565 Jeff Greenberg/PhotoEdit; 568 Carolyn A. McKeone/Photo Researchers; 569 Ron Kimball; 573 Peter Skinner/Photo Researchers; 576 (inset) Doranne Jacobson/International Images; 595A Phillip James Corwin/Corbis; 595A-595B Rich Iwasaki/Stone; 595B Richard Kaylin/Stone; H0 Tom McHugh/Steinhart Aquarium/Photo Researchers; H1 (t) Scott Camazine/Photo Researchers.;

All other photos by Harcourt Photographers: Weronica Ankarorn, John Bateman, Victoria Bowen, Ken Kinzie, Ron Kunzman, Alan Maxwell, Sheri O'Neal, Quebecor Digital Imaging, Sonny Senser, Terry Sinclair.

Chapter Opener Photography Credits by Chapter: 1 Earth Imaging/Stone; 2 W. Metzen/H. Armstrong Roberts; 3 Zena Holloway/FPG/Getty Images; 4 S. Nielsen/Bruce Coleman, Inc.; 5 Todd Warshaw/Allsport; 6 Transparencies, Inc.; 7 Roger Ressmeyer/Corbis; (inset) Stephen Agricola/Stock, Boston; 8 Robert A. Tyrrell Photography; 9 Suzanne Murphy-Larronde/PictureQuest; 10 Apopka Chief; 11 Harrison Shull/shullphoto.com; 12 AP Photo/Chuck Burton; 13 David Cavagnaro; 14 Stocktrek/Corbis; 15 Jeff Greenberg/Photo Edit; 16 Richard T. Nowitz/Corbis; 17 Harrison Shull/shullphoto.com; 18 Kevin R. Morris/Stone; 19 Michael Kevin Daly/Corbis; 20 Mark Richards/Photo Edit. Inc.; (inset) Harcourt; 21 Layne Kennedy Photography; 22 Michael Zito/SportsChrome; 23 Lance Nelson/The Stock Market; 24 502 Alese/MortPechter/The Stock Market; 25 David Forbert/SuperStock; 26 David Ball/The Stock Market; 27 Richard Nowitz; 28 William R. Sallaz/Duomo Photography; 29 Roy Corral/Stone; 30 Harcourt.